《老子》的公理化诠释

甘筱青 李宁宁 吴国富
曹欢荣 陈建军 柯镇昌 著

桑龙扬 顾丹柯 王俊超
田楚雨 陈腊春 梅君 译
万敏

Laozi: An Axiomatic Interpretation

Written by Gan Xiaoqing, Li Ningning, Wu Guofu, Cao Huanrong, Chen Jianjun, Ke Zhenchang

Translated by Sang Longyang, Gu Danke, Wang Junchao, Tian Chuyu, Chen Lachun, Mei Jun, Wan Min

中英文对照 Chinese-English Edition

外语教学与研究出版社
FOREIGN LANGUAGE TEACHING AND RESEARCH PRESS
北京 BEIJING

图书在版编目 (CIP) 数据

《老子》的公理化诠释 / 甘筱青等著；桑龙扬等译. -- 北京：外语教学与研究出版社，2023.12
ISBN 978-7-5213-5025-8

I. ①老… II. ①甘… ②桑… III. ①《道德经》- 研究 IV. ①B223.15

中国国家版本馆 CIP 数据核字 (2023) 第 257144 号

出 版 人　王　芳
责任编辑　周渝毅　陈　宇
责任校对　李亚琦
封面设计　李双双　彩奇风
出版发行　外语教学与研究出版社
社　　址　北京市西三环北路 19 号（100089）
网　　址　https://www.fltrp.com
印　　刷　北京盛通印刷股份有限公司
开　　本　710×1000　1/16
印　　张　33
版　　次　2024 年 1 月第 1 版　2024 年 1 月第 1 次印刷
书　　号　ISBN 978-7-5213-5025-8
定　　价　88.00 元

如有图书采购需求，图书内容或印刷装订等问题，侵权、盗版书籍等线索，请拨打以下电话或关注官方服务号：
客服电话：400 898 7008
官方服务号：微信搜索并关注公众号"外研社官方服务号"
外研社购书网址：https://fltrp.tmall.com

物料号：350250001

序

从2008年开始，九江学院甘筱青教授带领他的科研团队，对先秦儒家经典进行公理化研究，相继出版了《〈论语〉的公理化诠释》（中文初版、修订版，中英文对照版，中法文对照版）、《〈孟子〉的公理化诠释》（中文版、中英文对照版）、《〈荀子〉的公理化诠释》，成果丰硕，令人欣慰。

在长期的研究过程中，甘筱青教授每年数次来我这里，向我介绍研究的情况。这不仅因为我对家乡大学——九江学院的事业特别关心，更因为我从事的虽是工科研究，却热心关注人文学科的发展，关注用中华经典来推动大学生人文素质教育的事业。我曾跟甘筱青教授说，在中华传统文化中，儒道两家文化占有主流地位，而一部《论语》、一部《老子》就是两家最典型的代表，所以任继愈、涂又光两位先生在近十年间分别一再讲过，中国人一定要读两本书，一是《论语》，一是《老子》，这是很有道理的。对我自己来说，我喜欢《论语》，也喜欢《老子》。《老子》第三十三章说："知人者智，自知者明。胜人者有力，自胜者强。知足者富，强行者有志。不失其所者久，死而不亡者寿。"这是我经常吟咏的一段话。每次想起这段话，都有一种"于我心有戚戚焉"的感觉。这段话也是对历代人物事业成败的总结，古往今来的立功、立德之人，莫不具有如此的品性。我曾要求我的博士研究生能够背诵《老子》，因为这对于开展自然科学的研究也很有帮助。人首先要面对社会，有了关注社会、洞察社会的胸怀，才能做好具体的事情和具体的研究。

对于甘筱青教授及其学术团队从事的研究，我曾反复思考过。公理化方法作为一种科学的研究范式，在数学、物理学等自然学科的运用上，已经堪称经典。它运用于人文学科，虽然表面上看不像运用于自然学科那样贴切，但两者同样都有内在的规律，都可以去感悟与提炼其思辨逻辑与演绎推理，因而也都可以用公理化方法去研究。当然，从公理化角度去研究两者是有差别的，想完全解决公理化方法与人文学科的适配问题可能也很难，但可以尝试找出更好地诠释人文学科的公理化表达方式，这种创新性研究是很可贵的。这也正是我一直支持甘筱青教授这项研究工作的重要理由。

古人云"凡事问三老"。我年事已高，没有精力去从事很多具体的研究，但时常给他们一些鼓励，在一些重大的问题上帮助他们思考，也是我的责任所在。而甘筱青教授他们一路走来，把先秦儒家的三部代表作都做了公理化的诠释。学术界对他们的这项工作从开始的疑惑到逐渐认可，并且日益给予好评。2014年11月，季羡林基金会授予甘筱青教授及其学术团队"儒学传承与创新奖"，就是所结硕果之一。这可称得上"凡事慰三老"了。

在甘筱青教授他们从事研究的过程中，我曾几次希望注重对《老子》开展公理化诠释工作，因为老子是中华文化的代表性人物，在世界上的影响力很大。我也期待他们在完成对于先秦儒家经典的公理化诠释之后，才进行关于《老子》的公理化研究，因为这里头有一个"研究之序"。孔、孟、荀是面向社会讨论伦理，讨论修身、齐家、治国、平天下等问题，而《老子》的思想体系更庞大，老子是面向自然界与宇宙讨论"道"与"德"等问题，社会只是他讨论的部分论域。涂又光先生曾认为《老子》是根，孔子是从老子那里"问道"与发展而形成儒家思想体系的。所以，应该先学《论语》，再学《老子》；先熟悉社会，再掌握自然天地，才能踏着阶梯稳步前进。

甘筱青教授他们经过反复考虑，接受了我的建议，等到先秦儒家经典的公理化诠释系列完成之后，也等到公理化方法用得比较娴熟之后，再用公理化方法来诠释《老子》。于是，他们就有了比较厚实的基础与经验。甘教授说过，江西鹰潭的龙虎山是张道陵最早结庐炼丹之地，也是中国道教文化的发源地之一。第一代天师张道陵推崇老子为宗神，使"道"不仅是哲学上的最高范畴与天地万物的本原，而且也具有了人格神化的意义。作为江西的高校团队，从新的视野来从事"道神"老子的研究，是需肩负的使命。我对此表示赞赏与鼓励。

2014年下半年，甘筱青教授及其学术团队开始《老子》的会读与公理化诠释工作。2015年1月，甘教授来我这里，说他们经过多次探讨，觉得有两个重大问题不好解决：一是觉得用公理化方法来梳理儒家思想，容易切入并且是有效的，但用来梳理老子思想，似乎困难很大；二是道家思想的出发点与儒家思想的出发点大不相同，如何找准这个出发点，觉得比较困惑。我说，公理化系统是典型的形而上学，而《老子》哲理更多是唯物辩证的，这个矛盾不能回避。中国文化的显著特点之一是整体观，而西方文化的分割性则很明显，公理化方法也是注重分割性的。应当做到整体观与分割性的相互补充，而不是用分割性去肢解整体观。在这方面需要充分吸取唯物辩证的思想，从更睿智的角度看问题，突破"形而上"的某些缺陷。对于"出发点"问题，我觉得可以从儒家的"中庸"得到启发，围绕老子的"守中"去思考。因为孔子与老子是基于整体观同一体系的，只是孔子侧重于人文社会与伦理的层面，老子侧重于自然界与哲学的层面。儒家文化讲"中庸"，讲整体观，道家文化又何尝不讲整体观，如"知止不殆""物极必反""反者，道之动""人法地，地法天，天法道，道法自然"。老子的"守中"与孔子的"中庸"，本质上是相通的。

七年多的磨砺，使甘筱青教授及其学术团队具备了解决问题的能力，也使他们在面对《老子》的时候，再一次表现了坚韧不拔的精神，完成了《老子》的公理化诠释工作。从他们整理出来的老子思想的演绎系统来看，老子思想试图涵盖全面的程度，达到了人类认知的高端，它的系统观、整体观也达到了人类认知的高端，因而在指出人类认知和行为局限的时候，也就触及了根源性问题。在几千年的历史中，人类不乏对自我、对社会的深刻认知，但很少能把人类社会放在最大的系统中进行考察，因此也很难指出人类认知所存在的根本性、普遍性问题，往往表现出其片面与偏执之处。因此，用公理化方法来诠释《老子》，揭示其一以贯之的思想体系及认知高端，是一项富有创造性的成果。

甘筱青教授及其学术团队也较好地处理了辩证唯物思想与公理化方法之间的矛盾，注意到了以往谈矛盾的对立与统一、否定之否定时，着重从事物的包容与被包容关系、从个别事物与一切事物的本源谈问题。《〈老子〉的公理化诠释》的研究，将"守中"作为出发点，找到了这个"中"的两端——一端是本源性、整体性的"道"，一端是继发性、局部性的人间社会——等于是在系统与局部、整体与个别之间设立了解决矛盾的路径。这一设立兼有吸纳唯物辩证思想和运用公理化方法的作用，由此建立起老子思想的演绎系统，基本达到了预期的目标。

欣慰之余，援笔为序，以推荐他们的成果，并激励他们的前行。

杨叔子

中国科学院院士，华中科技大学教授

第一届、第二届、第三届教育部高等学校文化素质教育指导委员会主任

Preface

Since 2008, Professor Gan Xiaoqing of Jiujiang University has led his research team in the study of pre-Qin Confucian classics in an axiomatic way, the results of which have been the publication of a series of books with regard to the study of Confucian classics: *The Analects of Confucius: An Axiomatic Interpretation* (the Chinese edition, the revised Chinese edition, the Chinese-English edition, and the Chinese-French edition), *Mencius: An Axiomatic Interpretation* (the Chinese edition, the Chinese-English edition), and *Xunzi: An Axiomatic Interpretation* (the Chinese edition). Their academic endeavour has seen amazing achievements.

During his long-term research, Professor Gan Xiaoqing would come to me several times every year, telling me the progress of his research. This was not only a testimony to my special care of the development of Jiujiang University in my hometown, but also one to my enthusiasm in the development of humanities, though my major is engineering. I once said to Professor Gan Xiaoqing that in traditional Chinese culture, Confucianism and Daoism have been the two cultural mainstreams, of which the representative works are *The Analects of Confucius* and *Laozi* or *Dao De Jing* (*Tao Te Ching*). Ren Jiyu and Tu Youguang, the two experts in traditional Chinese philosophy and culture, had always been stressing in the past ten years that it was beneficial to every Chinese to read the two books, i.e., *The Analects* and *Laozi*. Personally, I like both of them. Chapter 33 of *Laozi* says, *"Those who know others are witty, and those who know themselves are wise. Those who defeat others are powerful, and those who overcome themselves are unyielding. Those who are content are rich. Those who are perseverant are ambitious. Those who keep their natural instincts last long. And those who have died with achievements left to posterity enjoy an immortal life."* I often quote this paragraph. I feel touched every time when I think of these words. It also tells how historical figures through the ages made great achievements. None of those of merits or virtue has failed to display such moral characters. I used to ask my PhD candidates to learn *Laozi* by heart, as it is also of great help to those who do research in natural science. As an individual, one should be concerned about his society and gain an insight into it before making any progress in his life or work.

I have repeatedly pondered upon the research Professor Gan Xiaoqing and his academic team are conducting. The axiomatic approach, as a classic paradigm of scientific research, is widely used in such natural sciences as mathematics and physics. It may have less relevance when applied to research in humanities. But in fact both natural sciences and humanities have similar inherent laws that can be understood, deduced, and ratiocinated, which makes it possible for them to be researched in an axiomatic way. Needless to say, there is a difference between axiomatic researches in humanities and those in natural sciences. Probably it is impossible to make the axiomatic approach fully match the researches in humanities, but the creative efforts to interpret humanities in an axiomatic approach are invaluable. So I have been in strong support of this attempt.

An old saying goes, "*You should consult the seniors whenever you have something in question.*" Now I am quite aged and lack energy for a specific research work, but more often than not, I will give them my sincere encouragement, and offer my own thinking upon some important issues. This is the duty on my part. With constant efforts, Gan Xiaoqing, together with his academic team, has completed the research in interpreting the three representative works of Confucianism of the pre-Qin period. To their joy, doubts in academic circles about their axiomatic research have gradually given way to recognition. There is also a growing amount of positive affirmation. In November 2014, Ji Xianlin Foundation conferred the "Prize for the Inheritance and Innovation of Confucianism" on Professor Gan Xiaoqing and his academic team. This is certainly a gratification to a senior citizen like me.

In the process of Gan Xiaoqing and his team's research, I suggested several times that they axiomatically interpret *Laozi*, because I think Laozi is a representative of Chinese culture, and has exerted a great impact both at home and abroad. I have been expecting them to work on *Laozi* when they finish their axiomatic research on the pre-Qin Confucian classics, as they should do it in an "orderly" manner because *The Analects*, *Mencius* and *Xunzi* aim at society and discuss ethics, which cover such issues as self-cultivation, administration of the household, governance, and world peace, while *Laozi* concerns the natural world and the universe, discussing the Dao (the Way) and the Virtue. Therefore, *Laozi* deals with a much wider scope of issues, with the human society as only part of his interest. Mr. Tu Youguang maintained that *Laozi* is the root while Confucius developed and formed the Confucian ideology by seeking the Dao from Laozi, the philosopher. Therefore, it is reasonable to study *The Analects* before *Laozi*, as you should get to know the society before you understand

Nature, Heaven and Earth, and gradually make progress.

They finally accepted my suggestion and started to work on *Laozi* after they had completed the series of the pre-Qin Confucian works. They have gained some experience and become skilled in interpreting Chinese classics in an axiomatic approach. Professor Gan once told me that Longhu Shan, or the Dragon and Tiger Mountain, in Yingtan City of Jiangxi, was the very first place where Zhang Daoling settled and made pills of immortality, and it was also one of the origins of Daoism. Zhang Daoling, the very master of the first generation of Daoism, regarded Laozi as the forefather of Daoists, thus not only making the Dao the highest philosophical category, but also the origin of everything between Heaven and Earth, and personified it. The axiomatic team led by Professor Gan from Jiujiang University in Jiangxi is bound to fulfil the mission of adding some fresh perspectives to the study of Laozi, the Daoist master. I appreciate their efforts and encourage them to do so.

In the latter half of 2014, Professor Gan Xiaoqing and his academic team started their intensive reading and the axiomatic interpretation of *Laozi*. In January 2015, Professor Gan came to me and said that two major problems had remained unsolved even though they had held several seminars to explore them. One was that it seemed more difficult and less effective to interpret Laozi's thought in the axiomatic way than to do Confucianism. The other was that it was bewildering to find the starting point of Laozi's thought, which was radically different from that of Confucianism. I told them that the axiomatic system is typically metaphysical, while the philosophy in *Laozi* is mainly materialistic and dialectic. This contradiction cannot be sidestepped. One of the obvious characteristics of Chinese culture is its holistic view, while the Western culture lays more emphasis on the separability. The holistic view and separability should supplement each other, but not use the latter to mutilate the whole. As far as this is concerned, it is good for us to absorb the materialistic and dialectic thought, and examine the issue from a wiser angle in order to overcome the pitfalls of the "metaphysical" defects. As to the "starting point," I thought we could be enlightened by the Confucian "doctrine of the mean" and Laozi's "keeping the moderate," because both Confucius and Laozi based their thinking on the same system of the holistic view, with the only disparity between Confucius' focus on the relation between human society and ethics, and Laozi's focus on the relation between Nature and philosophy. It is true that the Confucian "doctrine of the mean" lays stress on the holistic view, but Daoism does exactly the same thing, for instance, *"the knowledge of when to stop will not evoke danger,"* *"Things will develop in the opposite direction when they become extreme,"* *"The movement of the Way is in endless cycles,"* and *"Man models himself on Earth, Earth on Heaven, Heaven on the Dao, and the Dao on that which is naturally so."* Therefore, Laozi's "keeping the moderate" and Confucius' "doctrine of the mean" are practically identical.

More than seven years' collaborated efforts enabled Professor Gan Xiaoqing and his team to solve problems, and to finish the axiomatic interpretation of *Laozi*, persistent and dauntless in the face of such a difficult Daoism canon. From the deductive system of Laozi's thought, sorted out by the team, we can see that Laozi's thought seems to cover a wide range of things, and reaches the apex of human cognition. Its systematic perspective and holistic view also reach the apex of human cognition. Therefore, when it tries to point out the cognitive and behavioral limits of man, it also touches the root of the problem. Over the past thousands of years, man has profound self-recognition and that of society, but has hardly done anything to examine the human society on the basis of the largest system, and for that reason, it is hard for man to point out the fundamental and common problems existing in man's cognition, which tends to be partial or biased. Therefore, it is creative to interpret *Laozi* in an axiomatic way and to reveal its consistent ideological system and apex of cognition.

Professor Gan Xiaoqing and his academic team have fairly well tackled the contradiction between dialectical and materialistic ideology and the axiomatic approach. They have noticed that when people in the past discussed the contradiction and unity of opposites and the negation of negation, they focused on the relationship of being inclusive and included, and dealt with problems from the perspective of the origin of things. But when they worked on *Laozi: An Axiomatic Interpretation*, Professor Gan and his team started from "keeping the moderate," and found out the two extremes of "the mean": one being the Dao with its fontal nature and holistic nature; the other being the human society with its secondary nature and locality. That is to say, they have found a route to tackle the contradiction between the system and the part, the whole and the individual. This establishment plays the part of combining the materialistic and dialectical thought with the application of the axiomatic approach. And if the deductive system of Laozi's thought is constructed on the basis of this approach, the expected aim is achieved.

I am delighted to write this foreword, for one thing, to recommend their academic achievements, and for another, to encourage them to achieve more in the future.

YANG Shuzi

Academician of Chinese Academy of Sciences,

Professor of Huazhong University of Science and Technology, and

Director of the First, Second and Third Humanities
Quality Education Steering Committee for Higher Institutes,
Ministry of Education of the People's Republic of China

目　录

导读 001

第一章　引论 013

第二章　定义，基本假设，公理 145

第三章　明道篇 229

第四章　贵德篇 283

第五章　治国篇 335

第六章　摄生篇 405

跋一：人法地，地法天，天法道，道法自然 455

跋二：怀念萧树铁教授 482

后记：道法自然，顺势而为 488

英译说明 504

Contents

Readers' Guide 006

Chapter One: Introduction 013

Chapter Two: Definitions, Assumptions and Axioms 145

Chapter Three: On Understanding the Dao 229

Chapter Four: On Cherishing Virtue 283

Chapter Five: On Governance 335

Chapter Six: On Preserving Health 405

Epilogue One: Man Models Himself on Earth,

   Earth on Heaven, Heaven on the Dao,

   and the Dao on Nature 467

Epilogue Two: Professor Xiao Shutie Will Live in

   Our Hearts 485

Postscript: Dao Models on Nature and Follows the Trend 495

Translators' Notes 507

导　读

老子（约生活于公元前571年至公元前471年之间），姓李名耳，字聃，又称老聃，春秋时期楚国苦县厉乡曲仁里人。老子是中国古代的哲学家和思想家，道家学派的创始人，著有《老子》一书。司马迁在《史记·老子韩非列传》中记载，老子"居周久之，见周之衰，乃遂去。至关，关（令）尹喜曰：子将隐矣，强为我著书。于是老子……言道德之意五千余言而去，莫知其所终"。尹喜感动了老子，老子遂根据自己的生活体验，又总结了国家、社会治理的经验，写下《老子》五千言。

《老子》又名《道德经》或《道德真经》，它与《易经》和《论语》一道，被认为是对中国影响最深远的三部巨著。《老子》共八十一章，五千余字。前三十七章为上篇，属于"道经"；第三十八章及以后为下篇，属于"德经"。全文贯穿了"道是德的体，德是道的用"这一思想。老子认为"道"是世界万物的根本，提倡"自然""无为"，主张政治上的"无为"、道德上的"上德不德"、养生方面的清静寡欲等。

老子的著作和思想，早已成为世界的文化遗产。欧洲从19世纪初就开始了对《道德经》的研究。德国哲学家黑格尔说："中国哲学中另有一个特异的宗派，这派是以思辨作为它的特性。……这派的主要概念是'道'，这就是理性。这派哲学及与哲学密切联系的生活方式的发挥者（不能说是真正的创始者）是老子。"[1]同是德国哲学家的尼采曾评价说，《道德经》像一口永不枯竭的井泉，充满宝藏，放下汲桶，唾手可得。英国科学家李约瑟说，中国文化就像一棵参天大树，而这棵参天大树的根在道家。他晚年时则干脆自称是"名誉道家""十宿道人"。

《老子》对中国的哲学、科学、政治、宗教等产生了深远的影响，展现了古代中国人的一种世界观和人生观。而《老子》对学术思想方面的影响，最早

---

[1] 黑格尔，北京大学哲学系外国哲学史教研室译：《哲学史讲演录》第1卷，北京：生活·读书·新知三联书店，1956年，第125—126页。

体现于先秦诸子，其次是魏晋文学，再次是佛学，最后是宋代理学。但在中国近现代，对《老子》的异议多于赞美。人们对他的"无为而治""小国寡民"等思想都有较多的批判，被肯定的似乎只有"朴素的辩证法"这一点。近些年来，对于《老子》肯定较多的则在于"自然"方面，认为现代社会应当充分吸取老子主张的"人与自然和谐"的思想。可以说，中国近现代对《老子》的评价与西方世界对它的评价是不相称的。

在进行《老子》的公理化诠释之前，我们已经完成了《〈论语〉的公理化诠释》《〈孟子〉的公理化诠释》《〈荀子〉的公理化诠释》等著作。然后我们决定开始《老子》的公理化诠释工作。在会读中我们感到，《老子》虽然只有五千余字，但相比儒家经典，理解起来更为困难。其难点主要有三：（1）《老子》的思想体系面对整个天地自然，相比基本上面对人类社会的儒家思想，抽象程度更高；（2）《老子》以天地自然为镜子，照出了人类社会的种种偏颇之处，对于这些偏颇我们早已习以为常，因而要接受老子对人类社会的批判，事实上也在挑战我们自己的固有观念；（3）解释《老子》的著作浩如烟海，观点五花八门，"标准版本""权威版本"很难确定，相对于儒家经典而言，人们对于《老子》的看法更加不统一。近现代以来，对《老子》的阐释出现了与古代的种种不同，使它更显得扑朔迷离，面目难辨。当然，反过来说，如果能够努力克服这些难点，也正彰显了《老子》公理化诠释的价值。

对《老子》一书进行公理化诠释，就是要把书中体现的老子思想整理成一个演绎系统。展开这种演绎的方法简言之就是"转换表述形式，建立逻辑联系"。《老子》包含了各种思想观点，它们由众多概念、众多论断组成，我们用基本假设、公理、命题的形式来表述老子的各种论断，用定义的形式来表述老子的关键概念，这就实现了表述形式的转换。在《老子》一书中，表面上看起来孤立的各种概念和论断，实质上应该是有紧密的逻辑联系的。为此，我们从中先抽绎出一些论断作为基本假设，再形成由基本假设统摄的若干定义和公理，再用公理（基本假设可作为更大论域上的公理）把众多的命题推理出来，这样就在孤立的论断之间建立了紧密的逻辑联系，从而把老子思想整理成一个结构严密的演绎系统。如此一来，基本假设、定义、公理、命题以及推理的展开，就形成了《老子》公理化诠释的基本框架。

根据上述思路，我们在引论中按照"道经""德经"的分法，用八个部分阐述了《老子》思想的基本框架，在阐述中既注意吸收以往的众多研究成果，又结合了我们的研究视野与方法。首先，我们概述了老子、《老子》研究史，以及老子对后世政治思想和道教的影响，接着从多方面展开了对老子之"道"的解读，然后阐述了老子的天地自然观、老子的万物生成与运动方式观，从是"弃智入明"还是"由智入明"，到老子"天人观"的由来及旨归，展现了老子"破迷解惑"的理论和方法，体现了其"俯瞰人类"而不是"平视人类"的认识角度和高度；从老子之"德"与文明社会的理想形态，以及《老子》的水意象与为政之道，到老子的养生论，建构了老子指导人类组织行为和个体行为的思想体系。我们还概述了道家与儒家的互补及道家对人类社会发展的启示。

引论既要全面介绍《老子》的内容，又要为公理化体系的建构服务。对于老子的思想，我们的解读路径是："道"是一种"无限的无限性的综合"，"自然"是"道"的根本性质或"法则"，它支配着一切。在事物表现形态上，"自然"表现为"无为而无不为"，人类社会同样要遵循"无为而无不为"（或"顺势而为"）的原则。以此观察人类社会，有限的功德就不是合乎"自然"的功德，而执着于为欲望驱动的"智"，就形成了不合乎"自然"的种种观念，产生了种种不合乎"自然"的作为。

通过上述系统阐述，我们完成了公理化研究所需要的必要铺垫。接下来，我们在第二章中首先论述了《老子》的"守中"思想，将它作为基本假设的理论铺垫。在《〈论语〉的公理化诠释》中，我们将研究的逻辑主线定位在"矛盾的中庸状态"，但在诠释《老子》时，发现不能再从具有对等关系的矛盾双方引出逻辑主线，而是应当从具有包容与被包容关系的矛盾双方引出逻辑主线，前者就是指天地自然之"道"，后者就是指人类社会。如此一来，"守中"便成为处理好整体与局部关系的抽象概括。我们把研究的逻辑主线定位在人类认识世界、对待万事万物的"守中"状态，这就需要从世界生成论的层面阐述事物构成及其运动变化的规律，进而把人类世界放在这个系统的恰当位置，这样才能确定什么是"守中"状态，以及如何把握这种状态。这些原理对于人类的活动——下至修身与个人生活，上至治国与处理国家间关系，乃至把握当今社会的发展方向——均有重要的指导意义。

接下来我们提出了定义、基本假设、公理。在基本假设与公理中，我们主要从"道""自然""有无"这些展开天地自然之"道"的概念出发，阐述了老子的思想框架，进而过渡到人类社会，以及"自然观"对人类社会的指导作用等。定义则负责描述公理化诠释所涉及的核心概念，故而置于前面。我们一共给出了13个定义、5个基本假设、4条公理，进行了界定和说明，并配上与之对应的《老子》原文，为后面的命题、推理提供依据。

为了满足基本公理化研究的需要，我们必须将对《老子》的解读与基本假设对接起来。"守中"的提出就是由此及彼的桥梁，其核心就是明确矛盾的双方以及妥善处理矛盾的方法。我们认为，"道"的特性（即"自然"）与人类行为的"不自然"（偏离"道"）构成矛盾。而矛盾的根源是人类能"智"不能"明"，无法认识"道"的无限性，只凭借"智"去作为。如果不能处理好这个矛盾，就会使人类社会乱上添乱。故而人类必须化"智"为"明"，准确认识"道"，继而依照"道"的"自然"法则去作为，做到"无为而无不为"。如此人类就需要探索什么是合乎"自然"的"德"，如何按照"自然"法则去治国，去养生。这就衍生了四大方面的论述，命题也相应分为四大类，形成了"明道篇""贵德篇""治国篇""摄生篇"，这四篇用成组的命题分别展开论述，并通过例证和说明进行更具体的描述。

接下来的第三、四、五、六章是以公理化方法展开《老子》思想的命题组。

"明道篇"共21个命题，主旨是说明老子关于"道"的基本观念，以及人如何才能认识或体悟"道"。首先阐述"道"自身以及"道"与万物的关系；其次说明人的两种认知或体悟状态"智"和"明"以及它们之间的相互关系，指出由"智"入"明"才能正确认知或体悟"道"；再次说明体悟"道"的路径、方法和步骤。

"贵德篇"共23个命题，主旨是阐述顺应自然之德的方法，以及修德之方、修德之用。具体而言，顺应自然方为"德"，要具备这种"德"则应从偏执于"有为"转变为把握"无为"。在这方面，应当认识到贪欲、智巧为修德之害，而淡化二者的方法为知足、处下、柔弱、不争，这也是圣人得以修成的方法，圣人的特点为智之澄明、心之虚静，具有这种"玄德"，方能体现自然之道。

"治国篇"共28个命题，主旨在于论述遵循自然的治国之道，指出合乎自然的社会才是理想社会，而有道社会的特征是和谐自然，百姓安居乐业，无须繁苛的礼法；讨论良治的基本模式、表现及其实施路径。合乎自然的治国方式是循道、循古，不可过度崇尚智慧、贤能、仁义、礼法、功德、奇货等东西，而在用兵、外交、为君、行政、治民等方面均要遵循"守柔"之道，如此对于君主的修养提出了要求，也就是刚柔并济、修德修信。

"摄生篇"共22个命题，主旨是如何关爱自我的生命，实现关爱自我生命与关爱他人生命的统一，而真正实现这一点必须以"自然"为原则。养生的原则是效法"自然"，其根本在于保持虚静、淡泊、淳厚的心境以及节制自我的嗜欲。由此展开，需建立基于自然原则的财富观，正确对待财富与生命的关系；建立基于自然原则的祸福荣辱观，以知足不辱、为而不恃为核心；建立基于自然原则的强弱论、巧拙论，等等。基于"自然"的原则，其实也就体现了个体与万物共生的原则。

上述四篇，基本上涵盖了《老子》的主要内容。为了帮助读者理解命题，本书还采用"例证和说明"的方式加以补充阐释。它们与命题的关系为：

（1）命题是一般性、普遍性的论述，"例证"则是案例的论述。"例证"不能涵盖命题的全部内涵，但有助于了解命题的具体内涵；（2）"例证"可以是命题的延伸和扩展，从生活实践的不同侧面补充和丰富命题的含义，有的"例证"还有助于了解所阐释命题和其他命题的逻辑关系；（3）"说明"是以不同于命题推理的方式揭示命题的内涵和普遍性；（4）有些"说明"是为了揭示该命题与他人对《老子》某些解释的不同之处。

Readers' Guide

Laozi (also Lao-Tzu) (about between 571 BC and 471 BC) lived in the State of Chu in the Spring and Autumn Period. He was a philosopher and thinker of ancient China, the founder of the Daoist (or known as Taoist) School and author of *Laozi* (also *Lao Tzu* or *Dao De Jing*). In traditional accounts, his surname was Li and personal name was Er, and courtesy name was Dan or Lao Dan. Sima Qian in the *Records of the Grand Historian: Biography of Laozi and Hanfei* records that Laozi, who grew weary of the moral decay of life in the capital of Zhou Kingdom and noted the kingdom's decline, ventured west to live as a hermit in the unsettled frontier. At the western gate of the city (or kingdom), he was recognized by the guard officer Yin Xi. The sentry asked the old master to record his wisdom for the country before he would be permitted to pass. Moved by Yin Xi, Laozi wrote the book according to his own life experience and the lessons of the state and social governance as well as the success or failure of the dynasties for the well-being of the people. *Laozi* was said to be composed of two parts with a total of 5,000 Chinese characters.

The received *Laozi* or *Lao Tzu*, also known as *Dao De Jing* or *Tao Te Ching*, is a short text of around 5,000 Chinese characters in 81 brief chapters or sections. It is also known as the honorific Daode Zhen Jing (*True Classic of the Way and the Virtue*, or *Moral Scriptures*). Along with the *Book of Changes* and *The Analects of Confucius*, it is considered to be one of the three China's masterpieces which have had the most profound impact on China. It has two parts, the *Dao Jing* (the *Classic of Dao*; chaps. 1–37) and the *De Jing* (the *Classic of Virtue*; chaps. 38–81), which may have been edited together into the received. The two parts illustrate the thought "The *Dao* is the body of virtue and virtue is the utilization of the *Dao*." Laozi believes that Dao is the root of all things, encouraging "Naturalness" and "wuwei." Wuwei, literally meaning "non-action," "inaction" or "not acting," is a central concept of *Laozi*. The concept of *wuwei* is multifaceted, and reflected in the word's multiple meanings, even in its English translation; it can mean "not doing anything," "not forcing," "not acting" in the theatrical sense, "creating nothingness," "acting spontaneously," and "flowing with the moment." He therefore advocates "non-action" politically, and thinks that "a man of the superior virtue does not claim to be of virtue" on virtuous level and lives a "tranquil life devoid of fame and lusts."

Laozi's writings and thoughts have long been the cultural heritage of the world. As early as in the beginning of the nineteenth century, European scholars began to study *Dao De Jing* (*Tao Te Ching*). German philosopher Hegel said that there was another special school of philosophy in China, with speculation being its characteristics and Dao being its main idea, which was reason. He said that the initiator of the philosophy of this school and way of life of the Chinese closely linked to it is Laozi (though he cannot be said to be the real founder)[1]. Nietzsche, a German philosopher, commented that *Dao De Jing*, like an inexhaustible well full of treasures, is at one's fingertips. British scientist Joseph Needham said that Chinese culture is like a towering tree with roots in Daoism. In his later years, he simply described himself as an "honorary Daoist."

Laozi has a far-reaching impact on China's philosophy, science, politics, religion and so on, reflecting the world view and outlook on life of ancient Chinese people. The impact of *Laozi* on academic thinking was first reflected in the pre-Qin philosophy and literature of Wei and Jin dynasties, then in Buddhism, and finally in neo-confucianism of the Song Dynasty. But in modern China, *Laozi* has met with more objections than praises. There has been a lot of criticism of his idea of "inaction, or non-action" and "small country with small population." Only his "simple dialectics" is acclaimed. In recent years, for *Laozi*'s thoughts, the concept of "naturalness" is certainly accepted by Chinese people, who think that modern society should fully absorb the idea of "harmony between man and nature." It can be said that the evaluation of *Laozi* in modern China is not commensurate with that of the Western world.

Just after we had finished the three works *The Analects of Confucius: An Axiomatic Interpretation, Mencius: An Axiomatic Interpretation* and *Xunzi: An Axiomatic Interpretation,* we decided to start our axiomatic interpretation of *Laozi*. During our reading of *Laozi*, we found that although with only 5,000 Chinese characters, compared to Confucian classics, it is more difficult to understand. There are three main difficulties: (1) The ideological system of *Laozi*, which involves the Heaven, Earth and Nature, has a higher degree of abstraction compared to Confucianism, which basically involves the human society. (2) *Laozi*, with the Heaven and Earth and the natural world as a mirror, reflects the biases and wrongs of the human society, which we have long been accustomed to. In fact, it also contradicts our own inherent ideas to accept Laozi's criticism of human society. (3) There are numerous works including "standard version" and "authoritative version" on the interpretation and comments of *Laozi* with a wide variety of different

---

1 Hegel. *Lectures on the History of Philosophy (Volume 1)*, translated by Department of History of Foreign Philosophy, Department of Philosophy, Peking University. Beijing: Sanlian Bookhouse, 1956, pp.125-126.

views. It is difficult for us to determine which version is more reasonable. Compared to the Confucian classics, there is no uniform understanding of *Laozi*. In modern times, there have appeared many descriptions of *Laozi* different from the ancient ones so that the understanding of *Laozi* becomes confusing and difficult. Of course, on the other hand, if we can overcome these difficulties, the importance of *Laozi*'s axiomatic interpretation can also be highlighted.

To interpret *Laozi* in an axiomatic approach is to turn Laozi's thoughts into a deductive system. The way to start this interpretation is simply "to change the form of expression and to establish logical links." *Laozi* contains a variety of ideas, which are composed of many concepts and assertions. We use basic assumptions, axioms and propositions to describe the various assertions, and also use the definitions of the key concepts of *Laozi* to achieve the conversion of the form of expression. In the book *Laozi*, the various seemingly isolated concepts and conclusions, in essence, should have a close logical link. To this end, we first deduce some of the assertions as the basic assumptions, and then form a number of definitions and axioms based on these assumptions. Then we use these axioms (basic assumptions can be used as axioms in a larger domain) to deduce numerous propositions so as to establish a close logical connection among the isolated assertions, thus turning Laozi's thoughts into a well-structured deductive system. In this way, the development of the basic assumptions, definitions, axioms, propositions and reasoning becomes the basic framework for axiomatic interpretation of *Laozi*.

According to the above ideas, we expound the basic framework of the thought of *Laozi* in the chapter "Introduction" in eight sections in accordance with the two parts "Classic of Virtue" and "Classic of Dao." In the elaboration, we not only try to learn from previous research studies but also combine our research vision and methods. First of all, we summarize the research history of *Laozi* as well as its influence on political thoughts of later generations and Daoism, and then start the interpretation of Laozi's Dao. Then we elaborate his view of Heaven, Earth and Nature, and the view of the way all things generate and move. We discuss the ideas like "abandoning wisdom to become bright," "being wise before becoming bright" and the origin of Laozi's "view of Heaven and Man," which show Laozi's theory and ways of demystification and embody Laozi's unique way of understanding things, that is, "overlooking the human beings" rather than "observing human beings horizontally." We elaborate Laozi's De (virtue) and the ideal form of civil society, the water image and political way of *Laozi*, and preservation of health, which construct Laozi's ideological system in guiding individual behavior and the behavior of human community. We also outline the complementarity between Daoism and Confucianism and the enlightenment of Daoism on development of human society.

"Introduction" is written not only for a general survey of *Laozi* but also for the construction of axiomatic system. As for Laozi's thought, our interpretation path is: Dao is an "infinite synthesis of infiniteness" and "naturalness" is the fundamental feature or "rule" of Dao, which dominates everything. In the form of things, "naturalness" functions as "taking non-action but achieving everything." In human society, it is also necessary to follow the principle of "taking non-action but achieving everything" or "taking advantage of the situation." To observe the human society in this way, we will find that the limited merit is not in line with the "natural" merit, and that the obsession of "wisdom" driven by desire will form concepts that are not in line with "naturalness," resulting in a variety of actions that are not in conformity with "nature."

Through the above systematic elaboration, we have completed the necessary foreshadowing for the axiomatic research. Next, in the second chapter, we first discuss the concept "shouzhong" (keeping the moderate or taking the middle course), which is used as the theoretical foreshadowing for the basic hypothesis. In *The Analects of Confucius: An Axiomatic Interpretation,* we locate the logical main line in the "mean state of contradiction." But in the interpretation of *Laozi*, it is found that the logical main line cannot be drawn from the contradiction with reciprocal relations, but should be from the inclusive and included relationship between the two sides. The former refers to the natural way of the Heaven, Earth and Nature, and the latter refers to the human society. In this way, "keeping the moderate or taking the middle course" has become the abstract summary of dealing with the whole and partial relationship. We focus the logical main line of the study on "keeping the moderate" state of human's understanding of the world and treating all things. So it is required to elaborate the composition of things and the law of their movement from the perspective of generative theory so that the human world can be located in an appropriate position. In this way it can be determined what the moderate state is and how to grasp this state. These principles, for human activities, whether they are activities of self-cultivation and personal life, or activities of governance or handling relations between countries, even of grasping the direction of development of today's society, are of important guiding significance.

Next we propose definitions, assumptions and axioms. In the assumptions and axioms, we mainly start from the concepts like Dao, "naturalness" and "being or non-being" to expound the ideological framework of *Laozi*, then the human society and the guiding role of "view of naturalness" in human society and so on.

The definitions, which are used for describing the core concepts that axiomatic interpretation involves, are placed first. We have given a total of 13 definitions, five basic assumptions and four axioms, which are defined and explained, coupled with the corresponding original texts of *Laozi*, which provide the basis for the following propositions and reasoning.

To meet the need for axiomatic research, we must link the interpretation of *Laozi* with the assumptions. The concept "keeping the moderate" is the bridge connecting the two sides and its core is how to determine the two sides in contradiction and how to properly handle the contradiction. We believe that the feature of Dao is "naturalness," which constitutes a contradiction with "unnaturalness" (deviating from *Dao*). The root of the contradiction results from the fact that man can be wise but cannot be bright. Not knowing the infiniteness of Dao, man only takes action by virtue of "wisdom." If we cannot deal with this contradiction properly, it will cause chaos in human society. Therefore, we humankind must be "bright" rather than "wise" so that we can have an accurate understanding of Dao and follow closely the "natural way" of Dao to act by inaction. So human beings need to explore what is "virtue" that is "natural," and how to govern a state and how to preserve one's health in accordance with "natural rule." This is the formation of the four aspects of the discussion, and the propositions are divided into four categories, forming the four chapters "On Understanding the Dao," "On Cherishing Virtue," "On Governance" and "On Preserving Health." The series of propositions in these chapters are separately discussed with more specific descriptions by proofs and explanations.

The next chapters from Chapter 3 to Chapter 6 include groups of propositions which elaborate Laozi's thought in an axiomatic approach.

There are 21 propositions in Chapter 3 "On Understanding the Dao", whose main purpose is to explain the basic concepts of Laozi's Dao and how people can understand or realize the meaning of Dao. First of all, Daoism and the relationship between Daoism and all things are explained. Secondly, it elaborates the two kinds of cognition or enlightenment: wisdom and discernment or being bright as well as the relationship between them, pointing out that people can really understand or realize Dao only if they can be bright or have discernment rather than being just wise. It once again explains the path, methods and process of realizing Dao.

Chapter 4 "On Cherishing Virtue" has a total of 23 propositions, which intends to describe the way of adapting to the virtues of nature, as well as the way and application of virtue-cultivation. Specifically, it is virtuous to act in line with the nature. People can be virtuous when they turn from "youwei" (taking action) into "wuwei" (taking non-action). In this regard, it should be recognized that greed, wisdom and being crafty are harmful to virtue cultivation. To be less influenced by them, people should be content, low, weak, and not to contend. This is the way to become a sage because a sage is featured by clear wisdom and tranquil heart. With this profound virtue, the natural way can be reflected.

Chapter 5 "On Governance" has a total of 28 propositions, which intends to expound the way of governing the country by following the natural rule. It points out that the ideal society is the natural society, and the characteristic of a well-governed society is a harmonious and natural society where people live and work in peace and contentment without rigid rites and rules. Furthermore, this chapter discusses the basic mode, performance and its implementation of good governance. It points out on the one hand that good governance in a natural way is realized by following the Dao and ancient examples, not excessively advocating wisdom, talent, benevolence, righteousness, rituals, merits, valuable goods and other things. On the other hand, the ruler must follow the way of keeping soft and weak in military affairs, diplomacy, administration, governance of people and other aspects. Therefore, it is requested that a ruler maintain both hardness and softness, and improve cultivation in virtue and trust.

Chapter 6 "On Preserving Health" has a total of 22 propositions, which mainly discusses how to care for the self-life to achieve the unity of self-care and love of other people, pointing out that the real realization of this must follow principle of "naturalness". The fundamental principle of preserving health is to follow the nature and maintain the quiet, indifferent, pure and honest state of mind and control self-appetite, which is a natural basis of following the nature. In this way, we need to establish the concept of wealth based on the principle of naturalness, and "properly understand" the relationship between wealth and life; establish the concept of honor and disgrace based on the principle of naturalness, and be content all the time and do not take all the things as their own; build the concept of strength and weakness, and of cleverness and clumsiness based on the principle of "naturalness". The principle based on "naturalness" in fact embodies the symbiosis principle of the individuals and all things.

The above-mentioned four chapters basically cover the main contents of *Laozi*. In order to help readers understand the corollaries, this book has also adopted proofs and explanations as complementary illustrations, which include the following types:

(1) The propositions are general and universal elaborations. The proofs are the discussion of individual cases. They do not cover all the connotations of the propositions, but are helpful to the understanding of specific connotation.

(2) The proofs as extension and expansion of the propositions may complement and enrich the connotation of the propositions from different aspects of life. Some proofs can contribute to the understanding of the logical relationship between the interpreted propositions and other ones. (3) The explanations reveal the connotation and universality of the propositions in ways different from the approach used in propositional reasoning. (4) Some explanations are intended to reveal the differences between the proposition and other traditional explanations of *Laozi*.

第一章 CHAPTER ONE

引 论
Introduction

本章概述《老子》思想的基本框架。在对老子其人、《老子》其书及其对后世的影响进行简单介绍之后，我们从老子之"道"、老子的"自然"与"自然观"、老子论"智"与"明"、老子论"功德"、老子论"治国"、老子论"养生"六大方面阐述了老子的思想体系，最后指出了老子思想的价值和意义。基于公理化诠释的需求，我们必须在老子思想的各个方面找到明确的逻辑关系。简言之，"道"是万事万物的本体，它具有无限性；"自然"是"道"的一种重要的性质，它支配着万事万物的生成、存在与运动，"无为而无不为"。相比之下，人类的"智"却做不到，甚至妨碍了"无为而无不为"的"自然"法则，也就违背了"道"。为了做到这一点，我们必须对人类的"智"进行"破迷解惑"的工作，必须指出人类通常将"智"用于满足争名夺利、争强好胜的欲望。由此审视之，统治者将争名夺利、争强好胜所得视为"功德"，就是错误的。水意象是说明或描述"道"的最为重要的意象之一，老子认为水与"道"具有诸多相似之处，特别是治国理政所应遵循之道。接着，老子得出了"寡欲少死""清静柔弱"的养生原则，也就是追求"养生"与"养德"的合一。

一、老子、《老子》及其影响概述

孔子在历史上的形象是清晰的，除《论语》外，《孔子世家》与《仲尼弟子列传》中都保留了不少详细的记载。与此不同，老子在中国历史上的形象则显得模糊而且神秘，甚至对于老子是谁、生活于什么时代都不能确定。司马迁在《史记》中对老子的记载，十分简略："居周久之，见周之衰，乃遂去。至关，关（令）尹喜曰：子将隐矣，强为我著书。于是老子乃著书上下篇，言道德之言五千余言而去，莫知其所终。"而且，司马迁在后面还附了老莱子与太史儋两种异说。可见，即使是生活在西汉初年的司马迁，对于老子的了解也不多且不确定。先秦文献《庄子》《韩非子》和《礼记》中虽然有关于老子的少许记载，但其真实性往往受到质疑，传闻的色彩也很浓重。

1. 老子形象在后世的变迁及《老子》的流传

古代关于老子的记载大都源自传说。在有关老子的传说中,最有名的是说其母怀胎七十二年而生老子,老子生而白首。基于人类现有的认知水平,对这样的传说似乎没有证伪的必要。然而,这些传说的出现一定有其内在的文化与历史原因,而且这些关于老子的传说在产生与流传以后,又参与到此后中国文化的构建之中,产生了一定的文化影响。司马迁在《史记》中的一段记载,常被用来说明道家对儒家的影响:"孔子适周,将问礼于老子。老子曰:'子所言者,其人与骨皆已朽矣,独其言在耳。且君子得其时则驾,不得其时则蓬累而行。吾闻之,良贾深藏若虚,君子盛德容貌若愚。去子之骄气与多欲,态色与淫志,是皆无益于子之身。吾所以告子,若是而已。'孔子去,谓弟子曰:'鸟,吾知其能飞;鱼,吾知其能游;兽,吾知其能走。走者可以为罔,游者可以为纶,飞者可以为矰。至于龙,吾不能知其乘风云而上天。吾今日见老子,其犹龙邪!'"

东汉末年,张道陵在江西龙虎山结庐炼丹,逐步建立道教。张道陵的《老子想尔注》首次从宗教的角度诠释《老子》(道教常称之为《道德经》),对"道"及老子进行了神化:"一散形为气,聚形为太上老君,常治昆仑。"于是,老子变身为道教神仙系统中的太上老君。后来又由于道教与佛教论争的需要,出现了"老子入夷为浮屠"等传说。魏晋以后,随着道教发展的需要,神仙化了的老子形象被不断改造。于是,在不同的背景下、不同人的心目中,老子的形象便在智者与神仙的双重身份叠加下愈发神秘。参考古史辨派提出的"层累"的历史观,老子的形象在中国历史上也应该是不断被添加和改造的结果。

与老子的身份一样,《老子》一书的成书时间以及其作者是否为老子,同样是自古至今学者们一直争论不清的问题。目前可知的最早的《老子》版本,是1993年在湖北荆门楚墓中发现的郭店竹简本,据考古学研究,该墓的时间大致在公元前300年前后。从这一点来判断,《老子》成书的时间应该不会晚于战国中期。

《老子》篇幅虽小,但因其思想的深刻,在战国时期已引起关注,《韩非子》即有《解老》《喻老》等篇,对《老子》进行解说与例证。秦汉以后,《老子》得到更为广泛的流传,在流传的过程中形成了许多不同的版本。据学者统计,仅清代以前的《老子》版本就超过百种。历朝历代对《老子》进行研究和注释的很多,于是出现了大量的注释本,元代正一天师张与材曾说:"《道德经》八十一章,注本三千余家。"据学者调查,流传至今的《老子》注本约有一千余种。在这众多的古代注本中,影响最大的两个应该是王弼本与河上公注本。除传世本外,随着考古工作的开展,又在长沙马王堆汉墓出土了两种西汉帛书本,在湖北荆门郭店楚墓中出土了战国竹简本，为《老子》的研究提供了新的重要依据。

《老子》在流传的过程中，其文字的改变在有意或无意之中不断产生，从而出现了各种版本的差异、文本的分歧。虽然这一现象在中国古代的书籍中普遍存在，但《老子》的情况特别严重。近年发现的帛书甲乙本及竹简本，其文本差异应该大致可以体现出《老子》流传的情况。这一方面给我们的阅读和研究增加了难度，但另一方面，正如刘笑敢所言，也为我们在有些方面的研究提供了可用的资料。

据联合国教科文组织统计，在世界各国经典名著中，被译成外国文字而且发行量最多的，除了《圣经》以外就是《老子》。《老子》是有史以来译成外文版本最多、海外发行量最大的中国经典。《老子》在海外的影响远较《论语》为大。国外的许多著名学者如黑格尔、尼采、海德格尔等，都曾关注和重视老子的思想。老子的思想在西方的流传之久、流传之广，超出了许多当今中国人的想象。《老子》可以被视为中国体系中的"元文本"或"基因文本"，这些哲学基因在两千多年漫长的中国思想史及文化史的各个阶段上，均部分或全部地表达了出来。老子的思想不仅被看作中国人的精神财富，更被看成全人类的精神财富，其影响遍及全世界。

2. 《老子》对后世政治思想及实践的影响

先秦诸子百家面对的是春秋战国时期诸侯混战、礼崩乐坏的社会局面，因此他们各家的思想虽然不尽相同，但是都有为当时的社会现实寻找出路的意味，都有着明显的政治关怀。虽然老子的思想立足于一种很高的宇宙视野，但同样不乏对现实政治的关注与思考。《老子》一书根基于天道自然的哲学认识，表现出"常与善人"的人文关怀、"道法自然"的生态智慧、"若烹小鲜"的善治理念、"无为不争"的道德自觉、"神源于道"的深远影响、"重人贵生"的养生向往。[1] 特别是其中的"常与善人"的人文关怀、"若烹小鲜"的善治理念、"无为不争"的道德自觉，提供了一种不同于儒家、法家的政治思想。

老子主张对万物都应有一种慈爱的情怀，"天道无亲，常与善人"。这种人文关怀，是对人的尊严与符合人性的生活条件的肯定。老子的"无为不争"，在于遵道而行，亦即顺应自然和社会规律，不任意妄为，不扰民，不制造和激化矛盾，以达到"无为"而"无不为"的效果。老子的"治大国若烹小鲜"是一种非常高

---

[1] 夏维纪:《道家人文之光》,《江西日报・江西人文大讲堂》, 2015年11月11日。

明的善治理念。"小鲜"是指"小鱼",烹制时需小心慎作,不能随心所欲地翻搅,否则鱼肉就会烂糊一团。老子以此比喻在执政中不要折腾、不要扰民。汉初的司马谈在《论六家要旨》中评价道家"指约而易操,事少而功多",认为道家在六家中效率最高而弊端最少,极为推重。老子的这些政治思想,虽然没有成为后来官方依循的主流,但对后世社会产生了深远的影响。

老子的政治思想在西汉初年曾经得到很好的实践,并且显示出了明显的效果。西汉初年的几位统治者如刘邦、吕后、文帝和景帝等都信奉"黄老之学",尤其是文帝和景帝的统治,可以说是老子政治思想最好的实验范本。这段历史时期不仅政治清静平和,百姓安居乐业,而且经济上也得到了极大的恢复和发展,使西汉建立时"自天子不能具驷马,而诸侯多乘牛车"的局面得以改观,为后来汉武帝的征讨匈奴做好了政治与经济上的准备。

汉武帝采纳董仲舒的建议"独尊儒术",放弃了汉初的统治思路,开始采用"阳儒阴法"的政治治理策略,使之成为后来历代统治者主要奉行的政治思想。虽然老子的政治思想在此后的历史中没再出现类似于汉初这样的典型运用,但老子思想依然对后来的统治者的思路产生着或隐或显的影响。晋唐以后的统治者很多都尊崇老子,亲自参与祭拜老子。许多帝王如唐玄宗、宋徽宗、明太祖、清世祖等都曾御注《老子》,明显受过老子思想的影响。

道家思想对于后世政治思想及实践具有前瞻性。早在启蒙运动时期,它就已经为思想家设计现代世界的蓝图提供了强大的思想资源与参照坐标。它不仅在人类世界20世纪末产生出的软实力和反权力哲学思想方面,而且在全球良治和可持续发展理念方面均表现出了深刻的前瞻性。进一步而言,道家哲学思想正在改变我们的经济与社会生活实践方式,如反经济扩张模式、反消费主义社会形态,以及生活节奏之均衡、可持续发展目标之设定等。

3. 《老子》对道教的影响,道家与道教的关系

老子不仅是道家的创始人,对道教的创立和发展也产生了深远的影响。与世界上的其他宗教不同,作为中国本土宗教的道教,是在一个比较长的时期内,将中国文化中的一些文化元素杂凑而成的,其中包括了道家思想、民间信仰、神仙方术、阴阳学说以及中医中药、符箓之学等。在印度佛教扎根之前,中国并无真正意义上之宗教,仅有一些原始民间宗教信仰、巫术、萨满教,此一空白为印度佛教所填补。佛教之天然盟友乃是道家思想,佛教采取的本土化策略是援道入释,用以抵抗来自儒家思想的排斥。东汉末年至魏晋期间,张道陵、葛洪等人逐步创立了道教。从某种意义上说,道教是在面临佛教之竞争、针对民众欲望需求

而创立的一种宗教。《老子》一书由于具有较高的理论水准、独特的思想面目，遂被道教的创立者用作道教的基础理论。张道陵所著《老子想尔注》便是典型的代表。"神源于道"，老子被张道陵推崇为"太上老君"之后，道教便有了自己的能与孔子、释迦牟尼比肩的崇拜神尊。在道教发展和完善的过程中，葛洪更是借老子思想来构建道教的理论体系。因为道教并非由某个人集中创立，而是经由多人长时间逐渐发展构建而成的，为了增加在传播时的影响力，道教的创立者们不仅借用了《老子》中的理论，还把老子其人奉为道教的创立者。于是，老子便被动地成了道教的始祖，且被神化为太上老君，而《老子》一书也被奉为道教经典而成为《道德经》。同样道理，道家的另一重要人物庄子被道教奉为"南华真人"，《庄子》也被称作《南华经》。

因为道教在形成过程中与道家有着密切的渊源关系，两者在思想要素、主要人物以及代表经典上的共同性，使得它们在此后的中国文化中具有了千丝万缕的联系。很多时候，它们的界限是模糊的，不易区分。从学术的角度来看，道家和道教这两个词指称的内容应该是可以区分的。道家指的是由老子、庄子开创，出现于春秋战国并在后世流传的哲学思想流派，道教则是在两汉逐渐形成，后又有若干发展分化的一种宗教。虽然道教在理论上汲取了道家思想的大量元素，甚至奉老子为教主，但二者还是不能混为一谈，也不能说道教理论就是道家思想。道家作为一个哲学思想流派，其思想流变与代表人物应是它被解说时最重要的内容，由于没有成为官方主流的学术思想，魏晋之后道家思想的传承流变有些模糊而难以说清，但它对历代文人、学者的影响却仍是依稀可辨的。而道教作为一种宗教，具备了宗教的一些必备要素，有其神仙崇拜与信仰，有教徒与组织，有一系列的宗教仪式与活动，其主要派别的传承也是大致清楚的。

留法学者韦遨宇在2014年于庐山举行的中华经典的公理化诠释研讨会上，作了题为"老子、庄子与道家哲学思想"的系列演讲。他指出：道教之发展史显示出其对统治者而言为一柄双刃剑。以汉朝为例，道教教派黄巾军掀起的起义几使汉朝陷入崩溃之危机；唐朝为争正统，李渊托称老子后代，将道教奉为国教；北宋鼠疫期间，宫廷命国师作法消灾；元末，道教教派白莲教亦在推翻元朝之战争中起到相当大之作用；清末义和团曾经念着刀枪不入之符咒迎击密集射击之洋枪洋炮，由反清灭洋转至扶清灭洋。此等命运，令人唏嘘。然而在历史上的大部分时期，多数道教人士还是隐居于山林，道教在民间较有市场，并提供一些医疗服务和道场服务及从事其他一些活动。道教乃是中国历史上一个十分复杂且特殊的现象，道教史既有连续性亦有非连续性。它发展了系统性理论与实践，并对中国普通百姓之日常生活产生了重要、持久且深远之影响，如中医药、饮食文化、宗教仪轨、风水等，其影响亦延伸至东亚与南亚。

"道教"和"道家"这两个词在内涵上是大致清楚的，但在使用中并不易于区分，在很多的语境中它们常常被混用。特别在中国，儒、释、道三者常常并称，被认为是构成中国传统文化的三个重要支柱。这种简称中的"道"，往往是兼道教与道家两者而言的。在民间的观念和认识中，这一情况更加明显，作为历史人物的老子和被道教借老子形象塑造的太上老君往往混而为一。比如在河南鹿邑，人们对老子文化十分重视，但当地人口中所说和心中所认为的"老子""太上老君"和"老君爷"基本上是一回事。

道教借用了老子其人、《老子》其书以及老子的思想来完成自身系统的构建，可以说是对道家的许多文化内容进行了一种接管，这在某种程度上挤压了道家的生存空间。不可否认道教对老子在后世地位的提升和《老子》一书的流传所起到的积极作用，但道教对《老子》一书的传承和解释产生的负面影响则更需要引起警惕。道教虽然以道家特别是老子思想作为思想基础，但只是部分借用老子思想并对之进行了许多符合宗教需要的改造。出于与佛教论争的需要，道教将老子的形象不断神化，加之道教大量吸收了神仙方术、民间鬼神崇拜观念和巫术活动的内容，使得后世对《老子》的理解被附加了很多神秘化的内容。在这种文化背景下，我们回归文本对《老子》进行学理上的诠释，其意义就越发凸显出来。

4. 《老子》对后世学术思想的影响

先秦诸子著书立说的春秋战国时代，正是学者们所说的人类历史的轴心时代。先秦诸子的学说因为理论上的开创性，对中国后世的学术思想产生了极为深远而持久的影响。《老子》一书因其视野的开阔与哲思的深刻，对后世学术思想的影响尤其巨大。魏晋玄学与宋明理学是汉代以后中国学术发展中的两个最为重要的学术流派，在这两者的理论系统构建中，《老子》的思想都产生了至关重要的影响。

魏晋玄学是中国历史上一个重要的学术流派，也是魏晋文化的一个显著标志。玄学的产生和理论体系的建立，则与老子思想密切相关。玄学由王弼开创，由何晏建立理论体系，这两人的思想均与《老子》有重要关系。中国古代许多学者往往借注释经典来表达自己的思想，例如何晏和王弼。何晏的著作大都散佚，但从现在残存的一些材料中，可以看出他是曾经注过《老子》的。而王弼的《老子注》不仅至今尚存，而且是《老子》影响最大的两个古代注本之一，历来为学术界重视。何晏"以无为本"思想是在老子学说的基础上发展和改造而来，后又经王弼充实完善，成为玄学理论的核心内容。王弼借《老子注》建立了严密完整的玄学理论体系，《老子》作为"三玄"之一，为玄学提供了最为重要的"有""无"概念及理论基础。

理学也称新儒学，是由周敦颐、二程、朱熹等学者构建的一个学术体系。理学虽然以儒学为旗帜，但其思想体系却是儒、释、道融合的结果。周敦颐、朱熹等人在构建理学体系的时候，大量借用了道家思想特别是《老子》中体现的思想。周敦颐作为理学初创期的代表人物，他在奠定理学格局的《太极图说》中借用了《老子》一书中构建的宇宙模式，作为他的哲学认识的起点。二程和朱熹更是吸收了老子以道为宇宙本体以及"道生万物"的思想来完善儒家的本体论，又吸收了清静、无为和主静的修养思想。朱熹深受道家哲学的影响，他援道入儒，成为理学的集大成者。理学中"理"的概念在内涵上与老子的"道"有很大相似性，而朱熹"理-气-物-理"的思路，也与老子"道生一，一生二，二生三，三生万物"以及"人法地，地法天，天法道，道法自然"的思想类似。宋明理学将道家解决问题的起点、思路、方法、思维方式、概念模式、哲理框架、逻辑思辨等方面移植入儒家，提升了儒学的哲理思辨水平，促进了儒学的新发展，从而完成了理学理论体系的构建。不论从思想渊源还是理论特点看，宋明理学都深深地打上了老子哲学的烙印。

《老子》除了对玄学与理学产生了深远影响之外，对其他学者同样产生了或隐或显的影响。宋代的王安石、苏辙，清代的王夫之、魏源等人，都曾对《老子》做过深入的研究，深受《老子》思想的影响。

韦遨宇教授指出，道家哲学思想在中国影响最为直接且深远的学科领域还包括：（1）哲学与语言哲学。《老子》文中阐释的"反者道之动"的辩证法思想，对中国文化产生了深远影响。（2）宗教。道家自然哲学排除了在中国出现一元神论和超验性宗教的可能性，对印度佛教在中国的传播和道教的发生产生了影响。（3）政治学。无为而治的良治模式，小国寡民之理想及社会正义之理想，所倡导的"天之道，损有余而补不足"深入人心。（4）人与自然之关系。它尊重自然与回归自然之学说及实践，强调"宠辱皆忘"、无欲与无知、与宇宙自然精神的合一，因而中国古代未出现大规模的以开发自然为目标的科学探索，未出现消费主义的商业文化传统。（5）文学艺术领域。中国古代文学艺术浸透着象征思维，诗学与美学高度发达，成为历来抵抗各种权力的战场。

二、老子之"道"的解读

就文本形式而言,《老子》像散文、像诗歌、像格言,对这样一种面目多变的著作也就可以进行各种各样的解读。在《老子》的文本中,"道"这个字前后出现了七十三次,其含义和意义有不相同之处,研究者对"道"的理解和看法也很不统一。如胡适说"道"是"天地万物的本源",又说老子的"天道"就是"西洋哲学的自然法"(Law of Nature)。冯友兰说"道即万物所以生之总原理",又说"道或无就是万物的共相"(《中国哲学史》)。侯外庐说"道"是"超自然的绝对体"(《中国思想通史》)。张岱年早年说"道"是"最高原理",即"究竟所以";中年说"道"是"原始的混然不分的物质存在的总体,即混然一气";晚年则回到早年的立场,说"道还是指最高原理而言"(《中国哲学发微》)。吕振羽说"道的内容……是神话的东西","道是创造宇宙、统治宇宙的最高主宰"(《中国政治思想史》)。杨荣国说"(道)不是物质实体,是虚无,是超时空的绝对精神"(《简明中国思想史》)。徐复观说"道"是"创生宇宙万物的一种基本动力"(《中国人性论史》)。劳思光说"道"是"形上之实体,是实有义",又说是"道之为言,泛指规律"(《中国哲学史》)[1]。归纳各家的见解,"道"是一种虚无或物质的实体,也是一种原理或法则。但这样的解释似乎比较抽象,下面我们试图更具体地阐述"道"的含义。

1. 不可言说、难以命名的"道"

《老子》第一章说:"道可道,非常道;名可名,非常名。"按照这种句读,我们一般的理解是:第一个"道"是老子的特别概念,第二个"道"就是字面意思"言说"。可以言说的"道"不是常道,可以命名的"名"不是常名,综合意指用常规命名方式命名的"道"并非老子所说的"道"。

"道可道,非常道"给人的印象是"道"是"不可言说",或者说是难以言说的,或者说此"道"与通常所理解的"道"大不相同,说出来人们也不容易理解。然而即便是"不可言说"或"难以言说",也可以有多种意思。中国先秦时代还是一个人神混杂的时代,那些神秘的"鬼神"往往是不可言说的,似有似无,似乎能感觉得到又不能被清晰感觉到。那么,老子的"道"是不是这种神秘的"鬼神"?老子虽然说"道之为物,惟恍惟惚"(《老子》第二十一章),但说"道"像鬼神一般神秘,显然是不妥的。关于老子之"道"是否具有神秘主义色彩这一点,中

---

[1] 安蕴贞:《西方庄学研究》,北京:中国社会科学出版社,2012年,第49页。

外研究者有过很多探讨。如有人指出，老子关于"道"的无限性问题的阐述，与古希腊哲学家高尔吉亚提出的三个原则很是接近："第一个是：无物存在；第二个是：如果有某物存在，这个东西也是别人无法认识的；第三个是：即令这个东西可以被认识，也无法把它说出来告诉别人。"

美国本杰明·史华兹教授在《古代中国的思想世界》一书中指出：印度思想家认为"真实的依据"的含义或"无"的范围，不能被人类语言的门类所讨论，因为那是"一个超乎人类语言所描绘的所有决定、关系、过程的真实或真实范围"。西方和伊斯兰的中世纪哲学也同样强调"上帝就其本质而言是人类语言所不可知的和无法接近的"，因为"有限的人"处于无可改变的欠缺中，所以"永远不能知道上帝的内在本质"。

但是，所谓"真实的依据"或"上帝的内在本质"并不能等同于老子的"道"。本杰明·史华兹为此特别强调了老子哲学的无神论特征："老子的神秘主义确实并非建立于有神论的隐喻之上。对'道'的强调体现了对'天'的中心地位的惊人的背离。"因此，老子哲学的基本属性可以称为"无神的神秘主义"：一方面，由于超乎语言，无法言说，甚至不是人的理性所能达到的，所以笼罩着神秘主义的色彩；另一方面，因为纯任自然，无所崇拜，否定了外在于人的支配力量，所以又具有了无神论的特性。

既然如此，我们是否可以说"道"是一种纯粹的感觉，如同我们常说的"直觉"或"潜意识"，可遇不可求，感觉得到却无法清晰描述呢？这显然也不妥，因为老子又说"执古之道，以御今之有"（《老子》第十四章），指出"道"是可以把握的。《老子》第二十一章说"孔德之容，惟道是从"，这表明"道"是可以依从的。《老子》第八章说"处众人之所恶，故几于道"，明确指出"道"是可以接近或到达的目标。有了这些描述，"道"就已经不是纯粹存在于"直觉"或"潜意识"之中了。

在现象学理论中，也有所谓的"不可言说"。这种理论之所以要求"直面事物本身"，是因为事物的本质或真实的意义是不可言说的。这种"不可言说"，是指语言本身与事物无法精确对应。但实质上，这种"不可言说"的程度也是有区别的。对于寻常的事物，它们在人类可见、可感、可描述的范围之内，"可言说"的程度较高，"不可言说"的成分较少；如果这种事物大大超出了人类可见、可感、可描述的范围，则"不可言说"的程度较高，"可言说"的成分就较少了。从"道冲而用之或不盈"（《老子》第四章）、"天乃道，道乃久"（《老子》第十六章）这些提示中，可以想见"道"在空间上的广阔性以及在时间上的久远性，也可以想见"道"大大超出了人类可见、可感、可描述的范围,所谓的"不可言说"指的就是这方面的内容。

与"道"的"不可言说"有关的,还有"道"的难以命名:"名可名,非常名。"(《老子》第一章)在先秦儒家那里,"名"也是得到高度重视的。孔子重视"正名",并认为"名"关涉"礼"与"刑"之实,所指向的对象是伦理秩序,即立名分以定尊卑。当君向臣索取物质时应该说"取",而不是"假",这符合并标明君对臣的在财产和身份上的主宰。儒家代表人物之一荀子对正名有更多的论说和思考。"名"来源于传统或者约定。"名无固宜,约之以命,约定俗成谓之宜,异于约则谓之不宜。"(《荀子·正名》)区分"名"的根本依据是人的感官认识,"然则何缘而以同异?曰:缘天官"。"正名"的根本作用在于统一对"礼"的认识,"故王者之制名,名定而实辨,道行而志通,则慎率民而一焉"。由此可见,荀子在理论上深化了儒家的"正名"说,同时强调了"名"在伦理政治方面的社会性。在荀子看来,"名"不是事物先天固有的,而是约定俗成的,也可以说是人们易于理解的;而在儒家的"礼制"之中,"实"主要是指权力地位、对财产的支配权和分配权等内容,其范围是比较清晰的。荀子讨论"名"与"实"的关系,实质上就是在约定俗成的"名"与社会上一些事物、现象之间建立明确的关系。

按照形式逻辑的说法,概念是反映对象的本质属性的思维形式。人类在认识过程中,从感性认识上升到理性认识,把所感知的事物的共同本质特点抽象出来,加以概括,就成为概念。表达概念的语言形式是词或词组。概念都有内涵和外延,即其含义和适用范围。可以说,表达概念的语言形式就是"名",而它的内涵和外延都是比较明确的。儒家所说的"名",也有较为明确的内涵和外延,如"君"和"臣"。然而,对于老子之"道"这一概念来说,却难以用通常的"名"来指称。"道"是"听之不闻""搏之不得"的,难以把握它的本质属性;它既以一种事物或对象的形式存在,又不以任何事物和对象的形式存在。"无名,天地之始;有名,万物之母。"它可以用"大"的形式存在,也可以用"小"的形式存在。"万物归焉而不为主,可名为大","衣养万物而不为主,可名于小"。如果按照形式逻辑的说法,"道"的内涵和外延都是不确定的,这当然就不能用一个确定的"名"来指称它了。

姑且不论老子的常"道"和常"名"是否更"真"(从认识结果的"真""假"说),或是否更高(从认识阶段的不同层次说),把它与"言说"和"命名"关联起来表明老子是从"语言"的角度,或者说从反思"语言"的角度去阐发"道"和"名"的。反思"语言"就是语言哲学。

语言哲学作为一门学问有其"原"问题，比如语言的本质、功能和意义等。一般说来，语言哲学作为哲学的分支是存在于中西和古今思想家的思想内容中的，只有西方现代哲学中讨论语言转向的那种语言哲学才指一种特别的哲学旨趣和追求。西方传统哲学认为语言是理性思维的工具和形式，并以此来建立对象性的理论体系；西方现代哲学则认为所谓的"思"无非就是语言的真实意义，"语言是存在之家"（海德格尔语）。一般的语言哲学和现代西方语言哲学的反思"语言"思路为理解老子的"道"提供了一种角度。

　　现代语言学奠基人索绪尔有一个很著名的关于语言学研究的理论，他把"言语活动"分成两部分：语言和言说。索绪尔认为语言是社会现象，言说则是个人现象。语言以储存于每个成员大脑中的总和的形式存在于集体之中，有如一部词典，把它相同的印本分发给每个人。这是存在于每个人身上的某种东西，然而对所有的人来说仍然是共同的。它不受储存者意志的影响。而言说是人们说话的总和，包括：（1）从属于说话人意志的个人组合；（2）实现这些组合所必需的同样受意志支配的说话行为。这样，在言语中没有集体的东西，它的表现是个人的和瞬息的。

　　老子的"道可道"类似"言说"，"名可名"类似"语言"。"言说"是个体的，"语言"是社会的。先秦诸子大都不重视即时的、瞬间的"言说"，而重视社会的"语言"，但是老子反对或至少是轻视"语言"。如果说先秦其他诸子对于"名"的政治伦理及其社会性有大概相同的理解，那么老子反对"名"，实际上就是在反对当时流行的政治伦理观念。当社会中的"名"过多从而导致无穷的纷争时，老子选择了"不言"来对抗。

　　西方语言哲学的一个研究重点是探讨语言本身与语言所表达的意向及对象之间的关系，并发现在表达意向、描述对象方面，语言本身存在诸多缺陷。有人指出："为了获得对有关证实主义争端的一种更宽广的观点，让我们考虑下面的意见：我们的一切语词均不指称。我们的一切信念均非真。在英语和再现世界状况的那种语言之间无转译的可能。"[1]这种观点体现了一种否定语言之作用的倾向，我们不必完全接受，但却可以由此想到，"准确再现世界状况的那种语言"事实上是不存在的，也可以说，作为语言的"道"并不能准确反映作为对象的"道"。从另一个角度我们也可以看出这一点。如研究者指出，虽然语词的含义会随对象的变化而变化，但是每一种确定的含义（或者说每一个确定的概念）所指称的只能是

1　理查德·罗蒂：《哲学和自然之镜》，北京：商务印书馆，2011年，第320页。

一个（或一类）确定的对象。如果对象发生了变化，那么指称它的就应该是另外一个概念。在指称对象方面，概念自身并不存在什么灵活性，不可能存在同一个概念可以指称不同对象的情况。[1]以此而论，"道"这个语词只能指称一个（或一类）确定的对象，但事实上"道"并不局限于一个（或一类）确定的对象，而是代表了无数个（或无限类别）的对象。这样，用"道"这个语词或名称来指称"道"，当然就只能是勉强为之，事实上并不准确了。

其实，魏晋时期的哲学家早已对语言进行过辩证统一的思考，他们既肯定语言作为思想表达和认识世界工具的作用，又看到了语言表意的局限性，指出类似"道"等形而上的东西是难以通过语言的形式陈述和表达的。魏晋时期的"言意之辨"和现代西方语言哲学的探讨有契合之处。

2. 内涵与外延无限扩展的"道"

基于表达思想的需要，老子需要对"道"强名之；基于公理化研究的需求，更需要大致明确"道"的含义。正如德国哲学家海德格尔在谈论真理的本质时指出的："一位思想家的'学说'则是在他的道说中未被道说出来的东西……为了能够经验并且在将来能够知道一位思想家的未被道说出来的东西——不论它具有何种特性——我们必须思考它所道说出来的东西。"[2]

常规的概念，其内涵和外延都是"有限的"。而"道"恰好相反，其内涵和外延都是无限的，包括存在形式的无限性和运动形式的无限性。

从逻辑上理解，"道"是最大的抽象，不能被述说，只能勉强描述，"道法自然"中的"自然"是"无法述说""没有规定"的意思。但基于表达思想和建立一种理论体系的需要，老子抽取了"道"的一些特征进行重点描述。

其一是"道"对于天地间万事万物之生成的作用。"道生一，一生二，二生三，三生万物。万物负阴而抱阳，冲气以为和。"（《老子》第四十二章）这是老子对"道"的数理表达。"道"不能被述说，是"无、虚、静、朴"，是"自然"，但它却能述说万物。人的所有观念都是通过它而得到的，所以"道生一"以至于"万物"，而万物无非也就是"道"的述说。万物生成均有赖于它，这是"道"体现的"德"；无时无刻不在生成无处不在的万物，这是它的"功"。这也是"无限性"的一种体现，但依然不是"无限性"的全部。

---

[1] 胡泽洪、张家龙等：《逻辑哲学研究》，广州：广东教育出版社，2013年，第95页。
[2] 海德格尔：《柏拉图的真理学说》，见《路标》，北京：商务印书馆，2000年，第234页。

相比而言，人类自诩的功德不存在这种无限性。人类在主体上还是要依赖于"道"繁衍生息，传承不绝，从事一切生命活动，一切与外部环境有关的活动。夸大人类的作为，夸大人类的作用，其结果必然是忽视"道"的无限性。而脱离了无限性的滋养，"有限性"的固有缺陷会更加突出。实际上，也因为有限性较容易认识、较容易言说，无限性难以认识和言说，也使人类往往盯住有限性不放，用有限的认识来指导自己的行为。基于有限性的缺陷，人类却不知不觉地切断了许多无限性的滋养。例如，工具的制造、技术的开发，让人类不断获得无限的物质世界的滋养，但是，痴迷于这些人工的东西，却使生命失去了自然而然适应环境的许多可能性，人类已经变得离开自己制造的工具就无法前行一步了。政治、军事、经济制度的发展，一方面使人类的群体生活提高了质量，另一方面也使得人类在脱离社会的情况下就几乎无法存活。而对各种社会治理的依赖，又加重了人类社会的期望值，更加牢固地把人类捆绑在政治、军事、经济等各种社会管理之中。

其二是"道"与"天"的关系。从宇宙生成论的角度说，儒家的抽象止于"天"，天道就是最大的"道"，最根本的规律。这还是用具体的某种物质来替代真正的抽象，严格说来还不能算是"抽象"的结果，虽然在思考"天"的问题上运用了某种直觉抽象的方法。这就好比后来的唯物主义哲学家批评泰勒士一样，泰勒士虽然抽象出一句标志人类理性思维开端的结论——"世界是水"，但"水"依然是具体的某种物质。儒家以"天"来谈论世界，实际上也还是停留在具体的某种物质上。

老子虽然在抽象方法上与儒家是一致的，但抽象的深度却超越了儒家。老子认为在天地之先还有不可言说的"道"："有物混成，先天地生。寂兮寥兮，独立不改，周行而不殆，可以为天下母。吾不知其名，强字之曰道，强为之名曰大。大曰逝，逝曰远，远曰反。故道大，天大，地大，人亦大。域中有四大，而人居其一焉。人法地，地法天，天法道，道法自然。"（《老子》第二十五章）这样"道"就成了独立于任何具体物质的抽象。只有这种无形似有形、静止却运动的抽象才能在理论上说明万物的生成以及运行规律。万物都是有形的和运动的，如果要找到它们统一的起点，我们一般会在经验中断定那个起点也一定是有形的和运动的。然而经验在思考面前往往显得很苍白：如果断定起点也是有形的和运动的，那我们就找不到宇宙的起点，因为我们可以认为无数种有形的物质是起点。古希腊在泰勒士之后就有了"世界是气""世界是火"等相互抵触但也无法相互否定的自然哲学论断。老子洞察了这一点，所以提出了一个"恍惚"的"道"的世界观。

"道"是万物之母,道之功就成为"德"。所以,从宇宙生成论上看,"道"是万物生成的原料和动力。所谓"道法自然"中的"自然"指"无"和"有"的相互转化。"自然"是最为玄妙的宇宙规律。当然,老子关注宇宙,也意在为人确立行动规则。那么这种"道"的抽象世界观能为人的行动带来什么呢?儒家关注"天",并从天人相分和天人相合中找到了人的实践价值(指人不断进行自我修养,从而完成人生使命的过程)。老子关注"道",是从一个更为根本之处发现人的渺小和实践价值的虚无。所以人能够做的,或者说应该做的就是在看清楚"有""无"之变幻后,处下、守静、无为、不争。

老子的宇宙论贬低人的行为价值,但贬低不是否定。"无为"不会什么也不做。他只是告诫人必须要在任何作为的时候回想到自己作为的界限,回归到"道"的根本。也就是说,可以为,但不可以忘本。"无为"指的是不忘本的作为。有注释家也解释说老子的"无为"其真正含义是"不妄为",这是从宇宙生成论的角度来理解老子的"无为"思想。

三、老子的"自然"与"自然观"

在先秦的历史语境中,"自然"的意象并不是指与人的存在相分离的客观对象。在先秦文化中,不论儒家、道家或墨家,也不论哲学、文学或艺术,都把"天地自然"看作一个有机整体,人是其中的一部分,表现出人与自然的相互依存的认知与体验,把自然看作可以与人发生感应或共鸣的有情宇宙。因此,老子视域中的"自然"无论起点还是归宿都是人与社会。有学者指出,《老子》中的"自然"是一个富含人文性的概念。[1]

1. "自然"的三重意蕴

"自然"是老子思想的核心范畴之一,在其文本中一共有五处:"功成事遂,百姓皆谓我自然"(《老子》第十七章),"希言自然"(《老子》第二十三章),"人法地,地法天,天法道,道法自然"(《老子》第二十五章),"道之尊,德之贵,夫莫之命而常自然"(《老子》第五十一章),"以辅万物之自然而不敢为"(《老子》第六十四章)。

河上公对"我自然"的注解是:"百姓不知君上之德淳厚,反以为己自当然也。"吴澄注:"'然',如此也","百姓皆谓我自如此也"。而"莫之命而常自然"的意思是,圣人对万物的生长不加干涉,万物就能够自生自成。"以辅万物之自然

---

[1] 杨家友:《老子自然意蕴的再探讨》,《哲学分析》,2011年第4期。

而不敢为"则明确指出圣人对万物的生长应持"不敢为"的态度,以促使万物依靠自己的力量成就自己。这三处"自然"的基本意思是"自己如此"。因此,"自然"在《老子》文本中的一个基本意涵即是"自己如此",强调的是万物不依靠外在的力量自己成就自己的性质。

对于《老子》第二十五章"道法自然"的理解,尽管存在较大的分歧,但主要集中在对"道"以及"道与自然"的关系的理解上。河上公注"道性自然,无所法也",意思是"道"自己如此,不存在效法的对象。吴澄注"道之所以大,以其自然,故曰'法自然',非道之外别有自然也",意思是说"道"之所以能称为"大",在于它自己成就自己,而非在自身之外还有一可资效法的"自然"存在。也有人认为,此处之"自然"应为一名词,即自然界。从句法结构上看,"法"为"效法"之意,为谓语动词,因而此处的"自然"应作名词"自然界"解。而实际上,"道法自然"里的"自然"作"自己如此之性质"解,意为"道"效法的是万物自己成就自己的这种性质。"换句话说,道这个概念并非是老子凭空想象出来的,而是老子通过对万物依靠自己的力量成就自己的这种性质的观察之后抽象出来的,因而道最本初的含义即是万物生长之道。从这个角度来讲,道也是有效法对象的,效法的非其自身,而是万物自己如此之性质。"[1]因此,《老子》中"自然"的第一层意蕴是"自己如此"。

《老子》中"自然"的第二层意蕴,是在"希言自然"(《老子》第二十三章)中将"自然"作为一种原则来讲的。河上公对"希言自然"的注解是:"希言者,谓爱言也。爱言者自然之道。"也就是说,"希言"是符合自然原则的。很明显,这里的"自然"已经不能理解为"自己如此"之意了,而具有了老子之"道"的性质,成为万物需遵循的一种原则,与"道"是同一层级的概念。"希言自然"的意思即是"希言"是符合自然之原则的。"希言"就是少发号施令,也就是老子所谓"处无为之事,行不言之教",即老子主张的"无为"。与之相反的"多言",代表的是一种违背自然原则的"人为",这在老子看来只能招致"数穷"(机关算尽,濒临灭亡)。"无为"包含着"无欲""无技"和"不争"三个维度。"无欲"并非是对欲望的否定,而是要以自然为原则来界定欲望是否合于老子之"道",而为了实现这一点,就需要意识到欲望的边界。"无技"指明了遵循自然原则的具体方式,即"使有什伯人之器而不用……虽有舟舆,无所乘之;虽有甲兵,无所陈之。使民复结绳而用之"(《老子》第八十章)。"不争"则表明遵循自然原则的根

---

[1] 张敏:《老子文本中的自然观念》,《理论月刊》,2015年第2期。

本态度应如水一般,"善利万物而不争,处众人之所恶",方能"几于道"(《老子》第八章)。

《老子》中"自然"的第三层意蕴,是将"自然如此"的精神上升为"自然而然"的"爱民治国"的基本原则。同时,"自然"也是一种状态和境界,为老子对理想社会的终极追求。这种追求集中体现在老子对"小国寡民"的描述中:"小国寡民。使有什伯人之器而不用,使民重死而不远徙。虽有舟舆,无所乘之;虽有甲兵,无所陈之。使民复结绳而用之。甘其食,美其服,安其君,乐其俗。邻国相望,鸡犬之声相闻,民至老死,不相往来。"(《老子》第八十章)在这样的理想社会中,没有文字,没有战争,百姓的日常生活无须借助技艺,就能"甘其食,美其服,安其居,乐其俗"。这就是老子所追求的一种自然而然的社会状态。也只有摒弃一切"人为"的因素,高扬自然秉性,百姓才能够"不争""不为盗""心不乱""孝慈""自化""自正""自富""自朴",达到一种自然而然的状态和境界。

"自己如此",肯定万物依靠自身力量成就自己的性质,在老子看来这种性质是万物发展、变化的根本力量。如果我们肯定了万物、百姓自生自成这种性质的根本性,且能遵循自然原则,就能够达到一种自然而然的状态和境界。"自然"观念的这三层意蕴,可以视为老子整个思想的三个基石。

2. "自然"的人文寓意

就《辞海》"自然"条目的义项看,"自然"有三个义项:(1)天然,非人为的。如自然物、自然美。(2)不造作,非勉强的。如态度自然,文笔自然。(3)犹当然。也就是说,作为客观对象的存在,广义的自然物与自然界,指具有无穷多样性的一切存在物,与宇宙、物质、存在、客观实在等范畴同义,包括人类社会。狭义的自然界是指自然科学所研究的无机界和有机界。被人类活动改变了的自然界,通常称为"第二自然",或"人化自然"。而作为人和事物存在的状态,这里"自然"的寓意既指不受外界干预的人或事物发展变化的状态,也指人的自然本性和状态。除此以外,"自然"作为副词或连词的义项,是指人和事物发展变化的必然趋势,指人和事物长时间形成或习惯形成的理所当然。那么,老子语境中的"自然",又该如何定义呢?

刘笑敢在他的《老子古今》注释中,对老子语境中的"自然"做了系统的分析和界定:(1)"自然"属于名词;(2)"自然"不是大自然或自然界,因此不属于自然观、本体论或形而上学,"自然"也不是一般的伦理学、政治哲学、历史哲学的概念,更难以归入认识论或语言哲学或方法论。经过反复思考和比较,笔者发现将"自然"定义为中心价值,则比较符合西方哲学中的价值理论。还有一个原因是道的原则或根本是自然;(3)要将常识中的自然和老子之自然区别开,我们一般将老子之自然的核心意义定义为"人文自然",也就是说,老子的自然主要关心的是人类社会的生存状态;(4)概括说来,老子所说的自然包括了自发性(自己如此)、原初性(本来如此)、延续性(通常如此)和可预见性(势当如此)四个方面。可概括为两个要点,即动力的内在性和发展的平稳性。而更概括的说法则是总体状态的和谐[1]。《二十世纪中国老学》中提到,"自然"二字从字义上说是"莫使之然,莫使使之不然",而这一点是"自己如此"最古典的正式说明。

老子的"自然"并不是现代人所说的"自然界"或"大自然",而是指一种不受强制力量控制而顺应自然的状态,它是"自己如此""本来如此""自自然然""自然而然"的意思。在老子看来,宇宙是一个和谐的、平衡的整体,这种和谐、平衡的状态就是万事万物在不受外界干扰的情况下,都能发挥自己的最佳状态,都能与周围的其他事物保持着良好的关系,整个宇宙就在万物的最佳状态和良好关系中达到了和谐与平衡,发挥出最大的功能。这就是老子所谓的"自然"。

也有研究指出,老子的"自然"观念并非是一个意涵单一的范畴,而是包括了三个相互关联的层次:第一,自己如此之性质;第二,自然无为之原则;第三,自然而然之状态。"自己如此",肯定万物依靠自身力量成就自己的性质,且在老子看来这种性质是万物发展、变化的根本力量。而老子对万物的观察,并非如同古希腊哲学那样仅仅在于探究万物生成的规律,而是意图将其对万物生成的这种认识上升为"爱民治国"的根本原则。"自然"的第三层意蕴则是在前两者基础上生发出来的,如果我们肯定了万物、百姓自生自成这种性质的根本性,且能遵循自然原则,就能够达到一种自然而然的状态和境界。"自然"观念的这三层意蕴,可以视为老子的宇宙论、政治论、人生论。三者层层累进,凸显出《老子》的整个思想脉络。

老子的"自然"关心的是人类社会的生存状态,刘笑敢认为可以定义为"人文自然"。他认为"自然"的概念大体可以涉及行为主体与外在环境、外在力量的关系问题,以及行为主体在时间、历史的演化中的状态问题。

关于行为主体与外部世界的关系问题,"自然"的表述就是"自己如此"。(1)"自己如此"是自然的最基本的意涵,其他意涵都与此有关。"自然"的这一意义是指没有外力直接作用的自发状态,或者是外力作用小到可以忽略不计的状态。(2)关于行为主体或存在主体在时间延续中的状态问题是针对变化来说的,

---

[1] 刘笑敢:《老子古今》(上卷),北京:中国社会科学出版社,2006年版,第289—292页。

对此，我们可以用"本来如此"和"通常如此"来表述。自然是原有状态的平静的持续，而不是剧烈变化的结果。这就是说，一切源于内在动因的变化如果突然中断和改变，都是不自然的。（3）而"势当如此"是针对事物未来趋势而言的。也就是说，自然的状态，也包括事物自身的发展趋势，并且这种趋势是可以预料，而不是变幻莫测的。如果说，"自己如此"强调的是事物的内在动力和发展原因，"通常如此"则侧重于现状的持续，"势当如此"侧重未来的趋势。老子的自然包括了自发性、原初性、延续性和可预见性四个方面。这四个方面可以概括为两个要点：事物发展动力的内在性和事物发展的平稳性，而其本质是强调世界和事物总体状态的和谐。

那么，老子的"道法自然"的理想状态，可以理解为一种万物共生、共处的和谐目标。而人作为自然的一个部分，以自己的自然本性（"自己如此"）与外在的世界和历史保持和谐有序的发展节奏（"通常如此"），并维持自身发展的应有趋势（"势当如此"），这样的世界才是一个和谐的世界，这样的社会才是一个和谐的社会。而中国传统理念中"天人和谐"，是否便是要求尊重自然、保持自然和追求自然的最高理想和价值目标？

"自己如此"强调任何事物的天性。万事万物都有与生俱来的属于自己的本性，万事万物都应依顺这个本性发展，成为自己，这是万事万物的个性基础。同时，万事万物之所以能够"自己如此"，还有一个决定因素，那就是万事万物都有一个"通常如此"的客观条件。因为，世界是一个有机的整体，万事万物的个别性的存在与发展，必须与自我之外的其他事物的存在与影响发生关联，而这种关联既是决定能否实现"自己如此"的必要条件，也是促成万事万物"通常如此"的现实保证。也就是说，"自己如此"的自然天性，必须通过应对周遭环境的影响和变化，成为每一个事物"通常如此"的真实状态。而在老子看来，实现万事万物"自己如此"的自然天性，与促成万事万物自然天性发展的客观条件，原本是和谐有机的。人是自然之子，自然而然是人的生存与发展的理想境界。

3. 老子的"自然"与"道"的关系

就词语本身来说，用"自己如此""本来如此""通常如此"和"势当如此"来解释"自然"，差不多也穷极了它的意蕴；而用"人文自然"来描述它，也对"自然"的归属领域作了最大跨度的描述；然而，这里面还有一个问题没有解决，亦即"如此"到底是个什么样子？老子认为"人法地，地法天，天法道，道法自然"，于是也就不得不讨论"自然"和"道"的关系。朱晓鹏认为："自然"是"道"及一切万物的根本精神。它的基本含义有三层：一、事物存在及变动的天然状态；

二、事实存在（未被理性化）的本然状态；三、前两种融合的可能存在。[1]河上公注："道性自然，无所法也。"意思是，道自己如此，不存在效法的对象。吴澄注："道之所以大，以其自然，故曰'法自然'，非道之外别有自然也。"按照这些理解，"道"应该是无限事物及其运动演变状态之总和，是就事物层面而言的。"自然"就是"道"的根本性质、根本精神。

在前面，我们已经指出"道"在无限个方面都表现出"无限性"，那么，"自然"是不是就是这种"无限性"，还是在此之外别有性质与精神？老子并未对此做出明确的阐述。如果从人与天地并生同在这一关系来看，人是"自然"的人，人体现了"自然"，就无须法地、法天。因为从本体论与生成论来说，三者皆是"自然"的结果，都合乎"道"。这里讲"地法天，天法道"，不是老子的目的，老子的意图是"人要法道"。老子之所以提出"人法地，地法天，天法道，道法自然"，是因为他看到社会的人有不合乎自然之道的一面，主张人类要取法自然、遵循天道，以此作为解决社会、政治、人生问题的准则。

从"以辅万物之自然而不敢为"（《老子》第六十四章）一句中可以看出，人类的"不敢为"对于"自然"有辅助之功，也可以说就是"万物之自然"的一部分，是"自然"在人类身上的一种体现。而"不敢为"是就主观上而言的，反映在客观上就是"无为"。为此，人类的"无为"就是"自然"之根本性质的一种体现。老子关于"无为"的论述较多，如"上德无为而无以为"（《老子》第三十八章），可以说人类的最高德行就是"无为"——不但表现为客观上的"无为"，而且在主观意志上也没有"有为"的冲动意向和理由。不过，对于社会的统治者而言，"有为"也还是需要的，应当做到"有为"而不依赖于"有为"——"是以圣人为而不恃"（《老子》第七十七章），更不应为此去争功、争名、争利——"人之道，为而不争"（《老子》第八十一章）。而这一切，都是为了达到"我无为，而民自化"（《老子》第五十七章）、"无为而无不为"（《老子》第四十八章）的境界。

综上所述，人类的"无为"是"自然"的一种体现，为此"自然"的意义也相对比较清晰了。"自然"就是"道"的根本性质、根本精神，而"道"则在无限个方面都表现出"无限性"，圣人的"无为"就是为了做到人类之"为"的无限性，这既是"自然"的体现，也是合乎"道"的体现。

从"无为而无不为"一句来分析，它实际上体现了一种性质的两个方面：一

---

[1] 朱晓鹏：《智者的沉思——老子哲学思想研究》，杭州：杭州大学出版社，1999年，第331页。

方面是"无为",一方面是"无不为"。如果介入主体和客体,可以形成四个层面的关系:(1)主体无为,客体无不为;(2)主体既有为亦无为,客体既有为亦无为;(3)主体有为,客体无为;(4)主体有为,客体无不为。从老子本意来说,第二个层面是最接近他的思想的,而且主体的有为和客体的有为应该构成和谐关系而不是产生剧烈的冲突。当然,"无为而无不为"还只是"自然"一个层面的体现,也是从"道"的无限性中生发出来的一种性质。

四、从"智"到"明":把握"自然"的认识能力

先秦思想家中,关于"智(知)"的讨论几乎都涉及认识问题。他们对"智(知)"的不同理解(包括其含义、功能和意义等)反映了他们不同的认识论立场。例如,儒家强调"智"是人的重要德性,表现为"好学";墨家认为"智"是人的独特生存能力,重视技术发明;法家以及纵横家认为"智"是权谋机巧,以其来谋取权力和利益。相比之下,老子的认识论立场有点惊世骇俗,他说"绝智弃辩,民利百倍"(《老子》第十九章),且类似的说法在《老子》的文本中有多处重申。这些论断的确有些骇人听闻:自称"万物之灵"的人,居然连智慧也不要了吗?问题显然不是这么简单。只要看看老子思想对后世的影响就知道,老子正是用这种看起来极端的方式反对当时各种各样的智慧观(认识论),以澄清"谬说"的。老子同时提出并强调了一个关于认识论的新概念——"明"。老子说:"见小曰明,守柔曰强。用其光,复归其明,无遗身殃;是为袭常。"(《老子》第五十二章)由此需要明确的是,老子如何理解"智"和"明",以及它们之间的关系,他的认识论立场到底是"弃智入明"还是"由智入明"。

1. "智"(知)是为满足超出人正常生存需求的欲望而形成的认识能力

"智"是"知"的后起字,在经典中一般通用。知,从口从矢。清代段玉裁《说文解字》注:"识敏,故出于口者疾如矢也。"意思是认识、知道的事物,可以脱口而出。从词源上说,"智"(知)所表达的意义大致相当于今天我们说的认识能力(包括识别和表达两个方面)。从认识论的角度说,"智"(知)是认识方法、认识过程、认识成果以及由此而形成的认识能力的总称。思想者总是称他自己所总结、所宣扬或者所赞同的认识方法、认识过程、认识成果以及认识能力为"智"(知),称拥有这种"智"(知)的人为"智"(知)之人。当然,无论是"智"还是"知",还有很多其他义项和用法,而不同的思想者可以从不同认识论立场赋予它不同的含义。荀子为了表明他的认识立场,严格界定了"知"与"智"的区别,这在经典中恐怕是独一无二的。荀子认为人的感觉和情绪将影响人的认识,但起决定作用的是人的心,心是感官的主宰(天君),因此,荀子以"知"来概括

人的感知，以"智"来表达通过"心之虑"后的认识成果。《荀子·正名》云："所以知之在人者谓之知，知有所合谓之智。""智"是一种与物相合的认识，这一点与真理观中的"符合论"很接近。

先秦思想家对"智"（知）的含义固然有不一样的理解，但多数推崇"智"，主张"好学"。老子说"绝智弃辩"，往往被人视为"反智主义"。如果说"智"一般意义上指人的认识能力，那么，"反智"就是反对人拥有认识能力。然而通过分析可知，称老子为反智主义并不妥当，甚至有些武断地乱贴标签的意味。

在老子的思想中，"自然"在人类社会中的体现就是"无为而无不为"。而"智"之所以需要被批判，就是因为它违背"自然"，违背了"无为而无不为"的原则。老子云："使夫智者不敢为也。为无为，则无不治。"（《老子》第三章）"民之难治，以其智多。故以智治国，国之贼；不以智治国，国之福。"（《老子》第六十五章）"人多伎巧，奇物滋起。"（《老子》第五十七章）"常使民无知无欲。"（《老子》第三章）由此，"智"与"自然"形成了明显的对立，与人的所作所为联系在一起，所以老子对"智"的批判也就直接指向人的作为。在老子看来，人们通常将"智"运用于这些方面：一是争夺权力，要做主人，要做大人，因此老子主张"衣养万物而不为主"（第三十四章），"是以圣人终不为大"（《老子》第六十三章），"不敢为天下先"（《老子》第六十七章）。二是争名争利，争强争功，自夸自傲，因此老子主张"不尚贤，使民不争；不贵难得之货，使民不为盗"（《老子》第三章），"不以兵强天下，其事好还……不敢以取强"（《老子》第三十章），"人之道，为而不争"（《老子》第八十一章），"天之道，不争而善胜"（《老子》第七十三章），"不自伐，故有功"（《老子》第二十二章），"功成而弗居"（《老子》第二章）。三是自恃有"智"，高人一等，妄言妄作，因此老子指出"不知常，妄作凶"（《老子》第十六章），"不言而善应"（《老子》第七十三章），"多言数穷，不如守中"（《老子》第五章）。简言之，人们常常挖空心思去争权夺利、争强好胜、自是自夸，老子就是在这个层面上去"反智"的，反对将"智"用在上述各个方面。此外，老子还对"智"的内在驱动力作了分析，指出"智"之所以会用于上述各个方面，乃是因为"欲"的驱动，所以他说："咎莫大于欲得，祸莫大于不知足"（《老子》第四十六章），"不见可欲，使民心不乱"（《老子》第三章）。

综上所述，老子并不是在一般意义上反对人的认识能力的，而是反对那种单向的进取性和争夺性智慧。所谓单向的智慧，意思是从开始出发，不断增加某些东西，没有停留和回复（"周行"），从而完全脱离了出发点（"道"），是面目全非的智慧。这种单向的智慧带有强烈的进取性，也就是不断地去追求和把握外在的某种东西，或是名（"尚贤"），或是利（"贵难得之货"）。而这种外在的东西，除了不一定是生存所需（果腹）以外，也是稀缺的，从而造成无谓的争夺。

在人类历史的任何时代，以道德名义去支持和反对某些言论和行为，总是显得更具有正当性，更具有说服力和煽动性。道德评判的基本标准是"善"与"恶"（不善）。何为"善"这个标准本身是很模糊的和难以把握的。因此，去认识和把握这个标准需要"智"。先秦儒家正是在这个意义上肯定"智"对于个人修养的重要性。《论语》《孟子》以及《荀子》中的许多论述都强调了这一点。然而，老子认为这种关于善恶的智慧就是一种违背"道"与"自然"的单向性智慧。为什么呢？他说："天下皆知美之为美，斯恶矣；皆知善之为善，斯不善矣。"（《老子》第二章）对于这句，历代注家有不同解释。陈鼓应先生认为："一般人多把这两句话解释为：'天下都知道美之为美，就变成丑了。'老子的原意不在于说明美的东西'变成'丑，而在于说明有了美的观念，丑的观念也同时产生了。"一般人把"美"与"不美"当成相反的两端而相互依赖和相互转化，陈先生也不例外，只不过把"美"理解成"美的观念"。这样理解似乎很有依据，因为第二章这句话后面接着说："有无相生，难易相成，长短相形，高下相盈，音声相和，前后相随。"这都是在讲相反的东西相互依赖和相互转化。但继续往下读，便有重大疑问产生。下一句说："是以圣人处无为之事，行不言之教。"按照前面的理解，"无为"的对立面是"有为"，"不言"的对立面是"言"，既然对立面总是相互依赖和相互转化，那又何必强调圣人一定要"处无为之事"呢？也就是说，既然对立面都是相互转化的，那么应该有的态度便是，处于什么位置都无所谓啊！其实，《老子》第一章已经告诉我们如何去理解他的思想。"故常无，欲以观其妙；常有，欲以观其徼。""妙"指的是相生，"徼"指的是相成。相生就是"同"，相成就是"异"，"同谓之玄。玄而又玄，众妙之门"，因此，"同"和"妙"是根本，是源头，是整体，也是纯净的。而一般人却只懂得追求"异"和"徼"，这就背离了根本，从而导致一种单向性智慧，毫无疑问，这种抛弃了根本的单向性智慧具有强烈的进取性和争夺性。所以，老子教导我们要抓住根本，"无为"和"不言"才是根本，永远不能被遮蔽和抛弃。

其实，相反的东西相互转化和依赖并非是一个外在的客观规律，因为万物的生成并非是对立统一的结果。世界是一个无意识、无目的的"自然"过程。我们不能将老子的思想视为暗合当今流行的唯物辩证法。相反的东西相互转化和依赖是人认识的结果，所谓"有无""高下""难易"等表明的是认识角度，也就是说从一个角度看是"有"，从另外一个角度看是"无"。绝大多数有智慧的人只肯定事物的这一面或那一面，这本身就背离了根本（"道"），因为这个根本并不是一个点，而是一个整体，一个范围。如果对"天下皆知美之为美，斯恶已；皆知善之为善，斯不善已"（《老子》第二章）这句话做一个学理上而不是字面上的翻译，那就应该这样理解：天下的人都知道什么是美，如何才能美，并努力去追求这种美时，这种追求本身就是恶了；都知道什么是善，如何才能善，并努力去追求这种善时，这种追求本身就是不善了。相反相成是"自然"地浑然一体，当我们刻意追求我们所肯定的（也就是认为"有价值的"）那一面时，实际已经走向反面了（"不自然"，不自然就是恶），所以，不需要"智"的刻意追求。

老子在"道"的玄妙中，批评了那种单向的德性智慧。这种单向的德性智慧本身就是"恶"。老子说："大道废，有仁义。"冯友兰先生解释道："'大道废，有仁义'，这并不是说，人可以不仁不义，只是说'大道'之中，人自然仁义，那是真仁义。"¹至于由学习、训练得来的仁义，那就有了很多模拟成分，同自然而有的真仁义比较起来就差一点、次一级了。《老子》说"上德不德，是以有德"，就是这个意思。那种单向的德性智慧不仅是"次一级"的问题，根本就不是德性智慧，而是一种恶。老子认为真正的德行不是"智德"，而是"玄德"。"生而不有，为而不恃，长而不宰，是谓玄德。"（《老子》第五十一章）"玄德深矣，远矣，与物反矣，然后乃至大顺。"（《老子》第六十五章）玄德没有目的，没有追求，但深厚、阔远、周全，有了它才能大顺。

"地""天""人"和"道"都法自然。"自然"是混成一体的。当人在混成中区分出相反的东西，并刻意追求相反的东西中的一面时，就变成"恶"，变成"不自然"了。然而，人作为"域中四大"之一，为什么变得"不自然"呢？或者说人是如何形成了那种单向的智慧呢？其原因是人的对于外在东西的超出了生存需要的"欲"。"不尚贤，使民不争；不贵难得之货，使民不为盗；不见可欲，使民心不乱。"（《老子》第三章）尚贤就是好名，贵难得之货就是好利。如果社会以"好名好利"作为普遍追求，那么每个人都将挖空心思（智）去获取名利，这就违背了"自然"。因此对于统治者来说，一定要消除那多余的欲望（"不见可欲"），进而"虚其心，实其腹，弱其志，强其骨。常使民无知无欲。使夫智者不敢为也。为无为，则无不治"（《老子》第三章）。所谓"虚其心"就是抛弃那些单向的智慧，"实其腹"是满足他们的基本生存需要，"弱其志"是放弃刻意追求，"强其骨"是重视自身身体的生命力。做到这些，才能使民"无知无欲"。"无知"指的是消

---

1 冯友兰：《中国哲学史新编》（第2册），北京：人民出版社，1984年，第330页。

除那种单向的智慧,"无欲"指的是消除那些多余的欲望。《老子》中的第十二章强调"为腹不为目",这就是"无欲";第十三章强调"贵身",这就是"无知"。在第十九章和第二十章又再次强调"绝智"和"绝学",告诫"见素抱朴,少私寡欲"。人在刻意追求某个片面时就具有了私心,"私"也就是指"多余的欲望"("可欲")。因"可欲"而产生了单向的智慧,反过来说,因单向的智慧又增强了"可欲"。

有意思的是,先秦儒家荀子对"欲望"有着另外一番理解。荀子虽然认为放纵欲望会带来争斗,所以要用"礼"来规范,但是同时认为"欲"恰恰是构建社会秩序的原始依据,对于那些有德才的人就是要满足他们对于名利的欲望,贵贱高低的社会分层表现为社会对于欲望的不同满足程度。由此,消解多余的"欲"恰恰是对社会的反叛和对人性的扭曲。欲望是一种天性,不能放纵,所以须要体现"人道"的"礼"的规范,这就是天人相分;同时欲望也不能消解,是构建社会秩序的根据,这就是天人相合。"礼"的"分"与"养"的双重能力在人的"智"中得到完美结合。"智"以及由此而形成的"德"就得到了充分的肯定和张扬。老子并不认为人的欲望尤其是那些多余的欲望是天性,主张所有存在的"根本"特征是"自然",违背"自然"就是"恶"。所以在老子看来,那些人的"智"无非就是为满足超出人正常生存需求的欲望而形成的认识能力,这种能力是有害的,需要被超越的。

2. "明"是人的内在生命力的自我观照能力

老子对"智"(也就是人的认识)的反思是基于"本体"的、"形而上"的"域"。老子认为"域"中有四大:道大,天大,地大,人亦大。这种"本体"的"域"既超越了具体事物,也超越了"类"事物(天、地、人)。从这个"域"中反思人的"智",才能够发现这种"智"的单向性。道以"道冲而用之或不盈"(《老子》第四章)为大,天地以"天地不仁"(《老子》第五章)和"天长地久"(《老子》第七章)为大。那么,人何以为大呢?人虽然有"道"(言说)和"名"(命名)的认识能力,但恰是这种能力导致了相反的概念并片面肯定其中一面的后果。这些"可道"和"可名"的智慧之果远离甚至破坏了那不可道和不可名的"道"和"名"。只有了解那"玄之又玄"的"众妙之门"才是真正的人之大。老子说"知常曰明"(《老子》第十六章和《老子》第五十五章),因此,老子不是在一般意义上反对智慧,而是反对一般意义的智慧,并提出了真正的智慧是认识到"常",他称这种智慧为"明"。

何谓"常"?朱谦之说:"盖'道'者,变化之总名。与时迁移,应物变化,虽有变异，而有不易者在，此之谓常。"现代学者则称为"规律"，如陈鼓应解释为"万物运动变化中的永恒规律"。这种解释并未能显明"常"之真意。老子说："复命曰常"（《老子》第十六章），"知和曰常"（《老子》第五十五章）。"命"指的是初始之源，"和"是阴阳和合之流。以初始之源自然流淌出万物之和，不求有目的的添加和减少，不走向极端和邪路，就是"常"。相对于那种单向智慧来说，初始之源似"无"，似"虚"，似"静"，似"弱"，似"雌"，似"婴儿"。老子并不关心是否有所谓的"变化中的不变规律"，这种寻找客观规律的学问是物理学的目标。老子的目标是要为"人生"寻找到一个本体依据。因此，与其说"常"是变动中的不变规律，不如说"常"就是"平常""日常"的意思，也就是自然无为的状态。它不是什么特别的东西，不是那种一定要坚持、要追求，甚至要改变的东西。这种东西当然也不需要特别的"言说"和"命名"。如果抛弃那种单向的智慧，则它自存于心中。我们知道孔子特别重视"正名"，名不正则言不顺，言不顺则事不成。这种"名"，在老子看来就是"非常名"。"希言自然"（《老子》第二十三章），"常名"不"可名"，也无须"名"。

"常"是清楚明了于心的，本不需要去"知"。那老子又怎么说"知常曰明"呢？陈鼓应先生说："老子说到道体时，惯用反显法；他用了许多经验世界的名词去说明，然后又一一打掉，表示这些经验世界的名词都不足以形容，由此反显出道的精深奥妙性。"老子虽然没有区分哪些是经验世界的名词，哪些是非经验世界的名词，但确实总是在用"反显法"，可以说整个五千言都是在"反显"，在"强"说。老子强说"圣人为腹不为目"（《老子》第十二章）以及"贵身"（《老子》第十三章），听起来很消极，但实际上他在积极地告诉我们人生之"常"在哪里。《老子》第十章所说的"营魄抱一""专气致柔"，就是生命之"常"，那是人生的初始之源的自然流淌。我们也许可以称这种生命之"常"为人的内在生命力。拥有了它就拥有了"明"，便获得了照亮万物的"光"。"明白四达，能无知乎？"（《老子》第十章）如此这样还需要那些"知"做什么呢？"明"就是人的内在生命力的自我观照能力。

老子还反复从几个方面来"强说"人生之"明"境，这是一种真正的智慧之境：

第一，只有达到"明"境，才能没有私心。老子说："知常容，容乃公，公乃全，全乃天，天乃道，道乃久，没身不殆。"（《老子》第十六章）"知常"就是"明"，拥有"明"才能包容一切。人的"言说"和"命名"的智慧，实际上是"人为"的界限。一旦我们去命名，就将把对象标示为相互异化的类别，区分出远近亲疏，这样人就具有了私心，这个私心就将偏离常道。比如，当我们用"无"

来名天地之始，用"有"来名万物之母的时候，我们可能只看到"有"，而忽视"无"，更难看到"无"和"有"原来是"同出而异名"的。"同"才是根本，才是那"玄之又玄"的"众妙之门"。所以，老子在开篇就告诫道："故常无，欲以观其妙；常有，欲以观其徼"。老子的深意在于不要被"人为"的界限所限制，一定要超越这种限制。只有看到根本才具有真正的胸怀和眼界，以这种眼界去看万物，才能真正成就自身于万物之中。

第二，"明"者不自我夸耀和表现。老子说："不自见，故明"（《老子》第二十二章），"自见者不明"（《老子》第二十四章）。自我炫耀，努力去表现自己的智慧的人，是没有达到"明"境的。这种炫耀和表现中所显示的自信，是对某种片面的东西的盲目自信。比如，人对"善"很自信，并终身去表现和追求这种善，虽然从主观说是真实的、诚恳的，但其结果是"不善"。当某种"善"被追求时，它只是对某个界域内来说的，在这个界域之外，就是"弃人"或"弃物"。

第三，"明"者追求自我内在生命力的澄明，而不致力于去认识对象。老子说："知人者智，自知者明。"（《老子》第三十三章）如果追求去了解别人和对象，其内在动机是想去控制对象，而且越是追求知识广博，说明控制欲望越强。当人回观自我，让自我内在生命力不断地自然伸张，那才是"明"。内在生命力的澄明是不要"言说"的，"言说"是私心和欲望的孪生兄弟，所以真正的智者"不言"，"知者不言，言者不知"（《老子》第五十六章）；也不需要广博的知识，内在的澄明足以照亮一切，让一切都在无私的慈爱中蓬勃生长，"知者不博，博者不知"（《老子》第八十一章）。

3. "观"——"由智入明"之路

当"言说"（道）和"命名"（名）不能表达"常道"和"常名"时，我们只能在感官和抽象的认识面前去"观""常道"。这里的"观"不是眼睛的"看"，而是老子认识论中的一个特别概念。通过"观"而"明"的认识并不是完全抛弃"智"，而是"由智入明"。

按照老子的理解，"智"体现在两个方面：一是感官的感知；二是言说和命名的抽象。就认识成果来说，显然，言说和命名的抽象更能体现人的"文"（与"质""朴"相对）化。因此，老子在开篇中就从"有"与"无"这两个最抽象的"名"说起。既然常道不可道，常名不可名，那么，"无"和"有"两个最抽象的名也不是指称"道"的。多数人把"无"和"有"理解成为"道"的特征，"是表明'道'由无形质落实向有形质的活动过程"。这种理解是不够准确的。"无"和"有"是人的"智"的成果，虽然已经很抽象，也很深奥了，但那不是常道。怎么才能获得常道呢？老子说："故常无，欲以观其妙；常有，欲以观其徼。此两者，同出而异名，同谓之玄。玄之又玄，众妙之门。"（《老子》第一章）意思是我们应该从我们已经有的"名"——"无"和"有"中去观"常道"（众妙之门）。这是从言说和命名的抽象角度表明"观""道"之路是"由智入明"，而不是"弃智入明"。除此之外，从感官的感知角度说，感官是对外界对象的欲望之所，同时也从"可见""可听"以及"可摸"等方面分别对象。在"可见""可听"以及"可摸"等感知的极细微处，我们也可以"观""道"。老子说："视之不见，名曰夷；听之不闻，名曰希；搏之不得，名曰微。此三者不可致诘，故混而为一。其上不皦，其下不昧，绳绳兮不可名，复归于无物。是谓无状之状，无物之象。是谓惚恍。迎之不见其首，随之不见其后。"（《老子》第十四章）这个时候，"道"是不可名状的"恍惚"。从感官的感知角度表明"观""道"之路是"由智入明"，而不是"弃智入明"。

既然"观""道"之路是"由智入明"，那么，这个认识的道路就像是一种"反复"和"回归"。其实也确实是"回归"，由于人长期处于"智"的状态而忘记了内心的澄明，这个认识过程就是从关注外在的东西而转向关注内在的东西。因此，"观"的第一步是"涤除"（《老子》第十章），也就是消除那些导致妄为的欲望，心灵没有瑕疵，让身体和精神之气聚合，这是"玄览"的基础。第二步是放弃对"智"的盲目自信。老子说："知不知，尚矣；不知知，病也。圣人不病，以其病病。夫唯病病，是以不病。"（《老子》第七十一章）这是通过对人的智慧的反思而获得的一种必要的态度。这其实上是在告诫人们，认识的成果总是有限度的，不能固执己见和盲目追求。虽然人的认识是有限的，但只要我们认识到这种有限，我们还是可以通过内在生命力的澄明来获得完整的生命。当然，无论是"涤除"还是放弃对"智"的自信，都不是抛弃"智"，不是突然地遁入"明"。因此，从这个意义上说，老子的人生态度并不是"出世"，不是放弃现实的一切，而是一种试图拯救现世的态度。

这条"返复"的"观""道"之路，或者说是"由智入明"之路，最终到达"虚"和"静"。《老子》第十六章说："致虚极，守静笃。万物并作，吾以观复。夫物芸芸，各复归其根。归根曰静，静曰复命。复命曰常，知常曰明。""虚"和"静"是"明"的状态。所谓"虚"是内在生命力自我观照的若有若无、空灵缥缈的精微状态，所谓"静"是内在生命力在自我观照中的精气充沛状态。从对万物的感觉和抽象中，"观"到根本，这就叫"观复"，也就是从"异"和"同"中看到玄之又玄的"众妙之门"。这就叫"用其光，复归其明"（《老子》第五十二章）。这里的"光"是照亮万物的光,来自内在的"明",而借助这个光,又可以反过来观照内在的"明"。

这种认识过程,从方向上来说,是由外而内,从注重分析了解对象转而关注内心的澄明。内在生命力的精微和充沛才能显现"常道",才能无弃万物,才能成就人生。老子说:"不出户,知天下;不窥牖,见天道。其出弥远,其知弥少。是以圣人不行而知,不见而明,不为而成。"(《老子》第四十七章)天下万物,纷纭复杂,不在于能走多远,而在于内在的东西有多深,得道之人是可以照亮世间万物的;这种认识过程,从内容上说,是由多到少,或者说由大到小,一般的认识总是希望不断地积累,以达到博学而无所不通。不要说无所不通不可能达到,就算是达到了也没有意义,因为抛弃了根本。所以,老子说:"为学日益,为道日损。损之又损,以至于无为。无为而无不为。"(《老子》第四十八章)两条相反的道路,"为学"是加法,"为道"是减法。只有通过"减法"才能做到"无为而无不为"。

"观"是"由智入明"之路,但老子并没有说明和谈论"观法",也就是到底要怎样"观",才能达到"虚"和"静",从而"知常"。也许正因为"常道"本身是不可"言说"(道)的,因此"观""道"之法也是不可道和不可言的。或许老子的难以理解和难以领悟之处正是在这里。学者张岱年认为老子的"观"实际是一种直觉法:"老子讲'为道',于是创立一种直觉法,而主直接冥会宇宙根本,'玄览'即一种直觉。"[1]可备一说。

在道家的其他著作中,有不少说法与《老子》的"观"有关。如《列子》卷四所说的"内观":"务外游,不知务内观。外游者,求备于物;内观者,取足于身。取足于身,游之至也。""至观者,不知所视。物物皆游矣,物物皆观矣。"说"外游"的人到处跑想要看遍所有的事物,但看得再多也不可能看遍看尽,这不是"游"的最高境界,而从事"内观"的人,他不外出,只要向内看就足够,这才是"游"的最高境界。而最会看的人,不知道自己要看什么东西,但是却每个地方都游到,每件东西都看到。在《文子·道德篇》中又有所谓的"神听":"故上学以神听,中学以心听,下学以耳听。""凡听之理,虚心清静,损气无盛,无思无虑,目无妄视,耳无苟听。"在《庄子·人间世》中又有"心斋"之说:"无听之以耳而听之以心,无听之以心而听之以气。耳止于听,心止于符。气也者,虚而待物者也。唯道集虚。虚者,心斋也。"上述"内观""神听""心斋"都偏重于认识方

---

[1] 张岱年:《中国哲学大纲》,北京:中国社会科学出版社,1982年,第532—541页。

面，而在养生方面也有"内视"或"内观"之说，即目不外视、"内观"五脏，如同真有所见。这一点在道教中得到发扬，传承不绝。不管这些说法是否显得很神秘、是否具有实际的可操作性，仅从认识论的角度来看，"内观"的说法还是很有启发意义的。因为人通过五官认识、感觉到了万事万物，为思维器官——大脑——提供了素材，这就形成了知识、思想。但是，五官的认识、感觉能力是有限的，甚至是非常有限的；即便把所有的认识成果加起来，依然是非常有限的。"内观"的意义就在于提示人们不断突破、超越自身的认识能力，以便与"道"的无限性对接。

总之，老子认为人的"智"往往是为满足超出人的生存需要的欲望而形成的认识能力。这种智慧只看到了多样的、相辅相成的一面，并努力去追求，从而丢失了根本。人须在更大的范围和界域中来理解世界，这个界域就是"恍惚"的"道"。理解"道"的智慧被称为"明"。"明"当然不意味抛弃"智"，而是通过"观"而"由智入明"。老子的认识思想很可能从两个方向被误解：一是认为老子的认识思想是辩证法。老子文本中说了很多相对立的两面的依赖和转化，但老子认为这只是"智"的认识成果，不足以表达"常道"；二是认为老子的认识思想是神秘而消极的。其实从上文的分析中可以看出，老子的"观"具有神秘色彩，可能指的是一种直觉，但这种神秘还是以"智"为基础，不是完全从不可理解的空处而来的，因此神秘之中也有不神秘之处。他的认识论确实是一种"减法"认识论，但并不消极，"无为而无不为"一直是人的行为法则。老子对人的智慧的反思确实是具有理论成效的，主要表现在对智慧的有限性的认知以及对内心的重视，由此而得到的"无为而治"的理想对社群秩序的建立也有着重要启示。

五、体现"道"的"德"与文明社会

"道"尽管如此"玄远""无形"和不可琢磨，其在社会现实的影响和实现途径还是可以观察、描述和掌握的。这便是沟通"道"与万事万物的实践途径和中介——"德"。"德"同样是《老子》中的核心范畴，《老子》又称《道德经》。古代马王堆帛书版将《道德经》分为上篇《德篇》和下篇《道篇》，可见"德"这个范畴的地位和分量。那么，"道"与"德"是一种什么样的关系？

1. "德"是"道"的实现

老子说："孔德之容，惟道是从。"（《老子》第二十一章）这是说"德"的特征就是遵从"道"，是"道"的体现。进而言之，"德者道之舍……故德者得也，得也者，其谓所得以然也。无为之谓道，舍之之谓德，故道之与德无间"（《管

子·心术上》）。即谓"德"就是"道"的体现，万物依赖它而得以生长，心智依赖它而得以认识"道"的精髓，所以"德"就是"得"。所谓"得"，即是说所要得到的东西（"道"）已经实现了。无为叫作"道"，体现它就叫作"德"，所以"道"与"德"没有什么分别。当然，在不同语境中，"道"与"德"还是有区别的。唐玄宗《道德真经疏》说："道者德之体，德者道之用。"北宋陈景元《道德真经藏室纂微篇》说："道者，虚无之体；德者，自然之用。常道无名，唯德以显之；至德无本，顺道而成之。"这是用哲学上的体用范畴来说明"道""德"的体用关系。唐玄宗注《道德经》说："道之在我谓之德。"这表明"道"是总体，"德"是个体，德是指万物所含有的特性，故"道"和"德"又存在一种共性与个性的关系。这是说"道"与"德"的关系是分而有别，合而为一。这一切都充分说明了"德"与"道"有着密切关系。

　　陈鼓应对此解释说："'道'和'德'的关系是：（1）'道'是无形的，它必须作用于物，透过物的媒介，而得以显现它的功能。'道'显现于物的功能，称为'德'。（2）一切物都由'道'所形成，内在于万物的'道'，在一切事物中表现它的属性，亦即表现它的'德'。（3）形而上的'道'落实到人生层面时，称之为'德'，即'道'本幽隐而未形的，它的显现，就是'德'。"

　　老子强调"人法地，地法天，天法道，道法自然"以及"道常无为而无不为"。这里"道法自然"与"无为而无不为"也是一而二、二而一的，都是描述宇宙大化流行的特性，可以简称为"自然无为"。在老子看来，人类也应当效法这种自然无为而无不为的宇宙特性。这就是老子哲学中"道""德"作为本体论范畴所蕴含的理论价值与实践意义。在老子看来，"道"固然是万物的本根、根源，但宇宙万物的存在及其形成过程，还离不开"德"。老子说："道生之，德畜之，物形之，势成之。是以万物莫不尊道而贵德。道之尊，德之贵，夫莫之命而常自然。故道生之，德畜之，长之育之，亭之毒之，养之覆之。"（《老子》第五十一章）可见，"德"对于宇宙万物的存在及其形成过程来说，亦具有重要作用与意义。正是由于"德"与"道"有着密切关系，决定了"德"对宇宙万物的存在及其形成过程的重要作用与意义。特别是，对"人"而言，老子之"德"主要指人的纯粹本性——所谓"含德之厚，比于赤子"（《老子》第五十五章），以及修养境界——所谓"玄德深矣，远矣，与物反矣"（《老子》第六十五章）。

　　所以，老子之"道"不仅仅是一个自然哲学范畴，更是一个关于人的内在本体和价值的形上学范畴。对人而言，老子之"道"只是作为潜在的基础，要靠人的自觉实践、体验（即所谓"践道""体道"），才能把潜在变为现实，与"道"合一，获得自由。这就是老子之"道"作为本体论范畴所蕴含的"人道"意义，从中显示出其独特的理论价值与实践意义。

2. "德"是建立"道"和"物"关系的一条纽带

有的学者认为，《老子》的"道"之于"物"表现为非内在的不离不杂的超越关系，"德"是《老子》建立超越的"道"和"物"关系的一条纽带，是虚说的，起架构和组建的作用。道生万物，"道"与"物"的这种关系不仅导致了《老子》体系中"人为"义的丢失，也容易使仁义道德的积极意义也一起丧失。我们至少可以将《老子》的"德"字理解为两层意义。《老子·德篇》主要讨论人法天的人生政治哲学思想，这里讲的"德"多数有美德的含义。但是"德"字还有一种含义，"道生德畜"的"德"就与美德显得很不相干。问题是，这两种理解究竟是一种什么样的关系，是彼此隔绝的还是有着内在的逻辑相关性？流行的看法说后者是一种实然的宇宙创生论，而前者则是应然的人生哲学。对二者之间的关系，唐君毅先生认为："道虽生万物，而覆育万物，实未尝有仁于万物，亦非真含具价值之意义者也。""人之所以且求亦当求其生活之合乎道，在根底上惟依于人之不愿归于死之一念，此一念只有主观之意义，无客观之意义"。[1] 唐先生讲"道"未尝仁于万物，自然不是指"道"生万物之大德，而是讲"生之，畜之，生而不有，为而不恃，长而不宰，是谓玄德"，从"道"生万物这个意义上看，自然是"道"仁于万物。

事实上，《老子》"道生万物"的精神架构中，"道""物"之间的创生关系，非"物"对"道"有内在秉承，"道"为"天下之大公"，不为"物"内化、不为"物"私有，因此人、"物"对于"道"没有"内容"的体会。"道""物"的这种关系从理论上阻止了一切刻意、人为的可能。不管是为善还是为恶，人的一切刻意行为都在这条线索中没有大的区别。由于"道"和人的隔绝，人的作为就没有在"道"那里取得合法性。人本身的活动、作用、主宰义即丧失，这种人为义的丧失使得为善的合法性在《老子》的理路中自然被取消了。"善行无辙迹，善言无瑕谪"（《老子》第二十七章），只有"无为"才有大善。按老子的观点，只要人有所主宰刻意，道在人身上就处于遮蔽状态，所以唐君毅先生说："《老子》之言圣人之容、公与慈，如只是法此无情之道体，则未见此行为当然之善而行者矣，人之所以求其生活合乎道，在根上惟依于人之不愿归于死之一念，此一念只有主观之意义，无客观之意义。"所谓"客观意义"乃是指在《老子》系统中，人的"生活合于道"并

---

[1] 唐君毅：《中国哲学原论》，北京：中国社会科学出版社，2005年，第254页。

没有在内在理路中得到"道"的承诺。人要达成"生活合于道"的要求，要么是因为人本身"修身养性"、挣脱物累、洒脱自然的生活要求，要么就是统治者治国安邦的政治策略，而在混乱无序的社会做致虚守静的功夫以"复命"达到"知常"之明。(《老子》第十六章) 所以，人的行善去恶、致虚守静等"人法天"的行为都只是具有功夫论的意义，不具有本体意义，也不具有内在的必然性，其最终目的只是对"道"之"常"有所澄明、有所领会而已。在老子那里"道"具有绝对的地位，所以《老子》实际上暗含着"人应当与道在一起，但是由于'道'没有在人身上正面内在的落实下来，所以人要接近'道'，就只有作外在的'智'的观照"。

当然，这里的"智"不是指人的后天经验的认知，而是指人的本能的直觉。无"智"则"道"无以显，因此在老子这里"智"几乎获得了和"道"同等的地位，有绝对的优先性。马一浮先生对此有这样的描绘："任何运动不参加，任何伎俩都明白，看一切有为只是妄作，他只燕处超然，以佛语判之，便是有智而无悲。"[1] 这种静观的思路成就的是己物对待外物的哲学。故老子谓上善若水，其下者则刑名之察，权谋之机，皆崇智以废"德"。

但是老子究竟还是主张"绝圣去智"(此"智"是后天经验认识，而非老子注重的"智"之对"道"的领会)、"为道日损""致虚守静""少私寡欲""涤除玄览"等功夫，主张放下欲望与人为，以复返归根于大公至正之道，由"道"做主宰，让"道"无减损。所有老子的这些主张和功夫都在于维持与"道"的关系、保持对"道"的"智"的观照和领会。倘若人处在对外物的欲望中，处在对功名利禄的执着中，纷繁于见闻觉知，则人往往蔽于"物"而不知"道"。人为的积极功夫一旦被阻断，则所有功夫都在消极虚静的功夫中做，而这些功夫的落脚点最终都在"智"，这是唯一使人与"道"保持联络的方式。

那么，《老子》中的"德"的蕴含和功能有什么独有的意义呢?《老子》说："道生之，德畜之，物形之，势成之……长之育之，亭之毒之，养之覆之"(《老子》第五十一章)，"大道泛兮，其可左右，万物恃之以生而不辞，功成而不有。衣养万物而不为主"(《老子》第三十四章)。这里显示了"道"不但于物之生成见之，也于物之生长毁灭见之，"道"不仅使"物"得以生，也使"物"得以存活生长。"物得于道，道蓄养物"。"德"字的这个含义在《老子》的其他表述中可以得到验证。《老子》说"孔德之容，惟道是从"(《老子》第二十一章)，如果"德"是分有"道"

---

[1] 马一浮:《论老子流失》,《马一浮集》, 杭州：浙江古籍出版社、浙江教育出版社, 1996年, 第44页。

的实体字，那么自然"道""德"无异，自然不用蛇上添足、床上叠床，说"德"是"惟道是从"了。故以"德"为实体字是不恰当的，在此意义上，"孔"就成了"大"义，"德"没有增加新的意义。王弼对此有深刻认识，所以他说："孔，空也。惟以空为德，然后乃能动作从道"。这里，"空"字应为"德"不严格的引申义，"空"是用来解释强调"德"的含义的，二者是一种分析对应的关系。当然，于人而言，"空"字在这里还可理解为人的功夫，只有"空"除人为，"道"才不被遮蔽，才可以在人身上做主宰，同时在静虚无为的功夫下，人才可以对"道"有所观解。"德"起组建的功用，空出位置以由"道"的作用流出，对人而言，则是去除、"空缺"人欲或人为，由"道"做主宰。

我们也可以由此得出"德"的引申义"顺、守"的义项。之所以可以说"势成之"有"势"可言，乃在于其畅通无阻的顺，有阻则无势可言，"顺"对于万物之生有重要的作用，万物因"顺"因"势"而成，对人而言，人亦因顺道而为，去己之欲。"知其雄，守其雌，为天下溪。为天下溪，常德不离，复归于婴儿……知其荣，守其辱，为天下谷。为天下谷，常德乃足，复归于朴。"（《老子》第二十八章）《老子》里常用"谷""谷神""玄牝"比喻"道"。"谷神"来源于山谷的形象，"豁""谷"都是地势下陷的地方，只有下凹、有中空的空间才有可能承装，所以"豁""谷"等概念乃是对"德"字的说明，说明其架构组建义，保持"道"与人的关系。空去人为的因素，"道"的流行才具有条件。这样看来，"德"在这里便不是具有实存意义的道德名目，而是纯粹的架构、组建、虚说的动词，它是"道"和"物"维持关系的一种纽带，而这种纽带的作用并不是使物分有"道"的属性，而仅仅是使物不离"道"而已。[1]

3. 老子之"德"与其他"德"的差异

徐复观先生认为见于《尚书》中的周初"德"字，都应当指的是具体的行为，其原义亦仅能是直心而行的负责任的行为。这种行为（"德"）开始并不带有好或坏的评价意义，因而有了"吉德"与"凶德"的区分，故周初文献中的"德"，只有在前面加上一个"敬"字或"明"字时，才表示是好的意思，后来乃演进而为好的行为。[2] 李泽厚先生认为"德"的原义显然并非道德，而可能是各氏族的习惯法规。而后又对此提出修正说："'德'似乎首先是一套行为，但不是一般的行为，

---

[1] 吴小龙：《从老子的"道""德"到易传的"道德"——兼论儒家道德的先天性特点》，山东大学博士论文，2009年4月。
[2] 徐复观：《中国人性论史》（先秦篇），上海：上海三联书店，2001年版，第21页。

主要是以氏族部落首领为表率的祭祀、出征等重大政治行为。它与传统氏族部落的祖先祭祀活动的巫术礼仪紧密结合在一起，逐渐演变而成为维系氏族部落生存发展的一整套的社会规范、秩序、要求、习惯等非成文法规。"陈来先生根据甲骨文金文中"值-德-惪"的文字形体沿革，认为"'德'的原初含义与行、行为有关，从心以后，则多与人的意识、动机、心意有关。行为与动机、心意密切相关，故'德'的这两个意义是很自然的"[1]。

　　早期之"德"属于政治概念，其价值与功能主要体现在政治领域，"德"伴随着政治生活的出现而出现，而作为一种文化观念当形成于原始社会的尧舜禹时代，"德"的本义是"行为"，而主要是指为政者一套旨在惠民利民的政治行为。殷商时期帝神崇拜与祖先崇拜并存的宗教信仰，在总体上还未达到伦理宗教的水平，殷商时期的"德"观念是其宗教观的被动反应，并无伦理道德的内涵。当时的"德"主要是对殷王及其臣下政治行为的客观描述与概括，它有着较为具体的实指内容，尚未达到对人内在品格要求的维度，故殷商时代的"德"仍停留在其原始义的阶段。殷周之际的社会大变革，促使周人对殷人天命观进行了理性的改造，形成了以"惟命不于常"为核心的新天命观，周人开始自觉地反思自身的政治行为，将"德"视为受命之基和开国之本，"德"成为统治者的政治行为模式及治国理念，并通过创设各项政治制度来确保"德"的贯彻和实现，政治的伦理化使"德"开始有了道德的意义。尽管周初的统治者对"德"有了较为理性的思考，但尚未达到深入至人内在心灵的程度，周初之"德"所内蕴的道德义是指政治美德抑或政治伦理道德，主要是针对贵族阶层而言，并不具普适性的规范功能，与后世具有普遍意义的个体心性道德不可同等对待。在西周后期至春秋晚期较长的历史时段内，随着传统天命观的日趋动摇及人文思潮的日益兴起，加之宗法等级制度的日趋瓦解及血缘关系的日益松弛，"德"不再为贵族阶层所专享，它所面向的对象范围和所涉及的领域更为广泛，"德"的神圣性逐渐淡化，"德"观念中理性的、道德的因素在西周原有基础上进一步积蓄和成长起来，具有了更为普遍的道德规范意义。另外，"德"在春秋晚期以前虽然仍主要是一政治概念，它的具体功能仍局限于政治领域，但由于春秋时期"礼"之新观念的确立及其在政治思想领域引发的"礼治"思潮，致使"德"的政治功能与西周相比出现了弱化的态势，"德"逐渐地从政治层面抽离出来，在精神层面结合着各种抽象的"德目"而内向

---

[1] 陈来：《古代宗教与伦理——儒家思想的根源》，北京：生活·读书·新知三联书店，1996年版，第291页。

发展。因此，"德"观念在西周后期至春秋晚期的长时段中大致呈现出内向化、抽象化、世俗化的发展趋势，"德"的内涵渐向道德义倾斜，渐由政治范畴之"德"转向伦理范畴之"德"。而老子之"德"的精神寓意和形态，是处在"德"的政治功能向抽象化、世俗化的道德功能转化的过程当中。但是，在《老子》的语境中，无论是"以德合道"还是"以道释德"，其讨论的对象大都是圣人和君王的修养，而不是一般人的道德品质。

老子所说的"德"，与先秦时代对"德"的通常理解大不相同。

老子所说的"上德"或"玄德"与一般所谓的"德"存在"处下"与"处上"的区别，后者具有高高在上、雄视一切、掌管生杀大权的特点。"为天下溪，常德不离，复归于婴儿。"（《老子》第二十八章）"生而不有，为而不恃，长而不宰，是谓玄德。"（《老子》第五十一章）这有点像古代社会称皇帝为"九五之尊"，具有无与伦比的地位，谁也不敢仰视他；而现代社会则认为领导人是"人民公仆"，是为百姓服务的。

"上德"或"玄德"与一般所谓的"德"也有"不争"与"争"的区别。"善为士者，不武；善战者，不怒；善胜敌者，不与；善用人者，为之下。是谓不争之德。"（《老子》第六十八章）这是"上德"或"玄德"，是老子所肯定的。但是，一般的君主依靠的却是高高在上的位置，以及令人慑服的威武气概，若不顺从他，就采用强权和武力将人碾为齑粉，正如《战国策》中的名篇《唐雎不辱使命》记载秦王所说的话："天子之怒，伏尸百万，流血千里。"

"上德"或"玄德"与一般所谓的"德"还有用"智"与不用"智"的区别。"故以智治国，国之贼；不以智治国，国之福。知此两者亦稽式。常知稽式，是谓玄德。"（《老子》第六十五章）就历史现象而言，"以智治国"主要体现在两方面，一方面是按照君主的治国理想、治国模式去管理天下，强行将天下纳入自己的理想模式之中，例如两汉之交的王莽改制，包括土地改革、币制改革、商业改革和官名县名改革等，就是以"一己之智"强行治理天下的表现。另一方面是君主大玩权术，如韩非提出用"法""术""势"来管理天下的主张，其中的"术"即君主统治的手段和策略，内容包括任免、考核、赏罚各级官员的手段以及如何维护君主的权力，即所谓刑名之术、察奸之术等。它是统治者控制臣下的技巧，应当潜藏胸中，择机使用，不轻易示人。究其实质，这种"术"也是君主只相信自己、不相信别人，好逞"一己之智"的表现。老子极力反对这些"用智治国"的行为，主张"无为而无不为"的"上德"，也就是不用"一己之智"而尽量开发众生之智（当然是不违背"自然"的"智"）。

"上德"或"玄德"与一般所谓的"德"所产生的统治效果也是不同的。"玄德深矣,远矣,与物反矣,然后乃至大顺。"(《老子》第六十五章)"含德之厚,比于赤子。……和之至也。"(《老子》第五十五章)总结起来,用"上德"或"玄德"来管理社会,产生的效果就是"顺"和"和",而不是"逆"和"怨",这是因为用"上德"或"玄德"来管理社会,不会产生"一己之智""一己之私""一己之为"与社会成员的尖锐冲突,因而也就不会产生互相伤害的局面。"夫两不相伤,故德交归焉。"(《老子》第六十章)

4. 《老子》"道""德"合一的意义

首先,从万物本性之德看,万物都由"道"所构成,依靠"道"才能生出来("道生之")。生出来以后,万物各得到自己的本性,依靠自己的本性以维持自己的存在("德蓄之")。在此阶段中,"道"和"德"是最基本的。没有"道",万物无所从出;没有"德",万物就没有自己的本性。总之,在自然观上,所谓"德"即指"道"之在万物之中的下落,而由于"道"之"有"与"无"的层面,故万物之"德"也有"有"和"无"的两个方面。在"无"的层面万物有其虚玄之"德",而在"有"的层面,万物有其质性、气性之"德"。

其次,从圣人心性之"德"看,"道"落实到圣人内心世界,化为圣人之超越性的心性存在,此为圣人心性之"德"。而依据"道"的运行法则,圣人心性之"德"可分为两个层次:其一,反者"道"之动,弱者"道"之用,依反而动、以弱为用的心性之"德"是圣人之"常德"。其二,万物和"道"的运行不仅仅只是正反相生、各自向对立方向的运动,它们也是一种返回和回归式的运动,是循环,是圆圈,是"归根"和"复命"。而以"无"为用、以"无"为心,圣人之心的最高境界是复归"赤子之心",守候"赤子之德"。

再次,无为治道之"德"。"道"下落于社会政治领域,有无为治道之"德"。此"德"分两个层面,曰无为心性之"德",曰无为治术之"德"。见素抱朴,少私寡欲。在治术上,"德"之内涵就是圣人治国之"无为",所谓"以无事取天下"。而圣王无为之心性通常表现为居下不争之"德"、以愚治国之"德"和"啬"智无为之"德"。

最后,"道""德"合一的内在逻辑。一方面,"道"的超越性与君德的超越性,"道"的运行法则与君王之德的具体要求之间形成相互对应与统一。另一方面,万物德性与"道"之无为玄德,以及万物德性与臣民之德的相互对应与统一。中国哲学有天人合一的思想传统,在道家思想中,这一思想传统可以具体化为"道""德"之间的贯通与统一。

六、《老子》的水意象与为政之道

《老子》中出现的水及与水有关的字有20多种，并且分布于不同的地方，水的意象因此贯穿于《老子》的整个论述的内容。"道"是老子哲学的核心概念，在说明或描述"道"的意象中，水意象是其中最为重要的意象之一。老子认为水与"道"具有诸多相似，特别是治国理政所应遵循之道，"上善若水"。老子还通过水的意象来说明"道"在认识世界、管理社会、为人处世中的作用。

1. 水是用于言说"道"的意象

在老子的哲学中，"道"虽然在不同地方的表述和具体意义有所不同，但其主要内涵却是一致的。"道"在形态上是"虚"与"无"的，给人们的印象是"无为""不争""柔弱"的。在老子那里"道"本身是不可直接述说的。但要让人们认识到"道"，又必然需要一个意象来承载这样的一个间接的述说。

在《老子》中，水显然就是其进行"道"的言说的一个意象，通过水这个意象的隐喻意义，让人们间接地体会到"道"。"作为中国第一本体论范畴的'道'，其原型乃是以原始混沌大水为起点和终点的太阳循环运行之道。"[1] 从文化学的意义来说，水不仅是人的生命之源与文明之源，而且还是人们在日常生活经验基础上建立起具有深厚隐喻意义的原型，如中西方哲学思想中人们普遍用水来表达形而上意义的意象。从日常生活来说，水是人们日常所见之物，且变化多端，用水来隐喻哲学思想，能使人们更为清晰和容易地理解"道"所具有的深奥的内容。正如老子所言，"道可道，非常道；名可名，非常名。……故常无，欲以观其妙；常有，欲以观其徼……玄之又玄，众妙之门。"(《老子》第一章) 这样具有"众妙之门"的东西，如果不从人们熟悉的事物入手进行理解，其内涵很显然无法为人所知。从形态上来看，水既是有形的，但也是无形的，其既是空的，同时又孕育着万物，因此在形态上与"道"具有相似性。很显然，老子用水喻道不仅具有深刻的文化缘由，而且还是生活经验使然。

水的意象在本质上可以用来说明和描述"道"，因而也具有"道"的本体性意味。"视之不见""听而不闻""搏之不得""无状之状""无物之象""迎之不见其首，随之不见其后"，这是老子对"道"的描述，从其描述中可以明显地看出，人的视觉、听觉、触觉都无法感知"道"，但是"道"虽无可见、无可言、无可触，却无处不在，源生万物。在现实世界中，水在视觉、听觉、触觉方面最为微弱，但却

---

[1] 叶舒宪：《探索非理性的世界：原型批评的理论与方法》，成都：四川人民出版社，1986年版，第164页。

滋润了万物，所以水最接近于"道"。水只是用来说明"道"，而不是"道"本身，这一点从老子的言论中可以明确地看出："水善利万物而不争，处众人之所恶，故几于道。"（《老子》第八章）

"道"存在于世界的每一个地方，体现于事物各个方面，呈现为不同的样式，形成了一个以"道"为本体的系统。与之相应的是，水在《老子》中也呈现出不同的具体名称（如"视之不见""江""海"等）、不同的状态（如"深""淡""清""浊""混"等）。这些不同的名称与不同的状态共同形成了水的意象，从表面看来，它们一起构成了水的意象系统，从其意义来看，它们在一起通过对水的意象的描述完成了对"道"的表达和理解。

2. 水意象运用于治国理政与修身

在《老子》中，水的意象成为人们认识世界、治国理政以及循道修身的主要途径。

水意象首先体现在为政之道上，老子通过对水意象的表述所阐述的思想，深刻影响了中国古代的为政理念。"大邦者下流，天下之牝，天下之交也。牝常以静胜牡，以静为下。"（《老子》第六十一章）大国要像江河一样处于下流，只有在下流，才是天下交汇的地方。静柔的常能胜过雄强的，就是因为静柔处于下位的缘故。王弼对此作注："江海居大而处下，则百川流之；大国居大而处下，则天下流之。"位置处于下流，水往往汇聚，国家要想有大的发展，须像"川谷之于江海"（《老子》第三十二章）那样以"下"为善。

"江海之所以能为百谷王者，以其善下之，故能为百谷王。"（《老子》第六十六章）对于君王来说，要充分认识到水的这一特点并在为政之中体现出来，这是因为："天下莫柔弱于水，而攻坚强者莫之能胜，以其无以易之。弱之胜强，柔之胜刚，天下莫不知，莫能行。是以圣人云：受国之垢，是谓社稷主；受国不祥，是为天下王。正言若反。"（《老子》第七十八章）水虽然柔弱，但在应对刚强的东西方面却没有什么可以替代它，因为弱能胜强，柔能克刚。君王只有能承担国家的屈辱和祸难，才配做天下的王。只有认识到这一点，君王才能做到"贵以贱为本，高以下为基。是以侯王自称孤、寡、不谷。此非以贱为本邪？非乎？故至誉无誉"（《老子》第三十九章）。

对于官员来说也是如此。老子说："知其雄，守其雌，为天下溪。为天下溪，常德不离，复归于婴儿……朴散则为器，圣人用之，则为官长，故大制不割。"（《老子》第二十八章）深知雄强，却据于柔弱，这是天下所遵循的蹊径。只有认识到这些，才能回到真朴的状态，进而了解到真朴的"道"分散为万物。只有持真朴，才能不离"道"而为百官之长。所以完善的政治是不割裂的，对于"道"的理解，不仅君王如此，官员们也要如此。"道常无名，朴。虽小，天下莫能臣。侯王若能守之，万物将自宾。天地相合，以降甘露，民莫之令而自均……譬道之在天下，犹川谷之于江海。"（《老子》第三十二章）"道"虽然质朴，但却十分重要，为官者只有守住"道"，才可以使人们自然遵守。而"道"就像江海一样，是由河川流注而成。

对于普通人而言，水意象蕴含"守弱"的特质，而"守弱"在处事上体现为一种淡泊的心态。"俗人昭昭，我独昏昏。俗人察察，我独闷闷。澹兮其若海，飂兮若无止。众人皆有以，而我独顽且鄙。我独异于人，而贵食母。"（《老子》第二十章）世人光耀自炫，我独暗昧，世人精明灵巧，我独无所识别。沉静之态，如大海一样，飘逸之象，永远止境。老子在这里指出，只有像大海一样，淡泊心境，才可以不受外界的滋扰；只有坚持"道"，才可以在纷繁芜杂的世事中保持自身的正确坚持，做一个"善为士者"。除了淡泊的心态外，老子还用一系列的水的意象来隐喻守弱的行为。"古之善为士者，微妙玄通，深不可识。夫唯不可识，故强为之容。豫焉若冬涉川，犹兮若畏四邻，俨兮其若客，涣兮其若释，敦兮其若朴，旷兮其若谷，混兮其若浊，孰能浊以静之徐清，孰能安以动之徐生。保此道者，不欲盈。夫唯不盈，故能蔽而新成。"（《老子》第十五章）这一系列的水的意象是说，做人要像冬天过河一样小心谨慎，要像冰柱消融一样和蔼可亲，要像幽谷一样心胸开阔，要像浊水一样浑厚纯朴，在安定中如静水般澄清自己而不断去故更新。

3. 水意象的隐喻意义

很显然，老子的水意象系列具有十分丰富的隐喻意义，它们从各个不同的方面展示着"道"的存在。

第一，通过水的意象隐喻使人们理解"道"的存在。"道"在老子的哲学思想中处于本体的地位，因此，水意象在表达和阐述"道"时，体现出了本体性的意味。从这个意义上来说，水意象就是用来说明"道"的，所谓的"水德"本质上就是"道"。除此之外，在老子那里，水是最接近于"道"，同时又能被人从实践上把握的。"道"存于万物，普利万物，水也是一样，通过对水的观察与体悟就可以达到对"道"的观察与体悟。不难看出，老子是对"道"的理解，在很大程度上是依据水的意象展开的，在以水为中心的意象系列中达到对"道"的认识与理解，水成为"道"的隐喻。

第二，通过水的意象隐喻使人们理解治国之道。无论一个国家多么强大，都要虚怀若谷，江海之所以成其大，正是在于其所处下位。在《老子》中有多个与水有关的意象，如"冰""雨""甘露"等，这些意象体现出水的柔弱一面，但同时也揭示出水的万千变化与不可抵挡的力量，它柔软而坚强，内蕴着强大的力量。一个国家要虚心学习所有的于国有利的东西，不断积累，才可最终强大，成就自己的"百谷王"。水的意象在这里成为治国理念的隐喻。

第三，通过水的意象隐喻为官治理社会。君王要像大川、大海承载不同来源的水一样，要能承载各种不同意见，以及各种荣辱。无论是君王还是官员，首要在于坚持"道"，坚持"道"就须如江海一样收纳百川，同时处于守弱的位置。守弱即是守"道"，坚持质朴，无论世事怎么变化，基本的"道"是不会改变的。因此守弱并不是真弱，而是一种信念与坚持。只有守弱循"道"，才不会自乱方寸，才可以为社会治理树立起行为的标杆，从而使整个社会的运转处于正常状态。

第四，通过水的意象强调淡泊的心态。只有淡泊才能让人从各种事物的纠缠之中脱开身来，从而心胸豁达。"静之徐清"，老子也通过水的意象来强调"静"的心态，只有静，才可以像水静而清一样，使自己的精神得到不断的净化。要说明的是，老子强调淡泊与"静"，并不是要求人们真的无为，而是在达到心胸豁达、精神净化的过程中不断努力，这种努力的过程本身也就蕴含着有为。

七、"自然之道"与老子养生论

《史记》记载老子长寿："盖老子百有六十余岁，或言二百余岁，以其修道而养寿也。"[1]这可以算作老子善养生的证明。目前学界对老子养生论的研究主要集中在两个方面，一是探讨老子的养生思想，二是考察老子养生思想的影响。对于第一个方面，主要讨论了老子养生论的根本目标，亦即"长生久视"；根本原则，亦即"道法自然"；此外还有形神抱一、柔弱处下、恬淡寡欲、致虚守静、专气致柔等具体的养生方法。对于第二方面，主要讨论了老子的养生思想对道教、传统中医养生文化以及传统气功养生文化的影响。总体而言，这些研究虽然揭示了老子养生论的一些内容，但上升到哲学高度的认识成果较少，为此需要从老子的整体思想出发，进一步挖掘其养生论的思想结构。

1. 生命是"道"的体现

陈鼓应说："我们也可以视为'道'是人的内在生命的呼声，它乃是应和人的内在生命之需求与愿望所展开出来的一种理论。""道"就是内在生命力的表达，

---

[1] 司马迁：《史记》，北京：中华书局，1997年，第239页。

"自然"指生命力的勃发。"养生"也好,"摄生""卫生"也罢,首先应考虑生命的来源。有了"生",才有"养生"的问题。

《老子》一书中讲到许多起源问题,有的可以理解为宇宙起源,但也可以解释生命起源的问题。如《老子》第一章:"无,名天地之始;有,名万物之母。"《老子》第二章:"有无相生"。第四十章:"天下万物生于有,有生于无"。老子认为,生命作为"有",是生于"无"的。这个"无"当然不是绝对的虚无,什么都没有,而是"道"的本原状态,也即是"道"。所以《老子》第四十二章:"道生一,一生二,二生三,三生万物。"《老子》第五十一章:"道生之"。这就是说,"道"是一切的根本,当然包括"生命"。《老子》第三十九章进一步说:"万物得一以生"。

"道"不仅"能生",而且有"好生"之德。《老子》第五十一章有"道生之,德畜之"。因此,"道"完成生命的创造工作后,就由"德"来维持它。天有好生之德,《尚书·大禹谟》:"与其杀不辜,宁失不经,好生之德,洽于民心。"

虽然如此,但老子视生命为一个自然过程,有生即有死。虽然人们可以用"德"来维护生命(《老子》第五十章讲到"生生之厚"),但个体的生命终有结束之时,这是一个自然的过程。所以,《老子》第五十章说:"出生入死。生之徒,十有三;死之徒,十有三;人之生生,动之于死地,亦十有三。"第二十三章说:"故飘风不终朝,骤雨不终日。孰为此者?天地。天地尚不能久,而况于人乎?"

生命的结束是自然的,因而也是必然的。这就从根本上说明养生并不能够真正长生,所以,人不仅要追求生命的长短,更要追求死后的永恒。这大概就是《老子》第三十三章所说的:"不失其所者久,死而不亡者寿。"

2. "法自然"是养生的总原则

"法自然"是一切的法则,养生自然不能例外。《老子》第二十五章:"人法地,地法天,天法道,道法自然。"生命的最初状态没有做作,最接近自然状态,从人的生命阶段来说,孩童的状态最接近之,它的特点是柔、和。《老子》一书反复说之,如第十章:"载营魄抱一,能无离乎?专气致柔,能如婴儿乎?"第二十八章:"知其雄,守其雌,为天下溪。为天下溪,常德不离,复归于婴儿……知其荣,守其辱,为天下谷。为天下谷,常德乃足,复归于朴。"第四十九章:"百姓皆注其耳目,圣人皆孩之。"第五十五章:"含德之厚,比于赤子。蜂虿虺蛇不螫,攫鸟猛兽不搏。……终日号而不嗄,和之至也。"《老子》第三十章:"物壮则老,是谓不道,不道早已。"《老子》第四十二章:"强梁者不得其死。"《老子》第七十六章:"人之生也柔弱,其死也坚强。草木之生也柔脆,其死也枯槁。"

老子既然追求自然，因此反对刻意的经营，否定"求生之厚"(《老子》第七十五章)、"生生之厚"(《老子》第五十章)。《老子》强调："万物作而不为始，生而不有，为而不恃，功成而弗居。"(《老子》第二章)"生而不有，为而不恃，长而不宰，是谓玄德。"(《老子》第五十一章)"益生曰祥。心使气曰强。物壮则老，谓之不道，不道早已。"(《老子》第五十五章)

《老子》对于养生也提出了许多具体操作方法。比如"守静"："归根曰静，静曰复命。……没身不殆。"(《老子》第十六章)又如"寡欲"："五色令人目盲；五音令人耳聋；五味令人口爽，驰骋畋猎，令人心发狂；难得之货，令人行妨。是以圣人为腹不为目，故去彼取此。"(《老子》第十二章)"乐与饵，过客止。道之出口，淡乎其无味，视之不足见，听之不足闻，用之不足既。"(《老子》第三十五章)

《老子》谈到养生，实际上是有对象区分的，这里提出来作为探讨。上面讲的养生一般是针对圣人、官员等社会较高阶层人士。对于普通百姓，即"民"，《老子》也提出许多有启发性的问题。《老子》认为，民众如果不惧死亡，就很难管理，即："民不畏死，奈何以死惧之？"(《老子》第七十四章)"民之轻死，以其上求生之厚，是以轻死。"(《老子》第七十五章)反之，民众如果重视生死，社会就会保持稳定："使民重死而不远徙"(《老子》第八十章)。可惜，一般社会情况下，民众都挣扎在生存和死亡的边缘，哪里谈得上"养生"？这样的民众是社会不稳定的因素，也会影响圣人的养生。所以，《老子》主张圣人养生，不仅是养自己之生，也应养百姓之生，让民众生活无忧，社会就易于管理，趋于和谐稳定繁荣。"是以圣人之治，虚其心，实其腹，弱其志，强其骨。常使民无知无欲。"(《老子》第三章)"甘其食，美其服，安其君，乐其俗。邻国相望，鸡犬之声相闻，民至老死，不相往来。"(《老子》第八十章)

道家养生术与中医之世界观、自然观均需以语言之方式加以表达，医生与病患之间亦须进行沟通。然而因道家思想之语言哲学缘故，道家养生及医药学均以文学艺术思维方式和象征思维方式结构其语言，例如天池、天泉、上关与下关等。传统中医药学讲究天人感应，即自然能量与人体能量、气之互动；其表征为系统网络内部之穴位既为能量信息之发送者亦为接受者，并以连续不断之方式在穴位之间进行能量信息交流互动；讲究自然界阴阳五行与人体内脏之间的象征性对应关系等。这些都是在"法自然"总原则下的表现。总之，道家养生是中华民族养生学的一种自然健康疗法，它按五行相生相克的循环，以达到天地人的平衡和谐，顺天时者方健康长寿！

中国女科学家屠呦呦从中医古籍东晋道教先师葛洪《肘后备急方》里得到启发，通过对提取方法的改进，首先发现中药青蒿的提取物有高效抑制疟原虫的成分，她的发现在抗疟疾新药青蒿素的开发过程中起到关键性的作用。由于这一发现在全球范围内挽救了数以百万人的生命，屠呦呦于2011年9月获医学科学领域重要的大奖——拉斯克奖，2015年10月获诺贝尔生理学或医学奖。"法自然"的传统中医药学正走向世界。

由"道法自然"而发展起来的中国传统养生思想，逐步催生了一套旨在使人健康、幸福、长寿的认识体系与实践体系。"我命在我，不在天"这一口号首见于甲骨文，后被道教先师葛洪在《抱朴子》中加以引用，指的是人在遵循自然的前提下，可以通过自身努力，延续生命的长度，提高生命的质量。中国传统养生思想及体系，反映和促进了人类热爱生命、永葆健康的理性与追求，是人类文明发展的重要内容。

3. 寡欲促进"养生"与"养德"的统一

老子追求的是内在精神的澄明、完满和自由。寡欲、不言、守静都是从外在的东西转向内在的东西。寡欲是老子养生思想的特点。老子在"自然"原则的审视下，抓住"欲望""智巧""作为"三个方面，进行对症下药的引导。而通过前面的分析，我们也知道三个方面不是泛指一切的"欲望""智巧""作为"，而是有所特指的。其中，"欲望"体现为对名利、强大、世俗之功德的追求，这些目标演变到极致就是通常所说的"最有权、最有钱、最出名、最强势、最能干事"等概念。公允而论，人生当然少不了这些追求，可是无限度、无节制的追求，给生命本身带来了沉重的负担，因为个体生命所拥有的能量是有限的，每一种追求及其实现都要付出"辛劳""汗水"，无限度的付出等于是提前透支生命。为此老子提倡"寡欲""少智"，等于在提醒人们，在这些追求面前，何妨"悠着点""消极点"。而当人的追求淡化之后，"自然"赋予人生命的机能便能正常运转，生命与外部环境的关系便能常态化，这对于身体来说无疑是非常有益的。

寡欲可以促进"养生"与"养德"的统一，因为对名利、强大、世俗之功德的过分追求，不但损害了身体，损害了心理健康，也引起了纷争，制造了社会秩序的混乱。在社会生活中，人们苦苦追求的东西，通常都是"稀缺资源"，并不是每个人都能轻易得到的；如果每个人都能轻易得到，那么也就用不着苦苦追求了。例如，在一个国度里，君主只有一个，出将入相者不过寥寥数十人，而"首富""巨富"也少得可怜，"著名的、伟大的"之类称号，也只能是少数人所拥有的，而相比于日常的柴米油盐之事，天底下的"大事"也是少得可怜的。这种"稀缺性"导致人们在苦苦追求的时候互相算计、互相争斗，乃至互相残杀，所有的"智慧"和"才能"都被用在这些方面，于是引起了社会秩序的混乱，引发了严重的社会问题。这样一来，对名利、强大、世俗之功德的过分追求，就成为"恶"的行为，理当遭到万人唾骂。但是，社会上那些已经得到这些目标的人，却往往文过饰非，把这些追求打扮得冠冕堂皇，自诩有"解民于水火"之功，"再造苍生"之德，拥有"英主""明君"之名，把自己视若神明。诸如此类又从文化思想上造成了社会的混乱，这种混乱的恶劣影响更为长远，也更为可怕。为此老子提倡"寡欲""不争""柔弱"，实际上等于把这些对名利、强大、世俗之功德的过分追求"关进笼子里"，让人们看清其真实面目。从客观事实来说，社会大多数人都处于"弱势"的地位，想争名夺利、争强好胜也无能为力。从统治阶层的眼光来看，这大多数人本身就是"寡欲""不争""柔弱"的人。可是，这些人的存在、这些人的日常生活，却构成了社会的主体。如果既从物质利益、现实地位上压迫他们，又从文化观念上压迫他们，那么他们的生活就会变得更加艰难了。因此，从客观事实来看，老子的"寡欲""不争""柔弱"具有牵制、驾驭强者，保护弱者的积极意义，体现为一种高度的道德修养，也做到了"养生"与"养德"的统一。

八、道家与儒家的互补及道家对人类发展的启示

老子的思想，对后世产生了巨大的影响。在漫长的中国古代，儒佛道三足鼎立，互相渗透，互相补充，对传统文化思想的发展起到了重要的作用。

1. 老子思想与儒家的不同影响

虽然《老子》的作者与成书时间尚不能确定，但其思想产生的时代，应该与孔子思想出现的时代大体一致，也就是同在春秋战国时期。那是一个诸侯混战、礼崩乐坏的时代，长期的战乱使社会渴望新思想的产生，而价值评判体系的缺失和政治权力的分散又为思想繁盛提供了自由的空间。就是在这样的社会背景下，产生了中国历史上的百家争鸣。而以孔子为代表的儒家和以老子为代表的道家，则是诸子百家中影响最大的两个流派。

正是因为有着相同的社会背景，所以诸子百家的思想虽然各有特色，但也有着许多的互相关联，特别是各家都有着对社会现实的强烈关注，都有为当时的社会现实寻找出路的愿望和理论起点。曾有学者认为儒家源出于道家，细究老子思想与儒家思想，会发现它们之间确实有着一些相通的地方。当然，由于着眼点和思维方式的不同，两者之间的差异更为明显。虽然都立足于解决社会存在的问题，但两者有不同的理论起点。儒家的出发点是人伦亲情，而老子的出发点则是

包括天地人在内的整个世界的自然状态。由不同的起点出发，一个注重以伦理道德精神来调整现实的人伦关系，一个则强调回归原本就自然和谐的淳朴本性。虽然两者都指向改善现实社会的终极目标，但对于构成现实社会的人的理解是不同的，这种不同不仅体现在对人的本性的理论设定上，而且也体现在理解人的角度上。儒家是从现实的人伦关系中来理解人，这种人是一种社会的人；老子强调的是个体对于自己本性的觉悟与回归，所理解的人则是个体的人。

正是由于思想倾向和思维方式上的差异，老子思想与儒家思想在历史上的境遇和它们对后世的影响便有很大不同。儒家思想从践行出发，着力于构建一种以礼乐精神为准则的社会秩序，从社会个体的努力学习和自我修养出发，按一定的原则处理好各种社会关系，实现社会的和谐有序状态。这种思想虽然被司马谈（汉武帝时代的太史令）评价为"博而寡要，劳而少功"，然而因为其可操作性强，又比较符合统治者的需要，所以在汉代以后被统治者选中成为官方认可的主流思想，从而成为中国传统社会影响最大的思想流派。又因为儒家对教育的重视，使得其思想与中国古代的教育活动密切相关，渗透在教育的整个过程之中。于是，儒家思想便在中国古代的政统、道统与学统的构建中，都发挥了重要的作用。

相比于儒家的这种浓厚的官方化背景，老子及道家思想在中国古代则具有明显的民间化色彩，很多时候成为政治治理和个人修养的一种补充元素和调节手段。当然，这并非因为老子思想水平不高，恰恰相反，是因为老子的远见卓识，起点太高且思考深刻，理解和践行的难度较大。儒家的思想主要是源自知识的传承和生活经验的总结，给社会提供了一套易于操作的制度规范和处世原则；而老子的思想则更多依赖于直觉体验和对宇宙的整体感悟，提供的是一种对于政治和人生的全局思路。借用史学家评论史书特点的话来说，儒家的思想接近"方以智"，易于把握和实行；而老子的思想则接向"圆而神"，水平更高却难于理解和落实。这样的差异，大概也是造成儒道两家在古代境遇不同的一个重要原因。从另一方面来看，无数个体对"道"的感悟和把握，构成了一种强大的社会力量，又远非单纯的政治力量可比；而从民族的文化积淀来说，儒道两家可以说是难分高下的。

中国长期流传一个说法，说儒家积极入世，道家消极避世，进则儒家，退则道家。这其实包含着对于老子和道家思想的一种误解，儒家固然积极作为，甚至是知其不可为而为之，但道家却并不消极，只是一种更高层次的人生境界。南怀瑾曾有过一个比方，他认为在中国传统社会中儒家相当于粮食店，提供了日常生活的必需品；而道家则类似于药店，没病可以不需要，如果有病了则又必不可少。这是一个很有趣的比方，虽然这样的比方并非学术的严谨表达，却形象地传递出这两家的某种特点。虽然看起来老子思想在古代的影响力好像比不上儒家那么大，但却也有着极为重要的意义。而且在现代社会乃至人类未来，随着人类面对的难题的不断累积，老子思想的价值将会越发凸显。历史学家陈寅恪曾指出："中国儒家虽称格物致知，然其所殚精致意者，实仅人与人之间的关系。而道家则研究人与物之关系。故吾国之医药学术之发达出于道教之贡献为多。其中固有怪诞不经之说，而尚能注意人与物之关系，较之佛教，实为近于常识人情之宗教。"

当然，道家乃至道教与儒家在思想层面的相互影响与相互关联是错综复杂的，难以彻底厘清。上面的分析，只是我们力图作出的一种概括。

2. 《老子》的天人观及其对人类发展的启示

天人关系是华夏先民最早关注的问题，先秦典籍中此类记载很多。《尚书·周书·吕刑》有颛顼帝"命重黎绝地天通"的传说，《尚书·甘誓》有"恭行天罚"的战争，《史记·夏本纪》有"而致孝于鬼神"的祭祀活动，等等。在洪荒遍地，心智初开之际，先民们祈求上苍，以期子民安生，这样就形成了最初的天人关系。在对天人关系不断探究的过程中，天人思想也就成为中国古代思想文化中的一个主题，是思想家们不得不阐发的重要命题之一，老子也概莫能外。

此外，老子天人思想有其学术、思想的渊源——《周易》。首先，从老子的仕途经历来看，老子思想可能受到《周易》影响，其中，他的天人观应源自《周易》。《周易》形成于殷、周时期，是巫、觋用来沟通天人、揣摩天意的一种工具书。《易》中卦辞、爻辞是从先民祈祷上天、乞求神示时所得的经验中归纳、总结出来的，虽是一部占卜之书，但却包含了中国古人对天与人、自然与社会相互关系的最为朴素的认识，其成书者应是巫史。而道家出于史官。《汉书·艺文志》说："道家者流，盖出史官。历记成败祸福古今之道，然后知秉要执本，清虚以自守，卑弱以自持。此君王南面之术也。"古代巫史不分，老子本是史官出身，曾做过周朝"守藏室之官"，从职业角度考察，他应接触到《周易》，或对其比较熟悉。据此，可以推测老子思想来源于《周易》一书。

其次，从《周易》与《道德经》二者的天人思想比较来看，至少在以下几个方面存在相似性。其一，宇宙的系统意识。在《周易》中，卦的六爻就是天地人三才的符号。《系辞》说："《易》之为书也，广大悉备，有天道焉，有人道焉，有地道焉，兼三才而两之。"老子说："故道大，天大，地大，人亦大。域中有四大，而人居其一焉。"（第二十五章）《老子》与《周易》都认为宇宙是一个包含有天地人的整体系统。其二，宇宙的生生不已。《周易》认为"生生谓之易"，整个宇宙是一个生生不已、变动不居的世界。老子认为:"道生一,一生二,二生三,三生万物。万物负阴而抱阳,冲气以为和。"(《老子》第四十二章)"道"是万物之母,对万物"长之育之,亭之毒之,养之覆之"(《老子》第五十一章)。二者都认为宇宙是有机、生生不息的整体。其三,从天道推明人事。《周易·系辞》说:"古者庖牺氏之王天下也,仰则观象于天,俯则观法于地,观鸟兽之文,与地之宜,近取诸身,远取诸物,于是始作八卦,以通神明之德,以类万物之情。"通过占卜的象数来推导事物生成、发展、衰亡,并表现为一定的规律性,进而也可以预测人事的未来之吉凶祸福。尽管形式是直观的,思维是神秘的,"但却确立了一个对待与观察人与自然关系的基本准则:天人合一。天地人的合一实质即天人合一。在《周易》作者看来,体悟天人合一这一宇宙本质(通神明之德),使自己动合万物之本性(以类万物之情),实现天人合一,这就是人生的最高境界"[1]。老子则提出了"人法地,地法天,天法道,道法自然"的原则,认为人类社会应取法自然,这里显然继承了《周易》中天人一体观念,只不过他以理性主义取代了卜筮中的神秘思想。

老子的天人思想既有其文化的、历史的传统,也有其思想的、学术的根源。他的《道德经》把中国古代思想和哲学思维推到了一个前所未有的高度。其中,对天人合一思想做了一个系统的阐述,旨在主张人类要取法自然、遵循天道,以此作为解决社会、政治、人生问题的准则。

(1)人与天的并生、同在。老子说:"天下万物生于有,有生于无。"(《老子》第四十章)"道生一,一生二,二生三,三生万物。万物负阴而抱阳,冲气以为和。"(《老子》第四十二章)老子从宇宙生成论上说明了"道"生万物,但是老子在"生万物"后却没有说"生人"。我们认为,从"道"的本性来说,这里的生"物",就已包含了生"人",在老子看来,"人物同类""天人一体"。换言之,人与天(地)都是"道"的自然结果,人与天(地)都有"自然"的共性。这一思想可以从其后学庄子那里找到依据,比如"天地与我并生,而万物与我为一"(《庄子·齐物论》)。在庄子看来,人与天(地)是并生关系,人与天地万物同归于"道"。庄子的"万物为一体"主要从人与万物的自然性上说,也就是说,人在自然性方面与天(地)是一致的。

老子强调人与天(地)的共时性。"故道大,天大,地大,人亦大。域中有四大,而人居其一焉。"(《老子》第二十五章)其一,"道"与天地人同在,"道"的

---

[1] 解光宇、孙以楷:《老子与〈周易〉》,《孔子研究》,1997年第2期。

存在体现并蕴含在天、地、人中；其二，天、地、人也是同在，因为是同生，所以没有主次、先后，这一点与儒家不同。在儒家看来，"有天地然后有万物，有万物然后有男女，有男女然后有夫妇，有夫妇然后有父子，有父子然后有君臣，有君臣然后有上下，有上下然后礼仪有所错。"（《易传·序卦下》）天地万物到人的生成是有先后、等次的；其三，天的神性与德性（仁义道德）已经褪色了，这方面又不同于儒家，如孔子的"三畏"首先就是"畏天命"。"小人不知天命而不畏也"（《论语·季氏》），"天生德于予，桓魋其如予何?"（《论语·述而》），"天命之谓性"（《中庸》），等等，从中可以看到天的意志和天的德性；其四，人的地位得到提升。人在"四大"之中就占有"一大"，并加以突出，不再是"获罪于天，无所祷也"（《论语·八佾》）。由此可见，老子的天人认识不同于原始儒家。老子既看到了人的自然性（物性）一面，又看到了人的社会性（人性）一面，正是人的两面性与他的"道"产生了冲突，所以他主张以"人法自然"来消解这种对立。

（2）天、人皆"自然"。如果从人与天地并生同在这一关系来看，人是自然的人，人体现了自然，就无须法地、法天。因为从本体论与生成论来说，三者皆是自然的结果，都合乎"道"。这里讲"地法天，天法道"，不是老子的目的，老子的意图是"人要法道"，因为，在老子看来，天、地本自然，无须法"道"，甚至其"道"也是从天、地中抽象来的。

老子之所以提出"人法地，地法天，天法道，道法自然"，是因为他看到社会的人有不合乎自然之道的一面。在人身上，处处充满了社会性的"悖论"。如老子指出："和大怨，必有余怨；报怨以德，安可以为善?"（《老子》第七十九章）"名与身孰亲？身与货孰多？得与亡孰病？"（《老子》第四十四章）"咎莫大于欲得，祸莫大于不知足。"（《老子》第四十六章）人与人互相怨恨的矛盾，德与怨的矛盾，名利、财富与身体的矛盾，追求欲望满足与欲望导致罪恶的矛盾，等等，都是"社会性"给人带来的矛盾。而正是人的社会性存在，导致了对"道"的戕害，这是老子所不愿见到的。但从他所提倡"小国寡民"的社会思想来看，老子并不否认人的社会性存在，以及人与社会的种种关系，问题是人在社会性方面如何符合"道"？从"善者，吾善之；不善者，吾亦善之；德善。信者，吾信之；不信者，吾亦信之；德信"（《老子》第四十九章）、"夫礼者，忠信之薄，而乱之首"（《老子》第三十八章）来看，老子也讲德善、德信、忠义一类的伦理道德。这些社会伦理如何符合自然伦理（道）？其尺度又在哪里？老子的答案是"为无为"，以期追求、倡导自然的、内在的、自发的价值标准和社会行为。

庄子面对这一问题，处理更为简单："不以心损道，不以人助天"（《庄子·德充符》),"有人之形,无人之情"(《庄子·大宗师》),"古之至人,天而不人"(《庄子·列御寇》),等等。庄子直接摒弃了人的社会性(人之所以为人)而与天同一,把人"物化",真的人而不"人"。相对而言,庄子的"天人合一"牺牲了人的社会性,老子的天人思想中,则肯定人在社会生活中的自发行为。

(3)天之道即人之道。《周易》的思维特质就是从天道推演出人道,《四库全书总目提要·易类》曰:"故易之为书,推天道以明人事者也。"[1]老子也是从天道推明人道,但在天道与人道关系上,看法与孔孟不同。孔子说"性相近,习相远""唯上智与下愚不移",等等,却对"性与天道"语焉不详;孟子说要尽心、知性、知天,在心性上宏论迭出,至于如何知天,却未做申论。相较而论,孔孟以人类社会为中心,更多关注的是人如何社会化;而老子则以整个宇宙为视域,考虑的是人如何"自然"化。因此,从天到人、从天道推出人道,必然是老子的思维路径。

那么老子的天之道和人之道的关系如何?在这一问题上,老子主张天道自然,人道无为。"道常无为而无不为"(《老子》第三十七章),"道"永远是顺任自然的(无为),然而宇宙中却没有什么东西不是由"道"所为而成(无不为),即"道法自然"。因此,以"道"为法的天、地、人,也必须以"自然"为法,人一定要顺乎万物之自然,遵从天道的自然无为的必然趋势,不能人为地加以干扰。显然,老子是主张用"道"的"自然"这一法则取代儒家的人道——社会法则。

老子意识到天之道与人之道在现实中并不一致,他说:"天之道,损有余而补不足。人之道,则不然,损不足以奉有余。孰能有余以奉天下,唯有道者。"(《老子》第七十七章)只有遵循"天之道"的人,才能"损有余而补不足"以奉天下。他多次申明循道的好处——"是以圣人后其身而身先,外其身而身存。非以其无私邪?故能成其私"(《老子》第七章)、"古之善为士者,微妙玄通,深不可识……保此道者,不欲盈。夫唯不盈,故能弊而新成"(《老子》第十五章)等,并告诫人们要遵循"天道",做到"为而不争",这样也才能实现"没身不殆"(《老子》第十六章),要做到"人道"效法"天道",必须"惟道是从"(《老子》第二十一章),以天之道的无私("天地不仁,以万物为刍狗")行人之道的无私("圣人不仁,以百姓为刍狗")(《老子》第五章),以期实现他的天人合一:"天之道,利而不害;人之道,为而不争。"(《老子》第八十一章)人应取法天道,做到"不害"

---

[1] 永瑢、纪昀主编,周仁等整理:《四库全书总目提要》,海口:海南出版社,1999年,第13页。

而利万物、"不争"而为天下。

总之，老子的天人合一思想，是从"道"生万物出发，指出万物皆"自然"，主张天道与人道的合一，试图构建他的宇宙秩序、社会图景和人生路径，即"道"生万物的宇宙之中存在着一个无为而治之国，国中之民清心寡欲，过着与世无争、和谐共处的生活。

在中国古代的思想家特别是先秦诸子中，老子在哲学层面的思考是极具深度的。老子的独到之处在于他的视界与思维方式，老子的思想具有超越性和全局性，不是一时一地的简单考量，而是着眼于整个宇宙时空的全局把握。而且，老子眼中的世界不是静止的，而是在不断变动转化，事物之间不是各自孤立，而是密切关联互相影响。老子思想中蕴含的人生智慧，对我们思考现实问题乃至人类的未来命运有着重要的普遍意义。因为老子的智慧是较深层次的哲学思考，因此它的启示意义也就具有了一种普适性。无论是个人的自我修养与完善，国家的内政与外交，乃至整个人类的命运，都可以从中得到重要的启迪。

20世纪以来，人类进入了科学技术高速发展的时代，而且对于科技的依赖性也日益加强。科技给人们的生活带来了极大的便利和更多的可能性，但同时其负面影响也日益凸现。不仅是环境严重污染、资源日渐枯竭，更重要的是以科技为支撑的大工业生产带来的许多物质变化过程是不可逆的，使得地球上的物质越来越趋于不可用的无序状态。而且由于竞争的推动和利益的驱使，人类的贪欲被不断放大，过分地追求所谓发展和进步的速度，而没有考虑发展的空间和容纳度。在这样的背景之下，回过头来重新关注老子在两千多年前的思考，便有了很大的必要性。如何重新理解人在宇宙中的准确定位，回归人类生存的自然状态，重视生态保护和可持续发展，实现人与环境的自然和谐，成为当今人类面临的头等大事。

西方社会乃至波及世界的现代性危机，其根源在于个人主义以及工具理性的恶性膨胀。人们站在自我中心的立场上，从功利的角度来思考效率的最大化，借助于科学理性的工具，对自然进行全面的征服，对社会进行全面的控制，对人进行全面的管理，从而造成人与自然、人与人之间的对立，这样就使手段变成了目的，使科学理性成为套在人们身上的枷锁。老子所说的"智"与西方的工具理性有相似之处。"智"也是指向外物的，人类的生活实践需要认识外物，所以"智"是必不可少的。但是，随着人们对外物的认识，控制、占有外物的欲望往往也随之增长，这就会打破人们生活的自然状态，而导致争夺，社会秩序也会陷于混乱。老子对"智"怀有深深的警惕，其原因即在于此。而其通过对"自然""无为"

等概念的阐述所强调天地人之间的和谐发展，预示着人类未来的发展方向，对于现代人如何走出现代性的危机，如何在技术高度发展的今天不陷入技术至上的泥沼，提供了很好的启示。

总之，《老子》之思想乃是源于宇宙自然之道之德启迪而生发的哲学思想，其旨归为尊重自然，回归自然，建构人与自然之和谐。老子的思想蕴藏着人与自然和谐的生态智慧，凝聚成天地人融合的生态道德观，凝聚了目前后工业化历史发展阶段上人类社会的共识：生态环保与可持续发展。在人类文明发展的历史中，中华民族的祖先们积累了善待、善用生态资源与保护人居环境的丰富经验，使神州大地成为东方农业文明的重要发源地之一。老子创立的道家哲学思想之明灯将继续启迪我们，照亮我们，引导我们走向自由，走向智慧，走向政治、经济、社会、文化和环境诸方面均可持续发展之路。

CHAPTER ONE: Introduction

This chapter offers the main framework of the thought in *Laozi*. After giving a brief introduction to Laozi the person, *Laozi* the book, and the influence it has exerted on later generations, we expound the ideological system of Laozi from six aspects: his Dao, his "naturalness" and "outlook of nature," his ideas of "wisdom" and "cleverness," his ideas of "merits and virtues," his comments on "governance," and his ideas of "regimen, or the way of keeping good health." And finally, we point out the value and significance of Laozi's thought. Required by the axiomatic approach, we have to find out the logical relation from the different aspects of Laozi's thought. In brief, the Dao, as the noumenon of all the things and all the matters, is infinite. "Naturalness," one of the most significant features of the Dao, controls the generation, existence and movement of all the things and all the matters, "doing everything by doing nothing." By contrast, the human "wisdom" finds this impossible and even hinders the "natural" law of "doing everything by doing nothing," which is in opposition to the Dao. In order to explain this, we must "demystify" the human "wisdom," and point out that human beings apply their "wisdom" to covet fame and gain, or to excel over others. To examine this closely, we find that it is wrong for the ruling class to regard coveting fame and gain, or excelling over others as "merits and virtue." The image of "water," among other important images in Daoism, best explains or describes the Dao. Laozi maintains that water and the Dao are identical in quite a few ways, especially with the Dao that is to be followed to govern the country. In terms of regimen, Laozi puts forward two rules, i.e., "Fewer desires cause fewer deaths," and "It is good to stay in tranquility and weakness," which are actually the unity of "regimen" and the "nurture of virtue."

I. Laozi the Person, *Laozi* the Book and Its Influence

The image of Confucius is clear in history, as records of him can be found not only in *The Analects*, but also in *Kongzi Shijia* (*Saga of Confucius*), and *Zhongni Dizi Liezhuan* (*Profiles of Confucius' Disciples*), whereas Laozi's image in history is so blurry and mysterious that it is even not clear as to who he was, and when he lived. In Sima Qian's *Shiji*, or *Records of the Grand Historian*, there is a very brief record of Laozi: "He lived in the State of Zhou (the present-day Luoyang in Henan Province) for long, but when he saw the decline of the state, he left. When he got to Hangu Pass, Yin Xi, the Pass Officer, said to Laozi, '*You are going to live a secluded life, so I suggest that you write a book for me.*' So Laozi wrote a book entitled *Dao De Jing* in five thousand Chinese characters, and then left. Nobody knew what happened to him thereafter." What is more, two other records followed about Laolaizi and Taishizhan, so it is not hard to see that even Sima Qian, who lived in the early years of the Western Han Dynasty, knew very little about Laozi. Also in such pre-Qin documents as *Zhuangzi*, *Hanfeizi*, and *The Book of Rituals/Rites*, we find some records of Laozi, but they are often queried as to their authenticity, for they are more legends or anecdotes than facts.

1. The Changes of Laozi's Image in History and *Laozi*'s Handing Down

Most of the stories about Laozi recorded in historical documents are from legends, the most known of which is that his mother had been pregnant for seventy-two years before Laozi was born grey-haired. There is no need to prove such legends false with the present cognitive level of man. However, there must have been some internal reasons of culture and history for these legends. What is more, these legends, ever since their popularity, have contributed to the construction of the Chinese culture, and exerted a certain impact on later generations. There is a paragraph in Sima Qian's *Records of the Grand Historian*, which is often quoted to show the influence of Daoism on Confucianism:

"*Confucius went to the capital of the State of Zhou, and consulted Laozi on the rituals. Laozi said, 'The person you mentioned, who advocated the rituals, has been dead for long, and even his bones have decayed, what remains is only what he had said. Besides, when a person is lucky, he may go out in his chariot to work for the government, but when he is not fortunate, he may live a floating life like weed in the wind. I heard that good merchants tend to tuck away their goods as if they had no goods in stock at all, and virtuous people tend to appear as foolish. You should get rid of your conceit and your covetousness, your affection and ambition, for they will do you no good. That is all I can tell you, and no more.' Confucius left, and said to his disciples, 'I know birds can fly; I know fish can swim; I know beasts can run. I can catch running beasts with a bow and arrow, swimming fish with a fishing line, and flying birds with my net. But the dragon, I do not know when and how it rides the wind and soars up to the sky. Today, I saw Laozi, and he seemed to be such a dragon!'*"

During the last years of the Eastern Han Dynasty (25-220 AD), Zhang Daoling settled down and practised alchemy in Longhu Mountain or Dragon and Tiger Mountain, Jiangxi Province, thus establishing Daoism as religion. In his *Annotations to Laozi*, Zhang Daoling for the first time interpreted *Laozi* (*Dao De Jing* was a commoner title to Daoism as religion) from the religious perspective, and deified Laozi and his Dao: "When scattered, it is in the form of air/gas; when gathered, it is *Taishang Laojun*, or the very High Lord, who governs Kunlun Mountain." Laozi was thus turned into the very High Lord in the Daoist deity system. Later in the controversy between Daoism and Buddhism, there were other legends like "When Daoism was introduced outside China, it became Buddhism." After the period of Wei and Jin dynasties, and with the development of the Daoism, the deified image of Laozi was repeatedly altered. Therefore, under different backgrounds, in the hearts of different people, the image of Laozi became even more mysterious with his double identity of the wise and the deified. With reference to the historical outlook of "pile-up theory" put forward by the School of the Discernment of Ancient History, the present image of Laozi is also the result of continuous accumulation and adaptation.

Like the identity of Laozi the person, *Laozi* the book, with regard to its author and the time of its completion, has also been a source of constant controversies. Up till now, we can only know that the earliest edition extant of *Laozi* is the Guodian text written on bamboo slips excavated in the Chu Tombs in the Eastern Zhou Dynasty (770-256 BC) in Jingmen, Hubei Province. According to the results of archaeological research, the time of the tomb was roughly 300 BC. Judging from this, we can say for certain that *Laozi* was completed no later than the middle period of the Warring States period (475-221 BC).

Laozi is a small book, but it is a profound one, which had been paid attention to as early as in the Warring States period. In *Hanfeizi*, such passages can be found as *Interpreting Laozi*, and *Illustrating Laozi*, which interpreted and illustrated *Laozi* the book. After the Qin and Han dynasties, the circulation of *Laozi* was even wider, during which a lot of different editions appeared. According to scholarly statistics, there had been more than 100 editions of *Laozi* before the Qing Dynasty (1616-1911). During the different dynasties and periods, many scholars had worked on *Laozi*, and annotated it, so there appeared a large number of annotated versions. Zhang Yucai, a well-known Daoist master in the Yuan Dynasty said, "There are only 81 chapters in *Laozi*, but there are more than 3,000 versions of its annotations." According to an academic survey, even now there are more than 1,000 annotated versions of *Laozi* handed down from ancient times, two of which are the most influential: one is Wang Bi's version, and the other Master Heshang's version. Apart from the versions handed down from the ancient times, there have been unearthed, with the development of archaeology, three other editions: the two silk texts (A and B) unearthed in the Han Tombs in Mawangdui, Changsha, Hunan Province, and the bamboo edition unearthed in the Guodian Chu Tombs of the Warring States period in Jingmen, Hubei Province. These have provided new important additions to the literature of research on *Laozi*.

In the process of handing down from generation to generation, *Laozi* has undertaken many changes or alterations in its diction, whether consciously or unconsciously done, thus the different versions and the text disparities. Although it is a phenomenon not uncommon to Chinese classical books, *Laozi* is certainly of radical diversities. The text disparities in the silk texts (A and B) and the bamboo text discovered in recent decades show the changes of *Laozi* from one generation to another. This has made our research much more difficult, but at the same time, as Professor Liu Xiaogan put it, it has provided us with more available materials, to some extent, for our research.

According to the statistics of UNESCO, of all the world classics, apart from The Holy Bible, *Laozi* has been translated into the greatest number of foreign languages and enjoyed the largest amount of distribution. *Laozi*'s influence overseas is much greater than *The Analects*. A large number of scholars overseas such as Hegel, Nietzsche, and Heidegger did notice and study the thought of Laozi. The long and wide spread of Laozi's thought is beyond the imagination of most of the Chinese. *Laozi* the book can be regarded as the "meta-text" or "gene-text" of the Chinese system. These philosophical genes have been partially or wholly expressed at the different stages of the history of Chinese thought and culture in the past 2,000 years. Having influenced the whole world, Laozi's thought is not only deemed the spiritual treasure of the Chinese people, but also that of mankind.

2. *Laozi*'s Impact on the Political Ideology and Practice of Later Generations

The various schools of thought and their exponents during the pre-Qin period were faced with a social situation of tangled warfare among dukes or princes, and the destructed rite and music system during the Spring-Autumn and the Warring States period. Although having diversified thoughts, they all meant to find a way out for the then society and showed their political concerns. Much as Laozi's thought was established in a lofty cosmic vision, he still concerned and pondered over the political reality of the time. And *Laozi* the book is based on the philosophical cognition of heavenly law and Nature, and manifests its humanistic concern of "going with the good person," its ecological wisdom of "The Dao's coping the Great Nature," its governance ideology of "governing a big country just like cooking a small fish," its moral consciousness of "non-action and non-competition," its profound influence of "God created by the Dao," and its regimen expectation of "respecting man and treasuring life."[1] Among all these its humanistic concern of "going with the good person," its governance ideology of "governing a big country just like cooking a small fish," and its moral consciousness of "non-action and non-

---

1 Xia Weiji. Daoist Humanistic Light. *Jiangxi Daily·Jiangxi Humanities Lecture Hall*. November 11, 2015.

competition" are especially worth mentioning, as they provide the political ideology which is different from either Confucianism or Legalism.

Laozi maintains that we should hold a merciful heart towards everything in the universe, *"The law of nature is unbiased, and will go with the good person."* This humanistic concern is the affirmation for human dignity and is in agreement with the living conditions in accordance with human nature. Laozi's "non-action and non-competition" means acting according to the Dao, that is to say, to comply with Nature and social law, not to act recklessly or wildly, not to disturb the public, and not to create dissension or discord or intensify contradictions, so as to attain the results of "non-action," but "with everything done." Laozi put forward the idea of "governing a big country just like cooking a small fish," which is a very wise ideology of governance. When you are cooking a small fish, you should be very careful about it, and don't stir it in a reckless way, otherwise it will be in a mess. Laozi uses this figure of speech to signify that in governing affairs, the ruling class should not have z-turns (or have repeated abrupt changes), and not disturb the people. At the beginning of the Han Dynasty, Sima Tan, in his *Gist of the Six Schools of Thought*, comments on Daoism, "Concise commanding is easier to implement, and achieves more with fewer efforts," and thinks that of all the six schools of thought, Daoism is the most effective one with fewer defects, and highly praises it. Though Laozi's political thoughts did not become the essential aspect followed by the ruling class, they have exerted a profound impact on later dynasties and societies.

Laozi's political thought was put into practice in the first years of the Western Han Dynasty, and its results were obvious. The rulers in the first years of the Western Han Dynasty, such as Emperor Liu Bang, Empress Lü, Emperor Wen, and Emperor Jing, all believed in "Huang Lao Zhi Xue," or "Learning about the Emperor Huang and Laozi," a branch of Daoism, especially during the reigns of Emperor Wen and Emperor Jing, which can be said to be the model of Laozi's political thought. During their reigns, the political governance was clear and peaceful, and the people lived and worked in peace and contentment. What is more, the economy was greatly recovered and developed. And all these changed the situation "the state was so poor that even the emperor could not ride a coach-and-four, and the dukes or princes could only have carts drawn by oxen" when the Western Han Dynasty was first established, and enabled Emperor Wu to subjugate the Huns.

When Emperor Wu of the Han Dynasty (206 BC-220 AD) adopted the suggestion of Dong Zhongshu (179-104 BC, a philosopher of the Western Han Dynasty) of "exclusive reverence for Confucianism," he abandoned the political route of the early Han Dynasty, and started the political strategy of governance of "taking Legalism in the name of Confucianism," which later became the political ideology adopted by emperors or rulers of later dynasties. Although Laozi's political ideology was no longer taken as the dominant one as in the early years of the Han Dynasty, it still had some explicit or implicit influence on later emperors or rulers. Of the rulers after the Jin and Tang dynasties, many respected Laozi, and participated in the worshiping activities personally. Some of the emperors such as Emperor Xuanzong of the Tang Dynasty (618-907 AD), Emperor Huizong of the Song Dynasty (960-1279 AD), Emperor Taizu of the Ming Dynasty (1368-1644 AD), and Emperor Shizu of the Qing Dynasty (1616-1911 AD), had even annotated *Laozi* themselves. It is evident that they were influenced by Laozi's thought.

The Daoist ideology had the foresight with regard to the political thought and practice of later generations. As early as in the Renaissance period, it had offered ideological resources and reference coordinates for the thinkers to design the blueprint of the modern world. What is more, it shows its profound insight not only in the philosophical ideology with regard to the soft power and anti-hegemony, but also in global good governance and sustainable development. Furthermore, the philosophical ideology of Daoism is changing the practical mode of our economic and social life, in such aspects as the anti-economic expansion mode, the anti-consumerism social formation, the balance of living pace, and the goal-setting of sustainable development, etc.

3. Laozi's Impact on Daoism as Religion, Relationship between Daoism as Philosophy and Daoism as Religion

Laozi is not only the founder of Daoism as philosophy, but has also exerted great influence on the establishment and development of Daoism as religion. Different from all the other religions in the world, Daoism as an indigenous religion in China, has, in the relatively long period of time, been a mixture of different elements of Chinese culture, including the philosophical Daoist thought, folk faiths, deific arts of necromancy, astrology, medicine, the doctrine of Yin and Yang, even Traditional Chinese Medicine, and the magic incantation school. Before the Indian Buddhism had taken root in China, China had, in a real sense of the word, no religion, except some primitive folk religious faiths, witchcraft, and Shamanism. The situation changed when Indian Buddhism was introduced into China. Daoism was the natural ally of Buddhism. Buddhism adopted the strategy of naturalization and introduced Daoism into Buddhism, in order to oppose the repulsion from Confucianism. From the last years of the Eastern Han Dynasty to the period of Wei and Jin dynasties, Zhang Daoling, Ge Hong and others gradually developed Daoism into a religion. In a sense, Daoism as religion was established in face of the competition between

Daoism and Buddhism, aiming to meet the needs of the populace. As *Laozi* had reached a highly theoretical standard with its unique ideology, it was chosen as the fundamental theory by the founders of Daoism as religion, the typical representative being Zhang Daoling's *Laozi Xiang Er Zhu,* or *Annotations to Laozi.* "God was derived from the Dao." When Laozi was first worshipped by Zhang Daoling as *Taishang Laojun,* or the very High Lord, Daoism as religion had its own worshipped "God" on a par with Confucius and Sakyamuni, the founder of Buddhism. With the development and perfection of Daoism as religion, Ge Hong set up his theoretical system based on Laozi's thought. Daoism as religion was not founded by one single person at one time, but by a number of people during a long period of time. In order to enhance the influence in the spreading of the religion, the founders of Daoism as religion not only borrowed theory from *Laozi,* but also worshipped Laozi as the founder of Daoism as religion. Naturally, Laozi became the first ancestor of Daoism as religion, and was even deified as *Taishang Laojun,* while *Laozi* the book was deemed as the Daoist classic, with its title changed into *Dao De Jing.* Similarly, another important figure in Daoism as philosophy, Zhuangzi, was worshipped as "Nanhua the Immortal," and his book *Zhuangzi* was re-entitled *The Book of Nanhua the Immortal.*

Because Daoism as religion in its formation had close connection with Daoism as philosophy, and there were quite a few things in common—their elements of thought, major personages and representative classics—they had, in the later Chinese culture, all kinds of inextricable connections with each other. More often than not, they could not be clearly differentiated. Looking from the academic angle, the connotation of the two terms Daoism as philosophy and Daoism as religion is distinguishable. Daoism as philosophy was a school of thought and philosophy founded by Laozi and Zhuangzi in the Spring-Autumn and Warring States period, and handed down to later generations, while Daoism as religion gradually took its shape in the Han Dynasties, and finally became a religion undergoing a series of development and differentiation. Much as Daoism as religion theorized itself by taking much from the thought of Daoism as philosophy, or even worshiped Laozi as its hierarch, the two Daoisms cannot be confused with one another, and the theories of Daoism as religion are not those of Daoism as philosophy. The ideological changes and representatives of Daoism as a school of philosophical thought are its most important elements when interpreted. Although it didn't become the officially academic mainstream, and the heritage and transformation of the Daoist thought after the Wei and Jin dynasties were blurred and seemed hard to tell, its influence on the scholars and men of letters in later generations was still discernible. Daoism as religion had had the indispensable elements of a religion, such as deity worship and belief, believers and organization, a series of religious ceremonies and activities, and its major sects were roughly clear.

Wei Aoyu, a Chinese scholar in France, delivered in 2014 at the seminar on Axiomatic Interpretations of Chinese Classics, a series of lectures entitled *Laozi, Zhuangzi and the Ideology of the Daoist Philosophy*. In his lectures, he pointed out: The history of the development of Daoism as religion shows that it is a double-edged sword. Take the Han Dynasty as an example, the peasant uprising of the Yellow Scarves Rebellion raised by the Daoist sect, for several times brought crises to the Han Dynasty. In the Tang Dynasty, Li Yuan, the first emperor of the Tang Dynasty, in order to get the legitimacy of his rule, claimed to be the descendant of Laozi, and worshiped Daoism as the state religion. In the mice plague of the Northern Song Dynasty, the imperial court demanded that the state advisors hold religious rites to wipe out the mice. At the end of the Yuan Dynasty, the White Lotus Society, a Daoist sect, played a very important part in the war of overthrowing the Yuan Emperors. The Uprising Boxers in the last years of the Qing Dynasty fought against foreign invaders by reciting the invulnerable Daoist magic incantations, turning from overthrowing the Qing Dynasty to supporting it by wiping out the foreigners in China. Such influences made by Daoism were unbelievable. However, in the bulk of Chinese history, the majority of Daoist believers lived a secluded life in the forests. The religious Daoism was quite popular among the ordinary people, for the Daoist believers provided medical and religious services and some other activities. Daoism as religion is a very complicated and special phenomenon in Chinese history. It has developed intermittently with a systematic theory and ways of practice, and has had a lasting and profound impact on the ordinary people and their life, not only in China, but also in East Asia or South Asia, such as Traditional Chinese Medicine, Dietetic Culture, Religious Rituals, and *Fengshui*, or Geomancy.

Daoism as religion and Daoism as philosophy are theoretically clear in meaning and content, but, in practice, these two terms are often undistinguished. People tend to use either one or the other in the same context without discrimination. In China, "Confucianism," "Buddhism," and "Daoism" are often referred to together, as they are regarded as the three most important elements of Chinese culture. And here, it is really difficult to say this "Daoism" is Daoism as philosophy or Daoism as religion, or simply a mixture of the two. It is even more so in the ideology of the ordinary people. Laozi as a historical figure and *Taishang Laojun*, or the very High Lord, an image created based on Laozi in Daoism as religion, are more often than not, indiscriminate. For example, in Luyi, Henan Province, people lay special emphasis on Laozi culture, but when they speak of the person, their addresses of "Laozi," "Taishang Laojun" or "Laojun Ye (the very High Lord)" are practically the same.

Daoism as religion borrowed something from Laozi the person, *Laozi* the book, and Laozi's thought in the construction of its own system. It might be regarded as a sort of takeover of the culture of Daoism as philosophy, which, to some extent, displaced the existing space for Daoism as philosophy. Undeniable as it is that Daoism as religion played an important part in the promotion of Laozi's status in later generations and the circulation of *Laozi* the book, in the handing down and interpretation of the book, Daoism as religion has exerted some negative impact, which the readers should be vigilant against. Although Daoism as religion took the Daoists', especially Laozi's ideology as its ideological foundation, it only partially adopted Laozi's thought and readapted it for its religious purposes. Out of the necessity to debate with Buddhism, Daoism as religion not only deified the image of Laozi, but also absorbed a large amount of deific arts of necromancy, folk spirits worship, and witchcraft, adding much of mystification to the understanding of *Laozi* in the later generations. With this as a cultural background, we decide to return to the interpretation of the text of *Laozi* from the doctrinal point of view, and its significance is not hard to see.

4. *Laozi*'s Impact on Later Academic Ideology

The Spring-Autumn and Warring States period (770-221 BC) when the pre-Qin philosophers wrote books and put forward their doctrines, as maintained by some scholars, was the Axial Period in human history. Because of their theoretical creativeness and originality, their doctrines had a lasting and profound influence on the academic ideology of later generations. *Laozi* the book, due to its broad vision and philosophical profundity, has exerted especially great influence on later scholastic ideology. The Metaphysical School of the Wei and Jin dynasties and the Neo-Confucianism of the Song and Ming dynasties have been the two most significant schools of thought since the Han Dynasty, and the ideology of *Laozi* had its vital influence on them in the construction of their theories.

The Metaphysical School was an important school of thought in the Wei and Jin dynasties, and it was also a dominant sign of that period. The production of the School and the establishment of its theoretical system were closely related to the ideology of *Laozi*. The Metaphysical School was founded by Wang Bi, of which the theoretical system was established by He Yan. The thought of the two scholars was based on that of *Laozi*. Scholars in ancient China tended to express themselves by annotating classics, and He Yan and Wang Bi did the same. Most of what He Yan had written was no longer existent, but from the few extant materials, we can find that He Yan did annotate *Laozi*. Wang Bi was much luckier, as his *Annotations to Laozi* still exists today, which is one of the two most influential ancient annotated *Laozi*, and has long been treasured in academic circle. He Yan's thought of "centering on nothing" was developed and readapted on the basis of *Laozi*'s thought, which was later enriched and perfected by Wang Bi, thus becoming the kennel content of the Metaphysical Theory. Wang Bi constructed his own precise and complete theoretical system of Metaphysics by writing his *Annotations to Laozi*. As one of the "Three Metaphysical Works," it provided the Metaphysical School with the concepts of *you* and *wu* ("being" or "existence" and "non-being" or "non-existence") and its theoretical foundation.

Li Xue, alias Neo-Confucianism, was a Confucian school of idealist philosophy of the Song and Ming dynasties, set up by such scholars as Zhou Dunyi, Cheng Hao, Cheng Yi, and Zhu Xi. Though a claimed Confucian school of thought, Neo-Confucianism had an ideological system of the mergence of Confucianism, Buddhism and Daoism. When Zhou Dunyi, Zhu Xi, et al. first constructed the Neo-Confucian system, they borrowed much from the ideology of Daoism as philosophy, especially that embodied in *Laozi*. Zhou Dunyi, as a representative of Neo-Confucianism at its initial stage, in his *On the Taiji Picture* or *On the Diagram of the Universe*, a fundamental book of Neo-Confucianism, borrowed the universe pattern constructed in *Laozi* as the starting point of his philosophical cognition. The Cheng brothers and Zhu Xi went even further. On the one hand, they absorbed *Laozi*'s ideologies of taking the Dao as the noumenon of the universe, and "the Dao produces all the things in the universe" to perfect the ontology of Confucianism; and on the other hand, they also absorbed the ideology of cultivation of seeking quietness, calmness and non-action. Zhu Xi was greatly influenced by Daoism as philosophy, and his introduction of Daoism into Confucianism enabled him to epitomize the thought of Neo-Confucianism. The concept of "Li" in *Li Xue* or Neo-Confucianism is very much like Laozi's Dao, whereas the train of thought of Zhu Xi's "*Li-Qi-Wu-Li*" is also similar to Laozi's "*The Dao is unique, and from the Chaos there appear the Heaven and the Earth, which in turn produce the qi of Yin and Yang, or the material force of the Positive and the Negative. The union of Yin and Yang produces all things in the universe.*" and "*Man models himself on Earth, Earth on Heaven, Heaven on Dao, and Dao on that which is naturally so.*" "Song Ming Li Xue," that is, Neo-Confucianism, or the Confucian school of idealist philosophy of the Song and Ming dynasties, transplanted into Confucianism the starting point, the train of thought, the mode of thinking, the mode of pattern, the philosophical frame, logical thinking of Daoism, so as to enhance Confucian speculation and development, and finally perfected the construction of Neo-Confucian theoretical system. In short, whether it is from the origin of thought or from the theoretical features, Neo-Confucianism has undoubtedly stamped the marks of Laozi's philosophy.

Apart from its lasting influence on the Metaphysical School and Neo-Confucianism, *Laozi* has also exerted an impact on other scholars, whether implicitly or explicitly. Wang Anshi and Su Zhe in the Song Dynasty, and Wang Furen, Wei Yuan and some other scholars in the Qing Dynasty, all studied *Laozi* profoundly, so they were inevitably influenced by *Laozi*.

Wei Aoyu pointed out, the direct and lasting influence of the philosophical ideology of Daoism on China's academic fields includes: (1) philosophy and philosophy of language. The dialectical thought of "*the movement of the Dao is in endless cycles*" illustrated in *Laozi* has great influence on Chinese culture. (2) Religion. The Daoist philosophy of Nature rules out the possibilities of monotheism and other transcendental religions. The spread of Indian Buddhism in China had some influence on the appearance of Daoism as religion. (3) Political science. In political science, these concepts and ideals are internalizing: "government by doing nothing that goes against nature," "small population of small countries" and social justice, and "*It is the law of nature to reduce what is abundant, and replenish what is lacking.*" (4) The relationship between Man and Nature. The Daoist doctrine and practice of respecting Nature and returning to Nature lays special stress on "disregarding all favours or humiliations," freedom from desire and knowledge, unity of Man and the natural spirit of the Universe, which has resulted in the absence of large-scale scientific exploration based on the development of Nature in ancient China, and accordingly, the absence of the cultural tradition of consumerist commerce. (5) Literature and art. The classical Chinese literature is rich in symbolic thinking, with highly developed and mature poetics and aesthetics. What is more, it has for the past thousands of years the means of resisting all kinds of powers.

II. The Interpretation of Laozi's Dao

As far as its genre is concerned, *Laozi* is like prose, poetry, or maxims. This varied nature of the book makes it possible to interpret it in varied ways. In the text of *Laozi*, the character Dao (道) appears 73 times, with its different meanings or significances in different contexts. So it is not surprising to have diverse understandings or opinions of the term. Hu Shi said that the Dao was "the origin of all things in the universe," and that Laozi's "Dao of Heaven" was, in fact, the Law of Nature in Western philosophy (Hu Shi: *An Outline of Chinese Philosophy*). Feng

Youlan (Fung Yu-lan) said, "The Dao is the general principle by which all things come into being," and he also said, "The Dao and Wu (Non-being) is the universality of all the things" (*A History of Chinese Philosophy*). Hou Wailu said that the Dao is the "supernatural absolute" (*A General History of Chinese Thought*). Zhang Dainian said in his early years that the Dao was the "supreme principle," that is, "the whys and wherefores;" when he reached middle age, he said that the Dao was "the totality of material existence that is primitively chaotic, or the primal chaos;" however, in his later years, he returned to his early point of view, and said "The Dao is, after all, the supreme principle" (*Understanding Chinese Philosophy*). Lü Zhenyu said, "The content of the Dao is something mythological," "The Dao is the supreme control of creating the universe and governing the universe" (*A History of Chinese Political Thought*). Yang Rongguo said, "(The Dao) is not the entity of material, but emptiness, an absolute spirit which surpasses time and space" (*A Concise History of Chinese Thought*). Xu Fuguan said that the Dao was "a fundamental power to create all things in the universe" (*A History of Chinese Human Nature*). Lao Siguang said that the Dao was "the metaphysical entity, meaning the real existence of something," and he also said, "Generally speaking, the Dao means law" (*A History of Chinese Philosophy*).[1]

To summarize the viewpoints of the scholars, the Dao is an empty or materialistic entity, and it is also a principle or a law. But this explanation seems to be too abstract, and the following will be our attempts to interpret the significance of the Dao in a concrete way.

1. The Dao that Cannot Be Addressed or Hard to Name

Chapter I of *Laozi* says, "The Dao that can be worded is not the constant Dao. The name that can be named is not the eternal name." According to the punctuation in the original Chinese, we often understand it this way: The first character Dao (道) is a concept particular of Laozi, and the second Dao literally means "to speak, to express." The Dao that can be spoken or expressed is not the eternal Dao; the "name" that can be named or addressed is not the eternal name. To sum up, the Dao that is named in the ordinary way is not the Dao Laozi means.

"The Dao that can be worded is not the constant Dao." It seems to tell us that the Dao is "indescribable," or it is hard to describe, or this Dao is quite different from the Dao that we often understand, and it is still not easy to understand even if it is worded. Nonetheless, even though it is "beyond description" or "hard to

---

1　An Yunzhen. *Western Studies on Zhuangzi*. China Social Sciences Press, 2012, p.49.

describe," it may have more than one interpretation. The pre-Qin period in China was still a period of Man and Deities living together, and the mysterious "deity" was beyond description. At one time, it is there, and at some other time, it is gone. You may feel its existence, but is by no means clear. In that case, is Laozi's Dao such unearthly "deity?" Although Laozi said, "*Such a thing as the Dao is vague and eluding,*" (Chapter 21, *Laozi*), he also said that the Dao is as mysterious as the deity, which is not correct. Scholars at home and abroad have made numerous explorations with regard to whether Laozi's Dao is tinged with mysticism. Some pointed out that Laozi's illustration of the infiniteness of the Dao is quite the same as the three principles put forward by Gorgias (Γοργίας), a Greek philosopher, who said in English translation: "1) Nothing exists; 2) Even if something exists, nothing can be known about it; and 3) Even if something can be known about it, knowledge about it can't be communicated to others." Professor Benjamin L. Schwartz, a sinologist of the United States, pointed out in his *The World of Thought in Ancient China*,

Indian thinkers believe that the meaning of "the real basis" or the real range of "non-existence" cannot be discussed with any kind of human languages, because it is "a reality or real range about all the decisions, relationships and processes beyond descriptions with any kind of human languages." The west philosophy and the Islamic philosophy at medieval age also stressed that "The God is in essence unknowable and inaccessible with any human language" because "human beings of limited knowledge," in the immutability, "can never know God's essence."

But, the so-called "real basis" or "the intrinsic nature of the God" does not equate to Laozi's Dao. Benjamin Schwartz particularly puts emphasis on the atheism of Laozi's philosophy: "Laozi's mysticism is not based on theistic metaphor. The emphasis on Dao represents a striking departure from the centrality of 'Heaven'." So, the basic attribute of Laozi's philosophy can be called "atheistic mysticism." On the one hand, it is unspeakable and undescribable with languages, and not even achievable by human rationality, so it is filled with mysticism. On the other hand, it follows pure nature, worships nothing and negates the outside domination power of human, so it has the characteristics of atheism.

Since that is the case, can we say that the Dao is a pure perception, the same as what we often say, "instinct" or "subconsciousness," which can be chanced upon but not sought, and which can be felt, but cannot be clearly described or expressed? It is obviously not right, either. Laozi said, "*To administer the present situations, you can utilize the long-existent Dao.*" (Chapter 14, *Laozi*) It is certain that the Dao can be grasped. He also said, "*The manner of the Great Virtue varies with the* Dao." So it can also be followed. Laozi also said, "The perfect virtue is like water. Water is good at benefiting all things, but does not contend with them. It prefers to dwell in places that the masses of people detest, hence *it is closest to the Dao.*" (Chapter 8, *Laozi*) From this, we see that the Dao is the goal that can be approached or arrived at. From these descriptions, we can see that the Dao does not only exist in "instinct" or "subconsciousness."

In phenomenological theory, there is also the so-called "beyond expression." It is because the essence of things or the true meaning is so inexpressible that this theory requires "to face the thing itself." The degree of this "indescribability" differs. The ordinary things are within the human scope of seeing, feeling, and describability, that is, they are of higher degree of "describability," and lower degree of "indescribability;" if the thing is far beyond the scope of human ability to see, to feel, and to describe, it means that its "indescribability" is of higher degree, while its "describability" is of lower degree. According to the quotes from *Laozi*, "*The Way is vacuous and formless, but when you use it, its function is inexhaustible*" (Chapter 4, *Laozi*), and "*The person who is with Heaven is with the Dao; with the Dao, one can last long.*" (Chapter 16, *Laozi*), we can see the vastness in space and the remoteness in time of the Dao, and can find that the Dao is far beyond the human sight, the human feeling, and the human expression. Therefore, it is "indescribable."

Related to the "indescribability" of the Dao is the defied naming of the "Dao:" "The name that can be named is not the eternal name." (Chapter 1, *Laozi*) The pre-Qin Confucians laid great emphasis on the "Name." Confucius stressed the "rectification of name," as he thought that the "name" relates to the actuality of "rituals" and "punishment," with its orientation to the ethical order, that is, to the determination of superiority and inferiority by naming. When the emperor demands things from his subjects, it is to "*qu,*" meaning "to take," but not "*jia,*" meaning "to borrow", which is fit for and indicative of the emperor's manipulation of his subjects. Xunzi, another representative of Confucianism, has more ponderings and comments on the "rectification of name." "Names" either come from tradition, or from arbitrariness. "There is nothing to speak of the appropriateness of names, as they are arbitrary at the very beginning. But as soon as they are arbitrarily promissory, they became appropriate. Those that are different from the arbitrarily promissory are not appropriate." ("The Rectification of Name," *Xunzi*) The fundamental basis of differentiating "names" is the sensory awareness of man, "but where comes the difference? The answer is: It depends on Heaven." The fundamental function of "the Rectification of Name" is to bring unitary recognition of the "rituals," "so the emperor decides on the names, making it possible to distinguish the objects and carry out the way and policies, and finally carefully leading the subjects to unification."

From this, we can see that Xunzi deepens the theory of the Confucian "Rectification of Name," and at the same time, emphasizes the sociality of the "Name" in moral principles and politics. According to Xunzi, the "Name" is not the inherent but arbitrary part of objects, that is to say, it is easy to understand. However, in the Confucian "ritual system," "*shi*" or "nature, actuality" mainly indicates the power and social status, and the right to control and distribute property, of which the scope is quite evident. Therefore, the purpose of Xunzi's discussion on the relationship of "Name" and "Actuality" is to establish a definite relationship between the arbitrary "Names" and the things and phenomena in society.

According to formal logic, conception is a mode of thinking that reflects the essential property of the object. In the process of human cognition, when perceptual knowledge is promoted to rational knowledge, the concept is formed by abstracting and generalizing the common essential characteristics of the perceived thing. The linguistic form of expressing conception is the word or the phrase. The conception has connotations and denotations, or its significance and scope of application. You may say that the linguistic form of expressing conceptions is the "Name", and its connotation and denotation are relatively definite. The "Name" that Confucians denote also has quite definite connotations and denotations, such as "*jun*," or "king" and "*chen*," or "courtiers." But as to the conception of Laozi's Dao, it is hard to denote by using the common "Name." The Dao is what "*you listen to, but what you cannot hear,*" "*you try to catch it, but you fail to do it,*" the essential property of which is hard to grasp. It exists in the form of a thing or object, but does not exist in the form of anything or any object: "*I use 'Non-being' to mean the origin of Heaven and Earth; and I use 'Being' to indicate the root of all the things in the universe.*" It can exist in the form of "bigness" or in the form of "smallness:" "*all things in the universe submit to the authority of the Dao, but it does not want to dominate the world, therefore, you can call it 'da,' or 'the great,'*" "*It nurtures all things in the universe, but it does not want to dominate the world, therefore, you can call it 'xiao,' or 'a little.'*" If you follow formal logic, the connotation and denotation of the Dao are not definable, so naturally, you cannot use a definite "Name" to indicate it.

Let's not discuss for the present whether Laozi's eternal Dao and "Name" are truer (based on the cognitive result of "true" and "false"), or loftier (based on the different levels of the stages of cognition). When they are related to "speaking" and "naming," it shows that it is from the perspective of "language" or of rethinking "language" that Laozi illustrates the Dao and "Name." To rethink "language" is the philosophy of language.

The philosophy of language as a discipline of learning has its issues of "origin," such as the nature of language, the functions of language, and the meaning of language, etc. Generally speaking, the philosophy of language, as a branch of philosophy, exists in the thoughts of thinkers, Chinese or Western, past and present, but it is only the language philosophy that discusses the linguistic turn in modern Western philosophy that indicates the special philosophical purport and pursuit. Traditional Western philosophy maintains that language is the instrument and form of rational thinking, and establishes the objective theoretical system based on this. Modern Western philosophy maintains that the so-called "thinking" is no more than the true sense of language, "*language is home to existence*" (Martin Heidegger). The rethinking of "language" in the general philosophy of language and the modern Western philosophy of language provide another perspective of understanding the Dao of Laozi.

Saussure, founder of modern linguistics, has a very famous saying about the theory of linguistic research, which divides "speech acts" into two parts: *langue* and *parole*, or language and speaking. Saussure believes that language is a social phenomenon, while speaking is individual acts. Language exists in the form of a sum of impressions deposited in the brain of each member of a community, almost like a dictionary of which identical copies have been distributed to each individual. Language exists in each individual, yet is common to all. Nor is it affected by the will of the possessor. Speaking is the sum of what one utters, including: (a) individual combinations that depend on the will of speakers, and (b) equally wilful speech acts that are necessary for the execution of these combinations. As a result, there is nothing collective in one's speech; its manifestations are individual and momentary.

Laozi's "*The Dao that can be worded*" can be compared to "speech," while his "*the Name that can be named*" can be compared to "language." "Speech" is individual, while "language" is social. The majority of the scholars in the pre-Qin period laid little stress on the immediate and momentary "speech," but more on the social "language." However, Laozi objected or at least showed contempt for "language." If you say that other scholars of the pre-Qin period had more or less similar understandings of the political ethics and sociality of "Name,"

One of the key points of research in Western philosophy of language is to explore the relationship between language itself and the intention and object expressed or indicated through language, and find that language itself has quite a few defects with regard to expressing intention and describing objects. It is pointed out, "*In order to get a broader outlook with regard to the disputes on verificationism, let's consider the following opinion: none of our words or phrases is denotational. None of our brief is true. There is little possibility to convert between English and the language that re-creates the situation of the world.*"[1] This outlook shows a tendency to deny the function of language, which we do not have to take completely, but which will make us think that "the language that accurately re-creates the situation of the world" does, in actuality, not exist. That is to say, the Dao as language cannot accurately reflect the Dao as an object. We can see this from a different perspective. Studies show that the phraseological implication varies with the change of the object, but each definite implication (or each definite concept) can only denote one (or one category of) definite object. If the object has changed, the concept to denote it should be a different one. As for the denoted object is concerned, there is no flexibility in the concept itself: it is impossible to apply one single concept to denote different objects.[2]

From this, we can see that the term Dao can only denote one (or one category of) definite object. In fact, the Dao is not confined to one (or one category of) definite object, but represents numerous (or numerous categories of) objects. In this way, it is not accurate to apply the term Dao to denote the Dao itself, just making do with it.

Actually, philosophers in the Wei and Jin period (220-420) already pondered upon the language from the perspective of dialectical unity. They affirmed the effects of language as a means of expressing ideas and recognizing the world. At the same time, they were aware of the limitation of language in ideographical expression and pointed out that anything metaphysical like the Dao is hard to explain or express by means of language. The "dispute over speech and meaning" in Wei and Jin dynasties has something in common with the discussion of modern Western linguistics.

2. Dao with Its Infinitive Denotation and Connotation

For the sake of expressing thought, Laozi had to impose a name on the "Dao;" and for the sake of axiomatic research, we have to make clear the implication of the Dao, just as Heidegger, a German philosopher, pointed out in discussion of the nature of truth: a thinker's 'doctrine' is something that has not been expressed in what he said. In order to be able to experience and in the future to know what has

---

1 Richard Rorty. *Philosophy and the Mirror of Nature*. Commercial Press, 2011, p.320.
2 Hu Zehong, Zhang Jialong, et al. *Studies on Logical Philosophy*. Guangdong Education Press, 2013, p.95.

not been expressed by the thinker – whatever its nature – we must think about what he really expressed.[1]

With regard to the normal concept, its denotation and connotation are both "finite." But the Dao is just the opposite: its denotation and connotation are infinitive, including the infinity in the form of existence and in the form of movement.

Logically speaking, the Dao is the greatest abstraction, which cannot be expressed, but can only be constrainedly described. In "*the Dao just Models on Nature*," "Nature" is certainly "inexpressible," and "beyond prescription." But to meet the needs of expressing thought and establishing a theoretical system, Laozi abstracted some features of the Dao and emphatically described them.

One is the effect of the Dao on the generation of all the things between heaven and earth. "*Dao* begets one, one begets two; two begets three; three begets all things." All things carry on their backs the *yin* and embrace in their arms the *yang,* the opposites tending to harmony. (Chapter 42, *Laozi*) This is the mathematical expression of the Dao. The Dao cannot be recounted, as it is "non-being, emptiness, stillness, simplicity," and it is "Nature;" however, it can recount everything. All the ideologies of man are attained through it, therefore, "the Dao generates one" and it also generates "everything," and everything is no more than the recounting of the Dao. The generation of everything depends on it, which is the epitomized De of the Dao. To generate everything anywhere at any time is the power of the Dao. This is also a way of embodying "infinity," but it is not the whole of the Dao's "infinity."

By comparison, the deeds man claims to have done do not have this infinity. Basically, man depends on the Dao to live and multiply, and to take up all vital activities, and those that are related to exterior environment. It will not do to exaggerate the competence and performance of man, as it will lead to ignorance of the infinity of the Dao, and without the nurturing of the infinity, the innate defects of "finiteness" will be prominent. As a matter of fact, it is because finiteness is easier to recognize and recount, whereas infinity is harder to recognize and recount, people tend to cling to finiteness, and depend on their finite understanding to guide their own behavior. Owing to the defects of finiteness, man unconsciously cuts off the nourishment from infinity. For instance, the manufacturing of instruments and the development of technology enable man to obtain limitless nourishment from the material world, but indulgence in these artificial things will deprive man of the many possibilities of adapting himself to environment, and become dependent on

---

1 Martin Heidegger. *Plato's Doctrine of Truth. Wegmarken.* Commercial Press, 2000, p.234.

the instruments, without which he can do nothing. The development of political, military, and economic systems, for one thing, improves the living standard of man as a social species, and for another, deprives him of his ability to exist when isolated from society. Man's dependence on all kinds of social administration will enhance his expectation of human society, and makes him further fastened to the social administration of politics, military affairs, economy and living.

The other is the relationship between the Dao and "Heaven." From the perspective of cosmologic theory, the Confucian abstraction goes no more than "Heaven," and *Tian Dao*, the Dao of Heaven, or the natural law, is the greatest Dao, the ultimate law. It replaces real abstraction with some matter, which is, in the exact sense of the word, not the result of "abstraction," though some instinctive and abstract method is applied in the consideration of the issue of "Heaven." It is very much like the Greek philosopher Thales who held that all things originated in water — an abstracted conclusion that marked the beginning of human thinking. Nevertheless, "water" is also a concrete matter. Confucian scholars based their discussions of the world on "Heaven," which still focused on a certain matter.

Although Laozi was in agreement with Confucianism in the way of abstraction, his degree of abstraction surpassed that of Confucianism. Laozi thought that there had existed the indescribable Dao before the formation of Heaven and Earth: *"There was a chaotic lump that had been formed prior to the Heaven and the Earth. It is soundless and shapeless, but it exists independently for long and would never stop. It moves in endless cycles, and can be the origin of everything in the universe. I do not know its name, and make do with the mark the Dao, or the Way, and name it* Da, *or the Great. It is vast and flows round without stopping, and extends to the farthest, and then returns to its origin. Being great, it is receding further. Receding further, it is moving farthest. Moving farthest, it is returning to the very beginning. Therefore, the Dao is great, the Heaven is great, the Earth is great, and the Man is also great. In the universe there are four greats, and the Man is one of the four. Man copies the Earth as example, the Earth copies the Heaven as example, Heaven copies the Way as example, and the Way just copies Great Nature."* (Chapter 25, *Laozi*) In this way, the Dao becomes the abstraction which is independent of any concrete matter. Only this abstraction with formless form and still movement can explain, in theory, the generation of all the things and their law of movement. All the things have their forms and are in motion. If we want to find their common starting point, we tend, from experience, to assert that that starting point is tangible and in motion. But experience seems to be feeble: if we assert that the starting point is tangible and in motion, we will then miss the starting point of the universe, as we may think that the numerous tangible objects are the starting point. After Thales of ancient Greece, there appeared other assertions of natural philosophy, such as "the world is originated from gas," and "the world is originated from fire," but they were not mutually deniable. Laozi observed this, so he put forward his world outlook of the "confused and stupefied" Dao.

Dao was the mother of all the things in the universe, and its accomplishment turned into "De (virtue)." Therefore, judging from the cosmologic theory, the Dao is the raw material and momentum of the generation of all things. The "Great Nature" in *"the Way that just copies Great Nature"* is the reciprocal transformation of "non-being" and "being." "Nature" is the most mysterious law of the universe. Of course, Laozi paid close attention to the universe, but he also intended to establish rules and regulations of human conduct. Then, what can this abstract world outlook of the Dao bring to human conduct? Confucianism pays attention to "Heaven," and, from the "separation of heaven and man" and the "correspondence between heaven and man," finds out the human value of practice (indicating the process in which man constantly cultivates himself so as to accomplish human being's mission). Laozi paid attention to the Dao, as he wanted to discover the smallness of man and the emptiness of the value of human practice from a more fundamental angle. Therefore, what man could do, or rather should do, was to see through the illusion of "being" and "non-being," and then became accustomed to being at a lower and quiet place, where man took non-action and strove with none.

In Laozi's cosmology, the value of human conduct is depreciated, but it is not repudiated. And his "non-action" does not mean doing nothing at all. He only wanted to tell people that man should be, at any time of doing anything, clear about his own limit in action, and return to the fundamental Dao. That is to say, it is all right to do something, but the fundamental Dao should not be ignored or neglected. "Non-action" means doing something without forgetting the fundamental the Dao. Some annotators said that Laozi's "non-action" is, in fact, "not acting recklessly or wildly," which is an interpretation of Laozi's thought of "non-action" from the perspective of cosmologic theory.

III. Laozi's "Naturalness" and "Outlook on Naturalness"

In the historical context of the pre-Qin period, the image of "Nature" did not indicate the objective object isolated from the existence of man. In the culture of the pre-Qin period, whether it is Confucianism, Daoism, or Moism, or whether it is philosophy, literature or art, they all regard "Heaven, Earth, and Nature" an organic whole, of which Man is a part, thus, to embody the cognition and experience of the interdependency of man and Nature, and to regard Nature as a personalized universe which shows interaction with and sympathy for man. For this reason, "Naturalness" is, in Laozi's ken, man and his society, whether it is at the beginning or at the destination. Some scholars have pointed out that Laozi's "Naturalness" is a humanistic concept.[1]

1. The Three Layers of Significance of "Naturalness"

"Naturalness" is one of the core paradigms of Laozi's thought, which appears in his book five times all together: "When he accomplishes his tasks and finishes his affairs, the people all say, 'We are as we are.'" (Chapter 17, *Laozi*) "Little words conform to naturalness." (Chapter 23, *Laozi*) "Man models himself on earth, earth on heaven, heaven on Dao, and Dao on that which is naturally so." (Chapter 25, *Laozi*) *"The reason that the Way is respected and the Virtue is treasured is that they do not intervene but follow nature."* (Chapter 51, *Laozi*) *"The Sages just follow the law of nature, and do not intervene."* (Chapter 64, *Laozi*)

Master Heshang's annotation of *"wo ziran"* (we are as we are) is, "The ordinary people do not know the great virtue of the rulers, and think that it is naturally so." Wu Cheng explained, "'*Nature* (naturalness)' means it is so." and "the ordinary people say that they are naturally so." *"The Virtue is treasured is that they do not intervene but follow nature"* means that the sages do not intervene in the growth of all things and just let them grow naturally. *"The Sages just follow the law of nature, and do not intervene."* This shows the attitude of the sages towards the growth of all things, that is, "without intervention," so as to make things grow completely with their own strength. The basic significance of the term "Nature" in these three quotes is "doing things on their own (without human intervention)." Therefore, the basic significance of "Nature (naturalness)" in *Laozi* is "doing things by themselves," emphasizing the aptitude of all things that can make achievements by themselves free of other forces from without.

The understanding of *"the Way just models on Great Nature"* in Chapter 25, *Laozi*, in spite of radical controversies, mainly lies in the understanding of the relationship between the Dao and "The Dao and Nature." Master Heshang annotated: the significance of "Dao follows Nature, and nothing else" is that the Dao is as it is by nature, and there is nothing for it to imitate. Wu Cheng also said, *"The Dao is called 'great,' because it is natural, thus the saying 'models on Nature,'*

---

1 Yang Jiayou. Re-discussion on Laozi's Natural Implications. *Philosophical Analysis*, No. 4, 2011.

which does not mean there is Nature besides 'The Dao'." That is to say, the reason for naming the Dao "Great" is that it does everything by itself, without the imitation of "Nature" as an external force. Some other scholars believe that the term "Nature" here is a noun, meaning the natural world. Judging from the syntactic structure, "*fa*", which means "*xiaofa*," or "to imitate," is a predicate verb. Therefore, "*ziran*" should mean "the natural world." But the term "*ziran*" in "*xiaofa ziran*," as a matter of fact, means "something becomes so in a spontaneous way" or "to do something with its internal forces." That is to say, what the Dao imitates is the nature of all things' doing anything spontaneously with their internal forces. "*In other words, the concept of The Dao is not from Laozi's fantasy out of thin air, but from his abstraction after his close observation of the spontaneous growth of all things with their internal forces; therefore, the original meaning of The Dao was the Dao or law of growth of all the things in the world. From this, you may say that The Dao has something to imitate; however, it is not the thing itself that The Dao imitates, but the property of natural growth of all things.*" [1] All in all, the first implication of "*ziran*" in *Laozi* is "something develops as it is in a spontaneous way."

The second implication of "naturalness" in *Laozi* is found in "*xi yan ziran*" (Chapter 23, *Laozi*), which means the "principle." Master Heshang's interpretation of "*xi yan ziran*" is: "*Speaking little means speaking sparingly. And speaking sparingly is the Dao of Nature.*" That is to say, "speaking little" is in conformity with the natural principle. Obviously, "*ziran*" here cannot be interpreted as "doing something all on one's own," but has the nature of Laozi's Dao, and becomes a principle that all the things in the universe should follow. It is a concept that is in the same hierarchy with the Dao. The meaning of "*xi yan ziran*" is that speaking sparingly is in conformity with the natural principle. "*Xi yan*" means saying little or commanding little, that is, Laozi's "*the sages do by non-action and educate with non-speaking,*" which is Laozi's "non-action." The opposite of this is "speaking much," which represents "human intervention", opposed to the natural principle, which, in Laozi's opinion, can only invite the result that "*The more you show off, the faster you will decline.*" "Non-action" covers the three dimensions of "non-desire," "non-craftsmanship," and "non-competition" or "non-strife." "Non-desire" does not deny desire, but determines, according to the natural principle, whether the desire conforms to Laozi's Dao. In order to realize this, we will have to be aware of the boundary of desire. "Non-craftsmanship" demonstrates the concrete ways of

---

1 Zhang Min. Nature Concept in Laozi's Text. *Theory Monthly*, No. 2, 2015.

following the natural principle, that is, "*Even if there are dozens and hundreds of manual instruments, the people cannot use them,*" "*Even if there are many vehicles, the people cannot take them. Even if there are armours and arms, people have no chances to display them. They have delicious things to eat and drink, beautiful clothes to wear, comfortable houses to live in, and merry customs.*" (Chapter 80, *Laozi*) "Non-competition" or "non-strife" indicates that the ultimate attitude towards following the natural principle should be like our attitude towards water, "*A good person is like water, which moistens the world but never vies with the world, staying in the lowest place which everybody shows contempt for.*" Only in this way can you become "*closest to the Way.*" (Chapter 8, *Laozi*)

The third implication of "*naturalness*" in *Laozi* is to elevate the spirit of "it is natural to be so" to the basic principle of spontaneously "loving your subjects and governing your country." At the same time, "naturalness" is a state of things and mind, which is Laozi's ultimate pursuit for his ideal society. This pursuit is manifested in Laozi's description of "*xiaoguo guamin*" (small states with small population): "*Even if there are dozens and hundreds of manual instruments, the people cannot use them; and the people are made to treasure life so that they are unwilling to move away. Even if there are many vehicles, the people cannot take them. Even if there are armours and arms, people have no chances to display them. They have delicious things to eat and drink, beautiful clothes to wear, comfortable houses to live in, and merry customs. They can see what the neighboring countries are doing, and can hear the crows of poultry and barks of dogs, but there are not mutual visits on the part of the people of the two countries.*" (Chapter 80, *Laozi*) In such an ideal society, there will be no writing systems, no wars, and the ordinary people do not have to turn to craftsmanship for their daily life, but "*have delicious things to eat and drink, beautiful clothes to wear, comfortable houses to live in, and merry customs*" to enjoy. That is the social status of spontaneity that Laozi was pursuing. And only when all the "factitious" factors are abandoned, and naturalness is promoted, can the ordinary people be free from "competition," "robbery" and "disturbed heart," become "dutiful and affectionate," "self-actualizing," "self-rectifying," "self-enriching," and "self-simplifying," and reach the state (of mind) of being spontaneous.

Doing things on one's own affirms the nature that all the things accomplish things all by themselves, which, in Laozi's opinion, is the ultimate power of the development and change of all things. If we affirm the fundamentality of the self-generation and self-growth of all things in the universe, and follow this principle of Nature, we will reach the spontaneous state (of mind). The three implications of "naturalness" can be considered to be the three foundations of the complete ideology of Laozi.

2. The Humanistic Implication of *"Ziran"*

According to *Cihai*, a large-scale Chinese dictionary and encyclopedia, there are three entries for the term *"ziran"*: (1) natural, or not artificial. For example, natural objects, natural beauty; (2) unpretentious, or not imposing. For example, natural attitude, natural writing; (3) the same as *dangran* (as it should be; certainly). That is to say, as an objective object, natural things and Nature in a broad sense of the word, indicate all the things of infinite diversity, which are tantamount to such paradigms as the universe, matter, existence, objective entity, etc., including human society. The natural world, in a narrower sense of the word, indicates the inorganic world and the organic world studied by natural science. The natural world, which has undergone changes done by human activities, is usually called the "second nature" or "humanized nature." As the existing status of human and things, *"ziran"* here not only mean the status of the development and change of man and things, but also means the natural property and status of man. In addition, *"ziran,"* as an adverb or conjunction, also means the inevitable tendency of the development and change of man and things, and the matter of course formed in the long run by habit of man and things. In that case, how can "naturalness" be defined in Laozi's context?

Professor Liu Xiaogan, in one of his annotations to *Laozi: Past and Present*, has made systematic analyses and defining of *"ziran"* (*naturalness*) in Laozi's context: (1) *"ziran"* (*naturalness*) is a noun; (2) As *"ziran"* (*naturalness*) does not mean the Great Nature or the natural world, it does not belong to the outlook of Nature, ontology, or metaphysics. It is not a general concept in ethics, political philosophy, or historical philosophy, and it is even more improper to categorize it into epistemology, or philosophy of language, or methodology. After repeated considerations, comparisons and contrasts, the authors of the book have found out that it is more congruent with the value of theory in Western philosophy to define naturalness as the central value. The other reason is that the principle or essence of the Dao is naturalness. (3) To differentiate Laozi's naturalness from the common-sense naturalness, we will have to define the core meaning of Laozi's *naturalness* as "humanistic *naturalness*," that is to say, Laozi's *naturalness* mainly concerns the existent status of human society. (4) All in all, Laozi's *naturalness* includes the four aspects of spontaneity (doing things on its own), primitivity (being originally so), continuity (being usually so), and predictability (going to be so), which can be generalized into the following two: the internality of momentum, and the stationarity of development. A more generalized statement is that it means the harmony of the general condition.[1] *Laozi Studies in the Twentieth-Century China* mentions that the two Chinese characters *"ziran"* (自然) literally means "do not make it so, or do not make it not so," which is, actually, the most classical formal testimony to "it is so all by itself."

Laozi's *naturalness* does not mean the "Great Nature" or the "natural world" in the modern sense of the word, but a state conforming to nature that is free from control by external forces. It has the meanings of "It is naturally so," "We are as we are." According to Laozi, the universe is a harmonious, balanced whole, and the harmony and balance plays the best part in fostering all the things in the universe, without intervention from the outside world, to reach their best state, and to keep good relationships with all the other things around them. In this way, the whole universe, with all the things in their best state and in good relationship with each other, becomes harmonious and balanced. That is what Laozi calls *"naturalness."*

Other researches show that Laozi's *"naturalness"* is not simply a paradigm of one implication, but covers three aspects which are interrelated: First, the nature of being just so. Second, the principle of being natural and non-action. Third, the state of being spontaneous. "To be so on one's own" affirms the nature of all the things to make achievements all by themselves without any external force. According to Laozi, this nature is the ultimate power for the development and change of all things. And Laozi's observation of the generative laws of all things is different from that of ancient Greek philosophies, with the intention of promoting the knowledge of the generation of all things to the height of the ultimate principle of "loving the people and governing the country." The third implication of *"naturalness"* is generated on the first two implications. If we acknowledge the fundamentality of the nature of the self-generation of all things and all the people, and can abide by the natural principle, we can reach the state (of mind) of spontaneity. The three implications of Laozi's outlook of *"naturalness"* can be regarded as Laozi's Outlook of the Universe, of Politics, and of Human Life. These three implications with gradual step-ups will help us to see the whole thinking venation of *Laozi*.

Laozi's *"naturalness"* concerns the state of existence of the human society, and Liu Xiaogan thinks that it can be defined as "humanistic nature." He maintains that the concept of "naturalness" can roughly be said to cover the relationship between the doer of action and his external environment and external force, and the state of

---

1 Liu Xiaogan. *Laozi from Ancient to Modern Times (vol. 1)*, China Social Sciences Press, 2006 edition, pp.289-292.

the doer of action with regard to time and history of evolution.

As to the relationship of the doer of action with his external world, the illustration of *"naturalness"* is that "it is so on one's own." (1) That "it is so on one's own" is the very basic implication of *"naturalness,"* and other implications are related. The term *"naturalness"* here means the spontaneous state without the direct effect from the outside, or the state at which this effect is too small to be counted. (2) The agent of action or that of existence in the duration of time is in connection with change. For this, we can express it by means of "it is originally so" or "it is usually so." *Naturalness* is a continuation of the original tranquillity, not the result of radical change. That is to say, any change originated from within, if suddenly interrupted or altered, is not natural. (3) That "it must be so" is in connection with the future tendency. That is to say, the natural state should include the developmental tendency of the thing itself, and this tendency is predictable, instead of unpredictable. We can say that "it is so on one's own" lays stress on the inner force and developmental factor of the thing, "it is usually so" on the sustainable status quo, and "it must be so" on the future tendency. Laozi's *naturalness* should include the four aspects of spontaneity, originality, sustainability, and predictability, which can be summarized into the following two points: the internality of the developmental force of things and the stationarity of the development of things, which, in essence, stresses the harmony between the world and the general state of all things.

Therefore, Laozi's ideal state of *"the Dao or Way just models on the Great Nature"* can be understood as a harmonious goal of commensalism and coexistence of all the things in the universe. Man, as part of the Great Nature, with his own naturalness (it is so on one's own), keeps the harmonious and orderly development pace (it is usually so), and maintains the required tendency of self-development (it will be so) with the external world and history. In this way, the world will be a world of harmony, and the society will be a society of harmony. So is the traditional Chinese ideology of "harmony between Heaven and Man" the ultimate ideal and the value objective of respecting Nature, protecting Nature and pursuing Nature?

That "it is so on one's own" emphasizes the natural quality of all the things in the universe. Everything has its unique innate nature, and everything should follow it in order to develop and cultivate one's self. This is the individual foundation of all the things in the universe, besides which there is one decisive factor, that is, the objective condition of all the things in the universe of "being usually so." As the world is an organic whole, the individual existence and development of all the things in the universe must be linked with the existence and influence of other things, and this linking is not only the necessary prerequisite of the realization of "being so on one's own," but also the realistic guarantee of all the things in the universe to "be usually so." That is to say, the natural quality of "being so on one's own" must deal with the influence and change of the surrounding environment so as to become the real condition of each individual thing "being usually so." In the view of Laozi, to realize the natural quality of "being so on one's own" of all the things in the universe, and the objective condition of promoting the development of the natural quality of all the things were originally harmonious and organic. Man is the son of the Great Nature, and spontaneity is the ideal realm for man's existence and development.

3. The Relationship between Laozi's *"Naturalness"* and the Dao

As far as the word itself is concerned, it has almost exhausted the implications of *"naturalness"* by using "it is so on one's own," "it is originally so," "it is usually so," and *"shidang ruci"* (it will be so in the future). And when the term *"renwen ziran"* (humanistic nature) is used to describe *"ziran,"* it represents a broadly defined concept. However, there is one thing that remains unsettled: What is "so" like after all? But Laozi once said, *"Man models on the Earth, the Earth on the Heaven, the Heaven on the Dao, and the Dao just on Great Nature."* So we have to discuss the relationship between *"naturalness"* and the Dao. Zhu Xiaopeng thinks that *"naturalness"* is the ultimate spirit of the Dao and all the other things. It has three basic implications: (1) The natural state of the existence and change of things. (2) The primordial state of actual existence (before being rationalized). (3) The two states mentioned above.[1] Master Heshang annotated: "Naturalness is the quality of the Dao, so there is nothing to copy for it." Wu Cheng annotates: "The reason why the Dao is da or big, is that it is '*ziran*,' or natural, thus 'following naturalness,' but it does not mean that there is naturalness outside of the Dao." According to these explanatory notes, the Dao should be the sum total of all the things and their evolutionary changes or movements, which is based on the things as entities: "naturalness" is the quality and spirit of the Dao.

We have mentioned above that the Dao manifests its "infiniteness" in infinite aspects; then, is *"ziran"* just that "infiniteness," or some other quality or spirit? Laozi himself did not explain this clearly. Seen from the relationship between Man's co-generation and co-existence with Heaven and Earth, Man is Man of Nature, and embodies Nature, so there is no need for Man to copy Heaven or Earth. From the

---

1 Zhu Xiaopeng. *Study on the Philosophical Thoughts of the Wise Man Laozi*. Hangzhou University Press, 1999, p.331.

points of view of ontology and the generative theory, the three are all the results of Nature, and therefore, are all in conformity with the Dao. What is mentioned here is that "*Man models on the Earth, the Earth on the Heaven, the Heaven on the Dao, and the Dao just on Great Nature*" is not the purpose of Laozi, as Laozi's intention is that "Man should copy the Dao." The reason why Laozi puts forward "*Man models on the Earth, the Earth on the Heaven, the Heaven on the Dao, and the Dao just on Great Nature*" is that he saw there is something in disconformity with the natural Dao on the part of man in society. Therefore, he maintained that Man should copy Nature, and follow the law of Heaven, so as to make it the principle of settling social, political and life problems.

From "*The Sages just follow the law of nature, and dare not intervene with it.*" (Chapter 64, *Laozi*), we can see that Man's "*daring not intervene with it*" is in fact of help to "naturalness," which is part of "the *ziran* of all things," or the embodiment of "naturalness" in Man. And "*daring not intervene with it*" is subjective, but, from the objective perspective, that is "*non-action.*" Needless to say, Man's "*non-action*" is an embodiment of the ultimate quality of "naturalness." Laozi has made quite a few remarks on "non-action," such as "*The men of high virtue follow nature and intentionally achieve nothing*" (Chapter 38, *Laozi*), which can be said that "non-action" is the ultimate virtue of Man. Such "non-action" is not simply objective, but subjective as well: there is no intention of or reason for impulsive "action." However, "action" is necessary for the ruler of the state, who should take "action" but not be dependent on "action," "*Therefore, the Sages nurture the world but not capitalize on their achievements, ...*" (Chapter 77, *Laozi*); the ruler should take "action," but without laying too much stress on it; it won't do to compete for credit, fame, and profit: "*the conduct of a man of virtue is to do things without competition.*" (Chapter 81, *Laozi*) And the purpose of all these is to reach the state of mind of "*I resort to non-action, people will educate themselves*" (Chapter 57, *Laozi*), and "*If you reach the state of 'non-action,' there is nothing you cannot do.*" (chapter 48, *Laozi*)

To sum up, Man's "non-action" is an embodiment of "*naturalness,*" the meaning of which is, by now, made relatively clear. "*Naturalness*" is the fundamental quality and fundamental spirit, and the Dao is the "infiniteness" shown through infinite aspects. The sage's "non-action" is the infiniteness of Man's "action." This is not only the embodiment of "*naturalness,*" but also of the Dao.

To analyze "*If you reach the state of 'non-action,' there is nothing you cannot do,*" we can see that it is, in fact, a display of the two aspects of a quality: for one thing, it is "doing nothing," and for another, it is "doing everything." If the main body and the object are involved, there will be four relationships: (1) When the agent does nothing, the object does everything; (2) When the agent does something and nothing, the object does something and nothing as well; (3) When the agent does something, the object does nothing; and (4) When the agent does something, the object does everything. The real intention of Laozi is (2), which is the closest to his ideology, and what is more, the agent's doing something and the object's doing something should be in harmony rather than in conflict. As it should be, "doing nothing and achieving everything" is but the embodiment of one aspect of *"naturalness,"* that is, a quality that is generated from the infiniteness of the Dao.

IV. From "Wisdom" to "Brightness:" the Cognitive Ability to Master "Naturalness"

Almost all the studies of the pre-Qin ideologists on *"zhi"* (wisdom or knowledge) involve the issue of cognition. Their different understanding of "wisdom," including its implication, function and meaning, etc., reflects their different epistemological view of point. For example, Confucians lay stress on "wisdom" in that it is one of Man's important virtues, with its embodiment of "their love for study;" Moist scholars maintain that "wisdom" is Man's particular viability with emphasis on technological invention; the Legalists and the Political Strategists think that "wisdom" means political tactics for power or profit. By contrast, Laozi's epistemological standpoint seems to be peculiar to the world. He said, *"If the rulers could get rid of their sophistry, the people could have a hundred times of benefit"* (Chapter 19, *Laozi*), and similar remarks are found in quite a few passages in the text of *Laozi*. These inferences are indeed unique: He who claimed to be Man, "the wisest of all creatures", could do without wisdom? It is certainly not that simple. It can be known, from the influence of Laozi's thought on later generations, that Laozi used this seemingly extreme manner to oppose the variety of Wisdom Outlook (epistemology), in order to clarify the "absurd statements." At the same time, Laozi put forward and stressed the new concept of epistemology — *"ming"* (fair and just or bright) Laozi said, *"If you can observe the details of things, you are 'bright,' and if you can follow the tenderness of nature, you are 'strong.' By using the light of wisdom, and mirroring the inner brightness, you will not bring trouble to yourself. That is called the eternal Way."* (Chapter 52, *Laozi*) What needs explaining here is how Laozi understands "wisdom" and "brightness," and the relationship between them, and what his epistemological standpoint is, either "becoming clever by getting rid of wisdom" or "becoming clever by means of wisdom."

1. "Wisdom" (Knowledge) is the Cognitive Ability Formed to Meet Man's Unusual Desire for Normal Existence

"*Zhi*" (wisdom 智) came later than "*zhi*" (knowledge 知), both of which are the same in pronunciation, but different in written form, and in classical works they are often interchangeable. *Zhi* for knowledge (知), is composed by *kou* (口, mouth) and *shi* (矢, arrow) in Chinese. Duan Yucai, a Qing-dynasty linguist in his *Shuowen Jiezi*, or *Etymological Dictionary of Characters*, annotated, "*It indicates quickness, therefore, anything that comes out of the mouth is as quick as an arrow.*" This means that anything that you can recognize or know can be spoken out quickly. By etymology, the meaning that "*zhi*" (wisdom or knowledge) expresses is roughly the same as today's cognitive ability (including the two aspects of distinction and expression). From the epistemological point of view, "*zhi*" (wisdom and knowledge) is a generic term for cognitive ability, including the cognitive methods, process, and results that form it. Thinkers always regard "*zhi*" as the cognitive methods, cognitive process, cognitive results, and cognitive ability they themselves summarize, advocate or agree with, and call those in possession of this "*zhi*" (wisdom and knowledge) people of wisdom or knowledge. Of course, whether the "*zhi*" stands for wisdom or for knowledge, there are a variety of other meanings and usages for it, and different thinkers may give them different meanings from different standpoints. Xunzi, in order to show his standpoint, strictly differentiates the "*zhi*" for knowledge from the "*zhi*" for wisdom, which is unique in ancient classics. Xunzi thought that the human perception and mood or sentiment will affect human cognitive ability, but the decisive power is the human heart, which is the master of senses. Therefore, Xunzi summarized the human percipience by means of "*zhi*" for knowledge, and the cognitive result of "the thinking of the heart" by means of the "*zhi*" for wisdom. "The Rectification of Name", Xunzi says, "What Man knows is knowledge, and the sum total of knowledge is wisdom." The "*zhi*" for wisdom is cognition connected with things, which is quite close to the Correspondence Theory in the Truth Outlook.

It is true that the pre-Qin thinkers had different understandings of the implication of "*zhi*" for wisdom and knowledge, but most of them accorded great importance to "*zhi*" for wisdom, and advocated "loving study." Laozi said *"getting rid of their sophistry,"* which is often misunderstood as "anti-intellectualism." If "zhi" for wisdom is the generally acknowledged human cognitive ability, then, "antiwisdom" is to oppose the human cognitive ability. However, through analysis, we can see that it is not proper, if not dogmatical, to call Laozi one who advocated antiintellectualism.

In the thought of Laozi, the manifestation of *"naturalness"* in human society is *"doing nothing but achieving everything."* The reason why *"zhi"* for wisdom should be criticized is that it goes against the principle of *"doing nothing but achieving everything."* Laozi said, *"And make those who think of themselves as wise afraid of doing rash things. If you deal with worldly affairs by 'non-action,' there will be no trouble of government."* (Chapter 3, *Laozi*) *"Therefore, to govern with calculation is disastrous to the country,"* *"and to govern without calculation is a blessing to the country."* (Chapter 65, *Laozi*) *"The reason that the people are hard to govern is that they have too much calculation."* (Chapter 65, *Laozi*) *"The more intrigues the people have, the more evils there will be."* (Chapter 57, *Laozi*) *"And free the people of the cheating and stealing desire."* (Chapter 3, *Laozi*) From this, we can see that wisdom has become obviously opposite to *"naturalness,"* and is connected with human behavior. Therefore, Laozi's criticism of wisdom is directly pointed to human behavior. In Laozi's opinion, people often apply wisdom to the following aspects. First, it is used to vie for power, as everybody wants to be the master, or to be the big man. Therefore, Laozi stood for *"It nurtures all things in the universe, but it does not want to dominate the world."* (Chapter 34, *Laozi*) *"The sage never attempts to be great."* (Chapter 63, *Laozi*) *"It is not to be arrogant towards others."* (Chapter 67, *Laozi*) Second, it is used to vie for profit or fame, as people tend to be aggressive or fighting for profit, and they tend to sing their own praises and be conceited. Therefore, Laozi points out, *"If you do not flaunt the wise, the people will not strive for vanity or official ranks; if you do not treasure the things that are rare and precious, the people won't be lured to rob or steal."* (Chapter 3, *Laozi*) *"They must not flaunt their superiority by using force."* (Chapter 30, *Laozi*) *"Those who assist the rulers with the Dao do not rely on the power of the army. The use of military forces will end up in retribution."* (Chapter 30, *Laozi*) *"The conduct of the human world is to do things without competition."* (Chapter 81, *Laozi*) *"The law of nature is victory without fighting, responding without speaking."* (Chapter 73, *Laozi*) *"If you do not make brag of your skill, you can prove your attainment instead."* (Chapter 22, *Laozi*) *"When attainment appears, it does not claim credit for itself."* (Chapter 2, *Laozi*) Third, some people are self-assured for having *"zhi"* for wisdom, having a cut above others, and talking nonsense and going amuck. Therefore, Laozi pointed out, *"If you do not understand the eternal law, you will behave in haste and cause trouble."* (Chapter 16, *Laozi*) *"The law of nature is response without speaking."* (Chapter 73, *Laozi*) *"The more you show off, the faster you will decline. So it is better to keep vacuity and quietness in your heart."* (Chapter 5, *Laozi*) In a nutshell, people tend to rack their brains to vie for power and profit, and for self-conceitedness and their own praises, and to seek to excel over others. Therefore, Laozi based his "anti-intellectualism" on these things, and objected the use of wisdom in these aspects. In addition, Laozi also analyzed the innate driving force of wisdom, and pointed out that the reason why "*zhi*" for wisdom is used in the above-mentioned aspects is that it is driven by "desire." Therefore, he said, "*No disaster can be greater than that of insatiability; no sin can be greater than that of avarice.*" (Chapter 46, *Laozi*) "*If you do not show off the things that entice the greed of the people, they will not be lost in delusion.*" (Chapter 3, *Laozi*)

In conclusion, Laozi did not oppose the human cognitive ability in a general sense, but opposed the non-reversing, aggressive, and predatory wisdom. The so-called non-reversing wisdom means the distorted wisdom that tends to seek the accumulation of things from the very beginning in a progressive way without stop or without return (in a cycling way), and in the end, to be deviated from the original starting point (Dao). This non-reversing wisdom is possessed of strong aggressiveness, that is, pursuing and seizing extrinsic things nonstop, either fame ("flaunting the wise") or profit ("treasuring the things that are rare and precious"). Anything extrinsic, except for the necessities for life (food), will cause pointless contention.

At any stage of the human history, any support of or opposition to some remarks or conducts in the name of morality seems to be more justified, more convincing, and more seditious. The basic norm of moral judgment is "goodness" or "kindness" and "evilness" (lack of goodness). What is "goodness"? The norm itself is blurred and hard to grasp. Therefore, to get to know and grasp the norm requires wisdom. It is in this sense that the pre-Qin Confucians affirmed the importance of wisdom with regard to individual cultivation. Quite a large number of statements in *The Analects of Confucius*, *Mencius*, and *Xunzi* lay stress on this point. Nevertheless, in Laozi's opinion, wisdom concerning good and evil is a non-reversing wisdom deviating from the Dao and "naturalness." Why? He said, "*If the whole world knows why beauty is beauty, ugliness will appear; if the whole world knows why kindness is kindness, evil will emerge.*" (Chapter 2, *Laozi*) Annotators of the past dynasties had different annotations of the statement. Professor Chen Guying thinks, "*These two sentences are usually explained in this way: 'All the people in the world know how beautiful is beautiful, and thus it becomes ugly.' The original intention of Laozi was not to say what is beautiful 'becomes' ugly, but to show that when you have the sense of beauty, the sense of ugliness is formed at the same time.*" People often regard "beauty" and "non-beauty" as the interdependent and reciprocal transformation of the opposite extremes, and Mr. Chen is no exception, only that he understands "beauty" to be the "notion of beauty." This understanding seems to be well-grounded, for in Chapter 2 the sentence is followed by *"Therefore the 'Being' and the 'Non-being' generate each other, the difficult and the easy accomplish each other, the long and the short show each other, the upper and the lower complement each other, the sound and the voice harmonize with each other, the fore and the hind succeed each other."* All these emphasize the interdependency and reciprocal transformation of opposite objects. But when you read on, you will find doubts. The next sentence is: *"Therefore the sages do by non-action, and educate with non-speaking."* According to the previous comprehension, the opposite of "non-action" is "action," and the opposite of "non-speaking" is "speaking." As the opposite sides are always depending on each other and transforming from one to the other, so is it necessary to emphasize that the sages must "do by non-action"? That is to say, since the opposite sides transform reciprocally, then, the attitude we should hold is that it is not important what position you are in. As a matter of fact, Chapter 1 of *Laozi* has already shown us how to understand Laozi's thought. *"Therefore, with the constant 'Non-being,' I often observe the subtlety of the Way; with the constant 'Being,' I often observe the working of the Way."* "*Miao*" (Subtlety) indicates synergism, while "*jiao*" (working, superficialities) indicates complementing each other. Synergism means "sameness," which complements each other means "disparity," and *"both can be said extremely mysterious and profound. The mystery and profundity of the mysterious and profound is the real source of all mysteries and profundities."* Therefore, "sameness" and "subtlety" are the roots, the origins, which are holistic and pure. But ordinary people only desire to pursue the "disparity" and "superficialities," which is deviated from the root, which gives rise to the non-reversing wisdom. Needless to say, this non-reversing wisdom abandoning the root is possessed of strong aggressiveness and competitiveness. Therefore, Laozi taught us to grasp the root, that is, "non-action" and "non-speaking," which shouldn't be sheltered or abandoned.

In fact, the reciprocal transformation and interdependency of contrary objects is not an external objective law, for the generation of all the things in the universe is not the result of the unity of opposites. The world is a "natural" process, without consciousness and aim. We cannot think that Laozi's thought happens to coincide with the prevailing materialist dialectics. The reciprocal transformation and interdependency of contrary things is the result of human cognition, and the so-called "having and non-having," "highness and lowness," "difficulty and easiness" are the perspectives of human cognition, that is to say, from one angle, it is "having," and from the other angle, it is "non-having." Most of the people of wisdom only affirm the one side of a thing, which itself is deviated from the root (Dao), as the root is not just one dot, but an organic whole, a scope. If we explain doctrinally but not literally *"If the whole world knows why beauty is beauty, ugliness will appear; if the whole world knows why kindness is kindness, evil will emerge,"* the explanation should be like this: When all the people in the world know what beauty is and how they can be beautiful, they will make efforts to pursue this beauty, but the pursuit itself is ugly; when all the people in the world know what kindness is and how they can be kind, they will make efforts to pursue this kindness, but this pursuit itself is not kind. When two things oppose each other and yet also complement each other, they become a "naturally" unified entity. But when we intentionally pursue the positive (or some say "valuable") aspect, we actually go to the opposite side ("not natural," which is in fact evil). Therefore, we do not need this deliberate pursuit of wisdom.

In the subtlety of the Dao, Laozi criticized that non-reversing wisdom, as this non-reversing wisdom is itself "evil." Laozi said, *"When the natural Dao was discarded, benevolence and justice appear."* Mr Feng You-lan (Fung Yu-lan) explainsed "'*When the natural Dao is discarded, benevolence and justice appear,*' this does not mean that Man can be non-benevolent, it only means that in the 'Great Dao.' Man are naturally benevolent, and that is true benevolence." [1] As to the benevolence acquired through learning or training, it has much imitation in it, and is one level inferior to the true benevolence. Laozi said, *"The men of high virtue do not meticulously seek the Virtue, and get it."* The non-reversing wisdom in virtue is not only "one level inferior to true wisdom," it is simply not wisdom of virtue at all, it is evil. Laozi maintained that true virtue is not "the virtue of wisdom," but "virtue of profundity," *"Although the Dao generates them and the Virtue nurtures them, they do not take all things in the universe as their own, but let them grow naturally. That is the greatest virtue."* (Chapter 51, *Laozi*) *"The virtue of profundity is far-reaching. With the return to the very nature of simplicity, the country will harmonize with nature."* (Chapter 65, *Laozi*) The virtue of profundity denies purpose and pursuit, but it is profound, vast and holistic. With this, great harmony can be reached.

"The Earth," "Heaven," "Man" and the Dao all model on naturalness. "Naturalness" is a unified entity. When Man distinguishes the opposite things from the integrated entity, and deliberately pursues the one side of the opposite thing, that becomes "evil," and "not natural." However, why does Man, as one of the

---

1 Feng Youlan. *The New Book of Chinese Philosophy History, Volume 2.* People's Publishing House, 1984, p.330.

"Four Greats in the Universe," become "unnatural?" Or how has Man formed his non-reversing wisdom? It is just because Man has the "desire" for external things which is more than necessary for his living or existence. *"If you do not flaunt the wise, the people will not strive for vanity or official ranks; if you do not treasure the things that are rare and precious, the people won't be lured to rob or steal; if you do not show off the things that entice the greed of the people, they will not be lost in delusion."* (Chapter 3, *Laozi*) To flaunt the wise is to covet fame, and to treasure the things rare and precious is to covet profit. If the whole society takes "coveting fame and profit" as their common pursuit, everybody in the society will rack their brains (wisdom) to acquire fame and profit, which is deviated from *"naturalness."* Therefore, to the sovereigns, they must get rid of those superfluous desires ("see nothing desirable"), and *"to purify their soul, satisfy their needs of the stomach, reduce their selfish desire, and keep their health in good condition. And free the people of the cheating and stealing desire. And make those who think of themselves as wise afraid of doing rash things. If you deal with worldly affairs by 'taking non-action,' there will be no trouble of government."* (Chapter 3, *Laozi*) "To purify their soul" means abandoning those non-reversing wisdom; "to satisfy their needs of the stomach" means meeting their needs for basic existence; "to reduce their selfish desire" means abandoning their deliberate pursuit; and "to keep their health in good condition" means treasuring their own vigor and vitality. — If they can do all these, they will be able to make their subjects "ignorant and free from desire." "To be ignorant" means the elimination of that non-reversing wisdom; and "to be free from desire" means the elimination of superfluous desires. *"The Sage is only interested in not suffering from hunger or starvation, but not in physical pleasures"* emphasized in Chapter 12 of *Laozi* is "being ignorant," and *"To treasure your own body"* emphasized in Chapter 13 of *Laozi* is "being free from desire." In Chapters 19 and 20, Laozi once again stressed "abandoning wisdom" and "abandoning learning," and warned, *"try their best to retain simplicity and honesty, to discard selfish desires, and to be content with ignorance, and there will be no anxieties."* When people deliberately pursue something, they have a selfish heart. "To be selfish" means having "superfluous desires."And this "desirability" results in non-reversing wisdom, and vice versa, that is, the non-reversing wisdom enhances the "desirability."

The interesting thing is that Xunzi, a Confucian in the pre-Qin period, had another interpretation of "desire." Although Xunzi thought that hedonism would bring struggle and should be regulated by the "rituals." At the same time, he also thought that it is just the "desire" that is the original foundation for the construction of social order, so the society should try to meet the desire for fame and profit of those who have integrity and talent, and the social stratification of the respectable and the humble, the high and the low shows the degrees of the society's satisfaction of different desires. From this we can see that the elimination of superfluous "desire" is indeed a mutiny against society and a distortion of human nature. Desire is an inborn predisposition, which denies indulgence, therefore, it must be regulated by the "humanistic" "ritual," and that is the separation of Heaven and Man; at the same time, desire cannot be cleared up, as it is the basis of the construction of social order, and that is harmony between Heaven and Man. The double abilities of the "separation" and "cultivation" of the "ritual" is perfectly combined in Man's wisdom. Wisdom and "De (virtue)" shaped from it are amply affirmed and manifested. Laozi did not think that human desires, especially those superfluous desires, is an inborn predisposition, as the "basic" feature of all existences is "naturalness," or natural. Any violation of "naturalness" is "evil." Therefore, in Laozi's opinion, the wisdom of those people is no more than the cognitive ability developed to satisfy their desire for what is more than necessary for existence. This ability is harmful, thus wanting transcending.

2. "Fairness and Justice" is the Self-observation Ability of the Human Inborn Life-force

Laozi's meditation on "zhi" for wisdom (that is, human cognition) is based on "ontological" and "metaphysical" "domain." Laozi believed that in the "domain" there are four greats: the Great Dao, Great Heaven, the Great Earth, and Great Man. This kind of "ontological" "domain" transcends not only concrete objects, but also "similar" objects (Heaven, the Earth, and Man). Only when we reflect Man's "*zhi*" for wisdom from this "domain" can we find the unipolarity of this "*zhi*" for wisdom. "*The Dao is vacuous and formless, but when you use it, its function is inexhaustible.*" (Chapter 4, *Laozi*) This shows the greatness of the Dao. "*Heaven and Earth show no bias.*" (Chapter 5, *Laozi*) "*Heaven and Earth exist long and forever.*" (Chapter 7, *Laozi*) These show the greatness of Heaven and Earth. Then, what shows Man's greatness? Man has the cognitive ability to "*dao* (to speaking)" and "*ming* (to name)," but it is this ability that gives rise to the opposite concept and partially affirms the result of one side. The fruit of wisdom which "can be expressed" and "can be addressed" deviates from or even destroys the "Dao (the Way)" and "Ming (the name)" which cannot be expressed or addressed. Only when Man understands "*the real source of all mysteries and profundities*" of "*the mystery and profundity of the mysterious and profound*" can Man become truly great. Laozi said, "*To know the constant nature is known as fair and just.*" (Chapters 16 and 55, *Laozi*)

Therefore, Laozi does not oppose wisdom in a general way, but in its general sense, and furthermore, he put forward that the true wisdom is to realize "eternity," and this wisdom he call "discernment" or "fairness and justice."

What is "eternity"? Zhu Qianzhi explained, "The Dao is a general name of change. It changes with time, and it changes with things. Though there is change or alteration, there is something that is not changeable, and that is the 'eternity'." Modern scholars call it the "law," which Chen Guying explained as "the eternal law in the movement and change of all the things in the universe." This explanation does not show the true sense of the word "*chang*" (roughly eternal). Laozi said, "*It is the everlasting and eternal law that everything returns to its origin. It is called 'ming', or being fair and just.*" (Chapter 16, *Laozi*) "*The vital essence and the vigor and vitality are called 'chang' or eternity or constancy.*" (Chapter 55, *Laozi*) "*Ming*" indicates the original source, and "*he*" indicates the confluent flow of *Yin* and *Yang*. The sum total of all the things in the universe naturally coming out from the original source is "*chang*", or eternity or constancy, which does not seek any addition and deduction, and does not go to extremes or go on the evil ways. Compared with the non-reversing wisdom, the original source seems to be "nothing," "emptiness," "stillness," "weakness," "feminine," and "infants." Laozi did not care whether there is the "changing constant law." The learning in search of objective laws is the goal of physics. Laozi's goal is to find out an ontological basis for the "human life." Therefore, "*chang*" is not so much the changing constant law as "ordinary" and "daily," that is, the state of natural non-action. It is not something special, or something that should be maintained, pursued, or even changed. And this does not require special "expressing" or "addressing or naming." If you abandon that non-reversing wisdom, it will stay in the heart. We all know that Confucius laid special emphasis on the rectification of name. If the name is not right, the speech will not be in order, and if the speech is not in order, nothing will be accomplished. This "*ming*" (name), in the eye of Laozi, is "*not the eternal name.*" "*Few words conform to the natural Dao.*" (Chapter 23, *Laozi*) The "eternal name" cannot be "worded or named," or it simply needs no "wording or naming" at all.

"*Chang,*" meaning eternity or constancy, is clearly known, and there is no need to "know" it. Then why did Laozi say "*The recognition of eternity is called brightness?*" Mr Chen Guying said, "When Laozi talked about the body of Dao, he was used to using the reverse method; he used a large number of nouns in the experience world for his explanation, and then repudiated them one by one, in order to show that the nouns in the experience world are not sufficient to offer description, and from this we can see in a reversed way the subtlety and profundity of the Dao."

Although Laozi did not distinguish which are the nouns of the experience world, and which are those of the non-experience world, he actually used the "reverse method," to the extent that you can say the whole book composed of five thousand characters is said in a reversed way, and is said grudgingly. Laozi said grudgingly the Sage is only interested in not suffering from hunger or starvation, but not in physical pleasures. (Chapter 12, *Laozi*) And he also said that they love and treat their own bodies. (Chapter 13, *Laozi*) It sounds rather passive, but, in fact, he actively told us where the "*chang*" of human life is. What Laozi said in Chapter 10 "*The soul and the form can be combined as one,*" and "*Depend on the natural organism and gather the vital essence so as to be soft and tender*" is actually the "*chang*" of human life, which is the natural outflow of the first stage in human life. We may call this "*chang*" of human life is the human life-force, and when you possess it, you possess "fairness and justice" or "brightness", and possess the "light" which shines on all the things in the universe. "*If you are erudite and well-informed, can you have sense enough not to know anything?*" (Chapter 10, *Laozi*) With these, what is the point of knowing anything? "Brightness" is self observation ability of human innate life-force.

Laozi "made repeated efforts" to expound from various aspects the state of "*ming*" or brightness/cleverness of human life, which is a state of real wisdom:

First, only when you reach the state of "ming" (fair and just) can you become unselfish. Laozi said, "The person who knows the eternal Dao can be magnanimous towards everything, and anyone who can be magnanimous towards everything can be free of disasters throughout his life." (Chapter 16, *Laozi*) "To know the eternal Dao" is "discernment," and when you have "discernment," you can hold everything. The wisdom of human "speaking" and "naming" is, in fact, the "factitious" demarcation. Once we name something, we mark the named thing as different from those in other categories, and show the differentiation of far and near, intimate and distant. In this way, Man is possessed of selfishness, which deviates from the eternal Dao. For example, when we name Heaven and Earth by "non-being," and name all the things in the universe by "being," we can only see "being," but neglect "non-being," and can hardly see that "non-being" and "being" are actually "*both from the same origin, but only named differently.*" This "sameness" is the fundamental, and is the "*the real source of all mysteries and profundities*" with "*the mystery and profundity of the mysterious and profound.*" Therefore, Laozi, in the very first chapter of his book, said, "*Therefore, with the constant 'Non-being,' I often observe the subtlety of the Way; with the constant 'Being,' I often observe the working of the Way.*" Laozi revealed profoundly that Man should not be confined by the "factitious" limitation, and that Man should go beyond this confinement. Only when you see the fundamentality can you have the true bosom and vision, with which to see all the things in the universe, and achieve yourself among all the things in the universe.

Second, a person with "discernment" does not brag about himself or show off. Laozi said, "He is free from self-display, and therefore he has "discernment." (Chapter 22, *Laozi*) "He who displays himself is not conspicuous." (Chapter 24, *Laozi*) A person who brags about himself or expresses his own wisdom is one who has not reached the state of being *"ming"* or "discernment" The self-confidence shown in this self-bragging or self-expression is blind confidence in something biased. For example, when people are self-confident in "kindness," they will spend their whole life in expressing and pursuing this kindness. Though subjectively speaking, it is true and honest, its result is "unkindness." When a certain "kindness" is pursued, it is alright only within a certain boundary, and when it goes out of the boundary, it is an "abandoned person" or "abandoned thing."

Third, a person with "discernment" pursues the clarification of his innate life-force, but does not make efforts to get to know about objects. Laozi said, *"Those who know others are witty, and those who know themselves are wise."* (Chapter 33, *Laozi*) If you pursue the understanding of other people or other objects, your intrinsic motivation is to control them; moreover, the more you pursue, the stronger your desire to control them. When Man reflects on himself, and let the innate life-force stretch in a continuous and natural way, it is "discernment". The clarification of the innate life-force need not "speak out" and "speaking out" is the twin of selfishness and desire. Therefore, a truely wise person "speaks not," as *"the wise person is of few words, and the talkative person is not wise."* (Chapter 56, *Laozi*) A person does not need to be erudite, as the innate clarification can illuminate all, and let everything flourish in the unselfish kindness, as *"people with profound understanding are not erudite, and erudite people are not profound in understanding."* (Chapter 81, *Laozi*)

3. "Observation" — the Road "from Wisdom to Fairness and Justice"

When "wording" (Dao) and "naming" cannot express the "eternal Dao" and the "eternal fairness and justice," we can only resort to the sensory and abstract recognition in order to *observe* the "eternal Dao." The term "observation" here does not mean "seeing" with your eyes. It is a special concept in Laozi's epistemology. To become fairness and justice by means of "observation" does not mean abandoning wisdom or knowledge at all, but to "enter the state of fairness and justice from wisdom or knowledge."

According to Laozi's understanding, *"zhi"* is reflected in the following two aspects: one is the sensory perception; the other is the abstraction of speaking and naming. As to the cognitive achievements, it is obvious that the abstraction of speaking and naming can better reflect "*wen*" or cultivation (in contrast with "*zhi*" or plainness and "*pu*" or simplicity) aspect. Therefore, Laozi began his book with the two most abstract "names" of "being" and "non-being." Since the eternal Dao cannot be worded, and the eternal name cannot be named, then, the two most abstract names of "non-being" and "being" do not indicate the Dao. Most people think that "non-being" and "being" are the characteristics of the Dao, and are the active process of the Dao from formless substance to formed substance." This understanding is not correct. "Non-being" and "being" are the results of Man's "*zhi*." Though already abstracted and profound, that is not the eternal Dao. In that case, how can we acquire the eternal Dao? Laozi said, "*Therefore, with the constant 'Non-being,' I often observe the subtlety of the Dao; with the constant 'Being,' I often observe the working of the Dao. The two, i.e., Non-being and Being, are both from the same origin, but only named differently; both can be said extremely mysterious and profound. The mystery and profundity of the mysterious and profound is the real source of all mysteries and profundities.*" (Chapter 1, *Laozi*) That is to say, we should observe from the already known "names" of "non-being" and "being," the "eternal Dao" (*the real source of all mysteries and profundities*). From the perspective of the abstraction of wording and naming, it indicates the road observing the Dao is "from *zhi* to *ming* (discernment)," instead of "having discernment by abandoning *zhi*." In addition, from the perspective of the sensory conception, the sense organs are the habitat of desire for outside objects, and at the same time distinguish the objects by "seeing," "hearing," and "touching." From the almost impalpable minute points of senses including "seeing," "hearing," and "touching," we can also observe the Dao. Laozi said, "*You wish to look at the Dao, but you cannot see it, and this is called 'yi' or 'formless;' you wish to listen to the Dao, but you cannot hear it, and this is called 'xi' or 'silent;' you wish to feel the Dao, but you cannot touch it, and this is called 'wei' or 'minute.' The complete picture of the three phenomena, if approached in isolation, can be seen clearly, so they should be treated as an organic whole. There is no light above it, and there is no darkness under it either. It is continuous and hard to describe, and finally returns to the state of being imageless. The shape without shape and the image without image are called 'huhuang' or dimness. In front of it, you cannot see its head, and behind it, you cannot see its back.*" (Chapter 14, *Laozi*) At this time, the Dao becomes the inexpressible "trance." From the perspective of sensory perception, it indicates that the road observing the Dao is "from *zhi* to by abandoning *zhi*."

Since the road to observing the Dao is "from *zhi* to *discernment*," then, this cognitive road is like a kind of "repetition" or "regression." It is indeed "regression," as people have been in the state of *"zhi"* so long that they forget their innate purification, and this cognitive process is a shift from focusing on things external to that on things internal. Therefore, the very first step to observation is to *"clear your distracting thoughts"* (Chapter 10, *Laozi*), that is, to get rid of those presumptuous desires. In this way, there will be no blemishes in people's heart, and the vigor of the body and the spirit will get together, and that is the basis of *"reading into yourself."* The second step is to abandon the blind self-confidence in *"zhi."* Laozi said, *"It is your merit if you know your own ignorance; it is your demerit if you do not know but appear to know it. The person with the Way does not have demerits, because he regards his demerits as demerits. And just because of this, he has no demerits."* (Chapter 71, *Laozi*) This is a necessary attitude which is acquired through reflection of the human wisdom. It actually aims to tell people that human cognitive achievements are limited, so we should not be self-opinionated and blind in pursuit. However, in spite of the limitations in cognition, we can still acquire the wholeness of life by means of the clarification of innate life-force only if we are aware of this limitation. Without doubt, whether it is to *"clear your distracting thoughts"* or abandon your self-confidence in *"zhi,"* you should not abandon *"zhi"* itself, as you do not run into discernment all of a sudden. Therefore, from this sense we can see that Laozi's attitude towards human life is not to "be above worldly considerations," nor is it to abandon everything in the real world, but to attempt to save the present society.

This "repeatedly returning" road to observing the Dao, or this road "from *zhi* into discernment" finally reaches "emptiness" and "quietness." In Chapter 16, *Laozi* said, *"Stay empty and keep still. Everything grows all at once. I watch them return to their original state. Things come forth in great numbers; each one returns to its own root. Returning to roots means stillness, and also means a return to destiny. To return to destiny is known as the constant nature. To know the constant nature is known as discernment."* "Emptiness" and "quietness" is the state of "discernment." The so-called "emptiness" is the minute state of vagueness and ethereality of the innate life-force in self-observation. "Quietness" is the full state of vital essence and energy of the innate life-force in self-observation. If you can observe the root from the perception and abstraction of all the things in the universe, it is called observation of the truth of repeating itself in endless cycles, that is, to observe, from the "difference" and the "sameness," the *"real source of all mysteries and profundities"* with the mystery and profundity of the mysterious and profound. It is "*by using the light of wisdom, and mirroring the inner brightness.*" (Chapter 52, *Laozi*) This "light," the light that illuminates all the things in the universe, comes from the inner "brightness." And with the help of this light, the inner "brightness" can be mirrored.

This cognitive process, viewed from its direction, is from the outside to the inside, from analysing and understanding the object to caring for the inner clarification. It is the minuteness and profusion of the inner life-force that shows the "constant Dao," that does not abandon the things in the universe, and that helps to achieve a successful life. In Chapter 47, Laozi said, "*Without going out of the door, you can know what is happening in the world; without looking out of the window, you can see the law of nature. The farther you go, the less you know. Therefore, the Sages do not have to experience so as to know, they do not have to see with their own eyes to understand, and they succeed by non-action.*" All the things in the universe are complicated and complex, so what matters does not lie in how far you can go, but in how profound your innermost heart is. Those who have mastered the Dao can illuminate all the things in the universe. This cognitive process, seen from the content, goes from much to little, or from big to small, but generally speaking, human cognition is expected to be accumulating, so as to reach erudition or become knowledgeable in all the things. It is impossible to be knowledgeable in all the things. Even when that is possible, it is meaningless because it will abandon the root. Therefore, Laozi said, "*As to seeking knowledge, the desire should increase with each passing day; as to seeking the Way, the desire should decrease with each passing day. Day after day, it is finally reduced to the state of 'non-action.' If you reach the state of 'non-action,' there is nothing you cannot do.*" (Chapter 48, *Laozi*) The two roads are just opposite to each other. "To be knowledgeable" is an addition, while "to acquire the Dao" is a reduction. Only if you apply to reduction can you "*reach the state of 'non-action,' and there is nothing you cannot do.*"

Observation is the road that goes "from wisdom to discernment," but Laozi did not explain or discuss the "method of observation." That is to say, he did not tell how to observe to reach "emptiness" and "quietness," and "know what is the constant"? Perhaps it is just because the "constant Dao" itself is not "expressible," the method of observing the Dao is not expressible, either. And perhaps what denies understanding and interpretation on the part of Laozi lies just here. Zhang Dainian, a well-known scholar in China, said that Laozi's "observation" is, in fact, an intuitive approach: "Laozi emphasized 'following the Dao,' and established the intuitive approach, so as to directly coincide with the root of the universe. 'Reading into oneself" is an intuitive approach."[1] It might shed light on something here.

In other Daoist works, there are quite a few opinions which are related to "observation" in *Laozi*. For example, in *Liezi*, Volume 4, there is internal observation or introspection: *"People are often wild about going outing, but are negligent in introspection. Those who go outing desire to see all the scenes in the world; those who introspect pay much more attention to their own bodies and thoughts. If you pay much attention to yourself, you reach the acme." "For the ultimate sightseers, they may not know what to see, but they go to any places, and see everything."* Those who "love going outing" go everywhere to see all the things, but no matter how many they see, they cannot exhaust them. This is not the highest state. But those who pay attention to introspection don't have to go out, and it is enough to look inside, which is the highest state of "going outing." Those who can really enjoy going outing do not know what they want to see, but can reach every place and see everything. In the "On Virtue," *Wenzi*, you will find the so-called "listening with the soul:" *"the best learner listens with the soul, the mediocre learner listens with the heart, while the worst learner listens with the ear." "The principle of listening requires void and quiescence at heart, lessening of arrogance, and freedom from anxiety and care. Do not look at what you should not see, and do not listen to what you should not hear."* In "The Human World," *Zhuangzi*, it has the doctrine of "the fast of mind:" *"Do not listen with ears, but with your heart/mind; do not listen with your heart/mind, but with the spirit. The ears can do no more than listening, and the heart/mind can do no more than comprehension. But the spirit is a void ready to receive all things. The Dao abides in the void; the void is the fast of heart/mind."* The above-mentioned internal observation or introspection, "listening with the soul," and "the fast of the heart/mind," somewhat lays particular stress on epistemology, and in regimen, there are also such terms as "*neishi*" (looking inside) or "*neiguan*" (watching inside), that is, the eyes do not look at anything around you, but "introspect" the five internal organs, as if you could actually see these things. This is accepted by Daoism as religion, and is handed down to this day. Whether these sayings are mysterious or not, and whether they are in reality feasible or not, the statement of "*neiguan*" (watching inside) is quite enlightening, if seen only from the perspective of epistemology. Man recognizes and feels all the things in the universe through the five organs, which provides the brain, Man's thinking organ, with a large number of raw materials, thus forming human knowledge and thought.

---

1 Zhang Dainian. *An Outline of Chinese Philosophy.* China Social Sciences Press, 1982, pp.532-541.

However, the cognitive and sensory ability of the five organs is limited, or you may say very limited. Even if you put all the cognitive results together, it is still very limited. The significance of watching inside or introspection lies in the suggestion to Man to break through and surpass their cognitive ability, so as to reach the infinite end-to-end joint with the Dao.

All in all, the "*zhi*" for wisdom, in Laozi's opinion, is the cognitive competence formed by the human desire to covet for what is more than the needs for human existence. This kind of wisdom has lost its root as it only sees and pursues one of the diversified sides which complement each other. Man needs to understand the world from a bigger scope in a large domain, which is the "confused and stupefied" Dao. The wisdom of understanding the Dao is called discernment. "*Ming*" does not mean abandoning "*zhi* (wisdom)." On the contrary, it means "becoming bright from wisdom" through observation. Laozi's cognitive thought might be misunderstood in two aspects: one is that Laozi's cognitive thought is dialectic. Much as Laozi has said about the interdependence and transformation of the two opposite sides in his cognitive thought, Laozi thought that it is only the cognitive result of wisdom, which does not suffice to express the "eternal Dao." The other is that Laozi's cognitive thought is mysterious and passive. In fact, from the above analysis, we can see that Laozi's "observation" is somewhat mysterious, as it may denote the instinct, but this mysteriousness is based on the "*zhi*" for wisdom, and does not come totally from anything incomprehensible. Therefore, this mysteriousness has some non-mysteriousness. His epistemology is indeed "reductive," but it is not passive, "doing nothing and doing everything" has always been the principle for human behavior. Laozi's reflection on human wisdom has its theoretical effect, which is manifested in the cognition of the finiteness of wisdom and in the emphasis on the inner world. Besides, his ideal of "*government by doing nothing that goes against nature*" resulting from this is highly enlightening with regard to the establishment of social order.

V. De in Reflection of the Dao and the Polite Society

Much as the Dao is so "profound and lasting," "formless" and elusive, its influence and ways of realization in the social reality can be observed, described and mastered. That is the means or medium between the Dao and all the things in the universe — the De or virtue. The De is also one of the key paradigms in *Laozi*, which is also called *Dao De Jing* or *Tao Te Ching*. *Dao De Jing* on silk from Mawangdui, the ancient tome discovered in 1972, consists of two parts: On Virtue, the first part, and On Dao, the second part. From this we can see the position and importance of the De. Then, what is the relationship between the Dao and the "De (virtue)?"

CHAPTER ONE: Introduction

1. Virtue is the Realization of the Dao

Laozi said, "*The manner of the Great Virtue varies with the Dao.*" (Chapter 21, *Laozi*) That is to say, the feature of the "virtue" is to follow the Dao, and to give expression to the Dao. Furthermore, "*The virtue is the utility of the Dao, ... therefore, the virtue means getting. To get means that all the things in the universe get what is natural. Non-action is the Dao, and the utility is the De, so there is no disparity between the Dao and the virtue.*" (Xinshu Part I, *Guanzi*) That is to say, the De is the embodiment of the Dao, on which the growth of all the things in the universe depends, and on which the mind counts for the understanding of the essence of the Dao. Therefore, the "virtue" just means obtainment. De for obtainment means that you have got what you want to get (the Dao). "Non-action" is called the Dao, and the embodiment of the Dao is the De. Therefore, there is no difference between the Dao and the De. Certainly, in different contexts, there is some disparity between the Dao and the De. Emperor Xuanzong of the Tang Dynasty said in his *Commentaries on the True Canon of Dao and De*, "*The Dao is the substance of the Virtue, and the Virtue is the function of the Dao.*" Chen Jingyuan of the Northern Song Dynasty in his *Annotation to Moral Truths* said, "*The Dao is nothingness. Virtue is the use of nature. The constant Dao is nameless but obvious in virtue. The extreme virtue is rootless but takes shape by following the Dao.*" This is an explanation of the relationship between the Dao and the De by means of the philosophical paradigm of the relationship between essence and its use. Emperor Xuanzong of the Tang Dynasty in his *Annotations to Dao De Jing* said, "Dao is virtue to me." This indicates that the Dao is the whole, whereas the "virtue" is the individual, the "virtue" means the features common to all the things in the universe, as a result, the Dao and the "virtue" form the relationship of commonality and individuality. This shows that the Dao and the "virtue" are sometimes differentiated, and sometimes unified. That is to say, the relationship between the Dao and the "virtue" is very close.

Chen Guying explained in this way, "*The relationship between the Dao and the 'virtue' is: (1) the Dao is formless, and its function can be manifested only through the medium of an object when it acts on the object. The function of the Dao is called the 'virtue' when it is manifested through the object. (2) Everything in the universe is generated by the Dao, and the internalized Dao in all the things in the universe displays its nature, that is, displays its 'virtue.' (3) When the metaphysical Dao is applied to human life, it is called the 'virtue,' that is to say, the very nature of the Dao is hidden and formless, and its manifestation is the 'virtue'.*"

Laozi emphasized, "Man models himself on Earth, Earth on Heaven, Heaven on *Dao*, and *Dao* on Nature," "*the Dao just models itself on Nature*" and "*the Dao follows the course of Nature, but there is nothing it does not do*" also mean that one is two and two is one, and both describe the special features of the universe with regard to its nurturing and spreading. Therefore, it can be shortened into "natural non-action." According to Laozi, Man should also imitate the features of the universe of natural non-action and doing everything. That is the theoretical value and practical significance of the Dao and the De entailed in the ontological theory. In Laozi's opinion, it is true that the Dao is the root and origin of all the things in the universe, but in the course of their formation, they cannot go without the De. Laozi said, "*Dao generates them, virtue nourishes them, substance forms them, and circumstances accomplish them. Therefore all things revere Dao and honor virtue. Yet Dao is revered and virtue honored not because this is decreed by any authority but because it's naturally so on its own. Thus Dao generates them, and virtue nourishes them, makes them grow and ripen, and cares for and nurtures them.*" (Chapter 51, *Laozi*) Therefore, the De also has vital function and significance in the existence and formation of all the things in the universe. It is the close relationship between the "Virtue" and the Dao that decides the critical function and significance of the De in the existence and formation of all the things in the universe. Especially to "Man," the De in the implication of Laozi mainly indicates the pure nature of Man, that is, "*The person with profound virtue is just like an infant boy,*" (Chapter 55, *Laozi*) and the cultivation and state of mind of Man, "*... 'profound virtue'... far-reaching. With the return to the very nature of simplicity, the country will harmonize with Nature.*" (Chapter 65, *Laozi*)

Therefore, the Dao in Laozi's thought does not simply belong to the paradigm of natural philosophy, but also to the metaphysical paradigm concerning Man's inner ontology and value. As for Man, Laozi's Dao is no more than the potential foundation, and only through Man's conscious practice and experience ("practising the Dao" and "experiencing the Dao") can Man turn potentiality into reality, and become one with the Dao, so as to acquire freedom. That is the implied meaning of "humanistic Dao" of Laozi's Dao as an ontological paradigm, from which we can see its unique theoretical value and practical significance.

2. The De (Virtue) is a Link between the Dao and "Things"

Some scholars think, the Dao in relation to "things" in *Laozi* is embodied as an transcendental relation which is non-innate and neither separated nor mixed, while the De is a link between the transcendental Dao and things, which is hypothetical, but functions in structuring and construction. The Dao generates all the things in the universe. This relationship between the Dao and "Wu" not only results in the loss of "human action" in *Laozi*'s system, but also is liable to cause the loss of the active function of benevolence, righteousness, and virtue. At least, we can understand the De in *Laozi* from the following aspects: (1) The De chapters of *Laozi* mainly deal with the political and philosophical thought of Man, that is, Man models himself on the Heaven, and the De here has a number of meanings concerning virtue. (2) But the De has a second meaning, as in *"the Dao generates all the things in the universe, and the Virtue nurtures them,"* this De has nothing to do with virtue. So the question is: What is the relationship between the two understandings of the "De?" Are they completely isolated with each other or are they reciprocally relevant with its innate logic? The relatively popular opinion is that the latter is the actual universe creation theory, while the former is the normative philosophy of human life. As to the relationship between the two, Tang Junyi had his own understanding, "Although the Dao generates things, nurtures them and cares for them, it does not seek to be benevolent to all the things in the universe, nor does it have significance of any value." "The reason why people seek to own the life of their own in accordance with the Dao is that they are unwilling to die. This thought has only subjective meaning but not objective meaning."[1] Mr Tang said that the Dao is not benevolent to all the things in the universe. Naturally. it does not mean the virtue of the generation of all the things in the universe on the part of the Dao, but means *"Therefore, the Dao generates the things in the universe; and the Virtue nurtures them, ... Although the Dao generates them and the Virtue nurtures them, they do not take all things in the universe as their own, but let them grow naturally. That is the greatest virtue."* Seen from the significance of the Dao's generating all the things in the universe, it is natural that the Dao is benevolent to all the things in the universe.

As a matter of fact, in *Laozi*'s spiritual framing of "the Dao's generating all the things in the universe," the creative and growing relationship between the Dao and the "things," does not mean the things' innate heritance of the Dao, as the Dao is "the ultimate justice under Heaven," and does not internalize itself into things, or occupy things as its own. Therefore, Man and things will not have the realization of the Dao's "content." This relationship between the Dao and the "things," from theory, rules out all the possibilities of human deliberateness. Whether it is for good or for evil, all human deliberateness shows little difference in this line. Owing to the isolation between the Dao and Man, human action does not acquire its legitimacy from the Dao. With the loss of the significance of human activity, human function

---

[1] Tang Junyi. *The Original Theory of Chinese Philosophy.* Beijing: China Social Sciences Press, 2005, p.254.

and human mastery, the legitimacy of doing benevolence, according to *Laozi*, is certainly gone. "*Those who are good at walking will leave no traces; those who are good at talking will have no blunders.*" (Chapter 27, *Laozi*) Only when you take "non-action" can you be ultimately benevolent. According to Laozi, as long as Man resorts to deliberate mastery, the Dao in Man is in a sheltered state. Therefore, Tang Junyi said, "The reason why people seek to own the life of their own in accordance with the Dao is their unwillingness to die. This thought has only subjective meaning but not objective meaning." The so-called "objective meaning" indicates that in the system of *Laozi*, Man's "living in conformity to the Dao" does not find the promise of the Dao from the innate orderliness of the Dao. That Man wants to reach the requirement of his "living in conformity to the Dao" is either because of Man's own necessity of "cultivating his character and moulding his personality," so as to free his from the burden of materials and live a natural life, or because of the ruler's political strategies of governance and stabilization of the nation, and when the society is in chaos, he demands the country to keep void and empty, quiet and calm so as to "return to the origins" and reach the just and fair state of "*knowing the eternal Dao.*" (Chapter 16, *Laozi*) Therefore, Man's behavior of "modelling on the Heaven" by doing good and undoing evil, and keeping void and empty, and quiet and calm, only has the significance of making efforts, but not the significance of the thing-in-itself, and accordingly, has no innate inevitability. Its ultimate purpose is no more than getting to clarify and understand the constancy of the Dao. The Dao, in Laozi's opinion, has its absolute status, therefore, *Laozi* is, in actuality, implying that "Man should go with the Dao, but due to the absence of the Dao in Man himself, Man should get near to the Dao, and mirror it with the '*zhi*' (wisdom) from without."

Of course, the "*zhi*" here does not mean human cognition of acquired experience, but the intuition of human instinct. Without "*zhi*," the Dao cannot be embodied, so, for Laozi, "*zhi*" has almost gained its identical status as the Dao, and with absolute priority. Mr Ma Yifu has the following description: "*It is not involved in any motion, but knows any tricks, and sees that all actions are no more than presumptuous and vain efforts; he lives a secluded and detached life, and if we describe him in the Buddhist term, it may well be witted but free from grief.*"[1] This calm observation achieves the philosophy of your attitude towards outside things. That is why Laozi said "*The highest virtue is like water.*" The lower virtue lays stress

---

1 Ma Yifu. *On Laozi's Loss, Collection of Ma Yifu*. Zhejiang Ancient Books Publishing House, Zhejiang Education Publishing House, 1996, p.44.

on law and trickery, and emphasizes more on wisdom than on virtue.

However, Laozi still advocated the endeavour of *"getting rid of the zhi"* (This *"zhi"* here indicates acquired or postnatal experience and cognition, not Laozi's understanding of the *"zhi"* with regard to the Dao), *"seeking the Way, the desire should decrease with each passing day," "making yourself void and empty, quiet and calm," "discarding selfish desires, being content with ignorance, and freedom from anxieties,"* and *"clearing your distracting thoughts and reading into yourself."* He maintained that Man should be rid of his desire and efforts, returns to the great unselfish and just Dao, and let the Dao be the master, without lessening the Dao. All the advocates and efforts Laozi made lie in maintaining the relationship with the Dao, and in keeping the observation and understanding of the Dao. If Man indulges in coveting for material things, in the pursuit of fame and fortune, or in sensorial information or knowledge, Man will tend to keep the Dao in obscurity by material things. Once Man's active efforts are hindered, all his efforts will fade away into passive void and quietude, and all the efforts will finally be focused on the *"zhi"* for wisdom, which is the only way for Man to keep in contact with the Dao.

Then, what is the unique significance of the implication and function of the De in *Laozi*? Laozi said, *"Dao generates them, virtue nourishes them, substance forms them, and circumstances accomplish them... makes them grow and ripen, and cares for and nurtures them."* (Chapter 51, *Laozi*) *"The great Dao is spreading everywhere and vastly. All things in the universe depend on it for their growth and development, and it does not decline them; when attainment appears, it does not claim credit for itself. It nurtures all things in the universe, but it does not want to dominate the world."* (Chapter 34, *Laozi*) It is manifested that the Dao can not only be seen in the generation of things, but also in the destruction of things; the Dao not only generates things, but also makes them live and grow. *"All the things are generated by the Dao, and the Dao, in turn, nurtures them."* The De of this sense can also be testified in other enunciation in *Laozi*. Laozi said, *"The manner of the Great Virtue varies with the Dao."* (Chapter 21, *Laozi*) If the De is the entity word of the Dao, then, it is obvious that the Dao and the De are not different, and certainly it is superfluous and more than necessary to say that *"the manner of the Great Virtue varies with the Dao."* Therefore, it is not proper to regard the De as an entity word. In this sense, *"kong,"* or hole in its original sense, means *"da,"* or great, and the De does not add to any new meaning. Wang Bi has very deep understanding of this, and says, *"Kong is 'empty,' and only when the De is empty, can its action conform with the Dao."* Here, *"kong,"* void or emptiness, is acquisition. It is not very exact derivation, and the two show a relationship of corresponding analysis. Needless to say, as far as Man is concerned, "*kong*" can also be regarded as human efforts, and only when human efforts are empty, can the Dao be revealed and seen, and can it be the master of Man. And at the same time, with the efforts of being void and quiet, Man can better observe and understand the Dao. The De functions as a constructing or organizing force, and leaves the position to let the function of the Dao flow out, and to Man, it is to get rid of and "vacate" human desire or human action for the mastery of the Dao.

We can also, from this point, arrive at the derived meaning of the De as "to obey, to keep." The reason why we can say that *"circumstances accomplish them"* and circumstances result from "obeyance" or "smoothness," is that if there is hindrance, there will be no smoothness. "Obeyance" plays an important role in the growth of all the things in the universe. The growing and development of all the things in the universe depend on this "obeyance" and "environment," and in the same way, man should obey the Dao in doing things and abandon self-desire. *"You know the strength of the masculine, but keep the tenderness of the feminine, and are willing to be the ravine of the world. Being the ravine of the world, you will be accompanied by eternal virtue, and return to being a babe… You know the honor, but keep to the role of the disgraced, and are willing to be a valley of the world. Being the valley of the world, you will no longer lack the eternal virtue, and return to simplicity."* (Chapter 28, *Laozi*) In *Laozi*, there are metaphors of the Dao like "*gu*," "*gushen*," and "*xuanmu*." "*Gushen*" (the spirit of the valley) comes from the image of the valley, "*huo*" and "*gu*" refer to sunken or caved-in ground, because only places sunken or caved-in can contain things. Therefore, the concepts of "*huo*" and "*gu*" are explanatory to the De, illustrating the meaning of structuring and construction and keeping the relationship between the *Dao* and Man. The deprivation of the factor of Man makes possible the spread of the Dao. Given all that, the De here is not a noun equal to the Dao, which has its existent significance, but a verb of structuring, constructing and abstraction as it is a link to support the relationship between the Dao and "things;" however, the effect of this link does not make "things" share the property of the Dao, but simply keeps "things" attached to the Dao.[1]

3. Disparities between Laozi's De and Other De

Xu Fuguan thinks that the Chinese character De (德) in the early Zhou Dynasty

---

[1] Wu Xiaolong. *From Laozi's Dao and De to Yizhuan's "Virtue"– Concurrently on the Congenital Characteristics of Confucian Morality.* Ph.D. Thesis of Shandong University, April 2009.

CHAPTER ONE: Introduction

that appeared in *The Shangshu*, means concrete conduct, and its original meaning is only sincere and responsible conduct. This conduct (the De) at first did not have the commentary meaning of good or bad; therefore, there is the distinction between "*jide*" (auspicious De) and "*xiongde*" (ominous De). So the De in the documents of the early Zhou Dynasty means something auspicious only when it is added before the word "*jing*" (respectable or respectful) and "*ming*" (bright or honest), and later, it gradually gets the meaning of good conduct.[1] Li Zehou thought that the original meaning of the De has nothing to do with morality, but is likely to be the customary codes of individual clans. But later, he put forward his revision: "The De seems a set of conducts, first of all, but not ordinary conducts, which are mainly important political conducts when the chieftains hold sacrificial ceremonies or go to war. It is closely connected to the witchcraft rituals of ancestral sacrificial activities of the traditional clan tribes, which gradually evolves into a set of unwritten statutes concerning social standards, social order, social requirements, and social customs, which maintain the existence and development of clan tribes." Mr Chen Lai thinks, according to the morphological evolution of the character De (值 - 德 - 惪) of the inscriptions on bones or tortoise shells and on ancient bronze objects, "the original meaning of the word De (值) has something to do with action or conduct, and when the heart radical is applied (德 and 惪), it is related to human consciousness, motivation, and intention. Action or conduct has a close relationship with motivation and intention, so it is natural for the De to have these two meanings."[2]

The early De belongs to the political concept, with its value and function shown in political domains, and the De appears with the appearance of political life; but as a cultural ideology, it is formed in the eras of Yao, Shun, and Yu in the primitive society, and the original meaning of the De is simply "conduct," which mainly means the political conducts of the ruling class to bring benefits to the people. The religious conviction of emperor worship and ancestor worship during the Yin-Shang period (1600-1046 BC), has not, in general, reached the level of ethnic religion, and the ideology of the De in that period is only a passive response of its religious ideology, without any connotation of ethnical significance. The then De is no more than the objective description and generalization of the political conducts of the Yin-period king and his ministers, with somewhat concrete content, which has not

---

1 Xu Fuguan. *The History of Chinese Humanity (pre-Qin)*. Shanghai Joint Publishing Company, 2001 edition, p.21.
2 Chen Lai. *Ancient Religion and Ethics: The Roots of Confucianism.* SDX Joint Publishing Company,1996 edition, p.291.

reached the dimension of the requirements for innate human character. Therefore, the De in the Yin-Shang period is still at the primitive stage. The social revolution at the turn of the Yin and Zhou period, initiated the rational transformation of the Yin people's heavenly mandate on the part of the Zhou people, and formed the new heavenly mandate centred on the belief that *"human life is not eternal."* The Zhou people started consciously to reflect their own political conducts, and regard the De as the foundation of their mission and the establishment of their nation. Thus, the *De* becomes the mode of the ruling class's political conduct and government ideology, and establishes all kinds of political systems to ensure implementation and realization of the De. This ethicization of politics starts the moral sense of the De. In spite of the fairly rational consideration of the De on the part of the rulers at the beginning of the Zhou Dynasty, this De has by no means reached the innermost heart of the people. The morality significance of the De of the early Zhou Dynasty indicates the political virtue or political ethics, which is mainly directed towards the aristocracy of that time, without the regulating function for universal purposes. Therefore, it should be treated differently from the later individual moral standard on a universal scale. During the fairly long period of time from the late Western Zhou Dynasty to the late Spring and Autumn Period, with the traditional Heavenly Mandate on the verge of total collapse and the ever-increasing rise of the humanistic train of thought, coupled with the gradual disintegration of the patriarchal hierarchy and the increasing slackening of blood relationship, the De is no longer the exclusive right of the aristocratic class, of which the range and domain concerned is broader and the holiness of the De weakens. The rational and moral factors in the ideology of the De, accumulated and developed on the basis of that in the Western Zhou Dynasty have gained a broader sense of moral regulations. In addition, though the De remained a political concept before the late Spring and Autumn Period, its concrete function was still limited to the political domain. However, as a result of the establishment of the ideology of the "ritual" and governance by the "ritual" enticed by the "ritual" in the political and ideological domains in the Spring and Autumn Period, the political function of the De weakened compared with that in the Western Zhou Dynasty, and the De gradually dissociated from the political fields, but in the spiritual phase, was united to various abstract *"demu"* or items of the De and developed inwardly. So, the ideology of the De manifests its developmental tendency of internalization, abstraction, and secularization, in the long period between the late Western Zhou Dynasty and the late Spring and Autumn Period, and the connotation of the De is gradually deviated to its moral sense, thus turning from the politics-oriented De to the ethics-oriented De. And the spiritual connotation and form of Laozi's De is in the process of turning from its political function to its moral function of abstraction and secularization. But in the context of *Laozi*, whether it is "To show Dao by De" or "To interpret De with Dao," its subject of discussion is mostly the cultivation on the part of sages and rulers rather than the moral character of the common people.

Laozi's De is widely different from the De in the pre-Qin period.

"High virtue" or "the greatest virtue" as Laozi said, is different from the common De in the way of "*chuxia*" (staying under) or "*chushang*" (staying above), and the latter has the feature of being high above, overlooking downwards, and being empowered to decide the life and death of things. "Being the ravine of the world, you will be accompanied by eternal virtue, and return to being a babe." (Chapter 28, *Laozi*) "*Although the Dao generates them and the Virtue nurtures them, they do not take all things in the universe as their own, but let them grow naturally. That is the greatest virtue.*" (Chapter 51, *Laozi*) This is somewhat like the ancient society in which the emperor was called "the royal prerogative", who had the unparalleled status, and nobody was bold enough to look up at him; but in the modern society, the leaders are regarded as "public servants" and they should serve the common people.

"High virtue" or "the greatest virtue" as Laozi said, is different from the common De in the way of "non-contention" (not striving with others) or "contention" (striving with others). "*Those who are good at commanding do not resort to force; those who are good at fighting are not easily irritated; those who are good at subjugating the enemies do not fight battles with them; those who are good at using people are modest towards them. This is called the quality of not vying with others.*" (Chapter 68, *Laozi*) This is "high virtue" or "the greatest virtue," and is approved by Laozi. But the common rulers depend on their high position, and their awe-inspiring might. And if anyone who does not succumb, he will be ground to fine powder with the rulers' right and might, just as it was said by the first Emperor of the Qin Dynasty, in "Tang Sui Has Successfully Accomplished His Mission" of *The Strategies of the Warring States*, "When the Son of Heaven, or the ruler, is in rage, millions of lives will be lost, and their blood flows as far as a thousand miles."

"High virtue" or "the greatest virtue" as Laozi said, is different from the common De in the way of using wisdom or not using wisdom. "*Therefore, to govern with calculation is disastrous to the country; and to govern without calculation is a blessing to the country. It is the principle of government to distinguish these two differences. If you can abide by the principle, it is your 'profound virtue,' which is far-reaching.*" (Chapter 65, *Laozi*) History tells us that "*to govern with calculation*" mainly embodies the following two aspects: one is that the ruler should govern the country according to his ideal and mode of governance, and force the nation into his ideal mode. Just taking Wang Mang's reform at the turn of the Han Dynasties as an example, including land reform, currency reform, commercial reform, and reform in the names of officials and counties, etc., is a good example of forced governance with "one person's wisdom." The other is that the rulers play politics. For example, Han Fei put forward the proposition to administrate the nation with "*fa*" (law), "*shu*" (means, methods, tactics or strategies), and "*shi*" (power), of which the "*shu*" refers to the means and strategies of the rulers to govern the nation and the people, including the appointment and removal, evaluation and assessment, rewards and punishments of officials of all levels, and the means of securing the rulers' power, the so-called strategies of punishments and methods of detecting treacherousness. This is the strategy of the rulers to control their liegemen or subjects, which should be hidden from others and put into use as the chances come; it should be top secret. In essence, this "*shu*" shows that the ruler only believes himself and "his own wisdom," and does not believe others. But Laozi radically opposed this conduct of "*governing the nation with wisdom,*" and advocated the greatest or profoundest virtue of "*doing everything by doing nothing.*" That is to say, do not use your "own wisdom" but to make efforts to develop the wisdom of the public (of course, the "wisdom" that is not against "Nature").

"High virtue" or "the greatest virtue," as Laozi said, is different from the common De in the effect of their governance. "*If you can abide by the principle, it is your 'profound virtue,' which is far-reaching. With the return to the very nature of simplicity, the country will harmonize with Nature.*" (Chapter 65, *Laozi*) "*The person with profound virtue is just like an infant boy,... he has enough vigor and vitality.*" (Chapter 55, *Laozi*) To sum up, to administer the society with "*shangde*" (high virtue) or "*xuande*" (the greatest or profoundest virtue), the result of governance will be "*shun*" (to be in order) and "*he*" (to be in harmony), but not be rebellious and resentful. The reason is that to administer the society with high virtue or the greatest virtue, there will be no sharp conflict between the ruler's "own wisdom," "own selfishness," and "own conduct" and the members of that society, and accordingly, there will be no mutual harm. "*It is because the apparitions, the gods, the Sages and the people can treat each other with the Virtue, so they can live in complete harmony.*" (Chapter 60, *Laozi*)

4. The Significance of the Unity of the Dao and the De in *Laozi*

First, seen from the De of the nature of all the things in the universe: All the things in the universe are composed of the Dao, and are dependent on the Dao for their generation ("*The Dao generates all the things in the universe*"), and after their being generated, all the things in the universe acquire their own nature, on which they depend to support their own existence ("*the Virtue nurtures them*"); during these periods, the Dao and the De are the most fundamental. Without the Dao, all the things in the universe would not be generated; and without the De, they would not have their own nature. In short, as far as the Outlook of Nature is concerned, the so-called De is where the Dao belongs in all the things in the universe, and because of the "being" and "non-being" of the Dao, the De of all the things in the universe also has the two aspects of "being" and "non-being." On the level of the "non-being," all the things in the universe have their void and profound De, while on the level of "being," all the things in the universe have their qualitative and dispositional De.

Second, seen from the dispositional De of sages: When the Dao is conveyed into the inner world of the sages, and becomes the sages' super temperamental existence, it is the sages' De of disposition. According to the operational principle of the Dao, the sages' dispositional De can be divided into the following two levels: for one thing, the movement of the Dao is in endless cycles; the function of the Dao is in its soft and tender manner. The dispositional De that moves in circles and functions in its soft and tender manner is the "eternal De" of sages. For the other, the operation of all the things in the universe and of the Dao is not only the positive and negative operation that begets each other and that moves in opposite directions, but also a returning and recursive movement in circulations; it is "*to return to the origins*" and "*to return to the state of being quiet and calm.*" And when taking "non-being" as its function, and "non-being" as its heart, the loftiest realm of the heart of the sage is to return to the "innocent heart of a child," and keep the "innocent virtue of a child."

Third, the De with regard to the Dao of governance by doing nothing. When the Dao is applied to the domain of society and politics, it has the De of governance by doing nothing. And this De has two aspects: one is the De with a non-action temperament, and the other is the De with a non-action administration. The rulers should be plain and simple, with little selfishness and desire. With regard to the strategies of governance, the denotation of the De is the sages' governance by "doing nothing," which is the so-called "to win the world by doing nothing." But the sage's disposition of doing nothing is usually shown as the De that stays under and does things without competition, that governs the nation with fatuousness, and that "grudges" wisdom and does nothing.

Finally, it is the innate logic of the unity of the Dao and the De. For one thing, there will be mutual correspondence and unity between the transcendence of the Dao and that of the ruler's virtue, and between the operational principle of the Dao and the concrete requirements of the ruler's virtue. For the other, there will be mutual correspondence and unity between the dharma of all the things in the universe and the Dao's profound virtue of doing nothing, and the mutual correspondence and unity between the nature of the De of all the things in the universe and the De of the common people. The Chinese philosophy has the ideological tradition of the Unity of Heaven and Man, and in the Daoist ideology, this ideological tradition can be concretized into the linking-up and unity between the Dao and the De.

VI. The Image of Water in *Laozi* and the Dao of Government

In *Laozi*, the Chinese character "*shui*" (water) or any other characters that are related to water appears more than 20 times, and is scattered in various contexts. The image of water runs through the whole book of *Laozi*. The Dao is the core concept in Laozi's philosophy, and in the illustration or description of the image of the Dao, the image of water is one of the most important images. Laozi thought that water and the Dao are similar in many ways, especially the Dao that rulers should obey in governance and administration, i.e., "*A high virtue is like water.*" Laozi, also by means of the image of water, illustrated the function of the Dao in understanding the world, administrating the society, and bearing oneself.

1. Water Is the Image Used to Express the Dao

In Laozi's philosophy, the Dao may have different meanings in different contexts, but its main denotation is the same. In form, the Dao denotes "void" and "nothingness," and gives the impression of "non-action," "non-striving," and "being weak and delicate." In Laozi's opinion, the Dao cannot be directly stated or expressed. But in order to let others know the Dao, it is inevitable to turn to an image to express it in an indirect way.

In *Laozi*, it is obvious that water is an image applied to express the Dao, and let people understand the Dao indirectly through the metaphorical significance of the water image. "*The Dao is the first ontological paradigm, and its prototype is the mode of the sun's cyclical movement by taking the primitive chaotic flood as its starting point and its finishing point.*" [1] From the viewpoint of culturological significance, water is not only the source of human life and civilization, but also the metaphorical prototype based on the daily life of Man, and whether in Chinese philosophy or in Western philosophy, the image of water is widely used to embody

---

1   Ye Shuxian. *Exploring the World of Irrationality: Theory and Method of Prototype Criticism.* Chengdu: Sichuan People's Publishing House, 1986, p.164.

metaphysical significance. From the viewpoint of daily life, water is what people see daily, and it is changeable all the time. To use water to express philosophical ideology in a metaphorical way enables people to better and more easily understand the profound meaning of the Dao. Just as Laozi said, *"The Dao that can be worded is not the constant Dao. The name that can be named is not the eternal name. I use 'Non-being' to mean the origin of Heaven and Earth; and I use 'Being' to indicate the root of all the things in the universe. Therefore, with the constant 'Non-being,' I often observe the subtlety of the Way; with the constant 'Being,' I often observe the working of the Way. The two, i.e., Non-being and Being, are both from the same origin, but only named differently; both can be said extremely mysterious and profound. The mystery and profundity of the mysterious and profound is the real source of all mysteries and profundities."* (Chapter 1, *Laozi*) The thing, which is *"the real source of all mysteries and profundities,"* if not seen from something people are familiar with, makes it by no means easy to understand its profound denotation. Seen from its form, water has its shape, but at the same time it has no shape. It is empty, but it is also able to nurture all the things in the universe. Therefore, it is similar in form to the Dao. It is obvious that Laozi's metaphorical use of water is not only culture-based, but also experience-based.

The image of water in its essence is used to illustrate and describe the Dao; therefore, it also has the ontological implication of the Dao. *"You wish to look at the Way, but you cannot see it," "you wish to listen to the Way, but you cannot hear it," "you wish to feel the Way, but you cannot touch it," "the shape without shape," "the image without image," "in front of it, you cannot see its head, and behind it, you cannot see its back."* These are Laozi's descriptions of the Dao, from which we can see clearly that it cannot be seen, heard or felt by Man. Though the Dao is invisible, unspeakable, and untouchable, it is everywhere, and gives birth to all the things in the universe. In the real world, water is the weakest concerning the sense of sight, the sense of hearing, and the sense of touch, but it moistens all the things in the universe. Therefore, water is the closest to the Dao. Water is used only to illustrate the Dao, and it is not the Dao itself. This can be seen clearly from Laozi's statements, *"Water moistens the world but never vies with the world, staying in the lowest place which everybody shows contempt for. Therefore, it is the closest to the Dao."* (Chapter 8, *Laozi*)

The Dao exists in every place in the world, and is reflected in every aspect of things, which is shown in diverse forms, and makes up a system with the Dao as its noumenon. What is in accordance with it is that water in *Laozi* has a variety of names, such as *"yuan"* (abyss), *"jiang"* (river) and *"hai"* (sea) in different forms, such as *"shen"* (deep), *"dan"* (fresh), and *"qing"* (limpid), *"zhuo"* (muddy), and *"hun"* (dirty). These different names and forms together establish the image of water. Apparently, they combine to constitute the image system of water; and semantically, they together complete the expression and understanding of the Dao through describing the image of water.

2. The Image of Water Used in Governance, Administration and Self-cultivation

In *Laozi*, the image of water has become the main way for people to understand the world, govern the country, and follow the Dao.

The image of water is first embodied in the Dao of governance. The thought Laozi expounded with the expression of the image of water has exerted a profound impact on the ideology of governance in ancient China. *"The big states, feminine in nature in the world, should place themselves at the lower part in the same way as the big rivers where all the rivers converge. The feminine often prevails over the masculine in that the former is quiet by nature, because what is quiet is able to be at the lower part."* (Chapter 61, *Laozi*) A big country should be like the river that flows downwards. Only the lower reaches can become the place of confluence. The quiet and soft tends to beat the powerful and strong, just because the quiet and soft stays lower. Wang Bi (226-249 DC) in his annotations wrote: "Rivers and seas are vast, but stay in lower places, where all the other rivers and streams flow here; big countries are powerful, but not arrogant, so all the other nations pay allegiance to them." When the places are low, water will flow and converge there; and if big countries want to have rapid developments, they should be like *"the relationship of the streams with the rivers or seas"* (Chapter 32, *Laozi*) and keep themselves in "lower" places.

"Why is the sea a place where all the rivers converge? Because it stays low, and all the rivers can converge into it." (Chapter 66, *Laozi*) The kings and lords should amply realize this feature of water and apply it to their governance and administration. This is because *"In this world there is nothing softer than water, which has seen no rival in wearing away hard things, because there is no other thing that can take its place. The weak is stronger than the strong, and the soft is harder than the hard. There is nobody who does not know this in the world, but nobody will practise it. Therefore, the Sage says, 'Those who can bear the whole nation's contempt can be called the nation's true rulers; those who can stand the whole nation's disasters have the qualification of being the rulers of the nation.' What the Dao expresses seems to be just the opposite."* (Chapter 78, *Laozi*) Much as water is

weak, it can never be taken place in dealing with the strong and hard, because the weak can beat the strong, and the soft can subdue the hard. Only when the kings and lords take the responsibility for their nation's sufferings and disasters can they have the qualification of being the king. "*Nobility is based on humbleness, and highness is based on lowness. So the princes and marquises humbly call themselves Loneliness, Helplessness or Worthlessness. Isn't it based on humbleness? Is it? Therefore, the highest honor needs not honoring.*" (Chapter 39, *Laozi*)

Officials should act in the same way. Laozi points out, "*You know the strength of the masculine, but keep the tenderness of the feminine, and are willing to be the ravine of the world. Being the ravine of the world, you will be accompanied by eternal virtue, and return to being a babe... When the first natural Dao scattered into small things, it became the useful containers. Those who were possessed with the Dao would make use of them, and became the leaders of hundreds of officials. Therefore, the perfect political system was not separated.*" (Chapter 28, *Laozi*) Though aware of their own strength and power, they can make themselves seem to be weak and soft — this is the path that the whole world should abide by; and only when they realize these, can they return to the state of true simplicity, and further understand that the Dao of true simplicity is spread to all the things in the universe. And only when they stick to true simplicity, can they keep abreast with the Dao and become head of all the other officials. Therefore, perfect politics is an organic whole that cannot be severed, and the profound understanding of the Dao is not only a must to the kings and lords, but also to all the other officials. "*The Dao is forever nameless and simple in nature. Though simple and small, it is subject to no one in the world. Should lords and princes be able to obey it, all things in the universe will naturally follow. The combination of the qi of yin and yang between the Heaven and the Earth brings forth rain and dew. It is well-distributed free from the human force. Different names appear with all things that grow on earth, but there should be some limits. And when you know the limits, you can avoid danger. The Dao is to the world what the great rivers and seas are to the streams from the valleys.*" (Chapter 32, *Laozi*) The Dao is plain and simple by nature, but it is very important. Only when the officials keep the Dao, can they let the people automatically follow. And the Dao is like the river and the sea, which are formed by the flowing rivers and streams.

As to the common people, the image of water implies the feature of "remaining weak," which becomes a state of their psyche embodied in their behavior. "*The average people seem to live a rich and luxurious life, but I possess no material things and live in poverty. Only I am a real 'fool,' and muddle-headed. All the average people seem to be smart; only I am confused. My heart is of equanimity* like the unruffled sea surface without end. The average people are full of tricks and tactics; only I am stupid and ignorant. What I am different from the average people is that I think highly of the life with the Way." (Chapter 20, *Laozi*) The whole world likes to show off, but I keep myself in the dark; the whole world is smart and nimble, but I am slow and silly. My heart is as quiet and tranquil as the surface of the sea, and my ethereality is forever still. Here Laozi pointed out, only when you are as tranquil and satisfied as the sea, can you keep yourself from the outside disturbance of temptation, and only when you keep the Dao, can you keep yourself clear in the complicated world of the numerous troubles, and become a "kind person." Apart from the circumspect state of psyche, Laozi further described the conduct of remaining weak metaphorically by using a series of water images. "*The ancient people, deft in practising the Dao, were wondrously sensible and understood the ways of the world; and they were so profound that people felt difficult to understand them. It is because they were so profound that they can only be given a make-do description: They are hesitant and cautious, just as they are wading across the river; They are cautious and vigilant, just as they are afraid of the attacks from their neighbors; They are reserved and serious, just as they are visiting others as guests; They are lax in discipline, just as the thawing ice; They are honest and simple, just like the unpolished lumber; They are broad-minded and unprejudiced, just like the valleys and vales in the mountains; Their mind is in a whirl, just like the turbid water. Who can become quiet when in motion and gradually become crystal clear? Who can become calm and seek changes when everything is quiet? The people who abide by the natural Dao are not self-conceited. Just because they are not conceited, they are willing to eradicate the old and foster the new.*" (Chapter 15, *Laozi*) The series of water images show that people should be as circumspect in proper conduct as they are wading the river in winter, as amiable as the thawing icicles, as broad-hearted as valleys, and as simple and honest as turbid water. And in tranquil life, people should be like clear water to clear and refresh themselves.

3. The Metaphysical Significance of the Image of Water

Obviously, the series of water images of Laozi have profound metaphorical significance, and show the existence of the Dao from various aspects.

First, to help people understand the existence of the Dao by using the image of water metaphorically. The Dao in Laozi's philosophical thought holds the status of noumenon, therefore, when the image of water is used to express and expound the Dao, it embodies the significance of the noumenon. Seen from this significance, the image of water is used to explain the Dao, and "the so-called the Dao of water", is in essence the Dao. In addition, to Laozi, water is the closest to the Dao, and at the same time can be understood and grasped in practice. The Dao exists in all the things in the universe, and is beneficial to all the things in the universe, and so is water. By observing and experiencing water, we can observe and experience the Dao. It is not difficult to see that Laozi's understanding of the Dao is, to a large extent, based on the image of water. The recognition and understanding of the Dao is achieved through a series of images of water. Water becomes the metaphor of the Dao.

Second, to help people understand the Dao of governing the nation by using the image of water metaphorically. No matter how powerful the country is, it should be broad-minded like hollow valley. The reason why rivers and seas are so vast is that they remain in lower positions. In *Laozi*, there are quite a few images that are related to water, such as ice, rain and sweet dew. These images embody the soft and weak side of water, but at the same time disclose the constant changes and irresistible force. It is soft but strong, with strong potentiality. If a country wants to become strong and powerful, it should modestly learn all the things that are good to the benefits of the country, become powerful with constant accumulation, and finally establish itself as the "king of all valleys." The image of water here is the metaphor of governance and administration of the country.

Third, to help people be good officials and administrate the society by using the image of water metaphorically. The kings or lords should be generous enough to listen to different opinions and tolerate all kinds of humiliations in the same way as big rivers and seas accept water from different sources. Whether you are kings and lords or officials, the primary thing to do is to abide by the Dao, and if you want to abide by the Dao, you should accept all things in the same way as rivers and seas accept all the water from all sources, and at the same time keep yourself in a lower position. To keep yourself in a lower position is to keep the Dao and simplicity. No matter how the world changes, the basic Dao is constant. Therefore, it is not really weak when you keep the weak. It means faith and commitment, and only when you keep the weak and follow the Dao, can you keep yourself in a self-possessed manner, and become the conduct marker in social administration, thus keeping the society running in the right condition.

Fourth, to help people keep a plain and simple state of mind by using the image of water metaphorically. Only when you live a plain and simple life can you free yourself from all the entanglements of things, and become really broad-minded. *"What is motionless will gradually become clear and limpid."* Laozi emphasized the "tranquil" state of mind by using the image of water, because only when you are tranquil, can you be as still and clear as water, and make your mind continuously purified. What needs explaining is that Laozi's stress on simplicity and tranquility does not mean that people should do nothing. Instead, it means that people should endeavour to become broad-minded and spiritually purified; the process itself implies doing things.

VII. "The Dao of Naturalness" and Laozi's Regimen of Health

Records of the Grand Historian records the long life of Laozi, "It is said that Laozi lived to an age of 160, or, some even say, more than 200. It is most likely that his self-cultivation of the Dao enabled him to live to longevity."[1] This can be the testimony to Laozi's regimen. Nowadays, scholars' researches on Laozi's regimen mainly focus on the following two aspects: one is Laozi's ideas of regimen, and the other is the influence of Laozi's regimen. For the first aspect, discussions elaborate on the ultimate goal of Laozi's regimen, that is, "*and that is in agreement with the reason of lasting government;*" the fundamental principle, that is, "*the Dao just models itself on the Great Nature;*" in addition, there are other concrete ways of regimen, such as the soul and the form can be combined as one, be weak and stay under, be quiet in mind with few desires, keep void and tranquil, and concentrate on *qi* (spirit) and *rou* (softness). As to the second aspect, it focuses on the influence of Laozi's ideology of regimen on Daoism as religion, the regimen culture in Traditional Chinese Medicine, and the regimen culture in traditional *qigong*. All in all, although these researches disclose some content of Laozi's regimen, scarce are the epistemological results elevated to the loftiness of philosophy. Therefore, we need to start from the overall ideology of Laozi, and further discover the ideological structure of Laozi's regimen.

1. Life Is the Embodiment of the Dao

Chen Guying says, "We can also regard the Dao as the inner life's cry of Man, which is a theory that reflects the inner life's needs and desires of Man." The Dao is an expression of Man's inner life-force, and "*naturalness*" means the thriving of the life-force. Whether it is "health-preserving," "health-conserving," or "health-protecting," the priority should go to the origin of life. When there is "birth," there is "regimen."

There are quite a few issues discussed about origins in *Laozi*. Some are about the origin of the cosmos, which can explain the origins of life, for example, in

---

1 Sima Qian. *Records of the Grand Historian*. Zhonghua Book Company, 1997, p.239.

Chapter 1: "*Non-being is the name of the beginning of Heaven and Earth; being, the name of the mother of all things.*" In Chapter 2: "*Therefore the 'Being' and the 'Non-being' generate each other.*" In Chapter 40: "*All the things in the universe are generated from 'Being,' and 'Being' from 'Non-being.'*" Laozi maintained that life is generated from "Non-being." This "Non-being," of course, is not emptiness, or nothingness, but the original state of the Dao, and that is the Dao itself. Therefore, in Chapter 42, Laozi said: "*Dao begets one, one begets two; two begets three; three begets all things.* Chapter 51: "*The Dao generates all the things in the universe.*" That is to say, the Dao is the root of everything, and, of course, includs "life." So he further explained in Chapter 39: "*All things in the universe have got the 'one' and grow fast.*"

The Dao is not only "able to generate things," but also "loves to generate things." In Chapter 51, it says, "*The Dao generates all the things in the universe, and the Virtue nurtures them.*" Therefore, when the Dao finishes the generation of life, the De in turn begins to support it. Heaven has the De of loving to generate things, as is said in "The Counsels of the Great Yü," *Shangshu*, "*Rather run the risk of irregularity and error than put an innocent person to death. This life-loving virtue has penetrated the minds of the people.*"

In spite of all these, Laozi regarded life as a natural process: when there is birth, there is death. Although people can use the De to maintain life (In Chapter 50, Laozi said, "*still another three out of ten die an unnatural death*" and "*they treat themselves unduly*"), there will be an end to each individual life, which is a natural process. Therefore, in Chapter 50, Laozi said, "*As soon as a person was born, a life begins; and upon death, he is to be buried under the earth. Of all the people born, three out of ten survive, another three out of ten die at an early age, and still another three out of ten die an unnatural death. Why? It is because they treat themselves unduly.*" And he also says, "*Therefore, a fierce wind cannot blow the whole morning, and a rainstorm cannot last the whole day. What makes so? It is the Heaven and the Earth. The violence of the Heaven and the Earth cannot last long, let alone we human beings!*" (Chapter 23, *Laozi*)

The end of life is natural, and is also inevitable. This fundamentally shows that life cannot last forever, therefore, human beings should not only pursue the length of life, but also the eternity after life. This is what Chapter 33 of *Laozi* intends to convey, "*Those who keep their natural instincts last long. And those who have died with achievements left to posterity enjoy an immortal life.*"

2. "To Follow Nature" Is the General Principle of Regimen

"To follow nature" is the law of all things, and regimen certainly is no exception. Chapter 25 of *Laozi* says, "*Man models himself on earth, earth on heaven, heaven on Dao, and Dao on Nature.*" The primal state of life is not factitious, and is the closest to the natural state. As for the phases of human life, the infant stage is the closest, with its characteristics of being soft and harmonious. *Laozi* repeatedly mentions it. For example, Chapter 10, *Laozi* says, "*The soul and the form can be combined as one, but can they be forever combined and never severe? Depend on the natural organism and gather the vital essence so as to be soft and tender, but can it be like the baby?*" Chapter 28 says, "*You know the strength of the masculine, but keep the tenderness of the feminine, and are willing to be the ravine of the world. Being the ravine of the world, you will be accompanied by eternal virtue, and return to being a babe. You know the white, but keep to the role of the black, and are willing to be a model of the world. Being a model of the world, your eternal virtue will not go astray, and you return to the highest truth. You know the honor, but keep to the role of the disgraced, and are willing to be a valley of the world. Being the valley of the world, you will no longer lack the eternal virtue, and return to simplicity.*" Chapter 49, *Laozi*, says, "*And the common people carefully look at them and listen to them, while the sages treat them in the same way as they treat their children.*" Chapter 55, *Laozi*, says, "*The person with profound virtue is just like an infant boy, whom bees, scorpions and serpents cannot bite, and whom fierce birds and beasts of prey cannot attack. ... He cries all day long, but he does not lose his voice, that is because he has enough vigor and vitality.*" Chapters 30 and 55, *Laozi*, says, "*Excessive stimulation tends to make one age. This is against the Dao. What is against the Dao comes to an early end.*" Chapter 42, *Laozi*, says, "*A violent man will not die a natural death.*" Chapter 76, *Laozi*, says, "*When alive, the human body is soft, while dead, it becomes hard and stiff. In growing, the plants are soft and fragile, while dead, they become withered and dry. Therefore, what is hard and stiff belongs to Death, while what is soft belongs to Life.*"

Now that Laozi pursued Nature, he opposed deliberate operation, and denied "*leading a luxurious and dissipated life,*" and "*treating themselves unduly.*" (Chapters 50 and 75, *Laozi*) *Laozi* repeatedly mentiond, "*let all things grow and develop of their own accord, but do not initiate them; grow all things but do not possess them; bestow favours but do not require repayment.*" (Chapter 2, *Laozi*) "*Although the Dao generates them and the Virtue nurtures them, they do not take all things in the universe as their own, but let them grow naturally. That is the greatest virtue.*" (Chapter 51, *Laozi*) "*If you indulge in a comfortable life, you are inviting disasters, and if you give way to your carnal desires, you are stimulated. Excessive stimulation tends to make one age. This is against the Dao. What is against the Dao comes to an early end.*" (Chapter 55, *Laozi*)

In *Laozi*, there are also quite a few specific methods with regard to regimen. For example, "to keep tranquility:" "*To return to the origins is to return to the state of being quiet and calm, and the return to quietness and calmness is to return to the origins. ... and anyone who can be magnanimous towards everything can be free of disasters throughout his life.*" (Chapter 16, *Laozi*) And also "*to have few desires,*" "*Too many colors dazzle the eyes; too much music deafens the ears; too many tastes baffle his palate. Overindulging in hunting drives you crazy, and coveting too many material things tarnishes your conduct. Therefore, the Sage cares for bellies rather than senses, fending off material temptation and living a simple life.*" (Chapter 12, *Laozi*) "*Music and delicious food make the passers-by stop and enjoy them. But when the great Dao is expressed in words, it will be plain or even monotonous. When you listen to it, it cannot be heard; when you look at it, it cannot be seen. However, when you apply it, it can be limitless.*" (Chapter 35, *Laozi*)

Regimen in *Laozi*, in fact, aims at different targets. What we discussed above about regimen is for such people of upper classes as sages and officials. As to the common people, i.e., "*min*" in Chinese, *Laozi* also puts forwards quite a few instructive issues. *Laozi* maintains that if the common people are not afraid of death, they are hard to control, namely, "*The people do not fear death, so why do you frighten them with death?*" (Chapter 74, *Laozi*) "*The people do not take death seriously, because the rulers lead a luxurious and dissipated life; that is why the people do not take death seriously.*" (Chapter 75, *Laozi*) On the contrary, if the common people are very much concerned with life and death, the society will be stable: "*Make people unwilling to move away in spite of the danger of death.*" (Chapter 80, *Laozi*) But the pity is that, in most cases, the common people are struggling on the verge of death, not to speak of "keeping fit!" These people are the factors of social instability, which will affect the regimen on the part of the sages. Therefore, *Laozi* advocates sages' regimen, not only for their own, but for the common people as well. In that case, the common people will not be worried for their living, so it is easier to administrate the society, which will accordingly become stable and prosperous. "*Therefore, the sage, in the exercise of his government, empties their minds, fills their bellies, weakens their wills, and strengthens their bones. He always keeps them innocent of knowledge and free from desire...*" (Chapter 3, *Laozi*) "*They have delicious things to eat and drink, beautiful clothes to wear, comfortable houses to live in, and merry customs. They can see what the* neighboring countries are doing, and can hear the crows of poultry and barks of dogs, but there are not mutual visits on the part of the people of the two countries." (Chapter 80, *Laozi*)

The Daoist regimen and the Outlook of the World and the Outlook of Nature in Traditional Chinese Medicine all need to be expressed by means of language, and the doctor and his/her patients need to communicate by watching, hearing, asking and touching — a diagnosis method used in TCM. However, because of the linguistic philosophy of the Daoist thought, the language used in the Daoist regimen, medicine and pharmacy is mostly literary and symbolic. For example, the names of acupuncture points: *tianchi* (Heavenly Pool), *tianquan* (Heavenly Spring), *shangguan* (the Upper Pass), and *xiaguan* (the Lower Pass). The Traditional Chinese Medicine and Pharmacy pays particular attention to "*tianren ganying*", or interactions between Heaven and Mankind, that is to say, the interaction between the natural energy and the human energy and human spirit. Its manifestation is that the accupoints within the systematic network can be both the energy information senders and receivers, and perform continuous exchanges and interactions of energy information between acupuncture points. It also pays particular attention to the symbolically corresponding relationships between the yin-yang and five elements of the natural world and the viscera, or internal organs of the body. These are all the representations of the general principle of "following the Great Nature." In short, the Daoist regimen is a natural healthy therapy of Chinese regimen. It is a circulation based on the promotion and restraint among the five elements, so as to reach the balance and harmony between Heaven Earth and Man. Those who follow the order of nature shall enjoy good health and longevity!

Tu Youyou, a Chinese scientist and the 2015 Nobel Prize winner for medicine, got her inspiration from *Zhouhou Beiji Fang*, or *Prescriptions for Emergent Reference*, a TCM classic by Ge Hong, an Eastern Jin Dynasty Daoist master. By improving its extracting method, Tu Youyou (and her team) discovered, for the first time in human history, that the extraction from the Chinese herbal sweet wormwood (*Artemisia apiacea*) can successfully suppress plasmodium, which played a crucial role in the development of *artemisinin*, a new anti-malaria medicine. Thanks to her discovery, millions of lives are saved in the world. In September 2011, Tu Youyou was awarded the Lasker Prize in Medicine, which is, in the biomedical field, second to the Nobel Prize. And in October 2015, she was awarded the Nobel Prize in Physiology or Medicine. The Traditional Chinese Medicine with "modelling on the Great Nature" as its essence is becoming increasingly beneficial to the world.

The Chinese traditional regimen originated in the idea that "the Dao models itself on the Great Nature" gradually gives birth to a cognitive and practice system aiming at human health, happiness and longevity. *"My life/destiny depends on myself, not on Heaven."* This slogan was first seen in inscriptions on tortoise shells and animal bones, and was later quoted by Ge Hong, the Daoist master, in his book *Baopu Zi*, or *The Works of Master Baopu*, in which it means that human beings can, with following Nature as its prerequisite, elongate their life and better their qualities of living with their own efforts. The traditional Chinese ideology and system of regimen reflects and promotes the human rationality and pursuit of loving life and keeping fit, which is an important part in the development of human civilization.

3. Fewer Desires Promote the Unity of "Regimen" and "Virtue Nurturing"

Laozi pursued the clarification, perfection and liberty of the inner spirit. Continence, silence and keeping quiet represent a turn from the external to the internal. Having fewer desires or continence is a special feature of Laozi's idea of regimen. Laozi, under the scrutiny of the principle of the "naturalness" seized the three aspects of "desire," "ingenuity," and "deeds," provided a corresponding guidance. From the above analysis, we can see that the three aspects do not include all the "desires," "ingenuities," and "deeds," but are rather specific. "Desires" indicate the worldly pursuits of name, fame, and power. The extremities of these goals might be the common concepts of "the most powerful," "the most wealthy," "the most famous," "the most mighty," etc. It is justifiable that in the whole life people cannot go without these pursuits, but if people pursue things without limitation or containment, their life will be heavily burdened, as the energy each individual life possesses is limited, and each successful pursuit requires "hard work" and "perspiration." And an unduly pursuit without continence equals making excessive use of life. Therefore, Laozi advocated "fewer desires," and "less smartness," which seems to remind people that facing these pursuits, they should "take it easy" and "be more disciplined." When people do not ardently pursue these things, the life organism bestowed by "the Great Nature" will then turn for normal functioning, and the relationship between life and its external environment will return to normal, which is certainly highly beneficial to the body.

Continence can promote the unity between "keeping fit" and "nurturing virtue." The unduly pursuit of name, fame, power, and worldly deeds not only harms the body, but psychological health as well. Moreover, it causes conflicts and will finally result in the chaos of social order. In social life, what people strenuously pursue is usually "something scarce," which not everybody can get or possess; if it is within easy reach of anybody, there is no need to pursue them strenuously. For instance, any country has only one king or lord, some ten ministers, and very few "richest persons" or "millionaires." Titles like "famous" or "great" can only be conferred on a very few. Compared with the chief daily necessities like firewood, rice, cooking oil and salt, there are very few "important things" under the sun. This "scarcity" leads to mutual calculation, mutual fighting, or even mutual killing in their ardent pursuits, during which people exhaust their "wisdom" and "talent" causing social disorder, or even serious social problems. Thus, the excessive pursuit of fame, profit, power, and worldly deeds becomes an "evil" conduct, and will be harshly denounced by the public. Nevertheless, for those who have already gained all these goals, they tend to cover up their excessive pursuits and ill-deeds by saying that they are "saving the people from hardships" and "reengineering the livelihood." They have the fame of the "wise kings" or "fair kings," and are highly worshiped. All these bring about the ideological disorder in society, the baneful influence of which is far more lasting, and more destructive. Therefore, Laozi advocated "continence," "non-competition," and "being soft and weak," which is actually to "cage" their unduly pursuit of fame and profit, power and worldly deeds, and let people see through their true colors. From the objective side of the things we can see that the majority of the people in society are "disadvantaged and vulnerable," who are not able to pursue fame and profit or vie with others even if they want to. Seen from the perspective of the ruling class, they are "non-competitive," and "soft and weak" with "few desires," but these people do exist and their daily life constitutes the main social forces. However, if they are deprived of material gains and equality in society, or even suppressed culturally and ideologically, life will be made much harder for them. Therefore, objectively speaking, Laozi's "fewer desires," "non-competition," and "being soft and weak" are meaningful in that they curb and control the powerful but protect the weak, which manifest high moral cultivation, at the same time, bring "regimen" and "the cultivation of virtue" to unity.

VIII. The Complementation between Daoism and Confucianism and the Daoist Enlightenment to Human Development

The thought of Laozi has exerted a great impact on later generations. Over the past thousands of years, ancient China was long in a situation of tripartite confrontation: Confucianism, Buddhism, and Daoism. These three are mutually interpenetrating and complementary, and have played a very significant role in the development of traditional Chinese culture and ideology.

1. The Different Impacts of Laozi's Ideology and Confucianism

Although it is still uncertain as to the author and the time of completion of the book *Laozi*, it is almost certain that its thought first appeared roughly at the same time as that of Confucius, that is, the Spring and Autumn Period. It was a time of princes' melees, of rites collapsed, and music disintegrated. The long turmoil of war made the society long for the generation of new ideas, and the absence of value evaluation system and the scattering of political right provided room for the flourishing of creative and philosophical thought. It was in this social background that the contention of a hundred schools of thought was made possible. And Confucianism represented by Confucius and Daoism represented by Laozi were the two most influential of the hundred schools of thought.

Just because of the same social background, the hundred schools of thought, though each with its own characteristics, had many cross-correlations. Especially each school had its strong concern with the social reality, and each had its aspiration and theoretical starting point to find a way out for the then social reality. Some scholars thought that Confucianism came from Daoism, and when we study closely Laozi's thought and that of Confucianism, we can see that they indeed have something in common. Of course, from different focuses of attention and with different ways of thinking, there are obvious disparities between them. It is true that they both based their theories on solving social problems, but their theoretical starting points were different. The starting point of Confucianism was human relations and kinship, while Laozi's starting point was the natural state of the whole universe, including the Heaven, the Earth, and Man. Owing to the different starting points, i.e., one emphasizes readjusting realistic human relations though ethical and moral spirit, and the other stresses the pure natural character of spontaneity and harmony by returning to the original state. Although both are oriented to the ultimate goal of improving the realistic society, they have different understandings of the people who constitute the realistic society. This difference is not only embodied in the theoretical setting of human nature, but also in the perspective of understanding people. Confucians understood Man from the human relations, and this Man is social Man; while Laozi emphasized Man's own consciousness and returning of his nature, and this Man is individual Man.

Just because of the differences in the ideological inclination and ways of thinking, the thought of Laozi and that of Confucianism experienced different treatments in history, and their influence on later generations are also radically different. The Confucian thought started from experience and practice, aiming at the construction of social order with the spirit of rituals and music as its norm. In this society, each and every individual, starting from studying hard and self-cultivation, dealt with various social relationships according to a certain principle, so as to realize the harmonious and orderly state. This thought was remarked by Sima Tan (a Taishi Ling during the reign of Emperor Wudi in the Han Dynasty, a Han-dynasty official in charge of astronomy and calendar) as *"erudite but unimportant, working hard but achieving little,"* but as it was easy to operate and quite in conformity with the needs of the rulers, it was regarded as the main trend chosen by the rulers and became officially recognized, thus becoming the most influential school of thought in the traditional Chinese society. At the same time, the Confucian emphasis on education enabled its thought to be closely related to educational activities in ancient China, and became immersed in the whole educational process. In this way, the Confucian thought played a significant role in the construction of the standards in political tradition, orthodox Confucian tradition, and intellectual tradition in ancient China.

Compared with Confucianism which had a profound official cultural background, Laozi and the Daoist thought in ancient China were tinged with obvious folklore features, and on many occasions, Daoism became a supplementary element and modulation means in political administration and individual cultivation. Of course, it is not because that Laozi did not have high-level ideology, on the contrary, it is just because Laozi had foresight and sagacity, and because his starting point is lofty and profound. Therefore, it is more difficult for us to understand and put into practice. The Confucian thought mainly comes from the continuation of knowledge and summary of life experience, which provides the society with a set of systematic rules and regulations and the principles of the world; whereas Laozi's thought depends more on the intuitional experience and the holistic understanding of the universe, and provides the global idea with regard to politics and life. To borrow the comments from historians on the features of books of history, the Confucian thought is closer to "square and witty," which is easier to grasp and put into practice, while Laozi's thought tends to be "round and mysterious," which is on a higher plane but hard to understand and carry out. Such disparities may be a crucial factor that caused the two schools of thought to have different treatments in ancient China. Seen from a different aspect, the understanding and grasp of the Dao by numerous individuals formed a strong social force, with which no single political power could compare. However, as far as the national cultural deposit is concerned, it is hard to tell which is the better, Confucianism or Daoism; the odds are no better than evens.

In China, it has long been said that Confucianism is active and secular while Daoism is passive and retiring. To seek a life of higher social status, you need Confucianism, and to abjure from society, you resort to Daoism. This is, of course, a misunderstanding of Laozi and the Daoist thought. It is true that Confucianism is active in doing things, or even doing something in spite of its possible failure; however, Daoism is not passive, it is only on a higher plane of human mentality. Nan Huaijin once had an analogy. In the traditional society of China, Confucianism was something like a shop of provisions, where daily necessities were supplied, while Daoism was very much like a pharmacy, which was useless when you were healthy, but indispensable when you were ill. This is a quite interesting analogy. Though imprecise academically, it vividly reveals the special features of the two schools of thought. It seems that Laozi's thought was not as influential as Confucianism in ancient China, but in fact it had its crucial significance. What is more, in the present society or even in the future, with the accumulated issues that Man faces, the value of Laozi's thought will be increasingly prominent. Historian Chen Yinque once pointed out, "Although Chinese Confucians were said to study the phenomena of nature in order to acquire knowledge, their ultimate concentration is on the relationships between people. Daoists, on the contrary, studies the relationship between human beings and objects. Therefore, the highly developed traditional Chinese medicine owed much to Daoism. Although there are weird and uncanny statements in it, it can still pay attention to the relationship between Man and objects. Therefore, compared with Buddhism, it is a religion that is closer to common sense and human relationship."

Of course, the interrelationship between Daoism as philosophy, or even Daoism as religion and Confucianism as well as their ideological influence on each other is so intrinsic and complex that it is hard to be clarified. The above analyses are no more than a general conclusion we endeavour to draw.

2. Laozi's Outlook on Heaven and Man and Its Revelation on Human Development

The relationship between Heaven and Man was what the ancient Chinese were concerned about. Similar records can be found in quite a few pre-Qin classics: in *The Marquis of Lü on Punishments* in the *Books of Zhou*, *Shangshu*, the legend of Emperor Zhuanxu is recorded, "*Then he commissioned Zhong and Li to make an end of the communications between Earth and Heaven.*" *Speech at Gan, Book of History* has records of war of Heavenly Punishment. *Annals of Xia, Records of the Grand Historian* records the sacrificial activities of devotion to the gods and the spirits. In the very beginning of human beings, the ancestors prayed to the Gods for the peace of the people, thus forming the initial relationship between man and nature. In the process of constantly exploring the relationship between heaven and humanity, the idea of heaven and man has become a theme in ancient Chinese thought and culture, and it is one of the important propositions that the thinkers have to elucidate. Laozi is no exception.

Besides, Laozi's Integration of Heaven and Man has its academic and ideological origin — *Zhou Yi*, or the *Book of Changes*. First, seen from his official career, we find that the thought of Laozi might be influenced by *Zhou Yi*. Among other things, his Outlook on Heaven and Man certainly came from *Zhou Yi*. *Zhou Yi*, taking its shape in the Yin and Zhou dynasties, was a reference book used by witches and wizards to communicate between Heaven and Man, and to elicit the will of Heaven by careful study. The hexagram-records and the line statements in the *Book of Changes* were generalized and concluded from the experience of the ancestors' supplicating the Heaven for revelations. Though it is a book of divination, it contains the simplest understanding on the part of the ancient Chinese of the mutual relationships between the Heaven and Man, and between Nature and society. The book may have been written by some witch(es) or historian(s). And most historians came from Daoists, as *Art and Literature Records in the Books of the Han Dynasties* says, "Most Daoists were once historians, who recorded the success and failure, and weal and woe of the previous dynasties, and had a clear understanding of the rise and fall of these dynasties. Then they could grasp the essentials of the history, and maintain a humble and self-sustaining life. This is the way the kings should use in governance of the states." In ancient China, there was no clear demarcation between the witches and the historians. Laozi had been a historian, and had worked in the Zhou Dynasty as a "librarian." As far as his profession is concerned, he should have had the convenience to see the *Book of Changes*, or had been familiar with it. Based on this, we can deduce that the thought of Laozi had its source from the *Book of Changes*.

Second, seen from the comparison between the thoughts of Heaven and Man in the *Book of Changes* and *Dao De Jing* (*Laozi*), there are at least some similarities as follows: 1) The awareness of the universe system. In the *Book of Changes*, the six lines in the diagram are the symbols of "*sancai*" or the three talents, i.e., the Heaven, the Earth and Man. The *Interpretation of the Book of Changes* says, "*The* Book of Changes *as a book has stored a large amount of information, including the Dao of Heaven, the Dao of Man, and the Dao of the Earth; the three talents combine to form the two lines.*" Laozi said, "*Therefore, the Dao is great, the Heaven is great, the Earth is great, and the Man is also great. In the universe there are four greats, and the Man is one of the four.*" (Chapter 25, *Laozi*) Laozi and the *Book of Changes* both think that the universe is a holistic system that includes the Heaven, the Earth, and Man. 2) The lives of living beings go on without end. The *Book of Changes* says, "*the incessant generation of life is yi, or transformation,*" which means that the whole universe is a world of incessant generation and non-stop changes. Laozi said, "*The Dao is unique, and from the Chaos there appear the Heaven and the Earth, which in turn produce the qi of Yin and Yang, or the material force of the Positive and the Negative. The union of Yin and Yang produces all things in the universe. With the Yin in the innermost part, all things in the universe face the Yang, and the vigorous mutual agitation of Yin and Yang brings them into harmony.*" (Chapter 42, *Laozi*) The Dao is the mother of all the things in the universe, and as to all the things in the universe, the Dao "*nurtures them, makes them grow and ripen, and protects and cares for them.*" (Chapter 51, *Laozi*) They both think that the universe is an organic and all-generative whole. 3) To ratiocinate human affairs from the Dao of Heaven. "The Explanations of the Diagrams" in the *Book of Changes* says, "*In ancient China, when Paoxi, or Fuxi, was reigning, people kept observing the astronomical phenomena, the geographical phenomena, or even the textures of birds' wings and of the furs of animals, and what was suitable on Earth, and created the Eight Diagrams by taking from the bodies which were near and from materials which were far, so as to communicate with the De of the divinities, and to imitate the spirits of all the things in the universe.*" The ancient Chinese derived the generation, growth, withering and death of all the things in the universe by means of image-numerology used in practising divination, discovered some regularity in them, and further predicted human luck, good or bad, fortune and misfortune. In spite of its intuitionistic form, its way of thinking was mysterious, "*however, it set up the basic rules of treating and observing the relationship between Man and Nature: the Unity of Heaven and Man. The unity of Heaven, Earth, and Man was, in fact, the Unity of Heaven and Man. According to the authors of the* Book of Changes, *to understand and realize the universal essence of the Unity of Heaven and Man (the De of communicating with the deities), make their own actions in conformity with the nature of all the things in the universe (to imitate the spirit of all the things in the universe), and finally to realize the Unity of Heaven and Man is the highest of human state of mind.*"[1] Laozi, on the other hand, puts forward the principle that "*The Man models himself on the Earth, the Earth on the Heaven, the Heaven on the Dao, and the Dao just on the Nature.*" Laozi thought that the human society should imitate Nature, which is obviously inherited from the outlook of the Unity of Heaven and Man in the *Book of Changes*, only that he used rationalism instead of mysterious

---

1 Xie Guangyu, Sun Yikai. Laozi and Zhouyi. *Confucius Research*, No. 2, 1997.

thinking in divination.

Laozi's thought of Heaven and Man had its cultural and historical tradition as well as its ideological and academic origin. His *Dao De Jing* has certainly promoted to a higher sate the ancient Chinese thought and philosophical thinking. He especially made a systematic elaboration on the thought of the Unity of Heaven and Man, aiming at his avocations of Man imitating Nature, and following the Dao of Heaven, which were taken as the principle of solving the problems in society, politics, and human life.

(1) The intercrescence and co-existence of Man and Heaven. Laozi said, "*All things in the universe are generated from 'Being,' and 'Being' from 'Non-being.'*" (Chapter 40, *Laozi*) "*Dao begets one; one begets two; two begets three; three begets all things. All things carry on their backs the yin and embrace in their arms the yang, the opposites tending to harmony.*" (Chapter 42, *Laozi*) From the perspective of cosmologic theory, Laozi explained that the Dao generated all the things in the universe, but Laozi, after the "generation of all the things in the universe" did not say anything about the "generation of Man." We think that, from the Nature of the Dao, the "generation of all the things in the universe" should include the "generation of Man," as in Laozi's opinion, "Man and things are of the same kind," and "the Heaven and Man are one." In other words, Man and the Heaven (the Earth) are the natural results of the Dao, and have the commonality of "Nature." This concept can be backed up by what his successor Zhuangzi said. "*Heaven and Earth and I were born at the same time, and all life and I are one.*" (Working Everything Out Evenly, *Zhuangzi*) As in Zhuangzi's opinion, the relationship between Man and the Heaven (the Earth) is the relationship of co-generation, and Man and the Heaven, the Earth, and all the things in the universe are all ascribed to the Dao. His "*all life are one*" is mainly based on the naturalness of Man and all the things in the universe, that is to say, Man and the Heaven (the Earth) are in conformity with regard to their naturalness.

Laozi laid stress on the synchronicity of Man and the Heaven (the Earth). "*Therefore, the Dao is great, the Heaven is great, the Earth is great, and the Man is also great. In the universe there are four greats, and the Man is one of the four.*" (Chapter 25, *Laozi*) First, the Dao co-exists with the Heaven, the Earth, and Man, and the existence of the Dao is manifested in the Heaven, the Earth, and Man; second, the Heaven, the Earth, and Man are also co-existent. Just because they are co-generative, there is no difference in importance or time sequence, which is different from the idea of Confucianism. In the eyes of Confucians, "*When there are* the Heaven and the Earth, there are all the things in the universe; when there are all the things in the universe, there are men and women; when there are men and women, there are couples; when there are couples, there are fathers and sons; when there are fathers and sons, there are the monarch and his subjects; when there are the monarch and his subjects, there are the superiors and the subordinates; when there are the superiors and the subordinates, there are rituals to follow." (*Yizhuan*, or *Essays on the* Book of Changes) The generation of the Heaven, the Earth, and Man is in a good order and sequence; third, the divine nature and virtuousness (benevolence and morality) of Heaven have faded. This aspect is different from Confucianism. For example, Confucius's "Being in awe of three things" is first of all "in awe of the Decree of Heaven." "The small man, being ignorant of the Decree of Heaven, does not stand in awe of it." (Book 16, *The Analects of Confucius*) "Heaven is author of the virtue that is in me. What can Huan Tui do to me?" (Book 7, *The Analects of Confucius*) "That which is ordained by the Heaven is called our nature." (*The Doctrine of the Mean*), etc. From these statements still can be seen the will and virtues of the Heaven; fourth, the status of the human beings is elevated. The human beings, standing out as one of the four "Greats," are no longer the ones "who offend against *tian* (the Heaven) and have nowhere else to pray." (Book 3, *The Analects of Confucius*) It can be seen that Laozi's understanding of Heaven and Man is different from that of primitive Confucianism: Laozi not only saw the natural (physical) side of human beings, but also saw the social (humanity) side of human beings. It is the two sides of human beings that have caused conflicts with his Dao. Therefore, he advocated the idea "Man follows nature" which is a good way to resolve this opposition.

(2) The Heaven and Man are both *"ziran,"* that is, naturalness. Seen from the co-existent relationship between Man and the Heaven and the Earth, Man is natural Man, who manifests Nature, and there is no need to copy the Earth or the Heaven. From ontology and the generative theory, these three are the results of Nature, so they are all in conformity to the Dao. "The earth models on the Heaven, and the Heaven on the Dao" mentioned here is not the purpose of Laozi, as his true intention is that *"Man should model on the Dao."* In the eyes of Laozi, the Heaven and the Earth are Nature themselves, and there is no need to copy the Dao, or even his Dao is the Dao abstracted from the Heaven and the Earth.

The reason why Laozi put forward "Man models himself on earth., earth on heaven, heaven on Dao, and Dao on that which is naturally so" is that he saw Man as a social being has inconformity with the Great Nature. The human being is full of the societal "paradox." For example, Laozi pointed out, *"To mediate the deepest* enmity, there will still be enmity left after the mediation; and to return good for evil, can it be called the right way to solve problems if the Virtue is repaid with enmity?" (Chapter 79, *Laozi*) "Which is more intimate, fame or health? Which is more precious, health or wealth? Which is more harmful, the gaining of fame or the loss of health?" (Chapter 44, *Laozi*) "No crime can be greater than that of desire; no disaster can be greater than that of insatiability; no sin can be greater than that of avarice." (Chapter 46, *Laozi*) The contradictions of grudge against each other, the contradiction between virtue and enmity, between the body and other things like name, profit, and wealth, and between the pursuit of desire and the evil caused by desire, all these are the "societal" contradictions to Man. It is just the human societal existence that results in the injury of the Dao, which Laozi did not expect to see. But from his social ideology he advocated that "*the population of small countries is becoming smaller and smaller,*" Laozi did not deny the societal existence of Man, and the various relations between Man and society. The question is how man would conform with the Dao with his societal nature. "*The kind people, I treat them kindly; the unkind people, I treat them kindly as well. And in this way, I attain kindness. The trustworthy people, I trust them; the untrustworthy people, I trust them as well. And in this way, I attain trustworthiness.*" (Chapter 49, *Laozi*) "*The Ritual marks the insufficiency of loyalty and faithfulness, and the beginning of disasters.*" (Chapter 38, *Laozi*) In these two chapters, Laozi also dealt with moral principles, such as *deshan* (the virtue of kindness), *dexin* (the virtue of trustworthiness), and *zhongyi* (loyalty and righteousness). How can the social ethics become in conformity with the natural ethics (the Dao)? Where is the norm? Laozi's answer was "doing nothing," in order to pursue and advocate the natural, innate and spontaneous norm of value and social behavior.

Zhuangzi, in face of this issue, offered an even simpler solution, "*Do not damage the Dao with human wisdom, nor affect the Heaven with human efforts,*" (Signs of Real Virtue, *Zhuangzi*) "Having the form of Man, but having no feelings of Man," ("The Great Teacher", *Zhuangzi*) "In the past people paid attention to the Heavenly nature, not to the human." (Lie Yu Kou, *Zhuangzi*) Zhuangzi bluntly abandoned the sociality of Man (the nature of Man as Man) and advocated the oneness of the Heaven and Man, and "materialized" Man, so that Man can refrain from acting as "Man." Relatively speaking, Zhuangzi's "oneness of the Heaven and Man" sacrifices the sociality of Man, but in Laozi's ideology of the Heaven and Man, the spontaneous conduct of Man is ascertained in social life.

(3) The Dao of Heaven is the Dao of Man. The special feature of thinking in the *Book of Changes* is to deduce the Dao of Man from the Dao of the Heaven.

CHAPTER ONE: Introduction

The Category of Yi (changes) in *Siku Quanshu Zongmu Tiyao*, or *The Synopsis of the General Contents of The Complete Library of the Four storehouses* says, "*The purpose of the* Book of Changes *is to understand the human affairs from the Dao of Heaven.*"[1] Laozi also deduced the Dao of Man from the Dao of Heaven, but in understanding the relationship between the Dao of Heaven and the Dao of Man, Laozi's opinion is different from that of Confucius and Mencius. Confucius said, "*Human nature is much the same, and ways and habits make the difference.*" "*Only the wisest and the most foolish do not change,*" etc. But the "Nature and the Dao of Heaven" is not discussed in detail. Mencius said that one should follow one's mind, know one's nature and the nature of the Heaven. Mencius put forward a number of remarks on the mind and the moral nature, but he said nothing about how to know the Heaven. Comparatively speaking, Confucius and Mencius laid stress on the human society and are more concerned with Man's socialization; while Laozi saw the whole universe as an organic whole, focusing on Man's "Naturalness." Therefore, it is the inevitable way of Laozi's thinking to deduce the Dao of Man by starting from the Heaven to Man, and from the Dao of Heaven to the Dao of Man.

Then, what is the relationship between the Dao of Heaven and the Dao of Man on the part of Laozi? As far as this issue is concerned, Laozi maintained that the Dao of the Heaven is natural, and that the Dao of Man is doing nothingness. "*The Dao follows the course of nature, but there is nothing it does not do.*" (Chapter 37, *Laozi*) The Dao constantly follows Nature (doing nothing), but in the universe there is nothing that is not made by the Dao (doing everything), that is, "the Dao copies Nature." Therefore, the Heaven, the Earth and Man in imitation of the Dao, should imitate Nature as well. Man must follow the Nature of all the things in the universe, follow the Dao of the Heaven, that is, the inevitable tendency of being natural and of doing nothing without human intervention. It is obvious that Laozi's law is to substitute the Nature of the Dao for Confucian Dao of Man — the law of society.

Laozi realized that the Dao of the Heaven and the Dao of Man do not agree in reality. He said, "*It is the law of nature to reduce what is abundant, and replenish what is lacking. However, the human behavior is just the opposite: to exploit what is insufficient and supply what is abundant. Who can spare what he has more than enough to those in need? Only Sages can do this.*" (Chapter 77, *Laozi*) Only those who follow the "Dao of the Heaven" can "*reduce what is abundant, and replenish*

---

1 (Qing Dynasty)Yong Rong and Ji Yun(eds). *The Synopsis of the General Contents of Siku Quanshu*. collected by Zhou Ren. Hainan Publishing House, 1999, p.13.

what is lacking." He repeatedly explained the good points of following the Dao, "*Therefore, the Sages retreat to the back, but win the respect of others; they seldom consider for themselves, but keep themselves safe and sound. Isn't it because they are not selfish that they attain what they ought to attain?*" (Chapter 7, *Laozi*) "*The ancient people, deft in practising the Dao, were wondrously sensible and understood the ways of the world; and they were so profound that people felt difficult to understand them. ...The people who abide by the natural Dao are not self-conceited. Just because they are not conceited, they are willing to eradicate the old and foster the new.*" (Chapter 15, *Laozi*) He also admonished people to follow "the Dao of Heaven," and practise "*doing things without competition*" so as to realize "*freedom of disasters throughout their life.*" (Chapter 16, *Laozi*) He also advises that if one wants to make "the Dao of Man" copy "the Dao of the Heaven," he will have to "*follow only the Dao,*" (Chapter 21, *Laozi*) and with the unselfishness of the Dao of the Heaven ("*Heaven and Earth show no bias, and let all the things in the universe grow naturally*"), practise the unselfishness of the Dao of Man ("*the Sage shows no bias either, and let the people develop themselves*") (Chapter 5, *Laozi*), in the hope of realizing his oneness of the Heaven and Man: "*The law of nature is beneficial rather than harmful; the way of the human world is to do things without competition.*" (Chapter 81, *Laozi*) Man should learn from the Dao of the Heaven, become "harmless" and beneficial to all the things in the universe, and "not compete" but do things for the world.

In short, Laozi's thought of the oneness of the Heaven and Man, starting from the Dao of the generation of all the things in the universe, points out that all the things in the universe are natural, advocates the unity of the Dao of the Heaven and the Dao of Man, and tries to construct his universal order, social prospects, and life path. That is to say, in the universe where the Dao generates all the things, there is a state in which the government is doing nothing that goes against nature. In the state, the subjects live a life of a pure heart and few desires, with no strife with others and in harmony.

Of all the ancient Chinese thinkers, especially the pre-Qin thinkers, Laozi's philosophical thought is of great profundity. What is special of Laozi is his vision and way of thinking. His thought is transcendental and global, simply in consideration based on one place and one time, but with a view to the overall grasp of the whole universal time and space. What is more, the world in the eyes of Laozi is not still and motionless, but constantly changing and transforming; and things are not isolated, but closely linked and mutually influenced. The rich human wisdom implied in Laozi's thought has great universal significance in our thinking about the realistic issues or even the future destiny of Man. As the wisdom of Laozi is a relatively profound philosophical thinking, its enlightening significance has its universality. It has an significantly enlightening to individual self-cultivation or perfection, to the domestic affairs and foreign affairs of a nation, or even to the destiny of mankind.

Ever since the beginning of the 20th century, mankind has entered a speedy era of scientific and technological development, and people are showing increasing dependency on science and technology, which has brought to people great convenience and more possibilities in their living. But at the same time, its negative influences are becoming increasingly visible: the environment is seriously polluted and the resources are gradually exhausted. What is more serious is that many changes caused by the massive industrial production based on science and technology are irreversible, thus making the things on the earth more and more in disorder. Even worse, with the promotion of competition and the drive of profit, human greed is enhanced, and people excessively pursue the so-called speed of development and advancement, without considering developmental space and acceptance. Under this background, our attention back to Laozi's consideration more than 2,000 years ago, becomes very important. It is a matter of first priority as to how to understand afresh Man's precise orientation in the universe, return to the natural state of human existence, highlight the biological protection and sustainable development, and realize the natural harmony between Man and environment.

Modern crises in the Western society, even around the whole world, have their origin in egoistic individualism and the undesirable extension of instrumentality. Human beings, from the standpoint of the egocentricity, consider the maximization of efficiency from the perspective of utilitarianism, and with the help of the means of scientific rationality, completely conquer Nature, wholly control society, and globally administrate Man, which consequently brings Man to the opposite side of Nature and of Man himself, which turns the means into the purpose, putting scientific rationality fetters on Man. Laozi's "*zhi*" or wisdom is quite similar to instrumental rationality in the West. "*Zhi*" or wisdom directs at nonego, and human life needs to get to know nonego. Therefore, "*zhi*" is indispensable. Nevertheless, man's increasing understanding of nonego, the human desire to control and possess nonego also increases, which will break the natural condition of human life, bring about contention for material things and reduce social order to chaos. The reason why Laozi was quite vigilant against "*zhi*" lies here. Laozi laid emphasis on the harmonious development between the Heaven, the Earth and Man by elaborating on such concepts as "*ziran*" (Nature or naturalness) and "*wuwei*" (doing nothing or non-action), which foretells the developmental orientation of human future. It provides crucial enlightenment for modern people to go out of modernistic crises, and not to get into the trouble of putting technology the first priority in today's world with highly developed technology.

In conclusion, the thought in *Laozi* is the philosophical thought that originates from the enlightenment of the universal Dao of Nature, with its ultimate purpose of respecting Nature and returning to Nature, so as to construct the harmony between Man and Nature and The thought of Laozi is rich in the biological wisdom of the natural harmony between Man and Nature, coagulates the biological outlook of morality of harmonization of the Heaven, the Earth and Man, and coagulates the consensus of human society at the stage of present-day post-industrial historical development: biological environment protection and sustainable development. In the history of human civilization development, the ancestors of the Chinese nation have accumulated rich experience in making proper and good use of biological resources and in protecting the residential environment, so that China becomes one of the most important birthplaces of eastern agricultural civilization. The Daoist philosophical thought established by Laozi is like the beacon which illuminates us and guides us to move towards freedom, towards wisdom, and towards the sustainable development of politics, economy, society, culture and environment.

第二章 CHAPTER TWO

定义，基本假设，公理
Definitions, Assumptions and Axioms

我们用公理化的方法诠释《老子》，在考虑研究的逻辑主线时，把人类认识世界、对待万事万物的方法定位在"守中"状态，这就需要从宇宙生成论的层面阐述事物构成及其运动变化的规律，进而把人类世界放在这个系统的恰当位置，这样才能确定什么是"守中"状态，以及如何把握这种状态。这一原理对于把握人类的活动——下至修身及个人生活，上至治国及处理国家关系——以及把握人类社会的发展方向，均有重要的指导意义。我们给出了13个定义、5个基本假设、4条公理，进行界定和说明，并配上与之相应的《老子》原文，由此给后面的命题、推论提供基本的逻辑依据。

一、从"守中"出发理解《老子》的思想体系

对《老子》进行公理化诠释，首先必须找到老子思想的出发点，从而窥探老子整个思想体系的全貌，找出老子各种论述之间的逻辑关系。能做到这一点，就能根据它做出基本假设，选取定义，确定公理，为后面各篇的命题推理奠定基础。

中国古代向来有所谓的"尚中"精神，提倡中行、中道、中庸。它要求人们在待人处世、治国理政等社会实践中时时处处坚持适度原则，把握分寸，恰到好处，无过无不及，从而实现身心的协调、人与人的协调和整个社会的和谐。"中"的意思表示人类行为的质量，与"中正""正确""得当"等意思接近。如尧帝强调治理社会要"允执其中"（《论语·尧曰》），盘庚训导民众说"各设中于乃心"，周公倡行"中德"，并要求在折狱用刑时求"中正"等[1]；而《周易》里的"正中""刚中""得中""行中""中正""中行"等，亦是此义。

在公元前6世纪以后的几百年间，古希腊、以色列、古印度、古代中国等地先后出现了伟大的思想家如柏拉图、释迦牟尼、孔子等。这些先哲不约而同地提出了德性伦理的原则：以"中"为中心，强调"适中""适度"。亚里士多德的伦理学关键词是"中"（mean），在中文一般译为"中庸"和"中道"。毕达哥拉斯认

---

[1] 此三条分别见《尚书·盘庚》《尚书·酒诰》《尚书·吕刑》。

为"中庸"是一切事情的最佳境界，他在《金言》中指出："一切事情，中庸是最好的。"古希腊人有"凡事不要过度"的名言，亚里士多德也特别推崇"中道"和"适度"。而印度佛学大乘空观理论的基础——龙树的"中观论"，也在思想方法上提倡类似儒家的"执两用中"。龙树认为诸法之空性超越了一切观念，非有非无，泯灭一切分别，不可言说，乃是中道直觉之境。对之既不能执有，也不能执空，否则就会堕入"执有"或"执空"的"边见"。只有"遮破二边"，把"空""有"的执着都否定掉，才是中道。[1]

综观上述的"中"，笼统而言不外乎"认识之中""行为之中"，即在认识上不出现偏倚、行为上不走极端。但如同寻找一根线段的"中点"一样，所有对"中"的阐述都隐含着它的"两端"，没有两端，就无所谓"中"。而对于两端的不同认识，就会产生不同的"中"。

老子也提倡"中"，相关的论述有"至虚，恒也；守中，笃也""中气以为和""多言数穷，不如守中"等。但是对这个"中"，却有不同的理解。一种是把"守中"解释为"守冲"，就是保持一种虚静的心灵状态。另一种解释就是保持"中庸"："中，就是《中庸》中所说的'喜、怒、哀、乐之未发谓之中'的中，也就是道心的境界。'守中'就是保持道心之中庸的境界。对于道用的一动一静之间所具有的生发功能，无论用多少语言试图说明它或用多么高深的推测试图研究明白它，都不如保持在道心之中庸的境界而更能彻底地了解它。"[2] "多言数穷，不如守中。穷尽人类耳目观察，言语评述始终无法涵盖纷繁复杂的宇宙万象，倒不如守住道的能量本源化生万物这一根本。"[3] "俗话讲，有理不在言高，为政不在言多。政策出台过于频繁，会导致政策信号紊乱，百姓无所适从。大道'无名'也'无言'。如果管治者能按大道的自然法则守静、不言、无为、寡欲，社会自组织力量遵照大道的阴阳对立统一关系趋向平衡与'守中'。因为天地间有无穷的能量在不断地催生，少用政策干预，大道力量自动地反向运作将偏离的力量拉回正常轨道。"[4]

对于这两种不同的解释，我们暂不做过多的纠缠。其实还可以有一种理解，即"守冲"与"守中"并非毫无关联。在老子看来，保守虚静，方能得"中"，这

---

[1] 王路平：《略论龙树、提婆的中观哲学》，《浙江学刊》，2000年第3期。
[2] 冯家禄：《道德经三解》，北京：东方出版社，2013年，第36页。
[3] 王文明：《老子心声》，北京：九州出版社，2012年，第60页。
[4] 李国旺：《国学与新行为金融学——〈道德经〉行为策略启示录》，北京：中国金融出版社，2012年，第95页。

包括"中"的认识,"中"的作为;为此"守冲"与"守中"形成了"必由之径"与"必然结果"的联系。

事实上,还有不少人认为老子理论的核心就是"守中"。如赵俪生《儒道两家间存在争议的几种古籍之剖析》说,春秋时期,"当时大家都在谈'中'和'心'。孔子讲'时中',老子讲'守中';儒家讲'正心',道家讲'养心'(养成'金心')"[1]。张戬坤《圣贤智慧互通说》:"孔子讲'中庸',老子讲'守中',佛陀讲'中道',但'中'也不可执,执着'中'就将'中'作为一种极性观念而固定,那也是一种偏执。"[2]

吴重庆《儒道互补:中国人的心灵建构》一书说:"孔子讲时中,老子讲守中,释迦讲空中;如孔子讲一贯,老子讲得一,释迦讲归一,又因人同此'心',故每个人既可选择儒,又可选择道,亦可选择释,甚至儒道释可以同时选择。"[3]

那么,老子的"守中"意味着什么?这个"中"的两端在哪里?

在我们前面介绍的这些"中"之中,大多数的两端都设定在人间社会里。例如儒家之"中庸",就有"凡事不要过度"之意,而所谓的"事",基本上就是人间之事。只有佛教的"中观",它的两端分别设立在"天"和"人"之间。在这一点上,老子的"守中"有相似之处。首先,他力图从一体性来看整个世界,这个世界达到了人类认知、感觉和想象的极限,人类之外的天地万物和人间社会统统收罗其中,用来描述它的词语就是"道"和"自然"。

"自然"可谓是对"道"统辖范围内之万物运行状态、存在状态的最抽象描述,简言之就是从无到有,从有到无,浑然一体,不断演变。其次,他站在"道"的高度来看人类的一切,重点观察人类的自我认识和自我作为,这样就出现了认识的两端,即"道"的"全"和人的"偏"。也就是说,"道"是全面性和无限性的统一体,而"人"是片面性和有限性的统一体,"人"的认识和作为莫不如此。为此,老子的"中"就凸显出来了:人类的自我认识和自我作为必须做到"守中",即充分认识到自我的片面性和有限性、充分考虑到"道"的全面性和无限性。

论述到此,老子的"道""自然""有无"就可以进入人类社会,用来考察人类的认识和作为了。他的核心思想就是:人类在认识上、行为上保持"中"的态度,实现"自然"的状态,这才不会偏离"道"。

---

1 见曹峰编:《出土文献与儒道关系》,桂林:漓江出版社,2012年,第114页。
2 张戬坤:《圣贤智慧互通说》,北京:光大出版社,2010年,第272页。
3 吴重庆:《儒道互补:中国人的心灵建构》,广州:广东人民出版社,1993年,第281页。

第二章 定义，基本假设，公理
CHAPTER TWO: Definitions, Assumptions and Axioms

老子说"反者道之动"，其中的"反"有两层含义，一是"相反"的"反"，二是"复返"的"返"，意指往复回环的生命之道。通观《老子》所有的论述，皆会找出一般社会中认为是"正"的概念，而用"反"的概念来破除之，所谓"正言若反"。但是，他却又不执着于"反"，所谓的"反"不是通常意义上的"反"，其作用还是为了说明"中"的状态才是老子真正要描述的状态。

从层次上来看，老子的"破"和"立"大致分为两个层次：

第一层次是最抽象的"有"和"无"。老子认为，"道"是圆满而自足的，无所不包、无所不容的，而万物的生与灭，不过是"道"的一种体现形式，其运行的根本规律就是从无到有、从有到无、再从无到有，循环往复，生生不息，永无休止。从无到有，体现了"道"的无限可能性；而一旦变成了"有"，它的无限可能性就变成了有限性，因为在从"无"到"有"的过程中，也就被赋予了不全面的、偶然的、暂时的和难以长久的性质，人的认识和行为也是如此。

在这种情况下，人类在认识和行为上"守中"是必要的，这样才能自觉体现"道"又顾及人类的特性。具体而言，把握从"道"之"无"到生成万物之"有"的合适状态，就称为"守中"；实现这一状态，才算是常态，称为"常"（"恒"）；而属于人类的"常"（"恒"）是"自然"状态在人类社会中的个别体现。

第二层次是体现"道"的天地与"得道之一偏"的人类社会。人类相对于天地与"道"，其智慧、其能力是非常有限的，自诩为"万物之灵长"实在是狂妄自大而已。人类社会需要统治者，但统治者所能做的事情也是非常有限的，所谓国家之富、军事之强、功德之无量，与芸芸众生的自在自为乃至万物并作相比，都只是"偏功""偏德"而已。

从语言表述的角度来说，人类社会并没有创造出一套可供老子准确表达其"守中"思想的语言体系，这是因为人类一开始就专注于社会、专注于人本身，并不善于用"守中"的眼光认识世界，也就不可能用"守中"的语言去描述世界了。如此一来，就给老子表达他的思想造成了困难，也给我们准确理解老子的原意、准确转述他的论断造成了诸多困难。

就语言表述而言，老子只能选择"以破代立"的表达形式，而无法找到用来正面描述"守中"状态的词语。例如"道"，它是所有概念的综合体，在它那里"有"和"无"浑然一体，不断运动变化，有点像"宇宙"，它只能大致描述，而无法准确定义。又如"自然"，它描述的是一种万物自在自为的状态，而且什么状态都有，也没法准确定义。

而在人间社会里，他提倡"无为""不争""柔弱"，事实上，这并不是通常所说的"无所事事""一味退让""软弱无能"，而是一种不能用通常词汇来表达的状态。例如"无为"，并不是说要求人类一切无所作为，退回到蛮荒时代，而是说要求保持一种"有作为"和"无作为"的状态，其中"无作为"是为了更好地"有作为"，而"有作为"也包括"自己不作为以便让大家更好地作为"，还包括不要固执于偏于一隅的人类社会的"为"而要做出符合"道"的"为"；至于"不争""柔弱""素朴"，也可以同样理解。只有出现这种状态，才能做到"守中"，才算符合老子所说的"自然"。

在历史上，人们对老子的两种理解，就与这种语言表述方式有关。

一种是将老子的思想理解为"无"比"有"好，"弱"比"强"好，"朴"比"智"好。于是，统治者什么也不干，就比有所作为好；无德就比有德好，无功就比有功好，淳朴（甚至是愚蠢）就比聪明好，弱国就比强国好，放下武器就比加强军事好，等等。

这样老子就成了"反智主义者""反文明进步者""极度的消极厌世者"，等等。然而，如此就无法认识到《老子》一书在"无为"政治之后还描述了一种更理想的政治境界，在"无智"之后还描述了一种更为高明的智慧，在"不争"之后还描述了一种"莫能与之争"的强大境界。

另一种是将老子的思想理解为"辩证法"。"辩证法"一词源自古希腊，最初是指辩论的技巧，苏格拉底称之为"精神接生术"。但人们常说老子具有辩证思想，实际上是以马克思主义的唯物辩证法作为理论参照的。它主张用联系的、发展的、全面的观点来看待问题，基本内容包括：（1）三大规律：对立统一规律，质量互变规律，否定之否定规律；（2）五对基本范畴：原因与结果，形式与内容，现实与本质，必然性与偶然性，可能性与现实性。

人们说老子具有辩证思想，理由有三：

其一，老子揭示了"正与反的对立统一"。

老子提出了一系列正反的矛盾概念，如长与短、智与愚、巧与拙、大与小、高与下、前与后、生与死、难与易、进与退、古与今、始与终、正与反、美与恶、正与奇、敝与新、善与妖、强与弱、刚与柔、与与夺、胜与败、有与无、损与益、利与害、阴与阳、盈与虚、静与躁、张与歙、华与实、曲与全、枉与直、雌与雄、贵与贱、荣与辱、吉与凶、祸与福，等等。

老子认为，这些正反概念所揭示的矛盾双方并不是孤立的，而是相互依存的，每一方都以对方的存在作为自己存在的前提。所以他说:"天下皆知美之为美，斯恶已；皆知善之为善，斯不善已。有无相生，难易相成，长短相形，高下相盈，音声相和，前后相随。"(《老子》第二章)老子还认为，正反双方不仅相互依存，而且具有内在的统一性，所以要得到正面的结果，需要从反面去做。如其曰:"曲则全，枉则直，洼则盈，敝则新，少则得，多则惑。"(《老子》第二十二章)这就是所谓的"难易相成"。

其二，老子主张"反者道之动"。

老子不仅看到了对立面的普遍存在，而且看到事物的对立面会向相反的方面转化，由此他提出了"反者道之动"(《老子》第四十章)的命题，揭示了事物矛盾运动的这一普遍法则。对于这里的"反"字，一般有两种解释:一是"反"通"返"，返回复归之意，佐证如"万物并作，吾以观复。夫物芸芸，各复归其根"(《老子》第十六章)。二是相反、反面之反。"反者道之动"的意思就是事物向自己的反面转化，佐证如:"甚爱必大费，多藏必厚亡。"(《老子》第四十四章)"是以兵强则灭，木强则折。"(《老子》第七十六章)

其三，老子主张"柔弱胜刚强"。

在对待刚与柔、强与弱这些正反的对立面时，世人往往强调刚强的一面，认为这是正面的价值，老子则与之相反，他的价值取向是重视反面的意义，认为柔弱胜过刚强。所以他说:"人之生也柔弱，其死也坚强。草木之生也柔脆，其死也枯槁。故坚强者死之徒，柔弱者生之徒。是以兵强则灭，木强则折。强大处下，柔弱处上。"(《老子》第七十六章)"天下之至柔，驰骋天下之至坚。"(《老子》第四十三章)"天下莫柔弱于水，而攻坚强者莫之能胜，以其无以易之。弱之胜强，柔之胜刚，天下莫不知，莫能行。"(《老子》第七十八章)"守柔曰强"(《老子》第五十二章)。

以上就是人们用辩证法理解老子的基本观点。但是，这种理解总是难以面对以下质疑:

第一，老子说对立面会向相反的方面转，但不注重转化的条件性。

第二，"柔弱胜刚强"好像是由一些经验事实总结出的结论。人们可以提出其他一些经验事实，来得出相反的结论。如锋利的刀很容易割断柔弱的小草，类似的经验事实有很多，这样，人们是不是也可以得出一个"刚强胜柔弱"的结论?

第三，用辩证法解释老子的思想，从"正与反的对立统一"这一点看当然是合理的。但老子并不注重阐述正与反的差别。

如果从更广阔的视野来看，老子的思想很可能蕴含着高深的辩证法、彻底的辩证法。叶朗、朱良志认为：老子"反者道之动"里的"反"，有两层含义，一是"相反"的"反"，二是"复返"的"反"。两层意思又相互关联，反映出老子哲学的独特性。老子并不是强调事物的相反相成、互相转化，而是强调人们不能为相反而成的事物表象所遮蔽，要破除知识的妄见，契入往复回环的生命之道中。[1]这里，体现了老子的"守中"思想。

总而言之，一旦忽视了老子的"守中"，就会把老子放在反智、反文明、反人类的立场，会偏离与损害老子的思想价值。事实上，老子是一个建设性的思想家，他倡导建设人与自然和谐、人服从自然规律，并且人最终回归自然的理想社会。

二、公理化方法及其用于中华经典的诠释

古希腊哲学在方法论上有一个突出的特点，就是理性论证的原则。这就需要一些为人们所公认的出发点，这种最初公认的出发点就是"公理"（axiom），以后逐步发展成为公理化方法。公理化方法就是在尽可能少的基本假设、定义和公理的基础上，推导与证明出各种有意义的命题（亦称为定理），构成一个演绎系统。

在公理化体系中，基本假设是论述的前提，定义的作用是把公理、命题中所包含的核心概念加以清晰地描述，公理是不需要证明的共识。命题是从公理或其他已被证明的真命题出发，经过推导证明为正确的结论。

公理化方法是数学与系统科学经常采用的一种研究方法，它追求系统思维，证明严格明晰，富有逻辑力量。在公元前500年左右，人们已经从大量积累的实践中学会把一些图形的性质抽象为几何概念，以命题的形式研究其相互关系并进行推理论证。欧几里得运用公理化方法把几何命题整理起来，完成了数学史上的光辉著作《几何原本》。

牛顿在他的科学工作中经常运用公理化方法，体现他的光辉思想的《自然哲学的数学原理》一书，就是以公理化体系写成。爱因斯坦多次提出在物理学研究工作中也应当从少数几个基本假设及公理开始。他指出：近代科学的发展依赖于两种研究方法，一是公理化思维，二是可重复性实验。斯宾诺莎正是用公理化方法，写出了著名的哲学著作《伦理学》。总之，概念的清晰和逻辑的严谨，是公理

---

[1] 叶朗、朱良志：《中国文化读本》，北京：外语教学与研究出版社，2010年3月版，第12—13页。

化方法的优势，使之逐渐进入了数学以外的各种学科。

我们已经用公理化方法诠释了先秦儒家经典《论语》《孟子》和《荀子》。在这种诠释的应用中，我们发现公理化方法可以梳理出典籍的核心思想，有利于具有不同文化背景的人掌握经典的基本意思及其当代意义，并在一定程度上消除经典解释中的一些无谓的争论，从而在某些方面达成比较坚实的共识，对于中国传统文化的传承与传播具有基础性意义。

在诠释过程中，我们遇到了一些困难，也听到了一些疑问，主要集中于三方面：（1）人文科学领域的经典著作，能用"公理化方法"来诠释吗？（2）人文科学领域的经典著作，内涵丰富，用"公理化方法"来诠释，是不是会损害这种丰富性？（3）由于哥德尔不完全性定理，公理化方法自身也受到质疑，那么如何看待公理化诠释？

公理（axiom）一词，来源于古希腊语axioma，大概有三种意思：一是指有价值的事物，身价，名誉，地位；二是指认为合适的事物，决议，意图，目的；三是指哲学和数学上的自明之理或公理[1]。根据第三种意思，这是一个哲学和数学上的概念，在欧几里得的《几何原本》中得到很好的阐述。数学的产生是受到哲学推动的。当时的人论辩时，双方的论点乃基于某些大家都接纳的共识，这个共识也就是后来所说的公理。

在长期的研究过程中，我们发现对于人文领域的思想理论而言，只要它具备两个基本条件，就可以用公理化方法来研究：（1）著述者有自己的理论主张或独到的方法，足以贯穿他的整个思想体系；（2）论述时有主有次，能显出层次感，从主到次具有内在的逻辑关联性。当然，在研究的时候，不太适合用符号的形式来构建人文理论的框架，人文领域的抽象概括是一种综合性的抽象，比较适合用含义较为丰富的语言来描述。

用公理化来研究人文思想，都必须从一个层面、一个角度切入去抽绎它的内在体系，而不是、也不可能从所有层面、所有角度同时切入去观察它的内在体系。人文思想往往有一个综合性的架构，多种体系交叉并存。我们在用公理化方法研究经典的时候，关注的是它的主要思想体系。

在人们的印象中，像《论语》《孟子》《荀子》《老子》这类经典著作，内涵是很丰富的，历史上的各种注解众多（尤其是对于《老子》），而用"公理化方法"

---

1 罗念生、水建馥：《古希腊语汉语词典》，北京：商务印书馆，2010年版，第87页。

来诠释,是不是会损害这种丰富性?

对于这个问题,我们可以做两方面的分析。

第一,在《论语》和《老子》等经典中,往往一句话有多种解释。但人们在理解的过程中,只能取一种解释。至于别人问他为什么要取这种解释?则选取这种解释的人可以举出一大堆理由和证据,但他却没有办法证明这种选取是唯一合理的。由此一来,每个人都可以选取自己认为合理的一种解释,实际上等于在随心所欲地解读经典。

为此他人就可以问:"为什么要选取这些解释?"然而无限制的解释,表面上是丰富了经典的内涵,事实上对阅读者造成了极大的困难,就像摆在眼前的无数条路,还能起到指路的作用吗?公理化的诠释却不同。它必须做出唯一的选择,因为它跟整个思想体系构成逻辑关系。正因为具有明确的逻辑关系,阅读者从一句话中得到了启发,就可以从其他的话语中得到更多的启发,而且是从一个层面展开的系统性的启发。

第二,对于《论语》和《老子》这样的经典,一般的读者不乏敬畏之情,我们也不妨认为它们"字字千金""句句重要"。可是无限制的解释,往往造成了众多话语之间互相歧异、互相矛盾。如果全盘接受,那在读者脑海里留下的不过就是一大堆杂乱无章、互相冲突的印象,经典的作用也不过就是"以其昏昏、使人昏昏"而已。如果说"句句重要"的话语之中,也有特别重要、一般重要和不太重要的层次之分,那么无限丰富、无限可能的解释,恰好就不利于分清层次。

然而用公理化的方法诠释经典,就不得不特别关注经典的理论结构,就不得不把众多的论述安放在一个清晰的框架内。特别重要的观点或概念,应该是能统贯整个思想的;一般重要的观点或概念,是能在这个思想体系中统领一个方面的;具体的观点或阐述,是能找到其出发点和所依托的思想主体的。而经典的理论结构,又面向天地、面向人类,是自然现象、社会生活的总结和归纳,反过来又对社会生活起指导作用;它的丰富性、无限性就体现在这里,而不是体现在片言只语的丰富蕴含上。

以《老子》为例,我们首先要关注的就是老子思想的逻辑主线,这是老子的世界观和思想理论的基石。我们将老子思想的逻辑主线定位在"守中"上面,就是为了以严格的逻辑形式展开他的思想主干,将他的理论整理成一个演绎系统。

如果把人类赖以生存的外部世界统称为"天",人类和人间社会、人类的一切活动统称为"人",那么人类的认识和行为就总是在两个极端之间徘徊:一种是看到了人对天的依赖、天对人的制约,但没有看到人的作用和能力,可以叫作"蔽于天而不知人"；一种是看到了人的作用、强调人的能力，但没有看到天对人的制约、人对天的依赖，可以叫作"蔽于人而不知天"。

在前一种认识中，天就是神，就是佛，就是上帝，人在它面前毫无作为，只能顶礼膜拜；在后一种认识中，人就是自然的统治者，就是天地的征服者，就是全知全能的神。人类历史证明，无论偏向哪一个极端，都会造成严重的问题；而如果将这两个极端构成一对矛盾，则合理的状态就是保持矛盾之平衡的"守中"状态。老子思想的深刻之处，首先就在这里体现出来。

接下来老子就应当对天、地、人这一个大系统进行描述。他对天、地系统的描述，虽然很简要，但却达到了人类认知的极限。对于这个系统，他只能勉强称之为"道"，"道"囊括了一切事物的存在状态和运行规则。在"道"的统帅和滋养下，万物自在自为，自生自灭，从无到有，从有到无，不断演绎变化，而人类就是其中一个"产品"。如果说"道"是一棵参天大树，那么人类只不过是树枝上的一片树叶，他需要"道"给他定位，更需要"道"给他滋养。

正是因为对人类的深切关怀，才使老子不厌其烦地对人们谆谆教导。他认为，人类自身虽然是伟大的，但相比于"道"还是显得太渺小；人的作用是存在的，但时时刻刻需要"道"的滋养和校正。为此，他选择了"自然""有无"这些概念来对人类的认识和行为进行校正，由此出现了一系列的观点和理论。

他用"见素抱朴"来矫正人类之"智"的偏执，用"无为"来矫正人类对自我功劳的认识，用"玄德"来矫正人类对自我德行的标榜，用"弱"来矫正人类对"强"的迷信，用"寡欲"来矫正人类痴迷于自我欲望的疯狂行为，等等。得到矫正之后的人类行为方称得上是"自然"，得到矫正之后的人类认识方称得上是"守中"。

用老子的观点来观察人类行为，我们就可以看出它的指导意义了。人们通常痴迷于金钱、地位、名声，却忘了在欲火熏心的情况下，由"道"赋予自身的肉体、心灵已经受到了极大的戕害。当人间社会痴迷于科技、经济、军事的时候，却忘了由"道"赋予的芸芸众生已经处于不正常的生活状态。由此我们会想到，当人类还在继续前行的时候，是不是需要老子的思想来时时刻刻矫正我们的认识和行为？

在老子之后的两千多年中，人们往往一边说《老子》高深莫测、难以解读，或者可以有无限解读，一边又不断地阅读《老子》，接受它的影响。这样的做法，一方面无形中把《老子》"封杀"在金碧辉煌的神殿里，否认了它对人类社会的积极作用，另一方面又不加区别地接受《老子》的思想，不愿去反思它的长处和短处。

事实上，我们用公理化的方法解读《老子》，一方面展现了它的认识高度和深度，它对于人类文明的警示作用，另一方面又揭示了它的一些缺陷。从逻辑的角度来看，老子说"万物并作"也即万物的"自在自为"就是"自然"，那么人类的一切行为也就是万物的"自在自为"之一，也都是"自然"的。为什么他一方面肯定人类的一些行为（一般称为"正"），同时又否定人类的另一些行为（一般称为"奇"）？如果说被否定的这些人类行为（"奇"）不"自然"，背离了"道"，那么它们的根源又在哪里？是否在"道"之外还别有根源？如果在"道"之外还别有根源，那么"道"又何以称得上是"无所不包"？

这种逻辑上的缺陷是必须注意的。产生这种缺陷的根源就在于老子将"自然"描述为"万物并作"之时，注重"常态"的"万物并作"（"正"），而对"非常态"的"万物并作"（"奇"）则不够关注。若我们称前者为必然性，则后者为偶然性，而任何的"万物并作"都是必然性和偶然性的统一体。

"道"生万物是必然的，诞生出哪些形态和种类的万物，却是偶然的。人类社会也就在"奇""正"之变中不断交互运动。但老子对"奇"关注不够，于是将他的理论运用于社会实践时，就出现了论述上的一些偏差。例如在政治上，老子提倡"无为"，按照其"守中"的逻辑前提去理解，这实际上应该是"无为而无不为"。但老子强调说："我无为，而民自化；我好静，而民自正；我无事，而民自富；我无欲，而民自朴。"（《老子》第五十七章）

放在太平盛世来看，这种观点是很有道理的，但在战乱年代，就不见得正确了，因为这时候迫切需要统治者组织强大的军队来平定战乱。如果我们把战乱年代以及用武力平叛称为"奇"，把和平年代以及用不扰民的方式管理天下称为"正"，则老子的表述应当修订为"民未化而我有为，民自化而我无为"。

总之，如果将"守中"的原则贯穿到底，则人类应当在重视"正"的时候也善于正视"奇"，在保持"正"的时候也善于驾驭"奇"，在努力促成"奇"向"正"转化的时候，也善于发挥"奇"对"正"的积极作用。

最后，如何正确理解公理化方法以及哥德尔不完全性定理对它的质疑？

如前所述，公理化方法就是在必要的基本假设、定义和公理的基础上，推导与证明出各种有意义的命题（亦称为定理），以构成一个演绎系统。更加严格的公理化方法，则应归功于德国数学家希尔伯特，他在19世纪末明确给出了公理化方法在逻辑方面的要求和原则，即相容性、独立性和完备性。

（1）相容性是指在一个公理系统中，不允许证明某一命题的同时又能证明其否命题；（2）独立性是指在一个公理系统中，每一条公理都独立存在，不允许有的公理可以用其他公理推导出来；（3）完备性是指系统中的所有命题都能判断真伪，或理解成能从公理系统中推出体现其理论的全部命题。

1931年，德国数学家哥德尔提出了不完备性定理。他证明了任何一个形式系统，只要包括了简单的初等数论描述，而且是自洽的，它必定包含某些系统内所允许的方法既不能证真也不能证伪的命题。也就是说，公理化方法中的"相容性"和"完备性"是不能同时满足的! 这粉碎了希尔伯特关于公理化体系构建的信念，其影响远远超出了数学的范围。它不仅使数学、逻辑学发生革命性的变化，引发了许多富有挑战性的问题，而且还涉及哲学、语言学和计算机科学，甚至宇宙学。

但是，我们需要消除对哥德尔不完备性定理的误解。首先，该定理并不意味着任何有意义的公理系统都是不完备的。该定理需假设公理系统可以"定义"自然数，不过并非所有系统都能定义自然数，就算这些系统拥有包括自然数作为子集的模型。而欧几里得几何可以被一阶公理化为一个完备的系统（事实上，欧几里得的原创公理集已经非常接近于完备的系统）。

其次，要注意哥德尔不完全性定理只适用于较强的公理系统，有一些更弱的公理系统是相容而且完备的。在人文学科运用公理化方法而建立的系统，一般被认为是比较弱的公理系统。当我们试图对某一种学说（例如《论语》《孟子》《荀子》和《老子》）建立公理化系统时，其完备性中"推出体现该系统的所有命题"的要求往往难以达到，但是只要得出的命题涵盖这一学说的大部分内容，就可以在此基础上逐步完善。

三、从公理化的角度看"守中"与儒家"中庸"之区别

在采用公理化方法诠释先秦儒家经典时，我们从矛盾的分析出发，在此基础上建立基本假设，这不仅明确了研究的角度，也体现了公理化研究的需求。因为一个严格完善的公理系统对于公理的选取和设置，必须具备三个基本要求，第一个要求就是"相容性"，是指在一个公理系统中不允许同时能证明某一定理及其否定理。

反之，如果能从该公理系统中导出命题A和否命题非A（记作−A），从A与−A并存就说明出现了矛盾，而矛盾的出现归根到底是由于公理系统本身存在着矛盾的认识，这是思维规律所不容许的。因此，公理系统的无矛盾性要求是一个基本要求，任何学科与理论体系都必须满足这个要求。这就意味着，在诠释任何一种

思想理论的时候，从中抽绎出来的公理、命题，均不允许是相互矛盾的命题，也就是各个公理和命题之间，不能有模棱两可、无可无不可，甚至是互相否定的情况出现。

这一标准适用于公理，也就必然适用于从公理推导出来的全部命题，往上追溯也就是用于定义乃至于基本假设。如果在定义乃至于基本假设中出现了相互否定、相互冲突的现象，必定也会影响到由基本假设、定义、公理互相配合而推导出来的全部命题。由此可知，基本假设从矛盾的分析出发，进而将矛盾具体化，并借助于定义、公理，谈论更加具体的矛盾问题，既是对先秦儒家经典之思想体系进行解码的一种路径，也从一开始就贯彻了"公理的相容性"这一原则。

从"矛盾"的角度来看，先秦儒家经典的特色在于追求"矛盾的中庸状态"。按照辩证法的观点，矛盾是一种客观存在，矛盾的对立双方相互依存，矛盾从事物生成时就有了，直到事物本身的消亡。由此可知，矛盾的彻底解决意味着事物的消亡，在事物存续期间矛盾是不能被"彻底解决"的，但却可以达成一种动态平衡。

这一点也可以从辩证法的观点中推导出来。一般说来，事物的矛盾关系大致可以归结为三种状态：（1）无矛盾；（2）矛盾冲突尖锐，以至于不可调和；（3）处于相对协调状态。由"矛盾是事物固有的特性"可知，第一、第二种情况均不属于某一种事物存在期间的状态。从这个意义上来看，儒家追求"矛盾的中庸状态"，体现了人类借助于自己的智能对客观规律的一种自觉的把握。

事实上，我们也可以把"无矛盾""矛盾不可调和"看作事物存在的两个极端。如果把"无矛盾"看作是一种事物尚未产生之前的矛盾关系状态，则可以把"矛盾不可调和"看作是事物消亡之际的矛盾关系状态。假如将"事物"具体设定为"人类社会"，则上述推论也是成立的。

反言之，在人类社会这种特殊"事物"的存续期间，"无矛盾""矛盾不可调和"这两种绝对现象都是不存在的，而"矛盾的中庸状态"则是长期存在的。它是一种客观存在的状态，但也可以是一种主观自觉追求的结果。

然而，从不同的角度看待不同的矛盾关系，却可以看出人类社会这种特殊的现象乃是由众多的矛盾关系所构成的。囿于人类认知，我们观察到的矛盾关系总是有限的，由此建立不同的思想理论，也就因为观察角度的不同，可以得出不同的结论。而以孔子为代表的儒家和以老子为代表的道家，也因为对矛盾的观察角度不同，形成了不同的思想面貌。

关于儒道的区别，历来有许多阐述，但很难形成定论。李泽厚先生认为："表面看来，儒、道是离异而对立的，一个入世，一个出世；一个乐观进取，一个消极退避；但实际上它们刚好相互补充而协调。"[1]

又有人认为："道家主张复归于自然无为的社会状态，在原始的混沌中保持与维护人的纯真本性。老庄哲学、特别是庄子，倾向于以个体否定群体，以追求个体自我的精神自由为根本情趣。儒家则对自然往往抱有某种政治伦理上的功利主义态度，他们依据自己对自然的理解，来谋划一种君臣、父子、夫妇各安其分的宗法等级结构，主张人类社会的这种秩序体现着自然之道，因而是合理的、必然的。"[2]

简言之，就是儒家讲入世，道家讲出世；儒家讲个性修养，道家讲天性放纵。这两种观点具有代表性。但是，从社会矛盾的角度来看，这些观点还是值得商榷的。其一，道家与儒家，都具有强烈的批判世俗的精神，都看到了各种"欲望"所引起的纷争乃是社会问题、社会矛盾的焦点。

其二，道家与儒家，也都积极提出了解决社会问题的主张。儒家认为，若对欲望不加任何控制和调节，则会引起众多的社会纷争，导致社会的无序和混乱状态，为此就要提倡个体的修养，用"仁义礼智"来调节人的欲望与言行。

这种理论凸显了儒家所观察到的矛盾双方，一方是人的欲望，一方是社会的有道状态。他们主张把这一对矛盾调整到"中庸状态"，以防出现极端的"无道状态"，给民生带来严重的灾难。道家则认为，欲望出于天性，在"自然"的状态下，它是不会引起问题的；而人类偏离自然之道，人为制造了很多东西来刺激人的欲望，这样社会就乱了。

一方面用功名利禄、难得之货来刺激人的欲望和追求，一方面又要人们控制自己的欲望，这实际上形成了一种悖论。因此，还不如"不见可欲"使人做到自然"无欲""寡欲"，使之合乎自然之道，就用不着花那么大的力气来调节人们的欲望，人们也就完全可以任天而行了。

这凸显了老子所观察到的"矛盾双方"，一方是"自然之道"，一方是违背"自然之道"的社会欲望以及管理社会欲望的方法和制度。提倡"守中"，就是用"道"来审视人的社会欲望以及管理欲望的方法，消除它的偏颇，回归到"自然"的状

---

1 李泽厚：《美学三书》，天津：天津社会科学院出版社，2003年，第49页。
2 高晨阳：《阮籍评传》，见匡亚明主编《中国思想家评传丛书》，南京：南京大学出版社，2011年，第137页。

态，恢复社会的正常秩序。

从这个层面来看，老子也渴望人类社会的理想状态，并不主张人们恣意放纵自己的行为，也不希望看到天下大乱的状态，他只是追求一种类似于儒家的"随心所欲不逾矩"境界而已。因为在他看来，在合乎"自然"的状态下，人们的"随心所欲"是不会产生社会问题的。由此看来，老子对人类社会具有高度的关注之情和浓重的责任感，虽称为"出世"，但要说他撒手不管人间之事，这显然是不妥当的。

对孔子及老子思想进行公理化研究，就必然会涉及他们观察社会矛盾的不同角度。而上述的比较，也就呈现了儒家之"中庸"与道家之"守中"的不同之处。

其一，儒家之"中庸"、道家之"守中"，在层次及应用范围上是不同的。陈鼓应先生认为："老、孔为同一文化传统的继承者，所以他们的思想有颇多相似处，例如：（1）守中的观点，（2）以和为贵的心态——人和自然的和谐关系。"[1]

老子的思想体系和中庸的哲学基础与方法论具有同构性，而老子的守中思想和孔子的中庸之道都主张用中，反对过与不及，都主张以守中或中庸的方式把握矛盾双方的对立统一及其转化，以掌握正确认识世界和处理问题的根本。从这一点来说，守中与中庸是相似的。

然而，守中与中庸的层次是不同的，差异很大。一般说来，老子的守中思想，涵盖了天道与人事、自然与社会的所有方面，而孔子为代表的儒家中庸之道则多集中于道德与政治等人事方面，可以认为中庸之道是老子守中思想在道德和政治等人事领域的应用和发展。

作为方法论来说，中庸之道更多充满经世致用的色彩。儒家之"中庸"着眼于人类社会的内部矛盾，他们指出的"欲望""纷争"是人的欲望，是社会的纷争，而"有道状态"也是人类社会的有道状态。

而道家之"守中"所着眼的人类社会与天地自然（即人类所处的外部世界）的矛盾，是一种"内外矛盾"。他们指出人类的"欲望"并不全然是人的特性，更大程度上还体现了天地自然的"规定性"，而人们对此缺乏宏观的认识，因而在看待欲望、驾驭欲望以及处理欲望的社会行为上出现了偏差。

也就是说，对外部世界认识不足，对自身的自然属性认识不足，导致了治理社会时的种种偏差。研究者认为，老子的"不如守中"的"中"，是指遵守客观存

---

[1] 陈鼓应：《老庄新论》，北京：商务印书馆，2008年，第35页。

在于天地之间的万事万物所蕴含的宇宙总规律，万事万物发展过程中最原始本真的中庸状态，"中"的状态实质上也就是老子"道"的状态。因为宇宙、天地本身即是一个大中和，违反中和，天地尚且不能存在，何况于人类？世界中和不是人为的中间路线，或任意的调和、折中，而是天地的自然作为。[1]

基于对人类社会的不同视角，孔子和老子提出了不同的治理社会的主张。孔子主张的可以说是一种"自我平衡法"：病根子出在人类身上，手术刀也掌握在人类手上，人们只有靠自我修养、调节欲望，才能化解纷争，管理好人间社会。

而老子主张的可以称为是一种"自然平衡法"，因为从自然的角度来看，人类的"病症"严格来说并非真病，而是人类误以为它是一种病态，并施加了不恰当的治疗或实施了"过度治疗"。只要认识自然之道，按照它的法则和规律行事，就不会误以为人类有"病症"，而这种臆想出来的"病症"也不会带来致命的后果。相比之下，反倒是不恰当的治疗会给人类带来损害。

说到底，如同其他生物种群一样，人类社会也受一种"自然的平衡法则"所支配。这种"自然的平衡法则"是根本性的，作用更大，而人类"自我的平衡法则"只不过起到修修补补的作用。如果过于夸大人类"自我的平衡法则"，忽视乃至于破坏了"自然的平衡法则"，那将给人类带来灾难。而从层次来看，人类的"自我平衡法则"与其他生物种群的"自我平衡法则"，也都是要接受"自然平衡法则"驾驭的。

其二，从辩证法的角度来看，守中与中庸思想在阐述矛盾关系时，各有其优点和不足。以往的研究者也曾注意到守中与中庸思想的区别。研究者认为，老子的守中思想比儒家的中庸之道更注重矛盾的对立和相互转化，前者是辩证的、积极的，后者虽有辩证的因素，却也存在消极的成分。从本质上说，老子的守中思想更倾向于动态的和谐，强调世界的变动性及矛盾的转化和发展，主张通过不断地更新和斗争，达到更高层次的和谐。

而中庸之道对和谐的追求更多在静态的层面。"中庸"观虽有合理处理矛盾、保持和谐稳定的长处，但它忽略了对立面的斗争与转化，看不到事物的自我否定和质变，这是"中庸"观的主要缺陷。儒家把中庸之道所包含的合理因素加以绝对化，过分看重矛盾双方统一的一面而对其对立的特点及相互转化重视不足。在新旧制度更替时显得尤为突出，此时中庸之道带有一定的"守成"色彩。它虽然

---

[1] 史德新：《论老子守中思想与孔子中庸之道的异同》，《求索》，2010年第5期。

也承认发展，却并不主张发展就要超出量的限度，一如它虽然也承认矛盾，却力图使矛盾斗争保持在一定范围内。这样一种形而上学的痼疾，终究使它的辩证法大打折扣。这实际上反映了传统中庸思想辩证法精神的不彻底性。[1]

张岱年先生说："中庸的观念认为凡事都有一个标准，也就是一个限度，超过这个限度和达不到这个限度是一样的。这里包含对立面相互转化的观点，这是正确的。但是中庸观念又要求维护这个标准，坚持这个限度，防止向反面转化，没有促进发展变化的观点，这是中庸思想的局限。

"在日常生活中，确实需要无过无不及，如饮食衣着之类。但科学的发展有时需要突破传统观念，社会的进步更需要打破传统的束缚。在这些问题上，中庸观念就成为前进的阻碍了。我们现在要对中庸观念进行全面的分析。"[2]

其实，从"动态与辩证""静态与不够辩证"去谈"守中"与"中庸"的区别，未必能切中要害，而且带有用"斗争""发展"等眼光来评判的痕迹。事实上，中庸观念的不足主要跟它孤立地看待矛盾这一点有关。

按照辩证法的观点，矛盾不是孤立的，各种矛盾虽有主次之分，但它们之间是相互作用、相互关联的。按照宋儒的说法，儒家思想讲的主要就是"内圣"和"外王"，但内圣与外王的有机结合，总是显然不够紧密。我们在做先秦儒家经典的公理化研究时，也总是感觉到两者之间的逻辑关系显得不够顺畅自然。

儒家在谈个人修养时从个体的内在动机去找矛盾，等于是将"性善""性恶"作为矛盾的双方，这是合理的，但孤立地看待这一矛盾则是有问题的。按照马克思的观点，人是一切社会关系的总和，为此"性善""性恶"之矛盾与一切社会关系、现实生活的矛盾是交织在一起的，其他各种矛盾对"性善""性恶"之矛盾起到很大的作用，影响这一对矛盾的表现状态和发展状态。但儒家对这一点显然考虑不足，致使从"内圣"到"外王"缺乏紧密的逻辑关系。

因为"内圣"很大程度上并没有介入现实生活的种种矛盾，而"外王"则必须介入现实生活的种种矛盾，这等于是从单一矛盾出发来解决复杂矛盾，自然就不好处理了。儒学发展到宋明理学阶段，给人的感觉是专注于"内圣"，基本上抛弃了"外王"，或者说对"外王"的讨论显然有些虚无缥缈，就与上述的理论缺陷有关。反过来看，由于对现实生活的矛盾考虑不足，对人性之矛盾的讨论也就显

---

[1] 史德新：《论老子守中思想与孔子中庸之道的异同》，《求索》，2010年第5期。
[2] 张岱年：《中国古典哲学概念范畴要论》，北京：中国社会科学出版社，2000年，第179—180页。

得越发抽象了。

相比之下，老子的守中思想不存在孤立地看待矛盾这一问题。因为在守中思想之中，矛盾的双方分别是"自然之道"与"人类社会之偏"，实质上也是"无限性"和"有限性"的矛盾，两者其实就是无数矛盾的复合体，都不是单一性质的矛盾，已经把矛盾的总和考虑进来，自然就不会有孤立看待矛盾的问题了。就这一点来说，体现了"守中"的高明之处。

但是，老子的"守中"也难免有所疏忽。胡适指出："道家的流弊在于信天太过，以为人事全无可以为力之处，势必造成一种听天安命、靠天吃饭的恶劣心理。"[1] 后世的道教迷信画符念咒、吞刀吐火之术，表面看起来与道家思想关系不大，实际上也有"通天就可以出神入化、无所不为"的思想认识在内。从矛盾的对立统一关系来看，这是过于强调矛盾的对立关系而不注重其统一关系所造成的。

事实上，"自然之道"和人类社会是存在对立关系的，人类社会也的确有一意孤行、偏离自然之道的表现。但是，人类社会和"自然之道"本身又有统一关系，或者不由自主地按照"自然之道"去作为（任天而为），或者自觉地按照"自然之道"去作为（如遵循四季变化安排农业生产），并非总是一意孤行。

具体而言，人类的一切作为，如政治、军事、经济、文化等，也总是具有体现"自然之道"的一面，由此抽象出来的功业、道德等，并不是完全脱离"自然之道"而纯属人造的概念。上述这一切，鲜明体现了人类社会与自然之道的统一关系。

老子强调人类认知与行为之偏而努力纠正之，为此也就在很大程度上忽略了人类社会与自然之道的统一关系，结果造成了听天安命、靠天吃饭的心理，否定了人类认识并掌握自然规律、顺应自然规律的积极作为，给人造成一种反文明、反社会、反科学技术的印象。从这一点来看，老子的"守中"又不如高度重视人类作为的儒家"中庸"思想了。

四、《老子》的公理化诠释之框架

用公理化的方法诠释《老子》，提炼出道家思想的内在逻辑体系，是将《老子》众多语句整理成一个演绎系统，即在给出一些定义和基本假设以后，形成若干公理，并以逻辑推理的方法，推导和证明众多蕴含在《老子》中反映道家思想的系

---

[1] 胡适:《〈淮南子〉的哲学》,《胡适文集》（第1卷），广州：花城出版社，2013年，第183页。

列命题，从而将隐含在《老子》中的道家思想的逻辑体系凸显出来。

我们在给出定义、基本假设和公理的基础上，把《老子》的内容分为四个部分，分别是"明道篇""贵德篇""良治篇""摄生篇"，对每一篇的命题（定理）和推论进行梳理与论证，并作相应的例证与说明。它们是一个有机整体，各篇内部也有其内在严密的逻辑关系，图示如下：

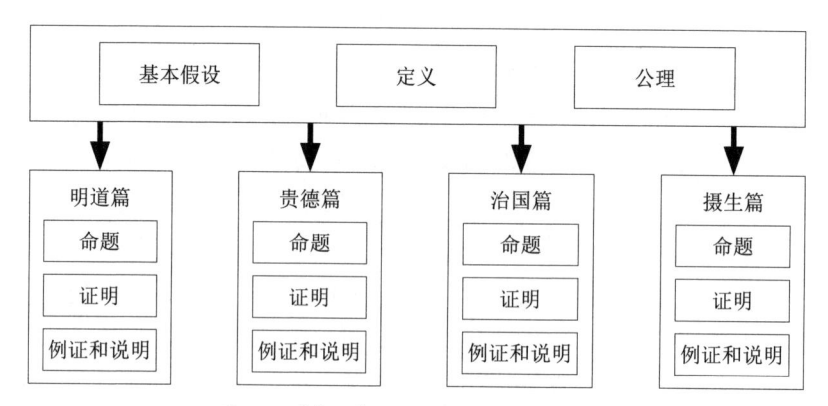

```
┌─────────┐    ┌─────────┐    ┌─────────┐
│ 基本假设 │    │  定义   │    │  公理   │
└────┬────┘    └────┬────┘    └────┬────┘
     │              │              │
     ▼              ▼              ▼
┌─────────┐  ┌─────────┐  ┌─────────┐  ┌─────────┐
│ 明道篇  │  │ 贵德篇  │  │ 治国篇  │  │ 摄生篇  │
│ ┌─────┐ │  │ ┌─────┐ │  │ ┌─────┐ │  │ ┌─────┐ │
│ │命题 │ │  │ │命题 │ │  │ │命题 │ │  │ │命题 │ │
│ └─────┘ │  │ └─────┘ │  │ └─────┘ │  │ └─────┘ │
│ ┌─────┐ │  │ ┌─────┐ │  │ ┌─────┐ │  │ ┌─────┐ │
│ │证明 │ │  │ │证明 │ │  │ │证明 │ │  │ │证明 │ │
│ └─────┘ │  │ └─────┘ │  │ └─────┘ │  │ └─────┘ │
│┌───────┐│  │┌───────┐│  │┌───────┐│  │┌───────┐│
││例证和 ││  ││例证和 ││  ││例证和 ││  ││例证和 ││
││说明   ││  ││说明   ││  ││说明   ││  ││说明   ││
│└───────┘│  │└───────┘│  │└───────┘│  │└───────┘│
└─────────┘  └─────────┘  └─────────┘  └─────────┘
```

图一　《老子》公理化诠释逻辑关系结构图

"明道篇"共有21个命题，主要是说明老子关于"道"的基本概念，以及人如何才能认识或体悟"道"，其中P1-1至P1-10，说明了道自身以及道与万物的关系；P1-11至P1-16，说明了人的两种认知或体悟状态"智"和"明"以及相互关系；P1-16至P1-21，说明了体悟"道"的路径、方法和步骤。

"贵德篇"共有23个命题，主要阐述顺应自然之德，以及修德之方、修德之用。P2-1至P2-3指出顺应自然方为德，以及如何做到这种德；P2-4至P2-10重点阐述贪欲、智巧为修德之害，而淡化两者的方法为知足、处下、柔弱、不争等；P2-11至P2-13阐述圣人之表象与心智状态；P2-14至 P2-23阐述实践"德"的诸多方面。

"治国篇"共有28个命题，主要论述遵循自然的治国之道。P3-1至 P3-2论述合乎自然、圣人引领的社会是理想社会；P3-3至P3-5阐述有道社会的特征是和谐自然，百姓安居乐业，无须礼法；P3-6至P3-8 讨论良治的基本模式、表现及其实施；P3-9至 P3-16指出治国方式是循道、循古，不可崇尚智慧、贤能、仁义、礼法、功德、奇货等；P3-17至 P3-24指出在用兵、外交、为君、行政、治民等方面均要遵循"守柔"之道；P3-25至P3-28指出君主的修养在于刚柔并济、修德修信。

"摄生篇"共有22个命题,主要阐述如何实现关爱自我生命与关爱他人生命的统一,而真正实现这一点必须以"自然"为原则。命题P4-1指出,根本原则是效法自然;命题P4-2至P4-6论述如何保持虚静、淡薄、淳厚的心境以及淡化自我的嗜欲,以之作为效法自然的基础;命题P4-7至P4-10指出基于自然原则的财富观,以及如何正确对待财富与生命的关系;命题P4-11至P4-14指出基于自然原则的祸福荣辱观,以知足不辱、为而不恃为核心;命题P4-15至P4-19指出基于自然原则的强弱论、争与不争、巧拙论;命题P4-20至P4-22指出个体与万物共生的原则。

我们可用树形图来描绘《老子》的公理化体系之框架,其中树的根部代表定义、基本假设,主树干代表公理,主枝代表根据基本假设及公理演绎推导出来的命题,分枝代表由命题演绎推导出来的推论,而枝叶代表与命题和推论相关的例证及说明。

图二 《老子》公理化诠释逻辑关系树形图

五、定义及其说明

这里提出相关定义的要求是:它们来自《老子》中的重要概念,符合《老子》的原意和当时的语境,并具有当代词语内涵的概括性。

1. 德

"德"是万物自在自为过程的总称,也指人对此过程的认识以及顺应此过程的品行。

【参见《老子》条目】

孔德之容，惟道是从。（第二十一章）

故从事于道者，同于道；德者，同于德；失者，同于失。同于德者，道亦德之；同于失者，道亦失之。（第二十三章）

知其雄，守其雌，为天下溪。为天下溪，常德不离，复归于婴儿。知其白，守其辱，为天下谷。为天下谷，常德乃足，复归于朴。朴散则为器，圣人用之，则为官长。故大制不割。（第二十八章）

上德不德，是以有德；下德不失德，是以无德。（第三十八章）

上德若谷……广德若不足。（第四十一章）

道生之，德畜之，物形之，势成之。是以万物莫不尊道而贵德。道之尊，德之贵，夫莫之命而常自然。故道生之，德畜之，长之育之，亭之毒之，养之覆之。生而不有，为而不恃，长而不宰，是谓玄德。（第五十一章）

含德之厚，比于赤子。（第五十五章）

常知稽式，是谓玄德。玄德深矣，远矣，与物反矣，然后乃至大顺。（第六十五章）

说明：《庄子·天地》说："物得以生，谓之德。"德指万物自在自为的过程。这个过程可描述为从"无"到"有"再到"无"，而不只是单从"无"到"有"。《老子》第二十一章说："孔德之容，惟道是从。"这描述了从"无"到"有"，道生无，无生有，有生万物。第五十五章说："含德之厚，比于赤子。"这描述了再从"有"到"无"，赤子、婴儿等都是"无"的意象。

人是具有认识能力的，能够认识到这个过程并顺应这个过程，这就是人的"德"。在《老子》文本中常将人的此种"德"称为"上德""孔德""玄德""常德"和"恒德"等。人的"德"突出体现在可以认识并主动顺应"德"。第二十八章说："知其雄，守其雌，为天下溪。为天下溪，常德不离。常德不离，复归于婴儿。知其白，守其辱，为天下谷。为天下谷，常德乃足。常德乃足，复归于朴。"这里强调了"常德"是知雄守雌，复归婴儿，就是对"德"的从"无"到"有"再到"无"的认识和顺应。同样，第五十一章和第六十五章也是在说明此意。

2. 欲

"欲"指人对财富、名声和权力的追求，这种追求可能违背"自然"。

第二章 定义，基本假设，公理
CHAPTER TWO: Definitions, Assumptions and Axioms

【参见《老子》条目】

不尚贤，使民不争；不贵难得之货，使民不为盗；不见可欲，使民心不乱。是以圣人之治，虚其心，实其腹，弱其志，强其骨。常使民无知无欲。使夫智者不敢为也。为无为，则无不治。（第三章）

见素抱朴，少私寡欲。（第十九章）

道常无为而无不为。侯王若能守之，万物将自化。化而欲作，吾将镇之以无名之朴。无名之朴，夫亦将不欲。不欲以静，天下将自正。（第三十七章）

咎莫大于欲得，祸莫大于不知足。故知足之足，常足矣。（第四十六章）

是以圣人欲不欲，不贵难得之货。（第六十四章）

说明：如果说道和万物（包括人）的自在自为过程是一个"自然"过程，那么人为什么会变得不"自然"呢？这是因为"人"有"欲"，且人的"欲"（对于富、名声和权力）可能违背"自然"。

老子并不主张"去欲"，而是主张"少欲"，这说明老子并非完全否定一切对财富、名声和权力的追求，而是否定可能导致不"自然"的过分追求。老子在绝大多数场合谈到的"欲"是特指那种将导致不"自然"的"欲"，包括"尚贤"（也就是追求名声）、"贵难得之货"（也就是追求财富）、"有为"（也就是追求权力）。

3. 智

"智"的一般意义指人对对象的认识能力和对个人行为的抉择能力，也特指人为满足"欲"的过分追求而产生的那种机巧智慧。后者往往对统治者而言。

【参见《老子》条目】

天下皆知美之为美，斯恶已；皆知善之为善，斯不善已。（第二章）

常使民无知无欲。使夫智者不敢为也。（第三章）

绝智弃辩，民利百倍。（第十九章）

说明：老子并不反对一般意义上的"智"，而是反对那种机巧智慧。这种智慧与人的"欲"的过分追求密切相关，或者说就是为了满足过分欲望而形成的智慧。所以，老子劝说"无知无欲"。《老子》第六十五章还说："古之善为道者，非以明民，将以愚之。民之难治，以其智多。故以智治国，国之贼；不以智治国，国之福。"管理民众就是不让民众有"智"，管理者自身也不以"智"治国。

4. 观，明

"观"是人知"道"的途径；"明"是人的内在生命力的自我观照能力。

【参见《老子》条目】

故常无，欲以观其妙；常有，欲以观其徼。（第一章）

致虚极，守静笃。万物并作，吾以观复。夫物芸芸，各复归其根。归根曰静，静曰复命。复命曰常，知常曰明。（第十六章）

知人者智，自知者明。（第三十三章）

见小曰明，守柔曰强。（第五十二章）

故以身观身，以家观家，以乡观乡，以邦观邦，以天下观天下。吾何以知天下然哉？以此。（第五十四章）

说明："观"是人知"道"的途径，也是达到"明"境的途径。老子对于"观"提出了一些角度和暗示，但没有详细说明"观法"，因此，老子的"观"带有一定的神秘感。"观"不是靠五官实现的，而是靠"心"的感知、体认等手段实现的，但与局限于人类之"有"的感知、体认、分析、思考形成本质上的区别。"明"是老子特别提出的一个概念，以区别"智"。它也是人能真正悟道这一认识能力的保证。

5. 静

"静"是涤除了过分的"欲"与机巧性的"智"的干扰而达到的内心澄明状态。

【参见《老子》条目】

虚其心，实其腹，弱其志，强其骨。（第三章）

致虚极，守静笃。万物并作，吾以观复。夫物芸芸，各复归其根。归根曰静，静曰复命。复命曰常，知常曰明。（第十六章）

说明："虚"就是"无"，到达虚的极致就是感悟到"道"的无限可能性。人的领悟和认识能力如果能达到如此，便是"静"。因此，"静"是特指人内在的"无"。

6. 身

"身"指人的内在生命力与外在欲望的统一体。

【参见《老子》条目】

是以圣人后其身而身先，外其身而身存。非以其无私邪？故能成其私。（第七章）

功遂身退，天之道也。（第九章）

载营魄抱一，能无离乎？（第十章）

宠辱若惊，贵大患若身。（第十三章）

欲先民，必以身后之。（第六十六章）

第二章　定义，基本假设，公理
CHAPTER TWO: Definitions, Assumptions and Axioms

说明：老子对人的认识分为两个方面：内在生命力和外在欲望，这两个方面的统一就是人。由于人是万物之一，因此这两个方面与"无"和"有"的概念是对应的，内在生命力精微，但充满力量，这就是"无"；外在欲望是身体感官的功能，这就是"有"。从人的认识角度说，内在生命力体现为"明"；外在欲望表现为"智"。不过，在阅读《老子》时需要注意的是，老子在某些地方谈到"身"侧重指内在生命力，如第十三章的"贵身"的说法；在某些地方侧重指"外在欲望"，例如第六十六章的"欲先民，必以身后之"，这里的"身"指个人欲望，也就是说，统治者想居民之上必先将自己的欲望放在民的欲望之后。其实，这种"后其身"的说法根本上依然是贵身，因为统治者需要更注重"内在生命力"的澄明，这才是真正的"贵身"。虽然欲望是不能消除的，但"贵身"不是贵欲望的满足。

7. 无私

"无私"指消除过分的"欲"和机巧性的"智"之后而达到的能包容万物的心理状态。

【参见《老子》条目】

天地不仁，以万物为刍狗，圣人不仁，以百姓为刍狗。（第五章）

是以圣人后其身而身先，外其身而身存。非以其无私邪？故能成其私。（第七章）

见素抱朴，少私寡欲。（第十九章）

是以圣人常善救人，故无弃人；常善救物，故无弃物。（第二十七章）

说明：人是万物之一，是"有"，因此就是"可名"的，只要人用自己的智去"名"，就意味着划分界限，这种界限对于人来说就是亲疏尊卑的表现。因此，儒家重视"正名"其目的也就是确立等级秩序。老子认为这种"名"是必要的，可以告诉我们行动的界限，但不是至高无上的，我们必须回到"无"，回到本初状态，才能真正不让这种界限成为生命力的束缚。消除过分欲望和技巧性智慧后而达到的能包容万物的心理状态就是"道"的状态。所以，圣人与"道"一样，以百姓为刍狗而无偏爱，这其实也是为了保存和尊重百姓那质朴的生命力不至于被扭曲。

8. 功

"功"指万物的自在自为状态，也指人自觉维护符合"自然"的社会秩序的活动。

【参见《老子》条目】

功成而弗居。（第二章）

功遂身退，天之道也。（第九章）

功成事遂，百姓皆谓我自然。（第十七章）

自伐者无功。（第二十四章）

说明："功"在一般意义上与"德"是对应的概念。"功"者，"德"也。对于人的"功"来说，由于人有认知能力，能主动去顺应自然，因此，人的"功"还着重强调了这种自觉活动。正是这种自觉的顺应"自然"的活动表明那些"居功""自伐"者由于违背自然而"无功"。

9. 圣人

"圣人"指有"德"的治国者。

【参见《老子》条目】

是以圣人处无为之事，行不言之教。（第二章）

是以圣人为腹不为目，故去彼取此。（第十二章）

是以圣人执一为天下式。（第二十二章）

圣人不积，既以为人己愈有，既以与人己愈多。（第八十一章）

说明："圣人"是老子提出的理想的治国者。这样的统治者能够认识到自然之过程，并努力地、自觉地在治国中顺应"自然"。

10. 无为

"无为"指顺应"自然"不刻意作为，更不妄为的行动原则。

【参见《老子》条目】

是以圣人处无为之事，行不言之教。（第二章）

为无为，则无不治。（第三章）

爱民治国，能无为乎？（第十章）

我无为，而民自化。（第五十七章）

为无为，事无事，味无味。（第六十三章）

说明：老子认为"道法自然""归根曰命"，"自然"就是万物的"命"。所以老子所谓的"命"与"原初状态"是一个意思。具有欲望和智慧的人脱离不开万物，因此，人的行动原则当然就是顺应"自然"。然而，"无为"不意味人没有行动，也不意味人可以不需要任何思考，像动物一样行动，而是将可能违背自然的刻意行动和妄加行动排除在有意义的行为之外。

11. 不争

"不争"指消除了过分的"欲"和机巧性的"智"后而形成的处世态度。

【参见《老子》条目】

不尚贤，使民不争；不贵难得之货，使民不为盗；不见可欲，使民心不乱。（第三章）

上善若水。水善利万物而不争，处众人之所恶，故几于道。（第八章）

夫唯不争，故天下莫能与之争。（第二十二章）

天之道，利而不害；人之道，为而不争。（第八十一章）

说明：老子认为"道"可"无"，表面上好像很"柔弱"，但精微处充满力量。万物都是自然的，没有被强迫，但却总是有着源源而来的活力。"不争"的处世态度就是对此的反应。"不争"不是退却、懦弱和胆小，反而是更有内在的力量。当欲望过分追求外在的财富、权力和名声，而"智"为满足这种追求却丧失了回归"无"的能力时，人不是变得更强大，而是变得更脆弱了，因为这个时候我们丧失了那充满力量的内在生命力，堵塞了滋养生命力的源泉。

12. 言

"言"指治国者的政令教化。

【参见《老子》条目】

是以圣人处无为之事，行不言之教。（第二章）

多言数穷，不如守中。（第五章）

不言之教，无为之益，天下希及之。（第四十三章）

知者不言，言者不知。（第五十六章）

天之道，不争而善胜，不言而善应，不召而自来，繟然而善谋。（第七十三章）

说明："道"不可名，也不可言；其实不需名，也不需言。治国者的"言"更要慎重，多言可能伤害百姓的"自然"，所以老子主张"贵言"，甚至"不言"。

13. 慈，俭

"慈"指柔和而不激烈的博爱品质，"俭"指坚韧而不孤傲的节制品质。

【参见《老子》条目】

绝伪弃诈，民复孝慈。（第十九章）

治人事天，莫若啬。（第五十九章）

我有三宝，持而保之。一曰慈，二曰俭，三曰不敢为天下先。慈故能勇；俭故能广；不敢为天下先，故能成器长。今舍慈且勇，舍俭且广，舍后且先，死矣！夫慈，以战则胜，以守则固。天将救之，以慈卫之。（第六十七章）

说明："慈"不是有差等的爱，而是表面上柔和、不激烈，内在却广博无边的爱，显示了得"道"之人的真正的"无私"境界。"俭"就是"道"之"不盈"在人身上的体现，诸如坚韧有力量、勇敢顽强、胸襟宽阔而不孤傲等。这两种品质是"圣人"的典型德性。从这两种德性可以看出，老子并不主张成为一个完全出世的隐士。

14. 柔弱

"柔弱"指不刻意展露自身强势的态度或行为，是一种高级的守中方式。

【参见《老子》条目】

人之生也柔弱，其死也坚强。草木之生也柔脆，其死也枯槁。故坚强者死之徒，柔弱者生之徒。是以兵强则灭，木强则折。强大处下，柔弱处上。（第七十六章）

说明：柔弱者，往往代表新生事物，具有充沛的生命力。它将克服与排除干扰，行进于自身的生命历程。老子揭示了"柔弱胜刚强"的道理，也表现为"阳刚阴柔"的守中方式，从而找出两者转化的条件，提炼事物发展变化的规律。

六、基本假设及其说明

基本假设是论述一个演绎系统的前提，可以作为形成公理与证明命题的依据。

第一，"道"是任何"某个（类）"的综合。它无特定含义，有指向但不指向任何"某个（类）"，也被称为"常""常道"等。"道"是天地万物的根源，具有无限的创造力。

第二，"道"可"无"，精微处充满力量；"无"生"有"，恍惚中混成迹象。精微而潜在的力量势在必发，为天地之始。道可"无"意味着道的无限可能性。"有"指万物之母，也就是万物的形成。"有"生万物，万物复归于"无"。万物需要"道"的滋养，"道"常在以助万物之生。

第三，"无"的无限可能性与"有"的有限现实性构成矛盾，矛盾是按量变到质变、"肯定-否定-否定之否定"的规律而发展的。"无"与"有"的统一才是"道"的圆满状态。

第四，任何事物与外部环境都构成矛盾的对立统一体。相比其他物种，人与人之间、人与外部环境之间的矛盾具有特殊性：（1）人类社会在不自为状态下出现的矛盾，通常处于稳定状态（称为"自然"或合乎"道"的状态）；（2）人类社会在自为状态下出现的矛盾，有可能处于不稳定状态（称为"不自然"或偏离"道"的状态）。在后一状态下，人类社会与外部环境冲突尖锐，社会内部动荡不安，最终可能毁灭自己。

第五，人的认知和行为的理想状态是"守中"，既看到"有"又坚守"无"。由"无"的无限可能性与"有"的有限现实性这一矛盾所决定，人类的思维和行为具有两面性：一面是不能正确认识"道"及其产生的"不自然"行为，另一面是能够正确认识"道"从而合乎"自然"的行为。"守中"可以促成人与人之间、人与外部世界之间的均衡。

关于基本假设的说明：

1. 基本假设1是从《老子》的以下各章中提炼概括出来的：

道可道，非常道；名可名，非常名。（第一章）

吾不知其名，强字之曰道，强为之名曰大。（第二十五章）

道常无名，朴。虽小，天下莫能臣。（第三十二章）

衣养万物而不为主，常无欲，可名于小；万物归焉而不为主，可名为大。（第三十四章）

基本假设1指出，"道"是"名字"，而不是"名"。名字就是一个符号，没有特定的内涵，无法说"道是什么"；名是概念，有特定的内涵，才可以说"某是什么"。然而，"道"并不意味着没有指向，只是不指向任何"某个（类）"。有指向但不指向任何"某个（类）"就意味着任何"某个（类）"的综合。"综合"不是"总合"。一般我们说"总合"是把一个个或一类的"某"加起来，就像用一粒粒的谷子堆成谷堆一样。

"综合"不是加起来，而是把任何"某个（类）"合进去，或者把任何"某个（类）"剥离开来，它既没有增加什么，也没有减少什么。为什么呢？因为它本身很"大"，可以包容一切，没有什么能给它增加；它本身又很"小"，小到无法感觉到它的存在，没有什么能给它减少。这个意义上的"道"，在《老子》中还被称为"常""常道"和"恒道"等。

2. 基本假设2是从《老子》的以下各章中提炼概括出来的：

无，名天地之始；有，名万物之母。（第一章）

道冲而用之或不盈。渊兮，似万物之宗；湛兮，似或存。吾不知谁之子，象帝之先。（第四章）

谷神不死，是谓玄牝。玄牝之门，是谓天地根。绵绵若存，用之不勤。（第六章）

视之不见，名曰夷；听之不闻，名曰希；搏之不得，名曰微。此三者不可致诘，故混而为一。其上不皦，其下不昧，绳绳兮不可名，复归于无物。是谓无状之状，无物之象。是谓惚恍。迎之不见其首，随之不见其后。（第十四章）

夫物芸芸，各复归其根。（第十六章）

道之为物，惟恍惟惚。惚兮恍兮，其中有象；恍兮惚兮，其中有物；窈兮冥兮，其中有精；其精甚真，其中有信。（第二十一章）

有物混成，先天地生。寂兮寥兮，独立不改，周行而不殆，可以为天地母。吾不知其名，强字之曰道，强为之名曰大。大曰逝，逝曰远，远曰反。（第二十五章）

衣养万物而不为主，常无欲，可名于小；万物归焉而不为主，可名为大。（第三十四章）

反者道之动，弱者道之用。天下万物生于有，有生于无。（第四十章）

道生一，一生二，二生三，三生万物。万物负阴而抱阳，冲气以为和。（第四十二章）

天下有始，以为天下母。既得其母，以知其子；既知其子，复守其母，没身不殆。（第五十二章）

基本假设2指出，"无"指天地之始，也就是一切的开端。"开端"必定储备着动力，也就是潜在的能量，不然就无以"开端"。没有什么能增加和减少"道"，表明它本身是有力量的。充满力量的"道"必然会成为万物的开端。精微而潜在的力量虽然势在必发，却还没有明确的指向，因此它的名是"无"。

当"无"用来指称万物之始时，道可"无"意味着道的无限可能性。"无"作为最抽象的"名"，完全是超越经验和可感现象之上的名。因此，"道"是形而上的"本"，"无"是形而上的"体"。《老子》中的"朴""虚""弱""雌""不盈"等说法以"水"和"婴儿"的喻相都指向这个形而上的"本体"。

"有"指万物之母，也就是万物的形成。"有"这个名不是超越经验和可感现象之上的名，而是对经验的和可感之万物的抽象，因此相比"无"来说，是次抽象的名。在本体意义上，蓄势待发的"无"创生出经验意义上抽象的"有"，这意味着完成了从本体论到宇宙论的合理过渡。虽然作为抽象的"有"依然是恍惚的，但混成中有了迹象。"无"和"有"不是直接指称"道"，但却表明了"道"在本体中的自我完成和向宇宙生成的转化。

"有"名万物之母，也可以说是对万物生成和发展过程的总称。万物虽然不能分割或者占有"道"，但其存在需要"道"的滋养。在从本体论过渡到宇宙生成论的过程中，万物似乎离开了"道"。然而，"道"总是常在，总在"周行"，以其"弱"（也就是充满力量的"无"的态势）辅助、成就万物之生。这样，万物就复归"无"而自生。

3. 基本假设3是从《老子》的以下各章中提炼概括出来的：

天地之间，其犹橐钥乎！虚而不屈，动而愈出。多言数穷，不如守中。（第五章）

三十辐，共一毂，当其无，有车之用。埏埴以为器，当其无，有器之用。凿户牖以为室，当其无，有室之用。故有之以为利，无之以为用。（第十一章）

知其雄，守其雌，为天下溪。为天下溪，常德不离，复归于婴儿。知其白，守其辱，为天下谷。为天下谷，常德乃足，复归于朴。朴散则为器，圣人用之，则为官长。故大制不割。（第二十八章）

基本假设3指出，"道"是圆满而自足的。"无"生"有"的过程总是不全面的、偶然的、暂时的和难以长久的。这种矛盾体现在万物上面，因为万物都是"无"生"有"的产物，人的认识和行为也是如此。为此，万物与人类均受到"无"的无限可能性与"有"的有限现实性这一矛盾的制约。

4. 基本假设4指出，在人类社会中，"无"的无限可能性与"有"的有限现实性这一矛盾有其特殊之处。一方面，人类不自觉不自为地接受了这一矛盾的支配，在这种情况下，矛盾自然而然地呈现出一种稳定状态。另一方面，人类借助于自己的思维和行为，对这一矛盾施加了各种作用力，在这种情况下，矛盾有可能依然保持稳定，也有可能因为人类的作用力变得不稳定。因为人类的作用力归根到底不能脱离"有"的有限现实性，故而加大这种作用力，有可能加剧"有"的有限现实性与"无"的无限可能性这一矛盾，其结果是人类社会与外部环境冲突变得尖锐，社会内部日益动荡不安，最终可能毁灭自己。

5. 基本假设5指出,在"无"的无限可能性与"有"的有限现实性这一矛盾面前,人类在认识和行为上保持"守中"(矛盾的平衡状态)是必要的,既自觉体现"道"又顾及人类的特性。具体而言,把握从"道"之"无"到生成万物之"有"的合适状态,就称为"守中";实现这一状态,就称为"常"("恒");属于人类的"常"("恒")是"自然"状态在人类社会中的特殊体现。

七、公理及其说明

以下公理是从道家思想的特性和《老子》的众多章节提炼而成。相对来说,它们是得到公认、不证自明的,是命题推导与证明的主要依据。

A1. "自然"是"道"从"无"到"有"再到"无"的自在自为过程。

【参见《老子》条目】

夫物芸芸,各复归其根。(第十六章)

悠兮其贵言。功成事遂,百姓皆谓我自然。(第十七章)

吾不知其名,强字之曰道,强为之名曰大。大曰逝,逝曰远,远曰反。……人法地,地法天,天法道,道法自然。(第二十五章)

衣养万物而不为主,常无欲,可名于小;万物归焉而不为主,可名为大。(第三十四章)

反者道之动,弱者道之用。天下万物生于有,有生于无。(第四十章)

天下有始,以为天下母。既得其母,以知其子;既知其子,复守其母,没身不殆。(第五十二章)

说明:公理A1指出,"道"是圆满而自足的。"道"的自我完成过程,并不意味着有任何对其本身的损伤或者补偿,从"无"到"有"再到"无"也不意味着"有"和"无"之间的直接转换和线性循环。"无"是起点,也是根本,是不可见却无处不在的精微。"道"可"无",是无限可能性;"无"生"有"的过程总是不全面的、偶然的、暂时的和难以长久的。从"有"再到"无"看似"回归""反复",其实根本就离不开"无"。这种以"无"为基点的过程就是"自然"。

A2. 由"智"入"明"就能悟"道"。

【参见《老子》条目】

天下皆知美之为美,斯恶已。皆知善之为善,斯不善已。(第二章)

视之不见,名曰夷;听之不闻,名曰希;搏之不得,名曰微。此三者不可致诘,故混而为一。(第十四章)

第二章　定义，基本假设，公理
CHAPTER TWO: Definitions, Assumptions and Axioms

致虚极，守静笃。万物并作，吾以观复。夫物芸芸，各复归其根。归根曰静，静曰复命。复命曰常，知常曰明。不知常，妄作凶。知常容，容乃公，公乃全，全乃天，天乃道，道乃久，没身不殆。（第十六章）

始制有名，名亦既有，夫亦将知止，知止可以不殆。（第三十二章）

知人者智，自知者明。（第三十三章）

天下有始，以为天下母。既得其母，以知其子；既知其子，复守其母，没身不殆。塞其兑，闭其门，终身不勤。开其兑，济其事，终身不救。见小曰明，守柔曰强。用其光，复归其明，无遗身殃；是为袭常。（第五十二章）

说明：老子反对那种以"正名"来确定社会秩序，并将此种作为当成是人的最高智慧的社会现实（也就是维护"礼"的现实）。由此，老子说："道可道，非常道；名可名，非常名。"在"可名"和"可道"之外才有真正的"道"。然而，老子对那种"可名"的智慧的反对并不是全然弃之，而是持一分为二的态度。

一方面，老子肯定了人对对象的认识能力和对行动的抉择能力的重要性；另一方面，当"智"成为满足过分欲望的工具而丧失了回到"无"的能力，也就是忘记了生命的原初状态时，老子给予坚决的反对。背离了原初状态的"智"没有了根本，失去了力量之源，也违背了"道"与"自然"。老子对"道"的认识具有强烈的思辨色彩，也就是说，他提出的"道"不再是经验概念，而是通过概念之间的转换而得到的。这种通过纯理论思维而提出的"道"否定了原始宗教的神秘观念。

然而，老子的"道"明显不是仅仅为否定原始宗教而提出的，更具有强烈的人文关怀。如果说天之道是从"无"到"有"再到"无"的周行，那么，人之道也是同样的，从充满力量的生命的"无"到把握和掌控对象的"有"，再回归到内在的"无"。这个过程可以概括为"由'智'入'明'"，通过这个过程就能悟"道"。老子在理解这个过程的时候没有完全否定"欲"和"智"，并认为人可以到达"明"，像"婴儿"一般的"明"就凸显了人的价值和意义，从而避免了消极的人生观。这是老子人文思想的重要表现。

A3. 治国的基本理念是"上善若水"，从"无为"达"有为"。

【参见《老子》条目】

是以圣人处无为之事，行不言之教；万物作而不为始，生而不有，为而不恃，功成而弗居。夫唯弗居，是以不去。（第二章）

为无为，则无不治。（第三章）

爱民治国，能无为乎？（第十章）

道常无为而无不为。侯王若能守之，万物将自化。化而欲作，吾将镇之以无名之朴。无名之朴，夫亦将不欲。不欲以静，天下将自正。（第三十七章）

故圣人云："我无为，而民自化；我好静，而民自正；我无事，而民自富；我无欲，而民自朴。"（第五十七章）

说明：《老子》对当时为追求"功业"而争夺的治国者有清醒认识。"有为"恐怕是所有治国者的梦想，无论"为"的方式和途径是什么。当主流意识认为国之强大关乎生死存亡时，人们总是在殚精竭虑寻找强大的策略。有的认为国之强大在于有"德"并能维护传统，有的认为国之强大在于有"力"并能震慑敌人，于是就产生治国的"王道"与"霸道"之争。

老子以其超常的理论思考能力和经验洞察力，提出了"无为"的治国思想。当然，我们需要明白的是："无为"不是什么都不做的完全消极状态，"无为"是不违背自然，不刻意行为和妄为。在一定程度上，"无为"确实有退让消极的表象，但这种退让消极本身不是目的，而真正回到"道"的不可言说的精微处，这个地方恰恰是力量之源。

A4. 圣人知"道"并"不争"。

【参见《老子》条目】

居善地，心善渊，与善仁，言善信，政善治，事善能，动善时。夫唯不争，故无尤。（第八章）

我独异于人，而贵食母。（第二十章）

夫唯不争，故天下莫能与之争。（第二十二章）

天之道，利而不害；人之道，为而不争。（第八十一章）

说明：老子肯定人的基本欲望和认知能力，这是在"人性"上确立人在万物中的主体地位。然而，老子对人性的肯定并不意味着是对每个个体的肯定，这表现在两个方面：（1）《老子》文本针对的是治国者，改变社会不"自然"的现状从根本上说依靠"治国者"的治理，即使这是一种"无为"的治理，它也还是治理而不是放任，完全不是依靠个体的力量和个体的觉醒；（2）从"人性"上确立人的地位不是为了争取个体的地位，而是为"圣人"（合格的治国者）的出现做理论上的铺垫。

当社会个体在许多方面都存在巨大的差距时，老子不可能贸然把"自然"社会的理想寄托在占大多数的个体民众身上。只有圣人知"道"并"不争"，理想社会依靠圣人的治理，这依然是等级制度下的社会意识。

A5. 摄生的基本方法是消除过分的"欲"和机巧性的"智"。

【参见《老子》条目】

常使民无知无欲。（第三章）

天长地久。天地所以能长且久者，以其不自生，故能长生。（第七章）

五色令人目盲；五音令人耳聋；五味令人口爽；驰骋畋猎，令人心发狂；难得之货，令人行妨。是以圣人为腹不为目，故去彼取此。（第十二章）

宠辱若惊，贵大患若身。（第十三章）

出生入死。生之徒，十有三；死之徒，十有三；人之生生，动之于死地，亦十有三。夫何故？以其生生之厚。盖闻善摄生者，陆行不遇兕虎，入军不被甲兵；兕无所投其角，虎无所用其爪，兵无所容其刃。夫何故？以其无死地。（第五十章）

说明：人是万物之一，是有形的，身体就是人的"形"。人也是"无"与"有"的统一，人的内在生命力就是人的"无"，人的身体感官欲望就是人的"有"。什么才是真正的摄生（养生）之道呢？既不是刻意去追求长生不老，当然也不是自我作死，而是顺应"自然"。顺应"自然"不一定长生不老，但比起刻意追求过分欲望（例如长生）和机巧性智慧（例如为了满足长生欲望而想尽各种办法），可能更能长生不老。

We adopt the axiomatic approach to interpret *Laozi*. When considering the logical thread of the research, we locate the ways in which men understand and treat the world in a state of "*shouzhong*" (keeping moderate or taking the middle course). It is required first to expound the law of composition and movement of things from the perspective of cosmogony theory, and then to put the human world in the appropriate position in this system. In this way, we can determine what the state of keeping moderate is and how to keep this state. This principle is very significant in guiding human activities, including cultivating one's morality and personal life, governing a nation and dealing with international relations, and grasping the direction of the development of human society. We have formulated 13 definitions, 5 basic assumptions, and 4 axioms, which are defined with explanations, coupled with the corresponding original quotations from *Laozi*, thus providing the basic logic basis for the propositions and reasoning that follow them.

I. To understand *Laozi*'s Ideological System from the Perspective of Keeping Moderate

In the axiomatic interpretation of *Laozi*, we must first find out the starting point of Laozi's thought so that we can have a close look at the picture of the entire system of Laozi's thought and find out the logical relationship among his various discussions. After we have completed it, we can make basic assumptions, select definitions, and determine axioms, which will lay the foundation for the propositions and reasoning in the following chapters.

Ancient Chinese laid emphasis on the spirit of "Upholding Middle" and advocated appropriate action, middle way, and the mean. It is required that people should adhere to the principle of moderation or proportionality, have the sense of propriety, and do not go to extremes in governance and social behavior in order to achieve physical and mental coordination, and harmony among people and in society as a whole. Chinese character " 中 " (*zhong*), which approximately means "central or middle," "correct or right," "appropriate and proper," "the mean," etc., indicates the quality of human behavior. For instance, Emperor Yao in ancient times stressed that the society should be governed by grasping everything sincerely in a middle way without deviations. Pan Geng (盘庚), a ruler of the Shang Dynasty (17th to 11th cent. BC), disciplined the people by saying that *"everybody must have the mean in his heart."*[1] Duke of Zhou (11th Century BC, a member of the royal family

---

[1] See the chapters *Pan Geng, Announcement about Drunkenness* and *Lü on Punishments* in *The Book of Documents*.

of the Zhou Dynasty) advocated "moderate virtue" and required an appropriate and correct judgment in criminal punishment. *Zhou Yi* (*The Classics of Changes*) has the terms such as "*zhengzhong*" (正中), "*gangzhong*" (刚中), "*dezhong*" (得中), "*xingzhong*" (行中), "*zhongzheng*" (中正) and "*zhongxing*" (中行). These terms contain either the meaning of "central, middle or mean," or "correct and right, or proper and appropriate."

During the several hundred years after the 6th century BC, great thinkers like Plato, Buddha, and Confucius, among others, appeared respectively in ancient Greece, Israel, ancient India, ancient China and other places. These sages invariably formulated the principle of virtuous ethics: "*zhong*" (中) is the center, stressing "moderate" and " appropriate." In Aristotle's *Ethics*, the key word is the mean, which is translated into Chinese as "*zhongyong*" and "*zhongdao*," meaning "moderate" and "middle way." Pythagoras believed that "*zhongyong*" (the mean) is the best state of all things, and he pointed out in *The Golden Verses of Pythagoras* that "*Of all things the mean is the best.*" Ancient Greeks had the saying that "all things should not go to extremes." Aristotle also highly valued "middle way" and "moderation." The basis of the Empty View Theory of Mahayana Buddhism in India – Nagarjuna's "Madhyamaka" also advocates "listening to both sides and choosing 'the middle course', a way of thinking similar to the Confucian idea." Nagarjuna believed that the emptiness of all phenomena (dhammas) is without any "own-being" and "self-nature," or "inherent existence" and thus without any underlying essence. It is empty of being independently existent. The emptiness of all phenomena transcends all concepts and is neither existence (being) nor non-existence (non-being). It can not hold to being nor non-being, otherwise, it will fall into bias. Eradicating all disparities, it is ineffable and is the middle way between two extremes. It can be called empty when being and non-being are negated.[1]

The above-mentioned "*zhong*," in the general term, is nothing more than the "middle or center" in cognition and behavior, i.e., we should do everything without bias and our behavior should not go to extremes. But just like looking for the "midpoint" in a line segment, all the elaboration of the "middle" implies its two "ends." Without the ends, there will be no middle. Due to different perceptions of both ends, different "*zhong*" will occur.

Laozi also believed in "*zhong*" (中), which is expounded in the sentences

---

[1] Wang Luping. On Madhyamaka Philosophical Outlook of Nagarjuna and Deva. *Zhejiang Journal*, Vol.3, 2000.

like "*Take emptiness to the limit. Maintain tranquility in the center,*" "*Through the blending of the unseen air, they arrive at a state of harmony,*" "*Too much talk leads to a dead end; it is better to hold fast to moderation and the void.*" However, there are different interpretations of the meaning of "*zhong*" in Chinese included in these discussions. In Chinese, "*shouzhong*" or "*shouchong*" means keeping a still and quiet state. It can also mean keeping "the mean or moderate:" in *Doctrine of the Mean*, "*zhong*" means an equilibrium or moderate in the sentence: "*It can be said 'zhong' while there are no stirrings of pleasure, anger, sorrow, or joy,*" which is the state of the heart of Dao. "*Shouzhong*" just means keeping a moderate or mean state in the heart. There is a kind of reproduction function resulting from the stillness and mobility of Dao. No words can explain and no inference can study and understand it. Only by keeping a mean state can people have a thorough understanding of it.[1] "*Too much talk leads to a dead end; it is better to hold fast to 'moderation.' Neither observance by human eyes and ears nor verbal comments have ever been able to offer solutions to the various complicated problems in the universe. Therefore, it is better to maintain the original power of Dao, the fundamental force for all things in the universe.*"[2] "*A saying goes that loud speech does not mean reasoning and many words can not ensure a good government. Too many policies will lead to disorder of policy signals. As a result, people won't know what to do. The great Dao means 'no name' and 'no words.' If the administrators can follow the natural laws, keep tranquil and void, and take inaction without too many words and with fewer desires, the society can organize automatically its own power and tend to balance and stay in the center in accordance with the unity of opposites of yin and yang because there is infinite energy between the Heaven and the Earth to produce new things. With less policy intervention, the power of great Dao will reverse the operation and draw the force deviated from the central way back on track.*"[3] We won't be entangled in these two different interpretations at the moment. In fact, there is also another understanding, that is, "*shouchong*" (守冲) and "*shouzhong*" (守中) are correlated.

Laozi thinks that we can have "*zhong*" (middle or center) only by maintaining tranquility and void, including the understanding of "*zhong*" and related actions. "*Shouchong*" (守冲) and "*shouzhong*" (守中) forms the relationship of the necessary way and inevitable result.

---

1 Feng Jialu. *Three Interpretations of Tao Te Ching.* Oriental Publishing House, 2013, p.36.
2 Wang Wenming. *Laozi's Aspirations.* Jiuzhou Publishing House, 2012, p.60.
3 Li Guowang. *Guoxue and New Behavioral Finance – Apocalypse of Behavioral Strategy of Tao Te Ching.* China Financial Publishing House, 2012, p.95.

In fact, many people believe that the core of Laozi's doctrine is keeping moderate. In *An Analysis of the Several Ancient Books Over which Confucianism and Daoism Have Disputes*, Zhao Lisheng said that in the Spring and Autumn Period, "*all the scholars were talking about 'zhong' (center or middle) and 'xin' (heart and mind). Confucius emphasized 'timely center,' and Laozi stressed 'maintaining central course.' Confucians believed in 'right heart' and Daoists 'cultivation of heart' (developing a 'golden heart')*."[1] Zhang Jiankun said in his *Interoperability Between Sages in Wisdom*, "*Confucius stressed the mean state, Laozi maintained center, and Buddha 'middle way.' However, 'zhong' (center or middle) does not mean too persistent. It is also a paranoid to hold fast to 'zhong' inflexibly and make it an extremely fixed concept concept.*"[2]

Wu Chongqing in his *Confucianism and Daoism in Complement: the Chinese People's Spiritual Construction* says: "Confucius emphasized 'timely center,' and Laozi stressed 'maintaining centeral course.' Confucians emphasized 'right heart,' Buddha empty center; Confucius stressed consistence, Laozi obtaining one, Buddha returning to one. As all people have 'hearts' of the same sense, everyone can have freedom to choose Confucianism, or Daoism or Buddhism, or even choose the three of them at the same time."[3]

So, what does "*shouzhong*" mean? Where are the both ends of "*zhong*?"

Of all the concepts concerning "*zhong*" previously described, in most cases, the two ends are set in the human society. For example, the "Mean" advocated by Confucianism indicates that we can not go to extremes to deal with matters, which are basically human matters. Only "*zhongguan*" (mid-view or Madhyamaka) of Buddhism has its both ends of "Heaven" and "humanity." At this point, Laozi's view of "*shouzhong*" is similar to Buddhism. First, he tried to see the whole world from oneness, which has reached the limits of human cognition, feelings and imagination. Because it includes all things in the universe other than human beings and human society, no words can describe it except Dao and Nature.

The word "Naturalness" is the most abstract description of the moving and existent state of all things within the scope of its domination. In short, it is constantly

---

1 Cao Feng. *Unearthed Literature and Confucianism and Daoism*. Lijiang Publishing House, 2012, p.114.
2 Zhang Jiankun. *On Interflow of Sage Wisdom*. Guangda Publishing House, 2010, p.272.
3 Wu Chongqing. *Confucianism and Daoism in Complement: the Chinese People's Spiritual Construction*. Guangdong People's Publishing House, 1993, p.281.

evolving from *"wu"* (non-being) to *"you"* (being) and then from "being" to "non-being," and finally becomes oneness. Secondly, he looked at all things of mankind at the height of Dao, focusing on observation of human self-awareness and self-act. Thus there appear the two ends of understanding, that is, comprehensiveness of Dao and bias (one-sidedness) of humankind. It indicates that Dao is the unity of comprehensiveness and infinity (limitlessness). Human's cognition and ability can not go beyond this. Therefore, Laozi's view of *"zhong"* is highlighted: human's self-awareness and self-act must be realized within the scope of *"shouzhong,"* namely, human beings must be fully aware of the one-sidedness and limitedness of themselves, and fully take into account the comprehensiveness and unlimitedness of the Dao.

At this point, Laozi's Dao, "naturalness," and *"you* and *wu"* can be used to examine the human cognition and behavior. The core of his thought is: we human beings will not deviate from the Dao if we can keep ourselves in the middle in cognition and behavior and remain in a "natural" state.

Laozi said "Recursion is the movement of Dao." Chinese character *"fan"* (反). that is, "recursion" has two meanings: one is "opposite" and the other is "reversal" or "turning back," meaning the cycling of the human life. Throughout all the discussions of *Laozi*, we can find out the general meaning of the concepts that are regarded as *"zheng"* (正) (correct, straight or upright) by the society, which can be matched by the concept meaning *"fan"* (reversal or opposite), just as in the sentence "Straight words seem to be expressed in their opposites." Or to say, "Correct words seem to say the reverse." However, Laozi did not cling to (not obsessed with) the so-called *"fan"* (reversal or negative) in its common sense, which is to illustrate the "mean state" Laozi really wanted to describe.

Laozi's *"po"* (break with) and *"li"* (establish) is roughly divided into two levels:

The first level is the most abstract being or existence and non-being or non-existence. Laozi thought that Dao is complete, self-sufficient and all-encompassing. The birth and death of all things are the forms reflected by Dao. It is its fundamental law to move and recycle endlessly from "non-being or non-existence" to "being or existence" and then from "being or existence" to "non-being or non-existence." To cycle from "non-being" or "non-existence" to "being" or "existence" reflects the infinite possibilities of Dao. Once the state of "being" or "existence" is reached, its infinite possibility will become finity, because Dao, in the very process, is endowed with incompleteness, accidentality and temporariness. This is also the case with human's knowing and behaving.

In this case, it is necessary for the humanity to take the middle course in cognition and behavior, which can consciously reflect Dao and take into account human characteristics. Specifically, it is regarded as "*shouzhong*" (to maintain or take a middle course) to maintain the appropriate state in which Dao changes from non-being to being that gives birth to all the things in the universe. This state is considered as a normal state, known as "normal" (or "constant"). And human's "normal" ("constant") is the "natural" state individually embodied in the human society.

The second level is the Heaven and the Earth, which is the embodiment of Dao, and the human society, which has just obtained a small part of the Dao. Compared with the Heaven and the Earth and Dao, man's wisdom and capacity is very limited. It is improper for man to claim arrogantly to be the supreme of all creatures. The human society needs rulers, but what the rulers can do is very limited. To human beings, it is significant to enjoy a prosperous country, strong military strength and immeasurable merit, but compared with the self-behavior and freedom and the functions of all things, these are nothing but partial merit and partial morality.

From the point of view of language expression, up to now, human society has not created a language system for Laozi to accurately describe his thought "keeping moderate." It is because, at the very beginning, human beings just focused on the human community and on the people themselves, not good at understanding the world with the vision of "keeping moderate." So, it is impossible for them to describe the world in language expressing "keeping moderate." Thus, it has not only caused difficulties for Laozi to express his thoughts, but also for us to have an accurate understanding of the original intent of Laozi and accurate quoting of his thesis and assertion.

As far as language expression is concerned, Laozi could only choose the words meaning "breaking up" instead of the words meaning "establishing." But he could not find a positive description for "keeping moderate." Dao, for example, is the complex of all the concepts, in which being and non-being are integrated. As it moves and changes constantly a bit like "the universe," it can only be given a general description and cannot be accurately defined. The other example is the "nature." It describes a natural spontaneous state of things for themselves, which contains various states and can't be accurately defined either.

As for human society, he advocated "wuwei" (literally meaning doing nothing, or taking non-action or inaction), "not to contend," and "to show softness and weakness." In fact, these are not the commonly defined meaning referred to as "idleness," "blind concessions" or "weakness," but the state which can not be expressed with commonly used vocabulary. Just take "wuwei" as an example. It does not require mankind to "do nothing" and return to the ancient barbarian times, but to maintain a balanced state between taking action or doing something and taking inaction or non-action, which intends for a better action. "Taking action" also includes the meaning "of doing nothing but let others do better." It also means that we should not be indulged in stubborns action of mankind, but actions that comply with Dao. "Not to contend," "to show softness and "weakness" and "simplicity" can also be understood like this. Only in this state, can we maintain "*shouzhong*" (keeping moderate) and act according to "naturalness" as Laozi described.

Historically, this kind of language expression resulted in two kinds of understanding of Laozi.

One kind of understanding is: Laozi thought that "*wu*" (non-being) is better than "*you*" (being), "weakness" is better than "strength," and "simplicity" is better than "cleverness." Hence, it is better for the rulers to do nothing than to do something; to be immoral is better than to be virtuous; to have merits is better than without merits; to be honest (even stupid) is better than to be clever; a weak country would be better than a powerful country; and to put down weapons is better than to strengthen the military forces; and so on.

If so, Laozi would have become the thinker who believed in "anti-intellectualism," "anti-civilization" and "the extremely negative misanthrope" and so on. However, with such understanding, we can not realize that behind the politics of "*wu wei*" advocated in the book *Laozi*, a more desirable political realm; and behind "ignorance of cleverness," he also described a more sophisticated wisdom; and behind the attitude "not to contend," he describes a powerful state: "nobody in the world can contend with him."

Another misunderstanding is: Laozi's thought is understood as "Dialectic." The term "dialectic" comes from ancient Greek, referring to debate skills at first, which was called by Socrates as "spiritual midwife surgery." But when people often say that Laozi has dialectical thinking, they are actually taking the Marxist materialist dialectics as the theoretical reference. It advocates the point of view of dealing with problems in a connective, developmental, and comprehensive manner. Its basic content includes: (1) three laws: the law of unity of opposites, the law of mutual change of quality and quantity, the law of negation of negation; (2) five pairs of basic categories: cause and effect, form and content, reality and the nature, necessity and contingency, and possibility and reality.

第二章 定义，基本假设，公理 187
CHAPTER TWO: Definitions, Assumptions and Axioms

People often say that Laozi's thinking is kind of dialectical for three reasons:

First, Laozi revealed "the unity of opposite of the positive and the negation."

Laozi put forward a series of contradictory concepts, such as long and short, wise and stupid, clever and clumsy, big and small, high and low, back and front, life and death, easy and difficult, advances and retreats, ancient and present, the beginning and the end, positive and negative, beautiful and ugly, positive and odd, worn and new, good and evil, strong and weak, hard and soft, giving and taking, victory and failure, having and not having, loss and gain, beneficial and harmful, *yin* and *yang*, full and empty (hollow), static and impatient, opening and shrinking, gaudy and practical, splendid and real, bent and straight, female and male, noble and humble, honor and disgrace, auspicious and ominous, misfortune and blessing and so on.

Laozi believed that both sides in contradiction disclosed by the positive and negative concepts are not isolated, but interdependent, and each side is the precondition of existence of anther side. So he said: *"When everyone in the world knows the beautiful as beautiful, ugliness comes into being; when everyone knows the good as good, then the bad comes into being. Therefore, being and non-being generate each other; the difficult and the easy complement each other; the long and the short offset each other; the upper and the lower incline towards each other; the tone and the sound harmonize with each other; the front and the back follow each other."* (Chapter 2, *Laozi*). Laozi also believed that both sides of the positive and negative are not only interdependent, but also have the inherent unity, as it is said in *Laozi*: *"To yield is to be preserved; to be bent is to be straight; to be hollow is to be full; to be worn out is to be renewed; to have little is to have more; to have too much is to be perplexed."* (Chapter 22, *Laozi*) So if we want to get a positive result, we need to do it from the negative side.This is what we call "the difficult and the easy complement each other."

Second, he advocated that "To turn to its opposite is the movement of Dao."

Seeing the pervasive existence of the opposite of things, which will be converted to the opposite side, he proposed the proposition "To turn to its opposite is the movement of Dao," (Chapter 40, *Laozi*) revealing the universal law of contradictory movement of things. Here, the Chinese character *"fan"* has generally two meanings: one indicates "return," as in "All things arise together, and I watch their return. Things come forth in great numbers, and each one returns to its own root. To return to roots means stillness." (Chapter 16) The other means "the reverse" or "going back to the opposite side." "To turn to its opposite is the movement of

Dao" means that all things will transform to their opposite side. It can be proved in *Laozi*: "*Too much love will cost much. Too much treasure will cause loses.*" (Chapter 44, *Laozi*) "*When military force is too strong, it will lose. Trees grown strong and stiff will break.*" (Chapter 76, *Laozi*)

Third, Laozi believed "the soft and weak is superior over the hard and strong."

In dealing with the contrary concepts of positive and negative opposites like the hard and soft, and the strong and weak, people tend to emphasize the strong side, thinking that this is a positive value. In contrast, Laozi's value orientation lays more emphasis on the negative side, thinking that "The soft and weak is superior over the hard and strong." So he said: "*While alive, a man's body is supple and soft; when dead, it becomes hard and stiff. While alive, grass and trees are pliant and fragile. When dead, they're withered and dried out. Thus, the hard and strong is the companion of death. The supple and weak is the companion of life. Therefore, if military force is too strong, it will lose. If a tree is strong and stiff, it will break. The strong and hard takes the lower position. The supple and weak takes the higher position.*" (Chapter 76, *Laozi*) "*The softest in the world can penetrate through the hardest object.*" (Chapter 43, *Laozi*) "*In the world, nothing is softer and weaker than water. And yet for attaching the hard and strong, nothing is better than water, because there is nothing you can use to replace it. The weak can overcome the hard. The soft can overcome the strong. Yet no one so far can put it into practice.*" (Chapter 78, *Laozi*) "*To keep modest and pliant is called 'strong.'*" (Chapter 52, *Laozi*)

These are basic concepts of Laozi understood by people from dialectic perspective. However, it is always difficult for people to face the following questions:

First, Laozi said that the antithesis would turn to its opposite side but he didn't stress the condition of the conversion.

Second, the proposition that "the weak can overcome the hard" seems to be the conclusions based on empirical facts. We can use some other empirical facts to draw the opposite conclusion. For example, a sharp knife can easily cut tender grass. As there are a lot of similar empirical facts, can people come to the conclusion that "the hard can overcome the weak?"

Third, it is, of course, reasonable to use dialectics to explain the thought of Laozi from the point of view of the unity of opposites. But Laozi did not try to explain the difference between the positive and negative.

If we observe Laozi from a broader perspective, we may find that Laozi's thought might contain profound and complete dialectics. "To turn to its opposite" in

"To turn to its opposite is the movement of Dao" includes Chinese character "*fan.*" Ye Lang and Zhu Liangzhi said, the Chinese character "*fan"* in Laozi's thought has two meanings: one is the opposite, and the other is to return. The two meanings are interrelated, reflecting the uniqueness of Laozi's philosophy. Laozi didn't stress the opposite, complementary and recycling features of things, but emphasized the fact that we should not be obscured by the appearance of things, and that we must get rid of the misperception of knowledge and get involved in the recycling life path,[1] which embodies Laozi's thought of "*shouzhong*."

All in all, if we ignore Laozi's thought of "*shouzhong*," we will think that Laozi has an anti-intellectual, anti-civilization and anti-human stance, and will deviate from and damage the value of the ideology of Laozi. In fact, Laozi is a constructive thinker because he advocated building the ideal society in which man obeys the laws of nature and eventually returns to the nature with which men live harmoniously.

II. Axiomatic Approach and its Application in the Interpretation of Chinese Classics.

Ancient Greek philosophy has a prominent feature in methodology: the principle of rational argument, which requires some commonly accepted starting points. These initially recognized starting points were "Axioms," which later gradually developed into axiomatic approach.

The axiomatic approach is to derive various meaningful propositions also known as theorems on the basis of a few basic assumptions, definitions and axioms to form a deductive system. In this system, basic assumptions are the premise of discussion, and the role of definitions is to clearly describe the core concepts. The axioms are the universally accepted consensus needing no proof (of course they can be illustrated). Propositions are correct conclusions that have been deduced from axioms or other proved true propositions.

Axiomatic approach is a kind of research method often adopted in mathematics and system sciences, which is characterized by systematic thinking, rigorous and clear proof, and logical force. Around 500 BC or so, people began to learn from a large amount of accumulated practice to convert concrete diagrams to abstract geometrical concepts, and studied their relationships and made deduction in the form of propositions. Euclid integrated geometrical propositions by using axiomatic approach and authored *Euclid's Elements*, the great masterpiece in the history of

---

[1] Ye Lang, Zhu Liangzhi. *Insights into Chinese Culture*. Foreign Language Teaching and Research Press, March, 2010, pp.12-13.

mathematics.

Newton often used axiomatic approach in his scientific work. His *Mathematical Principles of Natural Philosophy*, which embodies his brilliant ideas, was written by means of axiomatic system. Einstein often pointed out that the research work in physics should also be started with the basic assumptions and axioms. He pointed out that the development of modern science depends on two research methods: (1) axiomatic thinking; (2) the repeatable experiments. It is with axiomatic approach that Spinoza wrote the famous philosophical book *Ethics*. In a word, the clarity of the concept and the preciseness of the logic are the advantages of the axiomatic method, which has gradually entered into a variety of subjects other than mathematics.

We have used axiomatic approach to interprete the pre-Qin Confucian classics *The Analects of Confucius, Mencius*, and *Xunzi*. In the application of this interpretation, we find that axiomatic method can sort out the core ideas of classics, which is beneficial to those who have different cultural backgrounds to grasp the basic meaning of the classics and their contemporary significance, and to some extent, to eliminate some of the unnecessary arguments in the interpretation of the classics, so that a relatively solid consensus can be reached in some aspects. It is of fundamental significance to the inheritance and dissemination of Chinese traditional culture.

In the process of interpretation, we have encountered some difficulties and doubts, mainly in three aspects: (1) Can the axiomatic method be used to interpret the classic in the field of humanities? (2) The classics in the field of humanities are rich in content. Is the use of the axiomatic method in interpretation harmful to their richness? (3) Influenced by Gödel's incompleteness theorems, the axiomatic method itself has also been questioned, then how should we perceive?

The word axiom (axioma), derived from the ancient Greek, has three meanings: first, it refers to something of value, worth, reputation and status; second, it refers to the things, resolution, intent, purpose that are thought to be appropriate; third, it refers to philosophical and mathematical truism or axioms.[1] According to the third meaning, it is a philosophical and mathematical concept which is well expounded in Euclid's *Elements*. The development of mathematics was propelled by philosophy. At that time, the argument of both sides in debate is based on certain generally accepted consensus as a starting point, which is later called axiom.

---

1 Luo Niansheng, Shui Jianfu. *Chinese Dictionary of The Ancient Greek*. The Commercial Press, 2010, p.87.

In the long course of the study, we have found that axiomatic approach can be used in the researching the thoughts and theories in the field of humanities, as long as two conditions are met: (1) the author has his own theoretical proposition or unique method which can run throughout his entire ideological system; (2) the discussion can show the sense of hierarchy with inherent logical relevance from the primary to the secondary. Of course, symbols are not suitable for the construction of humanistic theory framework in the study. As abstract generalization in humanities is a comprehensive abstraction, it is more suitable to be described by more lively language.

When we use axiomatic approach to study humanistic theory, we must observe its internal system from one level and one angle, but not unravel its internal system from all levels and all angles at the same time, which is also impossible. The humanistic thought tends to have a comprehensive structure where a variety of systems coexist. When we use the axiomatic approach to study *Laozi*, we focus on its main system of thought.

In people's minds, such classics as *The Analects of Confucius*, *Mencius*, *Xunzi*, and *Laozi* have very rich connotations with various notes and interpretations throughout the history (especially so for *Laozi*). So does "the axiomatic interpretation" harm this richness?

For this question, we can make the analysis in two aspects.

First, any sentence in classics like the *Analects of Confucius* and *Laozi* has a variety of explanations. But in the process of understanding, people can only take one explanation. If others ask him why he should take this kind of explanation, the person who chooses this explanation can cite a lot of reasons and evidences, but he has no way to prove that it is the only reasonable choice. As a result, everyone can choose an explanation he thinks reasonable. In fact, this shows that he understands the classics at his own will.

So others may ask him: "Why do you prefer these explanations?" Although unlimited explanations may enrich the connotations of classics on the surface, in fact, they have caused difficulties for the readers because numerous roads in front of them lead to no way. Axiomatic interpretation is different. It requires to make the only option because it constitutes a logical relationship with the whole ideological system. It is precisely because of the clear logical relationship that the readers are inspired by one sentence and can get more inspirations from other sentences, which are systematic inspirations developed from one level.

Second, for such classics as *The Analects of Confucius* and *Laozi*, general readers usually are in awe of them. We might as well think that the words in these classics are very valuable and important. Unlimited explanations, however, tend to result in discrepancies and contradictions between many words. If completely accepted, they will leave in the readers' minds numerous chaotic and conflicting impressions, that is, these classics just make readers understand them hazily by their own hazy meanings. If we say that every word is important, there are also words particularly important, generally important and less important, and then infinitely abundant and infinitely possible explanations can not be easily distinguished in hierarchy.

However, in the interpretation of classics with axiomatic method, we have to pay special attention to their theoretical structures and put a lot of discussion within a clear framework. A particularly important point of view or concept should be consistent within the ideological system; a generally important point of view or concept should be able to be consistent in one aspect. As for specific point of view or exposition, it should be possible to show its starting point and the main body of the thought it relies on. And the theory structure of classics, which concerns the heaven and the earth and man, is the summary and induction of natural phenomena, which in turn serves as a guide in social life. Its richness and limitlessness are reflected in this aspect rather than in the isolated words and phrases with rich implications.

Take *Laozi* as an example. The first thing we need to focus on is the main logic line of Laozi's thought, which is the cornerstone of Laozi's view of the world and the ideological theory. We locate the main logic line of Laozi's thought at the concept "*shouzhong*" so that we can spread the trunk of his ideas in the strict logical form and arrange his theory into a deductive system.

If the outside world for the survival of humans is collectively referred to as "*tian*" (Heaven or nature), and all the activities of human beings and human society are collectively referred to as "*ren*" (Man or people), then human cognition and behaviors are always wandering between the two extremes: one is just to see man's dependence on "*tian*" (Heaven or nature) and the constraints of man by "*tian*," but not man's role and ability; the other one is just to see man's role and emphasize man's ability, but not the restriction of man by "*tian*" (Heaven or nature) and man's dependence on "Heaven."

In the first cognition, "*tian*" is spirit, the Buddha, and the God. Facing the heaven, man can do nothing. What man can do is only worship. In the latter cognition, man is the ruler of nature and the conqueror of heaven and earth, and is the almighty god. Human history proves that no matter which extreme man tends lean towards, it will cause serious problems. But if the two extremes are developed into a pair of contradictions, the reasonable state is to keep the state of *"shouzhong"* in which the contradictions are balanced. The profoundness of Laozi's thought is reflected in this way.

Then Laozi should describe the large system composed of the heaven, the earth, and man. Although it is very brief, his description of the heaven, the earth, and man reached the limit of human cognition. For this system, he could only describe it as the Dao, which includes the state of existence and operation rules of all the things. Due to the command and nourishment of Dao, all things move and act on their own in constant change from their birth to death. And man is just one of its products. If Dao is compared to a towering tree, then man is just a leaf on the tree. He needs Dao to give him direction and to nourish him.

Due to his deep concern for humanity, Laozi inculcated people patiently. He thought that man is great, but compared to the Dao, he still seems to be too small; the role of man does exist, but always needs to be nourished and corrected by Dao. To this end, he chose these concepts like "nature" and *"you wu"* (being or existence and non-being or nonexistence) to correct human's cognition and behavior, thus proposing a series of ideas and theories.

He tried to correct the paranoia resulted from man's "wisdom" with his idea "Keep plain outside and simple inside," to correct man's cognition of their self-merits with "wu wei" (inaction or non-action), correct self-advertised virtue with profound virtue, to correct human's superstition of "strength" with "weakness," and to correct the crazy behavior of men obsessed with self-desire with "few desires" and so on. The human behaviors after the correction can be called "natural," and the human cognition after the correction can be said to be *"shouzhong."*

When we observe human behaviors from Laozi's point of view, we can see its guiding significance. People are often obsessed with money, status, and reputation, but forget that our flesh and soul endowed by Dao are seriously harmed when we are obsessed with such desires. When the human society is obsessed with technology, economy, and military strength, we are usually unaware that the human beings produced by Dao are already in an abnormal state of life. From this we may ask, when man continues to move forward, is it necessary for us to use the thought of Laozi to constantly correct our understanding and behavior?

In the long history of more than 2,000 years after Laozi, people constantly read *Laozi* and accepted its influence while they thought that *Laozi* was enigmatic and difficult to interpret, or can have numerous interpretations. In this way, *Laozi* was on the one hand constrained in the magnificent temple with its positive role in human society was denied; on the other hand, people tended to indiscriminately accept *Laozi*'s thought and did not want to reflect on its strengths and weaknesses.

In fact, we use axiomatic approach to interpret *Laozi*, on the one hand, to show its height and depth in understanding and its serving as a warning for the human civilization; on the other hand, to reveal some of its defects. Logically, Laozi said that it is natural that "All things arise together," meaning that all things move and act freely on their own. Then all human behaviors, one of the actions of "all things which behave freely on their own," are "natural." However, why did Laozi deny some other human behaviors commonly referred to as "*qi*" (negative) while affirming some human behaviors commonly referred to as "*zheng*" (positive)? If such human behaviors are not "natural" and deviated from the Dao, then what are their roots? Are there any other roots besides the Dao? If there are other roots besides Dao, how can we say that Dao includes everything?

This kind of logical flaw cannot be ignored. The root cause of this defect is that Laozi pays more attention to its normal state when describing "nature" as "all things arise together" (positive), than to its abnormal state (negative). If we regard the former as inevitability, then the later has a nature of contingency, and any phenomenon that "all things arise together" is the unity of necessity and contingency.

It is inevitable that the Dao has given birth to all things, but it is accidental what forms and what kinds of things are born. Human society is in the constant interaction and movement in the change of "positive" and "negative." As Laozi paid little attention to "negative," some deviations in discussions occur when his theory is applied in social practice. In politics, for example, Laozi advocated "non-action," which means "doing all the things by doing nothing" if understood according to the logic premise of "keeping moderate." However, Laozi stressed "when I follow non-action, the people will be transformed. When I act little, the people will be naturally upright. When I am not meddlesome, the people will become rich. When I get rid of desire, the people will be simple and pure spontaneously." (Chapter 57, *Laozi*)

Of course, this view is reasonable in the peaceful period; but in the war time, it is not necessarily right, because the urgent need for a ruler is to organize a strong army to end the war. If we regard the war years and the use of force to repress the rebellion as "negative," and the era of peace and the non-intrusive way to manage the country as "positive," then the expression by Laozi should be amended and it should be expressed as "When the people are not transformed, I follow action; when the people are naturally transformed, I follow non-action."

In short, if we stick to the principle of keeping moderate through to the end, we should pay attention to "negative" while attaching great importance to "positive." We should make good use of "negative" while maintaining "positive," and should be good at giving full play to "negative" in "positive" while trying to turn "negative" into "positive."

Finally, how to correctly understand the axiomatic approach and the doubt from kurt Gödel's incompleteness theorem?

As previously discussed, the axiom approach is to deduce various meaningful propositions (or theorems) on the basis of a few basic assumptions, definitions and axioms, which can in general form a theoretic system, namely the axiomatic system. Hilbert, a German mathematician, who in the late 19th century clearly put forward the logical requirements and principles of the axiomatic approach, namely, compatibility, independence and completeness, contributed to the strict and delicate axiomatic approach.

(1) Compatibility: It means that in an axiomatic system, it is not allowed to prove one proposition with its negative proposition proved at the same time. (2) Independence: It means that in an axiomatic system, each axiom should exist independently and cannot be deduced by other axioms. (3) Completeness: It means that all propositions in the system can be proven to be either true or false by judgment, or all those propositions that reflect the theoretical content as a whole can be deduced from the axiomatic system.

In 1931, German mathematician kurt Gödel proposed incompleteness theorems. He proved that any formal system, as long as it includes a brief description of basic arithmetic and is self-consistent, contains certain propositions which can neither be proved true nor proved untrue by methods allowed within the system. That is, "compatibility" and "completeness" in the axiomatic methods can not be simultaneously satisfied. It has shattered Hilbert's faith in the establishment of axiomatic system. Its influence goes far beyond mathematics. It has caused not only revolutionary changes in mathematics and logic, but also a lot of challenging issues, involving philosophy, linguistics and computer science, and even cosmology.

However, we need to eliminate misconceptions about Gödel's incompleteness theorems. First of all, the theorem does not mean that any meaningful axiom system is incomplete. The theorems require, that an axiom system can "define" natural numbers, but not all systems can define the natural numbers, even if the systems include models of natural numbers as subsets. The Euclidean geometry can be axiomatically first-order and become a complete system (in fact, Euclid's original set of axioms is very close to the complete system).

Second, we must realize that Gödel's Incompleteness Theorem apply only to strong axiomatic systems, and some weak axiomatic systems are consistent and complete. The system etablished by using axiomatic approach in humanities is generally regarded as weak axiomatic system. When we try to establish axiomatic system for a certain theory (such as *The Analects of Confucius*, *Mencius*, *Xunzi* and *Laozi*), it is often difficult to meet the requirement in its completeness that "propose all the propositions reflecting this system." But as long as the propositions cover much of the content of the theory, it can be gradually improved on this basis.

III. The Difference between "Keeping Moderate" and "the Mean" from the Perspective of Axiomatic Approach

When using axiomatic approach to interpret pre-Qin Confucian classics, we start with the analysis of the contradictions and establish basic assumptions on this basis, which not only define the research perspective, but also reflect the needs of axiomatic study. For a strict and complete axiomatic system, the selection and setting of axioms must have three basic requirements and the first one is "compatibility," which means that it is not allowed that a theorem in an axiomatic system is proved true and the negative one is proved true at the same time.

Conversely, if proposition A and negative proposition non-A (denoted by -A) can be derived from the axiomatic system, it can be seen that there are contradictions because A coexists with -A. The emergence of contradictions is due to the contradictory understanding in the axiomatic system itself, which is not allowed by the laws of thinking. Therefore, non- contradictory nature in axiomatic system is a basic requirement and any disciplines and theoretical systems must meet this requirement. This means that it is not allowed that the axioms, the propositions derived from the interpretation of any ideological theory are mutually contradictory, that is, none of the various axioms and propositions can be ambiguous and contradict each other.

This criterion applies to axioms and also necessarily to all propositions derived from the axioms, and originally, to definitions and even basic assumptions. The mutual negation and conflict in the definitions and the basic assumptions, if there are, will also affect the propositions derived from the basic assumptions, definitions, and axioms which mutually cooperate with each other. It can be seen, starting with the analysis of the contradictions, the basic assumptions substantiate the contradictions and then discuss the more specific contradictions with the aid of definitions and axioms. This method is a decoding of ideological system of pre-Qin Confucian classics and also the implementation of the principle of axiomatic compatibility.

From the perspective of "contradiction," the pursuit of "the mean state of contradiction" is the characteristic of pre-Qin Confucian classics. In accordance with the dialectical view, the contradiction is an objective existence, and the contradictory opposites are interdependent and contradiction is generated at the birth of things until they themselves die out. From this, the complete eradication of contradiction indicates the demise of the things. The contradictions can not be "completely resolved," but it can reach a dynamic equilibrium during the existence of things.

This can also be deduced from the point of view of dialectics. In general, the contradiction between things can generally be attributed to three states: (1) no contradiction; (2) a sharp irreconcilable conflict; (3) in a relatively coordinated state. Because "contradiction is inherent in things," the first two cases are not particular state in which things exist. In this sense, the Confucian pursuit of "the mean state of contradiction" embodies man's conscious grasp of objective laws by means of his own intelligence.

In fact, we can also see "no contradiction" and "irreconcilability of contradictions" as the two extreme states at which things exist. If "no contradiction" is regarded as a state of contradictory relationship of things before they are produced, then the irreconcilability of contradiction is the state of contradictory relationship of things as they are dying out. If the "things" are specifically set as the "human society," the above reasoning is also established.

Conversely, during the duration of the existence of human society, which is regarded as a special "thing," "no contradiction" and "irreconcilability of contradiction," the two absolute states do not exist. However, the mean state of "contradictions" is long-standing. It is a kind of state of objective existence, and the result of subjective and conscious pursuit.

Observing the different contradiction relationships from different perspectives, however, we can see that this special phenomenon of human society is made up of many contradictory relationships. Conditioned by human cognition, the number of the contradiction relationships we have observed is always limited. Thus different thoughts and theories arise; and also due to different perspectives, different conclusions can be drawn. Confucianism represented by Confucius and Daoism represented by Laozi have established different ideologies because of different perspectives of observing contradictions.

Until now, there have been many elaborations on the difference between Confucianism and Daoism, but it is difficult to make a conclusion. Mr. Li Zehou so remarked, "On the surface, Confucianism and Daoism are separated and opposite, as Confucianism is about how man gets into the society and Daoism is about how man gets out of the society; the former is optimistic and progressive, and the latter is negative and seclusive. In fact, they just complement and coordinate with each other."[1]

It is believed that "Daoism advocates the return to the state of nature and inaction, and maintains and protects innocent nature of humanity in the original chaos. The philosophy of Laozi and Zhuangzi (Chuang-tzu), especially Zhuangzi, tends to emphasize individuals over groups, and to pursue the spiritual freedom of individual selves. Confucians have a certain utilitarian attitude of political ethics towards nature. They plan their own patriarchal hierarchy regarding the relationship between the monarch and his subjects, between father and son, and between husband and wife, according to their own understanding of nature, believing that this order of the human society embodies the natural way, which is reasonable and inevitable."[2]

In short, Confucianism emphasizes the accession to the society and personality cultivation while Daoism stresses retirement from the world and natural personality. These two views are representative. However, from the perspective of social contradictions, these views are still debatable. First, both Daoism and Confucianism have strong criticism on secular, and also realize that the disputes caused by a variety of "desires" are the focus of social problems and social contradictions.

Second, both Daoism and Confucianism have actively put forward the ideas of solving social problems. Confucianism believes that personal desires without any control and regulation will cause a lot of social disputes, leading to social disorder and chaos. Therefore, it is necessary to promote individual self-cultivation and to regulate people's desires and words and deeds with benevolence, righteousness, rituals and wisdom respectively.

This theory highlights the two sides of the contradictions observed by Confucians: one is the desire of human beings, and the other is the social state in which the society is in peaceful order. They advocate that this contradiction should be adjusted to "*zhongyong*" ("mean") state to prevent an extreme state in which the Way is abandoned to bring serious disasters to people's livelihood. Daoists think that man's desire, which comes out of nature, does not cause any problems when in a natural state; but the society will be in a chaotic state when human society is

---

1   Li Zehou. *Three Books of Aesthetics*. Tianjin Academy of Social Sciences Press, 2003, p.49.
2   Gao Chenyang. *Commented Biography on Ruanji*. In Kuang Yaming(ed.), *A Critical Biography of Chinese Thinkers*. Nanjing University Press, 2011, p.137.

deviated from the natural way and artificially create a lot of things to stimulate people's desires.

On the one hand, fame, fortune and rare goods are used to stimulate people's desires and pursuit. On the other hand, people are required to control their own desires. This has actually formed a paradox. Therefore, it is better to "refrain from displaying anything arousing desire" so that people can have "no desire" or "few desires" and people's behavior can comply with natural way. Thus, there is no need to make so much effort to regulate people's desires and people can do everything as required by the heaven.

Thus, the two sides in contradiction as observed by Laozi are highlighted: one side is the "way of nature," the other side is the social desires violating the way of nature and the methods and systems of managing them. The idea of "*shouzhong*" (keeping moderate) is the method of examining and managing social desires so as to return to the natural state and restore the normal order of society by eliminating such deviation.

From this perspective, Laozi also longed for the ideal state of human society. He did not advocate uninhibited indulgence of people's own behavior and did not want to see the state of chaos. What he desired was just the pursuit of a state similar to the one advocated by Confucianism: "I followed my heart's desire without overstepping the line." In his view, one can follow his heart's desire and do as he wishes in a state that complies with nature, which won't cause any social problem. From this, Laozi has a high degree of concern and a strong sense of responsibility for human society. "Though Laozi was known as being 'out of the world'," it is obviously inappropriate to say that Laozi did not like to take care of the worldly affairs.

An axiomatic study of Confucius' and Laozi's thoughts inevitably involves different perspectives in observation of social contradictions. And the above comparison also presents the difference between Confucian "maintaining the mean" and the Daoist "keeping moderate."

First, the Confucian "maintaining the mean" differs from Daoist "keeping moderate" in level and application range. Mr. Chen Guying said: "Laozi and Confucius are both the successors of the same cultural tradition and they have many similarities in their thoughts, such as: (1) the view of 'keeping moderate,' (2) and valuing harmony--the harmonious relationship between man and nature."[1]

---

1 Chen Guying. *New Commentary on Laozi & Zhuangzi*. The Commercial Press, 2008, p.35.

Laozi's ideological system and the philosophical basis and methodology of the doctrine of the Mean are similar in that both Laozi's idea of keeping moderate and Confucius' doctrine of the Mean emphasize impartiality, i.e., the thoughts and behaviors should be moderate in the middle of the two poles of the contradiction. They oppose excess and dificiency, and advocate the way of grasping the contradiction and unity of opposites and their transformation in order to grasp the root of correctly understanding the world and dealing with the fundamental problem. From this point of view, moderation and the doctrine of the mean are similar.

However, "keeping moderate" is quite different from the Mean in terms of level. Generally speaking, Laozi's thought of "keeping moderate" covers all aspects of Heaven and human affairs, and nature and society. The Confucian doctrine of the mean represented by Confucius mainly focuses on morality and politics. It can be said that The Doctrine of the Mean is the application and development of Laozi's ideology of "keeping moderate" in the field of worldly affairs, including morality and politics.

As a methodology, The Doctrine of the Mean is more of practical use. The Doctrine of the Mean advocated by Confucianism focuses on the inner contradictions of human society. The "desires" and "disputes" pointed out by Confucianism are human desires and social disputes. The state in which the society is in good order and well-governed is also the proper state of human society.

Daoism's "keeping moderate" focuses on the contradiction between the human society and the natural world (that is, the external world in which human beings live). It is a kind of "internal and external contradiction." Daoists point out that human desire is not entirely a human characteristic but also reflects the prescriptive property of heaven, earth and nature. Due to the lack of macroscopic understanding of this, there appears deviation in the social behavior of understanding, controlling and dealing with the desires.

In other words, the lack of understanding of the external world as well as the natural attributes of oneself leads to deviations in social management. According to some researchers, Laozi's *"zhong"* (meaning middle or moderation) in *"it is better to hold fast to moderation and void"* refers to the way of observing the general law of the universe implied by all things existing between heaven and earth objectively, the most primitive true state of the mean in the development of all things. The moderate state is essentially the state of Dao of Laozi because the universe or the world itself is a big *"zhonghe"* (the combination of moderation and harmony). Heaven and earth can not exist in violation of *"zhonghe,"* not to mention the human. *"Zhonghe"* of the world does not mean the artificial middle routes, or any random reconciliation or compromise, but the natural course of the world.[1]

Based on the different perspectives of human society, Confucius and Laozi proposed different ideas of governing the society. What Confucius advocated can be said to be a self-balancing method: the root cause is hidden in humanity, and the scalpel is also in the hands of mankind. Only by self-cultivation and regulation of desires can people resolve disputes and govern the society well.

What Laozi advocated can be called a "natural balance." From a natural point of view, the human "disease" is not a true disease in a strict sense. It is mistakenly regarded as a morbid state by human beings, who impose on it inappropriate treatment or over-treatment. As long as we understand the way of mature and behave in accordance with its laws and rules of action, we will not mistakenly think that we humans suffer from this kind of disease. This imaginary disease will not cause any deadly consequences; in contrast, inappropriate treatment will bring harm to mankind.

In the final analysis, as with other biological species, human society is also subject to the natural law of balance. This natural law of balance is fundamental and plays a greater role while human's self-balance law just plays the role of tinkering. Too much exaggeration of human's self-balance law, which ignores and even destroys the natural balance of the law, will bring disaster to mankind. From the perspective of level, man's "self-balance law" and other biological populations' self-balancing law are all under the control of the "natural law of balance."

Second, from the perspective of dialectics, both "keeping moderate" and "The Doctrine of the Mean" have their advantages and disadvantages in the elaboration of contradictory relations. Previous researchers have also noted the difference between Laozi's "keeping moderate" and the Confucian "doctrine of the mean." They think that the former, more focusing on the opposition and mutual transformation of contradictions, is dialectical and positive, while the latter, though having a dialectical element, has some negative elements. In essence, Laozi's idea of "keeping moderate" is more inclined to dynamic harmony, emphasizing the transformation of the world and the transformation and development of the contradiction, and advocating a higher level of harmony through constant renewal and struggle.

The Doctrine of the Mean lays stress more on the pursuit of harmony in the

---

1 Shi Dexin. On the Similarities and Differences between Laozi's Thought and Confucius' Doctrine of Mean. *Quest*, No. 5, 2010.

static level. Although the concept of "The Doctrine of the Mean" has the advantages in handling contradictions reasonably and maintaining harmony and stability, it ignores the struggle and transformation of the opposites and can not see the self-denial and qualitative change of things. This is the main defect of "The Doctrine of the Mean." Confucianism makes absolute the rational factors contained in "The Doctrine of the Mean" and puts too much emphasis on the unity of both sides of the contradiction but pays little attention to its opposite characteristics and the mutual transformation, which is particularly prominent during the transformation of the old system to the new one when The Doctrine of the Mean is a little conservative. Although it accepts development, it does not advocate that the development should exceed the limits of quantity, just as it admits contradictions, but it tries to keep the struggle in contradictions within a certain range. Such a metaphysical chronic illness, has, after all, greatly reduced the functions of the dialectics. This fact reflects the limitation of the dialectical spirit of the traditional Mean doctrine.[1]

Zhang Dainian said, "The Doctrine of the Mean holds that everything has a standard, that is, a limit. It is the same thing whether to go beyond or not to reach this limit, which shows the view of the mutual transformation of the opposites. This is correct. However, The Doctrine of the Mean tries to maintain this standard, to adhere to this limit, and to prevent it from turning into the opposite. It does not maintain the view of promoting the development and change. This is the limitation of The Doctrine of the Mean. "In daily life, we do need to behave in a limited way and avoid going to extremes, such as in food and clothing and the like. But the scientific development sometimes needs to break the traditional concept and social progress particularly need to break the shackles of tradition. For these issues, The Doctrine of the Mean has become an obstacle to progress. We now need to have a comprehensive analysis of The Doctrine of the Mean."[2]

In fact, it may not hit the mark to discuss the difference between "keeping the moderate" and "The Doctrine of the Mean" from the dynamic and dialectical or from static and non-dialectical perspectives, which seems to value things by struggle and development. In fact, the defect of The Doctrine of the Mean mainly lies in its one-sided viewing of contradiction.

1　Shi Dexin. On the Similarities and Differences between Laozi's Thought and Confucius' Doctrine of Mean. *Quest*, No. 5, 2010.
2　Zhang Dainian. *Outline of Conceptual Category of Chinese Classical Philosophy*. China Social Science Press, 2000, pp.179-180.

According to the dialectical point of view, the contradiction is not isolated. Although contradictions have primary and secondary ones, they are interactive and interrelated. Just as the Confucians of Song Dynasty (960-1279) pointed out, Confucianism mainly stressed "inner sage" and "outer king." But the organic combination of inner sage and outer king is not always close enough. When we make the axiomatic study of pre-Qin Confucian classics, we always feel that the logical relationship between the two is not smooth and natural enough.

When discussing individual cultivation, Confucianism seeks the contradiction from the perspective of intrinsic motives of individuals. It is reasonable to treat "goodness" and "evilness" as the two sides of a contradiction. But it is problematic to treat the contradiction separately. According to Karl Marx, man is the sum of all social relations. For this reason, the contradiction between "goodness" and "evilness" is intertwined with all social relations and contradictions in real life. The other contradictions play a great role in the formation of this contradiction and influence its performance and development. However, Confucianism is not fully aware of it, resulting in a lack of a close logical relationship between "the Dao which is within the sage and the Dao which manifests itself externally in the king."

Because "the Dao which is within the sage" to a large extent, is not involved in the contradictions of real life, while "the Dao which manifests itself externally in the king" must involve in the contradictions of real life; this is to solve complex contradictions starting from a single contradiction, which is not easily dealt with naturally. Confucianism in the period of the Neo-Confucianism of the Song and Ming dynasties after a long development gives us the impression that it focuses on the "inner sage" and has basically abandoned the "outer king," or that the discussion of "the Dao which manifests itself externally in the king " is obviously illusory, which is related to the above theoretical defects. Conversely, due to lack of consideration of the contradictions of real life, the discussion of the contradiction of human nature becomes more and more abstract.

In contrast, Laozi's idea of "keeping moderate" does not observe the contradiction in isolation. In the thought of "keeping moderate," the two sides of the contradiction, natural way and the deviation of human society, are essentially the contradiction between "infiniteness" and "finiteness," both of which are actually the complex of numerous contradictions, rather than the contradictions of single nature. Since the sum of contradictions has been taken into account, naturally there is no such problem as looking at contradiction in an isolated way. In terms of this point, "keeping moderate." is very particular.

However, there is still inadequacy in Laozi's "keeping moderate." Hu Shi (Hu Shih, Dec. 17, 1891-Feb. 24, 1962, Chinese scholar) pointed out, "It is Daoist defect to believe in the Heaven too much and think that human beings can do nothing about their affairs. This will inevitably lead to a bad mentality that humans can only depend on the Heaven and live at the mercy of elements."[1]

Daoism in later generations superstitiously believed in the power of drawing magic characters and chanting incantations, and swallowing knives and spitting fire. On the surface, this superstition did not seem to have much to do with the Daoist thought. In fact, in this superstitious thought, this exceptional ability can do everything by omnipotence. From the perspective of the unity of contradictory opposites, this concept is caused by too much emphasis on contradictory relationship without focusing on its unity.

In fact, there exist antagonistic relations between the natural way and the human society, which indeed goes its own way and deviates from the natural way. However, human society has a unified relationship with "Nature" itself, or involuntarily follows "the way of nature" (i.e., determined by the heaven), or consciously performs so (as in the case of following seasonal changes in agricultural production). It does not always doing things at will.

In concrete terms, all the actions of mankind, such as politics, military, economy, culture and so on, always have the side of "the way of nature." Thus, the abstracted merit, morality, etc., are not completely divorced from "natural way" and the purely artificial concept. All of these clearly reflect the unity of human society and natural way.

Laozi emphasized the deviation of human cognition and behavior, and strove to correct it, but also largely ignored the unity of the relationship between the human society and the way of nature, resulting in the psychology of depending and living on the heaven. It denies the positive actions of human beings who can know and master as well as conform to the laws of nature, leaving an anti-civilized, anti-social, and anti-science and technology impression. From this point, Laozi's "keeping moderate" is not as good as The Doctrine of the Mean of Confucianism which pays a high degree of attention to human beings.

1　Hu Shi. Philosophy of Huainanzi. *Collected Works of Hu Shi, Vol. 1*. Guangzhou: Huacheng Press, 2013, p.183.

IV. Frame of the Axiomatic Interpretation of *Laozi*

This book adopts the axiomatic approach to interpret *Laozi* and refines the inherent logic system of Daoism. The author(s) tries to establish a deductive system built upon the fundamentals of *Laozi*. That is, after making some basic assumptions and giving some basic definitions, the author(s) formulates a dozen of axioms, and proves through deduction the series of propositions contained in it by logical reasoning. In this way, the logical system of Daoism implied in *Laozi* is brought to light.

In the axiomatic interpretation of *Laozi* based on the assumptions, definitions, and axioms, we have divided it into four parts, namely, "On Understanding the Dao," "On Cherishing Virtue," "On Governance," and "On Preserving Health." We try to sort out and then prove the propositions (theorems) and corollaries of each part, and illustrate them with examples and explanations. These parts are actually a whole organic body with each of them having inner logic relationship.

Illustrated as follows:

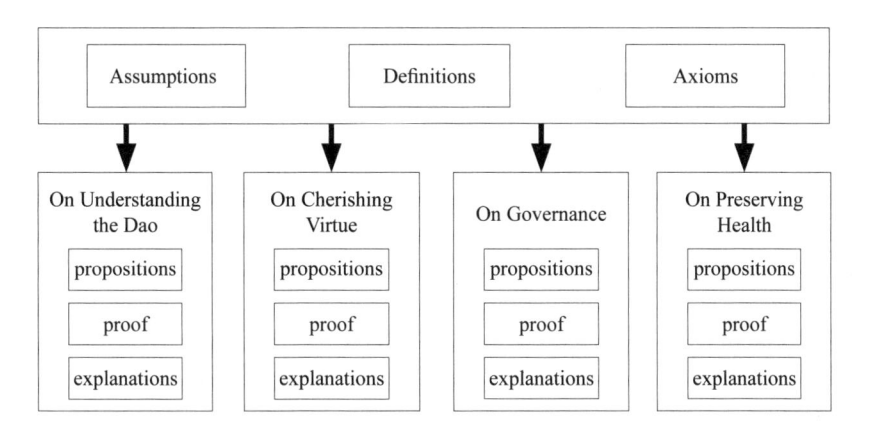

Assumptions	Definitions	Axioms

On Understanding the Dao	On Cherishing Virtue	On Governance	On Preserving Health
propositions	propositions	propositions	propositions
proof	proof	proof	proof
explanations	explanations	explanations	explanations

There are 21 propositions in the chapter "On Understanding the Dao", which mainly explains the basic concepts of Dao and the way people understand and comprehend Dao. P1-1 to P1-10 expound the meaning of Dao itself as well as the relationship between Dao and all things; P1-11 to P1-16 illustrate the two understandings or the cognitive state of man, i.e., "wisdom" and "insight," and their mutual relationship; P1-17 to P1-21 illustrate the path, methods, and procedures of understanding the Dao.

The 23 propositions in the chapter "On Cherishing Virtue" mainly discuss "*de*" (virtue) that conforms to nature and the way as well as the purpose of the cultivation of virtue. P2-1 to P2-3 point out what conforms to the nature is virtue and what ways are used to be virtuous. P2-4 to P2-10 mainly illustrate that greed, artifice, and deceit are harmful to the cultivation of virtue, and the ways to weaken them are contentment, willingness in low place, softness, and non-competitiveness. P2-11 to P2-13 elaborate representations of sages and their mental state. P2-14 to P2-23 elaborate how to practice "virtue" in different aspects.

There are 28 propositions in the chapter "On Governance" which mainly discusses the natural way of governance. P3-1 to P3-2 elaborate the ideal society is the one that is led by sages and conforms to nature. P3-3 to P3-5 elaborate the society characterized by a harmonious nature in which Dao is prevalent and the people live and work in peace and contentment without the application of rites and laws. P3-6 to P3-8 discuss the basic model, performance, and the implementation of good governance. P3-9 to P3-16 point out that governance must follow Dao and ancient examples, not cleverness, talent, benevolence, rites, merits, or valuable goods, etc.. P3-17 to P3-24 point out that people should abide by the principle of "softness" in wars, in diplomacy, in being a ruler, and in administration and governance of the people. P3-25 to P3-28 point out that the cultivation of the monarch is to follow the principle of being both hard and soft and strive for virtues and trust.

There are 22 propositions in the chapter "On Preserving Health," which mainly discusses how to achieve the unity of loving oneself and loving others, and points out that the unity must be achieved by following the principle of "nature." P4-1 points out that the fundamental principle is to follow nature. P4-2 to P4-6 point out how to keep quiet, tranquil, simple, pure, and honest in mind and soften one's addictions, which is the basis to follow nature. P4-7 to P4-10 point out that the concept of wealth must be established on the basis of principle of nature and it is important for people to learn how to properly deal with the relationship between wealth and life. P4-11 to P4-14 point out that we must build up our concept of fortune and misfortune, honor and disgrace, with contentment and modesty at its center in accordance with the principle of nature. P4-15 to P4-19 discuss the relationship between strength and weakness, between contending and not contending, and between skillfulness and clumsiness based on the principle of nature. P4-20 to P4-22 explain the principle of symbiosis of the individuals and all things.

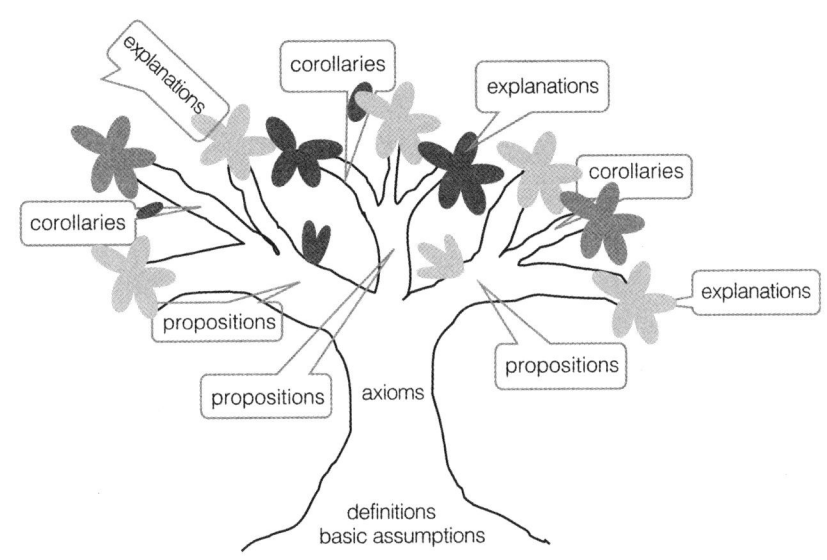

We depict the framework of the axiomatic system of *Laozi* with a tree diagram. The root symbolizes definitions, and basic assumptions; the trunk represents the axioms; the main branches signify propositions deduced and inferred according to those definitions and assumptions; the twigs stand for corollaries derived from those propositions and the leaves represent proofs and explanations related to the propositions and corollaries.

V. Definitions and Explanations

The requirements for relevant definitions presented here are: they are the important concepts derived from *Laozi*; they are in line with the original intent and context; and they have the generality of contemporary word meaning.

1. (*De*) *De*, literally meaning virtue or morality, is the generic term of the spontaneous process for all things that act without interference and also refers to man's understanding of the process and the conduct that adapt to this process.

Quotes from *Laozi*:

The character of the greatest virtue exclusively follows the Dao. (Chapter 21)

He who follows the Dao is with the Dao; he who follows the Virtue is with the Virtue; he who has lost the Dao and the Virtue will lose everything. If one is with the Virtue, the Dao will go with him; if he is in conflict with the Virtue, the Dao will go against him. (Chapter 23)

You know the strength of the masculine, but keep the tenderness of the feminine, and are willing to be the ravine of the world. Being the ravine of the world, you will be accompanied by eternal virtue, and return to being a babe. You know the white, but keep to the role of the black, and are willing to be a model of the world. Being a model of the world, your eternal virtue will not go astray, and you return to the highest truth. You know the honor, but keep to the role of the disgraced, and are willing to be a valley of the world. Being the valley of the world, you will no longer lack the eternal virtue, and return to simplicity. When the first natural Dao scattered into small things, it became the useful containers. Those who were possessed with the Dao would make use of them, and became the leaders of hundreds of officials. Therefore, the perfect political system was not separated. (Chapter 28)

A man of the superior virtue does not claim to be of virtue. Thus he is of the true virtue.

A man of the inferior virtue always holds fast to the virtue in form, thus he is actually of no virtue. (Chapter 38)

The great virtue resembles the valley; the abundant virtue appears insufficient. (Chapter 41)

Dao generates them, virtue nourishes them, substance forms them, and circumstances accomplish them. Therefore all things revere Dao and honor virtue. Yet Dao is revered and virtue honored not because this is decreed by any authority but because it's naturally so on its own. Thus Dao generates them, and virtue nourishes them, makes them grow and ripen, and cares for and nurtures them. Dao generates all things yet claims no possession; avails them yet takes no credit; and guides them yet not reigns them. Such is called the "greatest virtue." (Chapter 51)

Man of virtue in abundance is like a new-born baby. (Chapter 55)

If you can abide by the principle, it is your 'profound virtue,' which is far-reaching. With the return to the very nature of simplicity, the country will harmonize with Nature. (Chapter 65)

Explanation: "Heaven and Earth," *Zhuangzi* says, "In taking different forms, it brought life, and became known as Virtue." Virtue is the free process of all things developing from non-being and back to non-being not just from non-being to being. "The character of the greatest virtue exclusively follows the Dao." (Chapter 21, *Laozi*) This means that all things of the world develop from non-being to being. All the things are born from being and being from non-being and non-being from the Dao. Chapter 55 says: "Man of virtue in abundance is like a new-born babe," which describes the process from "being" to "non-being," and man of virtue in abundance and babe are the "image" of "non-being."

Being capable of understanding things, man can realize and comply with this process, which is man's "virtue." In *Laozi*, this kind of virtue is called superior virtue, great virtue, constant virtue, and eternal virtue, etc. Human's virtue is embodied in recognizing and actively complying with the Virtue. Chapter 28 says, "*You know the strength of the masculine, but keep the tenderness of the feminine, and are willing to be the ravine of the world. Being the ravine of the world, you will be accompanied by eternal virtue, and return to being a babe. You know the white, but keep to the role of the black, and are willing to be a model of the world. Being a model of the world, your eternal virtue will not go astray, and you return to the highest truth. You know the honor, but keep to the role of the disgraced, and are willing to be a valley of the world. Being the valley of the world, you will no longer lack the eternal virtue, and return to simplicity.*" It is emphasized here that constant virtue means knowing the male, but keeping to the role of the female, and returning to being a babe. This is the recognition of and compliance with virtue developing from "non-being" to "being" and then again to "non-being." Chapter 51 and Chapter 65 also illustrate this thought.

2. (*Yu*) *Yu*, literally meaning desire or lust, refers to people's pursuit of wealth, fame and power. This pursuit may violate "naturalness."

Quotes from *Laozi*:

Not to value and employ men of superior ability is the way to keep the people from rivalry among themselves; not to prize articles which are difficult to procure is the way to keep them from becoming thieves; not to show them what is likely to excite their desires is the way to keep their minds from disorder. Therefore, the sage, in the exercise of his government, empties their minds, fills their bellies, weakens their wills, and strengthens their bones. He always keeps them innocent of knowledge and free from desire, and disables the wise from taking any ill actions. If you deal with worldly affairs by "non-action," there will be no trouble of government. (Chapter 3)

Keep plain and simple; reduce selfishness and desire little. (Chapter 19)

Dao does nothing yet nothing is left undone. Should lords and kings be able to maintain it, all things will be transformed on their own. After they are transformed, they may grow avid. I will check the avidity with the nameless simplicity of Dao. Checked with the nameless simplicity, they will have no avidity. No avidity leads to serenity, hence the empire's stability. (Chapter 37)

No crime is greater than greediness. No disaster is greater than not being content. Therefore, be satisfied with what you have, and you will be content all the time. (Chapter 46)

The sage desires not to desire and does not value rare treasures. (Chapter 66)

Explanation: If free process of Dao and all things (including man) is a natural one, then why does man become unnatural? This is because "Man" has desire and this desire (for wealth, fame, and power) may go against Nature.

Laozi did not mean that people must give up desires but that they should desire little. This indicates that Laozi did not entirely deny all pursuits of wealth, fame, and power, but the excessive pursuit that does not comply with Nature. When Laozi talked about desires on many occasions, he meant the desires that are unnatural, such as honoring men of worth or paragons (that is, the pursuit of fame), valuing rare goods (that is, the pursuit of wealth), and taking active action (that is, the pursuit of power).

3. *Zhi* (meaning wisdom, intelligence, wit, cleverness) generally refers to a person's cognitive ability to understand the object and make choices about individual behaviors; it also refers specifically to the craftiness and wisdom in the excessive pursuit of desire. The latter is often true of the ruler.

Quotes from *Laozi*:

When everyone in the world knows the beautiful as beautiful, ugliness comes into being; when everyone knows the good as good, then the bad comes into being. (Chapter 2)

He always keeps them innocent of knowledge and free from desire, and disable the wise from taking any ill actions. (Chapter 3)

When the rulers abandon what is witty and what is sly, then the people will be truly benefited. (Chapter 19)

Explanation: Laozi did not oppose the wisdom in general sense, but the kind of craftiness in wisdom. This wisdom is closely related to the excessive pursuit of people's desire, that is to say, it is produced to meet the excessive desire. Therefore, Laozi asked the ruler "to steer the people out of knowledge." Chapter 65 of *Laozi* said, "*The person who was good at Dao in ancient times did not use it to enlighten the common people, but to keep them in ignorance. The reason the people are difficult to control is that they have too much intelligence. Thus, to govern a state with intelligence is always a disaster for the state. Not to govern the state with intelligence is a blessing to the state.*" Therefore, to govern the people is to keep the people in ignorance and the rulers themselves should not rule the state by wisdom.

4. (*Guan, Ming*) Guan literally means to view or observe things or examine oneself. It is the way to know Dao. *Ming*, **which means fairness and justice, discernment, or brightness, refers to the self-observation ability in inner human vitality.**

Quotes from *Laozi*:

One should gain an insight into the subtlety of Dao from the formless, and should gain an insight into the ultimate of all things from their forms. (Chapter 1)

Take emptiness to the limit and keep still. All things arise together, I watch their return. Things come forth in great numbers, and each one returns to its own root. Returning to roots means stillness, and also means a return to origin. To return to its origin is known as the eternal. To know the eternal is known as discernment. (Chapter 16)

He who understands others is wise; he who understands himself has discernment. (Chapter 33)

To be able to perceive the small is called discernment. To be able to keep pliant is called strength. (Chapter 52)

How do I know the empire is so? By observing other individuals through myself; observing other families through my family; observing other villages through my village; observing other states through my state; observing other empires through my empire. (Chapter 54)

Explanation: "To observe" is the way to know Dao and also the way to have discernment. Laozi proposed some angles and hints for "observation," but did not elaborate accurately how to achieve the effect of "observation." Therefore, Laozi's "observation" has a certain sense of mystery. "To observe" is not achieved by the five sense organs, but by the perception of one's "heart" and other means like recognition. However, it is fundamentally different from the perception, recognition, analysis, and thinking, which are limited to human's "being." "Discernment" is a concept put forward by Laozi in particular to distinguish it from "wisdom." It is also the guarantee for this cognitive ability of human's real understanding of Dao.

5. (*Jing*) *Jing*, stillness, means a state of mind purged of excessive desire and wit.

Quotes from *Laozi*:

Therefore, the way of the sages to govern the people is to purify their soul but fill their belies, reduce their selfish desire but strengthen their bones. (Chapter 3)

*Take emptiness to the limit and keep still. All things arise together, I watch their return. Things come forth in great numbers, and each one returns to its own root. Returning to roots means stillness, and also means a return to origin. To return to its origin is known as the eternal. To know the eternal is known as discernme*nt. (Chapter 16)

Explanation: "Emptiness" or "Void" is just "non-being" or "nothing." When a person reaches the limit of emptiness, he will understand the infinite possibilities of Dao. If a person's ability to comprehend and understand things can reach such height, it is called stillness, which specifically refers to the inherent non-being of a person.

6. *Shen*, literally meaning human body, oneself life or life, refers to the unity of humans inner vitality and external desire.

Quotes from *Laozi*:

The sage puts himself behind others yet finds himself before others. He completely disregards his own benefit yet it turns out that his own benefit is preserved. It is due to this selflessness that he can perfect himself. (Chapter 7)

When the deed is accomplished you retire; such is Heaven's Way! (Chapter 9)

The soul and the form can be combined as one, but can they be forever combined and never sever? (Chapter 10)

One is panic-stricken when he's favoured or humiliated. He is too much worried about his body as much as calamity. (Chapter 13)

To be head of the people, one needs to put himself behind them. (Chapter 66)

Explanation: Laozi's understanding of people is divided into two aspects: inner vitality and external desire. The unity of these two aspects is human being. Because man is one of all things, these two aspects correspond to non-being and being. The inherent vitality is subtle, but full of power, and, this is non-being. External desire, as the function of the body senses, is "being." From the perspective of human cognition, inner vitality is manifested as discernment; external desire is expressed as wisdom. However, in the reading of *Laozi*, it is important to note that when Laozi talked about "*shen*" on some occasions, he was focusing on the inner vitality, as he said, "*He is too much worried about his body as much as calamity.*" (Chapter 13) On other occasions, he focuses on external desire, or exactly to say personal desire, as he said, "*To be head of the people, one needs to put himself behind them*" in Chapter 66. That is to say, the rulers must first put their own desires after the common people's desires if they want to rule the people. In fact, if the ruler wishes to lead the people, he must place himself in the back because the ruler needs to pay more attention to the clarification of the "inner vitality." In this way he can really "be a head of the people." Although his desire can not be eliminated, his wish to be the head of the people does not mean satisfying his personal desire.

7. (*Wu Si*) *Wu Si*, literally meaning "selflessness," refers to the inclusive psychological state after the elimination of excessive "desire" and crafty "wisdom."

Quotes from *Laozi*:

Heaven and earth are unbiased, and let all things in the universe grow naturally; the sage is unbiased, and let the people develop themselves. (Chapter 5)

The sage puts himself behind others yet finds himself before others. He completely disregards his own benefit yet it turns out that his own benefit is preserved. It is due to his selfleness that he can perfect himself. (Chapter 7)

Keep plain and simple; reduce selfishness and desire little. (Chapter 19)

The sage is always good at saving others, and considers no one as abandoned. He is good at saving things, and, as a result, nothing is abandoned. (Chapter 27)

Explanation: Man is one of all things, and hence can be named. As long as man can be named with his own wisdom, it means dividing the boundaries, which are the relationships among people, close and distant, superiors and inferiors. Therefore, Confucianism's emphasis on "rectification" is to establish hierarchical order. Laozi believed that this "rectification" is necessary because it can tell us the boundary of action, but it is not the supreme, and that we must return to the non-being state, to the beginning of this state so that this boundary will not really become the shackle of vitality. The inclusive state of mind after the elimination of excessive desire and crafty wisdom is the state of Dao. Therefore, the sage, as a sample of Dao, treated the people without preference or bias. It is also to respect the simple vitality of the people and prevent it from being distorted.

8. (*Gong*) *Gong*, literally meaning task, action, function, achievement, accomplishment or credit, refers to the state of things on their own; it also refers to the activities of people consciously safeguarding social order in line with "nature."

Quotes from *Laozi*:

He succeeds, but does not claim credit for it. (Chapter 2)

When the deed is accomplished you retire; such is Heaven's Way! (Chapter 9)

When his task is accomplished and his work done, the people all say, "The things all happened to us naturally." (Chapter 17)

One who brags himself gets no credit. (Chapter 24)

Explanation: In the general sense, "*Gong*" is the concept corresponding to "*De*" (virtue), and sometimes it just means "*De*." As people have cognitive ability and can take the initiative to adapt to nature, people's "*Gong*" also stresses this conscious activity. It is this self-conscious adaptation to nature that shows he who claims credit for success and brags himself gets no credit.

9. (*Shengren*) *Shengren*, **literally meaning sages, refers to the virtuous people who administer the country.**

Quotes from *Laozi*:

Therefore, the sage manages things with non-action and practices wordless teaching. (Chapter 2)

Thus the sage does not satisfy his eyes with colors but satisfy his belly with enough food. (Chapter 12)

Therefore, the sage embraces the One (Dao) and is the example for the world. (Chapter 22)

The sage does not store up things for himself. Using more to help others, he obtains more himself. (Chapter 81)

Explanation: Laozi believed that sage is the ideal leader of the country. This kind of ruler can understand the process of nature, and try consciously to adapt to the "nature" in governing the country.

10. (*Wu Wei*) *Wu Wei*, **literally meaning inaction or non-action, refers to the principle that the governors must comply with nature, and should not take deliberate action or even reckless and ill action.**

Quotes from *Laozi*:

Therefore, the sage manages things with non-action and practices wordless teaching. (Chapter 2)

Though nothing is done, everything is done well. (Chapter 3)

If you are to love the people and govern a state, is it possible to do it by non-action? (Chapter 10)

I follow non-action and the people are transformed of themselves. (Chapter 57)

To behave with "non-action," to do things without disturbance, and to regard the tasteless as tasteful. (Chapter 63)

Explanation: Laozi thought that *"Dao takes what is natural as its models"* and *"All things return to roots, which are known as origin,"* and *"Nature is the origin of all things."* The so-called "origin" in Laozi's eyes means the same as "the original state." People with the desire and wisdom can not be separated from all things in the universe, therefore, the principle of human action is of course to comply with "nature." However, inaction or non-action does not mean that people do not act, Nor mean that people can act without any thinking like animals, but they should exclude any ill or blind actions that do not comply with nature from the meaningful actions.

11. (*Bu Zheng*) *Bu Zheng*, literally meaning not to contend, refers to the attitude towards life after the elimination of excessive "desire" and crafty "wisdom."

Quotes from *Laozi*:

Not to value and employ men of superior ability is the way to keep the people from rivalry among themselves; not to prize articles which are difficult to procure is the way to keep them from becoming thieves; not to show them what is likely to excite their desires is the way to keep their minds from disorder. (Chapter 3)

The perfect goodness is like water. Water is good at benefiting all things, but does not contend with them. It prefers to dwell in places the masses of people detest, therefore it is closest to the Dao. (Chapter 8)

One does not contend with others, so no one is in a position to contend with him. (Chapter 22)

The Dao of heaven benefits rather than harms all things; the Dao of the sage is to give rather than contend. (Chapter 81)

Explanation: Laozi thought that D*ao* can be nothing. On the surface, it seems to be "frail and weak," but is full of power in its subtlety. All things act naturally, not by force, but they always have a steady stream of vitality. "Not to contend" is the reaction to it. It does not mean retreat, cowardice and timidity, but more inherent strength. Any one, who has the excessive desire for the pursuit of external wealth, power and reputation, and has the "wisdom" to meet this pursuit, will lose the ability to return to nothing and will become more frail rather than more powerful, because if that happens, we will lose the inner vitality and the source of our nurturing vitality will be blocked.

12. (*Yan*) *Yan*, literally meaning words, refers to the governor's political decrees, policies and education.

Quotes from *Laozi*:

Therefore, the sage manages things with non-action and practices wordless teaching. (Chapter 2)

Too much talk leads to a dead end; it is better to hold fast to moderation and the void. (Chapter 5)

None in the world can match the wordless teaching and the usefulness of inaction. (Chapter 43)

He who is wise will not speak; he who speaks is not wise. (Chapter 56)

The way of Heaven is not to vie yet to be good at winning; not to speak yet respond skillfully; no one summons it, yet it comes on its own; to be at ease and yet good at decision. (Chapter 73)

Explanation: Dao is nameless and also wordless. In fact, it has no need for a name or words. People who govern the country must be careful in "words." Too many words may hurt the people's "naturalness." So Laozi advocated "less words," or even "no words."

13. (*Ci, Jian*) *Ci*, which literally means compassion or parental care, refers to philanthropic quality, soft but not intense; *Jian*, which literally means thriftiness or frugality, refers to the person's temperance, etc.; self-control of one's behavior, tough but not aloof.

Quotes from *Laozi*:

Discard hypocrisy and cheating and then the people will return to filial piety and parental care. (Chapter 19)

In governing the people and in serving heaven nothing's so good as being sparing... (Chapter 59)

I possess three treasures which I hold and cherish. The first is compassion, the second is frugality, and the third is not presuming to take the lead in the empire.

Being compassionate I therefore can be courageous. Being frugal I therefore can be magnanimous. Not presuming to take the lead in the empire I therefore can be the leader of those with complete talent. Now some people forsake compassion for courage, forsake frugality for magnanimity, and forsake the rear for leadership. Then they definitely end in death. When compassion is applied to war, one can win, and when it is applied to defense, one can guard. If Heaven helps one, it will protect him with compassion. (Chapter 67)

Explanation: Compassion does not mean the love of unequal difference, but the boundless inner love, soft but not intense on the surface, showing the real selflessness of the sage who has obtained Dao. Frugality is a kind of quality embodied in human beings, such as firmness and strength, courage and tenacity, broad-mindedness without aloofness, that is, "Dao does not seek fullness." These two qualities are typical virtues of a sage. It can be seen from these two virtues that Laozi did not propose to become a complete hermit.

14. (*Rouruo*) *Rouruo*, which literally means weak, pliant, supple or soft, is an advanced way of keeping moderate as it does not mean deliberately exposing one's strong attitudes or behavior.

Quotes from *Laozi*:

A man is supple and soft when living, but hard and stiff when dead. All things, grass and trees as well, are pliant and fragile when alive, but withered and dried out when dead. Thus, anything stiff and hard is the companion of death; anything supple, soft, weak and delicate is a companion of life. Therefore, if military force is too strong, it will lose. If a tree is strong and rigid, it will break. The strong and hard takes the lower position, and the supple and weak takes the higher position. (Chapter 76)

Explanation: The weak, with plenty of vitality, often represents new things and will overcome and eliminate interference with his own course of life. Laozi revealed the truth of "The weak conquers the strong," which is also expressed as the balance between "masculine and feminine" in the way of keeping moderate in order to find out the transformation of the two conditions, refining the law of the development of things.

VI. Assumptions and Explanations

The basic assumptions are the premise of a deductive system, which can be used as the basis of axioms and propositions.

1. Dao is the synthesis of any category. It has no definite meaning but does not point to any specific (category). It is called "eternal" or "eternal Dao." With infinite creativity, it is the root of all things in the world.

2. Dao can be expressed as nothingness or non-being and is full of power in its subtlety. Nothingness produces being. As its subtle and potential power will be certainly unleashed, it is the beginning of heaven and earth. That Dao can be expressed as nothingness indicates the infinite possibility of Dao. Being refers to the mother of all things, that is, the formation of all things. Being produces all things, which will return to non-being. All things need nourishment of Dao, which constantly helps the life of all things.

3. The infinite possibility of non-being and the limited reality of being forms contradiction, which develops according to the law of quantitative change to qualitative change, and of affirmation - negation - negative negation. The unity of being and nothingness is the complete state of Dao.

4. Anything and its external environment are contradictory unity of opposites. Contrary to other species, the contradiction between people, and between people and the external environment, has a special nature: (1) the contradiction of human society in the unspontaneous state exists usually in a stable state (known as "naturalness" or in line with Dao); (2) The contradiction of human society in its self-acting state may be in an unstable state (called "unnaturalness" or deviated from Dao). In the latter state, the sharp conflict between human society and the external environment, and the internal unrest of the society, may ultimately destroy itself.

5. The ideal state of human cognition and behavior is "*shouzhong*" (keeping moderate, middle or central). It combines both "being" and "non-being or nothingness." Determined by the contradiction between the infinite possibility of nothingness and the finite reality of "*you*" (being), human thinking and behavior have two sides: one is that they cannot correctly understand Dao and their "unnatural" behavior; the other is that they can correctly understand Dao and the "natural" behavior. "*Shouzhong*" can promote the balance among people, and between people and the outside world.

Explanations of Assumptions:

1. Assumption 1 is extracted from the following chapters of *Laozi:*

The Dao that can be worded is not the constant Dao. The name that can be named is not the eternal name. (Chapter 1)

I do not know its name. I might call it Dao or "Greatness" if you insist on naming it. (Chapter 25)

Dao is always nameless. Though small and simple, it is subject to no one in the world. (Chapter 32)

It breeds all things without claiming to be their lord and can be named Small. Everything submits to it, yet it never acts as master, and can be named Great. (Chapter 34)

Assumption 1 states that Dao is a symbol without specific meaning. So it is difficult to say what Dao really means. Name is just the concept with particular connotations. So we can say what is what. Name is just the concept with particular connotations. Only it does not point to a certain (category). Having orientation but not pointing to a certain (category), it means that it is the synthesis of any certain category. It is synthesis but not "aggregate." In general, "aggregate" is to add up more ones or categories together, like heaps of grains.

"Synthesis" is not a sum, but it integrates any category into it, or strips any category off it. By this means, it does not increase anything, nor reduce anything. Why? Because it itself is "big" and can accommodate everything, nothing can add anything to it; because it itself is very "small," small enough not to feel its existence, nothing can detract anything from it. In this sense, Dao is also known as eternal Dao in *Laozi*.

2. Assumption 2 is extracted and summarized from the following chapters of *Laozi*:

Non-being is the naming of the origin of Heaven and Earth; and being is the naming of the mother of all things. (Chapter 1)

Dao is invisibly empty, but its use is extremely infinite. Deep, it is like the mother of all things. Darkly visible, it only seems as if it were there. I know not whose son it is. It may be the forefather of God. (Chapter 4)

The spirit of the valley never dies. It is a deep womb. The gateway of the womb is called the root of Heaven and Earth. There it seems to exist and extend, to be used without end. (Chapter 6)

Looking without seeing is called Yi (the invisible); listening without hearing is called Xi (the inaudible); touching without feeling is called Wei (the formless). These three things can be in no way defined, thus blurred as one. Its upper part is not dazzling; its lower part is not obscure. Boundless, and formless, it cannot be named and return to nothing. This is called the formless form, shapeless shapes, and the substanceless image. To greet it, you don't see its head; to follow it, you don't see its rear. (Chapter 14)

Things come forth in great numbers, and each one returns to its own root. (Chapter 16)

As a thing the Dao is shapeless and formless. Formless and shapeless! Inside it there are images. Shapeless and formless! Inside it there are substances. Hidden and obscure! Inside it there are essences. These essences are very real, real with credence. (Chapter 21)

There was something formed out of chaos. That was born before Heaven and Earth. Soundless and formless, it does stand, extend, and recycle without stopping. It can be regarded as the mother of all things of Heaven and Earth. I do not know its name. I might call it Dao or "Greatness" if you insist on naming it.

"Greatness" suggests "without end," "without end" suggests "far away," and "far away" suggests "recursion." (Chapter 25)

It breeds all things without claiming to be their lord and can be named Small. Everything submits to it, yet it never acts as master, and can be named Great. (Chapter 34)

The movement of the Dao is in endless recursion and weakness is the function of Dao. Everything on earth is begotten from being, and being from non-being. (Chapter 40)

Dao begets one; one begets two; two begets three; three begets all things. With the Yin as the innermost part, all things in the universe face the Yang, and the vigorous mutual agitation of Yin and Yang brings them into harmony. (Chapter 42)

The universe has a beginning and the beginning could be the mother of all things. From the mother, you know the son; knowing the son, you go back to the mother, then you will be safe all your life. (Chapter 52)

Assumption 2 states that non-being refers to the beginning of heaven and earth, that is, the beginning of everything. Power, the potential energy, must be reserved in the beginning, otherwise, there is no beginning. Nothing can increase and reduce the Dao. That means that it itself is powerful. The Dao with power is bound to be the beginning of all things. The subtle and potential force in Dao, although bursting out abruptly, has no clear direction, so it is named non-being.

When non-being is used to refer to the beginning of all things, the nameless Dao indicates its infinite possibility. "Non-being," as the most abstract "name," is completely beyond experience and sensibility. Therefore, Dao is metaphysical foundation, and "non-being" is metaphysical body. The terms "simplicity," "emptiness," "weakness," "feminine," and "infiniteness" in *Laozi*, which are compared to "water" and "baby," all direct at this metaphysical "noumenon."

"*You*" (being) refers to the mother of all things, that is, the formation of all things. The name "*you*" is not the name that transcends experience and sensibility, but the abstraction of experience and sensible things, hence the name of sub-abstraction as compared to non-being. In the ontological sense, the ready-made non-being creates the abstract "being" in the sense of experience, which means the complete transition from ontology to cosmology. Although the abstract "Being" is still a trance, there are signs in mixture. Although not directly referred to as Dao, Non-being and being indicate the self-completion and transformation of the Dao into the universe.

"Being," the mother of all things, can be said to be the generic term of the generation and development of all things. Although all things can not divide or possess Dao, their existence need the nourishment of Dao. In the process of transition from ontology to cosmogony, all things seem to have departed from Dao. However, Dao is always there, and always recycling. With its "weakness" (that is, the tendency of mighty nothingness), it assists and supports all things in their growth. In this way, all things will return to nothingness and develop on their own.

3. Assumption 3 is extracted and summarized from the following chapters of *Laozi*:

Is not the space between Heaven and Earth like a bellows? It is empty but it is never exhausted. The more it works, the stronger wind it produces. Too much talk leads to a dead end; it is better to hold fast to moderation and the void. (Chapter 5)

Thirty spokes share one hub, the void of which makes the use of a cart. Clay is kneaded to make a vessel, the void of which makes the use of the vessel. Doors and windows are dug for the house, the void of which makes the use of the house. Thus, what we gain is Being, yet it is by virtue of Nothingness that this can be put to use. (Chapter 11)

You know the strength of the masculine, but keep the tenderness of the feminine, and are willing to be the ravine of the world. Being the ravine of the world, you will be accompanied by eternal virtue, and return to being a babe. You know the white, but keep to the role of the black, and are willing to be a model of the world. Being a model of the world, your eternal virtue will not go astray, and you return to the highest truth. You know the honor, but keep to the role of the disgraced, and are willing to be a valley of the world. Being the valley of the world, you will no longer lack the eternal virtue, and return to simplicity. When the first natural Dao scattered into small things, it became the useful containers. Those who were possessed with the Dao would make use of them, and became the leaders of hundreds of officials. Therefore, the perfect political system was not separated. (Chapter 28)

Assumption 3 points out that Dao is a complete and self-sufficient concept. The generation of "being" by "non-being" is not always comprehensive and long-lasting, and it is accidental and temporary. This contradiction is reflected in all things, which are the products when "non-being" produces "being," and so are the human cognition and behavior. For this reason, all things and mankind are subject to the limitless possibility of "non-being" and the limited reality of "being."

4. Assumption 4 points out that in human society, the contradiction between the infinite possibility of "non-being" and the limited reality of "being" has its special

features. On the one hand, mankind unconsciously accepts the domination of this contradiction; in this case, the contradiction naturally presents a stable state. On the other hand, human beings, by means of their own thoughts and actions, exert various forces on this contradiction, in which case the contradiction may remain stable or may become unstable due to human forces: the force of human being can not be separated from the limited reality of "being". Therefore, such forces may exacerbate the contradiction between the limited realism of "being" and the infinite possibility of "non-being." As a result, the conflict between human society and the external environment becomes acute, and the internal turbulence of the society becomes more and more destructive.

5. Assumption 5 points out that in the face of the contradiction between the infinite possibility of "non-being" and the limited reality of "being," it is necessary for human beings to keep moderate and mean (equilibrium of contradiction) in cognition and behavior, that is, conscientiously embodying Dao and at the same time taking into account the characteristics of human beings. Specifically, it is called "keeping moderate" or "taking the middle course" to grasp the proper state of Dao turning from "non-being" to "being," which produces all things. It is called "constant" (or eternal) to realize this state. The "constant" (or eternal) which belongs to humans is a special embodiment of state of "naturalness" in human society.

VII. Axioms and Explanations:

The following axioms are derived from the characteristics of Daoist thought and the chapters of *Laozi*. Relatively speaking, they are well-recognized and self-evident. They are the main basis for propositional deduction and proof.

A1. "Naturalness" is a natural process of Dao from "non-being" to "being," and then back to "non-being."

Quotes from *Laozi*:

Things come forth in great numbers, and each one returns to its own root. (Chapter 16)

He is so carefree and leisurely. He does not utter words lightly. He accomplishes his tasks and finishes his affairs. The people all say, "We are as we are." (Chapter 17)

I do not know its name. I might call it Dao or "Greatness" if you insist on naming it. "Greatness" suggests "without end," "without end" suggests "far away," and "far away" suggests "recursion." (Chapter 25)

Man models himself on Earth, Earth on Heaven, Heaven on the Dao, and the

Dao on Nature. (Chapter 25)

It breeds all things without claiming to be their lord and can be named Small. Everything submits to it, yet it never acts as master, and can be named Great. (Chapter 34)

To turn to its opposite is the movement of Dao. Weakness is the function of Dao. All things in the world are produced by Being, yet, Being has come forth from non-being. (Chapter 40)

The universe has a beginning and the beginning could be the mother of all things. From the mother, you know the son; knowing the son, you go back to the mother, and then you will be safe all your life. (Chapter 52)

Explanation: Axiom A1 points out that the Dao is a complete and self-sufficient concept. The self-fulfilling process of Dao does not mean that there is any damage or compensation to itself. The process of Dao from "non-being" to "being" and then back to "non-being" does not mean that there is a direct conversion and a linear loop between "being" and "non-being." Non-being is the starting point and is also fundamental. It is subtle, invisible but ubiquitous. Dao that can be regarded as "non-being" refers to its infinite possibility. The process of "non-being" producing "being" is always incomplete, accidental, temporary and short-term. All things, whose process from "being" to "non-being," seem to be returning and recycling, can not be separated from "non-being." Such a process based on "non-being" is "naturalness."

A2. A wise man who is fair and just can realize the truth of the Dao.

Quotes from *Laozi*:

When everyone in the world knows the beautiful as beautiful, ugliness comes into being; when everyone knows the good as good, then the bad comes into being. (Chapter 2)

Looking without seeing is called Yi (the invisible); listening without hearing is called Xi (the inaudible); touching without feeling is called Wei (the formless). These three things can be in no way defined, thus blurred as one. (Chapter 14)

Take emptiness to the limit and keep still. All things arise together, I watch their return. Things come forth in great numbers, and each one returns to its own root. Returning to roots means stillness, and also means a return to origin. To return to its origin is known as the eternal. To know the eternal is known as discernment. He who is ignorant of the eternal, if acting blindly, will be in great trouble. (Chapter 16)

As soon as we start to establish a system, we have names. Knowing when to stop, we can be free from danger. (Chapter 32)

He who understands others is wise; he who understands himself has discernment. (Chapter 33)

The universe has a beginning and the beginning could be the mother of all things. From the mother, you know the son; knowing the son, you go back to the mother, and then you will be safe all your life. Block the openings of intelligence, and shut the door of desires, and till the end of your life you'll not labor. Unlock the openings, meddle in affairs, and till the end of your life you'll not be saved. To perceive the tiny is called brightness; to hold fast to the pliant is called strength. Use the light, and return to what's bright, and you will be free from disasters. This is called following the constant. (Chapter 52)

Explanation: Laozi opposed the social reality (i.e., the reality of maintaining "rites") in which the social order is determined by means of "rectification of names," which is regarded as the highest wisdom of man. Therefore, Laozi said: "The Dao that can be worded is not the constant Dao. The name that can be named is not the eternal name." It is the real Dao that is beyond what can be worded and what can be named. However, Laozi's opposition to the wisdom of "name that can be named" does not mean completely abandoning it, but rather treat it in an objective and Mean way.

On the one hand, Laozi affirmed the importance of people's ability to understand the object and the ability to make decisions. On the other hand, when a person's *"zhi"* (intellect and wisdom) becomes a tool to satisfy his excessive desire, he will lose the ability to return to "non-being" and will forget the original state of life. Laozi firmly opposed this attitude. Deviated from the original state, *"zhi"* will have no fundamental, and will lose the source of power and go against Dao. Laozi's understanding of Dao has a strong speculative color. That is to say, his Dao is no longer a concept of experience, but obtained through the conversion between concepts. This Dao, which was put forward through purely theoretical thinking, negates the mystical idea of primitive religion.

However, Laozi's Dao is not proposed only for the denial of primitive religion, rather it has a strong humanistic concern. If the way of heaven recycles from "non-being" to "being" and back to "non-being," then so does the human's way, which recycles from "non-being" that is full of power of life to "being" that grasps and controls the object, and then returns to the internal "non-being." This process can be summarized as one recycling from wisdom to discernment or brightness, through which man will be able to realize the truth of Dao. In understanding this process, Laozi did not completely deny "desire" and "wisdom," but thought that man can have discernment as pure as a baby which highlights human value and meaning, thus avoiding the negative outlook on life. This is an important manifestation of Laozi's humanistic thought.

A3. The basic philosophy of governing a country is to follow the thought "the highest virtue is like water" and to accomplish everything by doing nothing or taking non-action.

Quotes from *Laozi:*

Therefore, the sage manages things with non-action and practices wordless teaching.... He lets all things grow without interference, and gives them life without claiming to be their owner. He benefits them yet exacts no gratitude. He succeeds without claiming merit. It is because of this that his merits last forever. (Chapter 2)

Though nothing is done, everything is done well. (Chapter 3)

If you are to love the people and govern a state, is it possible to do it by non-action? (Chapter 10)

Dao does nothing yet nothing is left undone. Should lords and kings be able to maintain it, all things will be transformed on their own. After they are transformed, they may grow avid. I will check the avidity with the nameless simplicity of Dao. Checked with the nameless simplicity, they will have no avidity. No avidity leads to serenity, hence the empire's stability. (Chapter 37)

The sage says, "When I follow non-action, the people will be transformed of themselves. When I act little, the people will be naturally upright. When I am not meddlesome, the people will naturally prosper of themselves. When I am free from desires, the people of themselves become simple and pure." (Chapter 57)

Explanation: Laozi had a clear understanding of the rulers who contended at that time in pursuit of "meritorious service." To do something for the country is probably the dream of all the people who are responsible for the governance of the country, regardless of the ways and methods. When people with the mainstream consciousness thought that the strength of the country was of vital importance to the survival of the country, people would always rack their brains in search of strategies for a strong country. Some believed that the strength of the country lay in "virtue" and maintaining the tradition; others believed that the strength of the country relied on the country's enough power to deter the enemy, resulting in the dispute of rule of the country by "kingly" way or by "overbearing" power to obtain dominant position.

Laozi put forward his thought of governance "*wuwei*" (doing nothing, inaction, and non-action) based on his exceptional theoretical thinking ability and experiential insight. Of course, what we need to understand is: "*wuwei*" is not a completely negative state of doing nothing but taking no deliberate and reckless action contrary to nature. To a certain extent, "*wuwei*" does have a negative appearance of retreat. This retreat is not an end in itself, but a real return to the unspeakable subtlety of Dao, which is precisely the source of strength.

A4. The Sage knows Dao but does not contend.

Quotes from *Laozi*:

He is ease with lowness in his dwelling. He is profound in his heart. He is faithful in his friendship. He is sincere in his speech. Like water, he never contends, so he is never at fault. (Chapter 8)

I alone am different from others because I take the greatest interest in obtaining Dao. (Chapter 20)

One does not contend with others, so no one is in a position to contend with him. (Chapter 22)

The Dao of heaven benefits rather than harms all things. The Dao of the sage is to give rather than contend. (Chapter 81)

Explanation: Laozi affirmed the basic desire and cognitive ability of human beings. This is to establish the subjective status of human beings in all things in "human nature." However, Laozi's affirmation of human nature does not mean affirmation of each individual, which is manifested in two aspects: (1) The text *Laozi* is directed at the leaders of the state. To change the "unnaturalness" of the society fundamentally relies on the governance of the leaders. Though it is defined as "inaction," it is still governance rather than laissez-faire. It is far from relying on the strength and awakening of individuals; (2) It is not to fight for the status of the individuals to establish the status of human beings from perspective of "human nature," but to foreshadow theoretically the emergence of the sage (qualified leader).

Since there is a huge gap among the individuals in the society in many ways, Laozi could not hastily place the hope of the ideals of "natural" society on the individuals of the majority of population. It is the sage who knows Dao and "does not fight," and the ideal society must rely on the governance of the sage. This is the social consciousness resulted from the hierarchical system.

A5. The basic method of conserving one's health is to eliminate excessive "desire" and crafty "wisdom."

Quotes from *Laozi*:

(To keep the people) innocent of knowledge and free from desire. (Chapter 3)

The heaven and earth can exit forever. The reason why they can exist forever themselves is that they do not exist for themselves. Hence they are able to be long-lived. (Chapter 7)

Too many colors dazzle the eyes; too much music deafens the ears; too many tastes baffle the palate. Overindulging in hunting drives you crazy, and coveting too many material things tarnishes your conduct. Therefore, the Sage cares for bellies rather than senses, fending off material temptation and living a simple life. (Chapter 12)

One is panic-stricken when he's favoured or humiliated. He is too much worried about his body as much as calamity. (Chapter 13)

We will certainly die, if we have no way to survive. There is a one third chance for people to survive, and another one third chance is for people to die. One third of them die from their own choices though they could have lived longer. Why is that? It is because they all have too strong a desire to live longer. It is said that one who is good at preserving his life would not be attacked by either rhinoceros or tigers on the road, nor be injured or killed on the battle-field. The rhinoceros would not have the chance to use its horns, the tiger would not have the chance to use its claws, and weapons would not have a chance to show their blades. Why is that? Because of their dodge of danger. (Chapter 50)

Explanation: Man, as one of all things, is tangible. The body is man's "shape." Man is also the unity of "non-being" and "being." The inner vitality of human is "non-being" and the sensual desire of man's body is "being." What is the real way of preserving one's health? It is not the deliberate pursuit of immortality, of course, nor self-inflicted death, but conforming to the nature. Conforming to the nature does not necessarily lead to immortality, but it is possible to live longer than to deliberately pursue excessive desires (such as the desire for longevity) and ingenious wisdom (like to use various means to live forever).

第三章 CHAPTER THREE

明道篇
On Understanding the Dao

在本章及后几章中，P表示Proposition（命题），D表示Definition（定义），A表示Axiom（公理）。

本章共21个命题，主要说明老子关于"道"的基本观念，以及人如何才能体悟"道"，其中P1-1至P1-10，说明了道自身以及道与万物的关系；P1-11至P1-16，说明了人的两种认知或体悟状态"智"和"明"及其相互关系；P1-17至P1-21，说明了体悟"道"的路径、方法和步骤等。本章及后续三章的命题或推论，是从《老子》原文中提炼出来的判断，需要对它们进行证明。这些命题中也蕴含着道家思想的现代价值。

P1-1 道自在，万物自在。

【参见《老子》条目】

道常无为而无不为。（第三十七章）

证明：依据基本假设1，"道"是任何"某个（类）"的综合。从定义1可知，"德"是万物自在自为过程的总称。再依据公理A1，"自然"是道从"无"到"有"再到"无"的自在自为过程。于是，道是"无"和"有"的统一，是自在自为的，且"道"统领着"德"，万物就是"无"和"有"的变换过程。因此，道自在，万物自在。

例证和说明："道"即是常道，是完全自在的规律性。这种自在的规律性不仅作为一种先于天地万物而存在的混成之物，而且贯穿于天地万物之中，成为客观世界的普遍法则，因此，天地万物也是自在的存在。在这两者的关系中，"道"只能以无为的方式来滋养万物，否则它就会破坏万物的自在的状态，而万物亦只能以无为的方式来顺应体现自在的"道"，否则它就会丧失自我存在的自在性，而成为自在之道的对立物。

西汉惠帝元年（公元前194年），曹参为齐国丞相。当时天下初定，齐国共有七十多座城池，是较大的封国，而齐悼惠王刘肥年纪较轻，尚没有能力治国理政，于是曹参代为摄政。为了制定正确的治国方略，曹参把齐国的老年人与儒生召来，向他们询问安定百姓的办法。而当时齐地的儒生数以百计，各有建言，曹参也不知该如何定夺。他听说胶西有位盖公，精研黄老之学，就派人以厚礼请之。盖公告诉曹参，治理国家贵在清静无为，这样百姓就会自己安定下来。曹参听取了盖公的建议，以黄老道家的无为而治的思想为指导，推行以轻徭薄赋、节俭省刑为主要内容的休养生息政策，不过多地干扰百姓，让他们有足够的时间来发展生产与安排生活。曹参相齐九年，齐国很快就出现了安定繁荣的局面，他也受到了百姓的赞扬，被称为贤相。

西汉惠帝二年（公元前193年），丞相萧何去世，曹参继之而为汉朝的丞相。接替萧何之后，曹参不做任何政治更张，史称"萧规曹随"。他为郡国选拔官吏，选拔木讷忠厚的长者为丞相史，并且斥退那些言辞苛刻、追求名声的官吏。他一天到晚喝着醇厚的美酒，而对政务无所用心。他接见卿大夫以下的官吏以及宾客，也不谈政务，而只是以美酒待之，不醉不归。受到曹参的影响，很多官吏也是每天饮酒唱和。丞相府的官员对此颇为不满，想让曹参加以制止，结果曹参见到他们，反而与他们一起饮酒歌呼。

汉惠帝对曹参不理政务也非常不满，就让曹参的儿子曹窋（时任中大夫）找机会劝谏一下。曹参听了儿子的劝谏，勃然大怒，用竹板打了曹窋一顿，告诉他说："赶紧入朝侍奉皇帝去，如何治理天下不是你能谈论的。"汉惠帝对此非常郁闷，自己派了一个说客，不仅没有劝动曹参，还被他打了板子，于是就在上朝时责备曹参。曹参赶紧谢罪，并反问惠帝："陛下与高皇帝相比，哪一个更圣明英武？"惠帝答："我怎么敢望先帝之项背呢！"曹参又问："陛下看我与萧何相比，哪一个能力更强？"惠帝答："你好像不如他。"曹参乘机进言："高皇帝与萧何平定天下，治国之法已经明确，现在陛下垂衣拱手于上，官员们恪守职责，遵循既定之法，不也是很好的吗？"惠帝理解了曹参的用意，就不再谴责他了。

曹参相齐以及萧规曹随的故事，说明了百姓其实具有自我发展的能力，统治者只要顺从民意，给他们自我发展的空间，他们能够自己解决经济发展和社会秩序等根本问题。统治者常常不明白这一点，总是想凭借手中的权力去强力妄作，给百姓套上种种枷锁，而结果往往适得其反。

P1-2 道是万物自在的根源。

【参见《老子》条目】

万物并作，吾以观复。夫物芸芸，各复归其根。（第十六章）

道生一，一生二，二生三，三生万物。万物负阴而抱阳，冲气以为和。（第

四十二章）

证明： 从定义1可知，"德"是万物自在自为过程的总称，而万物是"有"和"无"之间的转换。又依据基本假设2与公理A1，道可"无"，精微处充满力量；"无"生"有"，恍惚中混成迹象，而"自然"是道从"无"到"有"再到"无"的自在自为过程。"道"与万物同在，且万物自在自为的内在进程就是"道"。因此，"道"是万物自在的根源。

例证和说明： "道"作为自在的规律性，任何有为妄作都不能加以改变。天地万物作为客观的世界，正是因为遵循了"道"的自然无为的法则，才获得了自身存在的依据。所以《老子》曰："天得一以清，地得一以宁，神得一以灵，谷得一以盈，万物得一以生，侯王得一以为天下正。"（《老子》第三十九章）反过来说，如果天地万物丧失了"道"这个"一"，其自在的状态就会被打破，也就会丧失其存在的意义。

《庄子·逍遥游》中有这样一则寓言：在遥远的北海有一条大鱼，其名为鲲，其身体之大不知道有几千里。鲲变化而成一只鸟，其名为鹏，其背之大亦不知几千里。大鹏飞往遥远的南冥，翅膀扇动三千里的水面，扶摇直上九万里的高空。蜩与学鸠嘲笑它说："我们奋力飞出去，不过飞到榆树、枋树那么高，有时还飞不到那么高就落在了地上，你又何必为了飞向南冥而飞到九万里的高空呢？"在这则寓言中，蜩与鸠局限于自身条件，而不懂作为大鸟的鹏的逍遥。庄子认为，鹏、蜩、鸠因其自身的大小，实现其逍遥的条件也是不同的，蜩、鸠因其小，故不需高飞，鹏因其大，必须高飞以借风势，由此就形成它们对不同的逍遥的追求。而这种条件的差异，并不说明鹏所追求的逍遥就比蜩与鸠要高贵，它们的逍遥自在都是自然的。庄子借此所要表达的是，万物（包括人）之间的差别是客观存在的，但只要各安其性（道），也就获得了逍遥自在。

P1-3 道包容万物而不主宰万物。

【参见《老子》条目】

大道泛兮，其可左右。万物恃之以生而不辞，功成而不有。衣养万物而不为主，常无欲，可名于小；万物归焉而不为主，可名为大。以其终不自为大，故能成其大。（第三十四章）

证明： 依据基本假设1和2，"道"是任何"某个（类）"的综合。"有"生万物，万物复归于"无"。万物需要"道"的滋养，"道"常在以助万物之生。"道"与"万物"不可分离，万物从"道"来，又回归"道"。依据公理A1，"自然"是"道"从"无"

到"有"再到"无"的自在自为过程。万物是一个自在自为的"自然"过程，没有任何目的性。因此，道包容万物而不主宰万物。

例证和说明：道体之自身作为一种自在的存在，它的自在性就体现在它既不受他者的主宰，同时亦不主宰他者的存在。因此，"道"的自然无为，体现在对待万物的关系上，就是包容万物的差别，而不规定、主宰万物的发展方向，这样万物的发展就具有了无限丰富的可能性。

1953年，周恩来总理在接见印度代表团时，第一次正式提出了"互相尊重领土主权、互不侵犯、互不干涉内政、平等互惠、和平共处"的五项原则，后来修改为"互相尊重主权和领土完整、互不侵犯、互不干涉内政、平等互利及和平共处"。在中国的倡导下，和平共处五项原则在世界上获得越来越多国家的赞同，逐渐成为国际关系中处理分歧与争端的基本原则。1988年，邓小平提出以和平共处五项原则为准则，建立国际政治经济新秩序。这一主张实际上是针对美国在二战后所主导建立的国际政治经济旧秩序所提出的。旧秩序是以意识形态的区分来划定界限，不同意识形态的国家之间是你死我活的对立关系，而且大国与小国在地位上完全不平等，大国凭借其政治、经济、军事实力欺压小国，甚至侵略小国是常有之事。而通过遵守和平共处五项原则来建立国际政治经济新秩序，就是要尊重各国之间的差异，容纳多种多样的发展道路，而不是由大国去主导小国，甚至主宰其命运。由此可见，和平共处五项原则中既渗透着儒家以和为贵的精神，同时也体现了包容而不主宰的道家精神。

P1-4 道与万物的基本特征是自然。

【参见《老子》条目】

人法地，地法天，天法道，道法自然。（第二十五章）

道生之，德畜之，物形之，势成之。是以万物莫不尊道而贵德。道之尊，德之贵，夫莫之命而常自然。（第五十一章）

证明：依据基本假设2，"道"可"无"，精微处充满力量；"无"生"有"，恍惚中混成迹象。精微而潜在的力量势在必发，为"天地"之始，却还没有明确的指向。"道"可"无"意味着"道"的无限可能性。"有"指万物之母，也就是万物的形成。又依据公理A1，"自然"是"道"从"无"到"有"再到"无"的自在自为过程。无论是"道"还是"万物"其过程都是"无"与"有"的转换。所以，"道"与万物的基本特征是"自然"。

例证和说明："道"作为天地万物共同遵循的最高法则，在它之上没有更高的主宰，即"莫之命而常自然"。而万物的生成变化遵循"道"的法则，亦是一种"自然"的过程，没有任何目的论的因素贯彻其中。

《庄子·应帝王》讲述了这样一则寓言故事：在南海之域，其帝为倏；在北海之域，其帝为忽；而在两者的中央，其帝为浑沌。倏与忽经常相会于浑沌的地域，浑沌待他们非常友善。倏和忽商量，要报答浑沌的情谊。他们说："人人都有七窍以用来视、听、吃和呼吸，唯独浑沌没有，我们就试着给他凿开七窍吧。"于是，他们每天为浑沌凿一窍，七天之后，七窍成而浑沌死。倏与忽所犯的错误就是违背了"自然"而强行作为，结果害死了浑沌。

东汉著名哲学家王充的"天道自然无为"的思想也源于老子。王充认为天道是自然无为的，如果有为，那就违背了自然，也就不符合天道了。那么天道自然的根据在哪呢？王充认为，天不像人一样有嘴巴和眼睛，也就不像人一样具有欲望。天实质上是一团元气，天地合气，以生万物。在万物生成的过程中，天并不是像上帝那样有意识地去创造人和物，而是没有追求，没有索取，没有任何目的，它只是在元气运转中自然生成万物。正是因为天道是自然无为的，所以万物包括人，都不是天故意生出来的，而是元气自然生成的产物。

P1-5 道不能用言说和命名的方式去把握。

【参见《老子》条目】

道可道，非常道；名可名，非常名。（第一章）

有物混成，先天地生。寂兮寥兮，独立不改，周行而不殆，可以为天下母。吾不知其名，强字之曰道。（第二十五章）

道隐无名。（第四十一章）

证明： 依据基本假设1，"道"是任何"某个（类）"的综合。它无特定含义，有指向但不指向任何"某个（类）"。没有特定含义就不能构成概念。又依据基本假设2，精微而潜在的力量势在必发，为"天地"之始，却还没有明确的指向。"道"可"无"意味着"道"的无限可能性。"有"指万物之母，也就是万物的形成。"道"比我们使用的最抽象的名"无"和"有"还抽象。所以，"道"不能用言说和命名的方式去把握。

例证和说明： 老子的"道"虽然是一个哲学概念，但是它所指称的是贯穿于天地人之间的最高法则。虽然道体流行于万物之中，但它自身却超越于有形有象的万物，不是人类经验所直接面对的对象，也就无法用概念的方式去加以把握。就是说，"道"实际上是语言不能准确表达的。因为语言是在经验生活中形成的，它所

第三章 明道篇
CHAPTER THREE: On Understanding the Dao

能准确表达的，仅限于人们所能经验到的事物。如果语言要超越经验世界，而用来表达一个无形无象的"道"，那么所表达出的"道"实际上只是把握了"道"的某个层面，而不是"道"的全体，这就如盲人摸象，只能得其一端。在康德的哲学中，有所谓的"超越的本体界"，即上帝、灵魂与世界，理性如果超越经验世界而去试图认识这些本体之物，就会产生二律背反。这与老子对"道"的理解具有类似的特点。

在《庄子·天地》中有这样一则寓言：黄帝巡游到赤水北岸，登上昆仑之巅南望，在归途中不小心遗失了玄珠，便先后派遣"知""离朱""吃诟"去寻找，却都没能找到。最后，"象罔"找到了它。黄帝惊讶地说："奇怪呀，象罔这种人居然也能找得到？"在这个故事中，"玄珠"比喻"道"，而"知""离朱""吃诟""象罔"比喻四种不同的求道方式。"知"喻指有才智之人；"离朱"喻指视力好的人，能明察秋毫；"吃诟"喻指善于言辩的人；"象罔"则是无思虑、无明目、无言辩的完全自然的符合"道"的人。思虑、见闻和言辩的方式，都是将"道"作为对象来追求，结果是背道而驰。而"象罔"不是将"道"作为对象，他无心于求"道"，与"道"自然而然地合而为一，因而能够真正地得"道"。

P1-6 道体虚而用无穷。

【参见《老子》条目】

道冲而用之或不盈。渊兮，似万物之宗；湛兮，似或存。吾不知谁之子，象帝之先。（第四章）

天地之间，其犹橐籥乎！虚而不屈，动而愈出。（第五章）

弱者道之用。（第四十章）

证明：依据基本假设1与基本假设2，"道"是任何"某个（类）"的综合；"道"可"无"，精微处充满力量；"无"生"有"，恍惚中混成迹象。精微而潜在的力量势在必发，为"天地"之始，却还没有明确的指向，这表明"道"的"体"是虚的；进一步，"有"指万物之母，也就是万物的形成。"道"可"无"也意味着"道"的无限可能性，表明了"道"的"用"是永恒的。所以，道体虚而用无穷。

例证和说明：道体之虚并不是空无一物，而是道体之存在虚无形，不像具体事物那样具有特定的形象。正因为道体的虚而无形，是以守弱的方式发挥其功用，所以天地造化顺应"道"的法则，却不会消耗"道"的力量，也就是"道"的作用持续不断，永远不会穷竭。

在印度的奥修所著的《生命的真意》中，他用数学上0的概念来说明道体的空虚无物及其无穷之用。0的概念是印度人首先发明的，印度人认为每个事物都来自空无，来自0，而其消亡实质上又是回归到空无，回归到0。在数学中，0虽然只是一个数字，但却是其他所有数字的基础。也就是说，0虽然意味着空无一物，但却具有着无限的意义。当我们把0加在非0数字的后面，0的价值就不再是空无，而具有更加丰富的意义。依此，无限个0相加，其结果依然是0，但如果将无限个0加到1之后，就会变成一个无限大的数字。0的意义还不仅如此。在计算机语言中只有0和1这两个数字，所有数据都是以0和1的形式编码存储的，只要将0的位置加以改变，就会产生各种不同的数据。因此，如果用0来比喻"道"的话，0所产生的无限丰富之意义也就彰显了道体的无穷之用。世界发展的永恒的动力在哪里？就在于空虚的道体。因其体虚，所以才能产生无穷无尽的妙用。相比较之下，任何一个有形的事物，其存在都是有限的，其作用也是有限的。

P1-7 道无所不至，反复不息。

【参见《老子》条目】

　　有物混成，先天地生。寂兮寥兮，独立不改，周行而不殆，可以为天下母。吾不知其名，强字之曰道，强为之名曰大。大曰逝，逝曰远，远曰反。（第二十五章）

　　反者道之动。（第四十章）

证明：依据基本假设2，"道"可"无"，精微处充满力量；"无"生"有"，恍惚中混成迹象。"无"是力量，"有"是万物。再依据公理A1，"自然"是"道"从"无"到"有"再到"无"的自在自为过程。这里，"道"是万物的根源。"有"生万物，万物复归于"无"。万物需要"道"的滋养，"道"常在以助万物之生。因此，"道"无所不至，反复不息。

例证和说明：这里的"反"不是对立的意思，而是"返回"的意思，因此，老子说"反者道之动"的时候，意思是反复不息，而不仅仅是说"道"在向对立面转化。所以我们不能将老子的"反"简单理解为辩证法，老子也不是一概反对或者否认现实世界和生活领域中的对立现象与对立面的相互转化。

　　在《庄子·知北游》中有这样一段对话：东郭子问庄子："你所谓的道，究竟在什么地方呢？"庄子答："道无处不在。"东郭子追问："能不能说得具体点呢？"庄子说："在蝼蚁之中。"东郭子说："道怎么能在这样低下卑贱的地方呢？"庄子说："在稊稗之中。"东郭子说："怎么越来越低下了呢？"庄子又说："在砖瓦之中。"东郭子说："怎么又越来越低下呢？"庄子说："在大小便之中。"至此，东郭子不敢再问了，庄子的回答越来越不堪，完全超出了他的想象。这也表明，东郭子实际上对于宇宙万物做了高贵与低贱的区分，他认为低贱的事物中是没有"道"的。这种理解实质上扭曲了道家的思想，因为"道"作为贯穿于天地人之间的根本法则，落实于所有具体的事物，而完全不分高低贵贱。

"道在屎溺"的观点在清朝末年还被李鸿章拿来幽默了一把。李鸿章因为热心于办理洋务，进而对西方近代的自然科学理论产生了兴趣。一次，他问一个下属什么是抛物线，下属解释一通，李鸿章还是不明白。下属急中生智，问道："李中堂，你撒不撒尿？撒尿就是一条抛物线呀！"李鸿章一下子就理解了，他幽默地说："庄子说'道在屎溺'，说的就是这个道理啊！"

P1-8 道有象，却无定形。

【参见《老子》条目】

视之不见，名曰夷；听之不闻，名曰希；搏之不得，名曰微。此三者不可致诘，故混而为一。其上不皦，其下不昧，绳绳兮不可名，复归于无物。是谓无状之状，无物之象。是谓惚恍。迎之不见其首，随之不见其后。（第十四章）

道之为物，惟恍惟惚。惚兮恍兮，其中有象；恍兮惚兮，其中有物；窈兮冥兮，其中有精；其精甚真，其中有信。（第二十一章）

大象无形。（第四十一章）

证明：依据基本假设2，道可"无"，精微处充满力量；"无"生"有"，恍惚中混成迹象。"无"并非是"空"，而是精微，正是这种精微才具有无穷的力量。又依据基本假设1，"道"是任何"某个（类）"的综合。"道"不指向任何"个（类）"，表明它没有确定的对象，也就是没有"定形"。所以，"道"有象，却无定形。

例证和说明：老子常用水来喻"道"，水通常是有形和可观察的，但却没有固定不变的形态。唐代思想家刘禹锡曾说"古所谓无形，盖无常形尔，必因物而后见尔"，并提出"空者，形之希微者也"（《天论》）的命题。这些说法与老子之道的特性不谋而合。

《史记·老子韩非列传》记载，孔子向老子问礼后回到鲁国，告诉众弟子说："我知道鸟能在天上飞，鱼能在水里游，野兽能在地上跑。地上跑的野兽，可以用网来捉住它，水里游的鱼，可以用钩来钓它；天上飞的鸟，可以弓箭射下它；至于龙，我不知道用什么才能捉住它呢？龙乘风云而直上九天之上。我所见的老子，就像龙一样。他学识渊深而莫测，志趣高远而难以了解，就像蛇能够随着季节屈伸，就像龙能顺应时节而变化。老聃，真是我的老师呀！"孔子这里所描述的老子的形象，实质上正是老子的道之特性的体现。蛇与龙在古代被视为神物，它们都具有形象，但是其形象又不是固定不变的，它们都能顺应时节而加以变化。而"道"也是这样，它给人一种恍恍惚惚的印象，但正是因为其恍惚而无定形，使得它能流行于万物之中。

P1-9 道对任何事物都没有偏爱。

【参见《老子》条目】

天地不仁，以万物为刍狗。（第五章）

天道无亲，常与善人。（第七十九章）

证明：依据公理A1可知，"自然"是"道"从"无"到"有"再到"无"的自在自为过程。自在自为就是没有目的性，也无特别的偏爱。又依据基本假设1和命题T1-4，"道"是任何"某个（类）"的综合，它无特定含义，有指向但不指向任何"某个（类）"。而道与万物的基本特征是自然。所以，"道"对任何事物都没有偏爱。

例证和说明："道"作为贯穿于天地人之间的共同法则，万物皆依之而生，故对于任何事物都没有偏私，而具有最大的包容性。《老子》第十六章"知常容，容乃公，公乃全，全乃天，天乃道，道乃久，没身不殆"的说法虽是就人而论，实际上也揭示了"道"包容万物而无私的品格。《尚书·蔡仲之命》说："皇天无亲，惟德是辅。"这里的"皇天"，具有人格神的意味，而老子的"道"则超越于人格神之上，但是在无私的品格方面，两者又是相通的。在《史记·伯夷列传》中记载了这样一则故事：伯夷和叔齐是殷时孤竹国君的两个儿子，孤竹国君想立小儿子叔齐为接班人。等老国君死后，叔齐要将君位让给伯夷，伯夷以父命拒绝，并离开孤竹国以示决绝。而叔齐亦不愿违背长子继承君位的通行规矩，也弃位而去。伯夷、叔齐听说西伯侯姬昌尊重老人，老人都得到很好的赡养，就想到西岐去。等他们到了西岐，正赶上姬昌过世，武王载着文王的牌位，打着文王的旗号，起兵东伐商纣。伯夷、叔齐拦住武王的战马劝阻道："父亲死了尚未安葬，就动起干戈，这能称得上是孝吗？处于臣下的位置，却去杀害侍奉的君主，这能称得上是仁吗？"左右的将领非常愤怒，准备将他们俩拉出去杀了。姜太公赶忙加以阻止，告诉他们："这两人是义士呀！"哥俩互相搀扶着离去。等到武王平定殷商之乱后，天下的诸侯纷纷归顺，而伯夷、叔齐却以食周粟为耻，隐居于首阳山，采薇为食，终致饿死。临死前，他们作了一首《采薇》歌，指斥武王伐纣为"以暴易暴"。司马迁为此感慨说："常言道，天道无亲，常与善人。可是像伯夷、叔齐这样的人，难道不是善人吗？他们品行如此高洁，却不免于饿死。在孔门弟子中，颜渊最为好学，却是家徒四壁，连糟糠也吃不饱，终至早死。上天怎么能这样报答善人呢？盗跖每天杀害无辜之人，以人的心肝为食，凶狠残暴，并且聚集同类数千人横行为祸于天下，竟然活到高寿而死。如果这是符合所谓的天道，那么这天道是合理，还是不合理呢？"这里善恶之结局相反的例子，恰恰正说明了老子之"道"的包容性。因为"道"并不会主宰天地万物的命运，"道"对天地万物，包括人都没有偏爱，所以即使一个人做出恶行，"道"不会对他施加惩罚，一个人做出善行，"道"也不会奖励给他福报。

P1-10 符合"自然"就是善。

【参见《老子》条目】

　　上善若水。水善利万物而不争，处众人之所恶，故几于道。居善地，心善渊，与善仁，言善信，政善治，事善能，动善时。夫唯不争，故无尤。（第八章）

证明：从定义1可知，"德"是万物从"无"到"有"再到"无"的自在自为过程的总称，也指人对此过程的认识以及顺应此过程的品质，包括善言善行。依据公理A1和基本假设4，"自然"是"道"从"无"到"有"再到"无"的自在自为过程，而这时人类社会出现的矛盾通常处于稳定状态。在这种状态下，人类社会整体崇德向善，不会产生尖锐的外部冲突与内部动荡，因此，符合"自然"就是善。

例证和说明：自然是"道"的本质要求，符合自然的行为就是合于"道"的行为，也就具有善的价值。这可以说是老子的价值观。这种价值观反对人的强力妄作，要求把生命安顿在自然的状态中，即使生命终结，也是符合自然之道，而不应有过度的悲哀。

　　《庄子·至乐》有这样一则对话：庄子妻死，惠施去吊丧，却看到庄子蹲在地上，鼓盆而歌。惠施说："你不哭也就罢了，又鼓盆而歌，不是太过分了吗？"庄子说："不是这样的。她刚死的时候，我怎么能不伤心难过呢？不过，静下心来一想，她最初是无生命的，不仅无生命，而且连形体也没有，不仅没有形体，甚至连气也没有。恍惚之间，变化而有了气，气变化而生出形体，形体变化而有了生命。如今又变化而死去。这种变化与春夏秋冬四时的运行是一样的。现在她安静地躺在天地之间，而我却还哭哭啼啼，这不是太不通达生命之道了吗？想到这一层，我就停止了哭泣。"庄子将死时嘱托弟子把自己的尸体扔到野外。他认为埋地下让蝼蚁吃掉与弃于野外让飞禽走兽吃掉都一样，而野葬是以天地为棺椁，以日月星辰为陪葬的最好方式。可见，庄子将人的生命看成气之聚，而死亡则是气之散，也就是生死都是自然的，就像四季的运行一样。庄子这种崇尚自然的思想就源于老子。

《庄子·养生主》还记载了类似的一个故事：老子死了，好友秦失前去吊唁他，哭了几声就出来了。老子的弟子非常不满地问，你不是我们老师的朋友吗？秦失说，是呀。老子弟子责备说，那么你吊唁怎么能这样呢？秦失肯定地回答说，当然可以呀。开始时我认为你们都是得道之人，现在看来事实并不是这样。刚才我进去吊唁的时候，有老者哭他，像哭其子，有年少者哭他，像哭其母。大家聚集到这里，肯定有不想说的话却说了，不想哭却哭了。这样做是违背人的自然性情的。你们老师来到这个世间，是应时而生，而他的离去，也是顺应自然。既然如此，那又有什么可以悲哀的呢？庄子对生死的看法是一以贯之的，始终强调顺应自然。

P1-11 人如果将"智"用于追求过分欲望，则会导致善恶不分。

【参见《老子》条目】

天下皆知美之为美，斯恶已；皆知善之为善，斯不善已。有无相生，难易相成，长短相形，高下相盈，音声相和，前后相随。是以圣人处无为之事，行不言之教；万物作而不为始，生而不有，为而不恃，功成而弗居。夫唯弗居，是以不去。（第二章）

证明：从定义2可知，"欲"指人对财富、名声和权力的追求，这种追求可能导致违背"自然"的后果。又从定义3，"智"一般意义指人对对象的认识能力和对个人行为的抉择能力，也特指人为了满足对"欲"的过分追求所产生的那种机巧智慧，后者往往对统治者而言。依据命题T1-10，符合"自然"就是善。而人如果过分追求欲望的满足，其机巧智慧就会偏离"自然"。因此，人如果将"智"用于追求过分欲望，则会导致善恶不分。

例证和说明："智"是指向外物的，人类的生活实践需要认识外物，所以"智"是必不可少的。但是，随着人们对外物的认识，控制、占有外物的欲望往往也随之增长，这就会打破人们生活的自然状态，而导致争夺，社会秩序也会陷入混乱。老子对于"智"怀有深深的警惕，其原因即在于此。西方社会所出现的现代性危机，其根源即在于工具理性这种竞争性的"智"的过度膨胀。理性一方面使人摆脱了神学愚昧，促进了人类社会的发展，但是，另一方面，以理性为尺度为人与社会重新设计，从而导致理性的片面发展，使工具理性逐渐膨胀，于是人们以科学作为理性的工具开始对自然进行全面的征服，对社会进行全面控制，对人进行

第三章 明道篇
CHAPTER THREE: On Understanding the Dao

全面的管理，从而造成人与自然、人与人之间的对立，导致了现代性危机的产生。

在《列子·黄帝》中有这样一个故事：宋国有一个养猴的老人，人称狙公，家里养了一大群猴子。狙公能够了解猴子的想法，猴子也能够理解狙公的心意。为了满足猴群的需求，狙公宁可自己一家人节衣缩食。不久，狙公家里的粮食不足了，狙公只能限定猴子的食物数量，但又怕猴子们不服从自己的决定，就先与猴子们说，早晨给你们三颗橡实，晚上再给你们四颗橡实，够吃的吗？猴子们一个个都站了起来，非常恼怒。他又说，早晨给你们四颗橡实，晚上再给你们三颗橡实，够吃的吗？猴子们听了都非常高兴，一个个趴在了地上。

这个故事实际上是《庄子·齐物论》中"朝三暮四"故事的扩展版。猴子们的问题就在于以"朝四"为是，以"朝三"为非，而没有看到一天的食物总量是一样的。如果人执着于所谓的"智"，可能就会像故事中的猴子一样，无法把握事物的本来面貌。

P1-12 节制"欲"、超越"智"则心自"明"。

【参见《老子》条目】

不尚贤，使民不争；不贵难得之货，使民不为盗；不见可欲，使民心不乱。是以圣人之治，虚其心，实其腹，弱其志，强其骨。常使民无知无欲。使夫智者不敢为也。为无为，则无不治。（第三章）

专气致柔，能如婴儿乎？涤除玄览，能无疵乎？爱国治民，能无为乎？天门开阖，能为雌乎？明白四达，能无知乎？（第十章）

证明：从定义4可知，"观"是人悟"道"的途径，"明"是人的内在生命力的自我观照能力。又依据公理A2与命题P1-11，由"智"入"明"就能知"道"。对"欲"的过度追求，以及由此产生的"智"，都可能违背自然，与"道"背离，需要加以控制。而"观"才是知"道"的途径。所以，节制"欲"、超越"智"则心自"明"。

例证和说明：老子对正常的欲望是尊重的，但是，欲望的泛滥会使人迷失淳朴自然的本性，成为欲望的奴隶，所以，要对欲望有所节制，使其控制在一定的范围之内，即满足最基本的物质生活欲望。而"智"也容易把人的视野局限在外物上，引起物欲的膨胀，使人成为物化的人，所以要超越"智"的片面的单向度的认识。只有这样，人的认识能力才能实现飞跃，达到灵明的境地。

西汉文帝刘恒生性节俭，他即位以后，一件长袍穿了二十多年，皇宫里的日常用品也大都是前辈皇帝留下的。有一次，他打算建造一个露台，找来工匠一算费用，大约要一百两黄金，而一百两黄金在当时相当于十户中等人家的年收入。

考虑到国库的状况、百姓的生活，建设露台的想法就作罢了。不仅如此，汉文帝还虚心纳谏，闻过则改。一次，汉文帝出行，行至中渭桥，有一人突然从桥下走出，惊扰了汉文帝的御马。案件交给廷尉张释之审理。张释之仅仅判了该人挡马罪，令其交四两罚金。汉文帝很生气，认为判罚过轻。张释之则据理力争，强调法律是天下人共同遵守的，不能因为冲撞了皇帝的御马就要加重判罚。汉文帝思量良久，最终接受了这一判决。正是因为汉文帝能够节制自己的欲望，而且不私智自用，使其有通明之德。在他的统治下，汉朝的社会经济获得长足的发展，为后来汉景帝时期的经济繁荣奠定了坚实的基础，而他自己也作为一代名君被载入史册。

P1-13 有观照之"明"方能悟"道"。

【参见《老子》条目】

复命曰常，知常曰明。（第十六章）

知和曰常。（第五十五章）

证明：从定义4可知，"明"是人的内在生命力的自我观照能力。依据命题T1-4，"道"和万物的基本特征是"自然"，也就说，人对万物的内在观照本身和悟道是一致的。又依据公理A2，由"智"入"明"就能知"道"。"明"是与"道"相对应的认知境界。所以，有观照之"明"方能悟"道"。

例证和说明：人的认识能力达到灵明之境，所关注的不再是外物的存在对于人的意义，而是天地万物包括人在内的整个世界的和谐发展，其依据就在于万物依之而生并向其复归的常道。因此，"明"就是超越单个外物的局限而实现的对整个世界的本质的根本认识。就此来说，只有具备了"明"才可能彻底唤醒自己的淳朴自然本性，自觉地将自己的行为实践符合于常道。只有在"明"的观照下，人的生命实践才会脱去因小智而形成的小我，升华到与"道"为一的境界。

越王勾践是春秋时期的最后一位霸主，而他之所以能灭掉吴国成为霸主，既与他卧薪尝胆的坚强意志与信念有关，同时也离不开范蠡与文种两位大臣的辅佐。正是在他们的辅佐下，勾践带领越国军民励精图治，"十年生聚"，终于积聚了强大的国力。趁吴国主力北上争霸，国内空虚，勾践出兵灭掉了吴国，一雪前耻。勾践灭吴之后，出兵北上，与齐、晋等国诸侯在徐州会盟，被各诸侯尊为霸王。就在越国势力达到顶峰之时，范蠡突然离开越国，到了齐国。他从齐国写了一封信给文种，劝他说，飞鸟被打尽了，良弓就被藏起来了，野兔被打完了，猎狗也就被烹着吃了。越王人长得脖子长，嘴巴像鸟嘴一样尖，这种人可以一起共患难，不可以一起共享乐。你为什么还不离开呢？文种读了范蠡的书信之后，并没有听从他的警告，而是称病不上朝。于是，就有人向勾践进谗言，说文种有不臣之心，想要叛乱。勾践就把当年吴王夫差赐给伍子胥让其自杀的属镂之剑赐给文种，告诉他说，你教给我七种讨伐吴国的策略，我只用三种就打败了吴国，其他的四种还在你那里，就请你到阴间去帮我的先王谋划谋划，看看能不能打败吴国的先王？至此，文种悔之已晚，只得伏剑自杀。

在这则故事中，可以看出，范蠡显然有识人之明，也明白功成身退的道理，故在大功告成之日，不图加官晋爵，而是选择了悄悄地离开，最后保全了自己。而文种虽然擅于谋略，但却没有看透勾践，更不懂"功遂身退"的道家智慧，终致惨死。

P1-14 人达到"明"境，才能没有私心。

【参见《老子》条目】

知常容，容乃公，公乃全，全乃天，天乃道，道乃久，没身不殆。（第十六章）

证明： 由定义7可知，"无私"指消除过分的"欲"和机巧性的"智"之后而达到的能包容万物的心理状态。依据命题P1-12和T1-13，通过节制"欲"、超越"智"就能达到"明"，从而去除私心杂念，达到悟"道"。所以，人达到"明"境，才能没有私心。

例证和说明： "知常"就是"明"，"明"人才能包容一切。人的"言说"和"命名"的智慧，实际上是"人为"的界限。一旦我们去命名，就会把对象相互异化、分类，区分出远近亲疏，这样人就具有了私心，就会偏离常道。比如，当我们用"无"来名天地之始，用"有"来名万物之母的时候，我们可能只看到"有"，而忽视"无"，更难看到"无"和"有"原来是"同出而异名"的。"同"才是根本，才是那"玄之又玄"的"众妙之门"。所以，老子在开篇就告诫道："故常无，欲以观其妙；常有，欲以观其徼"。老子的深意在于不要被"人为"的界限所限制，一定要超越这种限制。只有看到根本才具有真正的胸怀和眼界，以这种眼界去看万物，才能真正成就自身于万物之中。

李泌是唐德宗时期的宰相，德宗怀疑太子有不臣之心，欲废太子而改立继子舒王李谊（实为其侄），李泌力言废子立侄之非，惹怒了德宗，德宗威胁他说："卿爱你的家族吗？"李泌正色曰："正因为我爱我的家族，所以不敢不尽言。如果畏惧陛下发怒而委曲顺从，一旦陛下明日后悔了，必然会埋怨臣说：我独任你为宰相，你却不谏言，导致这种局面。必定会杀臣的儿子。臣已经老了，死不足惜。

如果冤杀了臣的儿子，臣只能以侄为嗣了，臣不知能够得到他的祭祀吗？"德宗被感动了，哭着问道："事已经至此了，该怎么办呢？"李泌说："这是大事情，陛下要考虑清楚。自古父子互相猜忌，没有不亡国覆家者。"德宗问道："这是我的家事，为什么你要这样力争呢？"李泌答曰："天子以四海为家，臣现独自承担宰相这一重任，四海之内，一物不得其所，都是臣的责任。况且坐视太子遭受冤屈而不言，这样臣的罪责就大了！"最后总算解开了德宗的心结。隔了一天，德宗在延英殿独自召见李泌，哭着告诉他："如果没有卿直言极谏，我今天后悔都来不及了。太子仁孝，并无他心。今后军国大事及我的家事，都与卿商量谋划。"古训曰："疏不间亲。"正是因为李泌明白通达，所以才能不避忌讳地调解德宗父子之间的误会。

P1-15 "明"者不自我夸耀和表现。

【参见《老子》条目】

不自见，故明。（第二十二章）

自见者不明。（第二十四章）

证明： 从定义4可知，"明"是人的内在生命力的自我观照能力。"明"之境界的重点在于自我观照，其目标不是外部对象，也就不需要夸耀和表现。又依据命题T1-13，有观照之"明"方能悟"道"。"明"的对象是"道"，而"道"的特征就是"自然"，这也是没有外在目的性。所以，"明"者不自我夸耀和表现。

例证和说明： 自我炫耀，努力去表现自己的智慧的人，是没有达到"明"境的。这种炫耀和表现中所显示的自信，往往是对某种片面的东西的盲目自信。欧阳修的《归田录》中有一篇《卖油翁》，写的是一个卖油翁观看陈尧咨射箭的故事：北宋名臣陈尧咨是有名的神箭手，当时没有第二人能与他相比，他也因此自夸。有一次，他在自家的园子里练习射箭，有一个卖油的老人放下担子，斜着眼睛看他射箭，很久都没有离开。卖油的老人见陈尧咨命中率是十之八九，只是微微点点头。陈尧咨问老人，你也懂得射箭吗？我的箭法是不是很高明呢？老人回答说，没有什么特别的，只不过手法熟练罢了。陈尧咨气愤地说，你怎么敢轻视我的射箭本领呢？老人说，根据我倒油的经验就可以知道。于是他取了一个葫芦放在地上，将一枚铜钱放在葫芦口上，慢慢地用油杓舀油往葫芦里倒，油从钱孔注入葫芦，而铜钱上却没有沾上一滴油。老人告诉陈尧咨，我这里也没有什么奥妙，不过长期倒油，手法熟练罢了。最后，陈尧咨笑着让老人离开了。

在这个故事中，陈尧咨作为北宋时期的一位官员，仅仅因为擅长射箭就变得飘飘然，缺乏自知之明。而卖油翁向他展示了熟练的倒油技巧，并指出这不过是经验的积累。在此方面，项羽可谓是一个反面的典型。司马迁在《史记》中对他的评价是：居功自傲，师心自用而不效法古代，妄图靠武力征服天下以建立霸业，结果五年后兵败身死，即使到最后，仍然用"天亡我，非用兵之罪也"来作为自己失败的借口，真是荒谬。

P1-16 "明"者追求自我内在生命力的澄清。

【参见《老子》条目】

> 知人者智，自知者明。（第三十三章）
>
> 知者不言，言者不知。（第五十六章）
>
> 知者不博，博者不知。（第八十一章）

证明：从定义4可知，"明"是人的内在生命力的自我观照能力。这揭示了"明"的对象是内在自我。依据命题T1-12和命题T1-14，节制"欲"、超越"智"则心自"明"。人达到"明"境，才能没有私心，人的内在自我就达到了"自然"，获得了一种通达和静谧，抛弃了不必要的扰动和杂念。所以，"明"者追求自我内在生命力的澄清。

例证和说明：老子说："知人者智，自知者明。"如果追求去了解别人和对象，其内在动机是想去控制对象，而且越是追求知识广博，说明控制欲望越强。当人回看自我，让自我内在生命力不断地自然伸张，那才是"明"。内在生命力的澄明是不要"言说"的，"言说"是私心和欲望的孪生兄弟，所以真正的智者"不言"，"知者不言，言者不知"。也不一定需要广博的知识，内在的澄明足以照亮一切，"知者不博，博者不知"。

《庄子·知北游》中有这样一则故事：一个叫"知"的人向北游历到玄水的岸边，登上了一座名叫"隐弅"的山丘，碰巧遇到了一个叫"无为谓"的人，"知"向"无为谓"请教了三个问题：如何思索、考虑才能懂得"道"？如何居处、行事才能符合"道"？通过什么途径、采用什么方法才能获得"道"？对于这三个问题，"无为谓"一个都没有回答，不是他不愿回答，而是他不知道怎样来回答。

"知"不得所问，就返回到白水的南面，登上了一座名叫"狐阕"的山丘，见到了一位名叫"狂屈"的人。"知"问了他同样的三个问题，狂屈说我知道这些道理，一会儿就告诉你。等到他想说的时候，又忘记了想讲的话。"知"又不得所问，于是就返回帝宫，拜见黄帝，向他请教这三个问题。黄帝告诉他，没有思索、没有考虑才能够懂得"道"，没有居处、没有行事才能符合"道"，没有依从的途径、没有方法才能掌握"道"。

"知"问黄帝，我和你都知道了这些道理，而"无为谓"与"狂屈"却不知道，那么他们俩哪一个是对的呢？黄帝说，"无为谓"的做法是对的，而"狂屈"则接近于对，我们俩则未能接近于"道"啊。

"知"听了黄帝所说的一番道理，对黄帝说：我问"无为谓"，他不问答我，不是不愿回答我，而是不知如何回答我；我问"狂屈"，"狂屈"想告诉我而又没有告诉我，不是不愿意告诉我，是他想说的时候又忘记了。现在我来问你，你知道如何回答，为什么你没有接近于"道"呢？黄帝回答说："无为谓"是真的对，因为他完全不知晓如何言说"道"；狂屈接近于对，因为他忘记了对"道"的言说；而我们未能接近于"道"，因为我们已经在言说"道"。

这番对话虽然集中在言说与"道"的关系上，但可以看出，"道"对于人而言是一个体验的问题，而不是言说的问题，当你把注意力集中在言说上，那么你实际上已经远离了"道"。

P1-17 观"道"是对"智"的超越。

【参见《老子》条目】

道常无名，朴。虽小，天下莫能臣。侯王若能守之，万物将自宾。天地相合，以降甘露，民莫之令而自均。始制有名，名亦既有，夫亦将知止，知止可以不殆。譬道之在天下，犹川谷之于江海。（第三十二章）

天下有始，以为天下母。既得其母，以知其子；既知其子，复守其母，没身不殆。塞其兑，闭其门，终身不勤。开其兑，济其事，终身不救。见小曰明，守柔曰强。用其光，复归其明，无遗身殃；是为袭常。（第五十二章）

证明： 从定义3和定义4可知，"智"一般意义上是指人对对象的认识能力和对个人行为的抉择能力，也特指人为满足"欲"的过分追求而产生的那种机巧智慧；"观"是人知"道"的途径。又依据公理A2，由"智"入"明"就能悟"道"。获得"明"必须超越"智"，而"明"的对象就是"道"。所以，观"道"是对"智"的超越。

例证和说明： 老子说："为学日益，为道日损。"（《老子》第四十八章）但是，这两者之间又不是绝对对立的，不是为了获得"明"就要抛弃"智"。"智"的片面发展会导致物欲的膨胀，而只要超越"智"的思维局限，就会获得"明"。老子又说"涤除玄览"，就是将自己心灵的污垢扫除干净，也即是让自己的心灵不受外物的控制，这样，就从"智"而入"明"，天地万物的本相就会呈现于面前，而为人所认识。

在《庄子·逍遥游》中，庄子说：你没有见过野猫和黄鼠狼吗？它们低下身子匍匐于地，等待那些游荡的猎物出现；为了抓住猎物，它们东蹿西跳，不避高下；正是由此，它们往往就踩中了猎人所设下的捕兽机关，或者死于猎人布下的捕兽网中。庄子由此所表达的意思是，当你用"智"的眼光去看一个物时，你所看到的是这个物对你而言的利害关系。也就是说，"智"是出于人们趋利避害的竞争意识，所以庄子说"知出于争"（《庄子·人间世》）。而用这种竞争性的"智"来看物或人，当你做出对自己有利的选择时，最终的结果可能恰恰对你是不利的。因此，要想观"道"，必须超越这种竞争性的"智"。而这里的超越，是要在"智"的基础上超越对外在事物的利与害的划分，而去认识事物的本来的自然状态。

P1-18 从最抽象的"无"与"有"处可以观"道"。

【参见《老子》条目】

故常无，欲以观其妙；常有，欲以观其徼。此两者，同出而异名，同谓之玄。玄之又玄，众妙之门。（第一章）

证明：依据基本假设2，道可"无"，精微处充满力量；"无"生"有"，恍惚中混成迹象；"有"生万物，万物复归于"无"。"道"本身无法用概念来表达，但最抽象的概念"无"和"有"的转化能体现"道"的过程。又依据公理A2，由"智"入"明"就能悟"道"。最抽象概念的背后隐含着"道"，而"明"不是凭空而来的境界，是超越"智"的悟"道"境界。所以，从最抽象的"无"与"有"处可以观"道"。

例证和说明：道具有"无""有"之两面，"无"指称的是天地的本始，"有"指称的则是万物的根源。在天地未生之前，"道"是"无"的存在方式，而在万物生成的过程中及生成之后，"道"又以"有"的方式存在。因此，"无"与"有"是一体两面的关系，从两个不同的方式来揭示"道"的存在。

正因为道体具有这两面，所以可以通过两种不同的方式来观"道"：一种是"常无"，即观道体的"无"的状态，这时虽然天地未生，但其神妙莫测的生机已现；另一种是"常有"，即观道体的"有"的状态，这时虽万物纷纭，但其必归终于"道"。"无"与"有"作为道体之两面，都出于"道"，所以是同出而异名。"无"与"有"之两面都是幽昧难知的，而作为"无"与"有"所从出的道体自身更是幽昧，所以是"玄之又玄"。道体虽极其幽昧，但却是一切神妙莫测之用所产生的根源。

唐代的李公佐有一部著名的传奇小说《南柯太守传》，小说的主人公是唐朝的东平郡人淳于棼。他是位游侠之士，讲义气，爱喝酒。曾凭着武艺做过淮南军的副将，因为酒后触犯主帅，被撤了官职。自此，他行为放纵，终日以饮酒为事。有一次，他喝醉了酒，被人送回了家，躺在堂屋东面的走廊里小憩，一会儿他就进入了梦乡。

他梦见大槐安国的国王派人来接他，把二公主许配给他，还派他担任了南柯郡的太守。淳于棼到了南柯郡，勤政爱民，将南柯郡治理得井井有条。他守郡二十年，教化广被，老百姓歌谣赞之，并为其建功德碑，立生祠。国王非常看重他，赐给他食邑和爵位，使其居于台辅之位。他生有五男二女，儿子们都通过恩荫而被授予官职，两个女儿也嫁给了王侯，荣耀显赫之盛，无人能及。后来，檀萝国出兵攻打南柯郡，淳于棼的军队打了败仗。接下来，他的妻子也染病去世了。于是，淳于棼扶柩回到了京城。回京之后，他爱交游的本色又显现出来，整日结交宾客，结果遭到了国王的猜忌，被禁止结交宾客，并被软禁于私第之中。淳于棼过得非常郁闷。国王知道他不开心，就让他回乡省亲。等他被送回到广陵郡的老家，他就醒了，才知道曾经的荣耀显赫以及不幸俱是一场梦。淳于棼由此看透了人世的无常，就出家做了道士。

在这个故事中，淳于棼从富贵与落魄的两极对比中看透了人世的无常，在一定意义上，也可以说是从"有"与"无"之两端理解了"道"。

P1-19 从感觉的细微之处可以观"道"。

【参见《老子》条目】

视之不见，名曰夷；听之不闻，名曰希；搏之不得，名曰微。此三者不可致诘，故混而为一。其上不皦，其下不昧，绳绳兮不可名，复归于无物。是谓无状之状，无物之象。是谓惚恍。迎之不见其首，随之不见其后。（第十四章）

证明：依据基本假设2，道可"无"，精微处充满力量；"无"生"有"，恍惚中混成迹象；"有"生万物，万物复归于"无"。精微之处、恍惚之中，"无"与"有"的转化，既是"道"的表现特征，也是感觉的细微之处，这需要提升人的内在生命力的自我观照能力，后者即"明"（从定义4）。再依据公理A2，由"智"入"明"就能悟道。所以，从感觉的细微之处可以观"道"。

例证和说明："道"作为形而上的实存，其本身是无形无象的，故人的感官是无法捕捉到它的，即"视之不见""听之不闻""搏之不得""迎之不见其首，随之不见其后"。对于这个虚无缥缈、惚兮恍兮的道体，虽然无法直接加以名状，但却可以通过与具体事物的比较，用反显的方法揭示道体的实存，即"无状之状，无物之象"。就是说，道体的存在是恍恍惚惚、若有若无的，你不能像感知具体事物那样感觉到它的形象，但又不是什么都感觉不到。也即是说，恍惚是一种细微的感觉，在这种感觉中，你能够体会到"道"的存在。

在中国禅宗史上有一则著名的"香岩击竹"的公案：香岩智闲禅师本是百丈怀海门下的弟子，他虽聪明伶俐，问一答十，但总是不能顿悟。百丈怀海圆寂之后，香岩跟随沩山灵祐禅师继续参禅。灵祐禅师知道香岩聪明伶俐，且擅于辩论，就问了他一个问题，即在父母未生你之前，你是怎样的？香岩一脸茫然，不知该如何回答。

回房后，他将平日看过的书从头到尾翻了个遍，也没有找到一句适合做答案的话。他感叹地说，真是画饼不可充饥呀！香岩请求沩山灵祐为他解答，灵祐禅师告诉他，我如果现在为你解答，你以后会骂我的。而且，我告诉你的终究是我的见解，并不关你的事，对你又有何益呢？香岩一气之下，把平时看的书全烧了，长叹道：我这辈子再也不学佛法了，就做一个到处化缘乞食的和尚吧。

他哭着辞别了灵祐禅师，到处云游。一天，香岩在除草，见地上有一块瓦砾，就捡起来向竹林里丢去，瓦砾砸到了竹子，发出一声脆响，听此声音，香岩突然省悟。他对空拜道，师父大恩，如若当初为我说破，哪会有今天的顿悟呢？

听闻声音是一种感觉，香岩智闲禅师正是由此而悟到禅法的真谛。这虽是一个禅宗故事，但其中蕴含的观"道"方式与老子是相通的。在老子的思想中，通过一种细微而又不是那么具体的感觉，可以体会到道家之"道"的存在。

P1-20 消除妄为的欲望并放弃对"智"的迷信，是观"道"的前提。

【参见《老子》条目】

涤除玄览，能无疵乎？（第十章）

知不知，尚矣；不知知，病也。圣人不病，以其病病。夫唯病病，是以不病。（第七十一章）

证明：依据基本假设1，道是任何"某个（类）"的综合。又依据公理A2，由"智"入"明"就能悟"道"。又依据命题12，节制"欲"，超越"智"则心自"明"。可见，观"道"的基础是节制"欲"，超越"智"。因此，消除妄为的欲望并放弃对"智"的迷信，是观"道"的前提。

例证和说明：对"道"的认识需要具备一定的主体条件，首先要对欲望加以节制，使欲望的满足符合人的自然本性的需要；其次，要认识到"智"的局限，"智"是一种单向度的思维，很容易导致物欲的膨胀，因而不能陷入对"智"的迷信之中，以为凭借"智"就可以控制一切。达到了这两个条件,认识主体才能将注意力由外在的事物转向自己内在的生命实践,也才能具备对"道"的认识能力,即具备"明"。欲望归于自然,"智"的局限也得到克服,外物之来,物各付物,心灵就会归于虚静。在虚静的心灵的观照下,所呈现的不是万物纷纭复杂的差异性,而是其整体的归根复命的历程。这种观照,实质上就是对"道"的认识。

《庄子·秋水》有一则寓言说:秋雨绵绵,百川之水注入黄河,河水流量增大,河面变宽。于是河伯欣然自喜,以为天下最壮观的景色在自己这里。河伯顺着水流向东而行,到了北海边,向东一望,不见北海的尽头。于是河伯改变了之前洋洋自得的面目,对着北海之神慨叹说:"俗语说'听了很多道理,便以为没有谁比得上自己',说的就是我这样的人呀!开始时我还不相信你的浩瀚无边,现在我亲眼看到了,才真的服气了,要不然我肯定会受到嘲笑。"北海之神说:"井底之蛙,不能跟它们谈论大海,因为它们受到空间的限制;夏天的虫子,不能跟它们谈论寒冷,因为受到生活时间的限制;而乡曲之士,不能跟他们谈论大道,因为受到平时教养的限制。现在你从河岸的束缚中出来,看到了大海,而知道了自己的鄙陋,这样你就可以参与谈论大道了。"

在这则故事中,河伯的自我认识由最初的傲慢自大,到见北海之大而知其鄙陋,也即放弃了对其"智"的盲目自信。这也就具备了认识"道"的条件,所以北海之神说他可以参与谈论大道了。

P1-21 观"道"的最高境界是"虚"和"静"。

【参见《老子》条目】

致虚极,守静笃。万物并作,吾以观复。夫物芸芸,各复归其根。归根曰静,静曰复命。复命曰常,知常曰明。(第十六章)

证明: 从定义5可知,"静"是涤除了过分的"欲"与机巧性的"智"的干扰而达到的内心澄明状态。"虚"就是"无",意指人的内在状态就是空空如也,就是"静"。人的内在的"静"是一种内心澄明状态,也就是在认识和体悟上达到了"明"。依据公理A2,由"智"入"明"就能悟"道"。因此,观"道"的最高境界是"虚"和"静"。

例证和说明: 观"道"虽然是主体对"道"的认识,但是在这一过程中主体内部存在着两股张力,一股是随波逐流,顺从"智"与"欲"的要求,另一股则是截断众流,返归于"道"。只有涤除了过度的欲望与机巧性的"智",主体才能在虚静的状态中去直接把握"道"。在这种境界中,主体的心灵就像一块没有染污的镜子，空虚而宁静，万物在它面前呈现出自己的本来面目。

在《庄子·齐物论》中，开篇有这样一段对话：南郭子綦倚几案而坐，仰天而嘘气，那种忘我的样子，好像精神离开了身体。他的学生颜成子游陪在他跟前，问道："承载生命的身体，哪能使它像枯槁的木头？充满活力的心灵，哪能使它像死灰一样？您今天倚几案而坐，跟往常倚几案而坐的情形不大一样，让人惊讶啊。"

南郭子綦回答道：你这个问题问得很好！今天，我达到了忘我的境界。你听到过"人籁"，但没有听过"地籁"，即使你听过"地籁"，你没有听过"天籁"啊！颜成子游问：那我怎么才能听到"天籁"呢？南郭子綦说：大地吐出的气，其名为风。风不刮则已，一刮起来，则大地上的孔窍都随之而怒吼。你没有听过那呼呼的风声吗？陡峭的山陵上，百围大树上的窍孔，似鼻，似口，似耳，似圆柱上插入横木的方孔，似圈围的栅栏，似舂米的臼窝，似深池，似浅坑；风吹过所发出的声音，像湍急的激流声，像迅疾的箭镞声，像呵斥声，像呼吸声，像叫喊声，像嚎哭声，像幽怨声，像哀切声。前者唱而随者和，小风则小和，大风则大和。烈风突然停了，万窍也就寂然无声了。颜成子游问：那么什么是天籁呢？南郭子綦答道：天籁虽然也有万般不同，但其发作与停止都是其自己主宰，没有一个外在的主宰来控制它。

庄子这里通过南郭子綦与颜成子游的对话，强调进入物我两忘的虚静境界，就能听到天地万物的自然声音，即天籁，因为在这种境界中，人已经没有主宰万物的欲望，而万物都顺应其自然的本性，自作主宰。在这种境界中，与其说是观"道"，不如说是与"道"为一，因为此时"道"已经不是认识的对象，主体的心灵与"道"完全融合在了一起。

This chapter consists of 21 propositions that are mainly about the basic concepts of Dao and how people can perceive it. Specifically, the first ten propositions of this chapter deal with Dao itself and its relations with everything else; from P1-11 to P1-16 two perceptions of human beings – "knowing" and "enlightening," and their relations are provided; and the rest deals with the ways, steps and measures of perceiving Dao. The propositions and corollaries of this chapter and the next three ones, implying the values of Daoist thought in modern society, are judgments derived from the original text *Laozi*, and hence should be proved and illustrated.

In this chapter and following chapters, "P" stands for Proposition, "D" for Definition, and "A" for Axiom.

P1-1 Dao is free, and so it is with everything else.

Quotes from *Laozi*:

Dao does nothing yet nothing is left undone. (Chapter 37)

Proof: By Assumption 1, we know Dao is the sum of any category, and De (virtue) refers to the spontaneous and unrestrained process of free and all things (see Definition 1); besides, according to Axiom 1, the natural way is a spontaneous and unrestrained process where Dao comes into existence from nothingness and then disappears in nothingness. So, Dao, being free and unrestrained, is a unity of nothingness and existence and governs De. And everything is changing between non-being and being. Hence, we believe Dao is free, and so it is with everything else.

Explanation: Dao, namely the Way, is the rules that are completely free, which is not only a mixture prior to the existence of Heaven, Earth and all things, but also exists among them, becoming the universal rules of the objective world. Hence, Heaven, Earth and all things are free and unrestrained. In terms of their relations, Dao is nurturing all things by means of inaction, otherwise, it would destroy the unrestrained state of all things, whereas the latter can only get adapted to Dao in the way of inaction, or it would lose its spontaneity and become the opposite of Dao.

In the first year of Emperor Hui of Western Han Dynasty (194 BC), Cao Can was named the prime minister of the State of Qi, when the state had a total of over seventy walled cities and was a quite bigger state of the day. As the prince of Qi, Liu Fei, was rather young and incapable of governing, Cao Can governed the government on behalf of the prince; he summoned the aged and educated and consulted about the ways of making the people live in peace and order, with the aim of formulating the proper strategies of government. However, hundreds of the educated came up with varied suggestions, leaving Cao Can no decision. Learning that there was a Mr. Gai living in the west of today's Jiaozhou and that he was versed in the study of the thoughts of Emperor Huang and Laozi, Cao Can asked his subordinate to invite him with lavish gifts. Mr. Gai, after seeing Cao Can, suggested that the important thing for government be peaceful inaction and as such the people would live in peace and order. Taking this advice, Cao Can adopted the thought of inaction of Emperor Huang and Laozi and took such rest and recuperation measures featured by reducing taxes and punishment and promoting frugality, without disturbing people's living, which gave the grass-roots sufficient time to carry out farming. During his nine-year tenure as the prime minister, the State of Qi gradually became peaceful and prosperous, and Cao Can, highly praised by the locals, was called a virtuous minister.

When Prime Minister Xiao He passed away in 193 BC, Cao Can took his position and adopted no political initiative, which was historically called "Prime Minister Cao followed the rules of Mr. Xiao." While selecting officials, he would choose the faithful and slow-witted and repudiated those who were harsh and pursued fame. He was abandoned to drinking all day, cared little about political affairs, and would only meet and treat the subjects on low levels with wine, talking nothing about the governance. Under his influence, many officials would drink and dance all day long, making his subordinates rather unhappy. They asked him to stop it. However, when Cao Can summoned them. He instead drank and sang with them too.

Emperor Hui of Han was also very dissatisfied with Cao Can's ways of governance, and asked his son Cao Yong to advise his father when appropriate. After hearing the suggestion of his son, Cao Can burst into fury and beat him with a bamboo, scolding. "Go to serve the Emperor! It's none of your business as to the governance." Learning that his lobbyist failed and got beaten, Emperor Hui of Han was quite depressed and decided to blame Cao Can in his court; the latter immediately apologized and asked the emperor, "Who is more intelligent, you or Emperor Gaozu?" "How can I be more intelligent than the wise Gaozu?" Cao Can went on, "Who is more competent, Xiao He or I?" "I think Xiao He is more competent." Taking the opportunity, Cao Can explained, "Emperor Gaozu and Xiao He unified the state and formulated the laws, so now you and the officials fulfill the duty and abide by the laws, would this be not great?" The emperor grasped his intention, and blamed him no more.

The stories that Cao Can became the prime minister of Qi and followed the rules of Xiao He illustrate that the people have the competence for development and can solve such basic issues as economic development and social order, as long as the ruler follows the opinions of the public and gives full play to their potentials. Yet, more often than not rulers failed to practice this and would always use their power in an attempt to rule and confine the people, therefore the result was often counterproductive.

P1-2   Dao is the root of the freedom of all things.

Quotes from *Laozi*:

All things arise together, I watch their return. Things come forth in great numbers, and each one returns to its own root. (Chapter 16)

Dao begets one; one begets two; two begets three; three begets all things. With the Yin in the innermost part, all things in the universe face the Yang, and the vigorous mutual agitation of Yin and Yang brings them into harmony. (Chapter 42)

Proof: According to D1, De is the sum of any category, while all things can change between existence and non-being. Dao can be nothing but full of strength in subtlety and its nothingness brings forth fullness, the natural way is a spontaneous and unrestrained process where Dao comes into existence from nothingness and then disappears in nothingness (see P1-2 and A1). So Dao co-exists with all things whose free and unrestrained process is Dao per se. Hence, we say that Dao is the root of the freedom of all things.

Explanation: As the law without restrictions, Dao cannot be changed by any action or attempt. Heaven, Earth and all things that make up the objective world exist, because they follow the law of naturalness and inaction. Hence, it was recorded in Chapter 39 of *Laozi*, "*the sky has got it, hence clear and bright; the Earth has got it, hence staid and tranquil; the God has got it, hence effective; the river valley has got it, hence its brimming full; everything in the universe has got it, hence its growth and spread; the princes and marquises have got it, hence the states stable and secure.*" In turn, Heaven, Earth and all things would lose their free state and meaning of existence, if the One of Dao is ignored.

A story is told in "*A Carefree Wondering,*" *Zhuangzi*: In the far northern ocean there was a fish named Kun, and nobody know how many thousand miles it was in length. It changes into a bird called Peng, and nobody know how many thousand miles its back in breadth. When it flew to the far south, the water is smitten for a space of three thousand miles and the bird itself mounts upon a great wind to a height of ninety thousand miles. A cicada and a young dove sneered, "We would fly as high as the trees, if no efforts spared; sometimes we could not reach that high and would fall to the ground midway. What then can be the use of mounting upon ninety thousand miles to start for the south?" This story implies that the cicada and the dove only know their wondering as small birds while knowing about the wondering of such big birds as Peng. With this, Zhuangzi held that those three types of birds have different flying conditions: the first two do not need to fly high because of their small bodies, whereas Peng must fly high to take advantage of the wind, which determines their different manners of wondering. Such a difference does not mean that the wondering of Peng is superior, but that their ways of wondering are natural. Zhuangzi employed this story to illustrate this: the differences between all creatures, including man, are a true reality, and everything can enjoy carefree wondering, as long as it follows Dao.

P1-3 Dao is inclusive of rather than dominates all things.

Quotes from *Laozi*:

The great Dao is buoyant, going and extending everywhere. All things in the universe depend on it to thrive and it does not disown them, yet having produced them, it does not claim credit for itself. It nurtures all things in the universe, but it does not want to dominate the world, therefore, it may be called "xiao," or the little; all things in the universe submit to it, but it does not want to be their lord, therefore, it may be called "da," or the great. It does not think itself to be great, therefore, it becomes the great. (Chapter 34)

Proof: According to Assumption 1 and Assumption 2, Dao is the sum of any category, as "being" gives birth to all things that return to "non-being" and need the nurturing of Dao. Therefore, it is the return to nothing that leads to the nurturing of Dao. Dao and all things are inseparable, for the former gives birth to the latter and the latter returns to Dao. Also, the natural way is a spontaneous and unrestrained process where Dao comes into existence from nothingness and then disappears in nothingness (see A1), which means all things are in a "natural" process free from restrictions. Hence, we say that Dao is inclusive of rather than dominates all things.

Explanation: As a free existence per se, Dao shows its freedom in not dominating nor being dominated. So the naturalness and inaction of Dao are manifested in its relations with all things, namely, tolerant of all differences and determining not their directions of development, which in turn lets all things enjoy endless possibilities of development.

When meeting with the Indian delegation in 1953, Chinese Premier Zhou Enlai formally proposed the Five Principles — Mutual respect for territorial integrity, non-aggression, non-interference in internal affairs of each other, equality and mutual interest, and peaceful coexistence — for the first time, which was later amended as "Mutual respect for sovereignty and territorial integrity, non-aggression, non-interference in the internal affairs of each other, equality and mutual benefit, and peaceful coexistence." Initiated by China, the Five Principles of Peaceful Coexistence have been endorsed by more and more countries around the world and have gradually become the basic principles for handling differences and disputes in international relations. In 1988, Deng Xiaoping proposed to develop a new international political and economic order based on the Five Principles, which in fact was targeting at the old one formed by America after World War Two. In the old establishment defined by different ideologies, countries were in opposition and those of different sizes were unequal in status, that is, major powers oppressed smaller ones by means of their political, economic and military forces, and even invaded small countries. A new international establishment based on the Five Principles, requires that all countries should respect the differences in between and allow various ways of development, and that big powers should not dominate small countries. Therefore, we can see that the Five Principles hold not only the peaceful spirit of Confucianism, but also that of inclusiveness and naturalness advocated by Daoism.

P1-4   Nature is the basic feature of Dao and of all things.

Quotes from *Laozi*:

Man models himself on Earth, Earth on Heaven, Heaven on the Dao, and the Dao on Nature. (Chapter 25)

Dao generates them, virtue nourishes them, substance forms them, and circumstances accomplish them. Therefore all things revere Dao and honor virtue. Yet Dao is revered and virtue honored not because this is decreed by any authority but because it's naturally so on its own. (Chapter 51)

Proof: According to Assumption 2, Dao can be nothing, which means it is full of possibilities, but full of strength in subtlety; its non-being brings forth fullness, and chaos signs. Such subtle potential is bound to be given full play to and brings the beginning of Heaven and Earth, yet without clear directions. The fullness Dao brings forth is the mother of all things and also refers to the formation of all. Furthermore, the natural way is a spontaneous and unrestrained process where Dao comes into existence from non-being and then disappears in non-being (see Axiom 1), so the process of both Dao and all things are, as a matter of fact, changes between existence and non-being. Hence, we say that the basic feature of Dao and all things is natural.

Explanation: As the fundamental principle followed by Heaven, Earth and all things, Dao has no superior above it, that is, "*It is always natural and of itself so.*" So, all things follow the law of Dao, which is also a natural process, without any purpose in it.

There is a story in *Zhuangzi: Qualifications of Kings*, which goes like this: The kings of the South Ocean and the North Ocean were named Shu and Hu, while the king of the ocean in between named Hundun. As the first two kings often met in the land in between, Hundun would entertain them friendly. One day, Shu and Hu discussed how to repay his kindness, and agreed on this: "Everyone has seven orifices to see, hear, eat and breathe and so on. Hundun does not have these, so let's help him have them." Thus, every day they bored a hole into Hundun, yet Hundun died on the seventh day. The mistake they made was going against nature forcefully, which as a result killed Hundun.

Wang Chong, a famous philosopher of the Eastern Han Dynasty, drew on Laozi's thought and developed it into "The Way of heaven is naturally non-action," holding that action goes against nature and the Way of heaven. As for the basis of this, he pointed out that unlike human beings, Heaven has no mouth or eyes, and therefore has no desires. As a matter of fact, heaven is *qi* (vitality) and gives birth to all things with *qi* of the earth. In the development of all things, Heaven, unlike God, who creates man and things consciously, gives birth to all things naturally in the operation of *qi* without any purpose or aim. It is the actions of nature that make all things the creation of nature naturally rather than purposefully.

P1-5 Dao cannot be understood in terms of words or names.

Quotes from *Laozi*:

The Dao that can be worded is not the constant Dao. The name that can be named is not the eternal name. (Chapter 1)

There was something formless yet complete that existed before heaven and earth, without sound or substance, dependent on nothing, unchanging, all pervading, unfailing. One may think of it as the mother of all things under heaven. I do not know its name, and I might call it Dao or "Greatness" if you insist on naming it. (Chapter 25)

Dao is hidden and nameless. (Chapter 41)

Proof: According to Assumption 1, Dao is the sum of any category but defies the belonging to any "certain category;" it carries no specific definition, which means that it defies any conceptualization. Besides, its subtle potential is bound to be given full play to and brings the beginning of Heaven and Earth, yet without clear directions. The fullness Dao brings forth is the mother of all things and also refers to the formation of all (see Assumption 2). So, Dao is more abstract than such abstract terms as non-existence and existence we used. Hence, we say that Dao cannot be understood in terms of words or names.

Explanation: A philosophical concept as Dao is, it refers to the most vital law governing heaven, earth and man. It exists in all things, but it actually transcends all tangible creatures; it cannot be grasped by human's experience, or by concepts. That is to say, Dao in fact cannot be precisely expressed in words, because words with life experience and can only express the things embodied in reality. Even if words transcended the experiential world and were employed to express the intangible Dao, it would only reveal certain aspect of Dao but not Dao as a whole, which would be like the blind feeling the elephant and can only get a partial understanding. According to Kant's philosophy, among the so-called "transcendental noumenon" (i.e., God, soul and the world), any rationalist attempt to understand the noumenal things by transcending the empirical world would lead to antimony, which is similar to Laozi's understanding of Dao.

It was recorded in *Zhuangzi: Heaven and Earth* that Emperor Huang lost his Xuanzhu (literally Black Pearl) in his visit of Chishui River and Mountain Kunlun, so he sent Chi, Lizhu and Chigou to find it back respectively, but they failed. In the end, it was found by Xiangwang, while the Emperor said in surprise, "How Strange! People like Xiangwang should find it." In this story, Xuanzhu means metaphorically Dao, while Chi, Lizhu, Chigou and Xiangwang refer to four different ways of pursuing Dao; specifically, they refer to the intelligent, the one with sharp sight, the one with sharp tongue, and the carefree who has no sharp sight or tongue but totally follows Dao. Those who pursue Dao with concerns, sharp eyes or tongues are purposeful, and in the end will go against it. However, Xiangwang who did not seek Dao for the sake of pursuing Dao actually took its course and finally finds it.

P1-6 Dao in nature is empty but eternal in usefulness.

Quotes from *Laozi*:

Dao is invisibly empty, but its use is extremely infinite. Deep, it is like the mother of all things. Darkly visible, it only seems as if it were there. I know not whose son it is. It may be the forefather of God. (Chapter 4)

Is not the space between Heaven and Earth like a bellows? It is empty but it is never exhausted. The more it works, the stronger wind it produces. Too much talk leads to a dead end; it is better to hold fast to moderation and the void. (Chapter 5)

The function of the Dao is in its softness and tenderness. (Chapter 40)

Proof: According to Assumption 1 and Assumption 2, Dao is the sum of any category, as "existence" gives birth to all things that return to "non-being" and need the nurturing of Dao. Therefore, it is the return to nothing that leads to the nurturing of Dao; its subtle potential is bound to be given full play to and brings the beginning of Heaven and Earth, yet without clear directions, which shows that Dao in nature is empty, and by extension, the fullness Dao brings forth is the mother of all things and also refers to the formation of all. Also, Dao that can be nothing means it is full of possibilities, which shows that the usefulness of Dao is eternal. Hence, we say that Dao in nature is empty but eternal in usefulness.

Explanation: Dao itself is empty but it does not mean it's nothing; unlike concrete things, Dao is virtually shapeless and plays its role by means of being weak, which is the reason why Heaven and Earth would not exhaust its strength in the course of following Dao. That is to say, Dao can play its role in an endless and inexhaustible manner.

In *The True Meaning of Life* authored by Osho, he used a math concept (i.e., 0) to illustrate the emptiness and infinity of Dao. This very concept was first coined by the Indian who held that everything came from and returned to nothing or 0. Though it is just a figure mathematically, it serves as the basis of the rest figures; this is to say, empty as it is, it is of infinite significance. When it is added to the non-zero ones, it would be richer in meaning. By the same token, an adding of numerous zeros would still be 0, but that of zeros to one would result in an infinite number. In addition, in computer language all data is coded and stored based on 0 and 1, and different data will be generated, if the position of 0 is changed. Hence, provided zero is compared to Dao, the infinite significance produced by 0 will highlight the infinite role of Dao. The driver of the unstoppable development of the world lies in the empty Dao, and it is its emptiness that gives rise to infinite effects. Comparatively speaking, anything with a shape is finite and so it is with its role.

P1-7　Dao is nurturing all and unstoppable.

Quotes from *Laozi:*

There was something formed out of chaos. That was born before Heaven and Earth. Soundless and formless, it does stand, extend, and recycle without stopping. It can be regarded as the mother of all things of Heaven and Earth. I do not know its name. I might call it Dao or "Greatness" if you insist on naming it. "Greatness" suggests "without end," "without end" suggests "far away," and "far away" suggests "recursion." (Chapter 25)

The movement of the Dao is in endless recursion... (Chapter 40)

Proof: According to Assumption 2, Dao can be subtle but full of strength; it can be nothing that leads to being and chaotic signs, which means that non-being is strength while being all things. Besides, by Axiom 1, we know that the natural way is a spontaneous and unrestrained process where Dao comes into existence from nothingness and then disappears in nothingness, where Dao is the root of all things. "Being" brings forth all things that return to nothing and that need the nurturing of Dao. Hence, we say that Dao is nurturing all and unstoppable.

Explanation: Here "unstoppable" means repetitiveness, which is the reason for Laozi's "The movement of the Dao is in endless recursion," that is to say, Dao does not change into its opposite but change repetitively. Hence, we should not naively take his thought as something dialectal, because he did not deny the interchange of the opposites in life and the world alike.

According to "The North Tour of Mr. Zhi" in *Zhuangzi*: there was a dialogue between him and Dongguo Zi. "Where is the Dao you always advocate?" asked the latter. "It's ubiquitous." "Could you please put it more concretely?" "Among the ants." "How could it be in such an inferior and humble place?" "Among the bricks and tiles." "How could it be in a more humble one?" "Among the feces." Hearing this answer, Dongguo Zi did not dare to ask any more, for the replies went beyond his imagination. This reveals that Dongguo Zi actually distinguished all things into the superior and the inferior and there was no Dao in the latter, which in reality distorts the thought of Daoism. The reason is that Dao is the fundamental law existing in all things, regardless of their high or low status.

Speaking of "Dao exists among the feces," Li Hongzhang (1823-1901), a well-known senior official of the Qing Dynasty (1644-1912), once talked about it humorously. While carrying out the self-strengthening by learning from the West, he developed great interests in the science and technology of modern West. Once he asked his subordinate what a parabola was, but he failed to understand it after a detailed explanation. The subordinate was quick-witted and said, "My master, you know the trace of your peeing is what a parabola is!" Li Hongzhang got it immediately and laughed, "What you said is Zhuangzi's '*Dao exists among the feces.*'"

P1-8 Dao is of an image but free from vision.

Quotes from *Laozi*:

Looking without seeing is called Yi (the invisible); listening without hearing is called Xi (the inaudible); touching without feeling is called Wei (the formless). These three things can be in no way defined, thus blurred as one. Its upper part is not dazzling; its lower part is not obscure. Boundless and formless, it cannot be named and returns to nothing. This is called the formless form, shapeless shapes, and the substanceless image. To greet it, you don't see its head; to follow it, you don't see its rear. (Chapter 14)

Such a thing as the Dao is impalpable and shapeless. Impalpable and shapeless! Inside there are images. Shapeless and impalpable! Inside there are substances. Shadowy and obscure. Inside there are essences. These essences are very real and none the less efficacious. (Chapter 21)

The greatest image seems invisible. (Chapter 41)

Proof: According to Assumption 2, Dao can be subtle but full of strength; it can be nothing that leads to being and chaotic signs, which means Dao is subtle instead of void, and it is its subtlety that gives endless strength. Besides, by Assumption 1, we know that Dao is the sum of all categories but not a certain one, which implies that Dao is not of a certain object; nor is it visible. Hence, it is claimed that Dao is of an image but free from vision.

Explanation: To explain what Dao is, Laozi used water, which is observable but of no certain shape. Liu Yuxi, a great thinker of the Tang Dynasty (618-907), also said: "*The so-called shapelessness in ancient times means that it is of no certain shape and can only be visible in things,*" and proposed "*Emptiness is a miniature of shape.*" (*On the Heaven*) This is in conformity with the characteristics of Laozi's Dao.

It records in *Records of the Grand Historian: Biography of Laozi and Hanfei*: When going back to the State of Lu after inquiring Laozi about etiquette, Confucius told his disciples: "I know the birds that fly in the sky can be shot down, the fish that swim in the water can be angled, and the beasts that run around be netted, yet I don't know what can catch the dragon that rides the wind up to the sky. Laozi whom I saw was just like a dragon or a snake, being profoundly knowledgeable and cherishing high ambitions; like a dragon, he can be acclimated to the seasons. He is a teacher indeed!" The image of Laozi that Confucius described here is in fact manifestations of the Dao he advocated. Both dragon and snake in ancient China were deemed as holy creatures that had images but changing with the time. So does Dao. It gives an impression of being changeable, though, it is its changeableness together with formlessness that enables it to exist among all things.

P1-9   Dao holds no preference for anything.

Quotes from *Laozi*:

Heaven and earth are unbiased, seeing everything as a straw dog; the sage is unbiased, seeing everything as a straw dog. (Chapter 5)

It is Heaven's way, without distinction of persons, to keep the good perpetually supplied. (Chapter 79)

Proof: By Axiom 1, we know that the natural way is a spontaneous and unrestrained process where Dao comes into existence from nothingness and then disappears in nothingness, and where its spontaneity and freedom means Dao is free from any purpose or any preference. Also, according to A1 and P1-4, Dao is the sum of all categories but not a certain one, which implies that Dao defies any definition and together with all things is featured by being natural. Hence, we say that Dao holds no preference for anything.

Explanation: As the common law of Heaven, Earth and man, Dao, on which all things live, shows no preferences but the greatest tolerance. As it is recorded in Chapter 16 of *Laozi*, "He who has room in him for everything is without prejudice. To be without prejudice is to be kingly; to be kingly is to be of heaven, which is to be in Dao. Dao is forever and he that possesses it, though his body ceases, is not destroyed." This reveals the selflessness and tolerance of Dao in the real sense, though it is a comment on man. Also, *The Book of History: Life of Cai Zhong* reads, "Heaven, being fair and selfless, always helps the noble," in which "Heaven" sounds like a man, but Dao transcends God of a human character and is similar in selflessness. In *Records of the Grand Historian: Biography of Bo Yi*, there is a story like this: The king of Guzhu State had two sons named Bo Yi and Shu Qi, and he wanted his second son to take the throne. After his death, Shu Qi decided to give up the throne, but Bo Yi refused his brother in the name of going against their father's wish, leaving the state to show his determination. Shu Qi did not want to go against the rule that the eldest son should succeed to the throne and left the state too. Both heard that in Xi Qi there lived a marquis named Jichang who respected the old and let them well-cared, so they went there. On arrival, they learned that Jichang just passed away, while the son of Jichang (Emperor Wen of Zhou) launched an attack on King Zhou of Shang with his father's name on the banner. The two brothers stopped him on his way, and questioned, "You start the fight before your father being buried. Should this be called filial? You're going to kill the king whom you served. Should this be called benevolence?" The generals around were agitated and wanted to kill the two brothers in the way. Jiang Ziya, the prime minister of Zhou, tried to stop them immediately, saying that these two are righteous, so the two were let go in safety. When the prince won the war and was named Emperor Wu of Zhou, all the subjects came to him, while Bo Yi and Shu Qi were ashamed of the new emperor, persisting in being righteous and choosing to seclude themselves and live in Mountain Shouyang; the two lived on before death, they composed a song titled *Plucking Emerald Leaves*, which denounced Emperor Wu for taking the throne by violence. Sima Qian praised the two brothers with this: "It said well that 'it is Heaven's way, without distinction of persons, to keep the good perpetually supplied.' People like Bo Yi and Shu Qi are good; they have noble characters, but are died of starving. Among the disciples of Confucius, Yan Hui was the best at learning but starved to death due to poverty. How can Heaven repay the good in such a way? Pirates kill men every day and live on their flesh, which is viciously cruel; they even call up gangs of the same feather to kill the innocent, yet they enjoy longevity. If this is in line with Heavenly Way, should the latter be called reasonable?" Such contrary cases just illustrate the inclusiveness of Dao. Dao would not determine the fate of or show any preference for Heaven, Earth and all things. Therefore, Dao would not punish anyone who does evil, nor would it reward anyone who does good.

P1-10   What is consonant with "naturalness" is goodness.

Quotes from *Laozi*:

The perfect goodness is like water. Water is good at benefiting all things, but does not contend with them. It prefers to dwell in places the masses of people detest, therefore it is closest to the Dao. The person of perfect goodness is expert in choosing the right place for living, in keeping calm and quiet at heart, in treating others in a sincere and friendly manner, in making creditable and reliable promises, in doing sophisticated administrative affairs, in tackling businesses discreetly, and in taking action promptly. Because of the good person's virtue of being non-competitive, nobody will harbor resentment for him. (Chapter 8)

Proof: It can be seen from D1 that "virtue" is the generic term of the spontaneous process for all things in the universe from "non-being" to "being" and again to "non-being;" it also indicates the human recognition process and the quality of conforming to the process, including good words and good deeds. By A1 and Assumption 4, "naturalness" is the spontaneous and unrestrained process of Dao from "non-being" to "being" and then back to "non-being." Under this situation, contradictions in human society are usually in a stable state. In such a state, the human society as a whole is committed to virtue and goodness, without sharp external conflicts and internal instability. Therefore, it is goodness to be in conformity with "naturalness."

Explanation: Naturalness is the essential requirement of Dao, and the act in accordance with naturalness is the act that conforms to Dao, which has the value of goodness and can be said to be Laozi's values. This kind of values is against the force of human beings, requiring that life be settled in a natural state. Even if life ends, it is in line with the natural way, and there should be no excessive sorrow.

In the "Ultimate Bliss" of *Zhuangzi*, there is such a dialogue: Zhuangzi's wife died, and Hui Shi went to console him, only to find that Zhuangzi was crouching on the ground, beating a battered tub and singing. Hui Shi said: "You lived as man and wife. If you don't cry at her death, it's not too much. But you go too far as to bang the tub and sing. Isn't it too much?" Zhuangzi replied, "It's not like that. When she died, I certainly mourned just like everyone else! However, I then thought back to her death and to the very roots of her being, before she was born. At first, she was lifeless. She was not only lifeless, but also formless. Not only she was formless, she was also breathless. Through the wonderful mystery of change, she was given her life's breath. Her life's breath wrought a transformation and she had a body. Her body wrought a transformation and she was born. Now there was yet another transformation and she was dead. This change is the same as the altering process of the four seasons in the way that spring, summer, autumn and winter follow each other. Now she is lying still and quiet between the Heaven and the Earth. If I still sob and wail, it would appear that I could not comprehend the ways of destiny. Thinking of this, I stopped weeping." When Zhuangzi was dying, he asked his disciples to throw his dead body away in the wild. He believed that there was no difference between being buried in the earth and eaten by ants and mole crickets and being abandoned in the wilderness and eaten by birds and beasts. What was more, he also thought that it was the best way to be cast away in the wilderness with heaven and earth as coffin, and the Sun, the Moon and stars as mortuary objects. It is clear that Zhuangzi regarded human life as the gathering of *qi* (air or breath), while death the scattering of *qi*. That is to say, it is natural to have life or die just like the changes of the four seasons. Zhuangzi's idea of advocating nature stems from Laozi.

"Nurturing of Life" *of Zhuangzi* records a similar story: When Laozi died, his friend Qin Shi went to mourn for him. He wept for a very short time before he went out. One of Laozi's disciples was very frustrated about it and questioned him very dissatisfiedly, "Are you not a friend of our Master?" "Certainly," Qin Shi replied. The disciple reproached: "Then how can you express your condolences that way?" Qin Shi answered affirmatively, "Of course I can. To begin with, I thought you were all good students of Daoism, but now I find that you are not. Just now when I went in to express my condolences, I saw people weeping in their own ways. There were old men weeping as though they had lost a child; there were young people wailing as for the loss of a mother. People came here. They spoke what they had actually hadn't intended to, and they wept though they had actually hadn't prepared to. This goes against the natural disposition of man and violates the principles of Heaven. When the Master came to this world, it was because he was due to be born. When he left the world, it was also in conformity with Nature, or *ziran*. Then why not accept this and flow with it? Why do you need to weep and sorrow? Zhuangzi's view of life and death is always consistent and always emphasizes the conformity with Nature.

P1-11 If human beings apply "*zhi*" (intelligence or wisdom) to pursue excessive desire, it will result in the confusion of goodness and evilness.

Quotes from *Laozi:*

When everyone in the world knows the beautiful as beautiful, ugliness comes into being; when everyone knows the good as good, then the bad comes into being. Therefore, being and non-being generate each other; the difficult and the easy complement each other; the long and the short offset each other; the upper and the lower incline towards each other; the tone and the sound harmonize with each other.... He lets all things grow without interference, and gives them life without claiming to be their owner. He benefits them yet exacts no gratitude, and succeeds without claiming credit. It is because of this that his merits last forever. (Chapter 2)

Proof: According to D2, "desire" or "lust" refers to the pursuit of wealth, fame and power. And this pursuit may result in deviation from "naturalness." By D3, "*zhi*" (meaning wisdom, intelligence, smart, wit and cleverness) generally refers to a person's cognitive ability to understand the object and make choices about individual behaviors; it also refers specifically to dextrous smartness in their excessive pursuit of satisfaction of "desire," which is often applied to the ruling class. According to P1-10, conforming to "naturalness" is goodness. And if people excessively pursue the satisfaction of desire, their ingenuity and wisdom will deviate from "naturalness." Therefore, if people use "intelligence" to pursue excessive desire, it will result in confusion of good and evil.

Explanation: As intelligence or wisdom refers to the external things, and human life practice makes it necessary for human beings to understand the external things, intelligence or wisdom is essential. However, with the accumulation of people's understanding of external things, the desire to control and possess external things often increases, which will destroy the natural state of human's life, leading to competition and social disorder. This is the reason why Laozi was so deeply vigilant about intelligence or wisdom. The root of the modernity crisis that has emerged in Western society is the excessive expansion of the competitive wisdom of instrumental rationality. On the one hand, rationality has made people get rid of the theological ignorance and promoted the development of human society. However, on the other hand, rationality is used to redesign for people and society, leading to the one-sided development of rationality and the gradual expansion of instrumental rationality. As a rational tool, people have already begun to conquer nature on an overall scale, comprehensively control the society, and manage Man, thus giving rise to the confrontation between Man and nature and among human beings, and leading to the emergence of the crisis of modernity.

There is a story in "The Yellow Emperor" of *Liezi*: An old man in the State of Song raised monkeys. He was called Jugong, meaning the monkey keeper. As he raised a large number of monkeys, he could understand what the monkeys were thinking, and vice versa. In order to meet the needs of the monkeys, Jugong and his family members lived a very frugal life and the old man would rather have his family cut back on food and clothing. Before long, however, his family was running short of food, so he could only limit the amount of food the monkeys could eat. But he was also afraid that the monkeys might not accept what he had decided, so he talked with the monkeys. First he suggested that he give them each three acorns in the morning and four in the evening. All the monkeys stood up, furious. Then he suggested that he give them four acorns each in the morning and three each in the evening. Hearing this, all the monkeys lay on the ground on their stomachs, happy and satisfied.

This story is actually an extended version of "*Three in the morning, four in the evening*" in "On the Equality of Things" of *Zhuangzi*. The problem of the monkeys lies in their failure to know that the total amount of food of the day was exactly the same, based on their understanding that "four in the morning" was right and "three in the morning" was not right. If people cling to the so-called "*zhi*" (intelligence or wisdom), they would be like the monkeys in the story, failing to grasp the truth of the matter.

P1-12   When you check your "desire" and transcend your "wisdom," your mind will be "clarified."

Quotes from *Laozi*:

Not to value and employ men of superior ability is the way to keep the people from rivalry among themselves; not to prize articles which are difficult to procure is the way to keep them from becoming thieves; not to show them what is likely to excite their desires is the way to keep their minds from disorder. Therefore, the sage, in the exercise of his government, empties their minds, fills their bellies, weakens their wills, and strengthens their bones. He always keeps them innocent of knowledge and free from desire, and disables the wise from taking any ill actions. If you deal with worldly affairs by "non-action," there will be no trouble of government. (Chapter 3)

When breath is concentrated to utmost pliancy, can you become as supple as a tender baby? When you clear your distracting thoughts and read into yourself, can there be perfection and no blurs? When you love the people and administer the country, can you do it successfully by non-action? When you use your senses, can you be quiet and indifferent to the attraction of beauty? When you are erudite and well-informed, can you seem to know nothing? (Chapter 10)

Proof: From D4, we can see that "*guan*" (to observe or self-examine) is the means of human realization of the "Dao;" and "*ming*" (discernment or clarification) is the ability of the inner human life force to perform self-reflection. Also according to A2 and P1-11, you can comprehend the Dao going from "*zhi*" into "*ming*." The excessive pursuit of "desire," together with "wisdom" resulting from it, most likely runs counter to Nature, and deviates from the Dao. So it needs controlling. And the right means of knowing the Dao is to "*guan*" (observe or self-examine). Therefore, you should check your "desire" and transcend your "wisdom" to enable your mind to be "clarified."

Explanation: Laozi showed his respect for the normal desire. However, the unchecked desire will drive people away from the purely natural nature, and become the slaves of desire. Therefore, desire should be checked and confined within a certain limit, that is, to satisfy the desire for the fundamental material life. At the same time, wisdom tends to direct human attention to the external things, and cause human desire for material things to dilate, and make human beings materialized. Therefore, it is necessary to transcend the partial and one-way recognition of the *zhi* or wisdom. Only in this way can the human perceptual ability be radically improved and reach the state of purification.

During the Western Han Dynasty (206BC - AD24), Emperor Wendi was born provident. And after his enthronement, he kept wearing his robe for 20 years, and the articles for daily use in the royal court were mostly left by his predecessors. Once, he had planned to build an open stage, but when he budgeted with the artisan, he dismissed the idea, as the expenditure of building such a stage would be 100 taels of gold, equivalent to the annual income of about 10 middle-class households of that time. In the meantime, the public purse was almost empty, and the people lived a very miserable life. Besides, Emperor Wendi of the Han was also open-minded, and seeking advice, and happy to correct the mistakes pointed out. Once

Emperor Wendi went on a long journey, and when he travelled to Zhongwei Bridge, somebody suddenly turned up from under the bridge, and startled his horse. The man was arrested and was handed over to Zhang Shizhi, the main judicial officer of the time, for punishment. Zhang Shizhi only convicted him of the crime of horse-blocking, and demanded four taels of gold as forfeit. The emperor was very angry, as he thought the man was not duly punished. Zhang Shizhi argued strongly on just grounds, emphasizing that law was something that everybody was to obey, and that nobody should be more severely punished only because he blocked the emperor's horse. The emperor had done a lot of thinking before he accepted the judgment. It was just because Emperor Wendi of the Han Dynasty could check his own desire and did not apply his wisdom for his personal purposes that he had the virtue of being reasonable. During his reign, the society and economy of the Han Dynasty developed rapidly, which laid the solid foundation for the coming economic prosperity in the reign of Emperor Jingdi. And he was undoubtedly recorded in history as a wise ruler.

P1-13 Only with "discernment" of contemplation can one discern the Dao.

Quotes from *Laozi*

To return to the origin is known as the eternal. To know the eternal is known as discernment. (Chapter 16)

To know harmony is called eternal. (Chapter 55)

Proof: From D4 we can see that "ming," which means discernment, refers to the self-observation and self-contemplating ability of inner human vitality. According to P1-4, the basic feature of the Dao and all the things in the universe is naturalness, that is to say, the human inner contemplation of all the things in the universe itself is in agreement with the discernment of the Dao. According to A2, it is knowing the Dao to go from wisdom into "*ming*" (discernment). "*Ming*" is the cognitive state of mind in correspondence with the Dao. Therefore, only with "discernment" of contemplation can one discern the Dao.

Explanation: When the human cognitive ability reaches the state of purification, people will no longer be concerned with the significance of external existence to human beings, but with the harmonious development of the whole world, including all the things in the universe, human beings among them. Its basis is the eternal Dao on which all the things in the universe depend and to which all the things in the universe return. Therefore, "*ming*" is the fundamental awareness of the essence of the whole by transcending the confinement of the single external thing. So in this case, only when people are possessed of *"ming"* (discernment) can their simple nature be thoroughly aroused, and their actions consciously brought to the agreement with the eternal Dao. And only in the contemplation of the *"ming"* (discernment), can human life be quit of the small self formed with shallow wisdom, and be sublimated to the oneness with the Dao.

Goujian (520-424 BEC), king of the State of Yue (2032-222 BEC), was the last powerful leader in the Spring and Autumn Period. His success in defeating the Kingdom of Wu and becoming the powerful ruler was due to his strong will and belief, for one thing, of enduring hardships to accomplish his ambition, and, for another, due to the assistance of Fan Li and Wen Zhong, two of his ministers. It was because of their assistance that Goujian made great efforts to build a strong kingdom by leading the army and the people of Yue to accumulate the national might of Yue within ten years. So he took advantage of the time when the main strength of the army of the Kingdom of Wu went north to contend for hegemony, and sent troops to wipe out the Kingdom of Wu and, at the same time, to wipe out a disgrace. After Goujian obliterated the Kingdom of Wu, he led his army to go northward and met in Xuzhou other sovereigns of the Kingdoms of Qi and Jin, and he was honored as the Conqueror. The power of the Kingdom of Yue had reached its highest point when Fan Li left there. When he arrived at the Kingdom of Qi, Fan Li wrote a letter to Wen Zhong, and urged him to leave as well: When all the birds had been shot off, the bows should be hidden; and when the hares had all been hunted, the hounds would be cooked for meals. Goujian, the King of the Kingdom of Yue, had a long neck, and his mouth looked like the beak of an eagle. It was all right to share weal and woe with him, but it wouldn't do to share fair weather. Why didn't you leave? Wen Zhong read Fan Li's letter, but he did not listen to him. He only pleaded illness in order not to go to court. Somebody defamed Wen Zhong in front of Goujian, by saying that Wen was disloyal and tried to rebel. Goujian believed in the defamatory words and gave to Wen Zhong the sword in the name of Shulou that Fuchai, the King of the Kingdom of Wu, gave Wu Zixu to let Wu commit suicide. He said, "You have taught me seven strategies of crusading against the Kingdom of Wu, and I only used three of them to beat Wu. The other four are still in your hand. Now, I will ask you to help my deceased king in the netherworld and see if he could defeat the deceased king of Wu." By now, Wen Zhong regretted, but it was too late, so he had no other way but to kill himself with the sword.

We can see clearly from the story that Fan Li had the intelligence of knowing others, and he was also aware of the truth of retiring on his laurels. Therefore, at the time of his final completion of his mission, he chose to leave secretly without thinking of receiving official promotion. In this way, he saved himself. But Wen Zhong, on the contrary, did not see through Goujian in spite of his being good at stratagem, and knew even less the Daoist wisdom of "retiring after winning merit," so that he finally died a tragic death.

P1-14   Only when he reached the state of *"ming"* (discernment) could he become unselfish.

Quotes from *Laozi:*

To know the eternal Dao is to be all-embracing; to be all-embracing is to be impartial; to be impartial is to be kingly; to be kingly is to be with Heaven; to be with Heaven is to be with the Dao; to be with the Dao, one can be free of disasters throughout his life. (Chapter 16)

Proof: From D7, we can see that "unselfishness" means the psychological state of mind that is all inclusive after getting rid of excessive "desire" and cunning "wisdom." According to propositions P1-12 and P1-13, through abstention from "desire" and transcending "wisdom," you can reach "discernment," thus getting rid of your selfishness and distracting thoughts, and finally getting enlightened. Therefore, only when he reached the state of *"ming"* (discernment) could he become unselfish.

Explanation: "To know the eternal" is "being fair and just" or discernment, and only a pure-minded person can be all inclusive. The human wisdom of "addressing" and "naming" is, in fact, the "man-made" confinement. Once we try to name something, we will differentiate and classify what we name, so as to distinguish what is near or far, or what is close or distant. And when this is done, we start to have "selfishness," and will deviate from the Dao. For example, when we use *"wu"* or "non-being" to name the beginning of the Heaven and the Earth, and use *"you"* or "being" to name the mother of all the things in the universe, we may only see "being," but neglect "non-being." It is even more difficult for us to see that "non-being" and "being" are *"both from the same origin, but only named differently."* "Being the same" is fundamental and "the real source of all mysteries and profundities of the mysterious and profound". Therefore, Laozi warned at the very first chapter of his book, *"Therefore, with the constant 'Non-being,' I often observe the subtlety of the Dao; with the constant 'Being,' I often observe the working of the Dao."* The profound meaning Laozi tried to convey is that we should not be confined by the "man-made" confinement, but transcend this confinement. Only when we see the fundamental can we have true breadth and range of vision. And only with this vision to see all the things in the universe can we cultivate ourselves among all the things in the universe.

Li Bi was the prime minister during the reign of Emperor Dezong in the Tang Dynasty (779-805). Emperor Dezong suspected that the crown prince seemed to be disloyal, and tried to oust the prince from princedom and appoint Li Yi, his adopted son (he was, in fact, his nephew), as the prince. Li Bi made great efforts to dissuade Emperor Dezong from ousting his own son and appointing his nephew, and irritated the emperor. The emperor asked threateningly, "Do you love your family?" Li Bi replied in a serious manner, "It is just because I love my family that I dare not keep silent. If I feared that Your Majesty would be irritated and kept silent, you would lodge complaints against me, when you were remorseful the next day, and say, I appointed you as the prime minister, but you refused to offer any expostulation, which resulted in what it was now. Then you would certainly kill my son. I am old enough and do not feel sorry to die. But if you wrongly killed my son, I could only adopt my nephew, but I really don't know if I would get his sacrifice." Emperor Dezong was touched, and said, weeping, "But what should I do then, when what's done is done?" Li Bi replied, "This is a big issue. Your Majesty should have second thoughts about it. Since ancient times, mutual suspicion between father and son has, without exception, resulted in the downfall of the country or the destruction of the family." Emperor Dezong asked again, "It is a matter of our family, why are you so serious about it?" Li Bi answered, "You are the Son of Heaven, and the whole world surrounded is your family. I am now the prime minister of the kingdom, and around the four seas, it is my responsibility if there is anything wrong. Moreover, if I took no notice of the prince's sufferance of injustice, my guilt would be tremendous!" At last, the Emperor was no longer emotionally entangled. The day after the next, Emperor Dezong summoned Li Bi alone in Yanying Palace, and told him, crying, "If you had not frankly admonished me, it would have been too late for me to remorse. The prince was actually very filially pious, and had not at all been double-minded. And from now on, whether they are state affairs or my family affairs, I will consult you and seek your advice." There is an old saying, "Blood is thicker than water." It was just because Li Bi was a man of sensibility and understanding that he frankly mediated between Emperor Dezong and his son.

P1-15   One who has discernment does not boast or show off.

Quotes from *Laozi*:

He is free from self-display, and therefore he has discernment. (Chapter 22)

He who displays himself cannot see things clearly. (Chapter 24)

Proof: From D4, we can see that *"ming"* or discernment is the ability of one's inner life force to observe oneself. The key point of the state of "discernment" lies in self-observation. As its objective is not the external object, it does not need to boast or show off. In addition, according to the P1-13, only when you have the "discernment" of observation can you realize the Dao. The object of "discernment" is the Dao, of which the characteristic is *"ziran,"* or naturalness, that is, there is no external purpose. Therefore, anyone with "discernment" does not boast or show off.

Explanation: The person who shows off and tries his best to manifest his wisdom has not reached the state of "discernment." The self-confidence shown tends to be blind self-confidence in something that is partial. In his "The Old Man Who Sells Oil" from *Sketches after Returning to the Fields*, Ouyang Xiu wrote a story about an old oil-selling man watching Chen Yaozi shooting arrows: Chen Yaozi, a famous minister, was a well-known expert archer in the Northern Song Dynasty, and he was second to none at that time. Therefore, he often boasted about his archery. Once he was practising archery in his own garden, and an old man who was selling oil took off his carrying pole from his shoulder and made glimpses of him. He stayed there for a long time before he left. The old oil-selling man, seeing that Chen Yaozi hit his targets eight or nine times out of ten, nodded slightly. Chen Yaozi asked the old man, "Do you also know how to shoot? Isn't my archery good enough?" Hearing this, the old man answered, "There is nothing special about it; only you are a little skilful." Chen Yaozi flew into a fury and said, "How dare you be so disdainful of my archery skill?" The old man said, "I knew it on the basis of my experience in pouring oil." He then took out a gourd and put it on the ground. He put a copper coin on the mouth of the gourd and slowly scooped out oil with an oil dipper, and poured it into the gourd. The oil slowly flowed down into the gourd, but there was not even one drop of oil on the coin. The old man told Chen Yaozi, "It is no mystery of my pouring. It was all due to my daily practice." Eventually, Chen Yaozi, smiling, let the old man leave.

In the story, Chen Yaozi, as an official in the Northern Song Dynasty, behaved as if he was treading on air simply because he was good at archery. He lacked the wisdom to know himself. On the contrary, the old oil-selling man showed him the deft skill of pouring oil, and pointed out that it was nothing but deftness from experience. As far as this is concerned, Xiang Yu was also a negative example. Following is Sima Qian's comment on Xiang Yu in his *Records of the Grand Historian*: He plumed himself on his accomplishments. He trusted in his own measures without learning from the ancient ones. He attempted to establish his hegemony just with his might, only to find that both the kingdom and himself were defeated. Even before his death, he still said "It was Heaven that wanted to defeat me and it had nothing to do with the crime of wrong operation of military forces" as an excuse of defeat, which is so ridiculous!

P1-16 Persons with discernment will pursue a clarified self-intrinsic vitality.

Quotes from *Laozi*:

He who understands others is wise; he who understands himself has discernment. (Chapter 33)

He who is wise will not speak; he who speaks is not wise. (Chapter 56)

People with profound understanding are not erudite, and erudite people are not profound in understanding. (Chapter 81)

Proof: From Definition 4, we can see that discernment is the ability of self-reflection of human's intrinsic vitality. This reveals that the object of discernment lies in the inner ego. According to P1-12 and P1-14, he who can temper his "desire" and transcend "wisdom" will be discerning. Only when people reach the state of discernment environment can they have no selfishness, and will their inner self reach the "natural" state. They will be a kind of understanding and quiet because they have abandoned the unnecessary disturbance and distractions. Therefore, he who has discernment will pursue the clarified inner vitality of himself.

Explanation: Laozi said, "*he who understands others is wise; he who understands himself has discernment.*" When someone seeks to understand others and things, his intrinsic motivation is to control them. The more extensive his knowledge is, the stronger his desire to control others and things. When people look back at themselves and let their intrinsic vitality continue to extend naturally, it indicates that they have "discernment." The clarification of inner vitality needs not to be spoken. If someone wants to speak it out, selfishness and desires will occur. Therefore, the true wise does not speak, that is, "*He who is wise will not speak; he who speaks is not wise.*" He does not necessarily need extensive knowledge because his inner clarification is enough to illuminate everything, that is, "*People with profound understanding are not erudite, and erudite people are not profound in understanding.*"

There is such a story in "The North Tour of Mr. Zhi," *Zhuangzi*: a man named Zhi (meaning knowledge or wisdom) strolled north to the shores of the Dark Waters, climbed up a Mount of Secret Heights and happened to encounter a man called Wuweiwei (meaning Words of Non-action). Zhi asked Wuweiwei three questions:

What sort of thought and reflection is it to take to know the Dao? How to live and act to conform to the Dao? By what means and what methods can we obtain the Dao? For these three questions, Wuweiwei did not answer. It was not because he did not want to answer, but that he didn't know how to answer.

Zhi did not obtain any answers, so he travelled to the south of the White Waters, climbed up onto the top of a hill called Huque (meaning fox cave), and there caught sight of a man called Kuangqu (meaning wild and bending). Zhi put the same questions to Kuangqu, who said that he knew these truths, and would tell him later. When he wanted to say, he forgot what he was going to say. Zhi did not obtain any answers again, so he returned to the Imperial Palace to see the Yellow Emperor, and asked him these three questions. The Yellow Emperor told him that without thinking and reflection you could understand Dao, having no place to live in and taking no action you could act in accordance with the Dao, and having no plans and means, you could master the Dao. Zhi said to the Emperor, "You and I know these truths, but Wuweiwei and Kuangqu did not know, so which of them is actually right?" The Yellow Emperor answered, "Wuweiwei was truly right. Kuangqu is almost right. To this end, you and I are not close to the Dao." Having heard what the Emperor said, Zhi said, "When I asked Wuweiwei about these, he did not answer me. It was not because he did not want to answer me but because he did not know how to answer me. When I asked Kuangqu, he did not answer me either. It was not because he did not want to tell me, but he forgot what he was going to say when he wanted to tell me. So I'm puzzled why you say you are not close to the Dao when in fact you know how to answer my questions?" The Yellow Emperor said, "Wuweiwei was actually right, because he knew nothing. Kuangqu was almost right, because he forgot about how to describe the Dao. However, you and I are not close to the Dao, because we know it."

Although this dialogue concentrates on the relationship between speech and the Dao, it can be seen that the Dao is an experience rather than an issue of speaking. When you concentrate on speaking, then you actually stay away from the Dao.

P1-17   To observe Dao is a transcendence over "*zhi.*"

Quotes from *Laozi:*

The Dao has no constant name. Though simple and small, it is subject to no one in the world. Should lords and princes be able to obey it, all in the world will submit of their own accord. Heaven and Earth match and sweet dew will fall. They come naturally though nobody so decrees. A regime has various positions, hence various regulations, hence constraints and restraints, and with these one can be free from danger. The Dao is to the world what the great rivers and seas are to the streams.   (Chapter 32)

The universe has a beginning and the beginning could be the mother of all things. From the mother, you know the son; knowing the son, you go back to the mother, and then you will be safe all your life. Block the openings of intelligence, and shut the door of desires, and till the end of your life you'll not labor. Unlock the openings, meddle in affairs, and till the end of your life you'll not be saved. To perceive the tiny is called brightness; to hold fast to the pliant is called strength. Use the light, and return to what's bright, and you will be free from disasters. This is called following the constant. (Chapter 52)

Proof: According to Definition 3 and Definition 4, we can see that the general meaning of *"zhi"* (wisdom) refers to the ability of people to recognize the objective and to make choices in individual behavior, and also refers to the kind of cleverness produced by the excessive pursuit of people's desire. "Observation" is the way of knowing Dao. From Axiom 2, we can understand Dao by turning from wisdom into discernment. If we want to obtain discernment, we must first transcend "wisdom," and the object of discernment is Dao. Therefore, to view or observe Dao is to transcend the "wisdom."

Explanation: Laozi said: *"In the pursuit of learning one knows more every day; in the pursuit of the Dao one does less every day."* (Chapter 48, *Laozi*). But there is no absolute opposition between the two. We cannot abandon "wisdom" for "discernment." The one-sided development of "wisdom" will lead to the expansion of material desire. Only when one exceeds the mental limitations of "wisdom," will he be able to have "discernment." Laozi said, "Clear your distracting thoughts and read into yourself." It means that one must cleanse all the dirt of his own mind so that his own mind will not be controlled by the things outside. Hence, he can become discerning after being wise, and the true facts of all things in the universe will be presented in front of human beings.

In "Wandering Wherever You Will" of *Zhuangzi*, Zhuangzi said: Have you ever seen a wild cat or a weasel? It lies there, crouching down, in wait for its prey. East and west, it leaps about, not afraid of going high or low, until it is caught in a trap or dies in a net. What Zhuangzi thus expressed is that when you look at a thing with wisdom, what you see is the advantages and disadvantages of the thing. In other words, wisdom is the competitive consciousness of people seeking advantages and avoiding disadvantages. Therefore, Zhuangzi said that "Wisdom is out of contention." With this competing intelligence to view people or things, when you make a choice that is good for you, the end result may just be detrimental to you. Therefore, in order to observe Dao, we must surpass this competitive wisdom. The transcendence here is to go beyond the division of the interests and harms of the external things on the basis of wisdom, and to recognize the original natural state of things.

P1-18 Dao can be observed from the perspective of the most abstract "non-being" and "being."

Quotes from *Laozi*:

One should gain an insight into the subtlety of Dao from nothingness, and should gain an insight into the demarcation of all things from being. These two are of the same origin but different in name. The mystery and profundity of the mysterious and profound is the real source of all mysteries and profundities. (Chapter 1)

Proof: According to Assumption 2, the Dao can be nothingness, but in its subtlety it is full of strength; "being" is begotten from "non-being." Something was formed out of chaos. All things, begotten from "being," finally returned to "non-being." The Dao itself cannot be expressed in terms of concepts, but the conversion of the two most abstract concepts "nothingness" and "being" can reflect the process of Dao. By Axiom 2, one can realize Dao from "wisdom" to "discernment." Behind the most abstract concept is the Dao, and discernment is the realm obtained reasonably and is the realm of Dao enlightenment that is beyond the "wisdom." Therefore, Dao can be observed from perspective of the most abstract "non-being" and "being."

Explanation: Dao has two sides of "being" and "non-being." "Non-being" refers to the beginning of the heaven and earth, and "being" is the root of all things. Before heaven and earth appeared, Dao existed in the form of "non-being," while in the process of and after the creation of all things, Dao exists in the form of "being." Therefore, "non-being" and "being" are in the relationship of two sides of one body, revealing the existence of Dao in two different ways.

Just because Dao has these two sides, it can be seen in two different ways: One is "constant non-being," the state of "non-existence" of Dao as a body. Although the universe was not born at that time, its subtle vitality had already appeared. The other is "constant being," the state of the Dao in being as a body. The multitude of things, though confused in chaos, in the end, attains to Dao. "Non-being" and "being," the two sides of the body, are born out of the same Dao, but have different names. The two sides of "non-being" and "being" are so subtle and mysterious that they are difficult to be understood. Dao, which begot "non-being" and "being," is much more subtle and mysterious, and is the root cause of the magic of all things.

Li Gongzuo in Tang Dynasty wrote a famous legendary novel *The Chief of Nanke Prefecture*. The protagonist of the novel is a man named Chun Yufen in

Dongping Prefecture. As a ranger, he was a heavy-drinker, but chivalrous. With his martial arts, he once became the deputy general. Unluckily, he was removed from office because he offended his chief after alcoholic drinking. Since then, he acted indulgently, drinking alcohol all day long. Once, he was drunk and was sent back home, lying in the corridor east of the hall, where he fell asleep in a moment.

He dreamed of the King of the state of Huai'an, who sent someone to pick him up to the capital and betrothed the second princess to him, assigned him as the chief of Nanke Prefecture. After Chun Yufen came to Nanke Prefecture, he worked diligently and governed Nanke well. During 20 years of governance of the prefecture, he enlightened the people widely. The people praised him with songs and built monuments and temples for his merit. The king valued him very much and gave him land and title of nobility, and made him prime minister. He had five sons and two daughters. All of the sons were granted official positions and the two daughters were married to princes.

His family obtained glory and honor beyond comparison. Later, the army of a small kingdom called Tanluo attacked Nanke and defeated the army of Nanke led by Chun Yufen. Unfortunately, his wife died of disease. So he returned with his wife's coffin to the capital. When he was back in the capital, he resumed his love for playing games and making friends all day long. As a result, he was suspected by the king and was forbidden to make friends or leave his home. Chun Yufen was very depressed. The king knew he was unhappy and let him go back to his hometown. As soon as he was sent back to his home in Guanling County, he woke up to find that his glory and misfortune had been a dream. Understanding the impermanence of the world, he decided to become a Daoist priest.

In this story, Chun Yufen saw through the sharp contrast of inconstancy of the world between the two fates: the rich and the poor. In a certain sense, it can also be said that he understood Dao at both ends of "being" and "non-being."

P1-19   The Dao can be observed from the subtlety of senses.

Quotes from *Laozi*:

We look at it but cannot see it; we name this Yi (the invisible). We listen to it but cannot hear it; we name this Xi (the inaudible). We touch it but cannot hold it; we call this Wei (the minute). These three things can be in no way defined. Thus they merge together as one. Its upper part is not dazzling; its lower part is not obscure. Boundless, formless, it cannot be named and returns to the state of nothingness. This is called the formless form, the substanceless image. To greet it, you don't see its head; to follow it, you don't see its rear. (Chapter 14)

Proof: According to Assumption 2, Dao can be expressed as *"wu"* (non-being) and is full of power in its subtlety. *"Wu"* produces *"you"* and turns distinct in its indistinctness. Then *"you"* begets *"wu,"* and finally all things return to "wu." The conversion of *"wu"* and *"you"* in subtlety and indistinctness presents not only the characteristic of Dao but also the perceptual subtlety. For this reason, we need to enhance the self-observation ability of our inner vitality. This ability is just what we call "discernment." (by D4). By Axiom 2, we can understand Dao by turning from "wisdom" into "discernment." Therefore, we can examine Dao in perceptual subtlety.

Explanation: As a metaphysical real existence, Dao is formless and invisible, so our human senses are unable to catch it, that is, "We look at it but cannot see it. We listen to it but cannot hear it. We touch it but cannot hold it." "To greet it, you don't see its head; to follow it, you don't see its rear." This existence of Dao, which is indistinct, invisible and vague, though impossible to be described directly, can be compared with specific objects and can be revealed in an opposite way, i.e., "the formless form, the substanceless image." The existence of Dao is vague and indistinct. We can't feel its image as we feel the existence of specific things. However, it is not to say that we feel nothing. That is to say, it is a slight feeling in which you can experience the existence of the Dao.

In the history of Chinese Zen Buddhism, there is a famous legendary story "Xiangyan Clicking the Bamboo." It goes that Xiangyan Zhixian was a Buddhist monk, who was the disciple of a famous Buddhist abbot named Baizhang Huaihai. Xiangyan was very intelligent. When he was asked a question, he would give ten answers, but he never had an epiphany. After the death of Baizhang Huaihai, Xiangyan followed the Buddhist Master Lingyou of Mountain Wei to continue the meditation. When Master Lingyou knew that Xiangyan was intelligent and good at debate, he asked him the question, "How did you look like before your parents gave birth to you?" Xiangyan was so puzzled that he couldn't give a reply.

Back in the room, he turned over the books he had usually read from the beginning to the end, but didn't find a suitable answer. He said in a sigh, "Drawing a cake can never allay the hunger!" Xiangyan asked Master Lingyou to give him the answer. Lingyou said, "If I give you the answer now, you will scold me one day. And what I tell you is my opinion, not yours. What is its use to you?" In a rage, Xiangyan burned all the books he had read and said in a long sigh, "I will never learn Buddhism in my life, and I would like to be a monk travelling everywhere and begging for food.

Then he said good-bye to Master Lingyou, crying, and travelled everywhere. One day, when Xiangyan was weeding, he saw a stone. He picked it up and threw it away into the bamboo forest. The stone hit the bamboo and gave a crisp sound. Hearing this sound, Xiangyan had a sudden enlightenment. He knelt down and paid tribute to the Heaven, uttering thanks to Master Lingyou: "If I had been told the answer, how could I have today's epiphany?"

It is a feeling to hear the sound. It is just through the feeling that Master Xiangyan realized the true meaning of the Zen Buddhism law. Although this is a story about Zen Buddhism, the way Dao is observed is similar to that of Laozi. In Laozi's thought, we can experience the existence of Dao in Daoism through the subtle but not so specific feeling.

P1-20 To eliminate the desire for absurdity and to give up the obsessive belief in "wisdom" are the precondition for self-reflection of Dao.

Quotes from *Laozi*:

When you clear your distracting thoughts and read into yourself, can there be perfection and no blemish? (Chapter 10)

It is a gain if one knows something as if he doesn't know it; it is a fault if one doesn't know something as if he knows it. It is no fault just because one takes his fault as a fault. The sage has no fault. Just because he takes his fault as a fault, he has no fault. (Chapter 71)

Proof: By Assumption 1, Dao is the synthesis of any (category). By Axiom 2, a wise man who has discernment can realize the truth of Dao. According to P12, our mind is clear and bright if we can control our desire and go beyond "wisdom." It is obvious that self-reflection or observation of Dao is based on the control of "desire" and transcendence over "wisdom." Therefore, eliminating the absurd desire and abandoning the obsessive belief in "wisdom" are the prerequisite for "Daoism."

Explanation: The understanding of Dao needs to have certain subjective conditions. First, the desire must be tempered to make it conform to man's nature. Second, the limitation of "wisdom" should be realized. Wisdom is the unidimensional thinking which can easily lead to the expansion of materialism and therefore we cannot have blind faith in "wisdom," thinking that by virtue of "wisdom" everything can be controlled. When these two conditions are met, the subject of knowing can shift his attention from the external things to his intrinsic life practice, and only then can he have the ability to know the Dao, that is, to have the *ming* or discernment. As the desire goes to nature, the limitations of "wisdom" have also been overcome. Under the contemplation of a quiet mind, what is presented is not the complicated diversity of things, but the whole process of the reunification of the whole. This kind of observation is essentially a realization of Daoism.

There is an allegory in "Season of Autumn Flood" of *Zhuangzi*: The season of autumn flood had come, and hundreds of rivers were pouring into the Yellow River. The flow of water increased, and the rivers broadened. At this, the Lord of the Yellow River was immensely pleased, thinking that it is the most spectacular scenery in the world. Along with the water flow, he travelled eastward until he came to the North Sea. Looking east, he could see no end to the waters. The Lord of the Yellow Rive shook his head and was no longer overjoyed. He sighed and said to the God of the North Sea, "As the saying goes, 'The person who has heard of the Dao many times thinks that he is better than anyone else.' That's exactly who I am! At first I did not believe in your boundless vastness. Now I saw it with my own eyes, and I was convinced. Otherwise, I would certainly be mocked by other people." The God of the North sea said, "A frog in the well bottom cannot see the sea, because it is subject to space constraints; A summer insect cannot feel coldness because it is limited by the season of its life; and narrow-minded people cannot understand the Dao, because they are constrained by their knowledge. Now that you come out of the shackles of the river bank and have seen the sea, you know your own inferiority, and it is possible to discuss the great Dao with you."

In this story, the Lord of the Yellow River had an arrogant self-recognition in the beginning. When he saw the largeness of the North Sea, he realized his own inferiority, and at last gave up blind faith in his own "wisdom." And this also means that he had the conditions of knowing the Dao, so the God of the North sea said he could discuss the great Dao.

P1-21 The highest state of Dao is "Emptiness" and "Stillness."

Quotes from *Laozi*:

Take emptiness to the limit and keep still. All things arise together, I watch their return. Things come forth in great numbers, and each one returns to its own root. Returning to roots means stillness, and also means a return to origin. To return to its origin is known as the eternal. To know the eternal is known as discernment. (Chapter 16)

Proof: From Definition 5, "stillness" is the clarified inner state achieved by eliminating the interference of excessive "desire" and crafty "wisdom." "Emptiness" is "nothingness," meaning that the internal state of man is void. The inner "quietness" of a man is a state of inner clarification, that is, he realizes "discernment" in "cognition" and "understanding." According to Axiom 2, we can comprehend Dao from "wisdom" to "discernment." Therefore, the highest state of observing Dao is keeping "empty" and "still."

Explanation: Although observing Dao is the understanding of Dao by the subject, there are two tensions within the subject during this process. One is just to follow one's wisdom and desire, and the other is to cut off the general streams of common people and return to the Dao. Only by removing the excess desire and craftiness of wisdom can the subject directly grasp the truth of Dao in the state of emptiness and quietness. In this realm, the soul of the subject is like an unpolluted mirror, empty and quiet, and all things present their true colors in front of it.

In "Working Everything out Evenly" of *Zhuangzi*, Nanguo Ziqi sat by a table, staring up at Heaven and breathed gently, as if in a trance, forgetful of all around him even of his body. His disciple Yancheng Ziyou, who was in attendance on him, asked, "What is this? How could the body become thus like dry wood, and the mind like dead ashes? Surely the man here now is not the same as the one who was here yesterday."

Ziqi answered, "Ziyou, this is a good point to make, but do you really understand? Just now, I lost myself. Do you understand? You may have heard the music of pipes of man, but not the music of earth; you may have heard the music of pipes of earth, but not the music of Heaven." "Please explain this," said Ziyou. "The vast breadth of the universe," said Ziqi, "is called the wind. At times it is unmoving. When it moves, it makes every opening resound dramatically. Have you not heard the growing roar of a terrifying gale? On the steep mountainsides, the apertures and hollows in huge trees a hundred spans in girth are like nostrils, like mouths, like ears, like beam sockets, like fences, like mortars, like pools, and like puddles, sounding like a crashing wave, a whistling arrow, a screech; sucking, shouting, barking, wailing, and moaning. Some sounds are shrill, and some deep. Gentle winds make minor harmonies; violent winds major ones. When the fierce gusts pass away, all the apertures are empty and still again."

Yancheng Ziyou asked, "Then, what are the notes of the Heaven?"

"The winds as they blow," said Ziqi, "differ in thousands of ways, yet all are self-produced, not influenced by any other forces."

Through the conversation between Nanguo Ziqi and Yancheng Ziyou, Zhuangzi stressed that only when we are in the realm of emptiness, forgetful of all things and even unconscious of our own body, can we hear the natural sound of all things between heaven and earth, that is, the music of Heaven. In this realm, no one has desire to dominate anything and all things conform to their natural nature, self-dominated. In this state, it is better to say that we are not observing Dao but becoming one with Dao, for now the Dao is no longer the object of cognition and the mind of the subject is fully integrated with Dao.

第四章 CHAPTER FOUR

贵德篇
On Cherishing Virtue

本章的主旨是阐述顺应自然之德，以及修德之方、修德之用。P2-1至P2-3指出顺应自然方为"德"，以及如何具有这种"德"。P2-4至P2-10重点阐述贪欲、智巧为修德之害，而淡化两者的方法为知足、处下、柔弱、不争等。P2-11至P2-13阐述圣人之表象与心智状态。P2-14至P2-21阐述践"德"之行。P2-22至P2-23阐述"德"与"道"之关系。

P2-1 顺应自在自为的生命常态是"德"之体现。

【参见《老子》条目】

含德之厚，比于赤子。蜂虿虺蛇不螫，攫鸟猛兽不搏。骨弱筋柔而握固。未知牝牡之合而朘作，精之至也。终日号而不嗄，和之至也。知和曰常，知常曰明。益生曰祥。心使气曰强。物壮则老，谓之不道，不道早已。（第五十五章）

证明： 依据公理A1，自然是"道"从"无"到"有"再到"无"的自在自为过程；由此可知，自在自为乃生命之常态。从定义1可知，人对这个自在自为过程的认识以及顺应此过程的品质称为"德"。又依据基本假设5，人的认知和行为的理想状态是"守中"，从而促成人与人之间、人与外部世界之间的均衡。因此，顺应自在自为的生命常态是德之体现。

例证和说明： "德"是"道"在具体事物中的体现，是事物所以如此的内在根据。换言之，"德"是存在于万事万物之中的"道"，就万物的生成来讲是"道"，就万物的存在来讲则是"德"。"德是一物所得于道者。德是分，道是全。一物所得于道以成其体者为德。德实即是一物之本性。"[1] "道"与"德"是须臾不可离的二位一体。顺应自在自为生命常态就是顺应生命之自然。顺应生命之自然，能使生命处于最为和谐、平衡的状态。达到这种状态，正是"德"在人类社会的体现。《庄子·在宥》中说："君子如果不得已而君临天下，最好是顺任自然。顺任自然才能

---

1 张二平：《论老子哲学的体用观》，《商丘学院学报》，2007年第8期。

使大家安定性命的真情。因此老子说：'以尊重生命的态度去为天下，才可以把天下寄付给他；以珍爱生命的态度去为天下，才可以把天下托交给他。'所以君子如果不放纵情欲，不显耀聪明；安居不动而神采奕奕，沉静缄默而感人深切，精神活动都合于自然，从容无为，而万物的繁殖就会像炊气般积累上升。"[1]

P2-2 顺应自在自为的生命常态，在于把握"无"与"有"的统一。

【参见《老子》条目】

三十辐，共一毂，当其无，有车之用。埏埴以为器，当其无，有器之用。凿户牖以为室，当其无，有室之用。故有之以为利，无之以为用。（第十一章）

上德不德，是以有德；下德不失德，是以无德。上德无为而无以为，下德无为而有以为。上仁为之而无以为，上义为之而有以为，上礼为之而莫之应，则攘臂而扔之。故失道而后德，失德而后仁，失仁而后义，失义而后礼。夫礼者，忠信之薄，而乱之首。前识者，道之华，而愚之始。是以大丈夫处其厚不居其薄，处其实不居其华。故去彼取此。（第三十八章）

证明： 据命题P2-1，顺应自在自为生命常态是德之体现，而"德"是万物自在自为过程的总称，也指人对此过程的认识以及顺应此过程的品行（定义1）。又据基本假设3与基本假设5，"无"的无限可能性与"有"的有限现实性构成矛盾，"无"与"有"的统一才是"道"的圆满状态，人的认知和行为的理想状态是"守中"，既看到"有"又坚守"无"。因此，顺应自在自为生命之常态，在于把握"无"与"有"的统一。

例证和说明： "道"是有无的统一体。"无"具有超越和形而上的性质。对其把握，应从现实的在具体时空中存在的"有"入手。顺应自在自为生命常态其实就是遵循"道"。因此，要循道做到顺应生命之自然，其关键在于从"有"中把握"无"。在人生实践中，我们应当持之以恒地做到"有功"不居、"有才"不傲、"富贵"不骄等，这样才算是做到顺应自在自为的生命常态。关键在于我们能从"有"中把握"无"，知道这一切皆如昼夜更替、四季转换一般，不必过于执着与分别，这样就不会被自私和贪欲所奴役，也就使得自己的身心达到顺应自然的状态。如唐懿宗时，官场黑暗，杨牧贪鄙成性，为相期间贪银百万。杨牧有女嫁给尚书裴坦为儿媳，嫁妆豪奢。裴坦素性廉洁，令销毁嫁妆。不久杨牧获罪，先贬为端州司马，再流放欢州，继赐死。裴坦不追逐奢靡之风，不贪图非分之财。杨牧则没有

---

[1] 陈鼓应：《庄子今注今译》，北京：商务印书馆，2007年，第322页。

做到在"有"中把握"无",以顺应自在自为的生命常态,他贪赃枉法,结局凄惨。

P2-3 守静是践行"有"中把握"无"的根本。

【参见《老子》条目】

重为轻根,静为躁君。是以圣人终日行不离辎重。虽有荣观,燕处超然。奈何万乘之主,而以身轻天下?轻则失根,躁则失君。(第二十六章)

躁胜寒,静胜热。清静为天下正。(第四十五章)

大邦者下流,天下之交,天下之牝。牝常以静胜牡,以静为下。(第六十一章)

证明: 根据命题P2-2,顺应自在自为生命之常态要在"无"中把握"有"。又由定义5可知,"静"是涤除了过分的"欲"与机巧性的"智"的干扰而达到的内心澄明状态。人达到"静"的状态才能从"有"通于"无",感悟到"道"的无限可能性。因此,守静是践行"有"中把握"无"的根本。

例证和说明: "静"是心灵不受外物扰动的状态,指的是心灵的自然状态。正如南宋范应元所言:"致虚、守静,非谓绝物离人也。万物无足以扰吾本心者,此真所谓虚极、静笃。"庄子在《骈拇》中说:"小人牺牲自己来求利,士人牺牲自己来求名,大夫牺牲自己来为家,圣人则牺牲自己来为天下。这几种人,事业不同,名号各异,但是伤害本性,牺牲自己,却是一样的。""天下人都在牺牲自己啊!有的为仁义而牺牲,而世俗却称他为君子;有的为货财而牺牲,而世俗却称他为小人。"[1] 可见,世俗所谓"君子""小人"皆为外物所役所累,失去了生命和心灵之自然。通过守静,可从"有"中把握"无",从而得以体认大道。

P2-4 贪欲、智巧会使人类与自在自为的生命状态背道而驰。

【参见《老子》条目】

不尚贤,使民不争;不贵难得之货,使民不为盗;不见可欲,使民不乱。是以圣人之治也,虚其心,实其腹,弱其志,强其骨。常使民无知无欲。使夫智者不敢为也。为无为,则无不治。(第三章)

五色令人目盲;五音令人耳聋;五味令人口爽;驰骋畋猎,令人心发狂;难得之货,令人行妨;是以圣人为腹不为目,故去彼取此。(第十二章)

天之道,其犹张弓与?高者抑之,下者举之;有余者损之,不足者补之。天之道,损有余而补不足。人之道,则不然,损不足以奉有余。孰能有余以奉天

---

1 陈鼓应:《庄子今注今译》,北京:商务印书馆2007年,第280页。

下，唯有道者。是以圣人为而不恃，功成而不处，其不欲见贤。（第七十七章）

证明： 依据公理A1与基本假设2，"自然"是"道"从"无"到"有"再到"无"的自在自为过程；万物需要"道"的滋养。由此可知，自在自为乃生命之常态。又由定义2和3可知，对欲望的过分追求而产生的机巧智慧，往往是违背自然的。因此，贪欲、智巧会使人类与自在自为的生命状态背道而驰。

例证和说明： 贪欲、智巧及其交互作用而招致的纷争背离了"道"的精神，造成对人心自然状态的破坏。老子认为，通过致虚守静、涤除玄览的努力，在人物交接之时，就可以做到贪念不起，从而使心灵不受外界的惑乱，保持无私无欲的自然状态。世俗之人热衷于玩弄心机和诈伪，他们的心灵不再保有纯真朴实的自然状态。他们自以为聪明，实际上堵塞了体认"大道"的途径。贪欲、智巧及其交互作用而招致的纷争必然会导致与自然状态背道而驰。《庄子·马蹄》中说："在充满盛德的世代，人们和鸟兽同居，和万物并聚，又何必区分什么君子小人！大家都不用智巧，本性就不会丧失；人人都不贪求，所以都纯真朴实；纯真朴实便能保持人民的本性。可到了所谓的圣人出现之后，执着于求仁为义，天下人便开始迷惑了；制定了繁琐的礼乐，便出现人以群分的现象了。"[1] 在这种状况下，社会变得错综复杂，难以治理，其关键也就在于过多地杂糅了贪欲和智巧。

P2-5 少私寡欲、见素抱朴是达到自在自为生命状态的必由之路。

【参见《老子》条目】

载营魄抱一，能无离乎？专气致柔，能如婴儿乎？……天门开阖，能为雌乎？（第十章）

古之善为士者……敦兮其若朴。（第十五章）

绝智弃辩，民利百倍；绝伪弃诈，民复孝慈；绝巧弃利，盗贼无有。此三者以为文，不足。故令有所属：见素抱朴，少私寡欲。（第十九章）

为天下谷，常德乃足，复归于朴。（第二十八章）

道常无名，朴。（第三十二章）

化而欲作，吾将镇之以无名之朴。（第三十七章）

是以大丈夫处其厚不居其薄，处其实不居其华。故去彼取此。（第三十八章）

是故不欲碌碌如玉，珞珞如石。（第三十九章）

1　陈鼓应：《庄子今注今译》，北京：商务印书馆，2007年，第293页。

证明： 据命题P2-4，贪欲、智巧使人类社会与自在自为的生命状态背道而驰。由定义7可知，"无私"指消除过分的"欲"和机巧性的"智"之后而达到的能包容万物的心理状态。少私寡欲和见素抱朴都是消除过分的"欲"和机巧性的"智"所需要的行为。因此，少私寡欲、见素抱朴是达到自在自为生命状态的必由之路。

例证和说明： 欲望、智巧及其纷争是不符合大道精神的，也与自在自为生命状态背道而驰。通过少私寡欲、见素抱朴的修身功夫根除它们，可以恢复人心之自然。"少私寡欲""见素抱朴"是老子针对当时社会的道德状况提出来的，是一种矫正时弊的自我修养方法。老子看到，仁义等道德观念本来是用以劝导人的善行的，却流于矫揉造作、弄虚作假，有人更假借仁义之名以窃取名利。老子认为不如抛弃这些被人利用的外壳，而恢复人们天性自然的道德。《庄子·胠箧》中说："人们都内藏明慧，天下就不会迷乱了；人们都内敛聪敏，天下就没有忧患了；人们都内含智巧，天下就不会眩惑了；人们都内聚德性，天下就不会邪僻了。"[1]

P2-6 知足知止带来长久，贪得无厌招致祸咎。

【参见《老子》条目】

知足者富。（第三十三章）

甚爱必大费，多藏必厚亡。故知足不辱，知止不殆，可以长久。（第四十四章）

咎莫大于欲得，祸莫大于不知足。故知足之足，常足矣。（第四十六章）

证明： 据命题P2-5，少私寡欲、见素抱朴是达到自在自为生命状态的必然选择。知止知足是少私寡欲、见素抱朴的表现，而贪得无厌则与其背道而驰。又据公理A5，摄生的基本方法是消除过分的"欲"和机巧性的"智"，否则将对自身生活乃至生命带来伤害。因此，知足知止带来长久，贪得无厌招致祸咎。

例证和说明： 老子倡导的"少私寡欲"并不是要灭绝私欲，而是主张恬淡为上，把私欲控制在一定的限度之内，使心灵保持相对的"虚静"状态。不使私欲超过一定的限度，凡事都要适可而止，便是"知足知止"。在历史上，这样的教训很多。例如唐朝的长孙无忌，家世显赫，其妹妹即唐太宗的长孙皇后，长孙无忌则在太宗、高宗两朝为相，永徽年间又以元舅之亲辅政。然而，这位权倾一时的显赫人物却被武则天指使人诬告谋反，发配黔州，不久被逼自杀。长孙无忌下场凄凉，是他过分贪恋权势的结果。在封建社会，外戚当权，很容易成众矢之的。其妹文德皇后曾多次要其兄逊职，但长孙无忌没能真正理解胞妹的良苦用心，出于

---

1 陈鼓应：《庄子今注今译》，北京：商务印书馆，2007年，第308页。

私利，拥立庸才为帝。长孙无忌手握重权时，排除异己，打击同僚，到头来，自己也遭迫害。他因过分迷恋权势，极力维护和巩固自己的地位，其结果反而不得善终。

胡惟庸早年随朱元璋起兵，颇受宠信。洪武十年任丞相，位居百官之首。随着权势的不断增大，胡惟庸日益骄横跋扈，擅自决定官员人等的生杀升降。他得知大将军徐达对他不满、曾在朱元璋处奏其奸行时，竟诱使徐达家的守门人福寿谋害徐达，但因福寿揭发而未能得逞。胡惟庸还千方百计地拉拢因犯法受朱元璋谴责的吉安侯陆仲亨、平凉侯费聚，让他们在外聚集兵马，以图谋反。洪武十三年正月，朱元璋将胡惟庸处死。

P2-7 以柔弱处世是保全自在自为生命状态的方法。

【参见《老子》条目】

反者道之动，弱者道之用。（第四十章）

含德之厚，比于赤子。蜂虿虺蛇不螫，攫鸟猛兽不搏。骨弱筋柔而握固。（第五十五章）

证明： 从定义14可知，"柔弱"是不刻意展露自身强势的态度或行为，是一种高级的"守中"方式。依据基本假设5与命题P2-4，"守中"可以促成人与人之间、人与外部世界之间的均衡，而贪欲、智巧使人类社会与自在自为的生命状态背道而驰。因此，以柔弱处世是保全自在自为生命状态的方法。

例证和说明： 以柔弱方式处世，实际上就是要摒弃个人的贪欲、智巧诈伪和成心成见。朱元璋诛杀功臣可以说达到了极点，其中只有汤和一人得以幸免，为什么呢？因为他委曲求全，低调处世，而其他人之所以获罪被杀，多是因为他们飞扬跋扈，或者恃功自傲，或者直言谏诤，等等。徐达虽谦逊不自傲，但是他智勇过人，功高震主，朱元璋对他不放心，趁他得毒痈期间赏赐蒸鹅致死。因为常食鹅会得痈，如果已经得痈再食鹅，将毒发身死。

P2-8 柔弱方能生生不息，刚强导致枯槁易折。

【参见《老子》条目】

天下之至柔，驰骋天下之至坚。无有入无间，吾是以知无为之有益。不言之教，无为之益，天下希及之。（第四十三章）

人之生也柔弱，其死也坚强。草木之生也柔脆，其死也枯槁。故坚强者死之徒，柔弱者生之徒。是以兵强则灭，木强则折。强大处下，柔弱处上。（第七十

六章）

天下莫柔弱于水，而攻坚强者莫之能胜，以其无以易之。弱之胜强，柔之胜刚，天下莫不知，莫能行。（第七十八章）

证明： 依据命题T2-7，以柔弱处世是保全自在自为生命状态的方法。柔弱能够顺应自然，延年益寿；而刚强则往往耗竭生命，引发纷争。又据基本假设5与公理A5，"守中"可以促成人与人之间、人与外部世界之间的均衡，而摄生的基本方法是消除过分的"欲"和机巧性的"智"。因此，柔弱才能生生不息，刚强必然枯槁易折。

例证和说明： 子产临终时，在病榻之前把后事托付给心腹，并忠告说："我认为施政的方式不外柔与刚两者。刚与柔两者譬如水与火一般。火的性质激烈，故人民见之畏之不敢接近它，所以因火丧生的人极微；反观水，因为水是温和的，故而不易使人生畏，但因水而丧命的却不在少数。施行温和的政治看起来虽然容易，但实际上实行起来却极为困难。"子产自己就是因为掌握了刚与柔的平衡，才做到刚柔并济、治国有道。[1]

P2-9 "处下不争"是以柔弱处世的体现。

【参见《老子》条目】

上善若水。水善利万物而不争，处众人之所恶，故几于道。居善地，心善渊，与善仁，言善信，政善治，事善能，动善时。夫唯不争，故无尤。（第八章）

证明： 从定义11可知，"不争"指消除了过分的"欲"和机巧性的"智"后而形成的处世态度。据命题P2-7与基本假设5，以柔弱处世是保全自在自为生命状态的方法，而"守中"可以促成人与人之间、人与外部世界之间的均衡，这里"守中"将引导"处下不争"的行为。再据公理A4，圣人知"道"并"不争"。因此，"处下不争"是以柔弱处世的体现。

例证和说明： 老子有感于世人一味逞强好胜、不肯谦让而引起无数的纷争，于是提出"处下不争"的处世之道。《庄子·天下》说老子"以懦弱谦下为表"。谦下即谦恭处下，这不仅是避免祸患、保全自己的手段，也是消解社会纷争的有效方法。谦下的具体要求是：不自我表现，不自以为是，不自我夸耀，不自我骄矜。"不争"即不与人争，不争先，是老子崇尚的一种生活态度，也是老子全生避害、化解社会纷争的重要方法。"处下不争"是效法天道而来的。

---

[1] 常桦：《老子智慧书》，北京：石油工业出版社，2007年，第255页。

第四章 贵德篇
CHAPTER FOUR: On Cherishing Virtue

P2-10 坚守柔弱处世才是真正的自强不息。

【参见《老子》条目】

绝学无忧。唯之与阿，相去几何？美之与恶，相去若何？人之所畏，不可不畏。荒兮，其未央哉！众人熙熙，如享太牢，如春登台。我独泊兮，其未兆，如婴儿之未孩；儽儽兮，若无所归。众人皆有余，而我独若遗。我愚人之心也哉！沌沌兮！俗人昭昭，我独昏昏。俗人察察，我独闷闷。澹兮其若海，飂兮若无止。众人皆有以，而我独顽且鄙。我独异于人，而贵食母。（第二十章）

见小曰明，守柔曰强。（第五十二章）

慈故能勇；俭故能广；不敢为天下先，故能成器长。今舍慈且勇，舍俭且广，舍后且先，死矣！（第六十七章）

证明： 据命题P2-7，以柔弱处世是保全自在自为生命状态的方法。又据基本假设3与基本假设5，"无"与"有"的统一才是"道"的圆满状态，而人的认知和行为的理想状态是"守中"，既看到"有"又坚守"无"。以柔弱处世正是"守中"的体现，能够促成人与人之间、人与外部世界之间的均衡。因此，坚守柔弱处世才是真正的自强不息。

例证和说明： 老子从经验世界中观察到，貌似柔弱的东西可能是充满生机的和具有发展前途的，貌似刚强的东西可能是快要走下坡路的。天下没有比水更柔弱的，但是任何坚强的东西都不能改变水的本性；水是至柔的，又是至刚的。在人类社会，亦是如此。中国历史上深谙黄老之术、无论处于何种境况均能应对自如的是汉朝的陈平。他谙熟水之品德。当时刘邦身边谋士将才不少，能征善战者很多，但陈平一向受到高祖刘邦的重用。陈平的出身不如张良，张良是韩国贵族，而陈平家里很穷。一个出身平民家徒四壁的人如何获得一代英雄的垂青呢？只因为陈平性格如水，能吸纳知识，好读书，治黄帝、老子之术。陈平经常拜访请教一些前辈、社会上的名流，"读万卷书，行万里路"，以扩展见闻、增加阅历和丰富经验，从而匡扶汉室，消灭诸吕，历高祖、惠帝、文帝三朝而善终。

P2-11 贵德之士会表现出"守中"的人格。

【参见《老子》条目】

古之善为士者，微妙玄通，深不可识。夫唯不可识，故强为之容。豫焉若冬涉川，犹兮若畏四邻，俨兮其若客，涣兮其若释，敦兮其若朴，旷兮其若谷，混兮其若浊，孰能浊以静之徐清，孰能安以动之徐生。保此道者，不欲盈。夫唯不盈，故能蔽而新成。（第十五章）

证明： 由定义1可知，"德"是万物从"无"到"有"再到"无"的自在自为过程的总称，也指人对此过程的认识以及顺应此过程的人格品质。贵德之士即为尊道之士。依据基本假设5，人的认知和行为的理想状态是"守中"，这与顺应自在自为过程是一致的。因此，贵德之士会表现出"守中"的人格。

例证和说明： 贵德之士有较好的人格修养和心理素质，他们表面上清静无为，实际上蕴藏着很大的潜能，富有创造力，却不显山露水。在历史上，比较著名的是鬼谷子。鬼谷子姓王名诩，春秋时人，常入云梦山采药修道，因隐居清溪之鬼谷，人称鬼谷先生。他是孙膑和庞涓的老师，也是苏秦和张仪的老师，可谓声名赫赫。但是他除了有著作问世外，关于个人的生活记载非常少，可以说神龙见首不见尾。

P2-12 贵德之士能够通过"观"的方式达到澄明从而悟"道"。

【参见《老子》条目】

不出户，知天下；不窥牖，见天道。其出弥远，其知弥少。是以圣人不行而知，不见而名，不为而成。（第四十七章）

为学日益，为道日损。损之又损，以至于无为。（第四十八章）

证明： 由定义4可知，"观"是人知"道"的途径，"明"是人的内在生命力的自我观照能力，"观"是达到"明"的途径。依据公理A2与命题T2-11，由"智"入"明"就能知"道"。贵德之士会表现出"守中"的人格，从而由"智"入"明"，正确认识"道"。因此，贵德之士能够通过"观"的方式达到澄明从而悟"道"。

例证和说明： 妨碍人们悟"道"的主要有以下三大障碍：贪欲、智巧诈伪、成心成见。必须摒除以上三大障碍，使心灵从狭隘、封闭的局限性中提升出来，以广大的、超脱的、开放的心灵来观照万物和宇宙的真谛，如此才能悟"道"。心灵如一面镜子，宇宙万象都在镜中，镜面需经常抚拭、去其污垢才能明察世间百态。治理国家也是如此，要顺应自然本性及其规律，安定民心，才能收到较好的治理效果。[1]

P2-13 虚怀若谷是贵德之士应有之品行。

【参见《老子》条目】

古之善为士者……旷兮其若谷。（第十五章）

---

[1] 常桦：《老子智慧书》，北京：石油工业出版社，2007年，第38页。

知其雄，守其雌，为天下溪。……知其荣，守其辱，为天下谷。（第二十八章）

上德若谷。（第四十一章）

江海之所以能为百谷王者，以其善下之，故能为百谷王。（第六十六章）

知不知，尚矣；不知知，病也。圣人不病，以其病病。夫唯病病，是以不病。（第七十一章）

证明： 据命题P2-9，"处下不争"是以柔弱方式处世的体现，而虚怀若谷就是宽容大度、心胸豁达、处下不争的表现。又据命题P2-1，顺应自在自为的生命常态是"德"之体现，贵德之士需要有虚怀若谷的品行。因此，虚怀若谷是贵德之士应有之品行。

例证和说明： 大道有"虚""藏"的特性，能够包容万物，"善为道者"待人处世也应如空旷的山谷一样，胸怀广阔豁达，能够包容一切。《庄子·天下》说老子"常宽容于物，不削于人"。贵德之士应虚怀若谷，容天下难容之事，不苛求于人，使分歧与恩怨化解在自己宏大的度量之中，方能为众望之所归。[1] 西汉末年，王莽篡位，很快失去了人心，各地纷纷起义。人们思念汉室，所以在起义军中，有好几位都自称汉代的宗室。刘秀起兵，也打出匡复汉室的旗号，拥刘玄为帝。王郎原在邯郸城以占卜为生，现在也说自己是汉成帝的儿子，自立为汉帝，起兵攻取州郡，一时很有声势。刘秀这时正好以大司马的身份前往河北各州县巡抚，王郎就下令悬赏捉拿他，刘秀仓皇逃走。一时河北各郡纷纷望风归顺，尽属王郎。刘秀集结兵力，经过数番激战，最后一举攻取了邯郸，王郎战败被杀。刘秀搜查他的往来文件书信，发现里面有手下官员们写给王郎的上千封书信，内容很多是诋毁和诽谤刘秀的。左右劝他严加追查，好一网打尽。刘秀未置可否。一天，刘秀把手下官员召集到大殿，点起炉火，叫人烧掉那些书信，并且说："现在大家可以安心了！"大家拜伏在地上，庆幸自己逃过了这一劫，也很感激刘秀放过他们。[2]

P2-14 实现家、国、天下的德治，需要顺应自在自为的生命常态。

【参见《老子》条目】

修之于身，其德乃真；修之于家，其德乃余；修之于乡，其德乃长；修之于邦，其德乃丰；修之于天下，其德乃普。故以身观身，以家观家，以乡观乡，以

---

1 陈鼓应：《老子评传》，南京：南京大学出版社，2001年，第266页。
2 萧龙：《老子为人处世智慧全集》，北京：地震出版社，2007年，第121—122页。

邦观邦,以天下观天下。吾何以知天下然哉?以此。(第五十四章)

证明: 由定义1可知,"德"是万物从"无"到"有"再到"无"的自在自为过程的总称,也指人对此过程的认识以及顺应此过程的品行。家、国、天下都有各自的运行规律,呈现各自的生存状态。依据命题P2-1,顺应自在自为生命常态是"德"之体现。因此,实现家、国、天下的德治,需要顺应自在自为的生命常态。

例证和说明: 王弼对"以身观身,以家观家,以乡观乡,以邦观邦,以天下观天下"的注解是"彼皆然也",即是说我之身与他人之身之间存在着共性,就"身"而言,我之身如此这般,他人之身也是同样道理,因而由我之身出发,则可观照推知他人之身。同理,我之家与他人之家,我之乡与他人之家,我之邦与他人之邦,皆应作如是观。这种"以物观物"的类比推理方法使我们懂得,家、国、天下的治理需要顺应自在自为生命常态,帮助我们破除小我、超越自我,从更大范围看待万物、处理万事。

P2-15 圣人之功在于辅助民众回归自在自为之生命常态。

【参见《老子》条目】

圣人常无心,以百姓心为心。善者,吾善之;不善者,吾亦善之;德善。信者,吾信之;不信者,吾亦信之;德信。圣人在天下,歙歙焉,为天下浑其心。百姓皆注其耳目,圣人皆孩之。(第四十九章)

是以圣人欲不欲,不贵难得之货;学不学,复众人之所过,以辅万物之自然而不敢为。(第六十四章)

证明: 由定义8和定义9可知,作为有"德"的治国者,圣人之功表现为自觉维护符合"自然"的社会秩序的活动。又据公理A1与命题P2-4,"自然"是"道"从"无"到"有"再到"无"的自在自为过程,而圣人所致力的家、国、天下的德治,需要顺应自在自为生命常态。因此,圣人之功在于辅助民众回归自在自为之生命常态。

例证和说明: "圣人"是老子理想中的得道之人,他想百姓之所想,行百姓之所需。《老子》所倡导的"圣人常无心,以百姓心为心"是一种伟大的公仆意识,是光明正大的奉献精神。圣人仿效天地运行的自然规律,鄙弃一切束缚和影响人类身心自由活动的名教规范,以"无为"的态度和原则来处理世事,实行"不言"的教导,听任人们按照自己的自然本性去生活,从不横加干涉。圣人以这样的态度和原则治理社会,就不会给人们带来戕害,人们也不会感觉到权势的压迫,能够更好地自我发展、自我化育,因而能收到最好的效果,使社会得到最好的治理。《庄子·天地》叙述，伯成子高对大禹说："从前尧治理天下，不必行赏而人民却能勉励，不必刑罚而人民却能有所敬畏。现在你行使赏罚而人民却不仁爱，德行从此衰落，刑罚从此兴起，后世的祸乱从此开始了。"[1]

P2-16 圣人以无为成就其功。

【参见《老子》条目】

将欲取天下而为之，吾见其不得已。天下神器，不可为也，不可执也。为者败之，执者失之。故物或行或随，或嘘或吹，或强或羸，或挫或堕。是以圣人去甚，去奢，去泰。（第二十九章）

道常无为而无不为。侯王若能守之，万物将自化。化而欲作，吾将镇之以无名之朴。无名之朴，夫亦将不欲。不欲以静，天下将自正。（第三十七章）

不出户，知天下；不窥牖，见天道。其出弥远，其知弥少。是以圣人不行而知，不见而名，不为而成。（第四十七章）

证明： 由定义10可知，"无为"指顺应"自然"不刻意作为，更不妄为的行动原则。依据命题P2-15与公理A3，圣人之功在于辅助民众回归自在自为之生命常态，而其基本理念是从"无为"达"有为"，也是善为道者的境界。因此，圣人以"无为"成就其功。

例证和说明： 天道对于万物既有创生的功能又有养育的功能，但这些都是在自然而然中进行的，既不是有意的作为，也没有任何功利的目的。这种无为是一种美德，也是圣人治理天下的手段。在原始氏族社会中，生产资料归集体所有，氏族成员共同劳动，平均分配生活资料。远古的圣人管理生产和公共事务，却从不占有大家的劳动成果，他虽然有权做出决定，但却是代表着公众的意识。这与"道"的"生而不有，为而不恃，长而不宰"的精神相吻合。

P2-17 无私是圣人成就其功的必然要求。

【参见《老子》条目】

天地不仁，以万物为刍狗，圣人不仁，以百姓为刍狗。天地之间，其犹橐龠乎！虚而不屈，动而愈出。多言数穷，不如守中。（第五章）

天长地久。天地所以长且久者，以其不自生，故能长生。是以圣人后其身而身先，外其身而身存。非以其无私邪？故能成其私。（第七章）

---

[1] 陈鼓应：《庄子今注今译》，北京：商务印书馆，2007年，第362页。

证明： 据命题P2-16与公理A3，圣人以"无为"来成就其功，从"无为"达"有为"。这里的"无为"指顺应自然，不刻意作为，更不妄为。又由定义7可知，"无私"指消除过的"欲"和机巧性的"智"之后而达到的能包容万物的心理状态。在这种心理状态下，才能真正做到不刻意作为，更不妄为。因此，"无私"是圣人成就其功的必然要求。

例证和说明： 圣人的"无私"来源于其博大的慈爱之心。圣人将这种慈爱之心推及天下万物、形之于外就是"无私"。圣人无私，体现了"道"的基本精神，即辅助万物使其自我化育，而不居功不据为己有。如此无条件地付出而不求任何回报，可以称为"给予的道德"。只有真正的有道之人即圣人，才能具有这种"给予的道德"，才能倾其所有以奉天下。圣人"无执""无誉"，甚至"无身"，从不把自己放在心上，唯以天下为怀，"以百姓心为心"。

虽然不求任何回报，但却得到了众人的爱戴。心存无私，才能真正地拥有自己，才能得到他人的敬重。自私自利尽管能得到一时之小利，但会失去许多成就大事的机会。圣人的心中没有"自私"的概念，所以成就其功。春秋时，晋平公有一次问祁黄羊说："南阳县需要一位长官，你看，应该派谁去当比较合适呢？"祁黄羊毫不迟疑地回答说："叫解狐去，最合适了。他一定能够胜任！"平公惊奇地又问他："解狐不是你的仇人吗？你为什么还要推荐他呢！"祁黄羊说："你只问我什么人能够胜任，谁最合适。你并没问我解狐是不是我的仇人呀！"[1]可以说，祁黄羊的行为体现了一种"公而忘私"或者"无私"的精神。

P2-18 慈、俭、不为天下先，是圣人成就其功的日常实践。

【参见《老子》条目】

是以圣人欲上民，必以言下之；欲先民，必以身后之。是以圣人处上而民不重，处前而民不害。是以天下乐推而不厌。以其不争，故天下莫能与之争。（第六十六章）

我有三宝，持而保之。一曰慈，二曰俭，三曰不敢为天下先。慈故能勇；俭故能广；不敢为天下先，故能成器长。今舍慈且勇，舍俭且广，舍后且先，死矣！夫慈，以战则胜，以守则固。天将救之，以慈卫之。（第六十七章）

天下莫柔弱于水，而攻坚强者莫之能胜，以其无以易之。弱之胜强，柔之胜刚，天下莫不知，莫能行。是以圣人云：受国之垢，是谓社稷主；受国不祥，是

---

1 常桦：《老子智慧书》，北京：石油工业出版社，2007年，第18—19页。

为天下王。正言若反。(第七十八章)

证明： 从定义13可知，"慈"指柔和而不激烈的博爱品质，"俭"指坚韧而不孤傲的节制品质，而"不为天下先"是处下不争。"慈""俭""不为天下先"都是自在自为之生命常态，也是无私的表现。依据命题P2-15以及P2-17，圣人之功在于辅助民众回归自在自为之生命常态，而无私是圣人成就其功的必然要求。因此，"慈""俭""不为天下先"是圣人成就其功的日常实践。

例证和说明： "慈""俭"和"不敢为天下先"是老子的"三宝"，是圣人行为的信条，体现了为人处事的智慧。一次，晏子刚开始吃饭，齐景公派遣的使者就到了。于是晏子就将自己的饭食分给使者吃，结果使者没有吃饱，晏子也没有吃饱。使者回到官里后，便把这事告诉了景公，景公说："唉！晏子的生活竟然这么清贫，我怎么一点也不知道，这是我的过失啊！"于是派官吏送给晏子千镒（古代重量单位，一镒合二十两）黄金和市井的税收，让他用来款待宾客，晏子辞谢不受。景公又再三派人给他送去，晏子依然推辞，说："我的家并不贫困啊！君王您的赏赐、恩泽覆盖了我父、母、妻三族，还延及我朋友，我还用它来赈济百姓。君王给我的赏赐已是很优厚了！我听说，从君王那里得到过多的财物，而又施惠给百姓，那就是代替君王统治百姓，忠臣是不能这样做的。从君王那里得到过多的财物，而又不施惠于百姓，那就成了储藏钱财的竹箱子了，仁慈的人是不会做这种事的。先从君王那里接受财物，然后又得罪于士人，自己死后钱财又转移到别人手里，这就是为他人收藏钱财，聪明的人是不会做这种事的。粗疏的布衣，一豆（古代的计量单位，四升为一豆）的粮食，够我安家度日就可以了。"景公对晏子说："我的先君桓公，将五百社（古代一种居民组织，二十五家为一社）封赏管仲，他一点儿不推辞便接受了，您为什么辞谢我的赏赐呢？"晏子说："我听说，圣人千虑，必有一失；愚人千虑，必有一得。我想管仲失误的地方，或许正是我做得正确的地方吧，所以我再次拜谢您的恩典而不敢接受您的赏赐。"[1]

P2-19 一视同仁地善待事物，是圣人成就其功的关键。

【参见《老子》条目】

善行无辙迹，善言无瑕谪，善数不用筹策，善闭无关楗而不可开，善结无绳约而不可解。是以圣人常善救人，故无弃人；常善救物，故无弃物。是谓袭明。故善人者，不善人之师；不善人者，善人之资。不贵其师，不爱其资，虽智大

---

1 萧龙：《老子为人处世智慧全集》，北京：地震出版社，2007年，第73—74页。

迷，是谓要妙。（第二十七章）

圣人常无心，以百姓心为心。善者，吾善之；不善者，吾亦善之；德善。信者，吾信之；不信者，吾亦信之；德信。（第四十九章）

人之不善，何弃之有？（第六十二章）

大小多少，报怨以德。（第六十三章）

和大怨，必有余怨；安可以为善？是以圣人执左契，而不责于人。有德司契，无德司彻。天道无亲，常与善人。（第七十九章）

圣人不积，既以为人己愈有，既以与人己愈多。（第八十一章）

证明： 依据命题P2-18可知"慈""俭""不为天下先"是圣人成就其功的日常实践。其中排在首位的"慈"便是博爱，它意味着泛爱众生是圣人日常实践中的首要之义。又据命题P2-15，圣人之功在于辅助民众回归自在自为之生命常态，不必对各种事物有偏爱之心。因此，一视同仁地善待事物，是圣人成就其功的关键。

例证和说明： 以"慈"为宝，表明老子对人类充满爱心，对社会有着高度的责任感。"慈"的基本要求，就是与人为善。与人为善，难在善待不善之人。假如对不善之人也能善待之，往往会化解矛盾。刘向《新序》中有这样一个故事：梁、楚两国相邻，都在边亭种了瓜。梁人勤于灌溉，瓜长得好；楚人懒惰，瓜长得不好。楚人心生妒忌，半夜里把梁人的瓜弄死了很多。梁人的长官不但不许部下报复，反而让他们每天夜里偷着去浇灌楚人的瓜。楚人的瓜越长越好。他们发觉了是梁人所为，便把这事报告了楚王。楚王自感惭愧，派人前来谢罪，从此两国修好，边境相安无事。[1]

P2-20 把握"无"与"有"的统一，是圣人成就其功的法门。

【参见《老子》条目】

将欲歙之，必固张之；将欲弱之，必固强之；将欲废之，必固举之；将欲取之，必固与之，是谓微明。柔弱胜刚强。鱼不可脱于渊，国之利器不可以示人。（第三十六章）

为无为，事无事，味无味。大小多少，报怨以德。图难于其易，为大于其细。天下难事，必作于易；天下大事，必作于细，是以圣人终不为大，故能成其

---

[1] 陈鼓应：《老子评传》，北京：南京大学出版社，2001年，第270页。

大。夫轻诺必寡信，多易必多难。是以圣人犹难之。故终无难矣。（第六十三章）

其安易持，其未兆易谋。其脆易泮，其微易散。为之于未有，治之于未乱。合抱之木，生于毫末；九层之台，起于累土；千里之行，始于足下。为者败之，执者失之。是以圣人无为故无败，无执故无失。民之从事，常于几成而败之。慎终如始，则无败事。是以圣人欲不欲，不贵难得之货；学不学，复众人之所过，以辅万物之自然而不敢为。（第六十四章）

证明： 依据命题P2-15，圣人之功在于辅助民众回归自在自为之生命常态。又据命题P2-2与基本假设3，顺应自在自为生命之常态，在于把握"无"与"有"的统一；虽然"无"的无限可能性与"有"的有限现实性构成矛盾，但"无"与"有"的统一才是"道"的圆满状态。因此，把握"无"与"有"的统一，是圣人成就其功的法门。

例证和说明： 任何事物都有它的对立面，同时又都因着它的对立面而形成。如有无、美丑、善恶、成败、是非等。吴澄《道德真经注》曰："美恶之名，相因而有。"在老子五千言中，这种相反相成的概念多达80余对。从表面上看，对反的双方是相持不下、互不相容的，但老子经过深入的观察和思考后发现它们之间又是互相包含、互相渗透的。正是由于这种彼此相通关系，它们转化的必然趋势是向对立面转化，而不是转化为其他事物。[1]正因如此，我们应当从事物的精微处入手，抓住对立转换的契机，从而走向成功。事物总是向对立面转化，由有而无，由存而亡，由治而乱。老子正是从这一认识出发，提出未雨绸缪、防微杜渐、防患未然的问题，强调安而不忘危、存而不忘亡、治而不忘乱，要人们从难处着眼、易处入手、及时动手，"为之于未有，治之于未乱"。

这样，问题就比较容易解决，否则，等到问题拖到燃眉之急再动手解决，就十分困难了。我国历史上著名的政治家贾谊著有《论积贮疏》《治安策》《过秦论》，充分体现了老子提倡的居安思危的忧患意识。贾谊认为，当时的西汉虽然在汉文帝的统治下国家形势已经比较乐观，但是统治者应该看得更长远，居安思危，削诸侯、贮粮库，以安备不安，还应该从一些小事做起，如懂礼仪、知廉耻、爱民众，才能取得长治久安。汉文帝看了《论积贮疏》后，认为贾谊说得很有道理，便采纳了他的建议，接连两次发出通令，提倡发展农业，并且还制定了一些发展农业生产的措施，使西汉王朝逐渐富强起来。[2]

---

1 陈鼓应：《老子评传》，南京：南京大学出版社，2001年，第176—177页。
2 常桦：《老子智慧书》，北京：石油工业出版社，2007年，第205—206页。

> **P2-21** 功遂身退是圣人遵道而行的体现。

【参见《老子》条目】

持而盈之，不如其已；揣而锐之，不可长保。金玉满堂，莫之能守；富贵而骄，自遗其咎。功遂身退，天之道也。（第九章）

不自见，故明；不自是，故彰；不自伐，故有功；不自矜，故能长。（第二十二章）

企者不立，跨者不行，自见者不明，自是者不彰，自伐者无功，自矜者不长。其在道也，曰余食赘行。物或恶之，故有道者不处。（第二十四章）

证明： 依据命题P2-15，圣人之功在于辅助民众回归自在自为之生命常态。又据公理A1，"自然"是"道"从"无"到"有"再到"无"的自在自为过程。功遂即功业告成，意味着人类社会回归了"道"的自在自为过程，不再需要辅助之力，这时圣人可以适可而止，引身而退。因此，功遂身退是圣人遵道而行的体现。

例证和说明： 一般人在名利当头时，往往趋之若鹜。贪恋名利，富贵而骄，常常自取其祸，就像李斯做秦朝宰相时候，显赫不可一世，然而终不免沦为阶下囚。《史记·范雎蔡泽列传》记载，蔡泽见应侯范雎，劝其归还相印，退出政治舞台，对他大讲物盛则衰、功成身退的道理，又旁征博引，引用了"日中则移，月满则亏"以及"鉴于水者，见面之容，鉴于人者，知吉与凶""成功之下，不可久处"[1]等名言警句来告诫范雎。而老子则把历史上对于政治的经验之谈又提高了一步，上升到"功遂身退，天之道"的哲学高度。功遂身退体现了"道"的基本精神，也是圣人践行"德"的行为。

> **P2-22** 呵护人的生命常态并与万物同一，是德之本质。

【参见《老子》条目】

上德不德，是以有德；下德不失德，是以无德。上德无为而无以为，下德无为而有以为。（第三十八章）

生而不有，为而不恃，长而不宰，是谓玄德。（第五十一章）

玄德深矣，远矣，与物反矣，然后乃至大顺。（第六十五章）

证明： 从定义1可知，"德"是万物从"无"到"有"再到"无"的自在自为过程的总称，也指人对此过程的认识以及顺应此过程的品行。依据公理A1与命题

---

[1] 司马迁：《史记》，长沙：岳麓书社，2001年，第478页。

第四章　贵德篇
CHAPTER FOUR: On Cherishing Virtue

P2-1，"自然"是"道"从"无"到"有"再到"无"的自在自为过程，而顺应自在自为的生命常态是"德"之体现，这里蕴含着把人的生命常态融入万物之中的思想。因此，呵护自在自为生命常态并与万物同一，是"德"之本质。

例证和说明： 呵护人的自在自为生命常态，与天地万物息息相通，是"道"在人类社会的体现，这种体现就是"德"。春秋时期，孙武和伍子胥辅助吴王阖闾夺得国君之位后，孙武归隐，著成《孙子兵法》，但伍子胥不能及时隐退而自在自为，继续辅佐吴王夫差，导致结局悲惨。范蠡和文种共同辅佐越王勾践复国之后，范蠡及时引退，得以保全身家性命。文种贪恋权位，遭到身死名灭的结局。始终保有自在自为的生命常态，秉持平常心，不执着于名誉、地位、财富等外在事物，就能做到与万物同一，全生避害，这就与"德"的本质相吻合。

P2-23　"道"是万物的由来，"德"是万物的本性。

【参见《老子》条目】

孔德之容，惟道是从。（第二十一章）

故从事于道者，同于道；德者，同于德；失者，同于失。同于德者，道亦德之；同于失者，道亦失之。（第二十三章）

道生之，德畜之，物形之，势成之。是以万物莫不尊道而贵德。道之尊，德之贵，夫莫之命而常自然。故道生之，德畜之，长之育之，亭之毒之，养之覆之。生而不有，为而不恃，长而不宰，是谓玄德。（第五十一章）

证明： 依据基本假设2，"道"可"无"，精微处充满力量；"无"生"有"，恍惚中混成迹象。"无"意味着"道"的无限可能性，"有"指万物之母，也就是万物的形成。万物需要"道"的滋养，"道"常在以助万物之生。而从定义1可知，"德"是万物自在自为过程的总称，也指人对此过程的认识以及顺应此过程的品行。这里，"德"虽无"道"之创造力，却是"道"从"无"生"有"之后的具体落成。在万物之中的"道"就是"德"，它可以解释为万物本有的品质，也可以解释为在人伦关系中的德行。因此，"道"是万物的由来，"德"是万物的本性。

例证和说明： "道"具有形上性，但又真实存在；"德"具有形下性，但又无法用感官来把握。"道"创生万物，又存在于万物之中；"道"是万物的根源，又是万物的归宿。万物在创生之前，潜存在混沌未分的"道"中，与"道"一体；万物创生后，内在地包含着"道"，体现着"道"。"道"与万物仍然是一体。"道"是永恒的，万物的存在则是暂时的，都有生灭变化，万物消失后不是化为乌有，而是复归于"道"。"道"中又凝聚着新的生命力，集结着新的创造力，孕育着新的事物，酝酿着另一轮循环。返本是为了从本根处更生，获得新的生命。

"德"是"道"在自然界和人类社会中的体现，是万物本性的依据。如果将火比作为"道"，那火的光和热就是"德"；如果将水比作为"道"，那流淌的溪水、飘洒的雨露和浩瀚的大海就是"德"。"道"就像母亲，"德"就像母亲的乳汁。世间万物在"道"和"德"的生养和抚育下成形、成长、成熟、衰老直至死亡，然后再形成新的生命，万物就是在这种自然规律中循环往复的。

第四章 贵德篇
CHAPTER FOUR: On Cherishing Virtue

This chapter aims to illustrate the virtue of following Nature, and the ways and significance of cultivating the virtue. P2-1 to P2-3 deal with how to cultivate the virtue, how to follow Nature, and how to achieve virtue. P2-4 to P2-10 elaborate on what factors harm the cultivation of virtue, that is, greed and wrong manipulation of ingenuity, and the ways of weakening them by adopting contentedness, being low, being soft, and non-rivalry, etc. P2-11 to P2-13 illustrate the presentation and mind of sages. P2-14 to P2-21 tackle the practice of the "virtue". P2-22 to P2-23 explain the relationship between the "virtue" and the Dao.

P2-1 The embodiment of virtue lies in following the spontaneous and natural normality of life.

Quotes from *Laozi*:

The person with profound virtue is just like an infant boy, whom bees, scorpions and serpents cannot bite, and whom fierce birds and beasts of prey cannot attack. His bones are weak but his fists are firm. He is too young to know the copula of men and women, but his penis is naturally erect, which is because he has enough vital essence. He cries all day long, but he does not lose his voice, which is because he has enough vigor and vitality. (Chapter 55)

To know harmony is called constant. To know constant is called being fair and just. To indulge in carnal pleasures is to invite disasters. To let virility driven by desires is to bring violence. Excessive stimulation tends to make one age. This is against the Dao. What is against the Dao comes to an early end. (Chapter 55)

Proof: According to A1, naturalness is a spontaneous process from "non-being" to "being" and again back to "non-being"; from this we can see that spontaneity is the constant state of life. From D1 we can see that people's understanding of this spontaneous process and their character to follow this process are called the De (Virtue). According to Assumption 5, the ideal state of human cognition and behavior is "to keep moderate," so as to promote the balance between Man and Man, and between Man and the outside world. Therefore, it is the manifestation of the De to comply with the spontaneous and natural normality of life.

Explanation: The Virtue is the manifestation of the Dao in concrete things or matters, and it is the innate base of things' being naturally so. In other words, Virtue is the Dao that exists in all things in the universe. It is the Dao with regard to the generation of all things in the universe, but it is the De with regard to the existence of all things in the universe. "The Virtue is what a thing acquires from the Dao. The Virtue is partial, while the Dao is the whole. The Virtue is the realization of a *thing's acquisition of the Dao. The Virtue is in actuality the very nature of a thing."*[1] Therefore, the Dao and the "Virtue" are the two inseparable forms in one entity. To comply with the spontaneous and natural normality of life is to comply with the naturalness of life. To comply with the naturalness of life will bring life into a harmonious and balanced state. And the accomplishment of this state is just the manifestation of the De in human society. "Leaving the World Open," *Zhuangzi* says, "*So it is that the noble master who finds he has to follow some course to govern the world will realize that actionless action is the best course. By non-action, he can rest in the real substance of his nature and destiny.* [Translated by Martin Palmer, et al.] *So, Laozi said, 'If he appreciates his own body as he appreciates the world, then the world can be placed in his care. He who loves his body as he loves the world can be trusted to govern the world.' Therefore, if a noble man does not indulge in excessive desires and show off his wisdom; if he keeps peaceful and cheerful, quiet but touching, leisurely and carefree; if his spiritual activities are in harmony with nature, then all things in the world will accumulate and multiply.*"[2]

P2-2   To follow the spontaneous and natural normality of life, we should grasp the unity of "non-being" and "being."

Quotes from *Laozi*:

To put thirty spokes to form the hub of the wheel; but only when the hub is hollowed can the cart function properly. To smash clay to form vessels; but only when the vessels are hollowed can the vessels function properly. To build doors and windows in the house; but only when the house is emptied can the house function properly. Therefore, "Being" is convenience to people, but only when there is "Non-being" can "Being" function properly. (Chapter 11)

The man of the highest virtue does not claim to be of virtue, thus he is of the true virtue. The man of the lowest virtue always holds fast to the virtue in form, thus he is actually of no virtue. The man of the highest virtue never acts yet leaves nothing undone. The man of the lowest virtue acts but there are things left undone. The men of high benevolence act but unintentionally; the men of high uprightness act but intentionally. The men of high ethics act but obtain nothing in return, so they will raise their arms to call. Hence when the Dao is lost, virtue will be lost as well; when virtue is lost, benevolence will be lost; when benevolence is lost, uprightness will

---

1   Zhang Erping. On the View of Essence-function of Laozi's Philosophy. *Journal of Shangqiu University*, No.8, 2007.

2   Chen Guying. *New Annotated Translation of Zhuangzi*. Commercial Press, 2007, p.322.

be lost; when uprightness is lost; ritual will be lost. Ritual marks the insufficiency of loyalty and faithfulness, and the beginning of disasters. The presupposed norms are but the vanity of the Dao, and the beginning of fatuousness. Therefore, the true men should be honest and sincere, but not frivolous; and they should be honest and reliable, but not superficial. The true men should discard superficiality and keep sincerity. (Chapter 38)

Proof: According to P2-1, it is the manifestation of the De to follow the spontaneous and natural normality of life, and the De is a general name of the spontaneous and natural process of all the things in the universe, or the human recognition of the process, or quality of following the process (D1). Also according to the assumptions 3 and 5, the infinite possibility of "non-being" and the finite actuality of "being" are contradictory, the unity of "non-being" and "being" is the perfect state of the Dao, and the ideal state of human recognition and conduct is "keeping moderate," so as to see "being" but also abide by "non-being." Therefore, to follow the spontaneous and natural normality of life requires the unity of "non-being" and "being."

Explanation: The Dao is a unity of "being" and "non-being." "Non-being" is transcendental and super-organic. In order to grasp it, people have to start from "being" existent in the realistic and concrete time and space. In fact, it is the observation of the Dao to follow the spontaneous and natural normality of life. As a result, the key to the Dao of following the naturalness of life is to grasp "non-being" from "being." In human practice, we should not for even once claim credit for ourselves when we "have done some deeds" or become proud of our "talent," or be arrogant when we acquire "wealth." Only when we do all these can we say that we follow the spontaneous and natural normality of life. The key point is that we can grasp "non-being" from "being," and are aware that everything changes like the change of day and night and the four seasons, so we don't have to be so persistent and discriminative. In this way, we will not be confined to selfishness and greed, so as to make our body and soul follow the natural state. For example, in the reign of Emperor Yizong of the Tang Dynasty (833-873), the official circles were heinously dark. Yang Mu was truly corrupt by nature, and as a prime minister, he embezzled a million of silver. When Yang Mu married his daughter to Pei Tan's son, he prepared for her a luxurious dowry. Pei Tan was then a *Shangshu*, high official or minister in ancient China, and honest in performing his official duties, so he ordered to destroy his daughter-in-law's dowry. Before long, Yang Mu was accused of crimes, first demoted as a *Sima* (minister of war in ancient China) in Duanzhou Prefecture, then exiled in Huanzhou Prefecture, and finally ordered by the emperor to kill himself. Pei Tan was disinterested in extravagances and ill-gotten gains. By contrast, Yang

Mu failed to grasp "non-being" in following the spontaneous and natural normality of life, and took bribes and bent the law, only to have a wretched end of his own life.

P2-3   To keep quiet is the root of practising the "manipulation of 'non-being' in 'being.'"

Quotes from Laozi:

Heaviness is the root of lightness; calmness is the domination of restlessness. Therefore, the rulers move all day long without leaving their loaded chariots. Although they live a luxurious life and amuse themselves in sightseeing, they are peaceful and carefree, free of all material comforts and desires. Why do the rulers who own an army with ten thousand horses and chariots still govern the world in restless haste? If you act rashly, you will lose the root, and if you act restlessly, you will lose the domination. (Chapter 26)

Motion overcomes coldness; tranquility overcomes heat. By calmness and tranquility, you can be the model of the world. (Chapter 45)

The big states, feminine in nature in the world, should place themselves at the lower part in the same way as the big rivers where all the rivers converge. The feminine often prevails over the masculine in that the former is quiet by nature, because what is quiet is able to be at the lower part. (Chapter 61)

Proof: According to P2-2, if you want to follow the spontaneous and natural normality of life, you will have to grasp "being" from "non-being." Also according to D5, we can see that "peacefulness" is an innate clarified state of mind when the excessive "desire" and the intervention of the ingenious "wisdom" are eliminated. Only when Man reaches peacefulness or tranquility can he experience the infinite possibility of the Dao from "being" through "non-being." Therefore, keeping peacefulness is the very root of "grasping non-being through being."

Explanation: Peacefulness is a state in which the soul is free from external intervention, that is, the natural state of the soul. It is just like what Fan Yingyuan of the Song Dynasty says, "*To keep void and tranquil does not mean being secluded from people and separated from the material world. It just means that we should not let things disturb our hearts. This is really known as 'to take emptiness to the limit and keep ourselves in a state of tranquility.'*" Zhuangzi in his *Pianmu* (*Webbed Toes*) says, "*If someone makes sacrifices for reasons of benevolence and righteousness, people call such a person 'junzi' (a nobleman, gentleman, or man of noble character); if someone makes sacrifices for wealth and power, then people call such a person 'xiaoren' (a mean and a petty person). The action of sacrifice is the same,* yet we call one 'junzi' and the other 'xiaoren.' Both of the two can harm their true nature and sacrifice their lives." "Why should we make a difference of one being 'junzi' and other 'xiaoren'?" [1]

It is thus clear that the secular "*junzi*" or "*xiaoren*" are all encumbered with external things, and thus lose the naturalness in their life and soul. By means of keeping peacefulness, you will grasp non-being through being, and will be able to experience the Great Dao.

P2-4   Greed and ingenuity will make Man diverge from the spontaneous and natural state of life.

Quotes from *Laozi:*

Not to value and employ men of superior ability is the way to keep the people from rivalry among themselves; not to prize articles which are difficult to procure is the way to keep them from becoming thieves; not to show them what is likely to excite their desires is the way to keep their minds from disorder. Therefore, the sage, in the exercise of his government, empties their minds, fills their bellies, weakens their wills, and strengthens their bones. He always keeps them innocent of knowledge and free from desire, and disables the wise from taking any ill actions. If you deal with worldly affairs by "non-action," there will be no trouble of government. (Chapter 3)

Too many colors dazzle the eyes; too much music deafens the ears; too many tastes baffle the palate. Overindulging in hunting drives you crazy, and coveting too many material things tarnishes your conduct. Therefore, the Sage cares for bellies rather than senses, fending off material temptation and living a simple life. (Chapter 12)

Is the law of nature not just like the drawing of the bow? When the string is too high, it is lowered; when it is too low, it is raised; if there is too much, it will be reduced, and if there is not enough, it will be replenished. It is the law of nature to reduce what is abundant, and replenish what is lacking. However, the human behavior is just the opposite: to exploit what is insufficient and supply what is abundant. Who can spare what he has more than enough to those in need? Only Sages can do this. Therefore, the Sages nurture the world but not capitalize on their achievements, and not show off their cleverness or wisdom either. (Chapter 77)

Proof: According to A1 and Basic Assumption 2, naturalness is the spontaneous and natural process of the Dao from "non-being" to "being" and back to "non-being." All the things in the universe need the nourishment of the Dao. From this we can

---

1   Chen Guying. *New Annotated Translation of Zhuangzi.* Commercial Press, 2007, p.280.

see that spontaneity and naturalness are the constant state of life. According to D2 and D3 we can see that the ingenious wisdom resulting from the excessive pursuit of desire goes against naturalness. Therefore, greed and ingenuity will make Man run counter to the spontaneous and natural state of life.

Explanation: The dispute resulting from the greed and ingenuity and their reciprocation runs against the spirit of the Dao, which damages the natural state of the human heart. Laozi maintained that with the efforts of making Man's inner world extremely void and empty, and making Man's soul reach the extreme quietness and calmness, and of clearing Man's distracting thoughts and reading into Himself, Man will have no idea of greed when doing transactions with others, thus keeping Man's soul from the temptation of the outside world, and keeping the natural state of selflessness. Secular people are ardent in ingenuity and cheating, so their soul will no longer have the natural state of being pure and simple. They think they are smart, but, in fact, block the way leading to the "Great Dao." The dispute resulting from the greed and ingenuity and their interaction run against the natural state. In the "Horse's Hoof" of *Zhuangzi*, Zhuangzi said, "*In the time full of the profound virtue, Man lived harmoniously with birds and animals, and co-existed with all the things in the universe, and there was no need to distinguish between junzi (people of noble character) and xiaoren (mean people)! When nobody applied ingenuity, human nature was not lost; nobody was greedy, so everybody was pure and simple; purity and simplicity preserved human nature. But when the so-called sages appeared, who persisted in the pursuit of benevolence and righteousness, people in the world became perplexed; they formulated complicated and tedious rituals and music, then human discrimination emerged.*"[1]

Under this circumstance, the society became too intrinsically complex to be governed, the crux of which was that too much greediness and ingenuity were involved.

P2-5 Less selfishness, fewer desires and seeking plainness and simplicity are the inevitable course to the spontaneous and natural state of life.

Quotes from *Laozi*:

The soul and the form can be combined as one, but can they be forever combined and never sever? Depend on the natural organism and gather the vital essence so as to be soft and tender, but can it be like the baby? ... When you use your

---

1 Chen Guying. *New Annotated Translation of Zhuangzi*. Commercial Press, 2007, p.293.

senses, can you be quiet and indifferent to the attraction of beauty? (Chapter 10)

The ancient people, deft in practising the Dao ... are honest and simple, just like the unpolished lumber... (Chapter 15)

If the rulers could get rid of their sophistry, the people could have a hundred times of benefit; if the rulers could get rid of their falsity, the people's piety and affection could be recovered; if the rulers could forsake the swindling of material things, robbery and theft would vanish from this world. Sophistry, falsity and swindling are the three superficial embellishments, which could not be applied to governing the country. Therefore, if the rulers intend to make the people serve them willingly, they should try their best to retain simplicity and honesty, to discard selfish desires, and to be content with ignorance, and there will be no anxieties. (Chapter 19)

Being the valley of the world, you will no longer lack the eternal virtue, and return to simplicity. (Chapter 28)

The Dao is forever nameless and simple in nature. (Chapter 32)

If natural growth leads to greed, I will contain it by using the Dao. (Chapter 37)

(Therefore,) the true men should be honest and sincere, but not frivolous; and they should be honest and reliable, but not superficial. The true men should discard superficiality and keep sincerity. (Chapter 38)

So you should not desire the magnificence of the jade, but the firmness of the rock. (Chapter 39)

Proof: According to P2-4, greed and ingenuity make human society run against the spontaneous and natural state of life. And from D7 we can see that "being unselfish" means the psychological state of tolerating all the things in the universe Man reaches after eliminating excessive "desire" and ingenious "wisdom." Having less selfishness and fewer desires, and seeking purity and simplicity are all conducts needed in the elimination of excessive "desire" and ingenious "wisdom." Therefore, having less selfishness and fewer desires, and seeking purity and simplicity are the inevitable way of reaching the spontaneous and natural state of life.

Explanation: Greed and ingenuity and their interaction are not in conformity with the spirit of the Great Dao, and also run in the opposite direction of the spontaneous and natural state of life. When all these are eliminated through the self-cultivation of having less selfishness and fewer desires, and seeking plainness and simplicity, Man will recover his naturalness of the soul. "Less selfishness and fewer desires" and "seeking plainness and simplicity" are a way of self-cultivation. Laozi put forward to rectify the social and moral malpractices prevailing at that time. Laozi noted that such moral ideologies as benevolence and righteousness were originally used to persuade people into doing good, but in reality, they turned out to be pretentious and fraudulent, or even they were taken advantage of by some people to gain fame and wealth under their name. Laozi thought that it was better to get rid of the semblance taken advantage of by others and regain the natural morality of Man. In "Quqie (Stealing)" of *Zhuangzi*, Zhuangzi said, "*If all the people are wise enough, the world will not be in chaos; if all the people are restrained and clever, the world will not suffer hardships; if all the people are ingenious, the world will not be bewildered; and if all the people are virtuous, the world will not be pathogenic.*"[1]

P2-6 Being contented and knowing where to stop will result in long standing, while greed and insatiability will invite misfortune.

Quotes from *Laozi:*

Those who are content are rich. (Chapter 33)

Excessive covet for fame means the loss of wealth; and excessive amassment of wealth will give rise to great loss of health. Therefore he who is content need fear no shame, and he who knows when to stop incurs no blame. From danger free, long live shall he. (Chapter 44)

No disaster can be greater than that of insatiability; no sin can be greater than that of avarice. Therefore, the everlasting satiation is the satiation of the innermost being. (Chapter 46)

Proof: According to P2-5, being devoid of selfishness and desires, and keeping plainness and simplicity are the inevitable choice for reaching the spontaneous and natural state of life. And knowing contentment and where to stop is the manifestation of being devoid of selfishness and desires, and of keeping plainness and simplicity, while greed and insatiability go against this. According to A5, the basic way of keeping fit is to eliminate excessive "desires" and ingenuous "wisdom," or else there will be harm to one's own health or even to one's life. Therefore, knowing contentment and where to stop will result in long standing, while greed and insatiability will invite misfortune.

Explanation: "Less selfishness and fewer desires" advocated by Laozi does not mean eliminating all private desires, but asserting indifference to fame or gain

---

1 Chen Guying. *New Annotated Translation of Zhuangzi*. Commercial Press, 2007, p.308.

confining them within a certain limit so as to keep the soul in a state of relative "emptiness and tranquillity." We should confine private desires within a certain limit, and no matter what we do, we should know when and where to stop before going too far, and that is "knowing contentment and where to stop." Lessons of this kind were not few in history. For example, Zhangsun Wuji (594-659) of the Tang Dynasty was born to an eminent and powerful family. His sister was the empress of Li Shimin, Emperor Taizong of the Tang Dynasty. Zhangsun Wuji himself was twice prime minister during the reigns of Emperor Taizong and Emperor Gaozong. During the Yonghui period of the Tang Dynasty (649-655), he participated in imperial administration as the Emperor's maternal uncle. However, a false accusation was lodged against this powerful and distinguished man by Empress Wu Zetian. He was then exiled to Qianzhou, roughly present-day Guizhou Province, and forced to commit suicide. Zhangsun Wuji's doomed fate of death was the consequence of his own excessive greed for power. In the feudal society, any relative in power of a ruler or a king or an emperor on his mother's or wife's side was prone to be a target for attack. Empress Wende (Empress Zhangsun), his younger sister, repeatedly requested him to refrain from his post, but he did not quite catch her good intentions. Out of his personal gains, he supported a mediocrity to ascend the throne. When he was in office and power, he started to get rid of dissidents and attacked his fellow-officials. Eventually, he himself suffered persecution. He was obsessed with power, and spared no effort to secure and consolidate his position, only to suffer a miserable end of life.

Another example is Hu Weiyong in the Ming Dynasty. In his early years, he followed Zhu Yuanzhang, the first emperor of the Ming Dynasty, and received favour from the emperor. In the 10th year of Hongwu period (1377), Hu Weiyong was promoted to the prime minister, head of all the other officials. With the constant increase of his power, he became gradually overbearing and unbridled, and decided without permission who was to be promoted or demoted, and who was to be used or killed. When he learned that General Xu Da showed dissatisfaction with him, as Xu disclosed his evil deeds in a memorial to Emperor Zhu Yuanzhang, he enticed Fushou, Xu's janitor, into killing Xu Da. Fushou did not listen to him instead, and even disclosed it, so his plan failed. Hu Weiyong also drew by every possible means Lu Zhongheng, an official in Ji'an, and Fei Ju, an official in Pingliang, to his side. The two officials were both condemned by Emperor Zhu Yuanzhang because of crimes. Hu Weiyong ordered them to gather soldiers and horses and sought chances to rebel. In the first month of the 13th year of Hongwu period, Emperor Zhu Yuanzhang put Hu Weiyong to death.

P2-7 To conduct yourself in society in a soft and tender manner is the way to safeguard the spontaneous and natural state of life.

Quotes from *Laozi*:

The movement of the Dao is in endless recursion; the function of the Dao is in its soft and tender manner. (Chapter 40)

The person with profound virtue is just like an infant boy, whom bees, scorpions and serpents cannot bite, and whom fierce birds and beasts of prey cannot attack. His bones are weak but his fists are firm. (Chapter 55)

Proof: From D14, we can see that "to be soft and tender" is an attitude or conduct that does not deliberately make known your strength, which is a good way to keep moderation. According to Assumption 5 and P2-4, "keeping moderation" can help to keep the balance between Man and Man and between Man and his external world, while greed and ingenious wisdom make human society go against the spontaneous and natural state of life. Therefore, to conduct yourself in society in a soft and tender manner is the way to safeguard your spontaneous and natural state of life.

Explanation: To socialize in a soft and tender manner is, in fact, to eliminate personal desire, ingenious wisdom and prejudice. Zhu Yuanzhang went to extremes to kill his ministers with great achievements, of whom only Tang He alone narrowly escaped. How could Tang survive? Because he stooped to compromise and lived a life of obscurity. The reason why others were put to death was that they were either unruly and haughty, or arrogant and proud of their attainment, or criticized the emperor's faults frankly, etc. Xu Da was modest and not proud, but he was wiser and braver than most of his peers, with his achievements greater than those of the emperor. So Zhu Yuanzhang was not happy with him, and felt worried about him. When he was suffering from poisonous carbuncle, he was killed by eating the steamed goose offered by the emperor, because goose would make his carbuncle worse and spread to the whole body.

P2-8 To be soft and tender is the way to generate and regenerate, while to be hard and stiff is apt to break.

Quotes from *Laozi*:

The softest in the world can go through the hardest in the world. The formless force can penetrate anything that has no crevices. I thus know the benefit of "inaction." Few in the world can practice wordless instructions and the advantage of non-action. (Chapter 43)

When alive the human body is supple and weak, while dead, firm and stiff. So is

CHAPTER FOUR: On Cherishing Virtue

it with all things. When growing the plants are soft and fragile, while dead, withered and dry. Thus it is that firmness and strength are the concomitants of death; softness and weakness, the concomitants of life. Therefore, if you throw your weight and act violently in the battlefields, you will be destroyed, and if the tree is tall and strong, it will be felled down. Those that are strong will stay under, while those that are weak will stay above. (Chapter 76)

In this world there is nothing softer than water, which has seen no rival in wearing away hard things, because there is no other thing that can take its place. The weak is stronger than the strong, and the soft is harder than the hard. There is nobody who does not know this in the world, but nobody will practise it. (Chapter 78)

Proof: According to P2-7, to conduct oneself in society in a soft and tender manner is a way of keeping the spontaneous and natural state of life. To be soft and tender helps you to follow nature, and elongate your life; while to be hard and stiff is apt to exhaust your life, and cause conflicts. According to Assumption 5, "keeping moderation" can keep the balance between Man and Man, and between Man and the external world. The basic method to keep fit is to eliminate excessive "desires" and ingenious "wisdom." Therefore, to be soft and tender is the way to generate and regenerate, while to be hard and stiff is apt to break.

Explanation: On his deathbed, Zichan entrusted bosom friends his ideas of administration, and advised them, "There are no more than two ways of governance: the soft and tender way and the hard and stiff way. The nature of being hard and being soft is just like the nature of water and fire. Fire is fierce, so people hold it in awe and avoid approaching it, so that, few people die of fire; when it comes to water, things are different. Water is mild, and people are not afraid of it, so a large number of people die in water. In accordance, it seems to be easy to carry out mild politics, but, in fact, it is extremely difficult when you implement it." As a matter of fact, Zichan had already balanced the hard and stiff and the soft and tender, so he could govern the states with both force and mercy.[1]

P2-9 "To stay in the lowest place and be non-competitive" is the manifestation of conducting yourself in society in a soft and tender manner.

Quotes from *Laozi:*

The perfect goodness is like water. Water is good at benefiting all things,

---

1 Chang Hua. *A Book of Laozi's Wisdom.* Petroleum Industry Press, 2007, p.255.

but does not contend with them. It prefers to dwell in places the masses of people detest, therefore it is closest to the Dao. The person of perfect goodness is expert in choosing the right place for living, in keeping calm and quiet at heart, in treating others in a sincere and friendly manner, in making creditable and reliable promises, in doing sophisticated administrative affairs, in tackling businesses discreetly, and in taking action promptly. Because of the good person's virtue of being non-competitive, nobody will harbor resentment for him.* (Chapter 8)

Proof: From D11 we can see that "to be non-competitive" indicates the attitude of conducting yourself in society after the elimination of excessive "desires" and ingenious "wisdom." According to P2-7 and Basic Assumption 5, to conduct yourself in society in a soft and tender manner is the way to safeguard the spontaneous and natural state of life, and "keeping moderation" can help to keep the balance between Man and Man and between Man and his external world. "Keeping moderation" here will function as a guide to the conduct of "staying in the lowest place and being non-competitive." According to A4, sages know the Dao, but they "do not compete with each other." Therefore, "to stay in the lowest place and be non-competitive" is the manifestation of conducting yourself in society in a soft and tender manner.

Explanation: Finding that numerous conflicts were caused by people's excessive competition and lack of humility, Laozi put forward the way of treating others through staying in the lowest place and being non-competitive. In "Under the Heaven" of *Zhuangzi*, Zhuangzi said that Laozi *"thought that it is the external virtue to be soft and tender, to stay in the lowest place, and to be modest."* This is not only the means to avoid disasters, but also to protect ourselves. It is also an effective way to eliminate social conflicts. The detailed requirements of being modest and staying in the lowest place are: not showing off, or bragging, or being proud. "To be non-competitive" means not competing with others, nor being emulative, which is the attitude towards life that Laozi advocated. It was also Laozi's most significant method of keeping safe and avoiding disasters, and of defusing social contradictions. "To stay in the lowest place and be non-competitive" is an imitation of the Dao of Heaven.

P2-10 To behave in society in a soft and tender manner secures truly unremitting efforts to improve yourself.

Quotes from *Laozi*:

Eliminating learning and have no anxieties. Between the complimentary "Yea" and the absent-minded "nay" how much difference is there? Between the virtuous and the evil how great is the distance? What the average people fear is also what I fear. The difference between the average people and me is radical and unlimited! The average people go into raptures as if they were attending a sumptuous feast, or as if they were scaling the heights to get a better view of the scenery. I do not try to seek fame and wealth, nor do I live a noisy life. I have never experienced any indication of these, just like an infant baby who does not know what happiness is and what woe is. I am so unsociable as if I belonged nowhere. The multitude of people all have surplus. I alone seem to be in want. My mind is that of a fool—ignorant and stupid. The average people look bright and intelligent, only I am a real "fool" and muddle-headed. My heart is of equanimity like the unruffled sea surface without end. The masses all have their reasons for acting, while I alone seem stupid and incapable like a rustic. Thus I alone am different from other people, but I have the nursing Mother Dao with me. (Chapter 20)

If you can observe the details of things, you are fair and just, and if you can follow the tenderness of nature, you are strong. (Chapter 52)

Mercy makes me brave, thrifty makes me generous, and not being arrogant towards others makes me the leader of everything in the world. Therefore, if I discard kindness and pursue bravery, or discard thrifty and pursue generosity, or discard concession and pursue arrogance, there will be no way out for me! (Chapter 67)

Proof: According to P2-7, to conduct yourself in society in a soft and tender manner is the way to safeguard the spontaneous and natural state of life. According to Basic Assumptions 3 and 5, the unity of "non-being" and "being" is the perfect state of the Dao; and the ideal state of human cognition and conduct is "keeping moderation," that is, being aware of "being" while abiding by "non-being." To conduct yourself in society in a soft and tender manner is the manifestation of "keeping moderation," which promotes the balance between Man and Man, and Man and the external world. Therefore, to conduct yourself in society in a soft and tender manner secures truly unremitting efforts to improve yourself.

Explanation: From the empirical world, Laozi observed: anything that is seemingly soft and tender may be full of vitality and have the potentiality to develop, and anything that is seemingly hard and stiff may well go downhill. In this world, there is nothing that is softer and tenderer than water, but anything that is hard and stiff cannot change the nature of water; water is the softest but the hardest. In human society, it is also the case. In the Chinese history, the person who was versed in *Huang-Lao zhi Shu*, or the Art of Huangdi and Laozi, and in dealing with all kinds of situations was Chen Ping of the Han Dynasty. He was quite familiar with the nature of water. At that time, the counselors and talented generals were not few at the side of Liu Bang, Emperor Gaozu of the Han Dynasty, of whom some were valiant warriors, but only Chen Ping was put in an important position by Liu Bang. His family background was not as good as Zhang Liang's. Zhang Liang was an aristocrat, while Chen Ping's family was poverty-stricken. How could a young man of humble birth, and of a home with four bare walls, win the appreciation of a great hero? Only because Chen Ping had a soft and tender character of water, was able to absorb knowledge from reading, and was good at studying the art of the Yellow Emperor and Laozi. Chen Ping often visited and sought advice from senior scholars and celebrities, as he believed in the saying that "One should read a myriad books, and travel a myriad miles," in order to broaden his horizon, expand his vision, and enrich his own experience for the purpose of supporting the Han Imperial Family, and of wiping out the Lü's family. He successfully served the three emperors of Gaozu, Emperor Huidi and Emperor Wendi of the Han Dynasty, and ended well.

P2-11 Those who cherish virtue will show the human dignity of "keeping moderate."

Quotes from *Laozi*:

The ancient people, who were deft in practising the Dao, were wondrously sensible and understood the ways of the world; and they were so profound that people felt difficult to understand them. It is because they were so profound that they can only be given a make-do description: They are hesitant and cautious, just as they are wading across the river; They are cautious and vigilant, just as they are afraid of the attacks from their neighbors; They are reserved and serious, just as they are visiting others as guests; They are lax in discipline, just as the thawing ice; They are honest and simple, just like the unpolished lumber; They are broad-minded and unprejudiced, just like the valleys and vales in the mountains; Their mind is in a whirl, just like the turbid water. Who can become quiet when in motion and gradually become crystal clear? Who can become calm and seek changes when everything is quiet? The people who abide by the natural Dao are not self-conceited. Just because they are not conceited, they are willing to eradicate the old and foster the new. (Chapter 15)

Proof: From D1, we see that the "Virtue" is a general term of the spontaneous process of all the things in the universe from "non-being" to "being" and back to "non-being;" it also means the understanding of the process and the human personality of following the process. Those who cherish the Virtue are thus called the people who respect the Dao. According to Basic Assumption 5, the ideal state of human cognition and conduct is "keeping moderate," which is in agreement with the spontaneous and natural process. Therefore, those who cherish the Virtue will show the personality of "keeping moderate."

Explanation: Those who cherish the Virtue enjoy good personality cultivation and psychological diathesis, and they apparently seem to be quiet and do nothing, but, in fact, they have great potential, and are creative without showing off. In history, Guigu Zi, alias Wang Xu, was quite well-known during the Spring and Autumn Period. He often went up to Mount Yunmeng to collect herbs and to cultivate his spiritual and religious life up there. As he lived a hermit life in the place called Guigu near Qingxi, hence the name Mr. Guigu. He was the teacher of Sun Bin and Pang Juan, and of Su Qin and Zhang Yi, enjoying a high reputation. But except for masterpieces of his, little was known of his life.

P2-12 Those who cherish the virtue can reach clarification by way of "observation" so as to realize the truth of the Dao.

Quotes from *Laozi*:

Without going out of the door, you can know what is happening in the world; without looking out of the window, you can see the law of nature. The farther you go, the less you know. Therefore, the Sages do not have to experience so as to know, they do not have to see with their own eyes to understand, and they succeed by non-action. (Chapter 47)

As to seeking knowledge, the desire should increase with each passing day; as to seeking the Way, the desire should decrease with each passing day. Day after day, it is finally reduced to the state of "non-action." (Chapter 48)

Proof: From D4, we can see that the *"guan,"* meaning viewing or observing things or examining oneself, is the way to know Dao. *Ming*, which means discernment, refers to the self-observation and self-reflective ability of inner human vitality. And the path to human knowledge of the Dao. *"Ming"* is the self-reflective ability of the human innate life force. *"Guan"* is the path to *"Ming."* According to A2 and P2-11, if you start from the *"zhi"* into the *"ming,"* you can know the Dao; those who cherish the De will manifest the personality of "keeping moderate," so as to rightly know the Dao by going into the *"ming"* from the *"zhi."* Therefore, those who cherish the virtue or De can reach clarification by way of *"guan"* so as to realize the truth of the Dao.

Explanation: The three major obstructions to human enlightenment of the Dao are as follows: greed, ingenious counterfeiting, and intentional prejudice. We have to renounce the above-mentioned obstructions so as to upgrade our soul by doing away with the narrow, closed confinement, and observe all the things in the universe and the true meaning of the universe with a broad, detached, and open mind, and only in this way can we understand the Dao. The soul is just like a mirror, with all the things in the universe contained in it. So we will have to clean the surface of the mirror in order to clearly see the various aspects of the human world. It is also true to the government of the state: follow its nature and the law, stabilize the people, and you will result in better governance.[1]

P2-13 Open-mindedness and modesty are the required character of those who cherish virtue.

Quotes from *Laozi*:

The ancient people, deft in practising the Dao... are broad-minded and unprejudiced, just like the valleys and vales in the mountains. (Chapter 15)

You know the strength of the masculine, but keep the tenderness of the feminine, and are willing to be the ravine of the world...You know the honor, but keep to the role of the disgraced, and are willing to be a valley of the world. (Chapter 28)

The lofty virtue is like deep valley. (Chapter 41)

Why is the sea a place where all the rivers converge? Because it stays low, and all the rivers can converge into it. (Chapter 66)

It is your merit if you know your own ignorance; it is your demerit if you do not know but appear to know it. The person with the Way does not have demerits, because he regards his demerits as demerits. And just because of this, he has no demerits. (Chapter 71)

Proof: According to P2-9, "to stay in the lowest place and be non-competitive" is the manifestation of conducting yourself in society in the soft and tender manner, while open-mindedness and modesty are the manifestation of generosity, broad-mindedness, and staying in the lowest place without competition. According to P2-1, it is the manifestation of the virtue to follow the spontaneous and natural normality of life, so that those who cherish the Virtue should have the character of being open-minded and modest. Therefore, open-mindedness and modesty are the required

---

1 Chang Hua. *A Book of Laozi's Wisdom*. Petroleum Industry Press, 2007, p.38.

characters of those who cherish virtue.

Explanation: The great Dao has the characteristic of being "hollow" and "comprehensive," and is inclusive of all the things in the universe. "Those who are deft in practising the Dao" treat others in the same way as the open valley contains everything with its openness and comprehensiveness. "Under the Heaven" in *Zhuangzi* says that Laozi "is tolerant of things and does not haggle with others." Those who cherish virtue should be open-minded and modest, tolerate the intolerable, and not fastidious about others, so as to conciliate discrepancies and resentment with open-mindedness and generosity. Only in this way can they stand high in popular favour.[1] In the last years of the Western Han Dynasty, Wang Mang usurped the throne, but soon became unpopular. And uprisings took place here and there in succession. People still cherished the memory of the Han Dynasty, so in the uprising army, there were a number of people who claimed to be from the Han-dynasty imperial family. Liu Xiu revolted, also in the name of restoring the Han Dynasty, to set Liu Xuan up to the throne. Wang Lang, who had made a living by divination in Handan, now said that he was the son of Emperor Cheng of the Han Dynasty. He assumed the title of Emperor of the Han Dynasty and led his army to attack the neighboring cities and counties, causing an impressive momentum. At this time, Liu Xiu was on his way to the prefectures and counties in Hebei to make an inspection tour as the minister of the court on behalf of the New Emperor Liu Xuan. Wang Lang offered a reward to catch him, and Liu Xiu fled in haste. All the counties and prefectures in Hebei surrendered to Wang Lang. Liu Xiu then gathered his troops. Liu Xiu rallied his forces, and after several fierce battles, he finally captured Handan, where Wang Lang was defeated and killed. Liu Xiu checked his correspondence documents and found that there were thousands of letters written by his officials to Wang Lang. Many of them were apt to undermine and slander Liu Xiu. The officials around Liu Xiu advised him to find them out and punish them strictly. Liu Xiu didn't accept their advice. One day, he called them all together into the main hall and asked his subordinates to burn those letters, and said: "Now you can feel at ease!" Everyone bowed down on the ground, feeling very grateful to Liu Xiu for letting them go.[2]

---

1 Chen Guying. *Comments on Laozi's Biography*. Nanjing University Press, p.266.
2 Xiao Long. *A Complete Work of Laozi's Wisdom in Dealing with World Affairs*. Seismological Press, 2007, pp.121-122.

P2-14   It is required to follow the spontaneous and natural normality of life in the realization of virtuous governance of the family, the state, and the world.

Quotes from *Laozi*:

If you apply this principle to individuals, his Virtue will be true; if to families, his Virtue will be plentiful; if to villages, his Virtue will be respected; if to the whole nation, his Virtue will be abundant; and if to the whole world, his Virtue will be great. Therefore, we should scrutinize the individuals with the Way of cultivating personal moral character, the families with the Way of regulating families, the villages with the Way of living together in peace and unity, the nation with the Way of governing the state, and the world with the Way of making peace in the whole world. How can I know the affairs of the world? By using this principle. (Chapter 54)

Proof: It can be known from Definition 1 that De (virtue) is the generic term of the process for all things that act without interference from "non-being" to "being" and then back to "non-being," and also refers to man's understanding of the process and the conduct that adapt to this process. The home, the country, and the world all have their own operating rules, showing their respective living conditions. According to P2-1, conforming to the self-contained normal state is the embodiment of virtue. Therefore, to achieve the rule of virtue in governance of the family, the country, and the world, we need to conform to the normal state of life.

Explanation: Wang Bi's comment on "Use the individual to examine other individuals, use the family to examine the family of others, use the village to examine other villages, use the state to examine other states" is: There is a commonality between different individuals. As far as "my own individual" is concerned, my own individual is like this, and the other individuals are the same. Therefore, from my own self, I can inspect others. The same is true of my family and other families, of my villages and other villages, of my state and the state of others. All should be treated as such. This kind of analogical reasoning method of "observing things" enables us to understand the governance of the family, the country and the world. We need to conform to the principle of being at ease as the normal state of life, which helps us break the ego and surpass ourselves, so as to understand and deal with everything from a wider perspective.

P2-15   The success of the sages is to assist the common people to return to the spontaneous and natural normality of life.

Quotes from *Laozi*:

The Sages have no preconceived ideas; they will regard the ideas of the common people as their own. The kind people, I treat them kindly; the unkind people, I treat them kindly as well. And in this way, I attain kindness. The trustworthy people, I trust them; the untrustworthy people, I trust them as well. And in this way, I attain trustworthiness. In front of the common people, the Sages are amiable. And, for the sake of the common people, they appear to be slow-witted. And the common people carefully look at them and listen to them, while the sages treat them in the same way as they treat their children. (Chapter 49)

Therefore, the Sages pursue what the average people do not pursue, and do not covet rare goods; they learn what the average people do not learn, so as to remedy the faults of the average people. The Sages just follow the law of nature, and do not intervene it. (Chapter 64)

Proof: From Definition 8 and Definition 9, we can see that as a ruling person of virtue, the sage has his merits reflected in the activities that consciously maintain a social order conforming to "naturalness." According to A1 and P2-4, "naturalness" is the self-satisfaction and spontaneous process from "non-being" to "being" and again back to "non-being," while the rule of virtue in governance of the family, the country, and the world advocated by sages needs to be adapted to the self-contained normal state of life. Therefore, the merits of the sages are to help the people return to their own normal state of life.

Explanation: "Sage" is the one who is the right person in Laozi's ideal. He thinks about what the people think about and meets the needs of the people. *"The Sages have no preconceived ideas; they will regard the ideas of the common people as their own"* advocated by *Laozi* is the great consciousness of public servants and a dedication spirit of fairnes and grandeur. The sage emulates the natural law of the operation of the heaven and the earth, abandons all the regulations and norms that bind and influence the free movements of the human body and mind, handles the affairs of human life with the attitude and principle of "inaction," and implements the wordless teaching to let people follow their own natural nature. He never interferes with people's normal life. If the sage governs the society with such attitudes and principles, he will not bring harm to the people. People will not feel the oppression of power, so that they can better develop their own self-cultivation and the governance thus receives the best results. "Heaven and Earth," *Zhuangzi* so narrates the story: Bocheng Zigao, who had been made a governor in Yao's rule, resigned his commission and began farming when the throne was passed to Yu. When Yu asked why he resigned his commission, Zigao said, "In the past, when Yao ruled the state, people worked peacefully, although he gave no rewards; the people were in awe of him, although he gave out no punishments. Now, you exercise rewards and punishments but the people are not benevolent. Virtue will now decay and punishment will prevail. The chaos of the age to come has its origin here and now."[1]

P2-16 The sages make their accomplishments by inaction.

Quotes from *Laozi*:

If he does something grudgingly in order to govern the world, I don't think he will be successful. As the world is a sacred thing, no force can be placed on it, and no grasp can be placed on it. Otherwise it will cause failure or lose. People in the world have different dispositions. Some take the lead, or some follow others; some are slowpokes, or some are impetuous; some are strong, or some are feeble; some are self-loving, or some are feeble. Therefore, the Sage should dislodge the extreme, luxurious and excessive measures. (Chapter 29)

The Dao follows the course of nature, but there is nothing it does not do. If the princes and marquises want to maintain it, all things in the universe will grow naturally. If natural growth leads to greed, I will contain it by using the Dao. If I contain it by using the Dao, there will be no greed in the world. If there is no greed, they will become calm and quiet, and accordingly, the world will naturally return to the state of peace. (Chapter 37)

Without going out of the door, you can know what is happening in the world; without looking out of the window, you can see the law of nature. The farther you go, the less you know. Therefore, the Sages do not have to experience so as to know, they do not have to see with their own eyes to understand, and they succeed by non-action. (Chapter 47)

Proof: From D10, "inaction" or "non-action" refers to the principle of action that conforms to "naturalness" and is not deliberately and recklessly taken. According to P2-15 and A3, the sage's merit is to help the people return to their own normal state of life, and the basic idea is to achieve success from "non-action" and "action." Therefore, the sages make their accomplishments by non-action.

Explanation: Heavenly Dao has the function of both creation and parenting for all things, but these are carried out by nature, neither intentionally nor utilitarianly. This non-action is a virtue and a means for the sage to govern the world. In the primitive clan society, the means of production were collectively owned, and members of the clan worked together to distribute the means of subsistence equally. The ancient sages managed production and public affairs, but never occupied the fruits of the

---

1 Chen Guying. *New Annotated Translation of Zhuangzi*. Commercial Press, 2007, p.362.

people's labor. Although they had the right to make decisions, they represented public consciousness. This is consistent with the spirit of the Dao, "*Although the Dao generates them and the Virtue nurtures them, they do not take all things in the universe as their own, but let them grow naturally.*"

P2-17 To be unselfish is the inevitable requirement for the deeds of sages.

Quotes from *Laozi*:

Heaven and earth are unbiased, and let all things in the universe grow naturally; the sage is unbiased, and let the people develop themselves. It is very much like the bellows, the space between Heaven and Earth. The more vacuous it is, the more inexhaustible it will be; and the more it moves, the more air it will emit. The more you show off, the faster you will decline. So it is better to keep vacuity and quietness in your heart. (Chapter 5)

Heaven is long-enduring and earth continues long. The reason why heaven and earth are able to endure and continue thus long is because they do not live of, or for, themselves. Therefore, the Sages retreat to the back, but win the respect of others; they seldom consider for themselves, but keep themselves safe and sound. Isn't it because they are not selfish that they attain what they ought to attain? (Chapter 7)

Proof: According to P2-16 and A3, the sages make their accomplishments by non-action. The "non-action" here means adapting to nature, not deliberately acting, or not acting rashly. It is also known from D7 that "selflessness" refers to the mental state of being able to contain all things that is achieved after eliminating excessive "desire" and ingenious "intelligence." Under this state of mind, we can truly avoid acting deliberately and rashly. Therefore, selflessness is an inevitable requirement for sages to achieve their merits.

Explanation: The sage's selflessness stems from his great kindness. He extends this kind of loving heart to all things in the world. This selflessness of sage reflects the basic spirit of Dao, that is, to assist all things to develop by themselves, and not to take credit for his own. This kind of unconditional giving, without expecting anything in return, can be called the "giving virtue." Only the real virtuous people, the sages, can have this "giving virtue" and give everything they have to the people in the world. The sage has "no obsessiveness," "no fame" or even "no self." He never takes himself seriously but puts the whole country in his heart and does everything for the people.

Although he does not ask for any return, he is loved by the people. Only with selflessness can we truly own ourselves and gain respect from others. Selfishness, despite its petty gain, causes the loss of many opportunities for great things. There is no concept of "selfishness" in the heart of a sage, so he can accomplish his work. During the Spring and Autumn Period, Duke Ping of Jin once asked Qi Huangyang, the minister of Jin, "Nanyang county needs a governor, who is appropriate for it?" Qi Huangyang answered without hesitation, "Xie Hu is the most appropriate. He is sure to be competent!" "Isn't Xie Hu your enemy? Why do you recommend him?" Qi Huangyang answered, "You only ask me who is qualified and who is the best. You didn't ask me if Xie Hu was my enemy."[1] It can be said that Qi Huangyang's behavior reflects a kind of spirit of "Public business comes before private affairs" or "selflessness."

P2-18   Compassion, thrifty, and not presuming to take the lead in the world, are the daily practice of the sages to achieve their merits.

Quotes from *Laozi:*

Therefore, if the Sage is to be the leader of the people, he should be modest towards them; if he wants to be the model of the people, he must put his own benefit after that of the people. Therefore, the Sage rules over the people, but the people do not feel bearing a heavy burden; he stands in front of the people, but they do not feel exploited. Therefore, the people show respect to the Sage, but not detest or reject him. He does not compete with others, and there is nobody to compete with him. (Chapter 66)

I have three treasures which I hold tight and protect. The first treasure is mercy, the second is thrifty, and the third is not presuming to take the lead in the world. Mercy makes me brave, thrifty makes me generous, and not being arrogant towards others makes me the leader of everything in the world. Therefore, if I discard kindness and pursue bravery, or discard thrifty and pursue generosity, or discard concession and pursue arrogance, there will be no way out for me! If you put your kindness in the battle, you will be victorious; if you put mercy in defending the country, it will become consolidated. If Heaven determines to help anybody, it will protect him with mercy. (Chapter 67)

In this world there is nothing softer than water, which has seen no rival in wearing away hard things, because there is no other thing that can take its place. The weak is stronger than the strong, and the soft is harder than the hard. There is nobody who does not know this in the world, but nobody will practise it. Therefore,

---

1   Chang Hua. *A Book of Laozi's Wisdom*. Petroleum Industry Press, 2007, pp.18-19.

the Sage says, "Those who can bear the whole nation's contempt can be called the nation's true rulers; those who can stand the whole nation's disasters have the qualification of being the rulers of the nation." What the Dao expresses seem to be just the opposite.* (Chapter 78)

Proof: According to Definition 13, compassion defines the quality of universal love, which is soft and gentle. Frugality defines the quality of temperance, which is tough but not proud. Not presuming to take the lead means staying low and not contending. Compassion, frugality and not presuming to take the lead in the empire are the normal state of natural being. According to P2-15 and P2-17, the merit of the sage lies in assisting the people to return to the normal state of life in which they are free and independent, without having a preference for various things. Therefore, it can be seen that compassion, frugality and not presuming to take the lead in the empire are the daily practices of sages to accomplish their merits.

Explanation: The three virtues, "compassion," "frugality" and "not presuming to take the lead in the empire" constitute the "three treasures" of Laozi, which become the creed of the sages' behavior and the wisdom of treating things. Once, when Yanzi (578-500 BC), the famous prime minister of the State of Qi just started to have meal, the messenger sent by Duke Jing of Qi arrived. Then Yanzi shared his meal with the messenger. As a result, the messenger did not eat enough, and Yanzi himself did not eat enough either. After the messenger returned to the palace, he told Duke Jing about it. Duke Jing said: "Alas! Yanzi is living such a poor life. I don't know it at all. This is my fault!" So he sent an official to give Yanzi 1000 *yi* (ancient weight unit, one *yi* equals about one kilogram) of gold to entertain guests, but Yanzi rejected it. Duke Jing sent the money to him again and again, but Yanzi still refused to accept it, saying: "My family is not impoverished! Your reward reports my paternal clan, my maternal clan and my wife's clan, and also extends to my friends. I also use it to help the people. What you, my lord, has given me is very generous! I heard that if a minister get too much property from the lord, and give it to the people, it is to replace the lord to rule the people. A loyal minister can't do this. If we get too much property from the lord, and don't benefit the people with the property, we will be like a bamboo box for storing money. The benevolent people won't do this kind of thing. If one accepts too much property from the lord, then he will offend the scholars. After he died, the money would be transferred to other people's hands. This is to collect money for others. Smart people won't do this kind of thing. Now I have rough cloth and food enough for my living." Duke Jing said to Yanzi, "My ancestor Duke Huan rewarded his prime minister Guan Zhong five hundred *she* (an ancient community including 25 families), and he accepted it without hesitation. Why did you reject my reward?" Yanzi said: "I have heard that even the sage who thinks a thousand times must lose one. Even a fool who worries a thousand times will gain a penny. Maybe what Guan Zhong did wrong is what I'm doing right. So I thank you again for your grace and dare not accept your reward."[1]

P2-19   Treating things equally is the key to the achievement of the sages.

Quotes from *Laozi*:

Those who are good at walking will leave no traces; those who are good at talking will have no blunders; those who are good at calculating will not use chips in their counting; those who are good at closing will not open it without locks or keys; those who are good at binding will not undo it without ropes or cables. Therefore, the Sage is adept in giving full scope to the talents, and there is nobody who is abandoned; they will turn material resources to good account, and there is nothing that is discarded. And that is called "complying with the eternal Dao." Therefore, the well-doer can be well-doers' teacher, and the ill-doer can be the well-doers' wealth. Those who refuse to respect their teachers and do not treasure their wealth may think of themselves as being wise, but in fact, they are sheer blunderers. This is the truth that is comprehensive and profound. (Chapter 27)

The Sages have no preconceived ideas; they will regard the ideas of the common people as their own. The kind people, I treat them kindly; the unkind people, I treat them kindly as well. And in this way, I attain kindness. The trustworthy people, I trust them; the untrustworthy people, I trust them as well. And in this way, I attain trustworthiness. (Chapter 49)

How can the unkind man desert Dao? (Chapter 62)

What is serious comes from what is trivial, and what is plenty results from what is scanty. You should offer virtue in return for grudge. (Chapter 63)

To conciliate a great hatred, there is bound to be resentment left over. Therefore, the Sage keeps the stub of the receipt for the loan, not intending to demand its repay. The person with the Virtue is as rich as the person who keeps the stub of the receipt for the loan, while the person without the Virtue is as exacting as the person who is in charge of the taxes. The law of nature is unbiased, and will go with the good person. (Chapter 79)

The Sage who has gained the Way will not have private collection of things. He

---

1   Xiao Long. *A Complete Work of Laozi' Wisdom in Dealing with World Affairs*. Seismological Press, 2007, pp.73-74.

is willing enough to help others, thus making himself even more abundant; he gives as much as he can to others, thus making himself even richer. (Chapter 81)

Proof: According to P2-18, it can be seen that compassion, frugality and not presuming to take the lead in the empire are the daily practices of sages to make accomplishments. The first of these is fraternity, which means that universal love is the priority in the daily practice of sages. According to P2-15, the merit of the sage lies in assisting the people in returning to the normal state of life in which they are free and independent, without having a preference for various things. Therefore, treating things as equals is the key to a sage's achievement.

Explanation: Taking "compassion" as a treasure shows that Laozi was full of love for human beings and has an immense sense of responsibility for society. The basic requirement of "compassion" is to be kind to others. It is hard to be kind to people who are not good. If you are kind to people who are not good, you will often resolve conflicts easily. A story goes in Liu Xiang's *Xin Xu* or *New Preface*: Liang and Chu are two states adjacent to each other, and there were melons on the border of both states. People of Liang were diligent in irrigation, so their melons grew well. However, the Chu people were lazy and the melons did not grow well. The Chu people were jealous and destroyed many melons of the Liang people in the middle of the night. The chief officer of Liang did not allow their subordinates to retaliate. Instead, he secretly ordered them to water the melons of the Chu people every night. As a result, the melons of Chu grew better and better. They found out that it was the Liang people who did it and then reported it to the king of Chu. The king of Chu felt ashamed and sent people to Liang to plead guilty. Since then, the two countries resumed good relationship and the border was in peace.[1]

P2-20 Grasping the unity of "non-being" and "being" is the way for sages to make achievements.

Quotes from *Laozi:*

If you want to contract it, you should first expand it; if you want to weaken it, you should first strengthen it; if you want to discard it, you should first praise it; if you want to seize it, you should first offer it. That is the sign that is both faint and obvious. The tender is harder than the hard, and the weak is stronger than the strong. The fish cannot leave its water, and the weapons of a country cannot be shown to others. (Chapter 36)

---

1 Chen Guying. *Comments on Laozi's Biography*. Nanjing University Press, 2001, p. 270.

To behave with "non-action," to do things without disturbance, and to regard the tasteless as tasteful. What is serious comes from what is trivial, and what is plenty results from what is scanty. You should offer virtue in return for grudge. To deal with what is difficult, you should start from what is easy, and to aim high, you should be content in doing trivialities. All the great things in the world are done from the very tiny bits of things. Therefore, those with the Way will never be arrogant and conceited, and they can attain much. Those who make promise easily are sure to break their promises: if you take things as easy, you are sure to meet troubles. Therefore, the Sages would rather take things as difficult, and they will seldom be beaten by difficulties. (Chapter 63)

It is easy to control what is stable, and it is easy to deal with the situation before it has shown any sign. When it is weak, it is easy to break, and when it is small, it is easy to vanish. We have to make preparations before something actually takes place, and tackle it before a disaster has turned up. Huge trees grow from tiny seedlings; nine-storey towers are built with piles of earth; and a thousand miles of journey starts with the first step. If you want to achieve something, you may suffer defeats; if you want to seize something, you may lose it. Therefore, the Sages do not try to achieve anything, so that they will not suffer defeats; and they do not try to seize anything, so that they will lose nothing. For the average people, they often suffer defeats when it is almost done. Be as cautious about the end as about the beginning, and in this way, there will be no defeats. Therefore, the Sages pursue what the average people do not pursue, and do not covet rare goods; they learn what the average people do not learn, so as to remedy the faults of the average people. The Sages just follow the law of nature, and do not intervene with it. (Chapter 64)

Proof: According to P2-15, the merit of the sage lies in assisting the people in returning to the normal state of their own lives. According to P2-2 and Assumption 3, it is necessary to grasp the unity of "non-being" and "being" to conform to the normal state of life. Although the infinite possibility of "non-being" is in contradiction with the limited reality of "being," the unity of "non-being" and "being" is the perfect state of Dao. Therefore, to grasp the unity of "non-being" and "being" is the way for a sage to make accomplishments.

Explanation: Everything has its opposite, and at the same time it is formed by its opposite. Take the contradictory concepts for example: being and non-being, beauty and ugliness, good and evil, success and failure, right and wrong. Wu Cheng's *Annotations on Dao De Jing* says, "*The name of beauty and ugliness begets each other.*" In such a short book as *Laozi*, there are more than 80 pairs of these opposite and complimentary concepts. On the surface, the opposite sides are incompatible with each other. But after further observation and reflection, Laozi found that they are mutually inclusive and mutually infiltrating.[1] It is precisely because of this interrelationship that the inevitable trend of their transformation is to transform into each other, not to other things. For this reason, we should start with the subtleties of things and seize the opportunity of the opposite transformation to achieve success. Things always transform into opposites, from being to nothingness, from existence to death, or good governance to chaos. It is from this understanding that Laozi suggested that one should take precautions, check erroneous ideas at the outset and prevent problems beforehand. He emphasized that when at peace, we must be aware of the danger; when alive, we can't ignore death; when in good governance, we can't forget disorder. He asked people to start from difficulties and trivialities and take timely action. "Take measures before difficulties appear and take precaution before disorder comes."

In this way, it is easy to solve the problems. Otherwise, it will be quite difficult to solve the problem which becomes extreme urgency. *The Memorial to the Throne on the Accumulation of Resources*, *On Policies of Public Security* and *Disquisition Finding Fault with the State of Qin* (*Guo Qin Lun*), and *On the State of Qin*, and articles written by the famous politician Jia Yi (200-168 BC) in Western Han Dynasty, fully embody the sense of urgency that Laozi advocated, that is, to be prepared for danger in time of safety and aware of any eventualities in peace. Jia Yi believed that the national conditions in Western Han Dynasty were quite promising under the rule of the Emperor Wen, and that the rulers should have long-term view, reduce the power of the princes and dukes, increase grain storage, and be prepared for danger in safety and be alert to disorder in peace. They should start from some small things such as understanding etiquette, knowing shame and honor and loving the people so as to achieve long-term stability. After reading *The Memorial to the Throne on the Accumulation of Resources*, Emperor Wen of Han Dynasty thought that Jia Yi had made reasonable arguments and adopted his suggestion. He issued two orders in succession to promote the development of agriculture, and also took some measures to develop agricultural production. The Western Han Dynasty then gradually became stronger and prosperous.[2]

---

1 Chen Guying. *Comments on Laozi's Biography*. Nanjing University Press, 2001, pp.176-177.
2 Chang Hua. *A Book of Laozi's Wisdom*. Petroleum Industry Press, 2007, pp.205-206.

P2-21 It is to follow the Dao for the sage to withdraw when he has attained what he wants to attain.

Quotes from *Laozi*:

To keep full is not as good as to stop in time. To be pointed, it is hard to keep long. If the house is filled with gold and jade, nobody will be able to preserve them for good. If he is wealthy and arrogant, he will bring trouble to himself. It is only natural and rational that he should resign in a modest way when he has attained what he wants to attain. (Chapter 9)

He is free from self-display, and therefore he is illustrious; from self-assertion, and therefore he is distinguished; from self-boasting, and therefore he is meritorious; from self-complacency, and therefore he is enduring. (Chapter 22)

If you stand on your tiptoe, you cannot stand long; if you walk with big steps, you cannot walk far; if you stick to your own opinion, you cannot see things clearly; if you think you are always right, you cannot judge what is right and what is wrong. If you brag about yourself, you cannot achieve anything; if you are reserved, you cannot lead anybody. (Chapter 24)

Proof: According to P2-15, the sage's merit is to help the people return to their own normal state of life. By Axiom 1, "naturalness" is the spontaneous and self-satisfaction process from "non-being" to "being" and again back to "non-being." Success means achievements, and the return of human society to the spontaneous and free state of the Dao, in no need of any help. When all is accomplished, the sages can retreat. Therefore, to retreat after making achievements is the manifestation of the sages' following the Dao.

Explanation: In the face of fame and fortune, the common people tend to scramble for them. Greed for fame and fortune, and arrogance brought by wealth and a high position, often bring misfortune to them, just as what happened to Li Si. When Li Si was in office as the prime minister of the Qin Dynasty, he was extremely flaunting and arrogant, so he inevitably found himself in prison. *Records of the Grand Historian* writes that Cai Ze, a minister of the Qin State, met with Fan Sui, the prime minister of Qin, and persuaded him to withdraw from the political arena. He told him about the principles of "The full moon will wane and everything will decline at its prime." Cai Ze further warned him of the dangers of staying in high position and accumulating wealth for long time by quoting some famous epigrams like "In view of the water, we can see our faces. In view of the people, we can know the fortune and misfortune" and "One can't hold his power and wealth for long time when his work is accomplished."[1] Laozi took the political experience in history one step further, raising it to the philosophical height, that is: it is the Heavenly way to retreat after making achievements. Retreating after making achieve ments reflects the basic spirit of the Dao, and it is also the behavior of the sage's way to practice virtue.

P2-22　It is the nature of De (virtue) to conserve the natural normality of life and merge with all things in the universe.

Quotes from *Laozi*:

The man of the highest virtue does not claim to be of virtue, thus he is of the true virtue. The man of the lowest virtue always holds fast to the virtue in form, thus he is actually of no virtue. The man of the highest virtue never acts yet leaves nothing undone. (Chapter 38)

Although the Dao generates them and the Virtue nurtures them, they do not take all things in the universe as their own, but let them grow naturally. That is the greatest virtue. (Chapter 51)

The greatest virtue is profound and far-reaching. And together with things it returns. Thus we arrive at great conformity. (Chapter 65)

Proof: From D1, we can see that the virtue is a general term of the spontaneous and natural process of all the things in the universe from "non-being" to "being" and back to "non-being." It also indicates human understanding of the process and the character of following the process. According to A1 and P2-1, naturalness is a spontaneous and natural process of Dao in the universe from "non-being" to "being" and back to "non-being." It is the manifestation of virtue to comply with the spontaneous and natural normality of life. It means merging human life normality into all things. Therefore, it is the nature of virtue to conserve the natural normality of life and merge with all things in the universe.

Explanation: To conserve the spontaneous and natural normality of life, and to be closely related to all the things in the universe, are the manifestation of the Dao in human society, which is the virtue. During the Spring and Autumn Period, after Sun Wu and Wu Zixu helped Helü, the king of Wu, to ascend the throne, Sun Wu retreated and lived in reclusion, and wrote *The Art of War*. However, Wu Zixu was not able to retreat to live a carefree and natural life, but continued to assist Fuchai, the new king of Wu, and ended up in misery. After Fan Li and Wen Zhong helped Goujian, the king of Yue, to regain the state, Fan Li retreated to live a secluded

---

1　Sima Qian. *Records of the Grand Historian*. Yuelu Press, 2001, p.478.

life, thus protecting himself and his family. However, Wen Zhong clung to his post and status, which caused his final loss of life. If you can keep throughout your life the spontaneous and natural normality of life, and hold the usual mind, devoid of excessive pursuit of external gains like fame, status, and wealth, you will be in conformity with all the things in the universe, and will avert any potential disasters, thus reaching the unity with the nature of the De.

P2-23   The Dao is the origin of all the things in the universe, and the "Virtue" is the innate nature of all the things in the universe.

Quotes from *Laozi:*

The manner of the Great Virtue varies with the Dao. (Chapter 21)

All those who take up the Way conform to the Way; those who take up the Virtue conform to the Virtue; those who have lost the Way and the Virtue will lose everything and all. If their behavior is in conformity with the Virtue, the Way will go with them; if their behavior is in conflict with the Virtue, the Way will go against them. (Chapter 23)

Dao generates them, virtue nourishes them, substance forms them, and circumstances accomplish them. Therefore all things revere Dao and honor virtue. Yet Dao is revered and virtue honored not because this is decreed by any authority but because it's naturally so on its own. Thus Dao generates them, and virtue nourishes them, makes them grow and ripen, and cares for and nurtures them. Dao generates all things yet claims no possession; avails them yet takes no credit; and guides them yet not reigns them. Such is called the "greatest virtue." (Chapter 51)

Proof: According to Basic Assumption 2, the Dao can be "non-being," and is full of energy in its innermost part; and "non-being" generates "being," and forms traces in the chaotic world. "Non-being" means the infinite possibility of the Dao, and "being" indicates the mother of all the things in the universe, which is the formation of all the things in the universe. All the things in the universe need the nourishment of the Dao, which helps the generation of all the things in the universe. And by D1, we can see that the De is a general term of the spontaneous and natural process of all the things in the universe, which also indicates human understanding of the process and the character of following the process. Here, although the De does not have the creativity of the Dao, but is the concrete realization of the Dao which generates "being" from "non-being." The Dao in all the things in the universe is the De, which can explain the innate nature of all the things in the universe and the virtue in human relationships. Therefore, the Dao is the origin of all the things in the universe, and the De is the innate nature of all the things in the universe.

Explanation: The Dao is metaphysical, but it is also actually existent; the Dao is physical, but it cannot be grasped with the senses. The Dao creates all the things in the universe, and it also exists in all the things in the universe; the Dao is the root of all the things in the universe, and it is also the destination of all the things in the universe. Before creation, all the things in the universe lurked in the chaotic Dao, and formed unity with the Dao; and after creation, all the things in the universe contained the Dao in them, and manifested the Dao. The Dao and all the things in the universe are still an organic whole. The Dao is everlasting and eternal, but the existence of all the things in the universe is temporary and transitory, as they will all change from birth to death. But this does not mean that all the things in the universe become nothing, instead, they only return to the Dao, which gathers new life force and new creativity, generating new things and fermenting a new circle. Therefore, to return to the root or the Dao is to regenerate and give birth to new life.

The De (Virtue) is the manifestation of the Dao in the natural world and human society, and is the base of the nature of all the things in the universe. If we compare fire to the Dao, the light and heat of fire is the De (Virtue); if we compare water to the Dao, the flowing stream, the falling rain or dew, and the vast sea are the De. The Dao is like mother, and the De is like her breast milk. All the things in the universe take shape, grow, ripen, age and finally die in the production of the Dao and in the breeding up of the De. From this new life begins, and all the things in the universe run in the cycle under this natural law.

第五章 CHAPTER FIVE

治国篇
On Governance

本章论述遵循自然的治国之道。P3-1至P3-2论述合乎自然、圣人引领的社会是理想社会。P3-3至P3-5阐述有道社会的特征是和谐自然，百姓安居乐业，无须礼法。P3-6至 P3-16指出治国方式是循道、循古，不可崇尚智慧、贤能、仁义、礼法、功德、奇货等。P3-17至 P3-24指出在用兵、外交、为君、行政、治民等方面均要遵循"守柔"之道。P3-25至P3-28指出君主的修养在于教民守柔、修德修信、防微杜渐。

P3-1 合乎于道的社会是理想社会。

【参见《老子》条目】

人法地，地法天，天法道，道法自然。（第二十五章）

道常无名，朴。虽小，天下莫能臣。侯王若能守之，万物将自宾。天地相合，以降甘露，民莫之令而自均。始制有名，名亦既有，夫亦将知止，知止可以不殆。譬道之在天下，犹川谷之于江海。（第三十二章）

道常无为而无不为。侯王若能守之，万物将自化。（第三十七章）

道生之，德畜之，物形之，势成之。是以万物莫不尊道而贵德。（第五十一章）

治大国，若烹小鲜。以道莅天下，其鬼不神；非其鬼不神，其神不伤人；非其神不伤人，圣人亦不伤人。夫两不相伤，故德交归焉。（第六十章）

证明：根据基本假设1与基本假设2，"道"是任何"某个（类）"的综合。"道"可"无"，精微处充满力量；"无"生"有"，恍惚中混成迹象。"道"总是常在，总在"周行"。再根据公理A1与命题P1-2，"自然"是"道"从"无"到"有"再到"无"的自在自为过程，合乎"自然"的社会就是理想社会；而"道"是万物自在的根源。因此，合乎于"道"的社会是理想社会。

例证和说明：儒家也有他们的理想社会，如《礼记·礼运》篇所说"天下为公"的大同思想，即孔子所谓的"天下有道"的社会。但儒家的有道社会是人类社会为中心，以社会教化为手段，以社会伦理来维系整个社会，体现了人的主观意志和政治功利。与儒家的大同思想相比，老子从天人一体出发，认为理想的人类社会是回归到"道"的状态，既然万物是一种自然而然的状态，那么人类社会应像自然万物一样，这样的社会才是理想的社会。老子的理想社会也不同于古希腊柏拉图的理想国。柏拉图认为一个理想的国家，是一个依靠民主和正义的原则建立起来的，只有统治者、护卫者和生产者三种公民阶级组成的政体。

P3-2 圣人"无为而治"的社会应是理想社会。

【参见《老子》条目】

是以圣人处无为之事，行不言之教；万物作而不为始，生而不有，为而不恃，功成而弗居。夫唯弗居，是以不去。（第二章）

是以圣人之治，虚其心，实其腹，弱其志，强其骨。常使民无知无欲。使夫智者不敢为也。为无为，则无不治。（第三章）

是以圣人执一为天下式。不自见，故明；不自是，故彰；不自伐，故有功；不自矜，故能长。夫唯不争，故天下莫能与之争。（第二十二章）

故圣人云："我无为，而民自化；我好静，而民自正；我无事，而民自富；我无欲，而民自朴。"（第五十七章）

是以圣人方而不割，廉而不刿，直而不肆，光而不耀。（第五十八章）

非其神不伤人，圣人亦不伤人。夫两不相伤，故德交归焉。（第六十章）

是以圣人终不为大，故能成其大。（第六十三章）

是以圣人自知不自见，自爱不自贵。故去彼取此。（第七十二章）

圣人不积，既以为人己愈有，既以与人己愈多。天之道，利而不害；人之道，为而不争。（第八十一章）

证明： 从定义10可知，"圣人"指有"德"的治国者，这样的统治者能够认识到"自然"之过程，并努力地、自觉地在治国中顺应"自然"。根据公理A3和命题P2-15，治国的基本理念是"上善若水"、从"无为"达"有为"，而圣人之功在于辅助民众回归自在自为之生命常态。因此，圣人"无为而治"的社会应是理想社会。

例证和说明： 古代圣人是有"德"的领导者，他们治理国家的原则是通过"无为而治"而达到国泰民安。三代时，黄帝、尧、舜垂衣而治，一直被后人称道。老子认为古代圣人"无为而治"的社会往往是"小国寡民"，"甘其食，美其服，安其居，乐其俗"，当然应是理想社会。

圣人"无为而治"的理想社会不同于空想社会主义者的"乌托邦"社会。托马斯·莫尔（1478—1535）在《乌托邦》一书中，虚构了一位航海家到南半球时见到的一个岛屿国家。这个国家以公有制作为社会财产的基础，废除公民私有财产，人们在政治、经济、文化等领域一律平等，实行按需分配的原则。这里没有剥削，没有压迫，没有贫富差异，人人平等。

虽然老子的理想社会与"乌托邦"社会有一定程度相似，都是追求自在自为的小国，都是追求平等与自由。但是，他们提出的历史背景并不相同，批判的对象不同。莫尔处在西方殖民主义和圈地运动时期，批判的是资本主义扩张和资本的贪婪；老子处在礼崩乐坏的春秋末期，批判的是统治者的妄为乃至违背了人的自然本性。

P3-3 有道社会的根本特征是和谐自然。

【参见《老子》条目】

太上，下知有之；其次，亲而誉之。其次，畏之。其次，侮之。信不足焉，有不信焉。悠兮其贵言。功成事遂，百姓皆谓我自然。（第十七章）

人法地，地法天，天法道，道法自然。（第二十五章）

是以圣人欲不欲，不贵难得之货；学不学，复众人之所过。以辅万物之自然而不敢为。（第六十四章）

小国寡民。使有什伯人之器而不用，使民重死而不远徙。虽有舟舆，无所乘之；虽有甲兵，无所陈之。使民复结绳而用之。甘其食，美其服，安其君，乐其俗。邻国相望，鸡犬之声相闻，民至老死，不相往来。（第八十章）

证明： 从定义D11可知，"无为"指顺应"自然"不刻意作为，更不妄为的行动原则。根据公理A1和公理A3，"自然"是"道"从"无"到"有"再到"无"的自在自为过程，而治国的基本理念是"上善若水"、从"无为"达有为。这里，和谐自然的社会状态才是符合社会自身发展规律的一种自在自为状态。因此，有道社会的根本特征是和谐自然。

例证和说明： 在陶渊明的《桃花源记》可看到这一和谐而自然的社会。他讲述了东晋太元年间，一个以捕鱼为生的人，途经桃花林，奇遇了一个世外桃源的故事：那里土地平坦宽阔，房屋整整齐齐，有肥沃的土地，美好的池塘，桑树竹林之类。田间小路交错相通，村落间能互相听到鸡鸣狗叫的声音。村里面行人往来不绝，耕田种地的人劳作不止，男男女女的衣着装束完全像桃花源外的世人，老人和小孩都高高兴兴，自得其乐。他们为了躲避战乱，来此绝境，以致不知外面的世界了。

这是一个与世隔绝、顺应自然、自由自在、共同劳作、共同生活、没有教化、没有等级区分的群体，也就是老子所谓的"小国寡民"。这样一个人与万物的自在自为、和谐自然的社会，就是一个有道的社会。《桃花源记》是陶渊明的儒道思想交融的结晶。

P3-4 人民安居乐业是理想社会的根本表现。

【参见《老子》条目】

朝甚除，田甚芜，仓甚虚。服文彩，带利剑，厌饮食，财货有余，是谓盗夸。非道也哉！（第五十三章）

小国寡民。使有什伯人之器而不用，使民重死而不远徙。虽有舟舆，无所乘之；虽有甲兵，无所陈之。使民复结绳而用之。甘其食，美其服，安其居，乐其俗。邻国相望，鸡犬之声相闻，民至老死，不相往来。（第八十章）

证明：根据公理A1，"自然"是"道"从"无"到"有"再到"无"的自在自为过程。再根据命题P3-3，和谐自然是有道社会状态的根本特征。安居乐业是人民自在自为过程的必要基础，只有基本生活条件得到满足，百姓才能实现自在自为，社会才能达到和谐自然，由此才可能出现理想的社会状态。因此，人民安居乐业是理想社会的根本表现。

例证和说明：安居乐业虽是儒、道两家共同的政治目标，但存在着一些差别。老子认为，有道的社会应是和谐自然的状态，其表现为民众自在自为的安居乐业，而在儒家大同社会中的安居乐业，则是建立在"道之以德""天下为公""选贤与能""讲信修睦"等有为的政治实践基础之上，并且确立了一套伦理体系来规范人们的思想和行为。

在西汉初期，儒术未尊，黄老思想盛行，国家与民众得以休养生息。司马迁在《史记·平准书》中对此赞叹道："自汉朝建立七十多年之间，国家无大事，除非遇到水旱灾害，老百姓家给人足，天下粮食堆得满满的，官府仓库中还有许多布帛等货材。京城积聚的钱币千千万万，以致穿钱的绳子朽烂了，无法计数。太仓中的粮食大囷小囷如兵阵相连，有的露在外面，以致腐烂不能食用。"汉初七十余年"国家无事"，统治者政治上实行"无为而治"，百姓生活富足、安居乐业，在某种程度上实现了老子理想社会的目标。

P3-5 合乎于"道"的社会无须刻意倡导仁义礼法。

【参见《老子》条目】

大道废，有仁义。（第十八章）

上德不德，是以有德；下德不失德，是以无德。上德无为而无以为，下德无为而有以为。上仁为之而无以为，上义为之而有以为，上礼为之而莫之应，则攘臂而扔之。故失道而后德，失德而后仁，失仁而后义，失义而后礼。夫礼者，忠信之薄，而乱之首。（第三十八章）

其政闷闷，其民淳淳；其政察察，其民缺缺。（第五十八章）

证明：依据基本假设1，"道"是任何某个（类）的综合，"道"是天地万物的根源，具有无限的创造力。再依据命题P3-1与命题P3-3，合乎于"道"的社会是理想的社会，其根本特征是和谐自然，从而不需以"仁义礼法"等思想及制度解决严重的社会不公及纷争等问题。因此，合乎"道"的社会状态无须刻意倡导仁义礼法。

例证和说明：春秋之际，礼崩乐坏，社会处在急剧变革时期。在老子看来，正是由于社会"失道"，才会出现仁义礼法一类的教化。所以《老子》说："大道废，有仁义。"

"夫礼者，忠信之薄而乱之首。""法令滋彰盗贼多有。"其原因有三：首先，老子认为在理想的社会中，人们本性纯朴，彼此友好，互不伤害，因此，没有必要去提倡仁义礼法。仁义礼法这些概念的出现，就是社会无道的标志，恰恰说明了人类道德已在堕落。其次，老子反对仁义礼法是因为提倡仁义礼法时是带有功利目的的。儒家并不是从"百姓皆曰我自然"这一角度，提倡民本思想，宣扬仁义，实则是保民而王。更有甚者，一些统治者假仁假义，把仁义当作玩弄阴谋、实现自己利益的工具。第三，老子认为公开提倡仁义会破坏人的仁义本性，从而进一步破坏人类的美好生活。老子没有直接、明确地讨论人性的善恶问题，但根据其整个思想可以看出，他与孟子一样，都是性善论者。他认为人性本来就是纯朴厚道、相爱而不相害的。[1]

P3-6 顺应自然、无为而治是良治的基本原则。

【参见《老子》条目】

上善若水。水善利万物而不争，处众人之所恶，故几于道。（第八章）

---

[1] 张松辉：《老子研究》，北京：人民出版社，2006年，第194—197页。

人法地，地法天，天法道，道法自然。（第二十五章）

道常无为而无不为。侯王若能守之，万物将自化。化而欲作，吾将镇之以无名之朴。无名之朴，夫亦将不欲。不欲以静，天下将自正。（第三十七章）

治大国，若烹小鲜。（第六十章）

民之难治，以其上之有为，是以难治。（第七十五章）

证明：根据公理A3，治国的基本理念是"上善若水"、从"无为"达"有为"。在一定程度上，"无为"虽有退让的表象，但这种退让本身不是目的，而真正回到"道"的不可言说的精微处，才是力量之源。再根据命题P3-3，有道社会最根本的特征是和谐自然。因此，顺应自然、无为而治是良治的基本原则。

例证和说明：在老子看来，无为而治、顺应天道自然是社会良治的基本模式。这一模式在西汉初期得到了初步的实现。汉代初期，黄老思想是国家的政治思想，休养生息成为汉初的治国方略。文帝在位二十三年，宫殿御苑车骑服御无所增加。对内，当百姓感到不便时，他常放开禁令以利百姓。自己只穿黑色绨衣，所宠爱的慎夫人衣长也不拖地，帷帐不绣花，以表示自己的敦朴，为天下的表率。他修造霸陵陵墓都用瓦器，不准以金银铜锡装饰，因山起陵，不另选坟。对外，南越赵佗自立为帝，文帝嘉封赵佗兄弟，以德义感召，赵氏兄弟又重新称臣。汉朝与匈奴结为友好，不久匈奴背约侵扰，文帝只令边兵加强防守，却不发兵反攻其地，唯恐增加百姓负担。

文帝对内对外的无为、守柔政策，在景帝时继续实行。文景之治为汉代国力恢复奠定了基础。因此，司马迁、班固对此高度称赞。太史公说："汉兴以来，孝文皇帝广施大德，天下百姓怀恩而安。"班固赞叹道："孔子说过，'今时的人，也能像夏、商、周三代在政化淳一的情况下，直道而行。'这一看法是十分正确的。周、秦的弊端是因法网严密而律令苛峻，但违法犯罪的仍不可胜数。汉朝兴起，扫除繁苛，与民休息。至于汉文帝，加之以恭俭，景帝遵循前业，五六十年之间，至于移风易俗，黎民淳厚。周朝赞美成康，汉代称道文景，都认为那是美好的盛世啊。"

P3-7 良治的表现是社会公平、经济繁荣和民富国强。

【参见《老子》条目】

天地不仁，以万物为刍狗，圣人不仁，以百姓为刍狗。（第五章）

执大象，天下往。往而不害，安平太。（第三十五章）

小国寡民。使有什伯人之器而不用，使民重死而不远徙。虽有舟舆，无所乘之；虽有甲兵，无所陈之。使民复结绳而用之。甘其食，美其服，安其君，乐其俗。邻国相望，鸡犬之声相闻，民至老死，不相往来。（第八十章）

证明：根据命题P2-1与P2-14，顺应自在自为生命常态是德在人类社会之体现，而家、国、天下的治理与顺应自在自为生命常态的道理是一贯的。再根据命题P2-15，圣人之功在于辅助民众回归自在自为之生命常态；根据命题P3-4，人民安居乐业是理想社会的根本表现。因此，良治必然表现为社会公平、经济繁荣和民富国强。

例证和说明：在老子看来，理想的社会是老百姓过着自为自足的生活。这一思想在庄子那里得到进一步发挥。《庄子·胠箧》中也对古代良治社会进行了追溯。他说："你不知道至德的时代吗？从前容成氏、大庭氏、伯皇氏、中央氏、栗陆氏、骊畜氏、轩辕氏、赫胥氏、尊卢氏、祝融氏、伏羲氏、神农氏，在那个时代，人民结绳来记事，吃的饭菜很香甜，穿的衣服很美观，生活的习俗很顺意，休息的居室很安适，相邻的国家能互相看得见，鸡鸣狗叫的声音能互相听得着，人民之间直到老死也不互相往来。像这样的时代，就是高度的太平了。"

庄子认为，高居上位的人喜好智巧而摒弃大道，天下就会大乱。运用诳骗欺诈、坚白之论、同异之辩的权变多了，世俗之人就会被诡辩所迷惑，所以天下昏昏大乱，罪过便在于喜好智巧。舍弃淳朴的百姓而喜好奸猾的佞民，丢弃恬淡无为而喜好烦琐的说教，烦琐的说教已经扰乱天下了。庄子的论断也在《史记》中得到验证。《史记·殷本纪》中记载：在夏朝时，成汤还是一个方伯，有权征讨邻近的诸侯。葛伯不祭祀鬼神，成汤首先征讨他。成汤说："我说过这样的话：人照一照水就能看出自己的形貌，看一看民众就可以知道国家治理得好与不好。"伊尹说："英明啊！善言听得进去，道德才会进步。治理国家，抚育万民，凡是有德行做好事的人都要任用为朝廷之官。努力吧！"成汤对葛伯说："你们不能敬顺天命，我就要重重地惩罚你们。"由此可见，老庄对于垂裳而治、民风淳朴、百姓安居乐业的三代十分向往。司马迁所描绘的成汤治下的社会，就是一个良治的社会。

P3-8 文化认同、道义合法是良治的实施基础。

【参见《老子》条目】

昔之得一者，天得一以清，地得一以宁，神得一以灵，谷得一以盈，万物得一以生，侯王得一以为天下正。（第三十九章）

圣人常无心，以百姓心为心。（第四十九章）

大道甚夷，而人好径。朝甚除，田甚芜，仓甚虚。服文彩，带利剑，厌饮食，财货有余，是谓盗夸。非道也哉！（第五十三章）

以正治国。（第五十七章）

夫两不相伤，故德交归焉。（第六十章）

证明：根据命题P3-1和命题P3-6，合乎于"道"的社会自然是最理想的社会，循"道"是理想的治国方式。再根据P3-7，良治的表现是社会公平、经济繁荣和民富国强，因而在良治社会，人们必然趋同于相同的文化价值，并将道义置于合理合法的地位。可见，文化认同、道义合法是良治的实施基础。

例证和说明：老子一再强调，无为之道才是治理天下的法宝，圣人只有无为而治，才能化天下有为之民，这体现了贵柔、守慈、不争而有天下的思想。《史记·周本纪》中记载：西伯姬昌暗自行善，诸侯都来请他裁决是非。当时虞、芮两国的人有讼事不能裁决，故而前往周地。他们进入周的境域，看到种田的人都互让田界，人民都以谦让长者为美德。虞、芮两国的人还没见到西伯，已觉惭愧，相互说："我们所争的，正是周人所耻，还去干什么，去了只是自取羞辱罢了。"于是返回，互相谦让而去。诸侯听后都说："西伯是受有上天之命的君主。"虞、芮两国人民目睹了周文王治下社会，人民相互谦退自守，并以谦让为美德，以至于他们受到感染，自觉认同了周文王的治国理念。周文王也因此受到诸侯们的拥戴，赢得他们国家的民心，为周代的建立奠定了基础。

这种思想在今天仍然具有重要的现实意义。在企业国际化进程中，跨国企业都会面临来自企业内部和外部的挑战。对于外在的挑战，老子主张"以无事而取天下"。跨国企业的市场竞争，以老子思想观之，不仅仅是企业间的产品竞争，也是企业如何顺应当地市场规律、消费习惯、社会生活方式的问题。只有文化认同做得好的企业才可以不争而胜。用老子学说的观点来看，企业家在管理一个庞大的跨国企业时应当"无为而无不为"。著名企业家松下幸之助认为"所谓的无为就是人力本身的无所作为，但制度本身仍运行不违，这才是领导的真义，任何一个领导者不能不加留意。"[1]可见，老子思想有助于现代企业发展。

P3-9 循道而为是理想的治国方式。

【参见《老子》条目】

以道佐人主者，不以兵强天下，其事好还。（第三十章）

道常无名，朴。虽小，天下莫能臣。侯王若能守之，万物将自宾。天地相合，以降甘露，民莫之令而自均。（第三十二章）

---

1 袁剑峰主编：《松下经营管理学全书》，北京：地震出版社，2006年，第93页。

道常无为而无不为。侯王若能守之，万物将自化。（第三十七章）

上士闻道，勤而行之；中士闻道，若存若亡；下士闻道，大笑之。不笑不足以为道。故建言有之：明道若昧，进道若退，夷道若纇。上德若谷，大白若辱，广德若不足。建德若偷，质真若渝。大方无隅，大器晚成，大音希声，大象无形。道隐无名，夫唯道善贷且成。（第四十一章）

道生之，德畜之，物形之，势成之。是以万物莫不尊道而贵德。道之尊，德之贵，夫莫之命而常自然。故道生之，德畜之，长之育之，亭之毒之，养之覆之。生而不有，为而不恃，长而不宰，是谓玄德。（第五十一章）

道者万物之奥。善人之宝，不善人之所保。美言可以市，尊行可以加人。人之不善，何弃之有？故立天子，置三公，虽有拱璧以先驷马，不如坐进此道。古之所以贵此道者何？不曰：以求得，有罪以免邪？故为天下贵。（第六十二章）

证明： 根据基本假设1与基本假设2，"道"是任何"某个（类）"的综合。"道"既可以大到包容一切，又可以小到无法感觉到它的存在。"道"可"无"，精微处充满力量；"无"生"有"，恍惚中混成迹象。根据P3-1，合乎于"道"的社会才是最理想的社会。因此，只有遵循于"道"而为之，才是理想的治国方式。

例证和说明： 老子认为，天道是自然无为的，人道是天道在社会政治领域的落实，是对天道的效法，因而也应是自然无为的，无为才能无不为。老子说"我无为，百姓们就自我化育；我好静，老百姓就自然上正道"，是要求统治者在政治上能够做到清静无为，不去谋求功利，自然收到民自化、民自静的效果。他提出"治大国如烹小鲜"，是要求治理国家必须爱护民众，就像在烹调时谨慎地对待小鱼一样，如果不断翻腾，小鱼就会破碎不堪。老子以此强调：在治国的过程中，尽量不要繁杂的苛政，不要过分扰民，要以简约自然的手段达到国治民安的效果。

然而历史上大部分统治者却违背了循"道"而为的治理方式。春秋时期，天下大乱。面对社会现实，百家各持己见，主张不一。其中，不乏有人肆意地扩张一己的私欲和野心，导致了社会的危机和人民的苦难。老子"无为而治"的主张就是对这种违背天道的"有为"政治的反思和纠正。在《史记·老子韩非列传》中，司马迁指出："老子所推崇的道，本是虚无，以无为来应对变化。"

P3-10 宗圣循古有利于循道治国。

【参见《老子》条目】

执古之道，以御今之有。能知古始，是谓道纪。（第十四章）

善为士者，不武；善战者，不怒；善胜敌者，不与；善用人者，为之下。是

谓不争之德，是谓用人，是谓配天，古之极。（第六十八章）

是以圣人自知不自见，自爱不自贵。故去彼取此。（第七十二章）

证明：从定义D10可知，"圣人"指有"德"的治国者，这样的统治者能够认识到"自然"之过程，并努力地、自觉地在治国中顺应"自然"。根据公理A4与命题P2-15，圣人知"道"并不争，圣人之功在于辅助民众回归自在自为之生命常态。崇尚圣人，学习古代圣人的治国方式，就能更容易地顺应自然，趋向理想的社会状态。因此，宗圣循古有利于循道治国。

例证和说明：在先秦有关著述中，儒、道两家都崇尚古代的圣人之治。他们推崇上古传说时代的帝王品德，对早期人类的纯朴自然十分向往。陈鼓应认为，面对春秋时的世道衰微，儒家用现行的一套已经流于形式和工具化了的仁、义、礼、忠、信等道德观念和规范来矫治社会顽疾、挽救政治危局，这在老子看来不但无济于事，反而会越治越乱。因为，"古之真人"混沌蒙昧，无知无为，其心淳朴未散而合于自然，这是人类最美好的时代。后经伏羲、神农、黄帝乃至于唐尧虞舜，不断动用心智和增加人为的作用，渐渐背离大道，渐失"真蒙之心"。道德上的每况愈下，人心不古，致使社会步步陷入了不可解救的危机，人民遭受越来越深重的苦难。所以老子认为因循古代圣人的无为而治，是治理国家的最好方式。

老子虽然认为世道衰落，但并不悲观。他认为，社会陷入危机的最终根源，是人心质朴纯真的自然状态被破坏。因而在老子看来，返璞归真、返本复初，使人心恢复自然状态，既是人类的终极道德目标，又是解救社会危机的关键所在。[1]

P3-11 过度崇尚智慧，会使民心狡诈。

【参见《老子》条目】

不尚贤，使民不争；不贵难得之货，使民不为盗；不见可欲，使民心不乱。是以圣人之治，虚其心，实其腹，弱其志，强其骨。常使民无知无欲。使夫智者不敢为也。（第三章）

五色令人目盲；五音令人耳聋；五味令人口爽；驰骋畋猎，令人心发狂；难得之货，令人行妨。是以圣人为腹不为目，故去彼取此。（第十二章）

绝智弃辩，民利百倍；绝伪弃诈，民复孝慈；绝巧弃利，盗贼无有。（第十九章）

---

[1] 陈鼓应、白奚：《老子评传》，南京：南京大学出版社，2001年，第219—220页。

古之善为道者，非以明民，将以愚之。民之难治，以其智多。故以智治国，国之贼；不以智治国，国之福。知此两者亦稽式。常知稽式，是谓玄德。玄德深矣，远矣，与物反矣，然后乃至大顺。（第六十五章）

证明：从定义D3可知，"智"一般意义上指人对对象的认识能力和对个人行为的抉择能力；也特指人为满足"欲"的过分追求而丧失了回归"无"的能力的那种机巧智慧。根据公理A1，"自然"是"道"从"无"到"有"再到"无"的自在自为过程。如果过分崇尚智慧，就会使百姓步入非自在自为的过程，从而令人"不自然"，逐渐形成狡诈之心。因此，过度崇尚智慧，会使民心狡诈。

例证和说明：老子并不反对人们对知识与智慧的掌握。其一，"知常曰明"在《老子》中出现了两次，它告诉人们：理性思维能够使人获得对"道"的认识，并能指导人类的行为，如"无为""守中""抱一"等。其二，老子又认为"为学日益，为道日损"。一方面，经验知识的积累并不能使人获得对大道的体悟，亦不能使人的精神境界提高，相反，如果拘泥于生活的经验，局限于日常的知识，是不可能获得"大道"的，甚至有碍于"为道"；另一方面，老子指出了"为学"与"为道"的不同，"为学"靠的是"日益"，是生存经验的积累，"为道"却要"日损"，是对生活中经验机巧的抛弃。其三，老子明确反对人们在生活中用"智"使巧，以谋求个人的名利。他说："常使百姓没有欺诈之智，没有争夺之欲"，"百姓之所以难以统治，是因为他们心智太多"。为政者如果过度崇尚机智，就会使百姓处于"不自然"的境地。

《庄子·天地》中有这样一个故事：子贡从楚国返回晋国，路过汉阴，见一个老人正在整治菜园，用瓦罐取水浇园，用力很多而功效很低。子贡说："有种机械叫桔槔，一天可浇百畦，用力很少而功效很高。先生不想用它吗？"浇园老人冷笑着说："我听我老师说，使用机械的人一定会做投机取巧的事，做投机取巧之事的人一定会有投机取巧的心。投机取巧的心藏在胸中，心灵就不纯洁。心灵不纯洁，精神就摇摆不定，没有操守。精神没有操守，就不能得道。我不是不知道桔槔，而是感到羞耻而不用它。"当然，能够使用机械时而固执不用，是阻碍社会进步的。而如果对于"机巧"过度推崇，会使百姓心生伪诈，在老子看来，这是害"道"的。

P3-12 过度崇尚贤能，会使民趋争斗。

【参见《老子》条目】

不尚贤，使民不争；不贵难得之货，使民不为盗；不见可欲，使民心不乱。

第五章 治国篇
CHAPTER FIVE: On Governance

是以圣人之治，虚其心，实其腹，弱其志，强其骨。常使民无知无欲。使夫智者不敢为也。（第三章）

证明：贤能泛指为人推崇的具有很高智慧和很强能力的人。根据命题P2-8，过度崇尚智慧，就会使民心狡诈。根据公理A3，治国的基本理念是"无为"。从定义D11可知，"无为"指顺应"自然"不刻意作为，更不妄为的行动原则。过度崇尚贤能，必然导致人们膜拜智慧，强行"有为"，使得民众争强好胜。因此，过度崇尚贤能会使民众趋于争斗。

例证和说明：春秋时期，诸侯纷争，为了使国家强盛，各国大力延揽贤能，并给予他们丰厚的俸禄，显赫的身份。因此，一些人为了博取名利，用尽心机，如苏秦、张仪等舌辩之士，纵横列国，一时声名鹊起。在老子看来，这样的治国方式违背了"无为"的原则，也使民众为了名利而用尽心机，失去了他们的自然本性，引起不必要的纷争。

民间典故"头悬梁，锥刺股"讲述了苏秦发奋读书、出人头地的故事。苏秦外出游仕几年，潦倒而归。一家人暗地里都讥笑他不务正业。苏秦听到后，十分惭愧，头悬梁，锥刺股，埋头苦读。他说："读书人既然已经从师受教，埋头读书，可又不能凭借它获得荣华富贵，即使读书再多，又有什么用呢？"追逐名利，使苏秦失去了人的自然本性。

典故"负荆请罪"也是因崇尚贤能产生的。秦国、赵国举行渑池之会后，赵国蔺相如因功大被拜为上卿，位在廉颇之上。廉颇不高兴说："我是赵国的大将，有攻城野战的功劳，而蔺相如只凭口舌之辩，却位居我上，而且他出身贫贱，真是让我感到羞耻，不能忍受地位比他低。"他又扬言说："我见相如，必辱之。"蔺相如听说后，处处回避，不想与廉颇争夺名位。后来，廉颇领悟相如的良苦用心，负荆登门请罪，演绎了"将相和"的佳话。

P3-13 过度崇尚仁义，会使民众虚伪。

【参见《老子》条目】

大道废，有仁义。（第十八章）

上德不德，是以有德；下德不失德，是以无德。上德无为而无以为，下德无为而有以为。上仁为之而无以为，上义为之而有以为，上礼为之而莫之应，则攘臂而扔之。故失道而后德，失德而后仁，失仁而后义，失义而后礼。夫礼者，忠信之薄，而乱之首。（第三十八章）

其政闷闷，其民淳淳；其政察察，其民缺缺。（第五十八章）

证明：仁义是社会无道状态下倡导人们遵守的一种道德素质。根据命题P3-5，理想的社会状态下无须仁义礼法。根据公理A3与定义D11，治国的基本理念是"无为"，而"无为"是指顺应"自然"不刻意作为，更不妄为的行动原则。如果过度崇尚仁义，就会使得人们掩饰不德的行为，刻意表现有德的行为，因而难免虚伪。所以，过度崇尚仁义，会使民众虚伪。

例证和说明：春秋时期，大道不行，世风日下。为了化解社会危机，矫正人们的错误行为，便出现了仁、义、忠、信等伦理道德观念和社会规范。老子认为，仁义忠信的出现，违背自然之道，因为"道"不仅是自然界运行的普遍规律，而且也是人类的行为准则。

《淮南子·齐俗训》说："遵循天性而行叫作道，得到这种天性叫作德。天性丧失以后才崇尚仁，道丧失以后才崇尚义。所以仁义树立起来也就说明道德蜕化，礼乐制定施行也就说明纯朴散逸；是非显示反而使百姓迷惑，珠玉尊贵起来致使人们为之互相争夺。所以说，仁义、礼乐、是非、珠玉这四者的产生，说明世道衰落，是末世所利用的东西。"在老子看来，你不指出什么是仁义，人们也不知道什么是不仁不义，你一旦提倡仁义，人们反而会干出一些不仁不义的事情来。[1]例如，在儒家思想中，讲孝道是好的，但过分提倡孝道，甚至用许多名利来诱导，就很容易走极端，以至于出现"卧冰求鲤""郭巨埋儿"之类的荒诞现象（它们也可能是一些不接地气的"腐儒"编造出来的），反而成了对人性的摧残。

P3-14 过度崇尚礼法，会使民不聊生。

【参见《老子》条目】

上德不德，是以有德；下德不失德，是以无德。上德无为而无以为，下德无为而有以为。上仁为之而无以为，上义为之而有以为，上礼为之而莫之应，则攘臂而扔之。故失道而后德，失德而后仁，失仁而后义，失义而后礼。夫礼者，忠信之薄，而乱之首。（第三十八章）

其政闷闷，其民淳淳；其政察察，其民缺缺。（第五十八章）

证明：礼法是社会无道状态下要求人们遵守的社会规范。根据公理A3和公理A1，治国的基本理念是"无为"，而"自然"是"道"从"无"到"有"再到"无"的自在自为过程。如果过度崇尚礼法，就会强行推行一些社会规范，伤害"无为"而强行"有为"，使百姓步入非自在自为的过程，从而令人处于"不自然"的境地。

1　张松辉：《老子研究》，北京：人民出版社，2006年，第197—198页。

特别地，如果这些社会规范更多为统治者所利用，就会出现民不聊生的局面。因此，过度崇尚礼法，会使民不聊生。

例证和说明：老子提倡无为而治，"无为"是顺应"自然"而不刻意作为。在老子看来，推行礼法，就是"有为"而治，因为，礼法是一种社会约束性规范，一旦强加给百姓，必然使其丧失自然的本性，无法处于自在自为的状态，所以，老子说"礼是忠信不足的产物，是祸乱开始的根源"，"法令越是显著周密，盗贼就越多"。

《淮南子·道应训》里讲了这样一个故事：惠施为魏惠王制定国家法令，制定出来后，拿给德高望重的各位长者看，大家都称赞法令制定得好，于是惠施把法令上呈给魏惠王，惠王十分高兴，拿去给墨煎看。墨煎说："很好。"惠王说："既然法令制定得好，那么就拿出去颁布实行了吧？"墨煎说："不行。"惠王说："好却不能颁布实行，这是为什么？"墨煎说："你见过那些扛大木头的人吗？前面的呼喊'嗨哎'，后面的也同声应和。这是人们在扛举重物时为鼓劲而唱喊的歌声。他们难道不知道郑国、卫国那样的高亢激越的乐曲？他们知道的，但就是不用它，这是因为它不如那种号子歌声来得适用。同样，治理国家有原则，而不在于这法令的文辞修饰如何。"墨煎认为"举重劝力之歌"是劳动生活中自然产生的，而"郑卫之音"乃是礼乐，如果在劳动中演奏它就不合时宜了。

P3-15 过度崇尚奇货，会使民心惑乱。

【参见《老子》条目】

不尚贤，使民不争；不贵难得之货，使民不为盗；不见可欲，使民心不乱。是以圣人之治，虚其心，实其腹，弱其志，强其骨。常使民无知无欲。使夫智者不敢为也。（第三章）

五色令人目盲；五音令人耳聋；五味令人口爽；驰骋畋猎，令人心发狂；难得之货，令人行妨。是以圣人为腹不为目，故去彼取此。（第十二章）

证明：从定义D2可知，"欲"一般意义上指人对财富、名声和权力的追求；也特指人的违背"自然"的过分追求。根据公理A1，"自然"是"道"从"无"到"有"再到"无"的自在自为过程。崇尚奇货表现为人对财富的追求，会使人违背"自然"，产生欲望，形成私心，造成困惑。因此，过度崇尚奇货，会使民心惑乱。

例证和说明：《淮南子·道应训》说，饰伪品行的人互相吹捧抬高身价，施行礼义的人互相虚伪造作；车辆极力雕琢，器物竞相刻镂；求取财物的人争抢难得之物，并把它们当作宝贝；以文辞互相诋毁的人纠缠于冗长烦琐的事中而自以为聪明。官吏们互相争吵诡辩，将政务工作久拖而不处理，这些对治理国家毫无益处；工匠们殚精竭虑要制作奇异的器具，累月经年才完成，却不适合于使用。凡此种种，在老子看来，都是乱世的表现。

又如《史记·吕不韦列传》记载了吕不韦的经营之道。战国时，卫国商人吕不韦在邯郸做生意，知道秦国公子子楚在赵国做人质，认为他是"奇货可居"之人，决定做一次政治投机。他于是拿出五百金送给子楚，作为日常生活和结交宾客之用；又拿出五百金买珍奇玩物，自己带着东西去秦国游说。先拜见华阳夫人的姐弟，后把带来的东西统统献给华阳夫人，顺便谈及子楚聪明贤能，所结交的诸侯宾客遍及天下，常常说"子楚把夫人看成亲母一般，日夜哭泣思念太子和夫人"。华阳夫人听到很感动，收了子楚为养子。后来，秦昭襄王去世，太子安国君继位成了孝文王，华阳夫人为王后，子楚为太子。一年后孝文王突然暴毙，子楚即位，是为秦庄襄王。吕不韦被任命为丞相，获封文信侯，河南洛阳十万户作为他的食邑。吕不韦虽然得到了位极人臣的地位和富甲天下的财富，却引发秦廷内部的争权夺利。

P3-16 过度崇尚功利，会使民不自在。

【参见《老子》条目】

是以圣人处无为之事，行不言之教；万物作而不为始，生而不有，为而不恃，功成而弗居。夫唯弗居，是以不去。（第二章）

不尚贤，使民不争；不贵难得之货，使民不为盗；不见可欲，使民心不乱。是以圣人之治，虚其心，实其腹，弱其志，强其骨。常使民无知无欲。使夫智者不敢为也。为无为，则无不治。（第三章）

证明：根据公理A1，"自然"是"道"从"无"到"有"再到"无"的自在自为过程。功利与人们的欲望相关，过度崇尚功德表现为人对功名和权力的刻意追求，是一种违背"自然"的行为，不仅自身表现为"不自然"，更会对民众造成伤害。因此，过度崇尚功德，会使民不自在。

例证和说明："老子之政治理想，夫亦曰如何以善尽吾使民无知无欲之法术而已。然老子亦知必先以实民之腹为为政之首务，此则老子之智也。虚其心则无知，弱其志则无欲。而尚复有智者出其间，又必使之有所不敢为，夫而后乃得成其圣人之治。"[1]

---

1 钱穆：《庄老通辨》，北京：生活·读书·新知三联书店，2002年，第119页。

第五章 治国篇

CHAPTER FIVE: On Governance

一旦为政者崇尚功利，有人就会以此私心用"智"来争名逐利。汉武帝是好大喜功的人，上有所好，下必甚焉。据《汉书·汲黯传》记载，一次汉武帝招揽文学之士和儒生，对他们说，他想要做一些大事。汲黯便答道："陛下心里欲望很多，只在表面上施行仁义，怎么能真正仿效唐尧虞舜的无为而治呢！"

虽然武帝推崇儒术，公孙弘等人推行仁义教化，却导致天下事端纷起，官吏和百姓弄巧逞志的局面。汲黯认为他们心怀智诈，目的是取悦人主。酷吏张汤之流专门深究法律条文，巧言诋毁，陷人于罪，以此作为邀功的政治资本。在汲黯看来，他们的所作所为，只为私利，对上不能继承先帝无为而治的传统，对下不能遏止天下人的邪恶欲念。

P3-17 守柔而不轻敌，方能常胜不败。

【参见《老子》条目】

以道佐人主者，不以兵强天下，其事好还。师之所处，荆棘生焉。大军之后，必有凶年。（第三十章）

夫兵者，不祥之器，物或恶之，故有道者不处。君子居则贵左，用兵则贵右。兵者不祥之器，非君子之器，不得已而用之，恬淡为上。胜而不美，而美之者，是乐杀人。夫乐杀人者，则不可得志于天下矣。吉事尚左，凶事尚右。偏将军居左，上将军居右。言以丧礼处之。杀人之众，以悲哀泣之，战胜以丧礼处之。（第三十一章）

用兵有言：吾不敢为主，而为客；不敢进寸，而退尺。是谓行无行，攘无臂，扔无敌，执无兵。祸莫大于轻敌，轻敌几丧吾宝。故抗兵相若，哀者胜矣。（第六十九章）

人之生也柔弱，其死也坚强。草木之生也柔脆，其死也枯槁。故坚强者死之徒，柔弱者生之徒。是以兵强则灭，木强则折。强大处下，柔弱处上。（第七十六章）

虽有舟舆，无所乘之；虽有甲兵，无所陈之。（第八十章）

证明： 根据基本假设5，人的认知和行为的最高状态是"守中"。从定义D14可知，柔弱是指不刻意展露自身强势的态度或行为，是一种高级的"守中"方式。根据公理A3，治国的基本理念是"上善若水"，从"无为"达"有为"。这里，水意象蕴含"守弱"的特质。用兵时保持守柔之势，同时刚柔并济，不轻视敌方，充分备战才能保持常胜不败。因此，用兵守柔而不轻敌，方能常胜不败。

例证和说明： 春秋末期征伐频仍、杀戮惨重。老子对战争造成社会生产的破坏有着深切的忧虑，期望百姓能过上安然自适的生活，所以他对那时的战争持基本否定的态度。面对不可避免的战争现实，他主张不要轻易进行战争，更不能"以军事逞强天下"。

《孙子兵法·火攻篇》主张："没有利益不要行动，没有取胜的把握不要用兵，不到危急关头不要开战。不要因为自己的愤怒轻易开战，对自己有利就行动，不利于自己就停止。"孙子以此告诫明主和良将，因为人的愤怒是一时的，总可以转怒为喜，化愠为悦，但国家灭亡不可以复存，因战而死者不可以复生。所以，有道之君要慎之又慎，贤良之将要小心细察，这样的话，国家的安全才能得到保障，士兵的生命才能得以保全。《孙子兵法·军争篇》强调："战争是国家的大事，事关百姓生死、国家的存亡，不能不慎重！"

P3-18 辅君守柔而不耀武，方能常获威信。

【参见《老子》条目】

以道佐人主者，不以兵强天下，其事好还。师之所处，荆棘生焉。大军之后，必有凶年。（第三十章）

夫兵者，不祥之器，物或恶之，故有道者不处。君子居则贵左，用兵则贵右。兵者不祥之器，非君子之器，不得已而用之，恬淡为上。胜而不美，而美之者，是乐杀人。夫乐杀人者，则不可得志于天下矣。吉事尚左，凶事尚右。偏将军居左，上将军居右。言以丧礼处之。杀人之众，以悲哀泣之，战胜以丧礼处之。（第三十一章）

用兵有言：吾不敢为主，而为客；不敢进寸，而退尺。是谓行无行，攘无臂，扔无敌，执无兵。祸莫大于轻敌，轻敌几丧吾宝。故抗兵相若，哀者胜矣。（第六十九章）

人之生也柔弱，其死也坚强。草木之生也柔脆，其死也枯槁。故坚强者死之徒，柔弱者生之徒。是以兵强则灭，木强则折。强大处下，柔弱处上。（第七十六章）

虽有舟舆，无所乘之；虽有甲兵，无所陈之。（第八十章）

证明：从定义D14可知，柔弱是指不刻意展露自身强势的态度或行为，是一种高级的守中方式。根据命题P3-17，用兵守柔而不轻敌，方能常胜不败。同理，辅佐君王时也不能夸耀武力，不能恃强凌弱。"守中"不仅体现在和平时期的国家治理上，也体现在战争时期的取胜对策上，做到"守中"才能获得人们的信赖。因此，辅君守柔而不耀武，方能常获威信。

第五章 治国篇
CHAPTER FIVE: On Governance

例证和说明：循"道"是处理一切事务的原则，人臣也要顺应自然，不能以战争逞强天下。一旦通过战争解决争端，就会产生严重的后果。就如《韩非子·喻老》所说："天下不太平，战争频繁，相互防备着，几年都不能停止，将士的盔甲上都长出了虱子，燕雀在军帐上都筑起了窝，而军队仍不能返回。"老子认为，真正懂得战争危害的人，达到目的就会停止军事行动，绝不以军事实力来逞强称霸。这样的人取得了作战的胜利也不会自大，不会夸耀，不会骄傲。而侵略战争是得不到百姓支持的。

《淮南子·道应训》中有这样一个故事："吴国灭亡的原因是什么？"李克说："屡战屡胜。"武侯问："屡战屡胜，这是国家的福气，吴国偏偏为此而灭亡，这又是什么原因呢？"李克解释说："经常打仗，百姓必然感到疲惫不堪；而屡战屡胜必然导致君主骄傲；让骄横的君主去指挥、役使疲惫的百姓，不亡国这样的事情是很少见的。君主骄傲就会放肆，放肆纵欲就会穷奢极欲；百姓疲惫就会产生怨恨，怨恨多了就会去动足脑筋谋求摆脱疲惫痛苦，以致会用到谋反的手段。"从"道"的层面来看，事物过于壮盛就会走向衰老，这是自然规律。用战争逞强称霸天下，必然会加速自身的衰败。从治的层面来看，频繁的战争给百姓带来无尽的灾难，自然得不到百姓的拥护和支持。

P3-19 外交守柔而不凌弱，方能为人所服。

【参见《老子》条目】

柔弱胜刚强。（第三十六章）

反者道之动，弱者道之用。（第四十章）

大国者下流，天下之牝，天下之交也。牝常以静胜牡，以静为下。故大邦以下小邦，则取小邦；小邦以下大邦，则取大邦。故或下以取，或下而取。大邦不过欲兼畜人，小国不过欲入事人。夫两者各得所欲，大者宜为下。（第六十一章）

江海之所以能为百谷王者，以其善下之，故能为百谷王。是以圣人欲上民，必以言下之；欲先民，必以身后之。是以圣人处上而民不重，处前而民不害。是以天下乐推而不厌。以其不争，故天下莫能与之争。（第六十六章）

天下莫柔弱于水，而攻坚强者莫之能胜，以其无以易之。弱之胜强，柔之胜刚，天下莫不知，莫能行。是以圣人云：受国之垢，是谓社稷主；受国不祥，是为天下王。正言若反。（第七十八章）

证明：从定义D14可知，"柔弱"是指不刻意展露自身强势的态度或行为，是一种高级的"守中"方式。根据命题P3-14和命题P3-18，用兵守柔而不轻敌，方能常胜不败；而辅君守柔而不耀兵，方能常获威信。大国在外交上如能保持守柔之势，刚柔相济，又不恃强凌弱，才能为他国所敬服。因此，外交守柔而不凌弱，方能为人所服。

例证和说明：老子认为有无相生，强弱可以相互转化，任何事物一旦呈现出强势的一面，就意味着必将走向衰亡，因此，守柔的实质是维持着一种持久的向强转化的趋势，在处理国与国之间的关系时做到不刻意展示自身强大的一面，既避免加速自身的衰落，同时也能赢得人心，让人信服。

汉初文帝时在处理对南越和匈奴的外交上就采取了守柔政策。《汉书·文帝纪》说："文帝时，南越赵佗自立为南越王，文帝没有采用军事手段，没有兵临城下，来展示大汉的国威，而是采用怀柔的策略，以德怀之，感化了赵佗兄弟，使之臣服；对待匈奴采用和亲政策，在匈奴背弃汉朝、频频骚扰边境时，文帝舍攻取守，没有派兵深入匈奴，不愿意惊扰双方的百姓。"经过文、景两帝的无为而治，汉代国势日隆。至武帝时则在外交关系上采取强硬的方式，多次派遣卫青、霍去病、李广等征讨匈奴。司马迁对此批评说："兵祸不断，无法和解，天下人为此烦劳，叫苦不迭，而战争还是日甚一日。行走的为战事运载物资，居住的则忙于送行，到处扰攘骚动，都为战争而忙碌。"

P3-20 为君守柔而不滥权，方能长治久安。

【参见《老子》条目】

古之善为士者，微妙玄通，深不可识。（第十五章）

鱼不可脱于渊，国之利器不可以示人。（第三十六章）

证明：从定义D14可知，柔弱是指不刻意展露自身强势的态度或行为，是一种高级的"守中"方式。根据命题P2-14，家、国、天下的治理与顺应自在自为的生命常态的道理是一贯的。这里的"君"指君王，他既要具有不刻意展露自身强势的一面，又必须把握"守中"，韬光养晦，不随意滥用权力，才能国泰民安。因此，为君守柔而不滥权，方能长治久安。

例证和说明：《左传·郑伯克段于鄢》讲述了郑庄公韬光养晦的故事。隐公元年（公元前772年），郑国国君的弟弟共叔段，在其母亲武姜庇护下，谋划夺取哥哥郑庄公的君位。郑庄公发现后处处示弱，来满足共叔段的要求。共叔段则得寸进尺，愈加骄横，修治城廓，聚集百姓，修整盔甲武器，备好兵马战车，将要偷袭郑国。庄公获悉共叔段叛乱后，才率兵讨伐。由于共叔段的行为不得人心，百姓都离开了他，最后在鄢地他被打败。郑庄公在与段叔的对抗中，守柔而不逞强，以退为进，最终守住了自己的政治权力。

《淮南子·齐俗训》说："古代的君王能持守道体本性，因此能做到有令即行，有禁即止，名声留传后世，德泽遍及四海。……所以圣人君主是抓着这一'道体'根本而不丧失，于是万事万物的情理均在他掌握之中，四夷九州也就归顺降服。这说明'道体'这一根本是何等珍贵啊！掌握它就能无敌于天下。"

宋太祖在取得天下的第二年（公元961年），问宰相赵普如何巩固统治之道。赵普回答"削诸将兵权"。宋太祖深表赞同，采取了一个以柔克刚的办法。他宴请石守信等有功之将，于饮食谈笑间说："带兵真是一件辛苦的事，还容易引起君臣之间的猜忌。如果不必带兵，多买些良田美宅，颐养天年，才是人生最快乐的事啊！"石守信等人立即领会了其用意，便说"皇上顾念我们的辛劳，又为我们设想周到"。于是第二天，诸将纷纷称病请辞，交出兵权。历史上对于这次以和平手段解决权力分配、以柔性智慧解决人性贪婪欲望的重大事件，称为"杯酒释兵权"。

P3-21 行政守柔而不争功，方能长保平安。

【参见《老子》条目】

自见者不明，自是者不彰，自伐者无功，自矜者不长。（第二十四章）

证明： 从定义D14和定义D12可知，柔弱是指不刻意展露自身强势的态度或行为，而"不争"指消除了过分的"欲"和机巧性的"智"后而形成的处世态度。"不争"不是退却、懦弱和胆小，反而是更有内在的力量。根据公理A3，治国的基本理念是"上善若水"，从"无为"达"有为"，亦是"不争"。再根据命题P2-21，功遂身退是圣人尊道之行。因此，行政守柔而不争功，方能长保平安。

例证和说明： 在政治上，守柔是为了保持处下的姿态，不居功自傲，消除了自身好大喜功的欲望，即老子所说的"是以圣人为而不恃，功成而不处"。守柔也是"不争"，能打消政治对手的不满与猜忌，这样，才能使自己脱离危险的处境。

《史记·越王勾践世家》里说：春秋时期，范蠡竭力辅佐越王勾践，终于使得越国复兴。功成名就后，他不留恋功名，还劝诫大夫文种说："飞鸟尽，良弓藏；狡兔死，走狗烹。越王是长颈鸟嘴，只可以与之共患难，不可以与之共享乐，你为何不离去呢？"但大夫文种没有放弃高官厚禄，后被勾践杀死。范蠡急流勇退，却得以全身而退。

《史记·留侯世家》记载：汉初张良不居功自恃，婉拒高祖丰厚的赏赐。他说："现在凭三寸舌头做帝王的老师，封邑万户，位在列侯，这是平民的极致，对我来说已经足够了，希望放弃人间之事，跟赤松子云游。"张良以谦卑退守的态度，放弃应得官俸，真正做到了老子的"不自矜，故长"。相反，其同僚韩信没有做到功成身退，结果落个夷灭宗族的下场。在《史记·淮阴侯列传》里，司马迁对韩信评论道："假使韩信能够谦恭退让，不夸耀自己的功劳，不自恃自己的才能，那就差不多了。"韩信的悲剧在于其"伐己功""矜其能"，没有采用道家的谦让、守柔的态度，故而不得善终。

P3-22 与民守柔而不争财，方能长期获益。

【参见《老子》条目】

上善若水。水善利万物而不争，处众人之所恶，故几于道。（第八章）

夫唯不争，故天下莫能与之争。（第二十二章）

江海之所以能为百谷王者，以其善下之，故能为百谷王。是以圣人欲上民，必以言下之；欲先民，必以身后之。是以圣人处上而民不重，处前而民不害。是以天下乐推而不厌。以其不争，故天下莫能与之争。（第六十六章）

天之道，不争而善胜，不言而善应，不召而自来，繟然而善谋。（第七十三章）

民不畏死，奈何以死惧之？若使民常畏死，而为奇者，吾将得而杀之，孰敢？常有司杀者杀。（第七十四章）

天之道，利而不害；人之道，为而不争。（第八十一章）

证明： 从定义D14和定义D12可知，"柔弱"指不刻意展露自身强势的态度或行为，而"不争"指消除了过分的"欲"和机巧性的"智"后形成的处世态度。根据命题P3-4，人民安居乐业是理想社会的根本表现。安居乐业是人民自在自为过程的必要基础，只有基本生活条件得到满足，百姓才能实现自在自为。而君王不与民争财，社会才能达到和谐自然，民富国强。因此，与民守柔而不争财，方能长期获益。

例证和说明： 老子认为安居乐业是百姓自在自为的生活，是一种理想的社会状态。之所以这种理想社会没有出现，就在于行政者不能做到对民守柔，却与民争利。老子说："百姓遭受饥馑，是因为统治者收税太多，所以他们才陷于饥饿。人民之所以难于统治，是由于统治者任意妄为。"

《韩非子·解老》说："君主对内不用刑罚，对外不贪求民众的财物，这样的话，老百姓就安居乐业了。百姓安居乐业了，积蓄自然就会多，这就叫作有德。所谓作怪，就是丧魂落魄而精神错乱。精神错乱就是无德，反之，精神不乱，就是有德。君主使民众安居乐业，鬼也不来扰乱民众精神，那么德就在民众中了。"

《汉书·食货志》记载："汉初天下平定，生民疾苦，财物匮乏，连皇帝都找不到四匹同色的马车，文臣武将只能驾乘牛车。于是高祖颁布法令，禁止浪费，轻徭薄赋，节省开支，减轻百姓负担。"汉初政治上的无为而治、经济上的休养生息，为西汉奠定了二百多年的统治基业。守柔不与民争利，能使百姓安居乐业，过着安然自适的生活。

P3-23 教民守柔而不纵欲，方能长稳人心。

【参见《老子》条目】

是以圣人之治，虚其心，实其腹，弱其志，强其骨。常使民无知无欲。使夫智者不敢为也。为无为，则无不治。（第三章）

道常无为而无不为。侯王若能守之，万物将自化。化而欲作，吾将镇之以无名之朴。无名之朴，夫亦将不欲。不欲以静，天下将自正。（第三十七章）

圣人常无心，以百姓心为心。善者，吾善之；不善者，吾亦善之；德善。信者，吾信之；不信者，吾亦信之；德信。圣人在天下，歙歙焉，为天下浑其心。百姓皆注其耳目，圣人皆孩之。（第四十九章）

证明：从定义D14与定义D2可知，柔弱是指不刻意展露自身强势的态度或行为，是一种高级的"守中"方式，而"欲"特指人的违背"自然"的过分追求，也是为了私利而展露自身强势。根据基本假设5，人的认知和行为的最高状态是"守中"。让百姓守柔而不至于过多贪欲，就会让人保持自然本色，心态平和，不会出现人心混乱的局面。因此，教民守柔而不纵欲，方能长稳人心。

例证和说明：社会不稳定在于人心混乱，人心混乱是因为人们的欲望太多，欲望太多是因为人们没有做到守柔。《韩非子·解老》说："治理社会事务致力于根本，过度的奢侈就会被制止。一般说来，马的大用处是对外满足打仗需要，对内供给淫佚奢华的需要。现在有道的君主，对外很少用兵打仗，对内禁止过度的奢侈。君主不用马进行战争追击败敌，民众不用马到处运输货物，所积蓄起来的力量只用于农耕。"在韩非看来，圣人要做的是对外不征伐，对内禁淫奢。如果这样的话，百姓也就会一心一意去耕田。

P3-24 让百姓抱朴归真，可以使他们回归自然。

【参见《老子》条目】

是以圣人之治，虚其心，实其腹，弱其志，强其骨。（第三章）

是以圣人为腹不为目，故去彼取此。（第十二章）

圣人常无心，以百姓心为心。善者，吾善之；不善者，吾亦善之；德善。信者，吾信之；不信者，吾亦信之；德信。圣人在天下，歙歙焉，为天下浑其心。百姓皆注其耳目，圣人皆孩之。（第四十九章）

其政闷闷，其民淳淳；其政察察，其民缺缺。（第五十八章）

证明：根据P2-4，贪欲、智巧使人类社会与自在自为的生命状态背道而驰。再根据P2-5，从个人修养角度讲，少私寡欲、见素抱朴是根除欲望、智巧及其纷争从而达到自在自为生命状态的必然选择。在治理国家的过程中，让百姓保存真朴，是使其获得和谐自然状态的重要途径。因此，让百姓抱朴归真，可以使他们回归自然。

例证和说明：老子主张天道自然，倡导无为而治，不仅是针对统治者而言，也期望以此引导民众自在自为，安居乐业。有论者认为，老子主张圣人无为有两层意思：一方面它首先是社会治理者的无为，而不是普通人的行为准则；另一方面，圣人不仅是社会治理者的楷模，而且也是万民仰慕效法的对象，所以无为原则对普通人来说也有指导意义或启发意义。[1]

《淮南子·齐俗训》说："盛世太平国家的治理方法是，君王没有苛刻的法令，官吏没有烦琐的政务，士人没有虚伪的品行，工匠技艺没有淫巧的成分；事务合乎常规而不混乱，器物完美而不雕饰。……所以古代神农的法令这样说：'成年男子如果不从事耕种，那么天下就会有人因此而挨饿；年轻妇女如果不从事纺织，那么天下就会有人因此而挨冻。'因此神农自己亲自耕种，他的妻子亲自纺织，为天下人做出了榜样。神农教导人民，不要有意地珍贵难以得到的货物，不要过分器重无用的物件。所以那时代男子非得努力耕种不可，否则将要饿肚子；女子非得勤奋织布不可，否则将无法遮蔽身体；有余和不足，都直接关系到每个人自身；丰衣足食，邪奸就不会产生，大家安居乐业而天下太平。"

P3-25 行政者必须具有修德养真的心境。

【参见《老子》条目】

常使民无知无欲。使夫智者不敢为也。（第三章）

五色令人目盲；五音令人耳聋；五味令人口爽；驰骋畋猎，令人心发狂；难得之货，令人行妨。是以圣人为腹不为目，故去彼取此。（第十二章）

---

[1] 刘笑敢：《老子古今》，北京：中国社会科学出版社，2006年，第738页。

第五章 治国篇
CHAPTER FIVE: On Governance

绝智弃辩，民利百倍；绝伪弃诈，民复孝慈；绝巧弃利，盗贼无有。此三者以为文，不足。故令有所属：见素抱朴，少私寡欲。（第十九章）

是以圣人去甚，去奢，去泰。（第二十九章）

名与身孰亲？身与货孰多？得与亡孰病？甚爱必大费，多藏必厚亡。故知足不辱，知止不殆，可以长久。（第四十四章）

咎莫大于欲得，祸莫大于不知足。故知足之足，常足矣。（第四十六章）

是以圣人欲不欲，不贵难得之货；学不学，复众人之所过，以辅万物之自然而不敢为。（第六十四章）

证明： 根据命题P2-4，贪欲、智巧使人类社会与自在自为的生命状态背道而驰。又从定义D1和定义D10可知，"德"是万物从"无"到"有"再到"无"的自在自为过程的总称，也指人对此过程的认识以及顺应此过程的品质。根据命题P3-2，古代圣人领导下的社会是理想社会的典范，行政者如能学习古代圣人的治国方式，就能够更容易地顺应自然，使社会趋向理想状态。因此，行政者必须具有修德养真的心境。

例证和说明： 相传尧在位七十年后，年纪大了。有人推荐丹朱继位，尧不同意，因为他的儿子丹朱很粗野，好闹事。后来尧又召开部落联盟议事会议，讨论继承人的人选问题。大家都推举虞舜，说他是个德才兼备、很能干的人物。尧考验了三年才将帝位禅让给舜。后来，舜也是如此禅让给禹，没有留给自己的儿子商均。他们无私于民，开创了上古三代的黄金时期。这就是《周易·系辞》所说的"神农氏死后，黄帝、尧、舜氏开始，顺应天地之变，使百姓不怠倦，神妙地化育，使民众相适应。……黄帝、尧、舜垂衣拱手之间而天下大治。大概取象于乾、坤二卦"。

只有修德养真才能做到无为而治，才能"使民不倦、使民宜之"。《淮南子·齐俗训》说"（行政者）如果听觉迷惑于诽谤和赞誉，眼睛沉溺于五颜六色，却还想将事情办好，这是不大可能的"。

P3-26 行政者必须具有讲求诚信的品质。

【参见《老子》条目】

居善地，心善渊，与善仁，言善信，政善治，事善能，动善时。（第八章）

太上，下知有之；其次，亲而誉之。其次，畏之。其次，侮之。信不足焉，有不信焉。悠兮其贵言。功成事遂，百姓皆谓我自然。（第十七章）

夫轻诺必寡信，多易必多难。（第六十三章）

信言不美，美言不信。（第八十一章）

证明：从定义D1可知，"德"是万物从"无"到"有"再到"无"的自在自为过程的总称，也指人对此过程的认识及顺应此过程的品质。根据命题P2-22，行政者必须具有修德养真的心境，而"修德"的过程必然养成诚信的品质，绝不可以智巧欺骗于人。因此，行政者必须具有讲求诚信的品质。

例证和说明：老子认为，对为政者来说，循道而行就是要心怀诚信，诚信是为政者必备的品质。《淮南子·道应训》里有一个故事：春秋时期，晋文公征伐原邑，和大夫们约定三天攻克。但打了三天没有攻下，于是文公依约下令撤兵离去。身边的军官们就说了："再坚持一、二天，原邑人就会投降了。"文公说："我当初不知道原邑不可能三天内攻克，但我与大夫们约定三天内攻克，现在三天已过，如果继续攻下去，就会失去信用，这样即使得到原邑，我也不会做这样的事的。"这事被原邑的人得知后说："有这样讲信用的君王，还不投降干什么？"于是纷纷投降。

反之，失信于人，就会使为政者付出沉重的代价，在《史记·周本纪》里就有周幽王烽火戏诸侯的故事。幽王宠爱褒姒，见她整天没有笑容，就想方设法，为博美人一笑，但都没有效果。一天，幽王点起烽燧敲起战鼓，烽火通常是在敌寇来犯时才点燃，诸侯匆忙赶来后发现没有敌寇，褒姒于是露出笑容。幽王对此很高兴，又几次点燃烽火耍了诸侯们。此后诸侯们不再相信，再也不来勤王。等到申侯联络缯国、犬戎攻打幽王时，幽王再举烽火征召诸侯，就没有一人来救他了。

P3-27 行政者必须具有无私担当的胸襟。

【参见《老子》条目】

天长地久。天地所以长且久者，以其不自生，故能长生。是以圣人后其身而身先，外其身而身存。非以其无私邪？故能成其私。（第七章）

宠辱若惊，贵大患若身。何谓宠辱若惊？宠为下，得之若惊，失之若惊，是谓宠辱若惊。何谓贵大患若身？吾所以有大患者，为吾有身，及吾无身，吾有何患？故贵以身为天下，若可寄天下；爱以身为天下，若可托天下。（第十三章）

是以圣人欲上民，必以言下之；欲先民，必以身后之。是以圣人处上而民不重，处前而民不害。是以天下乐推而不厌。以其不争，故天下莫能与之争。（第六十六章）

天下莫柔弱于水，而攻坚强者莫之能胜，以其无以易之。弱之胜强，柔之胜刚，天下莫不知，莫能行。是以圣人云：受国之垢，是谓社稷主；受国不祥，是为天下王。正言若反。（第七十八章）

证明： 从定义D1和定义D8可知，"德"是万物从"无"到"有"再到"无"的自在自为过程的总称，而"无私"指消除过分的"欲"和机巧性的"智"之后而达到的能包容万物的心理状态。根据P3-22，行政者必须具有修德养真的心境。所以，行政者必须怀无私之心，以天下为己任，方能有效地治国理政。因此，行政者必须具有无私担当的胸襟。

例证和说明： 老子倡导为政者要无为而治，其终极目标仍是以天下苍生为念。在老子看来，百姓所想的就是圣人所思的，圣人对民众要言辞谦下，要把自己的利益放在他们的后面。这就要求统治者必须以天下为己任。

《淮南子·道应训》里有个故事。在宋景公时，荧惑星停留在心宿的位置，景公很害怕。太史子韦告诉他说："荧惑是表示上天惩罚的，心宿是宋国的分野。正因为这样，所以灾祸将要降落到君王身上。虽然如此，但可以将灾祸转嫁到宰相身上的。"宋景公说："宰相是任命来治理国家的，把死转移到他身上，不吉利。"子韦又说："那可以转嫁到百姓身上。"景公马上说："老百姓都死光了，我当谁的君主？我倒情愿我自己一个人死了。"子韦又说："可以转移到年成上。"景公接着话题说："年成是百姓的命根子，年成不好闹饥荒，百姓必定没活路，做人君的用百姓的死来换取自己的性命，那还有谁要我做君主？"于是，宋景公没有把灾祸转嫁给他人。正如老子所言，"能承受国家灾难的人，才配做天下的君王"，因为他们具有担当天下的胸襟。

P3-28 行政者必须具有防微杜渐的意识。

【参见《老子》条目】

祸兮，福之所倚；福兮，祸之所伏。（第五十八章）

图难于其易，为大于其细。天下难事，必作于易；天下大事，必作于细，是以圣人终不为大，故能成其大。夫轻诺必寡信，多易必多难。是以圣人犹难之。故终无难矣。（第六十三章）

其安易持，其未兆易谋。其脆易泮，其微易散。为之于未有，治之于未乱。合抱之木，生于毫末；九层之台，起于累土；千里之行，始于足下。为者败之，执者失之。是以圣人无为故无败，无执故无失。民之从事，常于几成而败之。慎终如始，则无败事。是以圣人欲不欲，不贵难得之货；学不学，复众人之所过，

以辅万物之自然而不敢为。(第六十四章)

证明：从定义D4可知，"观"是人知"道"的途径。根据命题P1-19和P2-12，"观道"的方法是从感觉的极细微处领悟，而贵德之士能够通过"观"的方式达到澄明从而体"道"的境界。行政者是"德"的践行者，必须关注细微，特别要注意"有""无"相生之际的各种征兆，才能有效预防"千里之堤，溃于蚁穴"。因此，行政者必须具有防微杜渐的意识。

例证和说明：对于行政者来说，要善于发现事物变化的征兆，在其萌芽状态时把问题解决掉。《后汉书·丁鸿列传》记载了一则故事。东汉和帝即位时年幼无能，便由窦太后执政，她的哥哥窦宪官居大将军。国政大权落入到外戚手中，他们为所欲为，密谋篡位。大臣司徒丁鸿对窦太后的专权十分气愤，决心为国除掉这一祸根。几年后，天上发生日食，丁鸿借此事上书和帝说："垂象见戒，以告人君"，"杜渐防萌，则凶妖可灭"。他建议趁窦氏家族权势尚不大时早加制止，以防后患，这样才能使得国家长治久安。和帝本来就有此心，于是采纳了他的意见，并任命他为太尉兼卫尉，进驻南北二宫，同时罢掉窦宪的官。窦氏兄妹情知罪责难逃，便自杀了，从而避免了一场可能发生的宫廷政变。和帝、丁鸿及时剪除外戚，得以维护国体。

《韩非子·喻老》讲述了扁鹊见蔡桓公的故事。春秋时，神医扁鹊拜见蔡桓公。他对桓公说："您有病在腠理，不治将恐恶化。"桓侯不以为然地说："医生喜欢医治没病的人，并以此当作自己的功劳。"过了些日子，扁鹊又见到桓公说："您的病已经恶化到肌肤，再不治疗的话，将会更严重。"桓侯不理他。如此这般多次劝说未果，直到桓公病入膏肓。扁鹊再见到桓侯时转头就跑，几天后桓公病死。

CHAPTER FIVE: On Governance

This chapter discusses how to govern the state by following the natural way. P3-1 and P3-2 are about an ideal society that follows the natural way and is led by the sage. P3-3 to P3-5 explain a society featured by Dao should be a harmonious one where people live and work in peace and are free from any restraints of rituals or law. From P3-6 to P3-16, it points out that the way to govern a state to conform with the Dao and the ancient way, rather than advocating the wise, the elite, the righteous, the rites, the virtuous or holding dear the rare. P3-17 to P3-24 make it clear that the soft way should be followed in terms of manipulating the troops, diplomatic relations, being the ruler, administrating and governing the people, etc. P3-25 to P3-28 elaborate that the accomplishment of the ruler lies in teaching his people the soft way, the cultivation of moral and good faith, and the importance of precaution.

P3-1   An ideal society is one that follows the Dao.

Quotes from *Laozi*:

Man models himself on Earth, Earth on Heaven, Heaven on the Dao, and the Dao on Nature. (Chapter 25)

The Dao is forever nameless and simple in nature. Though simple and small, it is subject to no one in the world. Should lords and princes be able to obey it, all things in the universe will naturally follow. The combination of the qi of yin and yang between the Heaven and the Earth brings forth rain and dew. It is well-distributed free from the human force. Different names appear with all things that grow on earth, but there should be some limits. And when you know the limits, you can avoid danger. The Dao is to the world what the great rivers and seas are to the streams from the valleys. (Chapter 32)

Dao does nothing yet nothing is left undone. Should lords and kings be able to maintain it, all things will be transformed on their own. (Chapter 37)

Dao generates them, virtue nourishes them, substance forms them, and circumstances accomplish them. Therefore all things revere Dao and honor virtue. (Chapter 51)

Governing a great state is like cooking small fish. When the Dao is with the world, the apparitions will not manifest their spirit. It is not that the apparitions will not manifest their spirit, but their spirit does not harm; not only does their spirit not harm, the sages do not harm. When the apparitions and the sages do not harm each other, they can live in complete harmony. (Chapter 60)

Proof: By Assumption 1 and Assumption 2, Dao is the sum of any category; it can be nothing but full of strength in subtlety; its nothingness brings forth fullness, and chaos signs. Dao is always there and always operates in circles. Besides, according to Axiom 1 and Proposition 1-2, the natural way is a spontaneous and unrestrained process where Dao comes into existence from nothingness and then disappears in nothingness, and a society that follows the natural way is an ideal one; also, Dao is the origin for the spontaneity of all things under heaven. Hence, we say an ideal society is one that follows the Dao.

Explanation: There is also an ideal society advocated by Confucianism. Take "Etiquette" in *Book of Rites* for example. The pantisocracy idea shown in "the whole world as one community" is what Confucius claimed a society "in a proper way." However, such a society advocated by Confucianism is human-centered and governed by means of social cultivation and sustained by social ethics, which highlights people's subjectivity and political utility. Compared with the pantisocracy idea of Confucianism, Laozi started with the idea of Heaven and human as one, and held that an ideal human society should return to the state of Dao; like everything else in nature, human society should develop in a natural and spontaneous manner, and thus can become ideal. This idea of Laozi is unlike that of Plato, the great philosopher of ancient Greece, who considered an ideal state a polity that consists of the ruler, the guardians and the producers, and is established in the principle of democracy and justice.

P3-2 A society where the sage governs by doing nothing can be an ideal one.

Quotes from *Laozi*:

Therefore the sages leave things as they are, and teach without inculcation; let all things grow and develop of their own accord, but do not initiate them; grow all things but do not possess them; bestow favours but do not require repayment. They achieve great successes but do not flaunt. Just because they do not brag, their achievements will be remembered forever. (Chapter 2)

Therefore, in governing the people, the sage purifies their soul, but fills their belies; reduces their selfish desire, but strengthens their sinews, and discourages the wise from doing rash things. Though nothing is done, everything is done well. (Chapter 3)

The sage embraces the One as the rule of the world. He is free from self-display, and therefore he is illustrious; from self-assertion, therefore he is distinguished; from self-boasting, and therefore he is meritorious; from self-complacency, and therefore he is enduring. It is because he is thus free from contending that therefore no one in the world is able to contend with him. (Chapter 22)

The sage has said, "I do nothing, and the people will be transformed of themselves; I keep quiet, and the people will be well-behaved. I am not meddlesome and the people will naturally prosper of themselves. I am free from desire and the people of themselves become simple and pure." (Chapter 57)

Therefore, those of the Virtue are square and upright, but they are not hurting; they are sharp and keen, but they are not stinging; they are straightforward, but they are not unbridled; they are bright and shiny, but they are not dazzling. (Chapter 58)

Not only does their spirit not harm, the sages do not harm either. The apparitions and the sages do not harm each other, so they can live in complete harmony. (Chapter 60)

Therefore, the sage fulfils his aim though he makes no claim. (Chapter 63)

Therefore, the sage knows himself but shows not himself, loves himself but values not himself. Therefore, he maintains the former and discards the latter. (Chapter 72)

The sage does not accumulate for himself. The more that he expends for others, the more he possesses of his own; the more that he gives to others, the more he has by himself. The law of nature is beneficial rather than harmful; the way of the human world is to do things without competition. (Chapter 81)

Proof: As shown in D10, the sage refers to the virtuous ruler who has knowledge of the process of naturalness and endeavors to govern his state in a natural way. The basic philosophies of statecraft, in accordance with A3 and P2-15, are "The highest excellence of humility is like that of water" and "do with non-action," while the accomplishment of the ruler lies in helping his people live a normal and free life. Hence, we know that a society where the sage governs by doing nothing can be an ideal one.

Explanation: With virtues, ancient rulers put their states in peace and prosperity by non-action. When Yellow Emperor, Emperor Yao and Emperor Shun were in the saddle, they governed the state through non-action, which has always been praised by later generations. Laozi held that the society governed by ancient sages with non-action tended to be "a small state with a small population," where "the people regard their (coarse) food as sweet; their (plain) clothes beautiful; their (poor) dwellings places of rest; and their common (simple) life sources of enjoyment." Such a society naturally is an ideal one.

The ideal society where the ruler governs with non-action is unlike the utopia claimed by the utopian socialists. In *Utopia*, Thomas Moore (1478-1535) invented an island discovered by a navigator in the Southern Hemisphere, a country where people enjoyed political, economic and cultural equality, and where the private ownership was subject to the public ownership of social property and the principle of distribution according to needs was followed. There, everyone was equal, with no exploitation, oppression or wealth disparities.

Although the ideal society conceived by Laozi and the utopia were similar to some extent, that is, both were small states in the pursuit of a small state of freedom and equality, they were proposed under different historical backgrounds with different targets of criticism. The latter was proposed under the backdrop of Western colonialism and the Enclosure Movement, which criticized capitalists' expansion and greediness, while the former came up during the late Spring and Autumn Period when social rituals collapsed, which criticized the recklessness of the rulers who even violated human nature.

P3-3 A society of Dao is essentially featured by being harmonious and natural.

Quotes from *Laozi:*

The best ruler, the people do not seem to know his existence; next comes the ruler whom the people are willing to get close to; next comes one awed by the people; next comes one they contempt. Short of credit, the rulers are not trusted. So leisurely and carefree, the best ruler is cautious in uttering words. When his task is accomplished and his work done, the people all say, "The things all happened to us naturally." (Chapter 17)

Man models himself on Earth, Earth on Heaven, Heaven on the Dao, and the Dao on Nature. (Chapter 25)

Therefore, the sage desires what the average people do not desire, not coveting rare goods; he learns what the average people do not learn, mending the faults of the average people. Thus he helps the natural development of all things, not intervening with them. (Chapter 64)

In a small state with a small population, the people have no use for the manual instruments they have; and they are unwilling to move away in spite of the danger of death; though having boats and carts, they have no need to use them; though having soldiers, they have no chance to deploy them. Let the people go back to the olden days to live a simple life, tying knots for records, fed well, dressed well, settled well, and happy with the way they are. They can see what the neighboring countries are doing, and can hear the crows of poultry and barks of dogs, but there are no mutual visits on the part of the people of the two countries. (Chapter 80)

Proof: Definition 11 shows that the principle of non-action means acting spontaneously rather than recklessly, as in the way of nature. Besides, according to A1 and A3, "nature" is the spontaneous and unrestrained operations of Dao from non-existence to existence and then back to non-existence, and the basic principle of statecraft is "The highest excellence of humility is like that of water" and "do with non-action." So, the natural state of a harmonious society is the way that meets the rules of social development. Therefore, a society of Dao is essentially featured by being harmonious and natural.

Explanation: In *Story of the Peach Blossom Valley* Tao Yuanming, the pastoral poet (365-427 AD) in ancient China, we can find an example of a harmonious and natural society. It is depicted that during the Taiyuan Period of Eastern Jin Dynasty (317-420 AD), a man living by fishing passed by a peach blossom valley and discovered a paradise on earth: there, the fertile land extends far and wide, and the houses sit in neat rolls, with amazing ponds, mulberry trees and bamboos; intersecting farm-roads are well-connected, with cocks crowing and dogs barking. The villagers are dressed unlike those outside the valley and have no communications with those outside but labor hard in the fields; both the old and the young are very happy and contented. To escape from war, they have fled to such a paradise for such a long time that they even know nothing new about the outside world.

Being characterized by an isolated and harmonious living without enlightenment or social caste, such a community is what Laozi called "a small state with a small population," and such a community where people are living naturally and harmoniously with all things is a society of Dao. Thus, Tao Yuanming blended the ideas of Confucianism and Daoism in *Story of the Peach Blossom Valley*.

P3-4 An ideal society manifests itself in social peace and prosperity.

Quotes from *Laozi:*

Their court shall be well kept, but their fields are ill-cultivated, and their granaries very empty. They shall wear elegant and ornamented robes, and have a superabundance of property and wealth; such princes may be called robbers and boasters. This is contrary to Dao surely. (Chapter 53)

In a small state with a small population, the people have no use for the manual instruments they have; and they are unwilling to move away in spite of the danger of death; though having boats and carts, they have no need to use them; though having soldiers, they have no chance to deploy them. Let the people go back to the olden days to live a simple life, tying knots for records, fed well, dressed well, settled well, and happy with the way they are. They can see what the neighboring countries are doing, and can hear the crows of poultry and barks of dogs, but there are no mutual visits on the part of the people of the two countries. (Chapter 80)

Proof: According to A1, "nature" is the spontaneous and unrestrained operations of Dao from non-being back to being and then to non-being; besides, P3-3 points out that a society of Dao is essentially featured by being harmonious and natural. Due to the fact that peace and prosperity are the basis for the people to live in a spontaneous and unrestrained way, only when this basic condition is met can the people live in freedom and the society operate in a harmonious and natural way, which makes an ideal society possible. Hence, an ideal society manifests itself in social peace and prosperity.

Explanation: Though both Confucianism and Daoism take social peace and prosperity as their common political goal, there are still some differences. In Laozi's mind, a society of Dao should be in a harmonious and natural state and is reflected in social peace and prosperity, while the whole world as one community advocated by Confucianism is built on such political ideas as "governing with morals," "serving for the state," "selecting the wise and competent" and "highlighting good faith and harmony," with an ethical system to regulate the thinking and behavior of the people.

Without the adoption of Confucianism, the early Western Han Dynasty (206 BC-24 AD) saw the popularity of Yellow Emperor and Laozi's thought, and thence the recuperation and recovery of the public. In *Records of the Grand Historian*: *On Stabilization*, Sima Qian praised, "Over the seventy plus years after the founding of the Han Dynasty, the state saw no sufferings, except floods and droughts, and the people lived in plenty, making granaries brimming and governmental barns full of materials including clothing. The capital witnessed an accumulation of uncountable coins in ropes that decayed later on. The public barns were bulged with piles of food supplies, some of which were exposed outward and gradually decayed." During the first seven decades of the Han Dynasty, the rulers adopted "government with non-action," making the state see no sufferings and the people live in plenty, peace and prosperity; to some extent, it realized the goal of an ideal society conceived by Laozi.

P3-5 A society where Dao prevails does not necessarily need the promotion of benevolence, righteousness, ritual or law.

Quotes from *Laozi*:

When the Great Dao ceased to be observed, benevolence and righteousness came into vogue. (Chapter 18)

The man of the highest virtue does not claim to be of virtue, thus he is of the true virtue. The man of the lowest virtue always holds fast to the virtue in form, thus he is actually of no virtue. The man of the highest virtue never acts yet leaves nothing undone. The man of the lowest virtue acts but there are things left undone. The men of high benevolence act but unintentionally; the men of high uprightness act but intentionally. The men of high ethics act but obtain nothing in return, so they will raise their arms to call. Hence when the Dao is lost, virtue will be lost as well; when virtue is lost, benevolence will be lost; when benevolence is lost, uprightness will be lost; when uprightness is lost; ritual will be lost. The Ritual marks the insufficiency of loyalty and faithfulness, and the beginning of disasters. (Chapter 38)

When the government is unwise, the people are simple; when the government is meddling, the people are troublesome. (Chapter 58)

Proof: From A1, we know that Dao is the sum of any category, the originator of all things under heaven, and brings forth infinite creativity. Moreover, a society that follows the Dao is an ideal one and is essentially featured by being harmonious and natural, in accordance with P3-1 and P3-3; therefore, it does not need to employ such ideas or systems as benevolence, righteousness, ritual and law to address severe inequality and disputes amongst other social issues. Therefore, a society where Dao prevails does not necessarily need the promotion of benevolence, righteousness, ritual or law.

Explanation: During the late Spring and Autumn Period (770-476 BEC), the society was subject to dramatic changes, with collapse of rituals. In Laozi's eye, it was the loss of Dao in the society that resulted in the promotion of benevolence, righteousness, ritual or law. Hence comes *"When the Great Dao ceased to be observed, benevolence and righteousness came into vogue"* in *Laozi*.

There are three reasons for the sayings that *"Propriety is caused by lack of loyalty and faith and results in chaos"* and *"The more display there is of legislation, the more thieves and robbers there are."* First, Laozi held that in an ideal society, the people are pure and simple, and friendly with each other, so there is no need to advocate benevolence, righteousness, ritual or law; on the contrary, the proposal of such concepts mentioned above reveals the loss of Dao in the society, and precisely shows the decadence of human morality. Second, Laozi opposed them, because he believed that benevolence, righteousness, ritual and law were promoted with a utilitarian purpose; Confucianism advocated the people-oriented idea, benevolence and righteousness, not from the view of "People all said 'We are as we are, of ourselves!'" but for the purpose of protecting the people so as to govern the state. Worse still, some rulers were hypocritical, and took benevolence and righteousness as the means to achieve their own ends. Third, Laozi held that public advocating of benevolence and righteousness would destroy human's virtue and even human's life. He did not discuss human's nature directly or clearly, but from his thoughts as a whole, like Mencius, he believed human in nature is good. He held that human nature is in fact pure and simple, as well as friendly and harmless.[1]

P3-6 Governing with non-action in a natural course makes the fundamental rule of good government.

Quotes from *Laozi*:

The perfect goodness is like water. Water is good at benefiting all things, but does not contend with them. It prefers to dwell in places the masses of people detest, therefore it is closest to the Dao. (Chapter 8)

Man is modeled on Earth, Earth on Heaven, Heaven on the Dao, and the Dao on nature. (Chapter 25)

Dao does nothing yet nothing is left undone. Should lords and kings be able to maintain it, all things will be transformed on their own. After they are transformed, they may grow avid. I will check the avidity with the nameless simplicity of Dao. Checked with the nameless simplicity, they will have no avidity. No avidity leads to serenity, hence the empire's stability. (Chapter 37)

Governing a great state is like cooking small fish. (Chapter 60)

The people are difficult to govern because of the excessive action of their superiors. It is for this that they are difficult to govern. (Chapter 75)

Proof: From A3, we know that the basic principle of statecraft is "The highest excellence of humility is like that of water" and "Do with non-action." In a sense, "non-action" marks a sign of concession, though, such concession is in itself not the purpose, and the unspeakable subtlety of Dao is the source of power. Besides, according to P3-3, the most essential nature of a society of Dao is being harmonious and natural, so governing with non-action and in a natural course makes the fundamental rule of good government.

---

1 Zhang Songhui. *A Study of Laozi*. The People's Press, 2006, pp.194-197.

Explanation: Non-action means following the natural course; in Laozi's view, it is the basic pattern for good government and has been basically practiced in the early Western Han Dynasty (206 BC-24 AD), a time when the thought of Yellow Emperor and Laozi, together with the policy of recuperation and recovery, became the national idea of government. For the twenty-three years in the reign of Emperor Wen, there was no increase of imperial gardens, royal chariots or robes in the court; when the people felt inconvenient, he would lift bans. He was always dressed in black clothing, and his beloved wife in clothes that should not fall to the ground, using curtains without embroidery, which was to indicate his simplicity and set an example for his people. His mausoleum was built upon mountains and merely with tiles and not decorated with any gold, silver, bronze or tin. Outwardly, when Zhao Tuo made himself a king in far southern territory, Emperor Wen canonized him as brother and hence made the latter concede as a minister with virtue; when the Huns broke the agreement not long after the alliance with the Han Kingdom, Emperor Wen only ordered the soldiers to defend the border rather than sending troops, for fear that it would cause burden to his people.

The non-action policy for internal and external affairs taken by Emperor Wen was picked up by Emperor Jing; as a result, those two emperors laid a foundation for restoring the power of the Han Empire, which was highly praised by historians Sima Qian and Ban Gu: the former commented that *"Since the prosperity of the Han Dynasty, Emperor Xiaowen governed with great virtues, and his people lived in peace and with gratitude,"* and the latter praised in Confucius' word, "The people of the day can live as those during the Xia, Shang and Zhou Dynasties when the politicization was pure;" this view is quite true. The late Zhou and Qin Dynasties saw innumerable crimes, because of their strict laws and harsh precepts, while the demolishment of laws and levies helped the people of the Han Dynasty live in peace and prosperity. Previous prosperity, combined with the humility and frugality of Emperor Jing, brought a change in morals and moves, and his people lived in simplicity and plenty during his reign. Later, people praised Cheng Kang of the Zhou Dynasty and Emperors Wen and Jing, believing that they created wonderful prosperity.

P3-7 Good government is reflected in social equality, economic prosperity and national wealth.

Quotes from *Laozi:*

Heaven and Earth show no bias, and let all the things in the universe grow naturally; the Sage shows no bias either, and let the people develop themselves.

(Chapter 5)

If you hold the great Dao, all in the world will come to you; when all come and do not cause harm, they will live with you in peace and ease. (Chapter 35)

In a small state with a small population, the people have no use for the manual instruments they have; and they are unwilling to move away in spite of the danger of death; though having boats and carts, they have no need to use them; though having soldiers, they have no chance to deploy them. Let the people go back to the olden days to live a simple life, tying knots for records, fed well, dressed well, settled well, and happy with the way they are. They can see what the neighboring countries are doing, and can hear the crows of poultry and barks of dogs, but there are no mutual visits on the part of the people of the two countries. (Chapter 80)

Proof: According to P2-1 and P2-14, one manifestation of De (attributes of Dao, literally meaning virtuous) in human society is following the spontaneity and freedom of life as it is, and this is also true of the management of household and the government of the state. Also, P2-15 shows us that the accomplishment of the ruler lies in helping his people live a normal and free life. Furthermore, an ideal society manifests itself in social peace and prosperity, according to P3-4. Hence, good government must be reflected in social equality, economic prosperity and national strength.

Explanation: In Laozi's view, in an ideal society people can live a self-sufficient life, an idea that was further explored by Zhuangzi. Good governance in ancient times was reviewed in *Zhuangzi: Pilfering*, where the author mentioned that "*Have you heard of the ages of the highest virtues? During the times of Rongcheng, Dating, Bohuang, Zhongyang, Lilu, Lixu, Xuanyuan, Hexu, Zunlu, Zhurong, Fuxi, and Shennong, people kept records by tying knots, their (coarse) food sweet, their (plain) clothes beautiful, their (simple) customs satisfying, and their dwellings comfortable; they could see each other from adjoined states, hear the crowing and barking, and never visit each other all their lives. Such times are of the greatest peace.*"

Zhuangzi held that a society would be in chaos, if the people of upper ranks abandoned Dao in favour of wisdom and smartness. The more deceptions, frauds and quibbles were employed, the more likely common people would be hooked, which in turn would cause disorder in society; the honest and simple people were rejected while reckless and eloquent people were well received, and non-action were dropped in favour of tedious moralizing, which would have already put the society in chaos. The theses of Zhuangzi were also verified in *Records of the Grand Historian*. It is recorded in *Records of the Grand Historian: Shang Dynasty* that when Chengtang was still a chief of the feudal princes in a region during the Xia Dynasty, he had the power to dominate the feudal princes nearby and chose to first attack Ge Bo, a feudal prince, who did not worship spirits. His reason was that "As I have said, one can know his own appearance by looking into the water, and the state governance at his people."

Yi Yin said that "How wise. He who can take in good advice can make progress with his virtues. For state governance and people cultivation, men of virtues and kindness should be appointed to serve in the court. Try to make it!" Chengtang told Ge Bo that "I will punish you for your disobeying of heaven and destiny." From above, we can know that Laozi and Zhuangzi were desperately eager for the Xia, Shang and Zhou Dynasties when the rulers governed through non-action there and the people lived a simple life in peace and prosperity. According to Sima Qian's description, the state under the governance of Chengtang was a society of good governance.

P3-8 The implementation of good governance is based on cultural identity and moral legitimacy.

Quotes from *Laozi*:

Since of old those that have got the "One," or the Dao, are: the sky has got it, hence clear and bright; the Earth has got it, hence staid and tranquil; the God has got it, hence effective; the river valley has got it, hence its brimming full; everything in the universe has got it, hence its growth and spread; the princes and marquises have got it, hence the states stable and secure. (Chapter 39)

The Sages have no preconceived ideas; they will regard the ideas of the common people as their own. (Chapter 49)

The Great Dao is even and smooth, but some people like to walk on the bypaths. Their court shall be well kept, but their fields are ill-cultivated, and their granaries very empty. They shall wear elegant and ornamented robes, and have a superabundance of property and wealth; such princes may be called robbers and boasters. This is not the Way! (Chapter 53)

To govern the state with justice. (Chapter 57)

It is because the apparitions, the gods, the Sages and the people can treat each other with the Virtue, so they can live in complete harmony. (Chapter 60)

Proof: According to P3-1 and P3-6, a society and the governance that follow the natural way are an ideal society and the ideal way of running a country respectively. According to P3-7, good governance is manifested in social equity, economic prosperity and national strength, and will create a society where people would have the same cultural values and observe the right way reasonably. Hence, we hold that the implementation of good governance is based on cultural identity and moral legitimacy.

Explanation: Laozi has repeatedly stressed that ruling with non-action is the key to governing the state, and that only by doing with non-action can the sage cultivate his people of actions; that is, he highlighted the idea of governing by being soft, kind and not competing. In *Records of the Grand Historian: History of Zhou Dynasty*, all the dukes turned to Jichang (i.e., Duke of Zhou State, later King Wen of Zhou Dynasty) for judging the right and the wrong, because he did good things secretly. When the people of the Yu and the Rui States failed to solve a lawsuit, they came to the Zhou territory, where they saw farmers were not arguing about the boundary between their pieces of land and the people there taking modesty as virtues. Not had they seen Jichang did the people from the two sides feel rather ashamed, confessing that "What we strive for is a shame in the eye of the people of Zhou; the meeting with Duke Jichang of Zhou would turn out to be a self-afflicted humiliation." They returned home after apologizing to each other modestly. Learning of this story, the dukes all praised that "Duke Jichang of Zhou is a God-disposed monarch." Seeing the society governed by King Wen — where people practiced mutual humility and considered modesty as virtues, the people of Yu and Rui were touched and came to identify with the governing philosophy of King Wen. As a result, the King won the support of his dukes and people, which laid a foundation for the establishment of the Zhou Dynasty.

Today, such an idea still carries practical significance. In the process of internationalization, multinational companies would be confronted with challenges, both internally and externally; as for external challenges, Laozi held that "to win the world by doing with non-action." Following this idea, international enterprises should focus not merely on product competition, but also on getting adapted to the rules, consumption habits and lifestyles of the local markets; only by cultural identity can they win out without striving. In terms of such internal challenges as how to manage a large multinational company, it seems to Laozi that "it should do nothing by doing something." Konosuke Matsushita, the famous entrepreneur, believed that "the so-called non-action is doing nothing in itself while running the system naturally, which is the true meaning of leadership and should not be ignored by any leader."[1] Thus, Laozi's thought is conducive to the development of modern

---

1   Yuan Jianfeng (ed.). *A Manual to Matsushita's Experiences in Managing*. Seismological Press, 2006, p.93.

enterprises.

P3-9 Doing by following the course of Dao is an ideal way of governance.

Quotes from *Laozi*:

He who would assist a ruler with Dao will not assert his mastery by force. Such a course is sure to end up in retribution. (Chapter 30)

The Dao is forever nameless and simple in nature. Though simple and small, it is subject to no one in the world. Should lords and princes be able to obey it, all things in the universe will naturally follow. The combination of the qi of yin and yang between the Heaven and the Earth brings forth rain and dew. It is well-distributed free from the human force. (Chapter 32)

Dao does nothing yet nothing is left undone. Should lords and kings be able to maintain it, all things will be transformed on their own. (Chapter 37)

The upper scholar, hearing the Dao, follows it; the mediocre scholar, hearing the Dao, shows his doubt; the lower scholar, hearing the Dao, simply laughs at it. If it were not laughed at, it could not be the Dao! Therefore, the ancient saying goes like this: The bright Dao appears dim; the forward Dao appears backward; the even Dao appears uneven; the lofty Virtue looks like deep valley; the great white seems black; the abundant Virtue appears insufficient; the vigorous Virtue appears cowardly; the simplest appears turbid; the ultimate square appears cornerless; the most precious object is always completed at the last moment; the loudest music seems silent; the greatest image seems invisible; the Dao is hidden and nameless. It is only the Dao that is good at starting and at completion as well. (Chapter 41)

Dao generates them, virtue nourishes them, substance forms them, and circumstances accomplish them. Therefore all things revere Dao and honor virtue. Yet Dao is revered and virtue honored not because this is decreed by any authority but because it's naturally so on its own. Thus Dao generates them, and virtue nourishes them, makes them grow and ripen, and cares for and nurtures them. Dao generates all things yet claims no possession; avails them yet takes no credit; and guides them yet not reigns them. Such is called the "greatest virtue." (Chapter 51)

The Dao is the shelter for all things in the world. The kind people treasure it, and the unkind ones are protected by it. Good words can buy respects; good deeds can attract people. If one is unkind, how can he abandon the Dao? Therefore, at the coronation of the lord and the appointment of the three ducal ministers, the tributes of gems followed by the four-horse chariot, are not as good as dedicating the Dao as a present. Why has the Dao been so treasured in the olden times? Isn't it said: seek it, and you'll have it; ask for redemption, and you'll be redeemed? Therefore, the Dao is treasured by all. *(Chapter 62)*

Proof: From Assumption 1 and Assumption 2, we know that Dao is the sum of any category; it can be so expansive that it includes all, and so tiny that nobody can feel it. It is nothing but full of strength in subtlety; its nothingness brings forth fullness, and chaos signs. Also, according to P3-1, an ideal society is one that follows the Dao; therefore, only by following the course of Dao can an ideal way of governance be achieved.

Explanation: In Laozi's eye, the way of Heaven is natural and non-action. The way of Man just follows the way of Heaven and is the implementation of it in social and political domains. So the way of Man should also be natural and non-action. By non-action, Man can achieve everything. Laozi said that "By non-action, the people would cultivate themselves on their own; in silence, the people would naturally embark on the right way;" it requires that the ruler do nothing and be silent rather than seek for achievements and profits, through which he naturally would achieve the effect of cultivation and peace. His proposal of "governing a great state is like cooking small fish" requires the ruler to care for his people, just like treating small fish tenderly in the cooking; otherwise, the small fish would be torn to pieces. As such, Laozi emphasized that the ruler should not levy heavy tax or over-disturb his people, but achieve governance and social peace through simple and natural means.

However, a majority of rulers in history went against the rule of governing by following the natural way. Take the Spring and Autumn Period. It was a time when there was great chaos in society and different schools of thoughts, among which some wantonly boosted their ambitions and desires that caused social crisis and sufferings to the common people. The governing with non-action proposed by Laozi was a political reflection and correction of the governance of actions that went against the way of Heaven. In *Records of the Grand Historian: Biography of Laozi and Hanfei*, Sima Qian said that *"The Dao advocated by Laozi is essentially nothingness, and it can be adapted to changes with its non-action."*

P3-10 Worshiping the sages and following their way of governance is conductive to governing the state with Dao.

Quotes from *Laozi*:

If you hold the long-existent Dao, you can administer the things today. And with the long-existent Dao, you can understand the origin of the universe. This is called the Law of the Dao. (Chapter 14)

Those who are good at commanding do not resort to force; those who are good at fighting are not easily irritated; those who are good at subjugating the enemies have no confrontation; those who are good at using people are modest towards them. This is the virtue of no contention; this is the ability to use people; this is in agreement with the Way of Heaven; and this is the ultimate norm since of old. (Chapter 68)

Therefore, the sage knows himself but shows not himself, loves himself but value not himself. Therefore, he maintains the former and discards the latter. (Chapter 72)

Proof: From D10, we know that "the sage" refers to the ruler of virtues, one who can grasp the natural process and try to follow it in his governance. Also, by A4 and P2-15, the sage knows Dao and hence he does not strive for anything; his achievement lies in helping the common return to the natural state of being spontaneous and unrestrained. By worshiping the sages and following their way of governance, one can follow the natural course and lead to an ideal society more easily and naturally. Therefore, we say that worshiping the sages and following their way of governance is conductive to governing the state with Dao.

Explanation: It is revealed in works concerning the pre-Qin period that both Confucianism and Daoism advocate the governance by ancient sages who held dear the emperors in legends and longed for the pure and natural state of men in the early era. Chen Guying holds that the moral concepts-benevolence, righteousness, propriety, loyalty and faith as a set of formalized tools-adopted by Confucianism to address social ills and eradicate political crisis are not only ineffective, but also would result in greater chaos according to Laozi. While "the real men in ancient times" were full of ignorance and inaction, but their honesty and purity were natural, making it the best age of humans. Later, as Fuxi, Shennong, the Yellow Emperor as well as Emperor Yao, Emperor Shun and Emperor Yu gradually used their intelligence and took action so that governance ran farther away from the Dao and gradually lost "the straightforward and unenlightened heart." Moral and honesty deterioration would send a society into a severe crisis and people into increasingly serious sufferings. This might be the reason why Laozi held that worshiping the sages and following their way of governance is conductive to governing the state with Dao.

Although Laozi believed that morals were deteriorating, he was not pessimistic, holding that the root cause of social crisis is the destruction of man's purity and innocence. So it seemed to him that returning to innocence and the natural state is not only the ultimate goal of human morals, but also the key to resolving social crisis.[1]

P3-11 Excessive worship of intelligence would make people more cunning.

Quotes from *Laozi*:

Not to value and employ men of superior ability is the way to keep the people from rivalry among themselves; not to prize articles which are difficult to procure is the way to keep them from becoming thieves; not to show them what is likely to excite their desires is the way to keep their minds from disorder. Therefore, the sage, in the exercise of his government, empties their minds, fills their bellies, weakens their wills, and strengthens their bones. He always keeps them innocent of knowledge and free from desire, and disables the wise from taking any ill actions. (Chapter 3)

Too many colors dazzle the eyes; too much music deafens the ears; too many tastes baffle the palate. Overindulging in hunting drives you crazy, and coveting too many material things tarnishes your conduct. Therefore, the Sage cares for bellies rather than senses, fending off material temptation and living a simple life. (Chapter 12)

If the rulers could get rid of their sophistry, the people could have a hundred times of benefit; if the rulers could get rid of their falsity, the people's piety and affection could be recovered; if the rulers could forsake the swindling of material things, robbery and theft would vanish from this world. (Chapter 19)

In olden days, those who followed the Dao did not make people wise and sophisticated, but made them simple. People are hard to govern if they are too intelligent. Therefore, to govern with wits is disastrous to the country; without wits, it is blessing to the country. Knowing the difference, you have the principle. If you can abide by the principle, it is your 'profound virtue,' which is far-reaching. With the return to the very nature of simplicity, the country will harmonize with Nature. (Chapter 65)

Proof: According to Definition 3, "*zhi*" (meaning wisdom, smartness, intelligence, wit, cleverness or craftiness) generally refers to cognition of objects and judgment of personal behaviors, and particularly to the smartness that drives men to excessively

---

1 Chen Guying, Bai Xi. *Comments on Laozi's Biography*. Nanjing University Press, 2001, pp.219-220.

meet desires so much that they lose the ability of returning to non-action. Besides, "Nature" is the spontaneous and unrestrained process of Dao from "non-being" to "being" and then back to "non-being." (see A1). Excessive advocacy of wisdom would lead the people onto the course of being not spontaneous and restrained, which would make people unnatural and gradually be reduced to be cunning. Hence, excessive worship of intelligence would make people more cunning.

Explanation: Laozi did not oppose people's mastery of knowledge and wisdom. First, "To know that unchanging rule is to be intelligent" appears twice in *Laozi*, which tells us that with rational thinking people can develop knowledge of Dao (like non-action, stillness and truth) and in turn use it to guide their behaviors. Second, Laozi also held that "He who devotes himself to learning seeks from day to day to increase his knowledge; he who devotes himself to Dao seeks from day to day to diminish his doing." For one thing, by accumulating experience and knowledge, people cannot grasp the meaning of Dao, nor can they improve their spiritual standard; on the contrary, the limitation of daily experience or life knowledge is unlikely to help them gain Dao and may even stop them from following the Dao; for another, Laozi pointed out the difference between devoting to learning and devoting to the Dao: the former is by the increasing accumulation of living experience while the latter is by doing less and less, namely, discarding daily experience. Third, he clearly opposed the pursuit of fame and fortune in daily life through smartness. Hence, he argued that "*it is necessary to free people from smart fraud or from competition*" and that "*the reason why it is difficult to govern is that people are too intelligent.*" If a ruler advocates intelligence excessively, his people would be reduced to a state of being unnatural.

There is a story in "On Heaven and Earth," *Zhuangzi*: On his way returning from Chu to Jin in Hanyin, Zigong saw an old man watering his garden with a jar, which called for onerous efforts but was ineffective. "With a machine named shadoof, you can irrigate hundreds of pieces of land per day. It is easier and more effective. Why not use it?" Zigong asked. The old man sneered, "My teacher once said, he who uses machine is bound to be opportunistic, and make gains by trickery. With trickery, his heart is not pure anymore, which would make his mind waver and unethical and then he would lose Dao. I don't use shadoof, not because I know not of it, but because I feel ashamed." Of course, he who stubbornly refused to employ machinery that was available hindered social development; however, an over-worship of opportunistic intelligence would lead people to fraud, which in Laozi's mind is detrimental to Dao.

P3-12   The overvaluing of men of superior ability would make people rival with each other.

Quotes from *Laozi*:

Not to value and employ men of superior ability is the way to keep the people from rivalry among themselves; not to prize articles which are difficult to procure is the way to keep them from becoming thieves; not to show them what is likely to excite their desires is the way to keep their minds from disorder. Therefore, the sage, in the exercise of his government, empties their minds, fills their bellies, weakens their wills, and strengthens their bones. He always keeps them innocent of knowledge and free from desire, and disables the wise from taking any ill actions. (Chapter 3)

Proof: Men of superior ability refer to those who have high intelligence and great competences that are respected. According to P2-8, excessive worship of intelligence would make people more cunning, and A3 tells us that the basic principle of statecraft is "do with non-action." Also, "non-action" means following the natural course and not acting deliberately or presumptuously. As an over emphasis of men on superior ability would inevitably lead to the worship of intelligence and forced "actions," which drives people to compete and rival with each other, it is thus claimed that overvaluing of men of superior ability would make people rival with each other.

Explanation: When the dukes competed against in the Spring and Autumn Period, all states strove to employ men of superior ability by offering a fat salary and prominent status in order to become prosperous and strong. As a result, those who were angling for fame and fortune made the most of trickery, such as canvassers Su Qin and Zhang Yi who lobbied all states and rose to fame. For Laozi, this ran against the principle of "non-action" and caused the trickery of the people, which would make the people lose their natural beauty and cause unnecessary disputes.

The folk story named "Tie one's hair on the house beam and jab one's side with a needle" tells the success of Su Qin who tried to keep himself awake by doing so in his painstaking study. After more than a decade of serving as a civil servant far from home, he returned to his hometown down and out. Hearing that someone laughed at his situation, he felt rather shamed and began to study hard by tying his hair on the house beam and jabbing his side with a needle. "Though being educated and working hard, one cannot become rich. So, what's the use of studying?" he questioned. The seeking of fame and fortune made Su Qin lose his natural character.

The famous story "Bringing a rod on one's back and asking for punishment" also derives from the overvaluing of men of great ability. After the meeting between the duke of Qin and the duke of Zhao at Mianchi, Lin Xiangru, Prime Minister of the State of Zhao was promoted to the official of the highest rank due to his contributions, a position over that of Lian Po, a famous general of Zhao, who complained that "As the general of Zhao, I made great contributions in battles, while Lin Xiangru was promoted over me merely because of his glib tongue; besides, he was born poor. It made me feel ashamed to be in a position lower than his." Later, he threatened, "Next time I see him, I would surely put him to shame." Learning this, Lin Xiangru tried his best to avoid seeing Lian Po, not wanting to rival with the latter. Lian Po gradually came to Lin Xiangru, and thus offered a humble apology with a rod on his back. Hence, there went the amazing story called "The General at Peace with The Prime Minister."

P3-13 Excessive advocacy of benevolence and righteousness would turn the people to be hypocritical.

Quotes from *Laozi*:

When the Great Dao ceased to be observed, benevolence and righteousness came into vogue. (Chapter 18)

The man of the highest virtue does not claim to be of virtue, thus he is of the true virtue. The man of the lowest virtue always holds fast to the virtue in form, thus he is actually of no virtue. The man of the highest virtue never acts yet leaves nothing undone. The man of the lowest virtue acts but there are things left undone. The men of high benevolence act but unintentionally; the men of high uprightness act but intentionally. The men of high ethics act but obtain nothing in return, so they will raise their arms to call. Hence when the Dao is lost, virtue will be lost as well; when virtue is lost, benevolence will be lost; when benevolence is lost, uprightness will be lost; when uprightness is lost; ritual will be lost. The Ritual marks the insufficiency of loyalty and faithfulness, and the beginning of disasters. (Chapter 38)

When the government is unwise, the people are simple; when the government is meddling, the people are troublesome. (Chapter 58)

Proof: Being benevolent and righteous is a moral quality advocated in a society without Dao. According to P3-5, an ideal society does not need benevolence, righteousness, ritual and law. Besides, it is said in A3 and D11 that the basic principle of statecraft is "do with non-action," which means acting naturally and not presumptuously. If benevolence and righteousness were excessively advocated, people would attempt to hide their immoral actions while showing their moral actions deliberately, which would inevitably make men hypocritical. Thus, we think that excessive advocacy of benevolence and righteousness would make people hypocritical.

Explanation: When the Dao failed and the society deteriorated during the Spring and Autumn Period, such moral concepts and social norms as benevolence, righteousness, propriety, loyalty and faith emerged in order to dissolve social crisis and correct people's misdoings. Their emergence ran against the Dao of nature in Laozi's eye, who believed that Dao is not merely the universal law in the operation of nature, but also the norm of men's behaviors.

It is said in "Respecting the Customs" of *Huainanzi:* "Acting by following the natural way is called Dao and the acquisition of the natural way is Virtue; benevolence is advocated when the natural way is lost and righteousness when virtue is lost. Thus, the prevailing of benevolence and righteousness means the deterioration of morals, and the establishment of rituals and music illustrates the loss of pure simplicity. As such, people were puzzled with right and wrong, and strove for priceless treasures. Thus, it is reasonable to hold that the emergence of benevolence, righteousness, rituals and music means social deterioration, something that only a state on the decline makes use of." In Laozi's view, if benevolence and righteousness were not proposed, people would have known nothing about it; once it was proposed, people would do unjust things.[1] For instance, it was good for to come up with filial piety. However, too much emphasis on it and using too much fame and fortune as temptation for it, which is why there were such absurd cases as "Wang Xiang climbed on the freezing ice to catch fish for his step-mother" and "Guo Ju attempted to bury his child so as to save food for his mother." Those might have been made up by some pedants, but did do wreck on human nature.

P3-14 Excessive advocacy of ritual and law would make people live in misery.

Quotes from *Laozi:*

The man of the highest virtue does not claim to be of virtue, thus he is of the true virtue. The man of the lowest virtue always holds fast to the virtue in form, thus he is actually of no virtue. The man of the highest virtue never acts yet leaves nothing undone. The man of the lowest virtue acts but there are things left undone. The men of high benevolence act but unintentionally; the men of high uprightness act but intentionally. The men of high ethics act but obtain nothing in return, so they

---

1 Zhang Songhui. *A Study of Laozi.* The People's Press, 2006, pp.197-198.

will raise their arms to call. Hence when the Dao is lost, virtue will be lost as well; when virtue is lost, benevolence will be lost; when benevolence is lost, uprightness will be lost; when uprightness is lost; ritual will be lost. *The Ritual marks the insufficiency of loyalty and faithfulness, and the beginning of disasters.* (Chapter 38)

When the government is unwise, the people are simple; when the government is meddling, the people are troublesome. (Chapter 58)

Proof: In a society without Dao, ritual and law are employed as social norms that men should observe. According to A3 and A1, the basic principle of statecraft is "non-action," and "nature" is the spontaneous and unrestrained operations of Dao from non-existence to existence and then back to non-existence. If ritual and law were over advocated, some social norms would inevitably be adopted and forced actions would harm those non-acted, making the common step into unspontaneous and restrained process, namely, an unnatural situation. This is especially true when such social norms are mainly employed by rulers, which will leave the people in misery. Thus, excessive advocacy of ritual and law would make the people live in misery.

Explanation: "Non-action" in "governing with non-action" proposed by Laozi means taking the course of nature rather than purposeful action. It seems to him that the practice of ritual is governing with "action," because ritual is a social norm with binding force, which once imposed on the people would lead to the loss of their nature and of their natural state. For this, Laozi had these sayings: "Ritual results from a shortage of loyalty and in troubles," and "The number of thieves increases with growing decrees."

It is told in "Following Dao" of *Huainanzi:* Hui Shi drafted the state laws for King Hui of the State Wei, and afterward showed the draft to the advanced with great virtue and high prestige, who appraised it. Thus, he submitted it to the King, who was very happy and took it to Mo Jian. "Great," King Hui then asked, "Since the laws are great, should we promulgate them?" "No," replied Mo Jian. "It's great. Why not?" "Have the Majesty seen people carrying wood? Those in the front would shout 'hey, hey,' to which those behind just corresponded. This is because they sang for encouragement while carrying wood. Did not they know that there are such rousing and inspiring music in the states of Zheng and Wei? They knew, but would not turn to it, because it is not as relevant as that chant. By the same token, governance should follow principles rather than rhetoric," explained Mo Jian. He held that "The chant for carrying" is a natural outcome of labor while the etiquette music played in Zheng and Wei would be inappropriate, if played when at work.

P3-15 Over-prizing of rare goods would confuse the mind of the people.

Quotes from *Laozi*:

Not to value and employ men of superior ability is the way to keep the people from rivalry among themselves; not to prize articles which are difficult to procure is the way to keep them from becoming thieves; not to show them what is likely to excite their desires is the way to keep their minds from disorder. Therefore, the sage, in the exercise of his government, empties their minds, fills their bellies, weakens their wills, and strengthens their bones. He always keeps them innocent of knowledge and free from desire, and disables the wise from taking any ill actions. (Chapter 3)

Too many colors dazzle the eyes; too much music deafens the ears; too many tastes baffle the palate. Overindulging in hunting drives you crazy, and coveting too much material things tarnishes your conduct. Therefore, the Sage cares for bellies rather than senses, fending off material temptation and living a simple life. (Chapter 12)

Proof: From D2, we know that "desire" means the pursuit of fame, fortune and power in general and particularly refers to over seeking that goes against nature. Also, it is said in A1 that nature refers to the spontaneous and unrestrained process where Dao comes into existence from nothingness and then disappears in nothingness. An overemphasis on rare goods is a manifestation of seeking for fortune, which would make people go against nature and have desires, selfishness, and consequently confusion. Hence, we claim that over-prizing of rare goods would confuse the mind of the people.

Explanation: It is told in "*Following Dao*," *Huainanzi*: that those who masquerade their actions would boast each other, and those who practice propriety be hypocritically affected; the over-decoration of vehicles and crafting of artifacts would give birth to rare things so that people would vie for them to make money and take as treasure; those who are quarreling with rhetoric would believe themselves to be smart. If officials are busy with arguing, they would have no time for work, which would be of no good for the governance; being devoted to rare instruments, craftsmen would spend years on something that would be of no use. Those, among other cases, are symptomatic of troubled times in the eyes of Laozi.

Another example is Lü Buwei from *Records of the Grand Historian*. It was recorded that Lü Buwei who was doing business in Handan, decided to speculate in politics after learning that Zichu, the prince of Qin, was held hostage by Zhao. Believing that Zichu was "rare and profitable," Lü gave him 500 *liang* gold for daily expenses, and spent another 500 *liang* buying rare playthings, which he took to lobby Qin. After visiting the siblings of Mrs. Huayang, he gave her all the playthings, while singing praise of the smartness and wide range of friends of Zichu; he also said that Zichu would often see her as his biological mother and missed her and her son day and night. Moved by his words, Mrs. Huayang adopted Zichu as her son. When King Zhaoxiang died, Price Anguo succeeded to the throne as King Xiaowen. As a result, Lady Huayang became queen and Zichu became prince. One year later when King Xiaowen died, Zichu took the throne to become King Zhuangxiang, and appointed Lü Buwei as Prime Minister, with the title of Duke Wenxin in charge of a hundred thousand of households in Luoyang. Although Lü reached the highest level both in rank and wealth, he triggered off an inner struggle in the court.

P3-16 Overvaluing of merits would make people uneasy.

Quotes from *Laozi*:

Therefore, the sage manages things with non-action and practices wordless teaching. He lets all things grow without interference, and gives them life without claiming to be their owner. He benefits them yet exacts no gratitude, and he succeeds without claiming merit. It is because of this that his merits last forever. (Chapter 2)

Not to value and employ men of superior ability is the way to keep the people from rivalry among themselves; not to prize articles which are difficult to procure is the way to keep them from becoming thieves; not to show them what is likely to excite their desires is the way to keep their minds from disorder. Therefore, the sage, in the exercise of his government, empties their minds, fills their bellies, weakens their wills, and strengthens their bones. He always keeps them innocent of knowledge and free from desire, and disables the wise from taking any ill actions. If you deal with worldly affairs by "non-action," there will be no trouble of government. (Chapter 3)

Proof: According to A1, nature refers to the spontaneous and unrestrained process where Dao comes into existence from nothingness and then disappears in nothingness. As merits and desires go hand in hand, overvaluing of merits and contributions would drive people to pursue fame and power, which runs counter to nature, being "unnatural" in itself and harming the people as well. Thus, excessive respect for merits would make people uneasy.

Explanation: Qian Mu once said: *"The political ideal of Laozi can also be put as a way of making people ignorant with no desire, though he knew well that government should take filling the belly of the people as the priority. This is the wisdom of Laozi. By making people humble and weakening their minds, the people would be ignorant* and cherish no desire; even though there would still be some smart ones, they would not dare anything. This is the governance of the sage."[1]

Once politicians advocate merits and contributions, there would be scheming for personal gains and fame. Emperor Wu of Han was overwhelmed by contributions, making his officials follow suit. In *History of the Han Dynasty: Biography of Ji An*, it was recorded when Emperor Wu recruited scholars, he made it clear that he would like to do some great deeds. "My lord, there is too much desire in your mind that you could barely practice benevolence; so how can you follow the governance with non-action by Emperor Tang, Rao, Shun and Yu?" asked Ji An.

While Emperor Wu advocated Confucianism, Gongsun Hong and other officials boasted of the enlightenment with benevolence, which led to national disorders, as officials and the grass-roots plotted to be ambitious. Ji An believed that the underlying purpose of such smartness was to delight the emperor. Another case is Zhang Tang, a ruthless official. He went all the way to study laws so that he could defame others with a silver tongue, and took this as leverage for his political career. It seemed to Ji An that such actions are nothing but for personal gains, which cannot carry on the legacy of governance with non-action from previous generations, nor would they help curb the evil desires of the people.

P3-17   Those who are soft and do not neglect the enemy can constantly win.

Quotes from *Laozi*:

Those who assist the rulers with the Dao will not assert his mastery in the kingdom by force of arms. The use of military forces will end up in retribution. Thistles and thorns spring up where the army has been stationed. There is sure to be a famine after a great battle. (Chapter 30)

Weapons are inauspicious objects, detested by all, therefore, not used by those who have Dao. The lords ordinarily consider the left hand the most honorable place, but in time of war the right hand. Weapons, inauspicious things, are not lords' tools, used only when they have no alternative. Even if they have won victory, they should treat it with indifference. They should not feel triumphant, and if they treat it triumphantly, it seems that they like killing people. And if one likes killing people, he cannot get his will in the world. Therefore, when one does auspicious things, he should stand on the left side, and when one does mournful things, he should stand on the right side. Therefore, those generals who are not in charge of killing should

---

1   Qian Mu. *Philosophy of Laozi and Zhuangzi*. SDX Joint Publishing Co, 2002, p.119.

stand on the left, while those generals who are in charge of killing should stand on the right, that is to say, the ritual of going out to war should be treated in the same way as one attends obsequies. When a great many people are killed, one should feel mournful towards them. When victorious in war, one should show mournful respects for the dead. (Chapter 31)

A master of the art of war has said, "I do not dare to be the host to commence the war; I prefer to act on the defensive. I do not dare to advance an inch; I prefer to retreat a foot." This is called marshalling the ranks where there are no ranks; baring the arms where there are no arms to bare; grasping the weapon where there is no weapon to grasp; advancing against the enemy where there is no enemy. There is no calamity greater than lightly engaging in war. To do that is near losing the gentleness which is so precious. Thus, it is that when opposing weapons are actually crossed, he who deplores the situation conquers. (Chapter 69)

Man at his birth is supple and weak; at his death, firm and strong. Trees and plants, in their early growth, are soft and brittle; at their death, dry and withered. Thus, it is that firmness and strength are the concomitants of death; softness and weakness, the concomitants of life. Hence, he who relies on the strength of his forces does not conquer; and a tree which is strong will fill the out-stretched arms, and thereby invite the feller. Therefore, the place of what is firm and strong is below, and that of what is soft and weak is above. (Chapter 76)

Though they had boats and carriages, they should have no occasion to ride in them; though they had buff coasts and sharp weapons, they should have no occasion to don or use them. (Chapter 80)

Proof: In accordance with A5, the best of cognition and behaving is "being defensive;" being soft and weak is a valuable way of being defensive, intentionally exposing one's strength (see D14). Also, it is said in A3 that the basic principle of statecraft is "The highest excellence of humility is like that of water" and "Do with inaction;" here the image of water reveals the quality of being soft. So in terms of employing armies, being on the defensive and not belittling the enemy can help the well-prepared keep undefeated. Therefore, we say that those who are soft and do not neglect the enemy can constantly win.

Explanation: During the late Spring and Autumn Period, there were endless wars and bloody slaughters. Being deeply concerned about the wreckage caused by war, Laozi was basically against the war of the day in the hope that the people could live a life comfortably. Confronted with the inevitable reality, he advocated that war should not be declared for any reason, and nobody should "dominate the world by force."

It is recorded in "Fire Attack" of *The Art of War*: No actions should be taken when there are no interests, no armies should be employed when victory is not guaranteed or needed. Do not get involved in war just because of anger; take actions when the situation is favourable, and stop when it is not. With this, Sunzi — the author of the book — warned the kings and generals that people's anger of the very moment can be changed, but a state once destroyed can never be restored, nor the dead can be brought to life. Hence, a king of the Dao should be cautious and a virtuous general be scrutinized, which can guarantee the security of the state and the life of soldiers. In the chapter entitled "Military War," it highlights *"War is a matter of national importance, a matter of life and death, and national survival; thus, it calls for caution."*

P3-18 Assisting the king by being soft and not displaying armies can win authority.

Quotes from *Laozi*:

Those who assist the rulers with the Dao will not assert his mastery in the kingdom by force of arms. The use of military forces will end up in retribution. Thistles and thorns spring up where the army has been stationed. There is sure to be a famine after a great battle. (Chapter 30)

Weapons are inauspicious objects, detested by all, therefore, not used by those who have Dao. The lords ordinarily consider the left hand the most honorable place, but in time of war the right hand. Weapons, inauspicious things, are not lords' tools, used only when they have no alternative. Even if they have won victory, they should treat it with indifference. They should not feel triumphant, and if they treat it triumphantly, it seems that they like killing people. And if one likes killing people, he cannot get his will in the world. Therefore, when one does auspicious things, he should stand on the left side, and when one does mournful things, he should stand on the right side. Therefore, those generals who are not in charge of killing should stand on the left, while those generals who are in charge of killing should stand on the right, that is to say, the ritual of going out to war should be treated in the same way as one attends obsequies. When a great many people are killed, one should feel mournful towards them. When victorious in war, one should show mournful respects for the dead. (Chapter 31)

A master of the art of war has said, "I do not dare to be the host to commence the war; I prefer to act on the defensive. I do not dare to advance an inch; I prefer to retreat a foot." This is called marshalling the ranks where there are no ranks; baring the arms where there are no arms to bare; grasping the weapon where there is no weapon to grasp; advancing against the enemy where there is no enemy. There is no calamity greater than lightly engaging in war. To do that is near losing the gentleness which is so precious. Thus, it is that when opposing weapons are actually crossed, he who deplores the situation wins. (Chapter 69)

Man at his birth is supple and weak; at his death, firm and strong. Trees and plants, in their early growth, are soft and brittle; at their death, dry and withered. Thus, it is that firmness and strength are the concomitants of death; softness and weakness, the concomitants of life. Hence, he who relies on the strength of his forces does not conquer; and a tree which is strong will fill the out-stretched arms, and thereby invite the feller. Therefore, the place of what is firm and strong is below, and that of what is soft and weak is above. (Chapter 76)

Though they had boats and carriages, they should have no occasion to ride in them; though they had buff coasts and sharp weapons, they should have no occasion to don or use them. (Chapter 80)

Proof: From D14, we know that being soft and weak is a valuable way of being defensive, and unintentionally exposing one's strength. According to P3-17, those who are soft and do not neglect the enemy can constantly win; by the same token, it is necessary that one should not display force or bully the weak when assisting a king. "Being defensive" is not merely required in peaceful time, but also in war, for with this one can win the trust of the mass. Hence, we think assisting the king by being soft and not displaying armies can win authority.

Explanation: Following Dao is the principle of doing, which is true for being ministers who should not dominate the world through wars. Once disputes are solved with military force, serious consequences would surely be incurred. As it is put in *Hanfeizi: On Laozi in Metaphor*, "During the years of wars, all states were on the defense; consequently, lice grew on soldiers' armors, songbirds built nests on the military camps, and armies cannot return home." It seems to Laozi that those who know the damage of war by heart would put an end to it when the aim was achieved, rather than dominating with military power, and they would not brag or be arrogant once taking the upper hand, as wars of aggression would not be supported by the people.

It is told in "Following Dao" of *Huainanzi*: Baron Wu of Wei asked Li Ke, "What is the reason for the demise of Wu?" The latter answered, "It won again and again." "It would be blessed if a state can win one after another of the wars; but should Wu

State demise for this?" asked Baron Wu. Li Ke explained, "Constant wars would make the people over-strained, and repetitive victory would inevitably make the monarch proud, so much that he would command and enslave the tired people; hence, it would be rather rare for a state not to perish. Being arrogant, the monarch would unbridle his lust and desire, while being tired, the mass would be resentful and then try to get rid of the suffering, and resort to rebellion." From the perspective of Dao, it is a natural rule that things would decline when they become too stronger. To dominate the world with wars would necessarily accelerate the pace of demise; administratively speaking, frequent wars would bring forth endless suffering to the people who would naturally never support them.

P3-19   Those who are defensive and not bullying others in diplomacy would be convincing.

Quotes from *Laozi*:

The soft overcomes the hard, and the weak, the strong. (Chapter 36)

The movement of the Dao is in endless recursion; the function of the Dao is in its sof and tender manner. (Chapter 40)

What makes a big state is its being like a low-lying, down-flowing stream, with the frailty of a woman, where all rivers converge; it becomes the centre to which tend all the small states under heaven. The feminine often prevail over the masculine by their stillness, their stillness being their lowness. Therefore, a big state can win the faith of a small state with its lowness, and a small state can win the favour of a big state with its lowness. Therefore, lowness wins or lowness reaps. However, the big state has to support the small states, and the small states have to serve the big states. Each gets what it desires, but the big state must learn to abase itself. (Chapter 61)

Why is the sea a place where all the rivers converge? Because it stays low, and all the rivers can converge into it. Thus, it is the king of them all. So it is that the sage, wishing to be above people, puts himself by his words below them, and, wishing to be before them, places his person behind them. The sage rules over the people, but the people do not feel weight. Therefore, the people show respect to the Sage, but not detest and reject him, because he does not strive with others, and there is nobody to strive with him. (Chapter 66)

In this world there is nothing softer than water, which has seen no rival in wearing away hard things, because there is no other thing that can take its place. The weak is stronger than the strong, and the soft is harder than the hard. There is nobody who does not know this in the world, but nobody will practise it. Therefore, the Sage says, "Those who can bear the whole nation's contempt can be called the nation's true rulers; those who can stand the whole nation's disasters have the qualification of being the rulers of the nation." What the Dao expresses seems to be just the opposite. (Chapter 78)

Proof: According to D14, being soft and weak is a valuable way of being defensive, and not intentionally exposing one's strength. According to P3-14 and P3-18, those who are soft and do not neglect the enemy can constantly win, and assisting the king by being soft and not displaying armies can win authority; hence, big states that can be soft and not bully the weak in diplomacy can win admiration. Therefore, it is claimed that those who are defensive and not bullying others in diplomacy would be convincing.

Explanation: Laozi held that both existence and non-existence, and strength and weakness are convertible; all things would definitely be doomed once they turn stronger, so being soft in essence is maintaining a lasting force. And not displaying strength in dealing with other nations can not only avoid a speeding decline, but also earn popularity.

In the Early Han Dynasty, the Emperor Wen adopted the policy of being soft in dealing with the Nanyue Kingdom and the Hun minorities. It is recorded in *Book of Han Dynasty: Biography of Emperor Wen of Han* that Zhao Tuo took himself as the King of the Nanyue Kingdom in the reign of Emperor Wen, while the latter did not choose to take military actions to show the power of Han but to enable Zhao Tuo to surrender by being soft; in terms of dealing with the Hun, he befriended the latter by marriage; even the Hun betrayed him and frequently harassed the border, the Emperor chose defense over invasion and did not send troops to the north, for fear of disturbing the people on both sides. Thanks to the governance with non-action by Emperor Wen and Emperor Jing, the Han Dynasty achieved greater national strength. During the reign of Emperor Wu, he adopted tough diplomat policies and sent such generals as Wei Qing, Huo Qubing and Li Guang to invade the Huns. For this, Sima Qian criticized, "The constant military disasters bring no reconcilability, and the commons are suffering a lot, while the war becomes increasingly worse. Soldiers are on the go for war supplies while the people are busy with sending off. All the hustle and bustle is for the war."

P3-20 By being soft and not misusing power, the monarch can achieve lasting peace and order.

Quotes from *Laozi*:

The skillful masters of Dao in old times, subtle and sophisticated, comprehended its mysteries, which were deep so as to elude men's knowledge. (Chapter 15)

Fishes should not be taken from the deep; sharp weapons of a state should not be shown off. (Chapter 36)

Proof: According to D14, being soft and weak is a valuable way of being moderate, rather than intentionally exposing one's strength. Also, according to P2-14, be it the governance of a household, a state or the world, the constant spontaneous law of life should be followed. Here, the monarch should not purposefully expose his strength on the one hand, and on the other, should be moderate; being in a low profile and not abusing power, he can achieve national peace and prosperity. Thus, we say that by being soft and not misusing power, the monarch can achieve lasting order and security.

Explanation: In "Duke Zhuang of Zheng Defeated Duan at Yan" of *The Spring and Autumn Annals*, there is a record about how Duke Zhuang of Zheng kept a low profile. In the first year of the reign of King Yin (772 BC), Gongshu Duan, the brother of Duke Zhuang of Zheng, attempted to take over the throne under the protection of his mother Wu Jiang. Discovering this, Duke Zhuang of Zheng tried to satisfy the demands of Gongshu Duan by being soft whenever necessary. However, the latter became all the more insatiable and arrogant, so much so that he built the fortress, gathered the crowd with armors and weapons and got ready chariots in an attempt to attack Zheng. Duke Zhuang did not make any attack until he was informed of the rebellion of Gongshu Duan, who lost the favour of the commons and was defeated in Yan. In this confrontation, Duke Zhuang kept soft rather than flaunting, took advance by retreating, and therefore maintained his political power in the end.

It is said in "Following Different Customs" of *Huainanzi* that those ancient monarchs who can keep the rule of Dao and thereby impose or lift bans when necessary were known by following generations and benefited the whole world. Hence, such sages can grasp the rule of Dao and the laws of all things in the palm of their hands, and as a result all the barbarians would surrender with allegiance. This shows how important the rule of Dao is, and that a full command of it can be invincible.

During the second year of his reign (961 AD), Emperor Taizu of Song asked his prime minister Zhao Pu about the way of governance, and was told, "Cut the military power of all generals." Emperor Taizu was in great agreement and adopted a soft way. He entertained generals of achievements, Shi Shouxin included, saying, "It is really tiring to command troops, which would also arouse mistrust; it would be the happiest thing to buy some fertile land to enjoy life rather than command the armies." Shi Shouxin and other generals immediately grasped his intention, replying "Thank you, your majesty, for worrying about our toil and being so thoughtful." The next day the generals resigned on the excuse of being ill and handed over their military power. This was a great event in history that distributed power by peaceful means and met man's desire with the wisdom of softness, which was called "Weakening military power with a cup of wine."

P3-21 He who is soft and does not claim credit for himself in administration would be safe and secure for a longer time.

Quotes from *Laozi*:

He who displays himself is not conspicuous; he who asserts his own views is not illustrious; he who brags himself is not meritorious; he who boasts of himself is not enduring. (Chapter 24)

Proof: From D14 and D12, we know that being soft and weak is a valuable way of being moderate, rather than intentionally showing one's strength, while "not striving" or "non-contention" is an attitude to dealing with the world after eliminating excessive desire and ingenious smartness, which is not coward retreat or timidity but an inward strength. Plus, what is claimed in A3 — the basic principle of statecraft is "The greatest virtue is like that of water" and "to do through non-action" — also shows the quality of not striving. And ancient sages advocated retreating after making achievements (by P2-21). Therefore, he who is soft and does not claim credit for himself in administration would be safe and secure for a longer time.

Explanation: Being politically soft is to keep a low profile and eliminate one's desire of claiming credit for himself, which is what Laozi called *"The sage acts without claiming the results as his; he achieves his merit and does not rest arrogantly on it."* Being soft is also "not striving" and can dispel the dissatisfaction and suspicion of the opponents, which can free one from dangers. According to "Family of King Goujian of Yue" of *Records of the Grand Historian*, with the joint efforts of Fan Li, King Goujian finally restored his state during the Spring and Autumn Period. Achieving fame, Fan Li did not abandon himself in the achievement, but persuaded Wen Zhong, "The arches won't be put away until all the rabbits are killed; good dogs would be cooked once foxy rabbits are dead. Like a long-beak bird, King Goujian is nothing but a fair-weathered monarch, so why not leave him?" Zhong Shu did not give up his high position or fat salary, and later was killed by King Goujian, while Fan Li stepped down gracefully and hence saved his own life.

It is also recorded in "Family of Zhang Liang" of *Records of the Grand*

Historian that during the Early Han Dynasty Zhang Liang did not claim for credits but politely turned down the generous rewards offered by Emperor Gaozu of Han, explaining "With a silver tongue, I served as an assistant to the monarch and was rewarded with ranks and land, which is the highest achievement by commons and is sufficient for me. So I'm willing to give up the ranks and travel around like Chisongzi, the ancient celestial being." With a humble and inoffensive attitude, Zhang Liang abandoned his ranks and salary, which is in conformity with what Laozi said, "With no arrogance, one lasts longer." In contrast, his colleague General Han Xin failed to step down and in the end got his clan killed. In *Records of the Grand Historian: Biography of Han Xin,* Sima Qian commented, "*If Han Xin were humble and stepped down rather than bragged about his achievements and talents, he would have been the same as Zhang Liang.*" His tragedy was incurred by his striving for merits and bragging of talent, and he did not end well, because he failed to follow the soft and humble attitude proposed by Daoism.

P3-22   Being soft with the people and not striving for fortune would bring long-term benefits.

Quotes from *Laozi:*

The perfect goodness is like water. Water is good at benefiting all things, but does not contend with them. It prefers to dwell in places the masses of people detest, therefore it is closest to the Dao. (Chapter 8)

One does not contend with others, so no one is in a position to contend with him. (Chapter 22)

Why is the sea a place where all the rivers converge? Because it stays low, and all the rivers can converge into it. Thus, it is the king of them all. So it is that the sage, wishing to be above people, puts himself by his words below them, and, wishing to be before them, places his person behind them. The sage rules over the people, but the people do not feel weight. Therefore, the people show respect to the Sage, but not detest and reject him, because he does not strive with others, and there is nobody to strive with him. (Chapter 66)

It is the way of Heaven not to strive, and yet to be good at winning; not to speak yet skillfully responding, not to summon, yet men come to it of themselves; to be at ease yet carefully plan. (Chapter 73)

The people do not fear death, so why do you frighten them with death? If the people were always in awe of death, and I could always seize those who do wrong and put them to death, who would dare to do wrong? It is the headsman that kills.

(Chapter 74)

The Dao of heaven benefits rather than harms; the Dao of the sage is to give rather than contend. (Chapter 81)

Proof: From D14 and D12, we know that being soft and weak is a valuable way of being moderate, rather than intentionally exposing one's strength, while "not striving" is an attitude to dealing with the world after eliminating excessive desire and ingenious smartness; besides, an ideal society manifests itself in social peace and prosperity (by P3-4), which is the fundamental basis for people's spontaneous and natural living, because the mass can behave freely only when their basic living is satisfied. On the part of the monarch, his no striving for wealth can make the society harmonious, strong and prosperous. Therefore, being soft with the people and not striving for fortune would bring long-term benefits.

Explanation: Laozi held that social peace and prosperity can make the people live spontaneously and naturally, and thus is an ideal state. The reason why such an ideal society did not come into reality is that the administrator failed to be soft but strove for interests. He also said, "*Heavy taxation reduced the people to starvation; it is the willfulness of rulers that makes the people a challenge to govern.*"

In "Explaining Laozi," *Hanfeizi* says, "*If the monarch does not employ penalty internally and strive for fortune externally, his people would enjoy social peace and security. As such, the commons would naturally have more accumulations, which can be called morals. The so-called misbehavior is in fact lifelessness, which is immoral. If the monarch creates social peace and security, even the ghost would not disturb people's life and morals prevail.*" It is recorded in "On Food and Goods," *Book of Han*: "*During the Early Han period, the people were suffering from food shortage after war. The Emperor could not get four horses of the same color for his chariot, and the ministers could only ride ox. In such a situation, Emperor Gaozu of Han issued a decree to prohibit waste and heavy taxation, which saved expenses and reduced people's burden.*" The political non-action and economic recuperation in the early Han laid a foundation for the two-hundred-year ruling of the Western Han Dynasty. Being soft with the people and not striving for fortune can bring forth social peace and security, and enable people to live comfortably.

P3-23 To teach the people to be soft and not to indulge in desires can keep their minds free from disturbance.

Quotes from *Laozi*:

Therefore, the sage, in the exercise of his government, empties their minds, fills their bellies, weakens their wills, and strengthens their bones. He always keeps them innocent of knowledge and free from desire, and disables the wise from taking any ill actions. If you deal with worldly affairs by "non-action," there will be no trouble of government. (Chapter 3)

Dao does nothing yet nothing is left undone. Should lords and kings be able to maintain it, all things will be transformed on their own. After they are transformed, they may grow avid. I will check the avidity with the nameless simplicity of Dao. Checked with the nameless simplicity, they will have no avidity. No avidity leads to serenity, hence the empire's stability. (Chapter 37)

The sage has no invariable mind of his own; he makes the mind of the people his own. The kind people, I treat them kindly; the unkind people, I treat them kindly as well. And in this way, I attain kindness. The trustworthy people, I trust them; the untrustworthy people, I trust them as well. And in this way, I attain trustworthiness. He abstains to make all men simple. The people all keep their eyes and ears directed to him, and he deals with them all as his children. (Chapter 49)

Proof: From D14 and D2, we know that being soft and weak is a valuable way of being defensive, rather than intentionally exposing one's strength, while "desiring" especially means an excessive desire that runs against nature and exposing one's strength for personal gains. According to A5, the best of cognition and behaving is being defensive, so teaching the people to be soft and not to indulge in desires can keep them true and peacefully-minded, rather than disturb their minds. Hence, to teach the people to be soft and not to indulge in desires can keep their minds free from disturbance.

Explanation: Being free from softness would make one desire too much, which in turn would disturb people's mind and cause social instability. In "*Explaining Laozi,*" Hanfeizi, "*Governing social affairs in essence involves the inhibition of excessive desire. Generally speaking, horses can meet the need of fighting, while it would be a luxury once used internally. Nowadays, kings of Dao seldom employ armies, and also curb excessive luxury; they would not use horses in fighting enemies, nor would the people use them for carrying military supplies; thus, all would be used for the purpose of plowing.*" In Hanfeizi's view, the sage should not start wars externally and should prohibit excessive luxury internally. As such, his people would be fully committed to farming.

P3-24 By rendering the people simplified, they can come back to the natural way.

Quotes from *Laozi:*

Therefore, the sage, in the exercise of his government, empties their minds, fills their bellies, weakens their wills, and strengthens their bones. (Chapter 3)

Therefore, the sage seeks to satisfy the craving of the belly, and not the insatiable longing of the eyes. He puts away from his the latter, and prefers to seek the former. (Chapter 12)

The sage has no invariable mind of his own; he makes the mind of the people his own. The kind people, I treat them kindly; the unkind people, I treat them kindly as well. And in this way, I attain kindness. The trustworthy people, I trust them; the untrustworthy people, I trust them as well. And in this way, I attain trustworthiness. He abstains to make all men simple. The people all keep their eyes and ears directed to him, and he deals with them all as his children. (Chapter 49)

When the government is unwise, the people are simple; when the government is meddling, the people are troublesome. (Chapter 58)

Proof: According to P2-4, greed and ingenuity would drive human society astray from the ease and spontaneous state of life. Also, it is said in P2-5 that a simplified mind with no desire is the natural choice for those who want to get rid of desire and ingenuity in order to return to the natural state. In the course of governing the state, making the people simplified is an important way of creating natural harmony. Thus, we claim that by rendering the people simplified, they can come back to the natural way.

Explanation: Laozi's advocating of the natural way is for governors to act with non-action and also for the mass to live an easy and happy life. There are views that his idea of sage's non-action has two meanings: on the one hand, it refers to the non-action of the social governors rather than the norm for the behavior of ordinary people; on the other hand, the sage not only sets an example for social governors, but also for the mass; hence, the principle of non-action serves as guidance or enlightenment for ordinary people as well.[1]

In "Following Different Customs" of *Huainanzi*, it records that "*To govern a state of peace and prosperity, the monarch gives no harsh decree, officials have no cumbersome tasks, scholars are free from hypocritical conduct and craftsmen from*

---

1 Liu Xiaogan. *Laozi from Ancient to Modern Times*. China Social Sciences Press, 2006, p.738.

wickedness, leaving everything in its natural way and things undecorated. Hence, the ancient decree of Shennong says: 'If a man does not engage in farming, there would be someone starving; if a woman does not work on weaving, there would be someone unclothed.' This is why Shennong engaged in farming by himself and his wife in spinning and weaving, setting an example for the people to follow. Shennong taught the people not to wittingly prize things difficult to get, and useless articles. As such, in that age men had to go farming, otherwise they would go hungry, and women had to do weaving, as abundance or shortage was tied to each person. If abundance emerges, there would be no evil behavior and everyone could live a happy and peaceful life."

P3-25   Administrators should have true virtue.

Quotes from *Laozi:*

He always keeps them innocent of knowledge and free from desire, and disables the wise from taking any ill actions. (Chapter 3)

Too many colors dazzle the eyes; too much music deafens the ears; too many tastes baffle the palate. Overindulging in hunting drives you crazy, and coveting too many material things tarnishes your conduct. Therefore, the Sage cares for bellies rather than senses, pleasures, fending off material temptation and living a simple life. (Chapter 12)

If the rulers could get rid of their sophistry, the people could have a hundred times of benefit; if the rulers could get rid of their falsity, the people's piety and affection could be recovered; if the rulers could forsake the swindling of material things, robbery and theft would vanish from this world. Sophistry, falsity and swindling are the three superficial embellishments, which could not be applied to governing the country. Therefore, if the rulers intend to make the people serve them willingly, they should try their best to retain simplicity and honesty, to discard selfish desires, and to be content with ignorance, and there will be no anxieties. (Chapter 19)

Hence, the sage puts away excessive effort, extravagance, and easy indulgence. (Chapter 29)

Fame or life, which do you hold more dear? Life or wealth, to which would you adhere? Keep life and lose those other things or keep them and lose your life, which brings sorrow and pain more near? Thus we may see, he who cleaves to fame rejects what is greater, he who loves large stores gives up the richer state, he who is content need fear no shame, and he who knows to stop incurs no blame. From danger free, long live shall he. (Chapter 44)

No disaster can be greater than that of insatiability; no sin can be greater than that of avarice. Therefore, the everlasting satiation is the satiation of the innermost being. (Chapter 46)

Therefore, the sage desires what the average people do not desire, not coveting rare goods; he learns what the average people do not learn, mending the faults of the average people. Thus, he helps the natural development of all things, not intervening with them. (Chapter 64)

Proof: According to P2-4, greed and ingenuity would drive human society astray from the free, unrestrained state of life. Besides, De refers to the spontaneous and unrestrained operations of Dao from non-existence to existence and then back to non-existence, and to the virtue that people learn and master in adaptation (By D1 and D10). By P3-2, ancient society under the leadership of sages is a paragon of an ideal society, which followed by administrators would lead to an ideal state that can easily be adapted to nature. Hence, we say that the administrators should have true virtue.

Explanation: Legend has it that Emperor Yao was advanced in age after reigning for seventy years, and he refused the recommendation of Dan Zhu, whom Yao believed to be rough and aggressive. Later, the Emperor held a tribal alliance meeting to discuss about the candidacy. People recommended Shun for his virtues and competences; after testing this candidate for three years, the emperor finally decided to give the throne to him. Years later, Emperor Shun gave his throne to Yu in the same way rather than to his son, Shang Jun. All of the three were generous to the people and created a golden age in ancient China. It is recorded in *Book of Changes* that "*After the death of Shennong, Emperors Huang, Yao and Shun took the course of Heaven and Earth, letting the people live easily and cultivating them marvelously. With this, the three emperors governed the state naturally. It is presumably by taking the image of Heaven and Earth, or Yang and Yin from Changes.*"

Only with true virtue can administrators make it with non-action and their people "tireless and adapted to it." "*Following Different Customs*" of *Huainanzi* has it that "*If administrators were confused by defamation and praise, or indulged in colorful things, it would be impossible for them to get things done.*"

P3-26   The administrators must have the quality of integrity.

Quotes from *Laozi*:

The excellence of a residence is in the suitability of the place; that of the mind is in abysmal stillness; that of associations is in their being with the virtuous; that of government is in its securing good order; that of the conduct of affairs is in its ability; and that of the initiation of any movement is in its timeliness. (Chapter 8)

The best ruler, the people do not seem to know his existence; next comes the ruler whom the people are willing to get close to; next comes one awed by the people; next comes one they contempt. Short of credit, the rulers are not trusted. So leisurely and carefree, the best ruler is cautious in uttering words. When his task is accomplished and his work done, the people all say, "The things all happened to us naturally." (Chapter 17)

He who lightly promises is sure to keep but little faith; he who is continually thinking things easy is sure to find them difficult. (Chapter 63)

Sincere words are not fine; fine words are not sincere. (Chapter 81)

Proof: By D1, we know that De refers to the spontaneous and unrestrained operations of Dao from non-existence to existence and then to non-existence, and to virtue that people learn and master in adaptation. Also, according to P2-22, administrators must have true virtue, which means they must also develop the quality of integrity and not cheat others with smartness. Thus, we say that the administrators must have the quality of integrity.

Explanation: Laozi held that administrators who follow the natural way should cherish integrity, one of the qualities that officials should have. There is a story in "Following Dao," *Huainanzi:* During the Spring and Autumn Period, King Wen of Jin discussed with his senior officials and decided on conquering Yuan Yi in three days, but failed. He gave the order of a withdrawal of the army. Officers on his side suggested that the people of Yuan Yi would surrender for one or two more days. King Wen answered: "I had never thought of this. As I had agreed with my senior officials, I would lose credibility if persisting in fighting, which is something I'd not do, even I could occupy Yuan Yi." When the people there heard of this, they all surrendered, saying "The king was so faithful to his words; why not surrender to him?"

On the contrary, there are also cases where administrators paid a heavy price for their loss of credibility. In "History of the Zhou Dynasty" of *Records of the Grand Historian*, it records that King You of Zhou made fun of the princes. King You endeared the beauty, Bao Si, who did not smile all day. Seeing this, he tried everything to bring a smile on her face but to no avail. One day, the king lit the beacon and beat the drums, which would only be done when there were invaders. The princes came hastily but saw no invasion at all, while this made Bao Si smile. King You was very delighted at the effect and then lit the beacon several times to make fun of the princes. From then onward, they did not believe the king, nor did they visit him. When the state was attacked by Prince Shen in liaison with Zeng State and Quanrong, King You lit the beacon tower but no princes came to help.

P3-27　The administrators should be selfless and responsible.

Quotes from *Laozi:*

Heaven is long-enduring and earth continues long. The reason why heaven and earth are able to endure and continue thus long is because they do not live of, or for, themselves. Therefore, the Sages retreat to the back, but win the respect of others; they seldom consider for themselves, but keep themselves safe and sound. Isn't it because they are not selfish so that they attain what they ought to attain? (Chapter 7)

One is panic-stricken when he's favoured or humiliated. He is too much worried about his body as much as calamity. What is meant by speaking thus of being favoured and humiliated? Favour itself is inferior. Getting that favour, one has the fear of losing it; losing it, one has the fear of still greater calamity. That's what is meant. And what is meant by saying that one is too much worried about his body as much as calamity? We have great worries because we have the flesh body. If we have no flesh body, what worries do we have? Therefore, he who values the empire as he values his own body can be entrusted with the care of the empire. He who loves the empire as he loves his own body can be given the custody of the empire. (Chapter 13)

So it is that the sage, wishing to be above people, puts himself by his words below them, and, wishing to be before them, places his person behind them. The sage rules over the people, but the people do not feel weight. Therefore, the people show respect to the Sage, but not detest and reject him, because he does not strive with others, and there is nobody to strive with him. (Chapter 66)

In this world there is nothing softer than water, which has seen no rival in wearing away hard things, because there is no other thing that can take its place. The weak is stronger than the strong, and the soft is harder than the hard. There is nobody who does not know this in the world, but nobody will practise it. Therefore, the Sage says, "Those who can bear the whole nation's contempt can be called the nation's true rulers; those who can stand the whole nation's disasters have the qualification of being the rulers of the nation." What the Dao expresses seems to be just the opposite. (Chapter 78)

Proof: From D1 and D8, we know that De refers to the spontaneous and unrestrained operations of Dao from non-existence to existence and then back to non-existence, and to the virtue that people learn and master in adaptation, while "selflessness" refers to the tolerance after eliminating excessive "desires" and smart "wits." Also, according to P3-22, administrators should cherish a mind of true virtues. This means that administrators should be selfless and shoulder the responsibility so much so that they can govern the state effectively. Hence, administrators should be selfless and responsible.

Explanation: By advocating governance with non-action, Laozi took into consideration the common people as the ultimate end. It seemed to him that the sage should think what the commons think, speak humbly, and put the interests of the people at first. So, rulers must be responsible for the people.

It is told in "Following Dao" of *Huainanzi*: Learning the Mars took the place of Antares, King Jing of Song was scared and told his historian, Zi Wei, who explained that "The Mars forebodes heavenly punishment while Antares the division of the state. By this way, it shows that disasters would fall onto the king, but I suggest you pass it onto the prime minister." "The prime minister is assigned to rule the country, and it would be unlucky to let him die instead," replied the king. Zi Wei then suggested that "Or you can pass it onto the people." The king refuted immediately, "If all the people died, who could be my people? I'd rather die instead." "What about pass onto the harvest?" The king continued, "Harvest is the lifeline of the mass, without which there would be starvation. If I save myself at the cost of the lives of the people, who would take me as the monarch?" In the end, King Jing did not pass the disaster onto others. Laozi had it: "He who can undertake the disasters of the state can be the king," because he was willing to take the responsibility for the state.

P3-28 The administrators should have a sense of prevention.

Quotes from *Laozi*:

Misery is what happiness is to be found by its side; happiness is what misery lurks beneath it. (Chapter 58)

To anticipate things that are difficult while they are easy, and do things that would become great while they are small. To deal with what is difficult, you should start from what is easy, and to aim high, you should be content in doing trivialities. Therefore, the sage, while he never does what is great, is able on that account to accomplish the greatest things. He who lightly promises is sure to keep but little faith; he who is continually thinking things easy is sure to find them difficult. Therefore, the sage sees difficulty even in what seems easy, and so never has any *difficulties.* (Chapter 63)

That which is at rest is easily kept hold of; before a thing has given indications of its presence, it is easy to take measures against it; that which is brittle is easily broken; that which is very small is easily dispersed. Action should be taken before a thing has made its appearance; order should be secured before disorder has begun. The tree which fills the arms grows from the tiniest sprout; the tower of nine storeys rises from a small heap of earth; the journey of a thousand li commences with a single step. He who acts with an ulterior purpose does harm; he who takes hold of a thing in the same way loses his hold. The sage does not act so, and therefore does no harm; he does not lay hold so, and therefore does not lose his hold. But people in their conduct of affairs are constantly ruining them when they are on the eve of success. If they were careful at the end, as they should be at the beginning, they would not so ruin them. Therefore, the sage desires what the average people do not desire, not coveting rare goods; he learns what the average people do not learn, mending the faults of the average people. Thus, he helps the natural development of all things, not intervening with them. (Chapter 64)

Proof: By D4, we know that people know "the Dao" by "observing." Also, the means of observing "the Dao" is by feeling the nuances and those who prize virtue can reach the realm of clarity and embody "the way" by observation. Administrators are practitioners of De, and they should pay attention to subtlety and particularly to signs in between existence and non-existence, so that they can guard against the risks of "A little leak will sink a great ship." Thus, administrators should have a sense of prevention.

Explanation: For administrators, they should be sharp in discovering the symptoms of changes and nip the problems in the bud. In "Biography of Situ Dinghong" of *History of the Later Han Dynasty*, it records that when the young incompetent Emperor He ascended the throne, Empress Dou actually ruled and promoted her brother Dou Xian as the general, making the national power fall into the hands of Empress Dou's families. They misbehaved and schemed to usurp the power and throne. Minister Situ Dinghong was rather angry with the autocracy of the empress and thus decided to remove the bane of the country. A couple of years later, seeing the eclipse, Dinghong reported it to the emperor, "The eclipse is a warning to the monarch" and "Your majesty can eliminate the disaster by preventing it beforehanded." He suggested that the power of the Empress should be put under control to guard against future troubles when it was not overwhelming, so that long peace and perpetuation of the state can be secured. As the emperor already had the determination, he took the advice of the minister, appointing the latter as senior official in charge of military and guarding affairs in the South and North Courts, and dismissing Dou Xian. Knowing they could not get rid of the punishment, the Dou families committed suicide, which helped prevent a likely palace coup in the end. The emperor and Dinghong eliminated the families of Empress Dou in time, and thus saved the state.

"On Laozi in Metaphor" of *Hanfeizi* tells the story of Bian Que the Doctor and King Cai Huan: In the Spring and Autumn Period, master Bian Que visited the King, and warned that "Your disease is just on the texture of the skin. I'm afraid it would be worse, if not cured." The king replied disapprovingly, "Doctors would choose to treat sound people, and take it as credits." After some time, Bian Que visited the king again and said, "Your skin gets deteriorate and would be more severe, if not treated," which fell upon a deaf ear. As such, he warned for some more times, but in vain. When the disease spread to the vital organs, Bian Que saw the king and left right away. The king died after a couple of days.

第六章 CHAPTER SIX

摄生篇
On Preserving Health

本章的主旨是，要关爱自我的生命，要实现关爱自我的生命与关爱他人生命的统一，必须以"清静自然"为原则。命题P4-1指出根本原则是效法"自然"；命题P4-2至P4-6指出如何保持虚静、淡泊、淳厚的心境以及淡化自我的嗜欲，以之作为效法"自然"的基础；命题P4-7至P4-10指出应基于自然原则的财富观，正确对待财富与生命的关系；命题P4-11至P4-14指出，基于自然原则的祸福荣辱观须以知足不辱、为而不恃为核心；命题P4-15至P4-19提出了基于"自然"原则的强弱论、巧拙论，以及争与不争的论题；命题P4-20至P4-22指出个体与万物共生的原则。

P4-1 遵循"自然"是养生的总原则。

【参见《老子》条目】

人法地，地法天，天法道，道法自然。（第二十五章）

证明：从定义2可知，"欲"指人对财富、名声和权力的追求，这种追求会违背"自然"，带来不良后果。根据公理A1与公理A5，"自然"是"道"从"无"到"有"再到"无"的自在自为过程，而摄生的基本方法是消除过分的"欲"和机巧性的"智"，以求做到不违背"自然"，摄生就是一个自在自为的过程。因此，遵循"自然"是养生的总原则。

例证和说明："道法自然"就是"道"效法（或遵循）"自然"。三国时代王弼对"人法地，地法天，天法道，道法自然"这句话及"法"字作了前后一贯的注解："法，谓法则也。人不违地，乃得全安，法地也。地不违天，乃得全载，法天也。天不违道，乃得全覆，法道也。道不违自然，乃得其性，法自然也。法自然者，在方而法方，在圆而法圆，于自然无所违也。自然者，无称之言，穷极之辞也。……道法自然，天故资焉。天法于道，地故则焉。地法于天，人故象焉。王所以为主，其主之者一也。"[1]

---

1 楼宇烈：《王弼集校释》，北京：中华书局，1980年，第65页。

我国东晋时的著名诗人陶渊明自号"五柳先生",他继承了老子"道法自然"的思想,顺应自己的本性,"不为五斗米折腰",弃官归田,为后人所称颂。他在《归园田居》一诗中写道:"少无适俗韵,性本爱丘山。误落尘网中,一去十三年。羁鸟恋旧林,池鱼思故渊。开荒南野际,抱拙归园田。方宅十余亩,草屋八九间。榆柳荫后檐,桃李罗堂前。暧暧远人村,依依墟里烟。狗吠深巷中,鸡鸣桑树颠。户庭无尘杂,虚室有余闲。久在樊笼里,复得返自然。"陶渊明通过几次做官、归田的反复,终于认识到自己"性本爱丘山",十几年的为官生涯实际是"误落尘网中",少年时期就流露出的"少无适俗韵"才是自己的真正本性。他从大自然中"羁鸟恋旧林,池鱼思故渊"的现象悟出养生的道理,只有在辞官之后他才感受到"复得返自然"的愉悦!陶渊明虽一生贫困,但由于他回归田园、回归自然,仍然得到了安定的生活。

P4-2 保持虚静之心才能回到生命的根本。

【参见《老子》条目】

致虚极,守静笃。万物并作,吾以观复。夫物芸芸,各复归其根。归根曰静,静曰复命。(第十六章)

天下有始,以为天下母。既得其母,以知其子;既知其子,复守其母,没身不殆。(第五十二章)

证明:根据基本假设2,"有"生万物,万物复归于"无",而万物需要"道"的滋养。所以,复归于"无"才能得到"道"的滋养。从定义5,"静"是涤除了过分的"欲"与机巧性的"智"的干扰而达到的内心澄明状态。只有虚静,才能回归于"无",才能得到"道"的滋养,从而颐养天年。因此,保持虚静之心才能回到生命的根本。

例证和说明:"万物并作,吾以观复",万事万物的发展变化都有其自身的规律,从生长到死亡、再生长到再死亡,生生不息,循环往复,以至于无穷。老子主张回归到一切存在的根源,这是完全虚静的状态,也是一切存在的本性。"归根曰静":归根是一种绝然的静,又是一种超然的"无"。"静曰复命":陈腐在"死一般"的寂静中消亡,但新生也在静中萌动。庄子对虚静也很重视,一再讲到虚静的重要性。他在《天道》中说:"夫虚静恬淡寂漠无为者,天地之平而道德之至,故帝王圣人休焉。无为则俞俞,俞俞者忧患不能处,年寿长矣。夫虚静恬淡寂漠无为者,万物之本也。"这就是说,虚静、恬淡、寂寞、无为,是天地的基准,是道德修养的最高境界,所以古代帝王和圣明的人都停留在这一境界上。虚静便能无为，无为也就从容自得，从容自得的人便不会忧愁与招致祸患，年寿也就长久了。在《刻意》篇中，庄子也谈到了类似的思想："夫恬淡寂漠，虚无无为，此天地之平而道德之质也"，"心不忧乐，德之至也；一而不变，静之至也；无所于忤，虚之至也；不与物交，淡之至也；无所于逆，粹之至也"。

从老子思想而发展起来的道教，倡导"我命在我，不在天""重人贵生"，将人的生命视作现实的存在，当作有形、有气、有神的统一，构造了一个比较完整的养生体系。张道陵追求长生仙寿，但修行的路依然沿着道家清静自然的情操为依归，强调遵"道"而行，结精自守。随着道教的传播，养生之道潜移默化地渗透进了广大民众的生活方式之中。

P4-3 养生的最高境界是保持"赤子之心"。

【参见《老子》条目】

载营魄抱一，能无离乎？专气致柔，能如婴儿乎？（第十章）

知其雄，守其雌，为天下溪。为天下溪，常德不离，复归于婴儿。知其白，守其辱，为天下谷。为天下谷，常德乃足，复归于朴。（第二十八章）

百姓皆注其耳目，圣人皆孩之。（第四十九章）

含德之厚，比于赤子。蜂虿虺蛇不螫，攫鸟猛兽不搏。……终日号而不嗄，和之至也。（第五十五章）

物壮则老，是谓不道，不道早已。（第三十章）

天下之至柔，驰骋天下之至坚。（第四十三章）

证明：依据公理A5，摄生的基本方法是消除过分的"欲"和机巧性的"智"。由定义7可知，"无私"指消除过分的"欲"和机巧性的"智"之后而达到的能包容万物的心理状态，"包容万物"的前提是消除过分的"欲"和机巧性的"智"（即表现为淳朴）。"包容万物"，也即让万物处于自在自为状态，不施加任何外在的强力作用。而"赤子之心"表现为淳朴、自在自为等。因此，养生的最高境界是保持"赤子之心"。

例证和说明：《庄子·庚桑楚》记载，庚桑楚的弟子南荣趎去请教老子养生的常规方法，老子告诉他说："你想知道养生的基本方法吗？那你要先问问自己，能够使身形与精神和谐浑一吗？能够不丧失本有的天性吗？能够不求助于卜筮而知道吉凶吗？能够满足于自己的本分吗？能够对消逝了的东西不做追求吗？能够舍弃仿效他人的心思而寻求自身的完善吗？能够无拘无束、自由自在吗？能够心神宁寂无所执着吗？能够回归到初生婴儿那样的纯真、朴质吗？婴儿整天啼哭咽喉却不会嘶哑，这是因为声音和谐自然达到了顶点。婴儿整天握着小手而不松开，这是因为在母腹内早已如此。婴儿整天瞪着小眼睛一点也不眨眼，这是因为内心世界不会滞留于外界事物。行走起来不知道去哪里，平日居处不知道做什么，接触外物随顺应合，如同随波逐流、听其自然。这就是养生的基本方法了。"南荣趎听完，迫切地问："那么这就是至人的最高境界吗？"老子回答："不是的，这只是所谓冰冻消解那样自然消除心中积滞的本能。道德修养最高尚的人，不因外在的人物或利害而扰乱自己，不参与怪异，不参与图谋，不参与尘俗的事务，无拘无束、自由自在地走了，又心神宁寂、无所执着地到来。这就是所说的养生的常识了。"南荣趎又问道："那么这就达到了最高的境界吗？"老子说："没有。我前面已经告诉过你，要像初生的婴儿那样纯真、朴质！婴儿活动不知道干什么，行走不知道去哪里。像这样的人，灾祸不会到来，幸福也不会降临，才是养生真正需要的境界。"

《庄子》中的"婴儿"即是"赤子"。《列子》中亦说："其在婴孩，气专志一，和之至也。物不伤焉，德莫加也。"可见，道家都将保持淳朴柔弱的"赤子之心"作为养生的最高境界。

P4-4 淡泊是"自然"的特性，也有益于生命。

【参见《老子》条目】

乐与饵，过客止。道之出口，淡乎其无味，视之不足见，听之不足闻，用之不足既。（第三十五章）

证明：依据公理A1，"自然"是"道"从"无"到"有"再到"无"的自在自为过程，而与"有"相对的"无"给人的感受包括"淡泊""宁静""空明"等自然特性。据公理A5，摄生的基本方法是消除过分的"欲"和机巧性的"智"，它所产生的特点就是"淡泊"等状态。因此，淡泊是自然的特性，也有益于生命。

例证和说明：《老子》一书多次提到"味"，如"道之出口，淡乎其无味"。有人指出，老子所说的"味""已经是一个美学范畴"。老子说的"味"，不是吃东西的味道，而"是一种审美的享受"。这种淡而无味又是最高境界的"味"，是"至味"。它强调对人们所易于沉迷的外在的物、财、权等妨碍人的身心健康的对象的摒弃和超越，而突出对精神上淡泊宁静、淳朴自乐的状态的追求。[1]明代的洪应明在《菜

1　叶朗：《中国美学史大纲》，上海：上海人民出版社，1985年，第33页。

根谭》中指出:"能忍受粗茶淡饭的人,他们的操守多半像冰一样清纯、玉一样洁白;而讲究穿华美衣服的人,多半都甘愿做出卑躬屈膝的奴才面孔。因为一个人的志向要在清新寡欲的状态下才能表现出来,而一个人的节操都是在贪图物质享受中丧失殆尽。"

梁漱溟是我国著名的思想家、教育家和社会活动家。他少年多病,但一生投身社会活动,经历坎坷,而这并没有影响到他的长寿。从清光绪十九年(1893年)出生到1988年逝世,梁漱溟活了95岁,这和他一生淡泊的人生态度有很大的关系。1928年,梁漱溟在河南进行过短期的村治实验,1931年又到山东的邹平,开展了长达七年的乡村建设运动,后来实验区逐步扩大到全省十几个县,在海内外产生了影响。他与毛泽东在1918年时即已相识,在后来的岁月中两人之间有共鸣,也有争论。无论在什么情况下,梁漱溟都保持了荣辱不惊的淡泊心态。曾有人在他晚年时询问他的长寿秘诀,梁漱溟回答道:"要说养生,我的经验可总结为:在生活上少吃多动,持之以恒,在精神上气贵平和,情贵淡泊。"

P4-5 无节制地追求感官享受有害于生命。

【参见《老子》条目】

五色令人目盲;五音令人耳聋;五味令人口爽;驰骋田猎,令人心发狂;难得之货,令人行妨。是以圣人为腹不为目,故去彼取此。(第十二章)

服文彩,带利剑,厌饮食,财货有余,是谓盗夸。非道也哉!(第五十三章)

治人事天,莫若啬。夫唯啬,是谓早服;早服谓之重积德;重积德则无不克;无不克则莫知其极;莫知其极,可以有国;有国之母,可以长久。是谓深根固柢,长生久视之道。(第五十九章)

证明:从定义2可知,"欲"指人对财富、名声和权力的追求,这种追求可能产生违背"自然"的后果。根据公理A5,摄生的基本方法是消除过分的"欲"和机巧性的"智"。无节制地追求感官享受就是过分的"欲"的表现,它违背了"自然",违背摄生的基本方法,不利于养生。因此,无节制地追求感官享受有害于生命。

例证和说明:能刺激人感官而产生愉悦的东西对于人来说实无益处,它们只是刺激人的欲望,使人"目盲""耳聋",甚至"心发狂",因而老子主张抛弃这些东西。老子提出"五色令人目盲,五音令人耳聋"的观点,尖锐地批判了富贵者对于声色之美的过分享受。不择手段地过分追求声色之美的享受,其结果只能导致对自身生命的损害。这种情况在当时的统治者中屡见不鲜。《左传·昭公元年》载晋侯有疾,求医于秦,秦伯派医和去晋,医和告诉晋侯不要"烦手淫声,慆堙心耳而忘平和"。君子虽然亲近琴瑟，但必定以仪节之。若无节制地沉溺于声乐享受，过度刺激生理感官，结果只会带来各种疾病，有害于人的生命健康。

《国语·周语下》中记载单穆公亦说："夫乐不过以听耳，而美不过以观目。若听乐而震，观美而眩，患莫甚焉。"近代魏源在《老子本义》中也指出："视久则眩，听繁则惑。"沉湎于声色之乐会使自己的理智感官受损害，甚至危及人的自身生命。老子提出了"圣人为腹不为目"，王弼《老子注》云："为腹者以物养己，为目者以物役己，故圣人不为目也。"圣人重身养己，保全自我生命，以自身生命价值为第一，使之不为外物所役使和损害。贪图感官享受，迷失了自己，就会让自身生命受损。

《吕氏春秋·本生》指出，水本来是清澈的，但因为搅进去了泥土，所以水无法保持清澈。人本来是可以长寿的，但因为有外物使他迷乱，所以人才无法达到长寿。外物本来是供养生命的，而不该损耗生命去追求它。可是如今世上糊涂的人多损耗生命去追求外物，这样做是不知轻重。假如有这样一种声音，耳朵听到它肯定感到惬意，但听了之后就会耳聋，人们一定不会去听。假如有这样一种颜色，眼睛看到它肯定感到惬意，但看了之后就会眼瞎，人们一定不会去看。假如有这样一种食物，嘴巴吃到它肯定感到惬意，但吃了之后就会声哑，人们一定不会去吃。因比，圣人对于声音、颜色、滋味的态度是，有利于生命的就取用，有害于生命的就舍弃，这是保全生命的方法。世上富贵的人对于声色滋味的态度大多是糊涂的。他们日日夜夜地追求这些东西，得到后就放纵自己不能自禁，如此，生命怎能不受到伤害？在这里，《吕氏春秋》指出外物是用来养性的，性为重，物为轻。凡是声色滋味，有利于养性则可适当获取，有害于养性就必须果断舍弃。

P4-6 大开嗜欲之门等于损害生命。

【参见《老子》条目】

塞其兑，闭其门，终身不勤。开其兑，济其事，终身不救。（第五十二章）

证明： 从定义2可知，"欲"指人对财富、名声和权力的追求。根据公理A5和命题P4-5，摄生的基本方法是消除过分的"欲"和机巧性的"智"，无节制地追求感官享受有害于生命。如果不仅仅在感官上，而是在各方面都过度贪欲，更是与摄生方法背道而驰的，等于是损害自己的生命。因此，大开嗜欲之门等于损害生命。

例证和说明： 司马承祯曾经发挥《老子》的思想说，道家所讲断缘，是指断绝有为俗事之缘。弃事则形不劳，无为则心自安，一天比一天恬淡，尘累一天比一天减少。行迹逐渐远离世俗，内心更加接近真道。所以《老子》说："塞其兑，闭其门，终身不勤。"有的人显露才能，保全自己；有的人遗问庆吊，人情往来；有的人隐居在山，却希望能够得到朝廷的征召；有的人请客吃饭，希望以后能派得上用场。他们都在行事中蕴藏心机，求取利益。所以《老子》说："开其兑，济其事，终身不救。"[1]《淮南子》中说得更为透彻，人要"约其所守，寡其所求，去其诱慕，除其嗜欲，损其思虑"，因为"约其所守则察，寡其所求则得"。（《原道训》）它认为"嗜欲"有害于"人性"，"好憎者，心之过也；嗜欲者，性之累也"（《原道训》），"欲与性相害，不可两立"（《诠言训》），"肥肌肤，充肠腹，供嗜欲，养生之末也"（《泰族训》）。人要损欲自养，才能恢复本性。

P4-7 物质追求以满足生命正常需求为度。

【参见《老子》条目】

名与身孰亲？身与货孰多？得与亡孰病？甚爱必大费，多藏必厚亡。故知足不辱，知止不殆，可以长久。（第四十四章）

咎莫大于欲得，祸莫大于不知足。故知足之足，常足矣。（第四十六章）

证明： 由定义1，"德"是万物从"无"到"有"再到"无"的自在自为过程的总称，也指人对此过程的认识以及顺应此过程的品质。根据基本假设5与公理A1，人的认知和行为的理想状态是"守中"，而"自然"是"道"从"无"到"有"再到"无"的自在自为过程，也就是"守中"的状态。人们对物质如果过度追求，就会破坏"守中"乃至损害生命的根本——"自然"。因此，物质追求以满足生命正常需求为度。

例证和说明： 名誉与生命，哪一个重要？生命与财富，哪一个珍贵？得到与失去，哪一个更有害？过分的吝啬必定会付出更大的耗费，聚财过多而不施以济众必然会引起众怨，最终会招致更惨重的后患和损失。所以，知足就不会受到屈辱，知道适可而止就不会遭到危险。古往今来，多少人由于贪得无厌，一步步陷入罪恶的泥潭，不能自拔。清朝的和珅就是典型一例。他十九岁世袭三等轻车都尉，由于他办事利落，又能察言观色，深得乾隆帝欢心，升迁很快，曾任户部尚书、兵部尚书，后为军机大臣。他的儿子还娶了公主，与皇帝成了亲家。和珅借乾隆的眷顾作威作福，大肆贪污受贿，而对他有意见的人则设法除去。嘉庆四年

---

[1] 司马承祯：《坐忘论·断缘第二》，据文物出版社、上海书店出版社、天津古籍出版社联合影印《道藏》本，1988年。

（1799）正月，乾隆帝去世，嘉庆帝根据给事中王念孙的揭发，逮捕了和珅，宣布和珅有二十大罪状，令其自尽。民间流传着"和珅跌倒，嘉庆吃饱"的笑谈。

简单主义正越来越成为一种新兴的生活主张，因为许多所谓的舒适生活，不仅不是必不可少的，而且是人类进步的障碍和悲哀。简单生活不一定是物质的匮乏，但一定是精神的自在。简朴、单纯的生活有利于清除物质与生命之间的樊篱。

P4-8 贪图丰厚的物质享受会伤害生命。

【参见《老子》条目】

出生入死。生之徒，十有三；死之徒，十有三；人之生生，动之于死地，亦十有三。夫何故？以其生生之厚。盖闻善摄生者，陆行不遇兕虎，入军不被甲兵；兕无所投其角，虎无所用其爪，兵无所容其刃。夫何故？以其无死地。（第五十章）

民之轻死，以其上求生之厚，是以轻死。夫唯无以生为者，是贤于贵生。（第七十五章）

证明： 根据命题P4-4，淡泊是"自然"的特性，也最有益于生命，而丰厚的物质会给人带来强烈的感官享受，也即与"淡泊"完全相反的感受。再根据公理A1和命题P4-1，"自然"是"道"从"无"到"有"再到"无"的自在自为过程，而遵循"自然"是养生的总原则。贪图丰厚的物质享受，不甘淡泊，就与"自然"背道而驰，破坏了养生的总原则。因此，贪图丰厚的物质享受会戕害生命。

例证和说明： "我姓钱，但是我不爱钱。"这是钱学森的至理名言，也是他的财富观。2001年12月7日，恰在钱学森90岁诞辰前夕，第二届霍英东奖在广东番禺市举行颁发仪式。钱学森因行动不便，不能亲自去领奖，便委托夫人蒋英和儿子钱永刚前去。临行前，钱学森看着穿戴得体的老伴，笑眯眯地说："你去领钱？"蒋英说："是的，我把支票领回来。"钱老又对儿子永刚说："你去领奖状，回来给我。"钱永刚说："是的。"钱学森又对蒋英说："那好，你要钱，我要奖。"秘书们尚未反应过来，钱学森先乐了。原来，九十高龄的钱学森在拿他和夫人蒋英的姓氏玩幽默呢！他说蒋英要的"钱"可不是金钱的"钱"，而是他这个姓"钱"的人，而他要的是姓"蒋"的蒋英，也不是奖状的"奖"。等秘书们回过神来，周围的人全都被逗乐了。其实，钱学森自回国以后，直至晚年，他除了将自己的知识和智慧奉献给了祖国和人民，还将他一生中较大笔的收入捐献了出去。

钱学森始终保持着一种简约朴素、不事张扬的人生态度。钱学森居住在20世纪50年代建造的那种红砖老楼里，室内陈设朴素大方，家具和地板因为年代久远，显得有些破旧。除了四壁书籍和一架当年从国外带回的钢琴外，一切都很简单，与普通老百姓的家几乎没什么两样。钱学森虽然是世界著名的科学家，但他在科技大学校园里只穿土布中山装，戴布帽，穿布鞋，在夏天还时而戴草帽，穿带补丁的短裤。在饮食方面，钱学森更是没什么讲究，认为"四菜一汤就挺好"。他从不抽烟，也不喝酒。钱学森于2009年逝世，享年98岁。长寿与他个人简约朴素、乐观平淡的人生态度有很大的关系。

P4-9 贪图突然发迹或者暴富会伤害生命。

【参见《老子》条目】

希言自然。飘风不终朝，骤雨不终日。孰为此者？天地。天地尚不能久，而况于人乎？（第二十三章）

咎莫大于欲得，祸莫大于不知足。（第四十六章）

证明：从定义10可知，"无为"指顺应"自然"不刻意作为，更不妄为的行动原则。又据公理A1，"自然"是"道"从"无"到"有"再到"无"的自在自为过程，而突然发迹或者暴富，都属于刻意作为或妄为的表现，是外在偶然因素产生的结果，不属于自在自为过程，背离了"道"的根本，不利于养生。因此，贪图突然发迹或者暴富会伤害生命。

例证和说明：中国古代向来有"暴富者不祥"的说法。《世说新语·贤媛十九》记载，陈婴是东阳县人，从小就注意道德品行的修养，在乡里很有名望。秦代末年，天下大乱，东阳人想拥护陈婴做首领。陈母对陈婴说："不行！自从我做了你家的媳妇后，从年轻时起就没遇到你家贫贱，一旦暴得富贵，不吉利。不如把军队交给别人。事成了，可以稍为得些好处；失败了，灾祸自有他人承担。"[1] 清代吴炽昌在《客窗闲话》中记载了刘智的故事。刘智不事生产而性好施舍，弄得家资荡然，流离失所，成为乞丐。有一次在一个破庙里看见别人开赌局，他不觉心动，乞得数钱，随意押了一宝，没想到赢了，于是又押，也是每局都赢了，一连十来天，赢了金钱数万。有人劝他成家做富人，刘智感叹说："余丐也，而暴富不祥，当思有以禳之。"于是决定将所有的钱拿来修庙，人们便把这座庙叫作"刘智庙"。[2] 这里的陈母和刘智，都是生活在百姓中的智者。

---

1 刘义庆：《世说新语》，长春：时代文艺出版社，2001年，第202页。

2 吴炽昌：《客窗闲话·续客窗闲话》，北京：文化艺术出版社，1988年，第126页。

P4-10 恃富骄纵，终将丧失财富。

【参见《老子》条目】

持而盈之，不如其已；揣而锐之，不可长保。金玉满堂，莫之能守；富贵而骄，自遗其咎。功遂身退，天之道也。（第九章）

证明：根据基本假设3，"无"与"有"的统一才是"道"的圆满状态。人的认知和行为的最高状态是"守中"，既看到"有"又坚守"无"。再依据命题P4-7，物质追求以满足生命正常需求为度。恃富骄纵者只看到"有"，不能坚守"无"，无法把握满足生命正常需求的度，等于是背离了"道"。因此，恃富骄纵者终将丧失财富。

例证和说明：功成名就急流勇退的人，就是顺应天道之人。"飞鸟尽，良弓藏；狡兔死，走狗烹"这句流传千古的名言，是范蠡写给文种的，听起来让天下有识之士非常伤感，但是其中蕴涵的哲理却非常发人深省。汉高祖刘邦诛杀异姓王，宋太祖赵匡胤杯酒释兵权，明太祖朱元璋火烧庆功楼等，不胜枚举。老子在这些事情还没有发生之前就看到了这一点，"功遂身退，天之道"。范蠡可以说是体现老子精神的典型代表，他辅佐越王勾践"卧薪尝胆"，打败吴国称雄诸侯的故事可谓家喻户晓。但是功成名就以后，他一叶扁舟飘然离去，从此开始经商。今天商人们供奉的"陶朱公"就是范蠡。陶朱公经商成功后，曾经散尽自己的钱财，然后重新白手起家。无论是从政还是经商，范蠡都取得了辉煌的成就，但他并不迷恋于成功的巅峰，是功成身退的典范。

P4-11 不知足容易招致祸患。

【参见《老子》条目】

故知足不辱，知止不殆，可以长久。（第四十四章）

咎莫大于欲得，祸莫大于不知足。（第四十六章）

证明：根据基本假设5，人的认知和行为的最高状态是"守中"，既看到"有"又坚守"无"。"不知足"就表现为不能"守中"，不能顺应"自然"，就会在自然之"道"面前碰壁，因而导致祸患。又据公理A5，摄生的基本方法是消除过分的"欲"和机巧性的"智"。不知足表现为过分的"欲"，违背了摄生的原则。因此，不知足容易招致祸患。

例证和说明：有一个青年总是感叹自己命运不济，生活多舛，既发不了财也求不到一官半职，终日愁眉不展。一天，他在路上偶遇了一个老和尚，当他看到老和尚一脸的平静祥和时不由得叹了口气。老和尚问他为何叹气，青年说："我看到你开心的样子觉得很羡慕。为什么我总有这么多的烦恼？为何我一贫如洗？"老和尚说："年轻人，你明明很富有啊！"青年问："富有？我除了烦恼什么也没有。"老和尚并没有急着解释，而是继续问他："那么，假如有人给你一千两银子，换你十年的寿命，你换吗？""当然不换！""给你五千两银子，换你的健康，你换吗？""不换！""给你一万两银子，换你的生命，你换吗？""不换！"老和尚顿时笑了："年轻人，到现在为止你至少拥有一万六千两银子了，难道还不够富有吗？"这个青年的烦恼来自未能真正认识到他自己所拥有的财富，而只是看到了自己缺少的东西。若能知足，则一切烦恼自会迎刃而解。

P4-12 知足会使"祸"转化为"福"。

【参见《老子》条目】

名与身孰亲？身与货孰多？得与亡孰病？甚爱必大费，多藏必厚亡。故知足不辱，知止不殆，可以长久。（第四十四章）

故知足之足，常足矣。（第四十六章）

祸兮，福之所倚；福兮，祸之所伏。（第五十八章）

证明： 根据公理A5，摄生的基本方法是消除过分的"欲"和机巧性的"智"，其表现就是知足，从而养生长寿。又据公理A1，"自然"是"道"从"无"到"有"再到"无"的自在自为过程。"知足"也表现为符合自然的自在自为的行为，人能知足就不会由于贪欲招致祸患，而会由于"常足"而感觉幸福。因此，知足会使"祸"转化为"福"。

例证和说明：《淮南子·人间训》中记载了塞翁失马的故事。在靠近边塞的人中，有一位精通术数的老人。他家的马自己跑到胡人那里去了，丢失了不少，大家都来安慰他。这个老人说："怎么就知道这不是一件好事呢？"过了几个月，他家的马带着胡人的骏马回来了，大家都来祝贺他。这个老人说："怎么就知道这不是一个祸患呢？"因为家里多了不少好马，他的儿子又喜欢骑马，有一次从马上摔下来折断了大腿，大家又都安慰他。这个老人说："怎么就知道这不是一件好事呢？"过了一年，胡人大举入侵边塞，青壮年男子都被征兵，拿起弓箭参战。靠近边塞的人很多都因战争而死去，唯独他的儿子因为腿摔断了的缘故免于征战，父子得以保全性命。塞翁失马的故事告诉我们，在生活中，如果满足于已有的成就，不做过分的追求，就能够保持长久的幸福与平和。

庄子说："鹪鹩巢于深林，不过一枝；偃鼠饮河，不过满腹。"人的饮食起居所需有限，何必以一生为代价去舍命追求。"功遂身退，天之道"，即使限于各种原因未能功遂名就，也不能执着强为，违背自然之道。正确对待的原则是：知足不辱，知止不殆。

P4-13 守静知足使人免于耻辱。

【参见《老子》条目】

化而欲作，吾将镇之以无名之朴。无名之朴，夫亦将不欲。不欲以静，天下将自正。（第三十七章）

名与身孰亲？身与货孰多？得与亡孰病？甚爱必大费，多藏必厚亡。故知足不辱，知止不殆，可以长久。（第四十四章）

证明： 由定义2，"欲"指人对财富、名声和权力的追求，这种追求可能违背"自然"，从而带来祸害与耻辱。依据命题P4-5与命题P4-12，无节制地追求感官享受有害于生命，而"静"能够涤除过分的欲望干扰带来的感官享受而使内心达到澄明状态；进一步，知足会使"祸"转化为"福"。因此，守静、知足令人免于耻辱。

例证和说明： 唐代大诗人白居易在《寄张十八》中抒发他的感想："饥止一箪食，渴止一壶浆，出入止一马，寝兴止一床。此外无长物，于我有若亡。胡然不知足，名利心遑遑。"白居易自从贬官浔阳后，与僧人、道士接触，吟诵陶渊明诗歌，逐渐体会到了守静知足的道理，不再追求高官厚爵，而是安然于自己的所得，从而心理安适，高寿而终。

宋代大文豪苏东坡有一篇脍炙人口的《前赤壁赋》，其中写道："且夫天地之间，物各有主，苟非吾之所有，虽一毫而莫取。惟江上之清风，与山间之明月，耳得之而为声，目遇之而成色，取之无禁，用之不竭。是造物者之无尽藏也，而吾与子之所共适。"苏轼屡遭贬官，但心胸坦荡，他以拥有人人都可以拥有的江上清风、山间明月为知足，守住内心的一分安静，尽管一生经历坎坷，却从未被击倒。

清代胡澹庵所编《解人颐》一书中有一首《知足歌》，其中写道："人生尽受福，人苦不知足。思量事劳苦，闲着便是福。思量疲厄苦，无病便是福。思量患难苦，平安便是福。思量死来苦，活着便是福。也不必高官厚禄，也不必堆金积玉。看起来一日三餐，有许多自然之福。我劝世人，不可不知足。"这首朴素易懂的诗歌，和白居易、苏轼的例子都告诉我们，人生不可能一帆风顺，只有守静、知足才能免于祸患耻辱。《菜根谭》中有"知足者仙境，不知足者凡境"的语句。进一步，若能守静知足才会体会到这首诗的意境："春有百花秋有月，夏有凉风冬有雪。如无闲事挂心头，便是人间好时节。"

P4-14 功成名就而不自傲是悟"道"的表现。

【参见《老子》条目】

功遂身退，天之道也。（第九章）

是以圣人不行而知，不见而明，不为而成。（第四十七章）

是以圣人为而不恃，功成而不处，其不欲见贤。（第七十七章）

证明：从定义8可知，"功"指万物的自在自为状态，也指人自觉维护符合"自然"的社会秩序的活动。功成名就的实质就是自觉维护了符合"自然"的社会秩序，维护了万物的自在自为状态。深知万物的自在自为构成了"功"的主体，而不是自我的作为构成了"功"的主体，当然就不会居功自傲。根据公理A4，圣人知"道"并"不争"，居功不傲。因此，功成名就而不自傲是悟"道"的表现。

例证和说明：东汉开国名将冯异，字公孙，颍川父城（今河南省宝丰县东）人，辅佐刘秀建立东汉。冯异为人处事谦虚退让，不自夸。出行与别的将军相遇，就主动把马车驶开避让。他的军队前进停止都有旗帜标明，在各部队中号称最有纪律。每到一个地方停下宿营，跟随刘秀的将领们常常聚在一起聊天，话题无非是自述战功，胡吹乱侃。冯异经常一个人默默地躲到大树下面，大家便给他起了个"大树将军"的雅号。攻邯郸时要重新分配士兵的归属，士兵们都说愿意跟随"大树将军"。刘秀称帝后，冯异被封为征西大将军、阳夏侯。刘秀特别派冯异回老家祭祀祖先，同时命令二百里以内的地方官和冯异宗族会聚饮宴，以宣扬冯异的荣耀。而冯异则更加谦谨，终其一生都得到光武帝的信任。

P4-15 顺应自然者能以柔克刚，强梁蛮横者必不得善终。

【参见《老子》条目】

柔弱胜刚强。（第三十六章）

强梁者不得其死。（第四十二章）

勇于敢则杀，勇于不敢则活。（第七十三章）

人之生也柔弱，其死也坚强。草木之生也柔脆，其死也枯槁。故坚强者死之徒，柔弱者生之徒。（第七十六章）

证明：从定义10与定义14可知，"无为"指顺应"自然"不刻意作为，更不妄为的行动原则，而"柔弱"指不刻意展露自身强势的态度或行为。强梁蛮横是刻意作为、恣意妄为的表现，是违背"自然"的。依据公理P2-7，以柔弱处世是保全自在自为生命状态的方法。强梁蛮横者乃是过分夸大自己现有的力量，并且过度消耗这种力量，就会很快地走向反面。因此，顺应自然者能以柔克刚，强梁蛮横者必不得善终。

例证和说明： 东汉末年的吕布擅长骑射，膂力过人，被称为"飞将"。但他喜好炫耀武力，自恃有功，十分骄恣，因不断遭受猜忌而频换阵营。他离开袁绍时，袁绍曾派兵追杀吕布，但那些士兵都害怕他，即使追上了也没有一人敢逼近。陈留太守张邈派人迎接吕布为兖州牧，占据濮阳。曹操知道后率领军队攻打吕布，双方多次交战，相持一百多天。建安三年（198年），吕布再次反叛朝廷依附袁术，派高顺、张辽等攻破沛城，俘虏了刘备妻儿，刘备败投曹操。曹操于是亲自率兵攻打吕布，送了一封信给吕布，向他陈述祸福。吕布想投降，但陈宫等人由于自己与曹操的关系问题而极力反对。陈宫对吕布说："曹公从远道而来，其局势不能持久，将军如果用步兵和骑兵驻守城外，我率领其余人马关了城门把守。曹操如果向将军进攻，我带领部队从后面进攻曹军；要是曹操只是攻城，将军就从外面救援。用不了一个月，曹军粮食全部用尽，发起进攻就可以打败曹操。"吕布暗中派人向袁术求救，又亲自率领一千多骑兵出城，结果，打了败仗后退回城内。袁术也未予施救。曹操围攻三个月，吕布军中上下离心，其部下缚了陈宫投降。吕布见大势已去，只得出城投降。吕布被捆到曹操面前，他要求松绑。曹操笑说："捆绑老虎不得不紧。"吕布又说："曹公得到我，由我率领骑兵，曹公率领步兵，可以统一天下了。"曹操颇为心动，但刘备在一旁说："明公您看见吕布是如何侍奉丁建阳和董太师的吧！"最终吕布被缢杀枭首。

P4-16 善待他人者不会争强好胜。

【参见《老子》条目】

上善若水。水善利万物而不争，处众人之所恶，故几于道。居善地，心善渊，与善仁，言善信，政善治，事善能，动善时。夫唯不争，故无尤。（第八章）

证明： 从定义11可知，"不争"指消除了过分的"欲"和机巧性的"智"后而形成的处世态度。根据公理A4，圣人知"道"并"不争"。悟道之人有包容万物的心理状态，能够善待他人，是形成"不争"品格的主要原因，而"不争"即包括不争强好胜在内。因此，善待他人者不会争强好胜。

例证和说明： 廉颇是赵国优秀的将领。赵惠文王十六年（前283年），廉颇率领赵军征讨齐国，大败齐军，夺取了阳晋，被封为上卿，他以勇气闻名于诸侯各国。蔺相如是赵国人，因为完璧归赵之功，被封为上大夫，又因为渑池之会的功劳被封为上卿，位在廉颇之上。廉颇说："我是赵国将军，有攻城野战的大功，而蔺相如只不过靠能说会道立了点功，可是他的地位却在我之上，况且相如本来是卑贱之人，我感到羞耻，排位在他下面我难以忍受。"并且扬言说："我遇见相如，一定要羞辱他。"相如听到后，不肯和他相会。相如每到上朝时，常常推说有病，不愿和廉颇去争位次的先后。没过多久，相如外出，远远看到廉颇，相如就掉转车子回避。于是相如的门客说："您与廉颇官位相同，廉老先生口出恶言，而您却害怕躲避他，您怕得也太过分了！我们这些人没出息，请让我们告辞吧！"蔺相如坚决地挽留他们，说："诸位认为廉将军和秦王相比谁厉害？"回答说："廉将军比不了秦王。"相如说："以秦王的威势，而我却敢在朝堂上呵斥他，羞辱他的群臣，我蔺相如虽然无能，难道会怕廉将军吗？但是我想到，强秦所以不敢对赵国用兵，就是因为有我们两人在呀，如今两虎相斗，势必不能共存。我之所以这样忍让，是把国家的急难摆在前面，而把个人的私怨放在后面。"廉颇听到此事后，感到羞愧，就脱去上衣，露出上身，背着荆条，来到蔺相如的门前请罪。他说："我是个粗野卑贱的人，想不到您是如此的宽厚啊！"二人终于相互交欢和好，成为生死与共的好友，保障了赵国的平安，其根本原因在于他们能够从他人的角度出发，善待彼此，善待国家，才能够做到不争强好胜。

P4-17 意气之争貌似保护自尊，实则伤害生命。

【参见《老子》条目】

道冲而用之久不盈。渊兮，似万物之宗；挫其锐，解其纷，和其光，同其尘，湛兮，似或存。吾不知谁之子，象帝之先。（第四章）

证明：据定理P4-16，善待他人者不会争强好胜。意气之争是争强好胜的一种体现，也是不能包容万物、不能善待他人的表现。如果不能包容万物与善待他人，则由于过分的"欲"和机巧性的"智"构成了自己的"私"，而"意气之争"争的就是这种"私"，往往导致他人用同样的态度和"欲""智"来对付自己，导致对自我的伤害。因此，意气之争貌似保护自尊，实则伤害生命。

例证和说明：齐景公时期，齐国有三位著名的勇士：公孙接、田开疆、古冶子。他们武艺高强，勇气盖世，为国家立下了赫赫功劳，但都自恃武艺高，非常骄横。晏子对齐景公说："这些人不讲究礼仪伦法，将会成为国家的危险和祸患！"于是晏子请齐景公召来三位猛将，说要赏赐他们两颗桃子。三人听说国君有赏，很高兴地前来。公孙接首先接过桃子，说："晏子真是聪明人。想当年我曾在密林捕杀野猪，也曾在山中搏杀猛虎，树木和风声都铭记着我的勇猛，我应该得到这颗桃子。"田开疆不甘示弱，抢到了第二个桃子，说："我曾经两次领兵作战，在纷飞的战火中击败敌军，捍卫齐国的尊严，守护齐国的人民。谁能像我这样勇敢呢？"古冶子看着两人说："我当年保护国君渡黄河，河水里突然冒出一只大鳖，一口咬住国君的马车，拖入河水中，我跳到水中，与这个庞大的鳖怪缠斗，一番激战才杀了大鳖。最后我浮出水面时，一手握着割下来的鳖头，一手拉着国君的坐骑，大家都吓呆了，以为是河神显圣。像我这样，难道不如你们勇敢吗？"说完，古冶子拔出自己的宝剑，要与二人比拼。公孙接、田开疆两人感叹道："我们勇猛和功劳都不及古冶子，却先抢了桃子，这是贪财啊。如果不死，那就是贪生，怎么是勇敢呢？"于是，他们两个放下桃子，自杀了。古冶子看到地上的两具尸体："两个朋友都死了，我独自活着，这就是无仁；做了错事，感到悔恨，却又不敢去死，这是无勇。"于是他也自刎而死。区区两个桃子，顷刻间让三位猛将都倒在血泊之中。这三人产生的意气之争，害了他们自己。

P4-18 顺应"自然"便能不争而强身。

【参见《老子》条目】

是以天下乐推而不厌。以其不争，故天下莫能与之争。（第六十六章）

善用人者，为之下。是谓不争之德。（第六十八章）

天之道，不争而善胜，不应而善应，不召而自来，繟然而善谋。（第七十三章）

证明：根据公理A4，圣人知"道"并"不争"。如果遵从圣人，就能知"道"而"不争"；如果背"道"而驰，与万物的自在自为状态去相"争"，这种"争"是不可能取胜的。再根据命题P1-4和命题P4-1，"道"与万物的基本特征是"自然"，而遵循"自然"是养生的总原则。因此，顺应"自然"就能做到不争而强身。

例证和说明："我和谁都不争，和谁争我都不屑；我爱大自然，其次就是艺术；我双手烤着生命之火取暖；火萎了，我也准备走了。"这是杨绛先生翻译的英国诗人兰德的一首诗，表达了对生命的"自然"态度。杨绛先生所说的"不争"是认识"自然"之后的不争，因而并不是盲目的。她面对记者谈到的"含忍"（即不争），也反映了老人的睿智。杨绛先生在百岁访谈《坐在人生的边上》中是这样说的："细细想来，我这也忍，那也忍，无非为了保持内心的自由，内心的平静。你骂我，我一笑置之。你打我，我决不还手。若你拿了刀子要杀我，我会说：'你我有什么深仇大恨，要为我当杀人犯呢？我哪里碍了你的道儿呢？'所以含忍是保自己的盔甲，抵御侵犯的盾牌。我穿了'隐身衣'，别人看不见我，我却看得见别人，我甘心当个'零'，人家不把我当个东西，我正好可以把看不起我的人看个透。这样，我就可以追求自由，张扬个性。所以我说，含忍和自由是辩证的统一。含忍是为了自由，要求自由得要学会含忍。"[1] 这里，杨绛先生所阐述的"含忍"与"自由"的道理，正是充分体认到"自然"的背景下，用含忍换得生命自由，以"不争"带来强身长寿。

P4-19 坚守根本者是大智若愚。

【参见《老子》条目】

众人皆有余，而我独若遗。我愚人之心也哉！沌沌兮！俗人昭昭，我独昏昏。俗人察察，我独闷闷。澹兮其若海，飂兮若无止。众人皆有以，而我独顽且鄙。我独异于人，而贵食母。（第二十章）

不自见，故明；不自是，故彰；不自伐，故有功；不自矜，故能长。（第二十二章）

证明： 从定义3可知，"智"特指人为满足"欲"的过分追求而丧失了回归"无"的能力的那种机巧智慧。依据公理A5，摄生的基本方法是消除过分的"欲"和机巧性的"智"，由此回归到"无"，也就是回归到根本——"道"，这是一种最高的智慧，但在表面看来就是"愚"。因此，坚守根本者是大智若愚。

例证和说明： 传说一位老翁对老子说："我今年已经一百零六岁了。我从年少时直到现在，一直是游手好闲地轻松度日。与我同龄的人都纷纷作古，他们开垦百亩沃田却没有一席之地，修了万里长城而未享辚辚华盖，建了无数房屋却落身于荒野郊外的孤坟。而我呢，虽一生不稼不穑，却还吃着五谷；虽没置过片砖只瓦，却仍然居住在避风挡雨的房舍中。是不是我现在可以嘲笑他们忙忙碌碌劳作一生，只是给自己换来一个早逝呢？"

老子听了，微然一笑，吩咐人说："请帮我找一块砖头和一块石头来。"老子将砖头和石头放在老翁面前说："如果只能择其一，您是要砖头还是愿取石头？"老翁得意地将砖头取来放在自己的面前说："我当然择取砖头。"老子抚须笑着问老翁："为什么呢？"老翁指着石头说："这石头没棱没角，取它何用？而砖头却用得着呢。"老子又招呼围观的众人问："大家要石头还是要砖头？"众人都纷纷说要砖而不取石。老子又回过头来问老翁："是石头寿命长呢，还是砖头寿命长？"老翁说："当然是石头了。"老子释然而笑说："石头寿命长人们却不择它，砖头寿命短人们却择它，不过是有用和没用罢了。天地万物莫不如此。寿虽短，于人于天有益，天人皆择之，皆念之，短亦不短；寿虽长，于人于天无用，天人皆摒弃，倏

---

[1] 杨绛：《坐在人生的边上》，《文汇报·笔会》，2011年7月8日。

忽忘之，长亦是短啊。"老翁顿然大惭。

P4-20 漠视自己的身体，也就不会珍惜万物。

【参见《老子》条目】

　　宠辱若惊，贵大患若身。何谓宠辱若惊？宠为下，得之若惊，失之若惊，是谓宠辱若惊。何谓贵大患若身？吾所以有大患者，为吾有身，及吾无身，吾有何患？故贵以身为天下，若可寄天下；爱以身为天下，若可托天下。（第十三章）

证明： 从定义6和定义1，"身"指人的内在生命力与外在欲望的统一体，而"德"指人对自在自为过程的认识以及顺应此过程的品质。根据公理A5和命题P4-18，摄生的基本方法是消除过分的"欲"和机巧性的"智"，而顺应"自然"便能不争而强身。表现为"爱身"的摄生，实质上就是将自我与万物同样纳入被包容的对象，既不因为自我而妨碍万物，也不因为万物而抹杀自我。对自己的"自在自为"的认识和顺应、对万物自在自为过程的认识以及顺应，两者是不可割裂的。因此，漠视自己的身体，也就不会珍惜万物。

例证和说明：《老子》说："故贵以身为天下，若可寄天下；爱以身为天下，若可托天下。"《庄子·在宥》继承了这种说法："故贵以身于为天下，则可以托天下；爱以身于为天下，若可以寄天下。"《庄子·让王》里还记载了这样的几个故事：尧把天下让给许由，许由不接受，遂让给子州支父。子州支父说："让我来做天子，是可以的。不过，我患有很深的病症，正打算认真治一治，没有空闲时间来治天下。"舜也曾让天下给子州支伯，子州支伯说："我患有很顽固的病症，正打算治疗，没有多余时间来治理天下。"如子州支父、子州支伯这样的人，虽然认为统治天下是地位最高、权力最重的了，却不能因此而妨碍自己的生命，更何况是其他的一般事物呢？

　　周人的祖先古公亶父居住在邠地的时候，狄人常来侵扰，古公亶父敬献兽皮和布帛狄人不愿意接受，敬献猎犬和宝马狄人也不愿意接受，敬献珠宝和玉器狄人仍不愿意接受，狄人所希望得到的是邠地的土地。古公亶父说："如果兴起战争，兄长就会失去弟弟，父亲就会失去子女，我不忍心这样做。而且我还听过这样的说法，不要因为争夺赖以养生的土地而伤害到土地上养育的人民。"于是古公亶父拄着拐杖离开了邠地，邠地的百姓则追随他，在岐山之下建立起一个新的都城。古公亶父正是因为看重人的生命，所以选择躲避战争，甚至不惜放弃君主的地位。

P4-21 与万物共生，才能成就人的养生。

【参见《老子》条目】

　　天长地久。天地所以能长且久者，以其不自生，故能长生。是以圣人后其身而身先，外其身而身存。非以其无私邪？故能成其私。（第七章）

证明：从定义7可知，"无私"指消除过分的"欲"和机巧性的"智"之后而达到的能包容万物的心理状态。根据公理A5与命题P4-1，摄生的基本方法是消除过分的"欲"和机巧性的"智"，而遵循"自然"是养生的总原则。养生的过程也就是包容万物的过程，需要逐步达到无私的心理状态，需要遵循"自然"。因此，与万物共生才能成就人的养生。

例证和说明：侗族是我国南方最大的人工林经营者，600多年来，原木外销一直是侗族获得现金的主要渠道。侗族在营林的过程中十分讲究复合型育林，他们在人工林中不仅种植经济价值很高的杉树，也精心养护其他树种并存。豆科、壳斗科、芸香科的乔木在侗族的人工林中随处可见，并且至少要占15%以上的比例。人工林中还拥有大量的草本植物和附生植物。他们的森林更新和培育往往与旱地农耕相兼容，在育林空地上，只要许可都混种各种旱生农作物，如做粮食用的小米、玉米、黄豆、红苕、荞子、洋芋等，做蔬菜用的黄瓜、南瓜、辣椒、红萝卜、白萝卜等，此外还混种西瓜、地瓜、蓝靛等水果、经济作物以及药用植物。他们并非只是追求商品木材生产的极大化。侗族村寨社区将河流、鱼塘、稻田整合为一个"连通器"，既种植水稻又养鱼、鸭。除了人工种、养的物种外，稻田中还生息着不胜枚举的野生动植物，包括茭白、水芹菜、莲藕等植物，螺、蚌、泥鳅、黄鳝等动物。一块稻田中，并生的动植物多达100多种。这些生物，包括一些被主流文化视为害虫、杂草的生物，都被作为生活、生产资源而培育利用。人类社会在自身发展的进程中会对原有的生态系统造成干扰，使其状态与原生状态发生偏离。侗族文化有意识地限制这种偏离，尽量保留原有的物种构成。这甚至引导了他们的生活习惯和价值标准，这种价值取向保护了原有的物种多样性，而原有的物种构成是上亿年演化形成的，是当地生态系统稳定延续的基础。

　　与之对比，如果简单地划分资源、废物、益虫、害虫、作物、杂草、好人、坏人……则长者数百年，短者数十年，原生物种构成就会被彻底改变，而新生的物种构成只能在人工养护下生存。人工养护的主要手段是耕作、灌溉、化肥、农药，不可避免地造成水土流失、土质变性、病虫害激增，这种人工生态系统已经暴露出高度的脆弱性。而在侗族的潜意识中，各物种都是同一个大系统中的成员，各成员相生相克，人类对生态系统的干预准则不是消灭一些种群，让另一些种群极大化，相反，要保持各种群的合理数量。"田里的黄鳝多了，就加强捕捉，少了，则将其他稻田中的黄鳝转放到稀缺的田块中。水蜈蚣对幼年期的鲤鱼有害，他们在放养鱼苗时，发现水蜈蚣太多，就捞捕水蜈蚣食用。但田里没有水蜈蚣时，又得人工放养。"可见，人"作为生物多样性的终极调节和制约力，只是控制其数量，并不会打乱它的生活习性和破坏它的生存空间"。这样的准则显然对生态系统的冲击更小，更有利于保存原有的物种构成，维护物种的多样性。人类社会系统必然对自然系统有所影响，但侗族努力保持自然系统的原状，力求实现共生共存，这样的价值观是人类社会与生态系统和谐共生的前提。[1]

"天人合一"代表着中华民族追求人与自然和谐统一的人生精神境界。道家把尊重自然规律、与万物共生看作是人类世界的最高法则，老子哲学特有的生态智慧指导人们努力实现"天地与我并生、万物与我为一"的和谐境界，从而真正成就人的养生。

P4-22 少私寡欲就是善待自我。

【参见《老子》条目】

见素抱朴，少私寡欲。（第十九章）

圣人不积，既以为人己愈有，既以与人己愈多。天之道，利而不害；人之道，为而不争。（第八十一章）

证明： 从定义7可知，"无私"指消除过分的"欲"和机巧性的"智"之后而达到的能包容万物的心理状态。根据公理A5和命题P4-6，摄生的基本方法是消除过分的"欲"和机巧性的"智"，而大开嗜欲之门等于损害生命。"少私寡欲"可以达到的能包容万物的心理状态，也即不损害生命、善待自我的目标，其实质就是让自己的生命在顺应自然、包容万物中得到滋长。因此，少私寡欲就是善待自我。

例证和说明： 张学良反对内战，曾同杨虎城一起发动震惊中外的"西安事变"，促成国共二次合作，结成抗日民族统一战线。西安事变后，他遭到长期软禁，失去人身自由。张学良的人生可以说是坎坷多变，然而他却能坦然地活到101岁，不能不说是个长寿奇迹。张学良早期曾患有严重的神经衰弱，导致睡眠不足。失去自由后他的失眠情况反而得到了真正的好转。正是在这种困境之中，张学良逐渐获

---

1 罗康隆、王秀：《论侗族民间生态智慧对维护区域生态安全的价值》，《广西民族研究》2008年第4期。

得了内心的安宁。在长期幽禁生活中，他远离了早期公子哥的奢华放纵生活，没有了战乱时期的操劳，没有了官场中的权欲角逐，也没有了让张学良烦躁不安的焦灼。张学良曾引用晋代道家学者嵇康的话说："人的养生有五难，一是名利不去为一难；二是喜怒不除为二难；三是声色不去为三难；四是滋味不绝为四难；五是神虑精散为五难。"排除这五难，就需要内心安静，少私寡欲。

第六章 摄生篇
CHAPTER SIX: On Preserving Health

The theme of this chapter is that to care for one's own life and realize the unity of caring for his own and others' life, one should abide by the principle of "seclusion and naturalness." P4-1 states that the fundamental principle is to follow nature; P4-2 to P4-6 dwell on how to keep a secluded, light and kind mind and make light of desires so as to form the basis of following nature. P4-7 to P4-10 elaborate on a nature-based philosophy on fortune and appropriate management of fortune and life. P4-11 to P4-14 state that nature-based philosophy of blessing and bane, honor and dishonor should take self-content and refusal of honor as the core. P4-15 to P4-19 discuss the nature-based theories of the weak and the strong, the smart and the clumsy, and contention and non-contention. Finally, P4-20 to P4-22 discuss the principle of symbiosis between individuals and all creatures.

P4-1   Following the Nature is the general principle of preserving health.

Quotes from *Laozi*:

Man models himself on Earth, Earth on Heaven, Heaven on the Dao, and the Dao on that which is naturally so. (Chapter 25)

Proof: According to D2, "desires" refer to man's seeking for fame, fortune and power, which would go against the Nature and thus bring adverse consequences. Also, by A1 and A5, the natural way is a spontaneous and unrestrained process where the Dao comes into existence from nothingness and then disappears in nothingness. So it is with life, as its basic rule is getting rid of excessive "desires" and tricky "smartness" so as not to go against the natural way. Thus we say, the general principle of life or preserving health is by modeling on Nature or taking law from Nature.

Explanation: "Taking Law from Nature" or "Modeling on Nature" means that the Dao models on or follows the Nature. During the Three Kingdoms Period, Wang Bi (226 AD-249 AD), a famous philosopher, made a consistent comment on Laozi's saying "Man models himself on earth, earth on heaven, heaven on Dao, and Dao on Nature." "The law means the rule. If man does not go against the law of the earth, he takes law from earth. If the earth does not go against the law of the heaven, the former can carry all for it takes the law of the heaven. If the heaven does not go against the Dao, it can cover all for it takes the law from the latter. The Dao is not contrary to nature, because it is its nature to take the law of the Nature, which means it takes the law of the square or the round once in case of the square or the round, and goes not against nature. The Nature can neither be named, nor put in any word ... The Dao takes law from the Nature, and therefore it is supported by heaven; the heaven takes law from the Dao, and therefore the earth follows it; the earth takes law from the heaven, and therefore Man model himself on it. The reason why the king becomes the master is that he is the only master."[1]

In the Eastern Jin Dynasty (317 AD-420 AD), Tao Yuanming (365-427), father of Chinese recluse and pastoral poetry, self-named "Mr. Wu Liu," or "Mr. Five Willows," modeled himself on "the law of nature" of Laozi, and abandoned his office rather than "bent for a shovel of rice;" and this story of him has always been praised in history. His poem *Back to Country Life* reads, "I've loathed the madding crowd since I was a boy, while hills and mountains have filled me with joy. By mistake I sought for the mundane careers, and got entrapped in them for thirty years. Birds in the cage would yearn for wooded hills, and fish in the pond would be desperate for flowing rills. So I reclaim the land in southern fields to suit my bent for reaping farmland yields. My farm contains a dozen acre of land; my cottage has eight or nine rooms around. The elm and willow cover backside eaves, while peach and plum trees shade my yard with leaves. The distant village dimly looms somewhere, with smoke from chimneys drifting in the air. In silent country lanes a stray dog barks, amid the mulberry trees, cockcrow with larks. My house is free from worldly moil or gloom, while ease and quietness permeate my private room. When I escape from bitter strife with men, I live a free and easy life again." Shuffling between official life and country life several times, Tao Yuanming finally came to realize his natural delights in hills and mountains, and that a dozen of years of his political career was actually "entrapped in mundane nets" and that his being loath to the madding crowd since childhood was his real nature. Seeing the natural phenomena of "Birds in the cage would yearn for wooded hills, and fish in the pond would be desperate for flowing rills," he got the law of managing life: Only by abandoning the official work can he get the joys of "living a free and easy life again" in the real sense. Although he had been poverty-stricken for a lifetime, he still obtained a stable life after returning to the country and to nature.

P4-2 The return to the root of life can only be obtained by keeping a vacant and peaceful mind.

Quotes from *Laozi:*

Take emptiness to the limit and keep still. All things arise together, I watch their return. Things come forth in great numbers, and each one returns to its own

---

[1] Lou Yulie. *Proof-reading and Noting the Collection of Wang Bi*. Zhonghua Book Company, 1980, p.65.

root. Returning to roots means stillness, and also means a return to origin. (Chapter 16)

Everything is rooted in the beginning and the beginning is regarded as the mother of everything. When you know the mother, you can get to know her children. After you have known the children, go back to holding fast to the mother. To the end of your life you will be free from all peril. (Chapter 52)

Proof: According to A2, "being" or "existence" gives birth to all things, which returns to "non-being" or "non-existence" and needs the nurturing of Dao. Therefore, it is the return to nothing that leads to the nurturing of Dao. Besides, by D5, "peacefulness" refers to the inner state of purity obtained by abandoning excessive desires and tricky smartness. Only by being vacant and peaceful can one return to nothingness and "non-existence" and be nurtured by Dao, and in return enjoy his advanced years. Thus we say, the return to the root of life can only be obtained by keeping a vacant and peaceful mind.

Explanation: By *"Everything grows all at once. I watch their return to their original state,"* Laozi meant that everything develops with its own law, which is observed from birth to growth and then to death in an endless way. He advanced the return to the roots of all existence, which is a state of total vacancy and stillness and the nature of all things. In *"Returning to roots means stillness,"* the returning to their roots is an absolute stillness and also a transcendent "non-existence;" and in *"and also means a return to destiny,"* decay vanishes in a dead silence, just as the new stirs in stillness. Zhuangzi also attached great importance to vacancy and stillness, and talked once again about their significance. In the chapter named "The Law of Heaven," he mentioned: *"He who is void, peaceful, secluded and doing with non-action sets the hallmark for heaven and earth, and the high realm of morals; thus, emperors and sages of ancient times can only reach this realm. Non-action brings calmness, which makes man free from sadness and disasters, and as a result brings longer life. So, the void, peace, seclusion and doing with non-action is the essence of all things."* That is to say, emptiness, tranquility, loneliness and inaction are the benchmarks of heaven and earth and the highest realm of moral cultivation. Therefore, emperors and sages of ancient times could stay in this realm. If a man can keep tranquil, he can do everything with inaction; with inaction, he will be contented. If he is contented, he will not feel sad or incur disasters. As a result, he can live a long life. In the chapter entitled "Being Tempered," Zhuangzi also talked about similar ideas: *"He who is tranquil, secluded, void and doing nothing sets the hallmark for heaven and earth and the essence of morals,"* and *"one can harbor* morality, once he cares not worries or joys; one who keeps the same and unchanged reaches the quietest quietness; one who has nothing to scare reaches the highest of vacancy; one who makes no desires for materials reaches the purest purity and he who is not rebelling reaches the finest paragon."

Daoism, originated in Laozi's thought, advocates "The fate is in my hand rather than in that of Heaven" and "Value body and life", and sees human's life as real existence — the unity of the tangible, the living, and the spirit, both of which constitute the system of valuing life that is quite complete. Zhang Daoling, who pursued longevity, followed the practice of being tranquil and natural proposed by Daoism, and emphasized the practice of Dao and the protection of one's life. With the spread of Daoism, the way of keeping healthy gradually found its way into the living of the mass.

P4-3 The highest realm of keeping fit is maintaining "utter innocence."

Quotes from *Laozi*:

When spirit and form are embraced as one, can it be kept from separating? When breath is concentrated to utmost pliancy, can it become as a tender babe? (Chapter 10)

You know the strength of the masculine, but keep the tenderness of the feminine, and are willing to be the ravine of the world. Being the ravine of the world, you will be accompanied by eternal virtue, and return to being a babe... You know the honor, but keep to the role of the disgraced, and are willing to be a valley of the world. Being the valley of the world, you will no longer lack the eternal virtue, and return to simplicity. (Chapter 28)

When things reached their prime, they become old. This is said to go against the Dao. What goes against the Dao will come to an early end. (Chapter 30)

The softest thing in the world dashes against and overcomes the hardest. (Chapter 43)

The people all keep their eyes and ears directed to him, and the sage deals with them all as his children. (Chapter 49)

Man of virtue in abundance is comparable to a new-born babe. Poisonous insects will not sting him, ferocious beasts will not seize him...All day long it will cry without its throat becoming hoarse. This is because his harmony is at its height. (Chapter 55)

Proof: By A5, the basic rule of managing life is getting rid of excessive desires and tricky smartness. "Selflessness" refers to the tolerance-of-all mentality after giving up excessive desires and tricky smartness, as defined in D7, so the premise of tolerance-of-all is the elimination of excessive desires and tricky smartness, namely, simplicity. Tolerance-of-all is putting all things in a free and independent state that is free from any external impact, and "a man of utter innocence" performs freely and simply. Hence, we say that the highest realm of keeping fit is maintaining "utter innocence."

Explanation: As it was recorded in "Gengsan Chu" of *Zhuangzi*, Nan Rongchu, a disciple of Gengsang Chu, went to ask Laozi about the normal way of keeping fit; in reply, Laozi answered, "If you want to know the basic way of keeping fit, then you should first ask yourself whether your body and mind are in harmonious unity. Can you hold onto your innate nature? Can you know about the good and bad turns without turning to fortune-tellers? Can you let the gone be gone without further pursuit? Can you give up imitating others' thought and seek for self improvement? Can you live in a free and unrestrained way? Can you enjoy a tranquil and free mind? Can you return to the simplicity and innocence of newly-born babies? Babies cry all the day but won't get hoarse throats, because their voice reach the top of harmony and nature; babies hold their little hands tight all the day, because they have done so since when they were unborn. Babies keep their small eyes open without blinkering all the day, just because their inner mind is free from the outside world. So, the basic way of keeping life is walking without knowing the destination, living without knowing what to do, and getting along well with external things by swimming with the drift and taking the natural course." Hearing this, Nan Rongchu immediately questioned, "So this is the highest realm of sages?" "No, this is the instinct of eliminating the inner stagnation, just as the so-called ice melting. The noblest person would neither be disturbed for other sake, nor participate in weird, worldly or contrive affairs, but come and go freely, unrestrained, and calmly. This is the common sense of keeping fit," Laozi replied. Then Nan Rongchu asked, "So this is the way of reaching the highest realm?" Laozi answered, "No. As I told you, it can be reached by being a simple and innocent infant. Infants have no idea of what to do or where to go. As such, neither happiness nor disaster would befall, which is the real realm of keeping fit." What was named babies in *Zhuangzi* is innocent infants. It was also mentioned in *Liezi* that "The highest harmony of spirit and ambition lies in infants who is free from harm and extra morality." Thus, we can see that Daoists take "utter innocence" — keeping simple and subtle — as the highest state of keeping fit.

P4-4 Indifference to fame and gain is a special feature of nature, and is beneficial to life as well.

Quotes from *Laozi*:

Music and delicious food make the passers-by stop and enjoy them. But when the great Dao is expressed in words, it will be plain or even monotonous. When you listen to it, it cannot be heard; when you look at it, it cannot be seen. However, when you apply it, it can be limitless. (Chapter 35)

Proof: According to A1, the natural way is a spontaneous and unrestrained process where Dao comes into existence from nothingness and then disappears in nothingness, whereas "nothingness," in comparison to "existence," has such natural features as indifference, peace and void. According to A5, the basic method of life preservation is to eliminate excessive "desire" and ingenuity "wisdom," which is characterized by such states as "indifference." Hence, we say that indifference to fame and gain is a special feature of nature, and is beneficial to life as well.

Explanation: In *Laozi*, "taste" has been mentioned several times, like "Once said, Dao becomes tasteless." Some pointed out that the "taste" by Laozi "is in the aesthetic category." So, what Laozi called "taste" does not mean that of eating food but "an aesthetic delight." Such thin tastelessness is the highest of taste, that is, "the highest of taste," which emphasizes discarding and overtaking of the things, property and power that people are apt to indulge in while they are harmful both physically and mentally, and the pursuit of mental indifference, peace and simplicity.[1] Hong Yingming, a writer of Ming Dynasty, pointed out in his *Tending the Roots of Wisdom*, "People who can stand coarse food would behave innocently, like pure ice and white jade, whereas a majority of those who wear fancy clothes are willing to act like groveling slaves, because one's ambition can only be manifested in the situation of being fresh and indifferent and lost in the indulging of materials."

Liang Shuming is a famous thinker, educator, and social activist of China. Though always ill in youth, he was devoted to social activities and went through ups and downs, which did not affect his longevity. He was born in 1893 and passed away in 1988, and such a long longevity of 95 years had much to do with his indifferent attitude to life. In 1928, he conducted a short-period experience on

---

1 Ye Lang. *Outline of Chinese Aesthetics History.* Shanghai People's Publishing House, 1985, p.33.

village management in Henan, and then in 1931 went to Zouping of Shandong Province, where he spent as long as seven years building the village; later, the experimental zone was expanded to over ten counties, which had extensive influence both at home and abroad. In 1918, he got acquainted with Mao Zedong. Their views resonated and differed. Whatever the situation, Liang Shuming always maintained an indifferent mentality; once being asked his secret of longevity, he answered, "Talking of longevity, I can summarize my experience like this: one should persist in eating less and having more exercise, and be calm and indifferent in mind."

P4-5 An unrestrained pursuit of sensual pleasure is harmful to life.

Quotes from *Laozi*:

Too many colors dazzle the eyes; too much music deafens the ears; too many tastes baffle the palate. Overindulging in hunting drives you crazy, and coveting too many material things tarnishes your conduct. Therefore, the Sage cares for bellies rather than senses, fending off material temptation and living a simple life. (Chapter 12)

The princes are dressed gaudily, equipped with sharp swords, fed up with delicacies, and having a super abundance of property and wealth. Thieves and robbers they are. This is not the way! (Chapter 53)

In governing the people and in serving heaven nothing's so good as being sparing with one's energy. Being sparing with energy is said to be well-prepared; being well-prepared is said to accumulate abundance of virtue; accumulating abundance of virtue, there is nothing he is not fit for; having nothing he is not fit for, his power will be immeasurable; with his immeasurable power, he will be qualified for the governance of the state; if he knows how to govern the state, he can govern it for long. This is called having deep roots and a firm base, the way of long life and long endurance. (Chapter 59)

Proof: From D2, we know that desire means the pursuit of fortune, fame and power, which is likely to go against nature. Also, by A5, the basic rule of managing life is getting rid of excessive desires and tricky smartness. As unrestrained pursuit of sensual pleasure is a manifestation of excessive desire against nature and the basic rule of managing life, it is harmful to health. Hence, we say that an unrestrained pursuit of sensual pleasure is harmful to life.

Explanation: Things that bring people sensual pleasure is detrimental, for they can only stimulate people's desires, making people "blind," "deaf" and even "mad."

Hence, Laozi advocated the discarding of those things. His view of "*Too many colors dazzle the eyes; too much music deafens the ears*" sharply criticized the rich who were indulged in the beauty of sounds and hues by all sorts of means, which can only damage their own lives in the end. Such cases were not uncommon to rulers of that time. For instance, it was recorded in "The First Year of King Zhao" of *The Spring and Autumn Annals* that being ill, Duke Jin sought for treatment from Qin; Qin Bo assigned Yi He who advised Duke Jin not to "indulge in dirty music, which would hurt the mind and make you lose peace." Though gentlemen love stringed instruments, they should play them with rites. If indulged in the musical enjoyment without restrictions, their senses would be excessively stirred, which would result in all kinds of diseases and harm to health.

It was recorded in "The Zhou Kingdom (II)" of *History of Chinese Kingdoms* that Duke Shan Mu said, "*Listening to music is just for amusement and seeing is merely for enjoyment. If the music was too resounding and the sight too dizzy, trouble would arise.*" In *The Real Meaning of Laozi*, Wei Yuan, a famous scholar and Chinese modern enlightenment thinker, pointed out, "*Seeing too long would make one dizzy, and listening too much would make one puzzled.*" Indulging in musical enjoyment would damage one's senses and even life. Laozi advocated that "The sage would act for filling the stomach, not for the eye," and Wang Bi in his *Notes on Laozi* also said, "*Those who act for filling the stomach feed on things, while those for the eye are controlled by things; this is why the sage would not act for the eye.*" The sage values his body and life, puts his life value in the first place, and is free from the control and damage of things, whereas he who indulges in sensual joys gets lost and would damage his health.

According to "On Preserving Health" of *The Annuals of The Lü's*, water in nature is clear, but it would be not, if mixed with dirt. Similarly, a human being could enjoy longevity, if he were not confused by outside things, which should be used for living rather than for damaging life. However, there are such a large number of people who are damaging life in their pursuit of outside stuff failing to get the point. If there was such a sound that would amuse the ear but cause deafness, people would never listen to it; if there was such a color that would amuse the eye but cause blindness, people would never see it; if there was such a food that would amuse the mouth but cause dumbness, then people would never have it. Therefore, the attitude to the sound, color and food by the sage is taking them for the sake of life and giving up if they cause harm, which is the way of preserving life. While most of the rich in this world are confused, they pursue such things day and night, and then abandon themselves in enjoyment; as such, how could their bodies bear it? As pointed out in *The Annals of The Lü's*, external things, which are of less importance, should be used to cultivate characters. As long as the sound, color and food are beneficial to life, they can be employed appropriately; otherwise, they should be discarded decisively.

P4-6   Opening the door to desires equals destroying life.

Quotes from *Laozi:*

Block the openings of intelligence, and shut the door of desires, and till the end of your life you'll not labor. Unlock the openings, meddle in affairs, and till the end of your life you'll not be saved. (Chapter 52)

Proof: By D2, desire means the pursuit of fame, fortune and power. Also, according to A5 and P4-5, the basic rule of managing life is getting rid of excessive desires and tricky smartness, and an unrestrained pursuit of sensual pleasure is harmful to life. If one was indulged not only in sensuality but also in all desires, he would go against the rule of managing life, which is nothing but damaging his life. Hence, we say that opening the door to desires equals destroying life.

Explanation: Sima Chengzhen once developed the thought of *Laozi* and said that cutting off karma proposed by Daoism refers to cutting off karma of worldly things. Discarding laborious exertion would make the body not dog-tired and doing nothing would make the mind calm, boost tranquility and reduce worldly boredom. The further one's behavior gets away from the worldly, the closer one's mind gets to the Dao; hence, as it goes in *Laozi*, "*Block the openings of intelligence, and shut the door of desires, and all his life he will be exempt from laborious exertion.*" Some people display their talents to protect their life; some are busy with interpersonal relations; others who live in seclusion hope that someday they would be summoned by the court; still others invite others to have meals in the hope that this would come to help later in life. All of those are done out of certain scheming and for certain interest. Hence, it is said in *Laozi*, "*Let him keep his mouth open and in the promotion of his affairs, and all his life there will be no safety for him.*"[1] While *Huainanzi* puts this more thoroughly: People should "simplify their possession and pursuit, and discard their desires and concerns," because "such simplifying would make them more perceiving and rewarding" (see *Doctrines of Dao*). It was believed

---

1   Sima Chengzhen. *On Cutting off Karma: Part Two* (Daoism Script Version). Joint Photo-printed by Cultural Relics Publishing House, Shanghai Bookstore Publishing House and Tianjin Ancient Books Press, 1988.

that "desires" are harmful to "human nature" and "The harbor of hatred is wrong mentally and the pursuit of desires is tiring sensually" (see *Doctrines of Dao*); "Desire is irreconcilable with sensuality" (see *Explaining the Doctrines*); "Satisfying desires to fill the belly and get fatty is the last thing to do for managing life" (*Doctrines of Tai Minority*). To return to human nature, people should preserve themselves by eliminating desires.

P4-7 The meeting of normal living requirements is the yardstick of material pursuit.

Quotes from *Laozi*:

Fame or life, which do you hold more dear? Life or wealth, to which would you adhere? Keep life and lose those other things or keep them and lose your life, which brings sorrow and pain more near? Thus we may see, he who cleaves to fame rejects what is greater; he who loves large stores gives up the richer state, he who is content need fear no shame, and he who knows to stop incurs no blame. From danger free, long live shall he. (Chapter 44)

No sin is greater than being insatiable; no disaster is greater than not being content; no misfortune is greater than being covetous. Hence, in being content, one will always have enough. (Chapter 46)

Proof: According to D1, virtue is the general term of the spontaneous and unrestrained process where all things come into existence from nothingness and then disappear in nothingness, and also refers to the cognition people have of the process and the quality cultivated through the adaptation. According to Assumption 5 and Axiom 1, the ideal of human cognition and behaving is "the middle way," so the spontaneous and unrestrained process of nature and where Dao comes into existence from nothingness and then disappears in nothingness is nothing but the middle way. Excessive pursuit of materials would destroy the middle way and even damage the essence of life, that is, nature. Hence, we say that the meeting of normal living requirements is the yardstick of material pursuit.

Explanation: Of fame, fortune and life, which is the most important? Of gaining and losing, which is more important? Excessive stinginess would necessarily cost more expense; an accumulation of wealth would inevitably cause mass hatred and eventually severe trouble and losses, if it was not used to serve the public. Therefore, contentment would neither result in humiliation nor in danger. Throughout the history, many people who were too greedy gradually got trapped in evil and couldn't help themselves. He Shen (1750-1799) of the Qing Dynasty is a typical example. He held the third-class chariot officer just at the age of nineteen; due to his efficiency and perceiving competence, he won the favour of Emperor Qianlong (1760-1820) and got promoted very quickly, from being the Minister of Revenue to that of soldiers and then to the Military Minister. His son married the princess, and therefore he became a family member of the Emperor. Taking advantage of the favours of the Emperor, He Shen took bribery wantonly and managed to dismiss others' suggestions. When Emperor Qianlong passed away in the first lunar month of 1799, He Shen, who was accused by the supervision official Wang Niansun (1744-1832), was arrested. Emperor Jiaqing announced twenty wrongs of He Shen and demanded the latter to kill himself; this gave rise to the folk saying, "The falling of He Shen, the filling of Jiaqing's people."

Simplicity is increasingly becoming a new lifestyle, because much of the so-called comfy life is not merely necessitated, but also becomes a hurdle and sadness to human advance. Simple life does not necessarily mean material shortage, but surely means mental freedom; simple life can promote the removing of the barriers between materials and life.

P4-8   Indulging in abundant materials would be harmful to life.

Quotes from *Laozi:*

Of all the people born, three out of ten survive, another three out of ten die at an early age, and still another three out of ten die an unnatural death. Why? It is because they treat themselves unduly. It is said that the one, who is good at preserving his health, will not be attacked by either rhinoceros or tigers when walking, and will not be wounded in the battlefields either. The rhinoceros will have nowhere to use their horns, the tigers will have nowhere to use their talons, and the weapons will have nowhere to show their blades. Why? It is because there is no place on his body that is fatal. (Chapter 50)

The people take death lightly because the rulers lead a luxurious life. Therefore, they take death lightly. Only those who are indifferent to fame or gain are wiser than those who lead a luxurious life. (Chapter 75)

Proof: According to P4-4, indifference to fame and gain is a special feature of the Nature, and is most beneficial to life as well, while abundant materials that would bring strong sensual enjoyment is contrary to indifference. Also, by A1 and P4-1, the natural way is a spontaneous and unrestrained process where the Dao comes into existence from nothingness and then disappears in nothingness, and following nature is the general principle of managing life. Indulging in material enjoyment and refusing indifference run against the Nature and thus damage the general rule of keeping healthy. Hence, we say that indulging in abundant materials would be harmful to life.

Explanation: "My surname is 'Qian' (i.e., money), but I don't like money." This is a famous saying and the philosophy of wealth of Qian Xuesen, a great Chinese scientist. On December 7, 2001, the ceremony of the 2nd Huo Yingdong Award was held in Panyu, Guangdong Province, which was just before the 90th birthday of Mr. Qian. As it was inconvenient for him to be present, he entrusted his wife Jiang Ying (the surname sounds the same as "award" in English) and his son Qian Yonggang to take the award. Before their departure, Mr. Qian, looking at his well-dressed wife, spoke in smiles, "Are you going to take the money (Qian)?" Jiang Ying answered, "Yes." He then said, "Well, then you take the money (Qian) and I'll take the award (Jiang)." Before the secretaries gave any response, Mr. Qian laughed. As a matter of fact, the ninety-year-old Qian Xuesen was playing a joke with their surnames; his "you take the money" does not mean money but his surname Qian and his "I'll take the award" does not mean award but his wife's surname Jiang. When the secretaries got the humor, the people around were all amused. In fact, after returning to China, Qian Xuesen not only devoted all his knowledge and wisdom to his motherland and Chinese people, but also donated a majority of his income till the end of his life.

For many years, Qian Xuesen had held a simple and unassuming attitude to life. He lived in an apartment in an old red-brick building built in the 1950s, barely decorated, with worn-out furniture and floor. Beside the books on four walls and a piano brought from abroad, everything else was all simple and not different from the houses of the commons. A world famous scientist though, he wore a Chinese tunic suit, a hat and a pair of cloth shoes on the campus of the University of Science and Technology of China. On summer days, he sometimes wore a straw-hat and patched pants. In terms of dieting, he was not particular about it and believed that "it's great to have four dishes and a soup." He never smoked, nor drank wine. When passing away in 2009, he was 98 years old. His longevity has much to do with his simple and optimistic attitude towards life.

P4-9   Seeking for overnight fortune or wealth would damage life.

Quotes from *Laozi*:

There is little description of the way of Nature. A violent wind does not last for a whole morning; a sudden rain does not last for the whole day. What makes so? It is the Heaven and the Earth. If Heaven and Earth cannot make such acting last long, let alone our human beings! (Chapter 23)

No sin is greater than being insatiable; no disaster is greater than not being content; no misfortune is greater than being covetous. Hence, in being content, one will always have enough. (Chapter 46)

Proof: D10 tells us that non-action means acting spontaneously rather than recklessly. Besides, according to A1, the natural way is a spontaneous and unrestrained process where Dao comes into existence from nothingness and then disappears in nothingness, while both overnight fortune and wealth are acting with purpose or recklessly, because they result from external factors rather than from spontaneous action; thus, they run against the essence of Dao and are harmful to keeping fit. Hence, we say that seeking for overnight fortune or wealth would damage life.

Explanation: In ancient China, it was always said that "He who becomes rich overnight is ominous." As it was recorded in *New Anecdotes of Social Talk: Virtuous Women*, Chen Ying, born in Dongyang County, attached great importance to cultivating his characters since childhood and enjoyed a good reputation throughout the town. When the society was thrown into chaos at the end of the Qin Dynasty, the people of Dongyang intended to support Chen Ying as their leader, but Chen's mother warned him: "Never! Since I married your father, we have been living a poor life. It would be ominous, if we got rich suddenly. Why not let others lead the army? If it succeeds, we can get some benefits; if not, we won't get into any trouble."[1] There was also a story recorded in *Talks beside Window* written by Wu Chichang in the Qing Dynasty. It talks about Liu Zhi, who didn't engage in laboring but in saving the poor, spent all his fortune and was reduced to a homeless beggar. One day, seeing there was a gambling in a broken temple, he begged for some coins, and then bet casually, only to find that he won it; he bet once again, and won all the betting; for over ten days, he earned a large amount of money in this way. Some people advised him to get married and live a rich life with the money, while he sighed, "I'm but a beggar, and it's ominous to become rich suddenly, so I should learn how to share it." In the end, he decided to spend all the money building a temple, which later was named "Liu Zhi Temple."[2] Liu Zhi and his mother were wise men among the mass.

---

1 Liu Yiqing (the Southern Dynasties). *New Anecdotes of Social Talk.* Times Literary Press, 2001, p.202.
2 Wu Chichang (Qing Dynasty). *Talks beside Window: Continued.* Culture and Art Publishing House, 1988, p.126.

P4-10 Wealth and arrogance would lead to the loss of fortune in the end.

Quotes from *Laozi*:

To keep it full is not as good as to stop in time. It won't be preserved long if it is too sharp. If the house is filled with gold and jade, nobody will be able to keep them for good. Arrogance and pride with wealth and rank will bring calamity upon oneself. To withdraw into obscurity when the work is accomplished is the way of Heaven. (Chapter 9)

Proof: By A3, the most ideal state of Dao is the unity of non-existence and existence, and the highest of human cognition and behavior is the middle way, that is, holding onto both non-existence and existence. Besides, according to P4-7, the meeting of normal living requirements is the yardstick of material pursuit. He who loves wealth and is arrogant holds so tight on existence that he misses non-existence, so his missing of the yardstick of material pursuit equals going against Dao. Hence, we say that wealth and arrogance would lead to the loss of fortune in the end.

Explanation: Those who get work done and then withdraw into obscurity are the wise who follow the way of Heaven. There goes a famous saying, "*After the flying bird is caught, the bow is stored away, and after the cunning hare is killed, the hound is boiled*," which was Fan Li's words to Wen Zhong; though it sounds sad to people of knowledge, it carries a profound philosophy and is very thought-provoking. Examples are not rare. Emperor Liu Bang of Han Dynasty killed the meritorious statesmen of different surnames; during the Song Dynasty, Zhao Kuangyin relieved the generals of their commands at a feast; Emperor Zhu Yuanzhang of the Ming Dynasty put the celebration building on fire. Before all of them came into being, Laozi had realized the truth, saying: "*To withdraw into obscurity when the work is accomplished is the way of Heaven.*" We may say that Fan Li was a typical representative of the thought of Laozi, for he assisted Gou Jian in defeating Wu and in coming into the throne, which is a household legend. After finishing these, Fan Li withdrew like a flowing boat and began to do business. "Master Tao" enshrined by businessmen nowadays is actually Fan Li. When succeeding in his business, Fan Li once distributed all his fortune and then started from scratch. He had made splendid success both in politics and in business; he became a model of withdrawing from credits, for he did not immerse himself in his achievements.

P4-11 The deficiency of contentment is apt to cause trouble.

Quotes from *Laozi*:

... he who is content need fear no shame, and he who knows to stop incurs no blame. From danger free, long live shall he. (Chapter 44)

No sin is greater than being insatiable; no disaster is great than not being content; no misfortune is greater than being covetous. Hence, in being content, one will always have enough. (Chapter 46)

Proof: By A5, the highest of human cognition and behavior is the middle way, that is, holding onto both non-existence and existence. The deficiency of contentment is manifested in neither following the middle way nor the nature, which would run against the Dao and incur trouble. Besides, the basic rule of managing life is getting rid of excessive desires and tricky smartness. Being unsatisfied is shown in excessive desires as well, and goes against the principle of managing life. Hence, we say that the deficiency of contentment is apt to cause trouble.

Explanation: There was a young man who was always lamenting about his ill-fated life, and was worried day and night about when he could make a fortune or get a good post. One day, he ran across an old monk who worn a peaceful appearance; seeing this, he sighed. The old monk asked why, and the youth replied, "I admire your being happy. Why should I always have so many worries, and why should I be so poor." The old man didn't rush to explain, but asked instead, "If someone wanted to buy ten years of your life with a thousand silvers, would you take it?" "Absolutely not." "What about five thousand for your health?" "No." "How about ten thousand for your life?" "No!" The old monk burst into laughter, "Young man, by now you've already got 16,000 silvers, aren't you rich?" The trouble of the youth is the fact that he did not recognize the wealth he actually owned, but focused on what he didn't have. If contented, he could have dismissed all his troubles easily.

P4-12 Contentment can transform misery into happiness.

Quotes from *Laozi*:

Fame or life, which do you hold more dear? Life or wealth, to which would you adhere? Keep life and lose those other things or keep them and lose your life, which brings sorrow and pain more near? Thus we may see, he who cleaves to fame rejects what is greater, he who loves large stores gives up the richer state, he who is content need fear no shame, and he who knows to stop incurs no blame. From danger free, long live shall he. (Chapter 44)

Hence, in being content, one will always have enough. (Chapter 46)

Good fortune lies within the bad, bad fortune lurks within the good. (Chapter 58)

Proof: According to A5, the basic rule of managing life is getting rid of excessive desires and tricky smartness, which is manifested in contentment and thus in longevity. Also, by A1, the natural way is a spontaneous and unrestrained process where Dao comes into existence from nothingness and then disappears in nothingness. Contentment is also shown in the behaviors that are spontaneous and unrestrained, free from troubles arising from greed, and thus brings happiness. Hence, we say that contentment can transform misery into happiness.

Explanation: "On Human Beings" of *Huainanzi*, there was a story about an old man at the frontier who lost his horses. Among the people living near the frontier, there lived an old master, whose horses ran away into where the Huns lived; seeing his great loss, the neighbors came to comfort him, while he replied, "Who knows this won't turn out to be unfortunate?" Several months later, his horses came back with many great horses of the minority people, and everyone else came to congratulate him. The old man then said, "Who knows this won't turn out to be unfortunate?" As there were so many handsome horses in his family and his son loved horse-riding, once his son fell off his horse and got a broken leg, then everybody else came to comfort the old man again. The old then said, "who knows this won't turn out to be fortunate?" A year later, the barbarians invaded their territory and all strong young men were conscripted to fight against them. A majority of the army lost their lives in the war, while only the son of the old man was exempted from the war and survived, due to his broken leg. This story tells us that we can enjoy long happiness and peace, if satisfied with the present and avoiding excessive demands.

Zhuangzi said: "Wrens are contented with having only one nest in the deep forest, and moles with drinking river water to fill the belly." What people need to live and eat is limited, so why we should pursue them excessively at the cost of life? There is great truth in "After the work is done, to withdraw into obscurity is the way of Heaven." Even if the work is undone for one cause or another, we should not persist and go against the natural way. The right principle to stick to is: Who is content need fear no shame; who knows to stop incurs no blame.

P4-13 He who is content and tranquil incurs no shame.

Quotes from *Laozi*:

Dao does nothing yet nothing is left undone. Should lords and kings be able to maintain it, all things will be transformed on their own. After they are transformed, they may grow avid. I will check the avidity with the nameless simplicity of Dao. Checked with the nameless simplicity, they will have no avidity. No avidity leads to serenity, hence the empire's stability. (Chapter 37)

Fame or life, which do you hold more dear? Life or wealth, to which would you adhere? Keep life and lose those other things or keep them and lose your life, which brings sorrow and pain more near? Thus, we may see, he who cleaves to fame rejects what is greater, he who loves large stores gives up the richer state, he who is content need fear no shame, and he who knows to stop incurs no blame. From danger free, long live shall he. (Chapter 44)

Proof: According to D2, "desires" refer to man's seeking for fame, fortune and power, which would go against the Nature and thus bring adverse consequences. Also, by P4-5 and P4-12, unrestrained pursuit of sensual pleasure is harmful to life and tranquility can help people get rid of excessive desires and reach a clear mind; by extension, contentment can transform misery into happiness. Hence, we believe that he who is content and tranquil incurs no shame.

Explanation: In his poem collection, Bai Juyi, a great poet of the Tang Dynasty, expressed his feelings: "Feeding on a bowl of food, drinking a pot of water, travelling with one horse, and on one bed he rests; outside things are out of sight, and fame and fortune are out of mind." After being dismissed from his office to Xunyang, Bai Juyi got the chance to communicate with monks and Daoists, chanting the poetry of Tao Yuanming and gradually realizing the significance of being contented and tranquil; he refused to seek for high office or fat payment, but was contented with what he owned and enjoyed a peaceful mind and a long life.

Su Dongpo, a great man of letters during the Song Dynasty (960-1279), wrote in his well-known *Boating at the Red Cliff*: "*All things under heaven have their separate owners. If a thing does not belong to me, not even a bit of it should be taken as mine. Only the refreshing breeze on the river and the bright moon over the hills, which generate in our ears a pleasant sound and in our eyes a dreamy color, are inexhaustible and can be freely enjoyed. They are an immeasurable treasure granted to us by our Creator as a grace, for our common happiness.*" Suffering from demotions time and again, Su Shi was magnanimous, and held dear to his inner peace by being content with the river breeze and the clear moon that are available to everyone else; though his life was full of ups and downs, he never gave it up.

Hu Dan'an of the Qing Dynasty (1644-1911) edited *Making You Happy*, in which there was the "Song of Contentment", reading: "Life is itself blissful, and if one isn't contented he will be painful. To ponder is painful, while leisure is blissful; to be ill is painful, while to be sound is blissful; to know disaster is painful, while to be secure is blissful; to die is painful, while living is blissful. Contentment comes not from office, fat pay, nor from gold or jade; it may come from a day of three meals. I advise people of the world to be contented." This simple and easy song, together with poems of Bai Juyi and Su Shi, tells us that life cannot be a smooth sailing, but being contented and tranquil can make people free from shame. There was such a saying in *Tending the Roots of Wisdom*: "He who is contented lives in a wonderland, while he who is not lives on earth." Further, he who is contented and tranquil can appreciate the real meaning of this saying: "There are flowers in spring and the moon in autumn, cool breeze in summer and white snow in winter; if the mind is free from worries, each season is a good time for man."

P4-14 The withdrawal from credits into obscurity is a manifestation of realizing the truth of Dao.

Quotes from *Laozi*:

Therefore, the Sages nurture the world but not capitalize on their achievements, and not show off their cleverness or wisdom either. (Chapter 77)

When the work is done, and one's name is becoming distinguished, to withdraw into obscurity is the way of Heaven. (Chapter 9)

The sages know without having to go, identify without having to see, and accomplish without having to act. (Chapter 47)

Proof: By D8, "achievements" refer to the free and spontaneous state of all things, and to maintaining the social order that is consistent with "naturalness." The essence of achievements with fame is to maintain the social order in line with nature and the natural state of all things. We need to know that the agent of merits lies in the free and spontaneous things rather than in the doings of one's own, and thus we would not rest in the merits. Moreover, by A4, the sage knows the Dao and thus would not fight for fame or credit. Hence, we say that the withdrawal from credits into obscurity is a manifestation of realizing the truth of Dao.

Explanation: Feng Yi, courtesy name Gongsun, was a famous general in the Eastern Han Dynasty. Born in Yingchuan (present day Baofeng in Henan Province), he assisted Liu Xiu in setting up the dynasty. Being a modest man, he never boasted. When meeting generals on the road, he would always be the first to give way; the army he led also had specific flags to march or stop, which became the most disciplined one. Wherever the armies camped, other generals would often brag about their success, while he would hide behind a tree by himself, hence the name "General by the Tree." When Handan was won over, the soldiers had to be rearranged and all of them begged to follow the "General by the Tree." After Liu Xiu came to the throne, Feng Yi was knighted as the General of the West and Marquis of Yangxia. The Emperor specially sent him back home to worship his ancestors and ordered the local officials within two hundred miles and his clans to gather together with the aim of glorifying him. Feng Yi became more modest and earned the trust of the Emperor through his lifetime.

P4-15   Those who follow nature can overcome the hard with their softness, while those who are rude and peremptory will not die a natural death.

Quotes from *Laozi*:

The soft overcomes the hard; and the weak the strong. (Chapter 36)

The violent and strong do not die their natural death. (Chapter 42)

He whose boldness appears in his daring (to do wrong) is put to death; he whose boldness appears in his not daring to do so lives on. (Chapter 73)

Man at his birth is supple and weak; his death, firm and strong. Trees and plants, in their early growth, are soft and brittle; at their death, dry and withered. Thus, it is that firmness and strength are the concomitants of death; softness and weakness, the concomitants of life. (Chapter 76)

Proof: From D10 and D14, we know that non-action means acting spontaneously and naturally rather than recklessly, and being soft means never deliberately displaying one's strengths. Arrogance and recklessness are manifestations of acting deliberately and wantonly, which run against the Nature. Besides, living by being soft is a way of protecting life, and the arrogant who exaggerates and overuses his strength would soon go to extremes. Hence, we say that the soft who follow Nature can overcome the hard, while the violent and strong do not die their natural death.

Explanation: Lü Bu, a famous general of the Eastern Han Dynasty, was proficient in riding and shooting, known as "Flying General." He loved to show off and take credits, which as a result incurred suspicion. After he left Yuan Shao, a lord in Northern China, the latter sent soldiers to kill Lü Bu; while those soldiers were so afraid of him that they didn't dare to approach him. Zhang Miao, a prefecture chief, sent subordinates to welcome Lü Bu as the head of Yanzhou Prefecture, and asked him to take Puyang. When learning this, Cao Cao led his army to attack Lü Bu and the fight lasted for over 100 days. In 198 AD, Lü Bu once again rebelled against the court, went to serve Yuan Shu, another local rebellious lord, ordering his subordinate generals Gao Shun and Zhang Liao among others to conquer Peicheng, and captured Liu Bei's wife and children. Liu Bei was the leader of one of the rebellious troops. He was just defeated and surrendered to Cao Cao, who thus led his troops on his own to attack Lü Bu and sent a letter to him about the bless and curse. Lü Bu would have surrendered, but his advisor Chen Gong and other subordinates opposed that strongly. Chen Gong said, "Cao Cao came for a long way and could not sustain for too long; it is wise of you to lead the infantry and cavalry to position out of the city and I will lead the rest to guard the gate; if Cao Cao attacked you, I would lead the troops to attack them from behind; otherwise, you could support me from the outside. As Cao Cao's provisions would last for less than a month, we can defeat them once we make the attack." Thus, Lü Bu agreed, but he secretly turned to Yuan Shu for help, and personally led more than a thousand of cavalry out of the city; he was defeated, and Yuan Shu did not do anything. Cao Cao besieged Lü Bu for three months, which made his troops lose trust and his subordinates surrender; seeing this, Lü Bu walked down and surrendered. He was tied and sent to Cao Cao, who asked the soldiers to tie him tightly while saying with a smile, "Tigers should be tied tightly." Lü Bu replied, "I'm in the hand of your Honor. If I led the cavalry and your Honor led the infantry, we can rule over the whole world." Hearing this, Cao Cao hesitated, while Liu Bei at his side advised, "Your Honor, you must have known about the story of Lü Bu who had once served general Ding Jianyang and the former Prime Minister Dong Zhuo." In the end, Lü Bu was beheaded.

P4-16 He who is kind to others would not seek to prevail.

Quotes from *Laozi*:

The perfect goodness is like water. Water is good at benefiting all things, but does not contend with them. It prefers to dwell in places the masses of people detest, therefore it is closest to the Dao. The person of perfect goodness is expert in choosing the right place for living, in keeping calm and quiet at heart, in treating others in a sincere and friendly manner, in making creditable and reliable promises, in doing sophisticated administrative affairs, in tackling businesses discreetly, and in taking action promptly. Because of the good person's virtue of being non-competitive, nobody will harbor resentment for him. (Chapter 8)

Proof: By D11, not fighting for gains means the attitude of life developed after getting rid of excessive desires and tricky smartness. Besides, the sage knows Dao and thus would not fight for gains. Those who know Dao can tolerate all things and treat others with kindness which helps them develop the character of not fighting for gains, which indicates not wanting to be outstanding or winning. Hence, we say that he who is kind to others would not seek to prevail.

Explanation: Lian Po was an outstanding general of the state of Zhao in the Warring States period (476-221 BC). In 283 BC, Lian Po led the troops of Zhao to attack Qi; after defeating it and taking Yangjin, he was given a high rank. Lin Xiangru, an official of Zhao as well, was granted the highest noble position because of his success in bringing the jade intact back to the state, and was further promoted to a position even higher than that of Lian Po for his feats in the Mianchi Meeting. Lian Po said, "I am a famous general of Zhao and have made great contributions in the wars, while Lin Xiangru was promoted above me just because of his lip service; besides, he is low and mean, which makes me shameful and unbearable." He also threatened, "I would humiliate him when seeing him!" Learning this, Lin Xiangru refused to meet him. He would pretend illness not to go to the court, unwilling to compete with Lian for rank. A few days later, Lin Xiangru went out and saw Lian Po from afar, and he asked to turn around his chariot to avoid him. As a result, his subordinates said, "Your Minister is equal to Lian Po in position; he often talks bad about you, yet your Minister was scared of him. As we feel humble, we'd beg to leave!" Lin Xiangru begged them to stay firmly, explaining "Whom do you think is more powerful, General Lian Po or King of Qin?" The subordinates replied, "The King of Qin." Their master then asked, "Although the King of Qin is powerful, I dared to criticize him and his officials. Could I be afraid of General Lian Po? I think the reason why Qin doesn't attack Zhao lies in General Lian and me. If the two of us fight like tigers, we would be doomed. The reason for my great tolerance of him is that I give the priority not to personal grievances but to our country." Hearing this, Lian Po felt ashamed. He carried a rod on his bare back to ask to be spanked at the front gate of Lin Xiangru, saying, "I'm a low and rude man, and I didn't know that your Honor should be so generous!" From then on, the two became life-and-death companions; the fundamental cause of the safety of Zhao was that they could put themselves in each other's shoes. As long as they gave priority to others and the State, they would not fight to be strong or victorious.

P4-17   Fighting on impulse seems to protect self-esteem, but is in fact harmful to life.

Quotes from *Laozi*:

The Dao is invisible and vacuous, but its use is infinite. How deep it is! It seems to be the origin of all things. Sharpness blunted, tangles untied, and brightness softened, it is mingled with the dust. Darkly visible, it only seems as if it were there. I don't know from where it comes, but it has been there earlier than Heaven. (Chapter 4)

Proof: By P4-16, those who treat others well would not contend to be strong or victorious. Contending without consideration is a manifestation of fighting to be strong and victorious, and also of intolerance of things or people; their excessive desires and tricky smartness would make them selflessness, and such selfishness is contending on impulse, usually resulting in others' selfishness, desires and tricks that can cause harm to them. Hence, we say that contending on impulse seems to protect self-esteem, but is in fact harmful to life.

Explanation: When Duke Jing was in power, there were three well-known warriors, namely, Gongsun Jie, Tian Kaijiang, and Gu Yezi in the state. All were proficient in martial arts and courageous, with great contributions to the State; all were arrogant and proud of their crafts. Yanzi told Duke Jing that they would turn out to be dangers and curses to the State, now that they paid no attention to ritual ethics! He asked the duke to summon the three generals, on the pretext that he would give them two peaches. Hearing this, the three generals followed the order. Gongsun Jie was the first to take the peach, saying "Yanzi is wise. I had hunted wild boars in the jungle once, and killed tigers in the mountain; both the jungle and wind witnessed my bravery, so I deserve this peach." Unwilling to show weakness, Tian Kaijiang grabbed the second peach, explaining, "I once led the troops to fight against and defeat the enemies twice, defending the dignity of the State and protecting our people. Who could be as courageous?" Looking at them, Gu Yezi argued, "Once I guarded our duke when crossing the Yellow River; when suddenly a big turtle bit our chariot, I jumped into the river and killed the turtle. In the end, I came to the surface of the river, with the turtle head in one hand and the reins in the other. Everyone else was startled and thought that I was God of River. Am I not as courageous as you are?" With this, he pulled out his sword and wanted to fight with the other two, who sighed, "We are no equals to Gu Yezi in bravery or in contribution, but we took the peaches first. We are greedy. If we keep living, we would be clinging to life and fearing death. How should we be called courageous?" Thus, the two put down the peaches and killed themselves. Seeing the two corpses on the ground, Gu Yezi cried, "Both of my friends are dead. If I keep living, I would be considered having no benevolence; if I feel no regrets and dare not to die for my wrong doing, I would be deemed a coward." Then he cut his own throat and died. Just for two peaches, the three brave generals died in a minute. They fought on impulse and consequently destroyed themselves.

P4-18   He who follows nature would not fight to win.

Quotes from *Laozi:*

Therefore, the sage obtains the people's love and respect, and not their detestation. Because he does not strive, no one can strive with him. (Chapter 66)

Those who are good at using people are modest towards them. This is the virtue of non-contention. (Chapter 68)

The way of Heaven is victory without striving; response without speaking; arrival without calling; and scheming without consideration. (Chapter 73)

Proof: By A4, the sage knows about Dao and thus would not fight for gains. It is wise to follow the sages and do not fight, while it is unfeasible to run against Dao, or all the spontaneous and free things. Or, according to P1-4 and P4-1, the basic feature of Dao and all things is nature, and following the natural way is the general rule of managing life. Hence, we say that he who follows nature would not fight to win.

Explanation: By translating the lines of British poet Walter Savage Landor, "I strove with none, for none was worth my strife; Nature I loved, and next to Nature, Art; I warmed both hands before the fire of 'naturalness' towards Life; It sinks; and I am ready to depart," Yang Jiang expressed her attitude of "naturalness" towards life. The "striving with none" in her eyes was achieved by knowing nature practicing it blindly, which also reflects her wisdom. In her book *Sitting on the Edge of Life*, she said, "In retrospection, I've tolerated this and that, just for keeping my inner freedom and peace. I would laugh off the cursing and refuse to fight back. If you want to kill me with a knife in hand, I would say, 'We don't have hatred, would you like to become a prisoner just for murdering me? How did I get in your way?' So tolerance is my cover for self-protection. Being covered, I can see through others who can't see me, and I'm willing to be a 'zero', which is nothing to others. As such, I can pursue freedom and personality. Therefore, I think tolerance and freedom are dialectical. Tolerance is for freedom while enjoying freedom requires tolerance."[1] Here, Yang Jiang elaborated the relation between tolerance and freedom, which fully reflects the freedom and longevity brought forth by tolerance when learning nature.

P4-19   He who follows Dao is the wise who seems as if stupid.

Quotes from *Laozi*:

Others all have surplus while I alone seem to be in want. I'm foolish and muddled. The average people seem to be intelligent while I alone seem to be benighted. They are all sharp and shrewd while I'm alone dull and confused. My heart is of equanimity like the unruffled sea and endless wind. All others seem to be clever and capable while I'm alone stupid and clumsy. Thus, I alone am different

---

1   Yang Jiang. Sitting on the Edge of Life. *Wenhui Daily*, July 8, 2011.

from others, but I have the Dao with me. (Chapter 20)

He is free from self-display, and therefore he is illustrious; from self-assertion, therefore he is distinguished; from self-boasting, and therefore he is meritorious; from self-complacency, and therefore he is enduring. (Chapter 22)

Proof: By D3, "wisdom" also refers specifically to the very smartness which keeps people from returning to non-being after meeting excessive desires. Also, according to A5, the basic rule of managing life is getting rid of excessive desires and tricky smartness; hence, it is the highest of wisdom that one returns to non-being and, namely, to Dao, which on surface seems stupid. Hence, we say that he who follows Dao is the wise who seems as if stupid.

Explanation: Legend has it that once an old man said to Laozi, "I'm 106 years old now. Since my boyhood, I've been living without much to do. My peers passed away one by one; they had no land of their own though they cultivated acres of fertile fields; they didn't enjoy comfy houses though they built the Great Wall; they were now buried in the wild though they built countless houses. While I who had never grew a bean have food to eat, and who had never lay a brick have a house to live in. Should I laugh at them for their busy life, only to end up earlier?"

After hearing this, Laozi smiled. He asked someone to bring a brick and a stone and put them in front of the old man, saying "If you can only choose one, which will you choose, the brick or the stone?" The old man took the brick and happily answered, "Of course the brick." Stroking his beard and smiling, Laozi asked, "Why?" The old man pointed at the stone, explaining "This stone is of no edge or point. What's the use of it?" Laozi then asked the surrounding people the same question. They all chose the brick over the stone. Laozi turned around and asked the old man, "Does the brick live longer or the stone?" "Of course the stone." Laozi replied with a relief, "People chose the brick over the stone, of which the former lasts shorter than the latter; this is just because of its usefulness. Everything else is no exception. However short it lasts, people would choose and miss it for its benefits, and vice versa." The old man felt ashamed at once.

P4-20 **He who ignores his body would treasure nothing.**

Quotes from *Laozi*:

One is panic-stricken when he's favoured or humiliated. He is too much worried about his body as much as calamity. What is meant by speaking thus of being favoured and humiliated? Favour itself is inferior. Getting that favour, one has the fear of losing it; losing it, one has the fear of still greater calamity. That's what is meant. And what is meant by saying that one is too much worried about his body as much as calamity? We have great worries because we have the flesh body. If we have no flesh body, what worries do we have? Therefore, he who values the empire as he values his own body can be entrusted with the care of the empire. He who loves the empire as he loves his own body can be given the custody of the empire. (Chapter 13)

Proof: According to D1 and D6, the body unifies the inner drive and outside desires, while virtue refers to the knowledge of the free and unrestrained process and the quality obtained from this adaptation. Also, by A5 and P4-18 we know that the basic rule of managing life is getting rid of excessive desires and tricky smartness and by following nature people can be strong without striving. Managing life that is manifested in loving body, in fact, is tolerating both self and all things, that is to say, we should neither get in the way of all things for the sake of ourselves nor degrading ourselves for the sake of all things; the knowledge of and adaptation to a free and unrestrained self is inseparable from those of the free and unrestrained processes. Hence, we say that he who ignores his body would treasure nothing.

Explanation: It was said in *Laozi* that "Therefore, he who values the empire as he values his own body can be entrusted with the care of the empire. He who loves the empire as he loves his own body can be given the custody of the empire." The same was said in *Zhuangzi*, "He who would govern the kingdom honors it as he does with his own person; he who governs the kingdom with love would be entrusted with love to his own person." It also records a couple of stories: When Emperor Yao gave the throne to Xu You, the latter refused to take it but gave it to Zhifu, who said, "It's Ok, but I am seriously ill and plan to cure it, so I have no time for governing the state." Emperor Shun also wanted to give the throne to Zizhou Zhibo, who refused with the same excuse as well. People like Zhifu and Zhibo, though knowing that governing a state was the greatest power and status one could enjoy, refused the honor after all, for it would damage their own lives, to say nothing of common things.

When Danfu, the forefather of Zhou, lived in Bin, the Dis were always invading; Danfu first offered them furs and clothes, and then hounds and smart horses and eventually jewelry and jade, but they refused all due to lust for the land of Bin. Danfu said, "If there were war, we would lose our brothers and fathers would lose their sons and daughters, so I would not launch it; besides, I've also heard that one should not harm his people just for the land that breeds the people." Thus, he left on his stick with his people following behind, and founded a new capital at the foot of Qishan. It was because of his love for people's life that Danfu chose to avoid war and even abandoned his throne.

P4-21   Only by living with all things can one manage his life.

Quotes from *Laozi*:

  Heaven is long-enduring and earth continues long. The reason why heaven and earth are able to endure and continue thus long is because they do not live of, or for, themselves. Therefore, the Sages retreat to the back, but win the respect of others; they seldom consider for themselves, but keep themselves safe and sound. Isn't it because they are not selfish so that they attain what they ought to attain? (Chapter 7)

Proof: By D7, "selflessness" refers to the tolerance-of-all mentality after giving up excessive desires and tricky smartness, and from A5 and P4-1, we know that the basic rule of managing life is getting rid of excessive desires and tricky smartness, and following nature is the general principle of managing life. The process of keeping fit is the tolerance of all things, which needs to maintain a selfless mentality step by step and to follow nature. Hence, we say that only by living with all things can one manage his life.

Explanation: The Dong Minority is the largest operator of artificial plantation in southern China, and for 600 years exporting logs has been the main channel for its people to earn a living. In the process of managing forests, the Dong Minority places great emphasis on developing compounded forests; in terms of artificial plantation, they not only plant cedars of economic value, but also preserve other trees carefully. Hence, leguminosae, fagaceae and rutaceae trees can be found here and there in their artificial plantation and account for at least 15% of the total. There are also a great number of herbs and epiphytes. Their forestation and cultivation are normally compatible with dry land farming, as all kinds of dry crops are planted on the vacant lots where they are available, including millet, corn, soybean, sweet potato, buckwheat and potato that can be used as grains, and such vegetables as cucumber, pumpkin, chili, carrot and white radish; besides, fruits, cash crops and herbs like watermelon, sweet potatoes and indigo indicum, are also planted not just for the maximized commercialization of timber production. In the village community of Dong Minority, rivers, fish ponds and rice fields are integrated into a "connector" that can irrigate the rice and feed the fish and ducks as well. Species of artificial breeding asides there are co-existing countless wild animals and plants, including wild rice, water celery, lotus root and snails, mussels, loaches and other fishes. There are over 100 species of animals and plants just within one paddy field. Among those creatures, some that are taken as pests and weeds by the mainstream culture are used and fed as living or producing sources. Some would interfere with the original eco-system with the advance of human society, and therefore are forced to separate, while such separation is consciously controlled by the Dong culture so as to preserve the original species. Such is what leads their living habits and values, which in turn protects the species diversity and lays a solid foundation for species diversity and composition.

In contrast, if there were a clear line drawn between resources and wastes, good worms and pests, crops and weeds, good and bad guys, then some would live as long as over hundreds of years while others would live as short as tens of years, which would change the original species totally. So new species can only be bred by artificial planting, which includes such major methods as cultivation, irrigation, fertilizer and pesticides; such means would inevitably cause soil erosion and degeneration, growing pests and diseases, which would make the artificial ecosystem highly vulnerable. Yet in the sub-consciousness of the Dong people, each species is a member of the system at large, where all members are co-existing. The rule for human intervention in the ecological system lies not in expanding some of the population at the cost of others, but in maintaining all species at a proper level. For example, "if there are too many eels, they should be caught; otherwise, they should be transferred to fields with a scarcity of them. Water centipedes are harmful to young carps, so they would be captured for foods when people find there are far too many centipedes around the small carps; otherwise, man should feed water centipedes." From this, we can find that "as the ultimate adjuster and controller of biological diversity, human won't disturb the living habits or destroy the living spaces of species, if they just control the number of species." Obviously, such a rule would exert little impact on the ecological system, and is more beneficial to preserving the composition and diversity of the original species. Although human society would inevitably affect the natural system in this or that way, the efforts of the Dong people on preserving the original natural state and maintaining co-existence are the very values that can be the premise of the co-existence between human society and the ecological system.[1]

"The unity of Heaven and Man" represents the highest realm of life in terms of Chinese's pursuit of the harmony between man and nature. The Daoists take the respect for natural rules and the co-existence of all things as the highest law of human being, which is also the ecological wisdom unique to Laozi's philosophy, guiding people to reach the realm of "I live with Heaven, Earth and All Things," and this is what managing life is in the real sense.

---

1 Luo Kanglong, Wang Xiu. On the Impacts of Dong Minority's Ecological Wisdom on Maintaining Regional Ecological Security. *Journal of National Studies of Guangxi*, 2008(4).

P4-22　When selfish ends and lusts are eschewed, one is well-treating himself.

Quotes from *Laozi*:

The rulers should retain simplicity and honesty, lessen self-interest and desires. (Chapter 19)

The sage does not accumulate for himself. The more that he expends for others, the more he possesses of his own; the more that he gives to others, the more he has by himself. The law of nature is beneficial rather than harmful; the way of the human world is to do things without competition. (Chapter 81)

Proof: By D7, "selflessness" refers to the tolerance-of-all mentality after giving up excessive desires and tricky smartness. From A5 and P4-6 we know that the basic rule of managing life is getting rid of excessive desires and tricky smartness, while opening the door to excessive desires would damage life. Besides, less selfishness and desire would make people tolerant and treat themselves well, which is in fact letting life grow in a natural and all-embracing way. Hence, we say that when selfish ends and lusts are eschewed, one is well-treating himself.

Explanation: Zhang Xueliang, who was against the civil war, had once initiated Xi'an Incident which astounded the whole world. It helped to promote the second cooperation between Kuomintang and the Communist Party so as to form a Chinese united front against Japanese aggression. After the Incident, however, Zhang was under long-term house arrest and lost his personal freedom. His life was full of ups and downs, but he lived 101 years, which is indeed a miracle. He suffered from severe neurasthenia at an earlier age, leading to lack of sleep. After losing his freedom in 1936, his sleep got better, so it was during such a difficult time that he gradually got a peaceful mind. In the long-term imprisonment, he got away from his previous luxury life and hard work during wartime, official scheming, and anxiety as well. Zhang Xueliang once quoted these words of Ji Kang, a Daoist scholar of the Jin Dynasty, "There are five difficulties in managing life: the first is the trap of fame and fortune, the second is the trap of happiness and sadness, the third sound and color, the fourth is taste, and the last anxiety." To overcome those five difficulties needs inner peace, selflessness and less desire.

跋一：人法地，地法天，天法道，道法自然

甘筱青教授与他的学术团队多年来筚路蓝缕，积极创新，以公理化方法诠释中华文化经典著作，其不懈的努力，赢得了国内外学术界的称道。他们在相继完成了《〈论语〉的公理化诠释》《〈孟子〉的公理化诠释》《〈荀子〉的公理化诠释》等力作之后，又对道家哲学的代表作《老子》进行了公理化诠释。在学术老前辈萧树铁、杨叔子、杜维明等先生的热情鼓励下，经过数年的反复论证和深度研讨，他们数易其稿，终于完成《〈老子〉的公理化诠释》这一著作，为创造性地弘扬传统文化做了贡献。笔者数年前曾为《〈论语〉的公理化诠释》一书作跋，指出运用公理化方式诠释经典体现了重要的认识论意义和方法论意义，本文再就《老子》的公理化诠释所体现的特殊意义展开探讨。

一、公理化诠释彰显了老子自然哲学和辩证法的独特面目

应该指出，《老子》的公理化诠释比《论语》《孟子》和《荀子》的公理化诠释具有更高的学术视野。首先，孔子、孟子和荀子的人本主义思想、民本主义思想等，既体现了中国先秦思想史的文化特征，又贯穿于两千多年的历史中，对中国文明和东亚文明产生了深远影响，具有较为明显的系统性和逻辑一致性。其次，孔子、孟子和荀子都特别注重其思想的经世致用，面对现实世界构建伦理道德规范和价值体系，因而以他们为代表的儒家思想有着不可置疑的认识论、方法论意义和实践理性的价值。而且这三位思想家的核心观点、逻辑思路，都是朝着实践理性的方向不断深入发展的，所以甘教授及其团队在完成《论语》的公理化诠释之后，接着进行《孟子》的公理化诠释、《荀子》的公理化诠释，能给读者以一气呵成和水到渠成的感觉，与先秦儒家在发展进程中所呈现出的连续性是一致的。

然而，《老子》在中国思想史乃至世界思想史中占有的历史地位更加独特，《老子》公理化诠释相对于儒学经典公理化的诠释，亦更为复杂和困难。

如果我们从全球的历史时空来分析老子的哲学思想，就会发现老子的自然哲学不仅包括了古希腊哲学中的本体论哲学，自古希腊直至19世纪欧洲哲学体系中的认识论哲学，还包括了19世纪末、20世纪初令西方哲学出现重大历史转折的语言哲学。换言之，贯穿于东西方哲学思想史的基本问题，《老子》

一书均做了精辟的阐述，在人类哲学思想发展史上可谓蔚为大观。虽然道家哲学在老庄之后出现过发展上的断裂，受到了佛教哲学的巨大冲击，经历了在近代传播到西方的考验，然而老子自然哲学的价值不仅没有出现丝毫的衰减迹象，而且在各个文明圈显示出强大的生命力和与日俱增的影响力，具有重要的现实意义。明确这一点，就能够说明用公理化方法诠释《老子》的必要性，更能说明此项工程的艰巨性。

老子不仅早于古希腊前苏格拉底学派，最先创立了一般意义上的哲学及辩证法，而且最先创立了以自然哲学为基础的否定性和批判性的哲学及其辩证法。在此需要加以强调的是，老子所揭示的自然哲学及其辩证法原理，以其前瞻性、艰深性、复杂性与丰富性，达到了人类今日尚难企及的高度、深度与广度，包括老子对自然宇宙世界发展规律的认识（即"道"的运动为第一推动力），对否定性辩证法与批判性辩证法的结论（"反者道之动"），以及对于人类自身所陷入的与自然世界无法克服与解决的矛盾、悖论和二律背反的思考，等等。

近代德国哲学家莱布尼茨第一次将老子的哲学思想精确地定义为自然哲学，另一位哲学家黑格尔对老子及其哲学系统亦敬佩有加。这种敬佩不是偶然的，而是因为黑格尔的哲学辩证法虽然博大精深，但其内部包含了时空的局限性和内在的矛盾性。就这一点而言，拿黑格尔的辩证法与老子学说比较，还不如将近代德国哲学家康德的思想与老子的思想进行比较。康德将其哲学认识论、哲学辩证法以及对于人类判断力、知解力和理性思辨能力的辩证批判，置于更广袤的空间尺度上和更久远的时间尺度上，使我们意识到康德与老子在哲学世界观和方法论上的心领神会。明确指出这一点，有助于我们理解对《老子》进行公理化诠释，需要更高的认识境界，绝非用某种辩证法来套老子思想那么简单，而甘教授及其团队对用简单辩证法来分析老子思想所得的结论，做出了种种反思。或许可以说，黑格尔的辩证法，是针对有限事物的辩证法，而老子的辩证法是面对无限事物、无限世界的辩证法。《老子》的公理化诠释彰显了《老子》自然哲学和辩证法的独特面目。

二、公理化诠释彰显了老子思想的丰富性、完整性和开放性

老子自然哲学和辩证法的丰富性，体现为其哲学思考与研究不限于一般意义上的对象范畴，而是一个包括了自然哲学、人本主义哲学、历史哲学、美

学和艺术哲学、法哲学、道德哲学与伦理学、生命哲学、政治哲学及政治科学，尤其是权力与反权力哲学、经济科学、社会科学、军事科学等对象的哲学及辩证法体系。

老子自然哲学和辩证法的完整性，体现为它不仅纳入了上述诸学科以及它们提出的问题，而且体现为它没有简单迎合人类在建构自然科学、艺术科学、人文科学和社会科学过程中所基于的人类中心主义的欲求。恰恰相反，老子用自己独特和高度睿智的自然哲学辩证法，对这些欲求加以分析批判，并将其置于被否定的地位。应该说，老子对于诸学科的独特批判甚至是否定性的评判，是基于老子的自然本体论、自然主体论和自然中心论作出的。为此，老子所论及的诸学科，并非人本主义哲学意义上的学科，并非人类中心主义意义上的学科，而是浸透了老子自然哲学思想的、体现了老子自然哲学概念的学科。他所运用的哲学辩证法，亦非普通的解释一切矛盾对立统一现象的辩证法，而是从自然哲学出发构建的辩证法，其中不仅有关于矛盾对立统一的阐述，更有对于悖论和二律背反原理的阐述。由于老子自然哲学体系与孔子、孟子等儒家哲学体系的差异，两个体系内"道"的基本概念就大相径庭。

老子自然哲学和辩证法的开放性，体现为它是向不同的文明圈和不同的文化系统开放的。因为，无论作为个体还是群体，在一定的时间空间尺度内，对于宇宙自然世界的奥秘、真实、真理性、科学知识和技术系统的认知与把握，均具有相对性。而老子创立的自然哲学和辩证法可以对所有的知识系统、文化系统开放。

甘筱青教授及其团队的研究彰显了老子自然哲学和辩证法的丰富性、完整性和开放性。我们既要理解人类所创造的各种学科，又不能简单切块式地用各种学科的理论来印证老子（这实质上是肢解老子），而是需要用老子思想来驾驭各种学科，指出各种学科在"道"的指导下所呈现的真正面目。做到这一点，不但是对团队成员自身学养的挑战，也需要对人类的认识与认识方法的全面反思。例如，作为一种否定性和批判性的哲学辩证法，老子对于人类所渴望拥有的主体性及其意识提出了批判，对于以孔子、孟子及儒家所代表的人本主义思想提出了批判。老子学说不同于以人为世界中心、以人为宇宙自然主体、以人为衡量万事万物尺度的古希腊人本主义哲学思想，他反复强调自然宇宙对于人类世界的主体地位是先天拥有的、无法质疑的、无法剥夺的。老子认为"道"作为宇宙自然发展运行的基本规律、基本理念与原则，不仅是无时无处不在的，而且是万事万物之本源，是其出发点，也是其归结点。他提出了"道生一，一生二，二生三，三生万物"的著名论断，并提出了与人本主义哲学有关人类认识并征服自然的观点截然相反的结论："人法地，地法天，天法道，道法自然。""道"乃是宇宙自然运行规律的某种表征，代表着宇宙自然的终极理念与理性，也是宇宙自然万物之本源。它不以人类的意志为转移，有别于按照人类中心主义设定的理念。为此，基于人类文明产生的各门自然科学、社会科学及人文科学，皆被推至"道"这一自然理性的法庭上接受审判，其存在的合理性必须重新得到审视。同样，人类对于自然界所表现出的征服、统治和开发利用的权力意志与权力哲学，也必须得到重新审视。通过甘教授及其团队的公理化诠释，我们可以清晰看到人类的权力意志与权力哲学退居到次要地位，成为"道"的一个组成部分，由此人类的知识系统和科学技术系统也从自我膨胀的状态变为"压缩饼干"。为征服与统治宇宙自然并以人类语言系统、符号系统或表征系统建构起来的理论学说体系，在"道"面前显示出它的不自量力和夸大失真。而通过"无为而无所不为""无知而无所不知""无欲则刚""柔弱胜刚强"来达到人类与宇宙自然的和谐共处、和谐共生的种种思想概念，在《老子》的公理化诠释中得到一以贯之的清晰反映。

三、公理化诠释彰显了《老子》在语言哲学、政治哲学、自然哲学以及艺术哲学等层面体现的价值

甘筱青教授及其学术团队用公理化方法诠释《老子》，也是为了揭示老子自然哲学及其辩证法所具有的公理性和普遍适用性。因篇幅所限，笔者仅从语言哲学、政治哲学、自然哲学以及艺术哲学等层面，去阐述对于《老子》开展公理化诠释的价值。

1. 从语言哲学层面

从古希腊与古罗马时期到18世纪启蒙哲学发展时期、19世纪欧洲古典哲学发展的高峰时期，无论是苏格拉底学派还是后来的柏拉图、亚里士多德，其关注点都在于本体论（探索宇宙自然、世界的起源与构成）和认识论（认识宇宙世界的辩证方法、逻辑方法）。19世纪末期，欧洲哲学家如维特根斯坦、

波普尔、索绪尔等开始专注本体论、认识论的基本结构要素，亦即语言的本质或称逻各斯的问题。西方哲学向语言哲学的转向，使我们得以重新审视作为语言现象的概念、定义与命题各自的特性及其相互关系，命题的逻辑推理及其所导致的结论，以及逻辑前提的假设，特别是先验的假设之间的关系问题，也使我们重新审视在使用由人类自身创造的、非自然的语言这一思维工具时，语言所表现的自我参照功能与自我循环论证功能，以及运用语言进行思维、逻辑推理所导致的结论是否可靠的问题。20世纪下半叶，法国的哲学家如德里达、福柯、拉冈等展开了对于西方语言逻辑系统的深度批判。

而《老子》一书对其提出的基本逻辑前提即"道"的概念（天道，或曰宇宙自然之道），在使用之前已展开了类似语言哲学层面的辩证批判。借用德国古典哲学的术语来说，即是在运用由语言构成的概念、定义与命题阐述哲理之前，首先对由语言构成的概念、定义和命题这些"用于批判的武器"进行了深刻批判。老子指出："道可道，非常道；名可名，非常名。"这12个看似简单易懂的字表明，老子在两千六百年前即已认识到，运用人类语言对宇宙自然之道进行言说、命名、假设并推理，均非具有绝对不变的性质，而是具有时空意义上的相对特征，具有人的主观认识、主观理性特征，而非纯然是客观理性的反映。为此，老子在运用语言描述概念时非常谨慎，例如他在界定"道"这个基本概念时，是采用多重定义法进而从各个层面、各个侧面去定义它，丰富并拓展其内涵与外延。钱锺书先生在《管锥编》一书中指出，老子的语言哲学及其辩证法向我们展示了一个"道本无名复多名"的定义、辨析、认识、推理与论证的过程。若借用法国20世纪下半叶的哲学家德里达的术语，便是解构主义哲学非常推崇的语义发散过程。老子在论述"德"的概念时，采用了相同的辩证方法。这种人类认识的多元性、多样性、多义性是符合宇宙自然客观规律的，它确保了历代读者在阅读理解时所面对的无限可能性，避免使其落入胶柱鼓瑟而死于句下的境地。

通常的概念、定义、判断及推理，都不可避免地带有它的局限性，然而，没有清晰界定又无从进行推理。为此，甘筱青教授及其团队在阐述老子思想的核心内容时，充分注意到概念的"可界定性"和"不可界定性"的统一，语言的有限启示能力和无限启示意义的统一，事物未产生阶段、存在阶段以及变化阶段的统一，因而较好地体现了老子思想的本色。在推导出哲学与一般科学的结论时,该结论的逻辑假设前提一般具有时间规定性、空间规定性、参照系的规定性,还有科研人员自身认识能力、思维能力与科研能力的规定性,以及分析推理时使用手段的规定性。这种种规定性往往导致了某种思想的局限。然而,如果充分考虑到语言哲学层面的问题,用恰当的方法展现老子的思想,就可以使之成为洞察人类认识之相对性、主观性与开放性的一面镜子,同时亦可以表现老子在阐述其思想时,已经充分考虑到自己也是在"强名之",从而避免误导读者。

2. 从政治哲学层面

在老子所处的春秋战国时期,如何结束各诸侯国之间持续不断的争霸之战,如何开出万世之太平,乃当时思想家们最为关切的现实问题。孔子基于其人本主义哲学思想,从人类的根本利益出发,设计了一个社会良治模式,意图通过教育途径培养仁人君子,通过仁人君子的个体价值在个人、家庭、社会、国家和人类诸空间的递进实现来达致全世界永久和平,即从诚意正心到修身齐家,进而治国平天下。为此,孔子提出了以公共利益和社会正义、社会公正为实现社会和谐目标的手段,并提出了"大道之行也,天下为公"这样的具有公理性质的基本原则。另一位中国战略学家孙子在《孙子兵法》一书中,亦基于其人本主义哲学的价值理念,提出了非战、慎战和速战的基本原则。而老子则提出了有别于孔子、力图以"圣人行无为之治"来实现永久和平的思想。老子从自然哲学的立场出发,立足于宇宙自然的高度,提倡按"道"来治理社会、国家与天下。自然宇宙运行的规律与法则乃是放手让一切存在形式根据其自身发展的客观规律自主、自由、自在与自为地运行、选择与运动,而宇宙自然则以无为的方式为一切存在形式提供客观条件。由此老子提出了独特的良治之道,即严格遵循无为而治之道行事。

对于实施国家、社会治理之一国君主的历史作用、存在理由及历史功过,老子亦以无为之治之道作为价值判断标准,提出了"太上,下知有之;其次,亲而誉之。其次,畏之。其次,侮之。"的衡量尺度。西汉时期汉文帝和汉景帝通过实践老子无为而治的政治理想,创造了中国历史上罕见的繁荣与社会进步,成为可资后世借鉴的楷模。文景之治与其后汉武帝实施穷兵黩武政策的国家、社会治理模式,恰好形成了鲜明对照。

然而,一般读者很难准确理解老子的"无为而治"的思想。人们很容易认为它是一种消极的主张，一种否定人类主观能动性的主张，甚至有可能是"反社会""反文明""反进步"的主张。甘教授及其团队的公理化诠释，能使我们更好、更准确地理解老子所说的"无为而治"，因为在公理化体系中，"无为而治"的内在逻辑性非常严密。老子用"道"这面镜子去照人类社会，发现了人类社会有"三虚"：即目标的"虚高"、功劳的"虚夸"和恩德的"虚构"。人类误以为良治社会单靠人的努力就可以实现，事实上，人的努力所起的作用是非常有限的，"靠道德修为实现万世太平"不过是一个"虚高"的目标。即使实现和平，自以为的"功莫大焉"、恩德无限，也不过是功劳的"虚夸"和恩德的"虚构"而已。更加危险的是，人类往往陶醉在自我的功德里，忽视"道"与"自然"的作用，甚至随意破坏这种作用，因此必须以"无为"来制止人类的妄为。老子认为权力哲学、统治与征服欲望是引发战争的根源。他还指出："天之道，取有余以奉不足；人之道，取不足以奉有余。"这就一针见血地揭示出社会公正、社会公平以及据此分配社会财富，乃是实现人类社会的正义、和谐的不二法门，是符合天道的表现。相反，对社会财富的创造者、劳动者群体与弱势群体巧取豪夺，乃是一种违背天道的暴政。此种"有为"就不仅是一种虚夸，而是对胡作非为的一种掩饰了。总之，政治的合法性来自"道"，即需要依据"道"来审视统治者的作用，规定统治者的作为，进而达到"无为而无不为"。这一结论在公理化诠释体系中得到了充分展示，而老子基于自然哲学的政治哲学也就此更加彰显了普遍性。

3. 从人与自然关系层面

老子的自然哲学向我们展示了其独有的大智慧。根据其自然哲学，自然为本体，为主体，为万事万物之本源和最终归宿。我们对于自然不仅应有敬畏之心与感恩之情，更应对它珍惜、珍爱有加，不能通过掠夺自然、竭泽而渔的方式来满足人类之无穷欲求，待将地球破坏殆尽再去破坏火星、月球或其他类地星球。老子的一项公理性的论断，即"人法地，地法天，天法道，道法自然"，对于我们正确认识并把握处理好人类与自然的辩证关系具有重大的指导作用，已经成为实现经济、社会、文化与生态环境可持续发展的指南。老子深刻分析了人与自然之间存在的矛盾和冲突，认为它们主要体现为"争功""争德""争智"，而公理化诠释彰显了这些论述的普遍性价值。

其一是"争功"。《老子》开篇指出，"道可道，非常道"。尽管"道"难以用人类语言加以精确定义与表述,然而充满智慧的老子却借助于艺术形象加以明喻:"上善若水。水善利万物而不争,处众人之所恶,故几于道。""居善地,心善渊,与善仁,言善信,正善治,事善能,动善时。夫唯不争,故无尤。""夫唯不争,故天下莫能与之争。""道"生万物、"道"养万物是自然界体现的机制,而人类往往贪天之功为己有,以为"人养人"远胜于"天养人",故而疯狂地开发、掠夺自然资源,导致地球的自然环境早已不堪人类无穷无尽欲求之重负。环境危机,生态危机,物种大规模消失之危机,气候灾害频仍之危机,已经危及现今地球上七十多亿人及其后代的生存。醉心于工业化、后工业化、科技革命与消费主义狂欢的人类,往往对此充耳不闻或行鸵鸟政策。笔者撰写本文之际,正是法国巴黎第二十一届全球气候峰会举行之时。人类若不能够从根本上辨析清楚自己与宇宙自然的客体与主体的辩证关系,那么人类像其他已经消失的物种那样从地球上消失只是一个时间问题而已。

甘筱青教授及其团队通过公理化诠释,揭示了老子哲学对人与自然之矛盾的本质性把握。"道"生万物,而万物的变化是一个从"无"到"有"、复归于"无"的过程。"有"和"无"是相伴相生、相应相和的,是无法分割的。由此,人类创造各种"有"的过程,也就是制造各种"无"的过程;创造的"有"越多,制造的"无"也越多;创造"有"的速度越快,制造"无"的速度也越快;对各种"有"的利用程度越高,各种"无"的不可利用程度也就越高。为此,疯狂开发利用自然资源的过程,也就是疯狂制造不可用物质的过程,最终会从"生养人类"的过程走向"毁灭人类"的过程。这一结论,是从老子思想体系的内在逻辑中揭示出来的,彰显了公理化诠释对认识老子大智慧的价值。

其二是"争德"。数千年以来,仁政与德政便一直是人本主义哲学家如孔子所追求的境界。然而老子振聋发聩地直言:"上德无德,下德有德。"换言之,对"德"的定义亦须以自然之德作为参照标准,而非以人本主义、人类中心主义有关"德"的概念与定义作为参照系。根据老子的自然哲学及其辩证法,自然之德在先,人为之德在其后。自然之德天然地维系着人们相互之间的关系,以及人与自然的关系。当自然之德遭到违背与践踏、自然理性遭到破坏时,人们才会对失去的乐园痛心疾首而倍加心向往之。人们之所以

跋一：人法地，地法天，天法道，道法自然
Epilogue One: Man Models Himself on Earth, Earth on Heaven, Heaven on the Dao, and the Dao on Nature

崇德，崇尚德政，乃是因为自然之德日渐丧失："大道废，有仁义；智慧出，有大伪；六亲失和，有孝慈；国家昏乱，有忠臣。"在此老子深刻地指出了人类创造的文明与自然之德、自然之理性、自然之秩序之间无法调和的矛盾与冲突，揭示了人类对于自然的异化以及自身的异化，也指出了消除双重异化现象、回归自然和谐状态的困难。老子进一步指出："天地不仁，以万物为刍狗，圣人不仁，以百姓为刍狗。"如果圣人能够奉行宇宙自然的无为之道，不去异化自然、异化自身，做到"百姓皆谓我自然"，那么人与自然的再度和谐共处并非完全不可能。

甘筱青教授及其团队用公理化方法诠释《老子》，是在阐述了"道"的本质内涵之后，坚持用"道"来审视人间的一切，也就对人类之德做出了理性的批判。在"道"的观照下，自然貌似无德而有德，"万物并作"且生生不息就是这种自然之德的呈现。同时，自然之德没有浮夸，没有人类的装饰，以本来面目呈现出来，但却居功至伟。而以"道"来观照人类之德，则常常是放大虚夸的结果。人类社会成就每一件大事，事实上大部分都要归功于"自然之德"加上一点人的作用，但人们却以为这全部是自己的功劳。如果不能像公理化诠释那样地分析，则很难理解老子为什么要颠覆"人类之德"。

其三是"争智"。老子指出："绝圣弃智，民利百倍；绝仁弃义，民复孝慈；绝巧弃利，盗贼无有。"这里的"圣"与"智"是指基于人类中心主义的工具理性，旨在征服自然、掠夺自然而建构的知识系统、科学技术系统、价值判断系统。欧洲18世纪著名启蒙思想家卢梭，对自然与文明的悖论关系进行了深入思考与批判，对基于工具理性的科技文明和知识系统提出了批判与否定，进而得出了必须消除人类异化和回归自然状态的结论，这与老子两千多年前推导出的结论具有异曲同工、相视莫逆的性质，证明了老子自然哲学所表现出的超越性以及前瞻性。在20世纪，西方哲学界对人类百年中所经历的以争夺自然资源、政治经济霸权为目的的两次世界大战，以及随之而来的冷战和局部战争作了深刻反思，并基于对工具理性、科技理性的辩证批判，发展出了反权力话语、反极权主义话语、反工业科技文明与消费主义文明、反人类异化现象的当代哲学思潮。

甘筱青教授及其团队的公理化诠释，再一次凸显了老子思想的价值。美国思想家约瑟夫·奈伊于20世纪末提出了软实力的概念。根据奈伊的观点，首先，软实力乃是对硬实力的辩证否定，硬实力以工业实力、经济实力、金融实力与军事实力为基础，是基于工具理性建构起来的；其次，软实力是对以国家政府及权力机构表现出的权力哲学尤其是霸权哲学的否定；再次，软实力是对人与自然具有亲和力的智慧系统的肯定。对于软实力的这些描述，符合老子于两千六百年前提出的知雄守雌、见素抱朴、负阴抱阳、专气致柔、以柔克刚等一系列的概念与范畴，以及由此推导出的逻辑结论。但是，要实现两种理论跨越时空的对接，不能依靠简单的比附，而需要内在的逻辑对接。公理化诠释从"道"这一核心概念出发，推导出符合"自然"之"道"是使万物生生不息的最强力量。明乎此，我们便能够充分地理解与把握老子自然哲学所具有的普遍意义和公理性质。

4. 从艺术哲学层面

老子于两千六百年前创立的艺术哲学，在当代艺术世界依然放射出耀眼夺目的光芒。老子以其自然哲学的辩证法逻辑推导出"万物生于有，有生于无"，换言之，自然宇宙世界的本源是"无"并最终会复归于"无"这一最高境界。在老子看来，至美至善至高的艺术境界乃是源于大自然的鬼斧神工。以音乐为例，人们所推崇的天籁乃是源于大自然的箫声，"大音希声，大象无形"。老子于此揭示出了艺术创作应该遵循的宇宙自然规律和以此为圭臬的人类艺术的发展规律。根据"道法自然"的原理，艺术之道亦须法乎自然之道。"五色令人目盲，五音令人耳聋，五味令人口爽。"老子这一阐述，指出了人类艺术的根本缺陷，回归到艺术哲学的根本。人为的艺术往往刻意以满足人类欲求为目的，违反自然之道，给人类带来精神境界的异化。痴迷于人类之美有可能令世人忘却万物之美，因而导致人与万物的对立。纯粹形式上的艺术追求总是与其对立面形影不离的，有"美"必然就有"不美"，有"善"必然就有"不善"。"天下皆知美之为美，斯恶已；皆知善之为善，斯不善已。故有无相生，难易相成，长短相形，高下相倾，音声相和，前后相随。"

甘筱青教授及其团队的公理化诠释，在一以贯之的逻辑推理中展现了老子艺术哲学的高度。从"道"出发，推理出"自然"为美的最高境界；而"自然"是"有""无"相生的，落实到人的感觉世界中，就是有形与无形、有色与无色。给人以强烈感受的功名利禄、大富大贵、金钱美色、美酒佳肴等，并非是"大美"的体现；而用"淡泊"来指导人的行为，培养人的德性，调节人的身体，就能体现自然之道而给人以莫大的益处。如此一来，老子的艺术哲学就不仅仅是"工匠"意义上的艺术哲学，而是贯穿整个人类社会、涉及人类生存之本的艺术哲学，人们从中可以得到无限的精神滋养。这一点对后世的中国及东亚诸国文人诗书画、音乐、造型艺术和建筑艺术产生了持续深远的影响，也对中国社会乃至世界的发展产生了深远影响。

时至今日，人类社会蕴含的巨大风险亦如达摩克利斯之剑，时时刻刻高悬于人类头上。只要我们回头看一看，地球上储藏了多少足令它毁灭数十次的热核武器和生化武器，历史上出现过多少与宇宙自然为敌、与全人类为敌的暴君与战争狂人，两百五十多年来工业化进程、科技化进程和现代化进程将自然环境毁坏到何种程度，就会不寒而栗，对人类发展的前景生出无限的忧思。本质上，哲学家往往是理想主义者。由于具有高瞻远瞩的认识能力与深刻的判断能力，哲学家对人类发展的前景多持悲观主义的态度，才会在其著作中表现出真诚的理想主义。老子亦不例外，他辞去了柱下史的官职，骑着青牛西出函谷关并消失于沙漠戈壁之中，直至与无限浩渺的宇宙自然融为一体。然而在西出函谷关之前，他给我们留下了集其自然哲学与辩证法智慧之大成的《老子》。

老子在两千六百年前撰写《老子》时所创立的自然哲学与辩证法体系，乃是人类哲学思想史上造山运动过程中形成的第一座像珠穆朗玛峰那样的高峰。其哲学体系之宏大，其否定与批判的辩证方法之高深，其自然哲学与辩证法体系对于不同时代、不同文明圈、不同哲学传统的开放性、对话性和启迪性，均为人类哲学思想史上所罕见。笔者在《〈论语〉的公理化诠释·跋》一文中曾论述，每当人类历史的发展到了特殊的转折关头时，人们都会自觉或不自觉地与先哲前贤对话，根据当下时空重新提出认识论、方法论和实践论的问题，以解决人们在现实中遇到的紧迫问题。这样经久不息的对话，不仅使我们每每能够拨云见日、豁然开朗，而且也能使先哲前贤的思想体系得以永葆青春活力，使其如灯塔一般四射的智慧之光能够不断延伸，进而普照千秋。只要宇宙自然尚在按照其自身规律不断演进，只要人类尚未因其与自然宇宙的矛盾冲突而提早步入自我毁灭的临终境地，老子的自然哲学思想体系以及高深的辩证法，同哲学思想史上诸多与老子相视莫逆的哲学家、思想家的智慧，就将继续烛照我们，引领我们走向一条尊重宇宙自然之道、与宇宙自然和谐相处的康庄大道。

然而，与先贤对话是艰难的。古往今来，关于老子的诠释是如此的纷繁复杂，又有多少能真正做到窥其堂奥？这同时也说明了甘筱青教授及其学术团队在进行《老子》的公理化诠释时，设立了高难度的学术标杆。我们应该向这一具有使命感并做出学术贡献的团队表达由衷的敬意。甘教授及其团队所作的公理化诠释工作告诉我们：那种视《老子》为神秘莫测的解说是不需要的，因为神秘莫测意味着与人类的需求隔绝；那种"我注六经"式的解说是不需要的，因为绝大多数注解者不会比老子更高明；那种片言只语的琐碎解说是不需要的，因为这样的解说还得依赖阅读者本身的接受与理解。公理化诠释是从简要的定义、基本假设和公理出发推导众多命题而建构起来的演绎体系，这个体系应当是老子思想的主干与精华，有助于读者比较准确而全面地洞窥《老子》的精髓，有助于道家思想的现代转型。

我唯愿老子自然哲学思想与高深辩证法智慧的光辉能够惠及地球上更多苍生，唯愿人类永远记取并躬行老子的谆谆教诲——"人法地，地法天，天法道，道法自然"。

是为跋。

韦遨宇
法国新索邦大学
2016 年初于法国巴黎

跋一：人法地，地法天，天法道，道法自然

Epilogue One: Man Models Himself on Earth, Earth on Heaven, Heaven on the Dao, and the Dao on Nature

For many years, Professor Gan Xiaoqing and his research team has been taking an axiomatic approach in interpreting Chinese classics, pioneering the field with innovative and vibrant reconstruction. Their tireless efforts have won acclaim from academics both at home and abroad. After successively completing such *tour de force* interpretations as *Analects of Confucius: An Axiomatic Interpretation*, *Mencius: An Axiomatic Interpretation* and *Xunzi: An Axiomatic Interpretation*, they began an in-depth axiomatic interpretation of the Daoist masterpiece, *Laozi*. With guidance from established scholars including Xiao Shutie, Yang Shuzi, and Du Weiming, Professor Gan's team has spent years honing their interpretations through numerous discussions and debates until finally they finished *Laozi: An Axiomatic Interpretation*, which is a truly unique contribution to the promotion of traditional Chinese culture.

When I wrote the epilogue for *Analects of Confucius: An Axiomatic Interpretation*, I discussed the epistemological and methodological importance of axiomatically interpreting classical works. In this epilogue, I shall further explore the unique significance of an axiomatic interpretation of *Laozi*.

I. Axiomatic interpretation manifests the unique features of Laozi's natural philosophy and dialectics

The axiomatic interpretation of *Laozi* arises from a higher academic vision than those of the *Analects, Mencius,* and *Xunzi*. First, the humanism and the people-oriented thought of Confucius, Mencius and Xunzi are major features of pre-Qin thought, illuminating the following two thousand years with a far-reaching impact both on Chinese and East Asian civilizations. Second, Confucius, Mencius and Xunzi all emphasized the practical use of their thoughts in society. They are systematic and logically consistent, having established ethical and moral norms and value systems for real world interaction. Confucianism has unquestionable epistemological and methodological significance as well as practical rational value. Third, the core viewpoints and logical thoughts of the three thinkers all develop along the lines of practical reason.

Logically, after completing the axiomatic interpretation of *The Analects of Confucius*, Professor Gan's team went on to interpret axiomatically *Mencius* and *Xunzi*. They have continued to work on the axiomatic interpretation of pre-Qin Chinese classics without delay, mirroring the continuity of the development of pre-

Qin Confucianism.

Nevertheless, *Laozi* occupies a more unique role in the history of thought in China and the world. The axiomatic interpretation of *Laozi* is also more complex and challenging than that of Confucian classics.

If we analyze the philosophy of Laozi from a global historical perspective, we will find that Laozi's natural philosophy offers a comprehensive view of the history of philosophical thought. It not only includes ancient Greek ontology, epistemology and arising in ancient Greek and continuing through the 19th century European philosophical systems, but also the philosophy of language which caused a turn of Western philosophy in the late nineteenth and early twentieth century. The fundamental problems that perplexed thinkers throughout the history of Eastern and Western philosophical discourse all find perceptive articulations within *Laozi*. After Laozi and Zhuangzi, the development of Daoist philosophy abruptly stagnated against the tremendous impact of Buddhist philosophy. In modern times, it has been spread to the west and come through many trials. However, the value of Laozi's natural philosophy does not betray even a trace of decline. In every civilization, it manifests strong vitality, an ever increasing impact, and practical significance. The necessity and challenge of interpreting *Laozi* axiomatically can only be discussed in the context of its ongoing significance.

Laozi was not only the first to establish philosophy in its general sense, prior to the pre-Socratic schools, but also the first to establish a philosophy of negation and critique and its dialectics based on natural philosophy. Due to its avant-gardism, complexity, richness, and profundity, the philosophical principle that Laozi revealed has reached a height, depth and magnitude unsurpassed by humanity even till today. When Laozi revealed the law of development of the natural universe, that is, the movement of Dao being the first mover, drew from this a conclusion of negative dialectics and critical dialectics of *"To turn to its opposite is the movement of Dao,"* he presented the insurmountable contradictions as well as dilemmas of paradoxes and antinomies that humanity encounters in the face of both the natural world and philosophy itself. This passage alone represents Laozi's unsurpassable achievements.

Early modern German philosopher Gottfried Wilhelm Leibniz accurately defined Laozi's philosophy for the first time as natural philosophy; another philosopher, George Wilhelm Friedrich Hegel, also admired Laozi's philosophical system. Their admirations are not groundless. Despite its profundity and vastness, Hegel's philosophy and dialectics carries a spatio-temporal limitedness and an internal contradiction. Hegel's dialectics focuses on limited things, but Laozi's emphasizes unlimited things in an unlimited world.

As compelling as the comparison of Hegel's dialectics to Laozi's philosophy may be, it is nowhere near as compelling as the intersection of modern German philosopher Immanuel Kant with Laozi's. Kant placed his epistemology, dialectics, and his critique of judgment, of cognition, and of reason on a broader timescale and vaster space scale, allowing for greater convergence with Laozi in worldview and methodology.

These philosophical comparisons underline the fact that axiomatically interpreting *Laozi* requires a higher level of comprehension than simply placing some dialectical framework on Laozi's thoughts. Professor Gan and his team have reflected in many ways on the conclusions reached using simple dialectics to analyze Laozi's thought. It can also be said that Hegel's dialectics is on limited things, but Laozi's is on unlimited things in the unlimited world. The axiomatic interpretation of *Laozi* makes evident the unique features of the natural philosophy and dialectics in *Laozi*.

II. The axiomatic interpretation demonstrates the richness, integrity and openness of Laozi's thought

The richness of Laozi's natural philosophy manifests not in the category of objects in a general sense, but a philosophical and dialectic system that includes natural philosophy, humanistic thought, philosophy of history, aesthetics and art philosophy, legal philosophy, moral philosophy and ethics, philosophy of life, and political philosophy and political science, especially philosophy of power and anti-power, economic sciences, social sciences, and military science.

The comprehensiveness of Laozi's natural philosophy manifests in his encyclopedic vision of all these disciplines and the questions they pose. Its refusal to cater to anthropocentrism in humanity's construction of natural sciences, social sciences, arts and humanities further distinguishes it as unique and sagacious. Laozi criticized these desires and tendencies, and even disapproved them. Most likely, Laozi's unique critique and even negative appraisal of these disciplines are based on his natural ontology, natural-subjectivity and natural-centrism. For this reason, Laozi's thought encompasses disciplines that are not disciplines in the sense of humanism and anthropocentrism, but rather disciplines infused with and embodying the concepts of his natural philosophy. He did not use the ordinary dialectics that explains contradictory but unified phenomena. Rather, he explored a dialectics that takes natural philosophy as its basis. There is not only exposition of contradiction and unification but also exposition of the principles behind paradoxes and antinomies. The difference between Laozi's natural philosophical system and Confucius and Mencius's Confucian philosophical systems means that the Dao inherent in the two is widely divergent.

The power of Laozi's natural philosophy and dialects manifests in its openness towards different civilizations and cultures. Whether individually or collectively, limited by time and space, the grasp of mysteries and truths as well as of knowledge and technologies is relative. Laozi's understanding of this fact renders his natural philosophy more accessible to all knowledge systems and cultural systems.

The research of Professor Gan's team underscores the richness, integrity and openness of Laozi's natural philosophy. We should understand the various disciplines of humanity, instead of using theories in various cookie-cuttered disciplines to substantiate Laozi's philosophy (this would in fact dismember Laozi's philosophy). True scholarship necessitates mastery of various disciplines in order to point out their real contour in light of Dao. To achieve this not only brings challenges to the team members' own learning and cultivation, but represents a comprehensive reflection of Humanity's cognition and cognitive methods.

As a negative and critical philosophical dialectics, Laozi's philosophy criticizes the aspirational subjectivity of humanity and the concomitant consciousness. He also critiques Confucian humanism, along with the Greek anthropocentric humanism, which renders humanity as the subject of the universe and as the measure of all things. Laozi repeatedly emphasized the priority of the natural universe over humanity as inherent, unquestionable, and unalienable. Laozi regarded "Dao (the Way)" as the basic natural law. It is not only omnipresent but also the root and source of all things, the start and end of all things. He famously proposed "Dao begets one; one begets two; two begets three; three begets all things." Diametrically opposed to humanism which encourages human conquest of nature and the study of nature, he proposed, "Man models himself on Earth, Earth on Heaven, Heaven on the Dao, and the Dao on Nature." Dao is a feature of the course of nature. It represents the ultimate idea and reason of nature. It is the root and source of all things in the universe. Differing radically from the perspective of anthropocentrism, Dao is not subjeted to human's will. All natural sciences, social sciences and human sciences have to stand trial in the court of the natural reason of Dao to reexamine the rationality of their existence. Humanity's will to power which fosters a philosophy to conquer, dominate and exploit nature necessitates reappraisal. Through Professor Gan's team's axiomatic interpretation, we can clearly see that, from Laozi's perspective, humanity's will and philosophy to power has receded to a secondary role to become a constituent part of Dao. This dynamic compresses the self-aggrandizing of humanity's knowledge system and scientific technological system. It should be said that humans have constructed epistemological, symbolic, and representational systems for the sake of conquering and ruling nature. They become fragile yet pompous in the face of Dao. All the thoughts and concepts for achieving the harmonious coexistence of humanity and nature find clear and consistent reflections in the axiomatic interpretation of *Laozi* through the expressions "To do by non-action," "Though ignorant, he knows everything," "A man without desire can be unbending," and "The soft and weak overcome the hard and strong."

III. The axiomatic interpretation underscores the value of *Laozi* in philosophy of language, political philosophy, natural philosophy and philosophy of art

Another goal of Professor Gan Xiaoqing and his research team's interpretation is to reveal the axiomatic nature and universality of Laozi's natural philosophy. Due to space constraints, the explication on the value of an axiomatic interpretation will be limited to philosophy of language, political philosophy, natural philosophy, and philosophy of art.

1. Philosophy of language

From Classical Antiquity to Enlightenment Philosophy in the 18th century and the European classical philosophy of the 19th century, all philosophers followed Socrates, Plato, and Aristotle and focused on ontology (exploration into the origination and composition of the universe and the world) and epistemology (the dialectical method and logical method to understand the universe and the world). By the end of the nineteenth century, European philosophers including Wittgenstein, Popper, and Saussure investigated the basic structural elements of ontology and epistemology, also known as the question of the essence of language or *logos*. With the linguistic turn, Western philosophy started to reexamine the characteristics and relationships between concepts, definitions, and propositions as language phenomena, including the logic in propositions and conclusions, as well as the presuppositions of premises, and, in particular, the relationship between *a priori* presuppositions. At the same time, it allows us to reexamine the functions of self-reference and self-circularity of languages, which are artificial and unnatural. It also calls into question the reliability of the conclusions achieved through thinking and deducing by languages. In the latter half of the 20th century, French philosophers such as Derrida, Foucault, and Lacan advanced profound critiques of the logic of languages.

The basic presupposition of *Laozi* is the concept of Dao, the Dao of Heaven, or the Dao of the universe and nature. Before using this concept, Laozi had already advanced a dialectical critique, similar to that of language philosophy. In the language of German Idealism, we find that before using concepts, definitions, and propositions to express philosophical thought, it criticized the language underlying the "weapons of critique." Laozi pointed out that "The Dao that can be worded is not the constant Dao. The name that can be named is not the eternal name." These seemingly simple phrases show us that as early as 2,600 years ago, Laozi already realized that using human language to speak, to name, to presuppose, and to reason the Way of the nature was not absolutely unchangeable. Instead, it had the feature of temporal-spatial relativity, a reflection of human subjective cognition rather than objective reason.

Thus, Laozi was very cautious when using language to capture concepts. For example, when he defined the basic concept Dao, he was using the method of multi-layer definition, and defining it on each level and in each facet; enriching and extending its connotation and extension. Qian Zhongshu points out in his masterpiece *Limited Views: Essays on Ideas and Letters* that Laozi's philosophy of language and dialectics shows us a process of definition, discrimination, cognition, reason, and argument of "Dao has no name but is multiple in names." In the phrase of late twentieth century French philosopher Derrida, it is the process of semantic divergence. When Laozi discussed the concept of De, he used the same dialectical method. The multiplicity, diversity, and polysemy of human understanding are reflected in the process in accordance with the law of nature. It ensures the infinity of possibility faced by generations of readers, helping them avoid a straitlaced understanding of sentences.

Usually concepts, definitions, judgment and reasoning inevitably carry finiteness. Without clear definition, there would be no reasoning. That is why when Professor Gan's team expounds the core contents of Laozi's thought, they present an honest reflection of Laozi's thought by paying sufficient attention to the unification of the definable and the undefinable, the unification of languages' finite and infinite ability to reveal, as well as the unification of the objects in pre-existing, existing and changing stages. When deducing general conclusions in philosophy and science, various factors including time, space, referential systems, the cognitive ability, reasoning ability, technology, and the means of reasoning employed by the researchers prescribe the premise. These prescriptions often lead to limitations in philosophical thinking.

Yet, if we fully take philosophy of language into account, and use appropriate methodology to reveal Laozi's thinking, then we can make Laozi's thought a mirror that reflects the relativity, subjectivity, and openness of human cognition. At the same time, this methodology also respects the fact that when Laozi expounded his thought, he had already fully realized that if people insisted on his naming it, he would just name it as Dao, in order to avoid any possibility of misinterpretation.

2. Political philosophy

In the Eastern Zhou Dynasty, the time when Laozi lived, the questions of the day were how to end the endless wars of hegemony and how to achieve eternal peace. Taking the fundamental interests of humanity into consideration, Confucius devised a humanistic model of benevolent rule, intending to nurture benevolent *Junzi* (an exemplary man of virtue) through education, and realize perpetual peace of the world through the realization of benevolent *junzi*'s personal value in the spheres of individual, family, society, state, and humanity. This is what *The Book of Great Learning* means by "*Their thoughts being sincere, their hearts were then rectified. Their hearts being rectified, their persons were cultivated. Their persons being cultivated, their families were regulated. Their families being regulated, their states were rightly governed. Their states being rightly governed, the whole kingdom was made tranquil and happy.*" For this, Confucius proposed using public interest and social justice as a means to realize social harmony. He also proposed the basic, axiomatic principle of "When the Grand course was pursued, a public and common spirit ruled all under the Heaven." The Chinese military strategist Sunzi proposed the basic principles of "avoiding war, being cautious in war and fighting a quick war" based on his humanistic philosophy. Laozi, however, proposed his unique method of realizing perpetual peace, which is embodied by the words "Therefore, the sage keeps to the deed that consists in taking no action and practices the teaching that uses no words." From the standpoint of natural philosophy, with the entirety of nature and universe in view, Laozi proposed the way of ruling the society, the state, and the whole empire in accordance with Dao. The rules and laws of the natural universe operate by allowing all forms of existence to operate, select, and move autonomously and freely for themselves in accordance with the laws of their own development, while the universe itself, by doing nothing, provides all forms of life with the material conditions. Based on this principle, Laozi proposed a unique way of governing, i.e., rigorously following the governance by non-action.

As for the historical role of monarchs, their *raison d'etre*, accomplishments, and crimes, Laozi also took "rule by non-action" as a normative yard-stick, putting forth the standard "The best ruler, the people do not seem to know his existence; next comes the ruler, the people are willing to get close to and praise; next comes one the people awe." In the Western Han Dynasty (206 BC-24 AD), through their practice of Laozi's political ideal of ruling with non-action, Emperor Wen and Emperor Jing achieved a level of prosperity and progress rarely seen in Chinese history, which server as a model for later generations. The reign of Emperors Wen and Jing, following Laozi's advice of peaceful development, stood in sharp contrast to the military exertion and belligerence of Emperor Wu of Han Dynasty (156BC-87BC), which led to the decline of Han Dynasty.

Yet, for the general readership, to precisely grasp Laozi's ideal of "rule by non-action" is quite difficult. They are likely to regard Laozi as advocating for something negative, something that negates humanity's creativity, and even something anti-society, anti-civilization, and anti-progress. The axiomatic interpretation of Professor Gan's team enables us to better and more precisely understand Laozi's "rule by non-action." They did it by showing that, in an axiomatic system, "rule by non-action" is marked by self-consistency. Laozi used Dao to mirror human society, finding three "vanities" in human society: the vain height of goal, the vain honor of achievements, and the vain fiction of kindness. Humanity wrongly thinks that merely from the striving of man an orderly society can be created. In fact, the role of human's endeavors is limited. Achieving peace for ten thousand generations through moral cultivation is a vainly high goal. Once peace is realized, those who take themselves to have "great achievement" and "infinite kindness" are the vain honor of achievements and vain fiction of kindness. More dangerously, humanity often intoxicates itself in its own achievement, neglects the functions of Dao and "nature," or even willfully destroys their functions. Humanity has to curb it by non-action. Laozi thought that the philosophy of power, government and the desire for conquest are the root cause of war. He also pointed out that "*It is the way of heaven to take from what is abundant, and replenish what is deficient. The way of man is just otherwise: to take from what is insufficient and offer this to what is abundant.*" It succinctly points out that fairness in wealth distribution is the only way to achieve social justice and harmony, a manifestation of the Dao of Heaven. Conversely, exploitation of the society's wealth creators, laboring community and disadvantaged community is a tyranny going against the Dao of Heaven. This kind of "doing or action" is not only a vain honor, but a disguise for misdeeds. In general, the legitimacy of politics comes from Dao, which is used to examine the rulers' impact and prescribe their deeds so that the governance of "*If you reach the state of non-action; there is nothing you cannot do*" can be achieved. This conclusion is fully explained in the axiomatic interpretation system. Laozi's political philosophy on the basis of natural philosophy thereby manifests its universality even more.

3. The relation between man and nature

Laozi's natural philosophy further reveals to us its unique wisdom. Based on natural philosophy, nature is substance, the subject, the ultimate source and the end of everything. We should be not only in awe of and grateful to nature, but also treasure it, rather than satisfy the infinite desire of humanity through rapine and "draining the pond to get all the fish" type of exploitation. We should stop dreaming of exploiting the Mars and the Moon after exhausting the resources on the Earth. Laozi offered an axiomatic judgment for this: "Man models himself on Earth, Earth on Heaven, Heaven on the Dao, and the Dao on Nature." It is of tremendous importance in guiding our understanding and handling of the dialectical relationship between man and nature. It has also become a compass for the sustainable development of the economy, the society, the culture and the ecological environment. Laozi deeply analyzed the conflicts between man and nature, mainly in the aspects of competing for achievements, competing for kindness, and competing for wisdom. The axiomatic interpretation reveals the value of these discussions.

The first is the competition for achievements. In the opening chapter of *Laozi*, it points out that "The Dao that can be worded is not the constant Dao. The name that can be named is not the eternal name." Although it is hard to accurately define and articulate Dao by human language, the sagacious Laozi told a poetic simile: "The perfect goodness is like water. Water is good at benefiting all things, but does not contend with them. It prefers to dwell in places the masses of people detest, therefore it is closest to the Dao." "He is ease with lowness in his dwelling. He is profound in his heart. He is faithful in his friendship. He is sincere in his speech. Like water, he never contends, so he is never at fault." "One does not contend with others, so no one is in a position to contend with him." That Dao gives birth to all and nurtures all is the basic mechanism of the natural world. Yet, humanity often greedily seeks to take the achievement of Heaven as its own, mistaking the power of "man's nurturing of man" as much greater than that of "Heaven's nurturing of man," thereby crazily exploiting and plundering natural resources, which leads to the overburdening of nature in the face of the endless desires of man. The environmental crisis, the ecological crisis, the crisis of wide-spread species extinction, and the crisis of meteorological disasters have endangered the survival of over seven billion people on earth as well as their descendants. Intoxicated in industrialization, post-industrialization, science revolution, and consumerist carnivals, humanity often turns a deaf ear or plays the ostrich. While I was writing this piece, the 21st Global Meteorological Summit was taking place in Paris. If humanity cannot clearly grasp its own dialectical relations with nature, its disappearance from the earth, like the disappearance of other species, is only a matter of time.

Through axiomatic interpretation, Professor Gan's team reveals Laozi's essential insight into the conflict between man and nature. Dao produces all things and the change of all things is a process from Non-being to Being and back to Non-being. Being and Non-being accompanies each other in arising. They coexist with each other and are indivisible from each other. Hence, the process of creating different Beings is also the process of creating different Non-beings. The more Being is created, the more Non-being is created. The faster Being is created, the faster Non-being is created. The more Being is utilized, the less Non-being is utilized. In this way, the exploitation and utilization of natural resources is the process of producing un-usable matter, ultimately going from nurturing humanity to destroying humanity. This conclusion, revealed by the analysis of the internal logic of Laozi's system, shows the value of the axiomatic interpretation in understanding Laozi's great wisdom.

The second is the competition for virtue. For thousands of years, humanist philosophers like Confucius have aimed at benevolence in government. Yet Laozi spoke with immense straightforwardness: "The men of high virtue do not show virtue and thus have virtue; the men of low virtue never stray from virtue and thus lose virtue." In other words, the definition of De also needs to take the virtue of nature as its reference frame. Based on Laozi's natural philosophy, the virtue of nature is prior to the virtue of man. The virtue of nature sustains the relationship not only between man and man but also between man and nature. Only when the natural virtue is disregarded, and natural reason disobeyed, will people yearn for the lost paradise with regret. The reason why people admire virtue and virtuous rule is that natural virtue is increasingly being forgotten: "When the great way falls into disuse, there are benevolence and rectitude; when cleverness emerges, there is great hypocrisy; when the six relations are at variance, there are filial children; when the state is benighted, there are loyal ministers." Here Laozi pointed out penetratingly that there is an irreconcilable conflict between human-created civilization and natural virtue, natural reason, and natural order. He revealed that humanity has alienated nature and alienated itself. He showed how difficult it is to overcome this double alienation, and to return to nature and a state of harmony. Laozi further asserted that "Nature is unbiased, seeing everything as a straw dog; the sage is unbiased, seeing everyone as a straw dog." If the sage can uphold the Dao of non-action, rather than alienate nature and humanity itself, and achieve such a state that "The people all say, 'it happened to us naturally,'" then the harmonious coexistence between man and nature is not impossible.

Professor Gan's team's axiomatic interpretation of *Laozi*, after explaining the essence of Dao, continue's to examine everything in the mundane world with Dao which rationally criticizes the human virtue. From the perspective of Dao, nature seems to be virtueless but is actually virtuous. "The myriad creatures all arise together" and grow vivaciously without rest, which is the manifestation of the natural virtue. At the same time, natural virtue is devoid of artificiality. It reveals itself in its originality, yet achieves the utmost accomplishment. To view human virtue through Dao, it appears to be an exaggeration. Everything great that is achieved by human society is in fact due to the virtue of nature and some work of man. Yet humanity takes it to be its own achievement. Without an axiomatic interpretation, it is hard for people to understand Laozi's intention in subverting the virtue of man.

The third is the competition for wisdom. Laozi pointed out that "When the rulers abandon wisdom and discard intelligence, the people will be truly benefited. When the rulers abandon humanity and righteousness, then the people will return to filial piety and parental care. When the rulers abandon skills and discard profits, thieves and robbers will disappear." Wisdom and intelligence here both mean anthropocentric instrumental reason, which aims at conquering nature and plundering nature, on which basis, epistemic, technological, and normative systems are constructed. Rousseau, the well-known thinker in Europe in eighteenth century, thought deeply and critically about the paradoxical relationship between nature and civilization. He criticized and denied the scientific and technological civilization and knowledge system based on instrumental rationality, thereby reaching the conclusion that man must eliminate alienation and return to nature. This is similar to the conclusion drawn by Laozi more than two thousand years ago, revealing the foresightedness of Laozi's natural philosophy. In the twentieth century, the Western philosophical circles made profound reflections on the two world wars and the subsequent cold war and regional wars, in which human beings had been fighting for natural resources, political totalitarianism, and economic hegemony for one century. On the basis of dialectical critique of the instrumental rationality and technological rationality, they developed contemporary philosophical trends: anti-power, anti-totalitarian, anti-industrial, anti-consumerist, and anti-alienation.

Professor Gan's team once more underscores the value of this aspect of Laozi's thought through axiomatic interpretation. American thinker Joseph Nye brought up the concept of soft power at the end of last century. According to Nye, first, soft power is the dialectical negation of hard power. Hard power is based on industrial power, economic power, financial power, and military power, and in a word, on instrumental rationality. Second, soft power is the negation of government regime and power agency's philosophy of power, especially power hegemony. Third, soft power is the affirmation of wisdom systems that have an affinity to man and to nature. These descriptions of soft power fit into the concepts and categories and their logical conclusions proposed by Laozi 2,600 years ago, such as "Know the male but keep to the role of the female," "Exhibit the unadorned and embrace the uncarved block," "The myriad creatures carry on their backs the *yin* and embrace in their arms the *yang* and are the blending of the generative forces of the two," "In concentrating on your breath, be as supple as a baby," "The submissive and weak will overcome the hard and strong." However, to achieve the matching between the two theories across time and space, one cannot rely on simple matching, but on internal logical matching. Starting from the core Dao, axiomatic interpretation infers that the best way for all things is to meet the natural Way or Dao. With this, we can form endless common power. Out of this, we will be able to fully understand and grasp the universal meaning and axiomatic nature of Laozi's natural philosophy.

4. Art Philosophy

The philosophy of art that Laozi established some 2,600 years ago still dazzles the contemporary world. Laozi, with the logic of its natural philosophy dialectics, deduced "*The myriad creatures in the world are born from Being, and Being from Non-being.*" In other words, the source of the universe is "Nothing or Non-being" and will return to "Non-being." From Laozi's point of view, the supreme beauty, supreme goodness, and supreme height of artistic achievement originate from the creation of nature. Take music for example. The sound of nature that people admire most is nature's bamboo playing; "*The great sound seems soundless; the great image seems formless.*" From this Laozi revealed that artistic creation should follow the natural patterns of the universe and the pattern of development of human art creation that takes this as a model. According to the principle of "the way models on that which is naturally so," the way of art shall also abide by the law of the way of nature. "*Too many colors dazzles the eyes; too much music deafens the ears; too many tastes baffle the palate.*" These words single out the fundamental deficiency in art and the importance of returning to the root of art. Man-made art often intentionally takes the satisfaction of human desires as its end, which is unnatural and anti-natural, bringing alienation to the spirit of humanity. Infatuated with the beauty of humans, one is more likely to forget the beauty of all things, leading to the conflict between man and all things. The artistic pursuit of pure forms can never get away with its own opposite side. Whenever there is beauty, there is ugliness. Whenever there is goodness, there is always evilness. So he said: "*When everyone in the world knows the beautiful as beautiful, ugliness comes into being; when everyone knows the good as good, then the bad comes into being. Therefore, being and non-being generate each other; the difficult and the easy complement each other; the long and the short offset each other; the upper and the lower incline towards each other; the tone and the sound harmonize with each other; the front and the back follow each other.*" (Chapter 2)

The axiomatic interpretation of Professor Gan's team reveals the height of Laozi's philosophy of art with dazzling internal consistency. Starting from Dao, he deduced the highest realm of beauty, "naturalness." Yet "naturalness" is a mutual production of Being and Non-being, which, in man's world of feelings, is manifested as form and formlessness, color and colorlessness. They point out that achievement, fame, profit and emolument, great wealth and great power, money and sexual attraction, wine and delicacies are not the embodiment of "great beauty." Rather, it will embody the way of nature and bring greater benefits to humans to guide human behavior, nurture human virtue, and regulate human body with "indifference." In this way, Laozi's philosophy of art is not only a philosophy of art in the sense of artisanship, but also a philosophy of art running throughout the entire human society and concerning the foundation of human existence, from which people can take infinite spiritual nourishment. This point has engendered a continuous and profound impact on Chinese and other East Asian countries' literary poetry, calligraphy, painting, music, plastic arts, and sculpture in later generations. It has also exerted a profound impact on the development of China and the world.

To this day, the huge risk within human society is like the sword of Damocles, hanging all the time above the head of humanity. If we simply look back upon how many nuclear weapons and bio-chemical weapons in the world are capable of destroying the earth tens of times, how many tyrant and warmongers inimical to nature and to the entire humanity have played a role in history, and how much the industrialization process, the scientification process, and the modernization process have jeopardized the natural environment, we would tremble with fear, and be sorrowful for the bleak prospect of human development. For the most part, philosophers are optimistic idealists. But just because of the clear foresight and profound judgment, philosophers often take a pessimistic view towards the prospect of human development, which is manifested in turn as a sincere idealism in their philosophical works. Laozi is no exception. After he resigned from the post as a court historian, he rode a horse westward out of Hangu Pass and disappeared in the Gobi, becoming integrated with the vast nature. Yet before he went out of Hangu Pass, he left us *Laozi,* a book that sums up his natural philosophy.

The philosophical and dialectical system established in the book *Laozi* written by Laozi about 2,600 years ago is the first Mount Qomolangma in human philosophical history. The vastness of its philosophical system, the profundity of its negative and critical dialectics, and the thought-provoking openness to dialogue with different eras, different civilization circles, different philosophical traditions exhibited by its natural philosophy and dialectical system are all rarely seen in the history of philosophical thought.

I have discussed in the epilogue of the book *The Analects of Confucius: An Axiomatic Interpretation* that, whenever human development has come to a critical turn, people often knowingly or unknowingly engage in dialogue with past sages, thereby reexamining the epistemology, methodology, and theory of practice based on the new historical circumstance, so as to solve the pressing problems human beings face in reality. This kind of long-lasting dialogue not only can offer us a clear, open view like the sun after dispelling the cloud, but also can revitalize the ideological systems of past sages, making their wisdom illuminate ever further like a lighthouse which will stand for thousands of years. As long as nature keeps progressing along its course, and as long as humanity refrains from the self-destruction resulting from its conflict with nature, the profound natural philosophy of Laozi and the wisdom of many philosophers and thinkers amiable to Laozi in the history of philosophical thought will continue to shine upon us, leading us to the right path of harmonious coexistence with nature.

Yet, it is difficult to converse with past sages. Ever since ancient times, the annotations to *Laozi* have been numerous and voluminous. But how many of them really penetrate into the very depth of its theory? Professor Gan Xiaoqing and his team of academics have truly set up a high standard for themselves during their axiomatic interpretation. With a sense of calling, the team has made contributions to scholarship and deserves our respect. From the point of view of the axiomatic interpretation of Professor Gan's team, the interpretation that takes *Laozi* as mysterious and unfathomable is unreliable because mystery means isolation from the need of humanity; the interpretation that expresses the annotators' own views while annotating classics is unreliable because most of them cannot be wiser than Laozi; the trivial interpretation that discusses scratches of phrases is unnecessary because this type of interpretation still relies on the readers' own acceptance and understanding. Axiomatic interpretation, starting from simple definitions, basic propositions and axioms, deduces numerous propositions and constructs a deductive system. As the stem and essence of Laozi's thought, this system is of great help to readers to gain a more accurate and comprehensive insight into the core of *Laozi* and is of great help to the modern transformation of Daoist thought.

I hope that the glory of the wisdom of Laozi's natural philosophical thought and his profound dialectics can benefit more living beings on earth. I hope that humanity shall always remember and put into practice Laozi's preaching, "*Man models himself on Earth, Earth on Heaven, Heaven on the Dao, and the Dao on Nature.*"

Thus shall be the epilogue.

Wei Aoyu
Professor, Université Sorbonne Nouvelle
Early 2016, Paris, France

跋二：怀念萧树铁教授

庐山上有一些挺拔高大的柳杉，它们通体浑圆，直插云霄，而周身的古干虬枝，如同张开的臂弯一般，护佑着树下的一方水土。它们屹立千年，至今郁郁葱葱。它们是庐山的标识，是庐山的精魂！

萧树铁先生的驾鹤西去，使我们这群庐山之麓的学生们无比悲伤。萧先生的形象就如同撑天的柳杉那样，高大挺拔，虬枝铁干，既令人敬仰，更让人缅怀。

萧树铁先生曾是清华大学数学系主任。在我们的心目中，萧先生是一位极具人文底蕴和家国情怀的数学家，也是一位极具探索精神和担当意识的教育家。先生的睿智通达，不仅表现在深厚的专业学养和造诣上，也表现为解决现实问题的勇气和眼光。特别是先生深厚的国学修养，既有家学的背景，也有童年读私塾的经历。

也许，正是积淀在老一辈知识分子身上共有的家国情怀和文化使命，使得先生将晚年的大部分精力和心血，花在如何有效地建立人文经典的演绎系统，实现对传统思想系统诠释的探究当中。尽管这样一种探究，不仅无助于增加先生作为数学家的声望，反而会隐含诸种非数学家能够承担的失败可能与风险，但是这么多年来先生却义无反顾，以巨大的热情投入这项以推动中西文化的对话和提升中华经典的国际影响力为目的的研究当中。

"中华经典的公理化诠释"无疑是一项跨越古今、融通中西、兼及文理并具有挑战性的研究探索，也是中国文化在期待重新崛起的时代语境下必须面对和回答的核心问题之一。先生的追求不是为了个人或某个小团体去追逐名誉和利益，而是发自内心深处对于民族和民族文化的热爱与担当，是老一代知识分子期盼"强国"和探求"强国之道"的世纪理想。

也正是基于对萧先生这份襟怀和理想的敬仰和感佩，我们这一群庐山之麓的"乡野儒生"这些年一直追随着先生的价值理念和文化理想，一步一步地登堂入室，持之以恒地在追求和接近我们的共同目标。由一开始的怀疑、迷茫和不解，到逐渐明白、熟知和确信，在先生的循循善诱和悉心指导下，我们先后用公理化的方法诠释了体现中国文化传统核心价值的几部重要经典：《论语》《孟子》《荀子》和《老子》。这些承载着中华文明思想精髓的先秦文化典籍亟须得到很好的现代诠释。对于先生而言，用公理化的方法诠释传统经典，是为解决国学传承和对外文化交流中的困顿，尝试跨越学科的突破和创新！而对于我们这些习惯于在历史、文学、哲学文献中获取感悟、尝试探索的研究者来说，这既是一个洗心革面、脱胎换骨的转变过程，也是不断反省自我、探求新知、提升成长的过程。

因此，我们的研究便是一个学习、探究和自我锤炼的进程。在这八年的研讨中，先生一直是我们这个团队的精神导师，我们在学习和研究过程中得到的启悟、乐趣和收获，要远远多于眼前可以看得到的这一本本研究成果。每一名团队成员在此过程中都感觉到自己的知识背景薄弱。学文学的觉得自己缺乏哲学知识背景，更缺乏对逻辑的深入理解；学哲学的又觉得自己缺乏对传统文化的深入了解。困顿迷茫之时，萧先生总是给予我们继续前行的底气和定力。

这几天我们在整理萧先生与研究团队在一起的照片和资料时，脑海中萧先生的音容笑貌再一次生动起来：精神矍铄的神情，深邃睿智的目光，亲切和蔼的笑容，有时些许调侃的话语。先生从不故作姿态，也不作好为人师的说教，虽持有教无类的态度，但对聪明好学的学生仍有所偏爱。先生看重一个人的德行，也看重一个人的才气，对学生的优点和才分从不吝惜夸奖的言语。先生在精神生活中追求自然、坦诚和质朴。或许，正是因为在生活中坚持不失自己的真性情，才能在事业上确保自己的真学问。先生一生追求才学与个性品质的统一，坚守简朴生活与纯净精神的一体，令人景仰，让人缅怀。

我们都非常庆幸和珍惜与萧先生的这一份"学缘"，更看重这份编外的师生情谊。尽管在得知先生患病以来，我们都真诚地期盼先生康复，期盼再一次在北京、在庐山聚谈，但残酷的现实只留给我们这份无尽的思念！好在我们每个人的身上都有先生留下的研究题目，而"中华经典的公理化诠释"这个课题还有待进一步的完善。我们这群人只有努力前行，以出色的业绩告慰先生！让这份编外学生的称誉变得名副其实。

"江南忆，牯岭作书堂。云外谈经无俗虑，山中开卷有清香，一笑余韵长。"

"江南忆，不畏楚天长。对雪横经重砥砺，临窗思远忽登堂，宛在老师旁。"

从2008年始，萧先生倾心指导九江学院"中华经典的公理化诠释"创新研究团队。这些年来，同样的情景都时常会浮现在我们每个人的眼前。深冬到了，又该到"对雪横经"的日子。还指望着形成许多想法，提出许多问题，到明年草长莺飞的时候，再一次到北京去，跟萧先生热烈地讨论。还想向萧先生汇报，我们总算悟出了他的用意，在"公理化""文化自立""文化自信""文化强国"之间建立了联系。然而，现在，我们已无法实现与萧先生的聚谈了，但我们每个人的心中都珍藏着这份永恒的师生情谊。

在《〈老子〉的公理化诠释》完稿之际，我们以此纪念研究团队公认的导师——萧树铁先生，寄托我们的无尽怀念。

九江学院"中华经典的公理化诠释"创新研究团队

李宁宁　吴国富　曹欢荣

2015 年 12 月 11 日

Epilogue Two: Professor Xiao Shutie Will Live in Our Hearts

On Mount Lushan, there are many towering cryptomeria with branches stretching like open arms, protecting what is under the trees. The green trees, some of which are about a thousand years old, are the symbol and the spirit of Mount Lushan!

We felt deeply mournful and sorrowful for the death of Mr. Xiao Shutie. We had been instructed and enlightened by him many times. He was like a gigantic tree and we respect him very deeply for his efforts, which are of great help to the innovative research on the "Axiomatic Interpretation on Chinese Classics."

Mr. Xiao was once dean of the Department of Mathematics of Tsinghua University. In our hearts, he was not only a mathematician, but also a man of immense erudition with regard to humanity and patriotism, and an educator with exploring spirit and responsibility. His wisdom and sensibility were reflected not only in his profound professional knowledge and accomplishments, but also in his courage and vision to solve real problems. His profound cultivation in traditional Chinese culture came from his family background and the experience of learning in private home school.

It's the patriotism and cultural mission that urged him to spend most of his energy and endeavour in his later life on how to build a humanistic classic deductive system effectively, and also on the exploration of interpretation of traditional thoughts system. Although such an undertaking will by no means add to his prestige as a mathematician, and is even likely to incur failure, over the years, Mr. Xiao showed great enthusiasm in the study, aiming to promote the dialogue between Chinese and Western culture and the international influence of Chinese classics.

"Axiomatic interpretation of Chinese Classics" is a cross-cultural study bridging the ancient and modern, and the east and the west. It is a challenge combining liberal arts and sciences. It is also the core problem we are facing in the context of the re-emergence of traditional Chinese culture. Mr. Xiao dedicated to it because of his love of and responsibilities for Chinese nation and Chinese culture, and the ideal of strengthening China, not for the sake of himself or his team.

Following Mr. Xiao's value and cultural ideal, we have been pursuing constantly and approaching gradually our common goals. At first we had doubt and were puzzled by this approach. But gradually we had better and deeper understanding of it. Finally we turned out to be confident. Instructed by him, we interpreted the Chinese classics with the axiomatic approach: *The Analects*, *Mencius*, *Xunzi* and *Laozi*, which reflect the core values of traditional Chinese culture. These pre-Qin classics carry the ideological essence of Chinese civilization and need to be interpreted in a modern way. For Mr. Xiao, the axiomatic interpretation of traditional classics is to solve the problems in traditional inheritance and cultural exchanges with other countries. It is also the attempt of interdisciplinary breakthrough and innovation. For us, the researchers, who are accustomed to the comprehension and thinking in the study of history, literature, and philosophy, this is a transformation process, a process of constant soul-searching, exploration of new knowledge and improvement of spiritual cultivation.

Therefore, our research is a process to learn, explore and temper ourselves. Mr. Xiao has been the spiritual mentor of our team during the past eight years of discussion and explanation. The enlightenment and gains we got in learning and research are the research achievements. We come from different disciplinary backgrounds, literature or philosophy. Some of us who majored in literature thought that they lacked the knowledge of philosophical thinking and sufficient logical understanding. Others who majored in philosophy might think that they lacked a deep understanding of traditional culture. In times of distress and confusion, Mr. Xiao gave us the confidence and vigor to go on farther.

These days, when we were sorting out photos of Mr. Xiao with us, we felt as if Mr. Xiao relived vividly in our company: hearty expression, deep and intelligent eyes and vision, kind smile, and a touch of humor. He had no prejudice on his students though he was fond of those who had talents and studied hard. He valued a person's virtue, and also his or her talent. He pursued a spiritual life: natural, honest and simple. It is his disposition that had made possible his success of learning. It is for his pursuit of the unity of intellect and personality, and the unity of a simple life and pure spirit that we admire and remember him.

It is our karma to have this close affinity with Mr. Xiao and we cherish it very much. When we heard the news that Mr. Xiao was ill, we felt very worried. We sincerely hoped that he would get well soon and that we could meet again in Beijing or Mount Lushan. But cruelly, we could just keep his memory in our mind! Fortunately, we all have research tasks assigned by him. The project of the "Axiomatic Interpretation of Chinese Classics" remains to be further improved. We must work hard to console Mr. Xiao with excellent performance. Only our achievements can make us worthy of the fame, as his students.

Southern China brought to mind,

We gathered at Cooling Street.

Discussing classics, without worldly worries of any kind,

Reading at the peak, we felt the books smelling sweet.

Laughter lingered on, you'd find.

Southern China brought to mind,

We were too lost in working to notice the long days.

Facing snow, we tried to make the project more refined,

Looking out, we felt, unblocked by the mountain haze,

That you were with us and giving counsel kind.

In 2008, Mr. Xiao began to instruct us in the research on "Axiomatic Interpretation of Chinese Classics." During these years, we have often recalled the scene we were together. Winter is coming, and it's time for us and Mr. Xiao to have a discussion as usual. We have many ideas and problems to discuss with him, and we wish we could visit him again in Beijing and tell him that we have realized his intention: to establish the link between axiomatic interpretation and "cultural self-reliance," "cultural self-confidence," and "cultural powerful country." We know that it is impossible for us to talk with him personally any more, but we will cherish the eternal friendship between teacher and students in our hearts.

We commemorate Mr. Xiao, mentor of the research team, with this draft *Laozi: An Axiomatic Interpretation* at its completion.

The Innovative Research Team on "Axiomatic Interpretation of
Chinese Classics" of Jiujiang University
Li Ningning, Wu Guofu, Cao Huanrong
December 11, 2015

后记：道法自然，顺势而为

冯友兰先生在《中国哲学史》的前言中指出，在诸子的著述中虽然没有"形式上的系统"，但有"实质上的系统"。从2008年5月以来，我与"中华经典的公理化诠释"研究及创新学术团队潜心庐山之麓，从先秦儒学切入，先后开展了关于《论语》《孟子》和《荀子》的公理化诠释之研究。在遵循原意的基础上，我们以基本假设、定义、公理为基本要素，推导证明了众多蕴含在《论语》《孟子》和《荀子》中的客观命题，从而将隐含在其中的逻辑体系凸显出来，便于东西方人士超越不同文化语境的局限，共同地用理性的方式理解和准确把握儒家思想。我们先后出版了《〈论语〉的公理化诠释》（第一版、修订版、中英文对照版、中法文对照版）、《〈孟子〉的公理化诠释》（中文版、中英文对照版）和《〈荀子〉的公理化诠释》，并获国家出版基金资助。2014年11月，季羡林基金会组织专家对上述工作进行评审后，在千年学府白鹿洞书院为九江学院"中华经典的公理化诠释"创新研究团队颁发了"儒学传承与创新奖"。

在上述研究过程中及专著出版后，我们收获了很多专家与读者的厚爱和鼓励，越来越多的同仁希望我们继续用公理化方法诠释《老子》，因为中华传统文化中儒道两家文化占有主流地位。《老子》又名《道德经》，其著者老子是中国古代的哲学家和思想家、道家学派的创始人。老子认为"道"是世界万物的根本，提倡"自然""无为"；老子期望治国应遵"道"而行，即顺应自然和社会规律，不能任意妄为；其清静寡欲的思想也给养生以基本理念。道家思想曾给西方启蒙运动时期的思想家以启迪和借鉴，而且对于当代可持续发展理念方面表现出深刻的前瞻性。《老子》是有史以来译成外文版本最多、海外发行量最大的中国经典。用公理化的方法诠释《老子》，需要将《老子》的众多语句整理成一个演绎系统，即在给出一些定义和基本假设以后，形成若干公理，并以逻辑推理的方法，推导和证明众多蕴含在《老子》中反映道家思想的系列命题，从而将隐含在《老子》中的道家思想的逻辑体系凸显出来。

2014年8月16日至20日，由九江学院庐山文化研究中心举办的"中华经典的公理化诠释研讨会"在庐山成功召开。此次会议特邀旅法著名学者韦遨宇先生为主讲嘉宾。他以"老子、庄子与道家思想"为主题，讲解了道家哲学与西方自然哲学、本体论哲学、认识论哲学及语言论哲学的关系，道家哲学思想与道教之间错综复杂的关系，二者之异同与对立等内容。韦教授广征博引，纵横捭阖，结合自己的多年研究和在国内外的丰富阅历娓娓道来，参加研讨会的学者边听讲边讨论，为各人先聚力于通读《老子》和即将开始"《老子》的公理化诠释"展开了广阔的视野。

我们在2014年11月确定开始会读《老子》。《老子》文字不过五千有余，但包含的内容博大精深。在会读《老子》的过程中，我们对之前先秦儒学的会读方式做了一些改造，亦即将"分篇阅读"改变为"抽取专题阅读"。每位成员选取《老子》思想的一至二个主题担当主讲，结合《老子》的整体思想，着重阐明每一主题的基本内涵，并以整体切入思想框架的方式斟酌命题。其他成员则提出各种问题，然后大家进行深入的讨论。

目前存在多种《老子》的注释本，如竹简本、帛书本、傅奕本、严遵本、想尔注本、敦煌本、范应元本、景龙碑本，以及通行本（河上公注本和王弼注本）等，我们选择主要参考王弼之注和香港中文大学的刘笑敢教授所著的《老子古今》（它对五种主要的版本作了对勘与评析）。同时，在文本注释与思想的阐发上，陈鼓应的《老子注译及评介》《老子今注今译》体现了老学研究的较高造诣，是我们会读《老子》的重要参考。在为期4个月的会读（每周保持2个集中研读单元，寒假连续8天）后，我们对《老子》文本作了逐章逐句的研讨。

2015年5月，我与几位团队成员怀着虔诚的心情前往老子故里——河南鹿邑学习、考察，与周口师范学院和位于鹿邑的"中国老子文化研究中心"的同仁展开学术交流。鹿邑以太清宫景区、老君台、明道宫景区和老子文化广场为组合，充分发挥其人文景观优势，向人们展示了一个民间流传的老子形象。其后，为了进一步理清道家与道教的关系，我与吴国富教授还访问了庐山仙人洞道院的王理天道长，更多地了解了道教的思想起源、祖师崇拜、历史作用及其局限。

2015年8月16日至20日，由九江学院庐山文化研究中心和庐山文化传承与传播协同创新中心举办的2015年"《老子》的公理化诠释研讨会"在我校成功召开。法国新索邦大学教授、著名旅法学者韦遨宇先生围绕《老子》及《〈老子〉的公理化诠释》初稿，就"方法论""老子哲学的否定特征""老子哲学中的辩证法""老子哲学中的反权力思想"等问题进行了精彩阐述。他还结合当前西方哲学发展的特点，从全球化的视角对《〈老子〉的公理化诠释》初稿进行了点评。

清华大学程钢教授结合西方诠释学和中国考据学对《〈老子〉的公理化诠释》书稿进行了评析，他认为书稿在研究中注意到了文本问题，也注意到了诠释的多种途径，即语言哲学、宇宙生成论、逻辑学、生命哲学等，期待团队能够探索出对中华经典解读和诠释的新范式。鹿邑"中国老子文化研究中心"陈大明研究员结合老子在民间千年传承中的形象演变，指出《老子》一书在千年传承中也有较大变化，团队利用公理化方法诠释《老子》一书，可以帮助理解《老子》中的许多概念和命题。参与书稿撰写的我校学者就书稿及暑期修改部分进行了交流和讨论。研讨会还就团队前期开展的《论语》《孟子》《荀子》公理化诠释的成果进行了回顾和探讨，讨论了公理化方法应用于人文学科，特别是"文化"研究，应注意的问题。

2015年9月12日至13日，应北京大学高等人文研究院院长杜维明先生邀请，我与柯镇昌博士参加了在河南省登封市举行的第四届"嵩山论坛——华夏文明与世界文明对话"。"嵩山论坛"是由中国国际文化交流中心、北京大学高等人文研究院、河南省华夏历史文明传承创新基金会联合主办的国际性高端文化论坛，论坛为华夏文明与世界文明的对话提供了良好平台，我已受邀连续出席了四届论坛。第四届论坛的主题是"和而不同——共建人类命运共同体"。会议期间，我同国际哲学院院士、国际哲学学会联合会名誉主席、丹麦奥胡斯大学彼得·肯普教授探讨了中华经典公理化诠释的相关问题。彼得·肯普教授对于这一研究课题产生了浓厚的兴趣，并对我校在东西方文化交流方面所做的工作给予了肯定。会议期间，我还与杜维明先生围绕"《老子》的公理化诠释"进行了研讨。

2015年10月31日至11月1日，由九江学院"庐山文化传承与传播协同创新中心"举办的"《老子》的公理化诠释研讨会"在我校成功召开。来自中国社会科学院、南昌大学、江苏理工学院等单位和我校的学者共16人出席了研讨会。在研讨会上，陈霞研究员从诠释学的角度审视公理化诠释方法，指出了公理化的独特价值以及需要解决的一些问题，并对公理化研究团队的学术氛围表示由衷的赞赏。顾丹柯先生从翻译的角度提出拟定命题需要注意简洁的要求，并就中华经典公理化诠释研究的英译工作提出有价值的建议。杨柱才教授、谌贻庆教授对书稿进行细致的分析和论述，推动书稿的进一步完善。研讨会议日程紧凑，讨论热烈，成果丰硕。来自不同领域的学者对中华经典公理化诠释工作的意见和建议，为《〈老子〉的公理化诠释》书稿的不断完善提供了有力的支撑。

2015年11月，我赴中央党校参加为期2周的"全国高校领导专题研讨班"，深入学习习近平总书记系列重要讲话精神，进一步增强思想政治素质和治校治教能力。恰逢中国共产党十八届五中全会闭幕不久，这次会议审议通过了国家发展"十三五"规划建议，该建议突出了创新、协调、绿色、开放、共享这五大发展理念。这些发展理念是中国特色社会主义理论体系的重要组成部分，与老子学说的一些内容有相当程度的契合。《习近平谈治国理政》第一卷中有篇文章是《"治大国若烹小鲜"》，其中指出："这样一个大国，这样多的人民，这么复杂的国情，领导者要深入了解国情，了解人民所思所盼，要有'如履薄冰，如临深渊'的自觉，要有'治大国若烹小鲜'的态度，丝毫不敢懈怠，丝毫不敢马虎，必须夙夜在公、勤勉工作。"习总书记的殷切教导激励我们为国家分忧，为人民担当。

2016年元月，我与课题组同仁前往江西鹰潭市龙虎山。这里是中国道教文化的发源地之一，第一代天师张道陵在龙虎山结庐炼丹，逐步建立道教，并从宗教的角度诠释《老子》（道教改称《道德经》），老子成为道教神仙系统中的太上老君。我们深入考察了"道教祖庭"嗣汉天师府、上清宫等名胜古迹，分别访问了中国道教协会副会长张金涛道长、鹰潭道教协会副会长张贵华道长、鹰潭道文化研究中心主任夏维纪先生、龙虎山道教文化研究所所长薛清和先生，特别与他们探讨老子、道家思想与道教的关系及异同，得到不少启迪。

我与张金涛道长一起回顾了在2014年11月25日于鹰潭召开的第三届国际道教论坛大会上，第九、第十届全国人大常委会副委员长，现任世界汉语教学学会会长许嘉璐先生的讲话。许嘉璐先生精辟地指出：当代的道学道教需要改革和开放，落在具体面上，可以概括为三个拟人化的"对话"，包括古今对话、"教""科"（宗教与科学）对话、中外对话。"在对话中，我们完全有资格奉献道教道学的伟大智慧，例如中国'三教'相克相融的经验，足可供自古及今因宗教问题而未停杀戮的国家和民族参考；再如，我们自古对自然、对地球、对宇宙的关怀，完全可以成为人类共同挽救地球的精神支柱；又如，我们'法自然'式的自由，可用来纠正新自由主义的偏差。"

夏维纪先生认为：道家思想是一棵树，道教是这棵树上的花和果。谈到道教，对一般老百姓而言大部分都是道神、教派、教义等问题，即看到花和果而忽视了树，没有看到哲学的问题。我们就是追根寻源，要挖掘出道教背后的老子哲学渊源。中国文化不能没有宗教文化，而道教为传承老子的道家哲学做出了贡献。

老子思想的核心，简约地说，就是人们耳熟能详的"人法地，地法天，天法道，道法自然"和"道生一，一生二，二生三，三生万物"等精辟论说。老子以"道"为核心展开他的全部学说。张岱年先生曾说："老子的道论是中国哲学本体论的开始，这是确然无疑的"，"在中国哲学本体论的发展过程中，道家学说居于主导地位"。老子推崇"道法自然"，即要遵循事物发展的内在法则，根据实际条件采取适宜方式，顺应自然，就会事半功倍。"无为"是老子思想中的重要概念。这里的"无为"并非消极不做，而是不违背其本意，乃是不乱为，不妄为；也是"上善若水，水善利万物而不争"，从而顺势而为。

润色稿子之际，我漫步在庐山之麓的白鹿洞书院，感悟着崇德祠取自于《中庸》的一副楹联：致广大而尽精微，极高明而道中庸。冯友兰先生在《新原道》一书中，曾以"极高明而道中庸"为标准来评价儒道学说。他认为：儒家思想的特点在于"道中庸"，于伦理道德的领域见长；而道家思想的特点则在于"极高明"，于形上哲学的领域见长。儒道两家的文化，可见仁见智，各有千秋，既有差异，又可互补。

我们感谢杨叔子院士长期以来对于"中华经典的公理化诠释"研究工作的倾心指导。杨院士近年来身体欠佳，但依然时常关心和鼓励我们的研究进展，并为著作赐序。同时我们感谢韦遂宇教授，连续两年利用暑假从法国来到庐山讲学，使我们受益匪浅。他以深厚的学术功底，从中西文化交流的视野出发，为本著赐跋，堪称美文。

中华民族在五千多年的文明发展进程中，创造了博大精深的中华文化，积淀了中华民族深沉的精神追求和根本的精神基因，是中华民族生生不息、发展壮大的丰厚滋养。以儒道为主要代表的中华优秀传统文化，是中华民族团结奋进的重要精神支撑，是我们深厚的文化软实力。回顾近些年来"中华经典的公理化诠释"创新研究团队不畏艰辛、奋力前行的历程，我不由感慨万千。在团队同仁几番讨论的基础上，我撰写对联一副以总结我们的研究工作：老子孔子孟子荀子诸子皆圣，天理道理伦理公理顺理成章。

2015年12月5日，我到上海参加全球孔子学院大会。清华学友传来噩耗，萧树铁先生辞世西去。遥望东方明珠之塔，追思先生风范之碑，悲伤哽咽难表思念。我连续三晚不能入睡，恩师的高尚情怀、音容笑貌涌现心头，历历在目。萧先生一生致力于教育事业，主持了清华大学数学系恢复重建，培养了一批批杰出学子，在微分方程及非线性扩散等领域的研究上取得丰硕成果。先生创建了中国工业与应用数学学会，创办了全国大学生数学建模教育及竞赛，为中国工业化进程和应用数学发展留下了不朽的足迹。先生主持撰写了《21世纪中国高等教育改革——非数学专业高等数学改革研究报告》白皮书，为高校数学教育及素质培养描绘了蓝图。先生在晚年还对中国文化的国际传播思考不止，提出了"从公理化体系看中西文化"的思路，不辞辛苦多次来九江学院指导"中华经典的公理化诠释"创新研究，在庐山白鹿洞书院、在濂溪湖边，与我们热烈讨论中西方文化比较与中国文化的国际传播话题。

1986年，我追随萧先生进入清华大学的知识殿堂，一直得到恩师品德的熏陶、学术的引领、悉心的呵护。先生博学睿智，淡泊名利，正直做人；先生充满激情，任劳任怨，大公无私；先生谦虚谨慎，平易近人，和蔼可亲；先生爱生如子，舐犊情深，德艺双馨。萧先生的一生，树撑苍穹，铁铸学魂，是爱国爱民的一生，是让后世学人敬重的一生，永远激励我们开拓进取。我与"中华经典的公理化诠释"创新研究团队的同仁商定，谨以本书纪念尊敬与爱戴的萧树铁先生。萧先生驾鹤西去之后，九江学院"中华经典的公理化诠释"创新研究团队成员纷纷撰文表示深切哀悼，综合成文"怀念萧树铁教授"，以作"跋二"。

在《〈老子〉的公理化诠释》的研究、讨论与撰稿的过程中，课题组又扩增了不少志同道合之士。这部书稿的问世是我们认真会读、反复研讨和通力合作的结晶。具体各章撰写的分工如下："导读"由甘筱青执笔；第一章"引论"由甘筱青、李宁宁、吴国富执笔；第二章"定义，基本假设，公理"由曹欢荣、吴国富、甘筱青执笔；第三章"明道篇"由曹欢荣执笔；第四章"贵德篇"由陈建军执笔；第五章"治国篇"由柯镇昌执笔；第六章"摄生篇"由吴国富执笔；文献校对：吴国富；全书总撰：甘筱青、吴国富。

甘筱青

2016年2月8日，丙申年春节

Postscript: Dao Models on Nature and Follows the Trend

In the preface to *A History of Chinese Philosophy*, Mr. Feng Youlan held that although there isn't a system in form, there is a system in essence in ancient philosophers' books of the pre-Qin period. Since May 2008, the academic team of research and innovation on the axiomatic interpretation of Chinese classics and I have concentrated on the axiomatic interpretation of *The Analects of Confucius*, *Mencius* and *Xunzi*, in Jiujiang University. By following the original intent, we have used basic assumptions, definitions and axioms as fundamental elements and verified many objective propositions in *The Analects of Confucius*, *Mencius* and *Xunzi* to highlight the logical systems implied, so that readers in both Western and Eastern countries can surpass the limitations arising from different cultural backgrounds and linguistic contexts to understand and grasp Confucianism in a rational way. Subsidized by the National Press Fund, we have published *The Analects of Confucius: An Axiomatic Interpretation* (first edition, revised edition, Chinese and English version, and Chinese and French version), *Mencius: An Axiomatic Interpretation* (Chinese version, and Chinese and English version which was published in 2016) and *Xunzi: An Axiomatic Interpretation*. In November 2014, after evaluating the above works, experts from Ji Xianlin Foundation came to Jiujiang to award the prize of the Inheritance and Innovation of Confucianism to the Research and Innovation Team of Jiujiang University on axiomatic interpretation of Chinese Classics in Bailudong, or the White Deer Cave Academy, which has a history of over 1,000 years.

In the course of research, especially since the publication of the above mentioned monographs, we have been praised and encouraged by many experts and readers, and most of them hope that we can interpret *Laozi* in an axiomatic way as Confucianism and Daoism take up the equally important positions in traditional Chinese culture. *Laozi*, also known as *The Book of Dao and Its Virtue* or *Dao De Jing*, was written by Laozi, who was not only a philosopher and thinker in ancient China, but also the founder of Daoism. Laozi considered the Dao as the root of all things in the world, and advocated a theory of "naturalness and inaction or non-action." He expected a country could be ruled by following the Dao, which means ruling the country by the laws of Nature and society, and avoiding all wayward behaviors. Moreover, his thought of living a quiet life with controlled desires is also the underlying rationale for health-preservation theory. In addition, the Daoist theory once provided enlightenment and references for Western thinkers in the

Enlightenment period, and showed a forward-looking vision in terms of the concept of sustainable development in the contemporary world. As a Chinese classic, *Laozi* has been translated into various languages with the highest number of different versions in foreign languages and the highest circulation abroad. To interpret *Laozi* in an axiomatic way, it is necessary to arrange numerous statements in *Laozi* into a deductive system, which means forming a number of axioms on the given definitions and basic assumptions, and deducing and proving a series of propositions reflecting the Daoist thought in *Laozi* by logical reasoning, so as to highlight the logical system of the Daoist thought implied in *Laozi*.

From 16 to 20 August, 2014, the Seminar on Axiomatic Interpretation of Chinese Classics, held by Lushan Culture Research Center of Jiujiang University, was successfully convened in Mt. Lushan, China. Mr. Wei Aoyu, a famous scholar living in France, was invited to present a keynote speech on the relationship between Daoist philosophy and Western natural philosophy, ontological philosophy, epistemological philosophy and philosophy of language, and their influences, as well as the complicated relationship between Daoism as philosophy and Daoism as religion, the similarities, differences and conflicts between them, etc. Concerning the theme of Laozi, Zhuangzi and Daoism, Professor Wei combined quotations of various theories and made a wonderful speech based on his long years of study and broad experience at home and abroad. The scholars, who attended the seminar, discussed relevant topics during the speeches, which expanded a broad field of vision for us to read through *Laozi* and interpret *Laozi* axiomatically.

Laozi contains abundant and profound content in about 5,000 Chinese characters. In November, 2014, we decided to get together to study it. During the process, we modified the ways of reading the pre-Qin Confucianism by dividing the book into several parts. Every member of the team selected one or two topics on the thoughts in *Laozi*, combined with the whole thought of the book, to give a lecture, focusing on illuminating the basic connotation of every topic, while other participants presented the speaker with various questions and made in-depth discussions including the selection of the version of *Laozi*.

As there are various versions of *Laozi*, such as the bamboo slips, the silk manuscripts, the Fu Yi version, the Yan Zun version, the Xiang'er annotated version, the Dunhuang version, the Fan Yingyuan version, the version of Jinglong Tablet, the popular editions annotated by Heshang Gong and Wang Bi, and so on, it is difficult for us to decide which versions we should choose. After serious discussions on the selection of versions, we decided to use *Laozi Gujin (Laozi, Ancient to Modern)* written by Professor Liu Xiaogan of the Chinese University of Hong Kong and

Wang Bi's *Commentary on Laozi with Critical Text and Translation* as a primary reference. In *Laozi Gujin*, the author proofreads and analyzes five major versions. We also selected *Laozi: With Annotations and Evaluation* and *A Newly Annotated Translation of Laozi* by Chen Guying as important reference for us to read *Laozi*. Mr. Chen Guying shows great academic achievements in studying *Laozi*, in terms of text annotations and idea elucidation. After a four-month's study of *Laozi*, we continued our research on the text of *Laozi*, chapter by chapter and sentence by sentence.

In May, 2015, several members of the team including me went on a study and investigation tour to Laozi's hometown, Luyi in Henan Province, and communicated with researchers from Zhoukou Normal University and Chinese Research Center for Laozi Culture in Luyi. Luyi enjoys the scenic spots of Taiqing Palace, Laojuntai (Memorial Platform of Laozi), Mingdao Palace and Laozi Cultural Square. With such humanistic landscapes, the city has successfully made Laozi known to the public, which provides the convincing evidence of the profound influence of Daoism and the popular saying "Laozi is the most important under the sun," and helps you to have thorough comprehension of the Daoist theory. Subsequently, in order to further clarify the relationship between Daoism as philosophy and Daoism as religion, Professor Wu Guofu and I visited Wang Litian, the Daoist priest of the Fairy Cave, a Daoist temple in Mt. Lushan, to know more about the origin of Daoism as philosophy, the way of worshiping its founder, its role in history, and the limitations.

From 16 to 20 August 2015, a Seminar on Axiomatic Interpretation of *Laozi*, sponsored by Lushan Culture Research Center of Jiujiang University and the Collaborative Innovation Center of Lushan Cultural Inheritance and Transmission, was held in Jiujiang University. Mr. Wei Aoyu, professor with University Sorbonne Nouvelle, in discussion of *Laozi* and the first draft of *Laozi: An Axiomatic Interpretation,* made a wonderful exposition on the methodologies, feature of negation of Laozi philosophy, dialectics of Laozi philosophy, anti-power thought of Laozi philosophy, and so on. He also made comment on the first draft of *Laozi: An Axiomatic Interpretation* with a global vision by combining the characteristics of current development of Western philosophy.

Professor Cheng Gang from Tsinghua University, combining Western hermeneutics and Chinese textual criticism, made an analysis of and comment on the manuscript of *Laozi: An Axiomatic Interpretation.* He thought that the research team paid attention to the text versions in the study and the multi-approaches in the interpretation of classics, namely, using linguistic philosophy, the theory of cosmology, logic, life philosophy, etc., hoping that the team can explore a new paradigm to interpret and annotate Chinese classics. Chen Daming, a research fellow from Chinese Research Center for Laozi Culture in Luyi, based on the evolution of Laozi's folk images, argued that there was a relatively significant change of the book *Laozi* in thousands of years of heritage, and that it was helpful to illustrate numerous concepts and propositions in *Laozi* to interpret *Laozi* in an axiomatic way. Besides, scholars of Jiujiang University, who co-authored the manuscript, discussed the manuscript and the part revised previously with other attendees. The attendees of this seminar also had a review and discussion of the achievements in the axiomatic interpretation of *The Analects of Confucius*, *Mencius* and *Xunzi*, and the problems to which attention should be paid, when the axiomatic method was employed in humanities, especially in cultural research.

On 12 and 13 September 2015, Dr. Ke Zhenchang and I were invited by Mr. Du Weiming, director of the Institute for Advanced Humanistic Studies of Peking University, to attend the Fourth Songshan Forum—Dialogue between Chinese Civilization and World Civilization, held in Dengfeng City, Henan Province. Songshan Forum is a high level international cultural forum, co-sponsored by China International Culture Exchange Centre, the Institute for Advanced Humanistic Studies of Peking University, and Henan Foundation of Innovation and Inheritance of Chinese History and Civilization. It provides a good platform for the communication between Chinese Civilization and World Civilization, and I have been invited to attend the forum for four times in succession. The theme of the fourth Songshan Forum was "Harmony but not Uniformity—Working Together to Create a Community of Shared Future for Mankind." During the conference, Professor Peter Kemp from Aarhus University in Denmark, an academician of the Institute of International Philosophy and the honorary chairman of International Federation of Societies of Philosophy, and I talked about some related problems about the axiomatic interpretation of Chinese Classics, and Professor Peter Kemp took a keen interest in this research subject of our university, thinking highly of our efforts in the cultural exchange between the East and the West. Besides, Mr. Du Weiming and I also held a discussion on the axiomatic interpretation of *Laozi* during the conference.

From 31 October to 1 November 2015, the Seminar on the Axiomatic Interpretation of Laozi, organized by the Collaborative Innovation Center for Lushan Cultural Inheritance and Publicity of Jiujiang University, was held in Jiujiang University. Sixteen scholars from Chinese Academy of Social Sciences, Nanchang University, Jiangsu University of Technology, Jiujiang University and other organizations attended this seminar. Professor Chen Xia from Chinese Academy of Social Sciences pointed out the unique value of axiomatization and some problems that needed to be solved from the theoretical perspective of hermeneutics, and expressed sincere appreciation for the academic atmosphere of our research team. Mr. Gu Danke from Jiangsu University of Technology put forward valuable suggestions for developing propositions and translating the research achievements of the axiomatic interpretation of Chinese classics into English. Besides, Professor Yang Zhucai and Professor Shen Yiqing from Nanchang University analyzed the manuscript thoroughly for further improvement of the work. The seminar achieved fruitful result after brief and vigorous discussions. The opinions and suggestions on the axiomatic interpretation of Chinese classics presented by scholars from different fields have provided strong support for continuous improvement and perfection of *Laozi: An Axiomatic Interpretation*.

In November 2015, I attended the National Seminar for College Leadership in the Party School of the Central Committee of the CPC, which lasted for two weeks, and I learned more about the essence of a series of important speeches by General Secretary and President Xi Jinping, and further improved my ideological and political quality as well as my capability of management and teaching. This seminar came soon after the closing of the Fifth Plenary Session of the 18th CPC Central Committee, which reviewed and adopted the proposals for the 13th five-year plan for China's development, highlighting the five development concepts of innovation, coordination, green development, openness and sharing. In terms of the axiomatic interpretation of *Laozi*, I think that the above conceptions of development are important parts of the theoretical system of socialism with Chinese characteristics, which have improved the thought of Laozi greatly and agree with some contents of Laozi's theory. In *Xi Jinping: The Governance of China*, which quotes from the sixtieth chapter of *Laozi*, President Xi points out as China is such a big country with so many people and such complex situation, the leaders should understand thoroughly the realities of the country as well as and wishes of its people, and should be careful and diligent in official working with self-consciousness of walking as if on eggs and the attitude of "*To govern a big country is very much like frying a small fish in a pan* (do not stir it too often)." The ardent teaching by President Xi inspires us to share concerns for the country and bear our responsibility for the people.

In January 2016, colleagues of our research group and I went to Longhu Mountain in Yingtan City of Jiangxi Province. Longhu Mountain is one of the places where the Chinese Daoist culture originated, and where Zhang Daoling, the first-generation Daoist master, practiced alchemy and founded Daoism gradually. He interpreted *Laozi* (renamed *Dao De Jing*) from the religious point of view. Laozi the person was called *Taishang Laojun*, the very High Lord in the Daoist immortals system. We conducted a thorough investigation of some places of interest, including the Dragon Tianshi Mansion, the ancestral home of Daoism, and Shangqing Palace, We also visited Priest Zhang Jintao, vice chairman of China Daoism Association, Priest Zhang Guihua, vice chairman of Yingtan Daoism Association, Mr. Xia Weiji, director of the Centre for Yingtan Daoist Cultural Studies, and Mr. Xue Qinghe, director of Longhu Mountain Daoist Culture Research Institute respectively. We particularly discussed the relationship, similarities and differences between Laozi, Daoism as philosophy and Daoism as religion, and got remarkable enlightenment.

Priest Zhang Jintao and I looked back at the speech in the Third Forum of International Daoism on November 25, 2014, delivered by Mr. Xu Jialu, the ninth and tenth vice chairman of the Standing Committee of the National People's Congress and president of the International Society for Chinese Language Teaching. Mr. Xu made a penetrating analysis and pointed out that reform and opening up were necessary for Daoism both as philosophy and as religion, which, more concretely, contained three kinds of anthropomorphic dialogues, including dialogue between ancient and modern, dialogue between religion and science, and dialogue between China and other countries. In the dialogues, we are well qualified to contribute great wisdom of Daoism to the world. For instance, the experience of inter-restriction and integration among three Chinese representative religions—Buddhism, Confucianism and Daoism can provide reference for countries or nations involved in the killings due to religious conflicts. Secondly, our concern for nature, the earth, and the universe starting from ancient times can become the emotional anchor for all humanity to save the planet. Thirdly, our freedom in following the "law of Nature" can be used to correct the deviation of neo-liberalism.

Mr. Xia Weiji holds that Daoism as philosophy is like a tree, and Daoism as religion is the flowers and fruit of the tree. When talking about Daoism, the common people will mainly think of Daoist immortals, denominations, religious dogmas, and so on. They just pay too much attention to the flowers and fruit, ignoring the tree or the issue of philosophy. We are tracking the source to dig out the origin of Laozi's philosophy behind Daoism. Chinese culture cannot develop without religious culture, and Daoism has made contributions to the transmission and inheritance of Daoist philosophy of Laozi.

Briefly speaking, the core concept of Daoism as philosophy can be reflected in the well-known saying: "Man models himself on Earth, Earth on Heaven, Heaven on the Dao (the way), and the Dao on that which is naturally so," and "Dao begets one; one begets two; two begets three; three begets all things." Laozi expanded all his theory with Dao as its core. Mr. Zhang Dainian said, "It is no doubt that the

Dao theory of Laozi is the beginning of Chinese philosophy ontology," and "In the development of Chinese philosophy ontology, Dao theory is in a dominant position." Laozi praisesd highly "The Dao models on that which is naturally so," which means everything must be done by following the inner principles of the development, adopting proper methods according to actual conditions, and complying with nature, so that twice as much can be accomplished with half the effort. Besides, there is an important concept of Laozi's thought—"wuwei" (non-action or inaction), which does not mean being negative and doing nothing, but means not doing foolish things against one's instinct and not violating the original intention. It also means "The perfect goodness is like water. Water is good at benefiting all things, but does not contend with them." Thus, people should follow the existing trend.

In embellishing the manuscript, I strolled along the path in White Deer Cave Academy at the foot of Mt. Lushan, comprehending the implication of a couplet from *The Doctrine of the Mean* in the Virtue-upholding Temple, "Being profound while paying attention to the details; being noble while following the golden mean." In the book *The New Original Way*, Mr. Feng Youlan appraises the theories of Confucianism and Daoism for taking "being noble while following the golden mean" as a norm. He holds that Confucianism is characterized by "following the golden mean," and by ethics and morality, while Daoism is characterized by "being noble," and by metaphysical philosophy. Different people can have different views on Confucianism and Daoism, and both have their own advantages. They are different, but they can be complementary.

It is appreciated that Yang Shuzi, an academician of China Academy of Sciences, has provided long-term guidance to us for the axiomatic interpretation of Chinese classics. Although Mr. Yang has suffered from health problems in recent years, from time to time, he encouraged us and showed his concern in our research, and has written the forward to our book. Besides, we are also very grateful to Professor Wei Aoyu for his lectures during the two summer vacations. We are very much appreciated for his epilogue based on his profound academic knowledge from the perspective of cultural communication between China and the West.

In more than 5,000 years' development of civilization, the Chinese nation has created the extensive and profound Chinese culture, which has accumulated the spiritual pursuit deep in our hearts and the fundamental spiritual gene, greatly nourishing our Chinese nation in constant growth and development. Excellent traditional Chinese culture with Confucianism and Daoism as the main representatives is an important spiritual support for the Chinese nation to unite and forge ahead, and is also our strong cultural soft power. In recent years, our research team on the axiomatic interpretation of Chinese classics has taken a challenging and arduous journey, so I have all sorts of feelings well up in my mind. On the basis of several rounds of discussions with colleagues in our team, I have written a couplet to summarize our research work: By learning Laozi, Confucius, Mencius and Xunzi, the young can be edified; by following justice, truth, ethics and principles, the ideal will be vivified.

On 5 December 2015, when I was attending the Confucius Institute Conference in Shanghai, I heard the sad news of Mr. Xiao Shutie's death from a schoolmate of Tsinghua University. Looking at the Oriental Pearl Tower and recalling Mr. Xiao Shutie's elegant demeanour, I felt it hard to express my feeling of missing him and my voice choked with sadness. I could not sleep for three consecutive nights, and the nobility, voice and smiling face of my mentor emerged in my mind, with scenes of the past appearing before my eyes. Mr. Xiao devoted himself to the cause of education all his life. He presided over the restoration and reconstruction of the Department of Mathematics at Tsinghua University, cultivated a group of outstanding students, and made substantial achievements in the fields of differential equations and nonlinear diffusion. He established China Society for Industrial and Applied Mathematics, and developed national collegiate mathematical modelling education and competition, leaving an immortal footprint in Chinese industrialization advancement and the development of applied mathematics. Besides, he presided over writing the white paper "China's Higher Education Reform in the 21st Century: A Report on the Study of the Reform of Higher Mathematics in Non-mathematics Majors," which provided a blueprint for mathematics education in colleges and universities and for quality training. In his later years, Mr. Xiao always thought about the international publicity of Chinese culture, presenting his thought of "Looking at Chinese and Western Cultures from the perspective of the Axiomatic System." He frequently put himself out of the way to provide guidance for the innovation research on the axiomatic interpretation of Chinese classics in Jiujiang University, and had heated discussions with us in Jiujiang on topics of comparison between Chinese culture and Western cultures and the international spread of Chinese culture.

In 1986, when I entered Tsinghua University, Mr. Xiao became my supervisor. Since then I have been influenced by his virtue, and have always received his academic guidance and tender care. He was a wise and knowledgeable man, being indifferent to fame or wealth. He was also an upright and passionate man, affable and approachable. Besides, he was modest and prudent, without complaining and selfishness. He was affectionate toward his students and loved them as if they were his own children. In brief, he was excellent in both work performance and moral integrity. With firm learning belief and ardent love for the motherland and for the people in his whole life, he is so great that he will be respected by future generations, and his spirit will always inspire us to forge ahead. After discussion with colleagues in our research team on the axiomatic interpretation of Chinese classics, we agree to honor the memory of our highly esteemed and deeply beloved Mr. Xiao Shutie, by this book. Since his passing away, the members of the research team on the axiomatic interpretation of Chinese classics of Jiujiang University have written articles to express our deep condolence, and completed the article "Professor Xiao Shutie Will Live in Our Hearts" as a second Epilogue.

In the course of studying, discussing and writing *Laozi: An Axiomatic Interpretation*, many people of like mind have joined our research group. The publication of this book is the fruit of our careful study, numerous discussions and full cooperation. The writing of each chapter is as follows:

Readers' Guide, written by Gan Xiaoqing;

Chapter One: Introduction, written by Gan Xiaoqing, Li Ningning, Wu Guofu;

Chapter Two: Definitions, Assumptions and Axioms, written by Cao Huanrong, Wu Guofu and Gan Xiaoqing;

Chapter Three: On Understanding the Dao, written by Cao Huanrong;

Chapter Four: On Cherishing Virtue, written by Chen Jianjun;

Chapter Five: On Governance, written by Ke Zhenchang;

Chapter Six: On Preserving Health, written by Wu Guofu;

Literature collation: Wu Guofu;

Writers-in-chief: Gan Xiaoqing and Wu Guofu.

Gan Xiaoqing

February 8, 2016, Spring Festival of the Monkey Year

英译说明

《老子》，又名《道德经》，成书年代大约在公元前6世纪左右。一般认为，《老子》(《道德经》)的作者为老子。老子又名李聃，生活在春秋时期，但有关老子本人的记载很少，据说他曾做过朝廷中很小的文官（管理周王朝的文书）。

《老子》全书仅八十一章，五千余字，分《德经》和《道经》两部分，是道家思想的代表作品，也是中国本土宗教道教的思想基础。该书篇幅虽然不大，然而思想博大精深，自诞生至今两千五百多年来对中国文化和国人思想的形成和发展一直有着深远的影响。老子所开创的道家学派是与儒学齐名的中国古代主要哲学流派之一。近代以来，随着东西方文化交流的深入，道家思想引起了西方学者的广泛关注，《老子》译本也层出不穷，早在15世纪《老子》(《道德经》)就开始被译介到西方，成为被译介得最多的中国哲学典籍之一。

2012年10月，九江学院成立了国学译馆。我们的主要工作就是将甘筱青教授领衔的"中华经典的公理化诠释"研究团队的系列研究成果翻译成英语和其他语言。我们想通过翻译，使当代读者，特别是外国读者从新的角度审视和理解中国经典。

到目前为止，我们先后翻译出版了甘筱青教授等学者的力作《〈论语〉的公理化诠释》《〈孟子〉的公理化诠释》中英文版，以及《〈论语〉的公理化诠释》中法文版、中日文版，这些中外文双语对照版均由外语教学与研究出版社正式出版。《〈老子〉的公理化诠释》是"中华经典的公理化诠释"研究团队的第四项研究成果。本书依然从文理交融、中西贯通的角度，对中华经典进行新的解读。我们从2016年6月开始着手翻译，经过多次探讨修改，在2018年7月完成了译文定稿。

本书英译主要由九江学院、广东外语外贸大学、江苏理工学院教师和哥伦比亚大学在读博士生共同完成。具体章节分工如下：序、第一章、第三章（P1-10至P1-15）及第四章（P2-1至P2-12）由江苏理工学院顾丹柯先生翻译；导读、第二章、第三章（P1-16至P1-21）及第四章（P2-13至P2-23）由桑龙扬教授翻译；第五章、第六章和第三章（P1-1至P1-9）由广东外语外贸大学翻译学博士王俊超副编审翻译；跋一由哥伦比亚大学在读哲学博士生田楚雨翻译；跋二由九江学院陈腊春老师翻译；后记由九江学院梅君老师和万敏老师翻译。

桑龙扬教授除担任部分章节的翻译之外，还负责全书翻译工作的策划、各部分译文初稿和终稿修改，以及全书译文的编辑工作。桑龙扬教授作为九江学院国学译馆馆长，先后主持翻译出版了《〈论语〉的公理化诠释》《〈孟子〉的公理化诠释》。现为中国翻译协会专家会员，中国先秦史学会国学双语研究会常务理事，中国英汉语比较研究会翻译传译专业委员会常务理事，中国中医药研究促进会传统文化翻译与国际传播专业委员会常务理事，九江市翻译协会会长。翻译出版了美国长篇科幻小说《红火星》和两部汉语诗集，曾赴美国路易斯维尔大学做访问学者，在英国安格利亚鲁斯金大学学习。

顾丹柯先生除了承担翻译任务外，还参与了前期准备、部分译文的修改和审校等工作。顾丹柯，中国典籍英译研究会常务理事，长期从事中国典籍的英译，有译作《老子说》《孝经·二十四孝·弟子规》和《图说中国文化》等。其中，《孝经》英译本收入《大中华文库》。顾丹柯先后在英国爱丁堡大学东亚系及加拿大多伦多大学东亚学系做访问学者。

本书翻译工作是九江学院国学译馆与九江学院庐山文化研究中心的合作项目，纳入了九江学院省级"庐山文化传承与传播协同创新中心"的规划。本书作者团队，特别是甘筱青教授，为我们理解原文提供了很有价值的帮助。甘筱青教授在《〈老子〉的公理化诠释》的基础上，给我们提供了特色鲜明、便于理解的精简文本，统筹了中英文对照本的编撰、出版等环节。上海大学赵彦春教授对本书的翻译工作提出了宝贵的意见，我们深表感谢。

在本书的翻译过程中，我们参考了大量的国内外有关《老子》或《道德经》的英译成果和相关文献。《老子》所引用的条目主要参考了理雅各、刘殿爵、Robert G. Henricks、赵彦春、辜正坤、任继愈、顾丹柯等不同的《老子》或《道德经》汉英对照本或英译本。这些研究和译本有助于我们准确理解《老子》原文的含义，我们从中获益匪浅，对于其中不敢苟同之处我们也做了深入推敲。同时，我们还参考了其他相关著作，如外语教学与研究出版社出版的冯友兰《庄子》英译本和企鹅出版社出版的Martin Palman与Elizabeth

Breuilly、Chang Wai Ming、Jayramsy的合作译本。在公理化方法的英语表达方面，我们参考了斯宾诺莎所著的英文版《伦理学》等。本译著中《老子》条目的部分英译引自这些翻译名家的《老子》或《道德经》译本。在此，我们对这些研究者和译者表达诚挚的感谢。

诚望读者诸君不吝赐教，对译文不当之处给予批评指正，以便我们不断改进。

桑龙扬　顾丹柯
2018年7月

Translators' Notes

The book *Laozi*, also known as *The Classic of the Way and Virtue* (*Dao De Jing* or *Tao Te Ching*), was written around the sixth century BC. The extant version of the book consists of slightly over 5,000 Chinese characters. Li Dan, or Laozi, a recluse who lived during the Spring and Autumn Period (770 BC-476 BC), was accredited with the authorship of the book. Few records have survived about Laozi, who was said to have once held a low civil position in the royal court, in charge of the archival records of the Zhou Dynasty (1046 BC-256 BC).

Its 81 chapters are divided into two parts, *the Dao* (*the Way*) and *the De* (*Virtue*). Short as it is, the book has played a tremendous role in the development of Chinese history and culture. It has become the basis of Daoism as philosophy, parallel to Confucianism in ancient China. The thought of *Laozi* formed the foundation of Daoism as religion, the most influential indigenous school of religion in China. It has also exerted a direct impact on the characteristics, trends of thought, and aesthetic sensibilities of the Chinese nation. Today *Laozi* still plays a role in the development of Chinese thinking. *Laozi* was first introduced into Europe possibly as early as the 15th century and has been one of the most translated philosophical works of ancient China.

In October 2012, the Translation Institute for Guouxe (Traditional Chinese Classics) of Jiujiang University was set up. Its main task is to translate into English the series of research achievements made by the Research Team of Jiujiang University on the "Axiomatization of Chinese Classics." We intend to translate these classics with axiomatic interpretation into English and other major languages, so that contemporary readers, especially foreign readers, can read and understand the Chinese classics from a new perspective.

Up to now, we have respectively published the Chinese-English version, Chinese-French version and Chinese-Japanese version of *The Analects of Confucius: An Axiomatic Interpretation*, and the Chinese-English version of *Mencius: An Axiomatic Interpretation* written by Professor Gan Xiaoqing and other scholars. All the above-mentioned bilingual books were published by Foreign Language Teaching and Research Press. *Laozi: An Axiomatic Interpretation* is the fourth research achievement made by the Research Team of Jiujiang University on the "Axiomatization of Chinese Classics." This book also attempts to interpret Chinese classics from different perspectives based on different disciplines. We began our translation in June, 2016, and completed the final drafting in late 2018 after many discussions and revisions.

This translation is a collaborative work mainly by teachers from Jiujiang University, Jiangsu University of Technology, and Guangdong University of Foreign Studies, and PhD. candidates of Columbia University. The specific division of the work goes as follows: the Forward, Chapter One, Chapter Three (P1-10—P1-15) and Chapter Four (P2-1—P2-12) are translated by Professor Gu Danke from Jiangsu University of Technology; Readers' Guide, Chapter Two and Chapter Three (P1-16—P1-21) and Chapter Four (P2-13—P2-23) by Professor Sang Longyang; Chapter Three (P1-1—P1-9), Chapter Five and Chapter Six by Wang Junchao (PhD in Translation Studies) from Guangdong University of Foreign Studies; Epilogue One by Ms. Tian Chuyu (PhD candidate in Philosophy) from Columbia University; Epilogue Two by Mr. Chen Lachun, and the Postscript by Ms. Mei Jun and Ms. Wan Min from Jiujiang University.

Mr. Sang Longyang, Professor of the Foreign Language School of Jiujiang University and also professor of the Foreign Language School of Guangdong Technology College, is responsible for the design and revision of the whole translation of the book as well as its editing. As the head of Translation Institute for Traditional Chinese Classics of Jiujiang University, he is the chief translator of *The Analects of Confucius: An Axiomatic Interpretation* and *Mencius: An Axiomatic Interpretation*. He has published the Chinese version of American science fiction *The Red Mars*. He once studied as a visiting scholar in University of Louisville, Kentucky, USA and was trained as language teacher in Anglia Ruskin University, UK.

Mr. Gu Danke, apart from completing the arranged translation tasks, took part in the preparatory work before the translation actually began. He also revised and proofread some of the translations of this book. He has been translating Chinese classics into English for over 30 years and has published a number of translation works, such as *Tao Te Ching*, *The Book of Filial Piety*, and *Dos and Don'ts for Children*. He worked as a visiting scholar in the Departments of East Asian Studies in the University of Edinburgh, the UK, and in the University of Toronto, Canada.

This bilingual book is a cooperative project of Chinese Classics Institute of Jiujiang University and Lushan Culture Research Center of Jiujiang University, and is a planned program of the Collaborative Innovation Center of Lushan Cultural Inheritance and Transmission at Provincial Level.

We're indebted to the scholars of the research team of the Chinese version, especially Professor Gan Xiaoqing, who has offered us much help in our understanding of the Chinese edition. Professor Gan has not only provided us with the revised Chinese version of *Laozi: An Axiomatic Interpretation*, but also its condensed version. He has contributed a lot to all the necessary processes including the compilation and publication of the Chinese-English version. We are thankful to Professor Zhao Yanchun of Shanghai University, who has offered constructive ideas on the translation of the book.

Finally, we'd like to thank all of the research scholars or translators of *Laozi* or *Dao De Jing* and other relevant Chinese classics, especially James Legge, D. C. Lau, Robert G. Henricks, Zhao Yanchun of Shanghai University, Gu Zhengkun of Peking University, Professor Ren Jiyu, and Professor Gu Danke, from whom we have benefited much. Their different English versions of *Laozi* or *Dao De Jing* turn out to be good references for us to determine the appropriate English expression of *Laozi* itself. We have also consulted *Zhuang Tzu* which is translated by Fung Yulan (Feng Youlan) and published by Foreign Language Teaching and Research Press, and *The Book of Chuang Tzu* translated by Martin Palman with Elizabeth Breuilly, Chang Wai Ming and Jayramsy and published by Penguin Classics. We have quoted some of the items of *Laozi* from the translations of these translators, to whom our deep thanks should be expressed. In translating the axiomatic terms, we have mainly consulted the English version *The Ethics* by Benedictus Spinoza, to whom we owe a debt of gratitude.

We sincerely hope that the readers would not hesitate to give us suggestions, instructions or even criticisms for the improvement of our translation, of which the translators will be most appreciative.

Sang Longyang & Gu Danke
July, 2018